Archaic States

The publication of the Advanced Seminar Series
is made possible by generous support from
The Brown Foundation, Inc., of Houston, Texas.

SCHOOL OF AMERICAN RESEARCH ADVANCED SEMINAR SERIES

Douglas W. Schwartz, General Editor

Archaic States Contributors

John Baines
Faculty of Oriental Studies
University of Oxford

Richard E. Blanton
Department of Sociology and Anthropology
Purdue University

Gary M. Feinman
Department of Anthropology
University of Wisconsin–Madison

Kent V. Flannery
Museum of Anthropology
University of Michigan

Joyce Marcus
Museum of Anthropology
University of Michigan

Craig Morris
Department of Anthropology
American Museum of Natural History

Gregory L. Possehl
Department of Anthropology
University of Pennsylvania

David Webster
Department of Anthropology
Pennsylvania State University

Henry T. Wright
Museum of Anthropology
University of Michigan

Norman Yoffee
Department of Near Eastern Studies
University of Michigan

Archaic States

Edited by Gary M. Feinman and Joyce Marcus

School of American Research Press ■ Santa Fe ■ New Mexico

ST CHARLES COMMUNITY COLLEGE
LIBRARY
WITHDRAWN

School of American Research Press
Post Office Box 2188
Santa Fe, New Mexico 87504-2188
www.sarweb.org

Director of Publications: Joan K. O'Donnell
Editor: June-el Piper
Designer: Deborah Flynn Post
Indexer: Andrew L. Christenson
Typographer: G&S Typesetters, Inc.
Printer: Thomson-Shore, Inc.

Library of Congress Cataloging-in-Publication Data:
Archaic states / edited by Gary M. Feinman and Joyce Marcus.
p. cm. — (School of American Research advanced seminar series)
Includes bibliographical references and index.
ISBN 0-933452-98-5 (cloth). — ISBN 0-933452-99-3 (pbk.)
1. Political anthropology. 2. State, The—Origin. 3. Civilization,
Ancient. I. Feinman. II. Marcus, Joyce. III. Series.
GN492.6.A72   1998
306.2—dc21   97-50302
                                                        CIP

© 1998 by the School of American Research. All rights reserved.
Manufactured in the United States of America. Library of Congress
Catalog Card Number 97-50302. International Standard Book
Numbers 0-933452-98-5 (cloth) and 0-933452-99-3 (paper).
Second paperback printing 2000.

Cover: Lintel 8 from the Classic Maya center of Yaxchilán, showing
the Yaxchilán ruler Bird Jaguar (far right) and a subordinate lord (far
left) taken captives. This event took place in May, AD 755. Drawing by
John Klausmeyer, courtesy of Joyce Marcus.

ST. CHARLES COMMUNITY COLLEGE
LIBRARY

Contents

Illustrations

Tables

Preface

One of the most challenging problems that faces contemporary archaeology concerns the operation and diversity of ancient states. Because archaeologists, historians, and other social scientists have tended to focus on the rise and decline of early polities, questions concerning how archaic states worked (or broke down) have been given less attention. It can be argued, however, that it is difficult to understand a state's rise or fall if we do not comprehend what it looked like at its peak. Furthermore, can we evaluate general explanations of state origins if we do not apprehend the full range of variation in how states operated?

We proposed this session to the School of American Research in the fall of 1989. At that time, there had not been a major comparative seminar on the operation and structure of ancient states for more than 15 years. That gap in the recent literature on archaic states remains as significant now as it was when the meeting was held in November 1992. As the cycle from conference papers to finished chapters nears completion, we believe that the articles in this book collectively take significant strides in addressing questions of state diversity and operation, as well as in helping define key avenues for research and discussion in the decades ahead.

The participants in this session were selected to provide both broad geographic coverage and a range of theoretical viewpoints. We wanted to include diverse scholars, including several who work principally with documents, others who mostly examine the archaeological record, and a third group who studies both. In regard to archaic states, there is relatively little that we all would agree on other than the deep interest that we share in the topic. It was this passion and the wealth of experiences we brought to the seminar table that kept our discussions going far into the night.

As editors, we wish to thank all the participants for their thoughtful presentations and papers. We also are grateful to them for responding quickly and with good humor to Gary's bibliographic queries as we readied the book for press. George L. Cowgill and an anonymous reviewer provided valuable reviews of the entire volume. It is a better book as a result of their suggestions. Linda M. Nicholas, Sandra Austin, Lane Fargher, and Steve Germain assisted in numerous ways as we edited and prepared the manuscripts for publication. We also appreciate the great care and comfort generously provided by Doug Schwartz and the entire School of American Research staff in Santa Fe, as well as the production and editorial support given us by Joan O'Donnell and the staff of the SAR Press.

We dedicate this volume to Robert McCormick Adams, a pioneer in the comparative analysis of Old and New World states.

Archaic States

1
Introduction
JOYCE MARCUS and GARY M. FEINMAN

During the past 25 years, ancient states have been the subject of numerous volumes and conferences around the world. Two dominant themes of this work have been the "origins" and "collapses" of such states.[1]

Believing that many other themes—including the operation and behavior of ancient states through time—had not been exhaustively treated, we assembled ten scholars at the School of American Research between October 30 and November 6, 1992. One of our goals was to produce a volume that could be used in conjunction with previously published books on the origins and collapses of ancient states. We hoped to do this by providing new comparative studies of early states in the Old and New Worlds, emphasizing similarities and differences. We also hoped to shed new light on a number of theoretical issues. Included among those issues are the operation and structure of ancient states, their scale and territorial extent, the nature of state-level political and economic institutions, the diversity of ancient states, and the value of their systematic comparison. These topics are ones we share with other scholars, such as Southall (1991:77), who recently wrote, "I am now more interested in how states work, what basic similarities in their working (processes) can be found (a) at different *eras* of world history, (b) at different *stages* of their development, (c) in different climates and ecologies, and (d) in different *historical streams.*"

Given that most of the seminar participants were archaeologists, we decided to focus on *archaic states,* those that arose early in the history of their particular world region and were characterized by class-endogamous social strata with royal families, major and minor nobles, and commoners. Most of the states we consider were first-, second-, or third-generation states in their region. We have not included more recent states with democratic institutions, presidents, parliaments, and global market economies.

Among the themes discussed in this volume are the scale, size, and organization of ancient states (Gary M. Feinman); an evaluation of state typologies and corporate political economy (Richard E. Blanton); a comparative study of the ground plans of buildings in archaic states, aimed at helping the archaeologist determine if a state is in fact present and whether certain institutions and groups of personnel have emerged (Kent V. Flannery); the strategies of state expansion, the incorporation of autonomous polities in the state, and their subsequent governance (Joyce Marcus, Craig Morris, Henry T. Wright); evidence for warfare and status rivalry in chiefdoms and states (David L. Webster); evidence for order, legitimacy, and wealth in ancient states (John Baines and Norman Yoffee); and the political and social complexity of states (Gregory L. Possehl). World regions represented include the Near East, India and Pakistan, Egypt, Mesoamerica, and the Andes.

Another theme discussed by various participants at the seminar was the relationship between "state" and "civilization." The former was seen as a political or governmental unit, while the latter was seen as the cultural sphere associated with that political or governmental unit. In this volume, "the state" is *not* considered to be isomorphic with "civilization" in the Indus region (Possehl), the Near East (Yoffee and Baines), or the Maya region (Marcus). Even for Egypt, it is only during the politically more centralized periods called "kingdoms" that there was a reasonably close areal fit between "state" and "civilization."

Such historical differences were a central theme in seminar discussions. We pondered why in some regions several states arose that shared a single ethos of civilization, while in other areas the boundaries of a state and its civilization were roughly coterminous. Although we could not explain this historical variation, all seminar participants agreed that this diversity would be an interesting question to examine in the future.

TERMINOLOGY

One of the first topics discussed at the seminar was, "What is an archaic state?" Although definitions varied among participants, many believed that in contrast to modern nation-states, archaic states were societies with (minimally) two class-endogamous strata (a professional ruling class and a commoner class) and a government that was both highly centralized and internally specialized. Ancient states were regarded as having more power than the rank societies that preceded them, particularly in the areas of waging war, exacting tribute, controlling information, drafting soldiers, and regulating manpower and labor (Flannery 1972, 1995; Marcus 1976a, 1993a; Sanders 1974; Wright 1977, 1978). For some well-known states where texts are available, one could add to this the stipulation that archaic states were ruled by kings rather than chiefs, had standardized temples implying a state religion, had full-time priests rather than shamans or part-time priests, and could hold on to conquered territory in ways no rank society could. For less well known states, where texts are absent, perhaps the best definition is the most general and simple, so as to encompass marked historical variability.

One source of disagreement was over such terms as "chiefdom" and "state," which archaeologists have borrowed from ethnology and political science. Many participants argued that such terms have been used in very productive ways for a long time (Carneiro 1970a, 1970b, 1978, 1981, 1987; Drennan and Uribe 1987; Earle, ed. 1991; Flannery 1972, 1995; Kirch 1984; Krader 1968; Marcus 1983a; Sahlins 1958, 1970; Sahlins and Service 1960; Service 1975; C. Spencer 1987, 1990, 1993). Other participants see less value in such typologies, including Service's (1962) more specific band, tribe, chiefdom, and state, and Fried's (1967) more general egalitarian society, rank society, and stratified (or political) society.

Critics such as Crumley (1987, 1995); Ehrenreich, Crumley, and Levy (1995); Mann (1986); and Patterson and Gailey (1987) have previously attacked the notion that each stage of evolution (chiefdom, states, etc.) is "uniform," that each type is "static" or "restrictive," and that each type is the "inevitable product" of another stage. Other participants (e.g., Flannery and Marcus) responded that all these criticisms were based on problematic assumptions. They stated that few evolutionary anthropologists had ever suggested that such stages were uniform, static, or inevitable; if such assumptions had been made, it was by archaeologists who had tried to use the scheme like a cookbook. Paleontologists, they argued, never complain that the stage "reptile" is too "uniform"; they know it includes animals as different as lizards, snakes, and turtles, and that none of those categories have been static in an evolutionary sense. Nor do paleontologists see "mammals" evolving from all "reptiles"; the evidence suggests that early mammals arose from only one type of reptile, the cynodonts, and that subsequent mammals arose from those first mammals (see Flannery 1995).

Just as paleontologists are aware of the diversity within the categories of fossil animals they use, so, too, evolutionists are aware of heterogeneity within categories such as "state" and "chiefdom" (Carneiro 1970a, 1991; de Montmollin 1989; Easton 1959; Feinman and Neitzel 1984; Ferguson 1991; Flannery 1995; Johnson and Earle 1987; Marcus 1983a; Marcus and Flannery 1996; McGuire 1983; Shifferd 1987; C. Spencer 1990, 1993; H. Spencer 1967; Trigger 1993). Simply put, zoologists and anthropologists use typologies because the creation of such categories facilitates general comparisons and contrasts.

Anthropologists who use the category "state" are generally aware of the dynamic qualities that each state displays during its specific history and time span (Claessen 1984; Claessen and van de Velde 1987, 1991; Earle, ed. 1991; Erickson 1973, 1975; Marcus 1989, 1992a, 1993a; Schreiber 1992). Furthermore, such scholars do not believe in inevitability; they know that not every autonomous village society gave rise to a chiefdom, nor did every group of chiefdoms give rise to a state. A set of necessary conditions must be present before a state is formed; even when such conditions are present, a new state may be very short-lived and difficult to detect archaeologically. Among the questions discussed at the seminar were, What allowed one state to adjust and survive for long periods of time while another broke down quickly? Following a period of breakdown and decentralization, what conditions allowed a second-generation state to form? How does a second-generation state differ from the first state in the same region? How do third- and fourth-generation states differ from first- and second-generation states? Wright and Marcus, whose research has included several generations of states, and Blanton and Feinman, who have looked at the settlement patterns from multiple generations, were particularly interested in such questions.

Although not necessarily agreeing on answers, many participants singled out three problems that they saw as particularly thorny: how to classify a transitional society that seems to lie part way between a chiefdom and a state (Skalník 1983; Southall 1952, 1965, 1988, 1991); what to call the smaller polities that sometimes follow the collapse of a centralized state (Ferguson 1991; Kristiansen 1991; Marcus 1989; Snodgrass 1977, 1980); and what to call the polities on the periphery of a state when they acquire some of the trappings of that state but are never really incorporated into it.

Most seminar participants believed that it was important to call attention to some of the differences that have been used to distinguish rank societies (including chiefdoms), on the one hand, and states, on the other. Suggestions included (1) a change in the settlement hierarchy from three to four levels; (2) a change in the decision-making hierarchy from two to three (or more) levels; (3) a fundamental change in the ideology of stratification and descent, such that rulers were conceded a sacred supernatural origin (establishing their divine right to rule) while commoners were seen as having a separate descent of nondivine origin; (4) the emergence of two endogamous strata, the result of severing the bonds of kinship that had once linked leaders to followers in a branching continuum of relationships; (5) the evolution of the palace as the ruler's official residence; (6) the change from a single centralized leader (e.g., a chief) to a government that employed legal force while denying its citizens the use of personal, individual force; and (7) the establishment of governmental laws and the ability to enforce them. Although not all participants concurred with each of these criteria, a degree of support generally was found for each.

Participants also agreed that ancient states were dynamic political systems that changed throughout their specific historical trajectories. Each state is, therefore, different in some respects from other states, but early states as a group do display similarities. In this volume some authors tend to emphasize the similarities among states, while others emphasize both similarities and differences.

SOME POINTS OF AGREEMENT

Although the seminar participants chose to disagree on a number of topics, many felt that the use of two terms—"segmentary states" and "city-states"—was problematic. The first is an oxymoron, resulting from the ill-advised phrase originally applied to a nonstate society. The second is a term coined for the Greek polis and indiscriminately applied to dozens of other societies that are not similar.

Let us consider "segmentary states" first. The concept can be traced back to *African Political Systems,* a volume edited by Fortes and Evans-Pritchard (1940). Fortes and Evans-Pritchard contrasted noncentralized lineage groups (acephalous societies) with centralized hierarchical governments (unitary states). They noted that stateless societies displayed many structurally equivalent segments, and "if one segment defeats another it does not attempt to establish political dominance over it; in the absence of an administrative machinery there is, in fact, no means by which it could do so" (Fortes and Evans-Pritchard 1940:14).

The African ethnologist Aidan Southall (1956) was unable to fit the Alur into Fortes and Evans-Pritchard's categories of "unitary state" or "acephalous society," so he created an intermediate category he called a "segmentary state." Southall thought that this concept would be useful in describing the interaction between the Alur and their political economy; eventually other scholars (such as Burton Stein [1977] in his historical analysis of the Chola "empire" of medieval south India and Richard Fox [1977] in his account of the Rajput states of north India) adopted the segmentary state concept in their studies.

Unfortunately, however, the phrase "segmentary state" misled many scholars because they took it to refer to a "state-level" society when the Alur are no more than a rank society at best. Eventually Southall (1991:91) himself recanted: "Although I called it [the Alur polity] a segmentary state, it was *hardly* a state, hardly a two class society, and it could not prevent secession."

He unfortunately made things worse by adding, "I think it is permissible to refer to kings and kingdoms in these cases, terms which are appropriately flexible, rather than chiefs and chiefdoms, in order to avoid discriminating against them simply because they are not Western, although politically they were not fully states." Most seminar participants rejected this attempt to avoid "discriminating" against the Alur, and lamented the application of terms like "king," "kingdom," and "state" to what are actually rank societies without social stratification, kingship, and centralized government.

The phrase "segmentary state" was embraced unwisely by some scholars working in the Maya area (and elsewhere) before Southall had a chance to take it back. They apparently did not realize that the phrase is derived from "segmentary lineage system," an expression that describes the act of fissioning, with lineages being the units undergoing fission; and that those societies were liable to fission precisely because they were *not* states. One author who made this very clear was Marshall Sahlins (1961:323), who wrote that "a segmentary lineage system is a social means of intrusion and competition in an already occupied niche. More, it is an organization confined to societies of a certain level of development, the *tribal* level, as distinguished from less-developed *bands* and more advanced *chiefdoms* . . . It develops specifically in a tribal society which is moving against other tribes, in a *tribal intercultural environment.*"

More than a decade ago, Ronald Cohen (1981) argued that fissioning characterized *non*-states, and he regarded "antifission institutions" as *the* criterion for statehood. For Cohen, a "segmentary state" would be impossible; a society is either segmentary or a state, not both. Peter Skalník (1983) also added his misgivings about the application of terms such as "segmentary state" and "state" to societies in Africa that are really "chiefdoms and chieftaincies," *not* states. We also believe the term "segmentary state" is too much an oxymoron to be useful in the future.

Another term many participants would like to see phased out is "city-state." This term came into widespread use as a kind of English synonym for the Greek polis (Burke 1986; Griffeth and Thomas 1981; Jones 1981). There are two problems with its use: (1) many Aegean specialists do not believe the polis was a state at all, and (2) many of the polities all over the world to which the term has been applied do not resemble the Greek polis. The polis has been defined as a democratic and self-sufficient polity in which the majority of towns and villages had a high degree of autonomy and very little economic control over their citizens (Snodgrass 1977, 1980). Almost no society to which this term has been applied in Mesoamerica (for example) fits this definition.

Many of the seminar participants (and indeed, many of our colleagues elsewhere) would gladly scrap the term. As Peter Burke (1986:151) writes,

"The choice is between giving the concept up or resigning oneself to using it imprecisely." Tom Jones (1981:x) has described the term "city-state" as "an awkward one for which, regrettably, there is no acceptable alternative. . . . Part of the difficulty with city-state is that one must include in this category small towns that cannot qualify as cities in the modern sense. Further, citizens of city-states were not in every instance residents of the population centers where the governments were housed, nor did such cities or centers of government always rule the surrounding countryside. Even worse, city suggests to many persons urbanization as we know it today." Other scholars point out that many of the clusters of small polities that have been called city-states are simply the product of the breakdown of larger states (Marcus, this volume). When those states break down, their former provinces become autonomous polities who for a time lack the power to incorporate their neighbors into a new state. What develops is a kind of stand-off between roughly equal small polities. The rulers of those polities may continue to behave like kings (and be addressed as if they were kings), but the territories they control are no larger than a chiefdom and may have no more than a two- or three-tiered settlement hierarchy. They are de facto chiefdoms yet have stratification rather than ranking; several seminar participants believe they belong in their own category.

Seminar participants suggested a variety of labels for these groups of small polities that have appeared in various parts of the world. "Balkanized provinces," "petty kingdoms," and "principalities" were but a few of the terms considered. Several participants suggested that the local terms for each world region might be the best: *hesps* or nomes (Egypt), *altepetl* (Aztec region), *cuchcabalob* (Maya region), *cacicazgos* (Mixtec region), *curacazgos* (Peru), and so forth. Many of these local terms share a common root origin: they mean "the territory controlled by a native lord" (Marcus 1983b). In virtually every case, this local term is a more accurate description of the polity than "city-state."

The term used for the petty kingdoms of Mexico's Mixtec region at AD 1300–1500 is a good example. In certain ways, many *cacicazgos* (Spores 1967, 1974) were not typical states because they had only a two- or three-tiered hierarchy and displayed the de facto size and administrative structure of chiefdoms. On the other hand, they were not chiefdoms either, because class-endogamous social strata had survived from the preexisting large states of which they had been parts; their "kings" still lived in palaces.

The term "principality" has been used by Colin Renfrew (1972:369) to refer to Aegean polities that he describes as "something more than chiefdoms, something less than states." Nicholas Dirks (1993) has used a similar term, "princely state," to refer to those areas of India (roughly a third of the country) that were not conquered by the British. "Princely states" were, however, ruled indirectly by the British through the traditional agencies of maharajas and chiefs, the latter destined to be incorporated into the empire through a "political economy of honor" (Dirks 1993:xxv).

One common aspect of these principalities, petty kingdoms, or so-called city-states is that many seem to be the breakdown product of former states (Charlton and Nichols 1997; Hodge 1984; Marcus 1989). We could find few areas of the world where they were not preceded by a large territorial state, such as Moche, Teotihuacán, Monte Albán, Tikal, Calakmul, or Egypt's "Dynasty 0." "Peer polities" may *precede* the first state in a region (which is exactly what Renfrew and Cherry [1986] meant when they introduced the term), but the first state usually does not appear as a lot of little "peer statelets." The creation of the state often involves the act of consolidation of many small polities into one large whole, which is what can create the additional hierarchical level identified by Wright and Johnson (1975). Usually, that results in the first state for each region being large and unitary, rather than a cluster of "statelets."

It should be noted, however, that Yoffee (this volume and elsewhere) still likes the term "city-state," applying it to virtually every archaic state in the world except Egypt. Yoffee's definition of a city-state is unlike that of the other seminar participants, since he uses it to refer to huge unique metropoli like Teotihuacán, rather than to groups of small polities like the Greek poleis. Certainly Yoffee is using the term differently from Bruce Trigger (1993:8), who draws a contrast between large, unitary states like Teotihuacán and the clusters of small polities usually referred to as "city-states."

THE COMPARISON OF ARCHAIC STATES

This volume builds on the work of many previous investigators. Meyer Fortes and Edward Evans-Pritchard (1940) argued that one value of isolating general patterns in states is that it facilitates worldwide comparison. Since then, scholars such as Julian H. Steward (1949), Shmuel N. Eisenstadt (1965), Robert McCormick Adams (1966), Paul Wheatley (1971), Elman R. Service (1975), Henri J. M. Claessen and Peter Skalník (eds. 1978, 1981), Richard E. Blanton et al. (1993, 1996), and Bruce Trigger (1993) have undertaken comparative studies of states with the goal of isolating regularities and differences. All these authors found the general concept of "state" useful, although they have argued for great diversity in the *kinds* of states that existed in ancient times—alternatively calling them bureaucratic, despotic, expansionist, inchoate, mature, mercantile, or militaristic (Bargatzky 1987; Britan and Cohen 1980; Claessen and Skalník, eds. 1978, 1981; Claessen and van de Velde 1987; Cohen 1978, 1981; Cohen and Service 1978; Earle, ed. 1991; Flannery 1972, 1995; Flannery and Marcus

1983a; Folan, Marcus, and Miller 1995; Gledhill, Bender, and Larsen 1988; Marcus 1973, 1992a, 1993a; Pattee 1973; Service 1975; Willey 1991; Wright 1977, 1978). This broad menu contradicts any notion that evolutionary categories like "state" are "rigid" or "mask diversity."

Seminar participants did little to reduce the variety of state types in their discussions. One source of diversity is the fact that states may have multiple hierarchies with nonisomorphic or only partially overlapping functions (see Marcus 1983a, 1983b). For example, a given site may be the political capital but *not* the economic or religious capital for its region. A second-tier political center may be a first-tier religious center; a fourth-tier political center might be a first-tier craft production center.

To deal with such situations, Crumley (1987) and others (Ehrenreich, Crumley, and Levy 1995) have embraced the concept of "heterarchy"—a term that goes back to at least 1945, when it was used to describe the relationships among parts of the human brain. Then McCulloch (1945) used the term to assert that the brain and its functions were not hierarchically structured. Heterarchy, however, is not the opposite of hierarchy; it simply means that different functions can exist in a system without their arrangement being hierarchical. Archaic states were both heterarchical *and* hierarchical.

Another comparative theme touched on during seminar discussions was that even those aspects of the archaic state that are hierarchical can be volatile. Although it is common for archaeologists to depict ancient states as powerful and centralized, many rulers, in fact, had a great deal of trouble controlling their subordinates. In this volume, Blanton as well as Baines and Yoffee discuss the diverse strategies and arrangements that were designed to link principal rulers with more local elites. This difficult dynamic is certainly one reason that ancient states seem to oscillate between periods of successful centralization and loss of control. As noted by Fortes and Evans-Pritchard (1940:11), it was difficult for rulers to achieve a perfect balance between centralized authority and regional autonomy. If a king abused his powers, subordinate leaders were liable to secede or lead a revolt against him. If a subordinate leader got too powerful and independent, the central authority might call on other subordinate leaders to help suppress him. Fortes and Evans-Pritchard (1940:11) note that kings often tried to buttress their own authority by playing subordinates off against each other. Their ultimate goal was to keep the power of the ruler and that of his subordinates in balance. That balance could not be maintained if all subordinates allied against the ruler. When they acted collectively, subordinates could pose a real threat to the ruler, as we see in the Maya and Egyptian cases discussed in this volume.

Yet seminar participants also recognized that power in archaic states was not always as tightly focused on individual rulers as was the case for the Maya and in Egypt. Cross-cultural variation in the strategies of state rulership, and

the relationship between these differences and variability in economic production and exchange, was often discussed. Likewise, we considered the nature of the relationship between the spatial extent of archaic states and the
degree of centralization. Many participants agreed in a general sense with
Southall's (1988:81) observation that, other things being equal, "it is easier
for a small than for a very large state to centralize."

Finally, we discussed a number of topics at the seminar that we could not
resolve. One was the question of whether or not there were fundamental
differences between primary or first-generation states and the second-
generation states that followed them. On the most specific level, one can see
differences of detail. Some first-generation states had palaces but lacked standardized temples; others had standardized temples but lacked palaces. The
second-generation states in such areas often had both, suggesting to some of
the participants a level of "maturity" in state institutions that was not found
in primary states. Other participants emphasized the organizational differences between specific states, however, and did not see these distinctions as
necessarily developmental in nature. In this organizational material, no
member of the seminar saw a universal pattern or sequence from which we
could draw unilineal conclusions. Furthermore, all participants recognized
that in any given region the degree of political integration did not increase
steadily or uniformly through time.

One reason such diachronic questions are hard to resolve is that our current chronologies are too coarse-grained to allow us to see the order in
which various institutions appeared. Archaeologists have "gross chronologies" based on ceramic phases and C-14 dates; "medium-grained chronologies" based on the stratigraphic superimposition of floors and buildings; and
(in some regions) "fine-grained chronologies" based on texts with calendric
dates. Often each of the three chronologies suggests a different political scenario for the same region, and even when all are present the three rarely fit
together as snugly as we might wish (Smith 1992).

Parenthetically, we might add that chronology can obscure the transition
from chiefdom to pristine state. At the seminar, Henry Wright pointed out
that immediately prior to state formation in southwest Iran, one of the area's
largest chiefdoms collapsed, creating a competitive situation that may have
led to consolidation. If the same process happened in the Valley of Oaxaca,
he argued, we cannot see it because the process of state formation was so
much more rapid there than in southwest Iran. This is probably another way
of saying that, for certain regions, we need a much more fine-grained
chronology to detect whether (and the degree to which) general processes
do indeed exist.

One impression we all took away from the seminar is that archaic states
were a lot more fragile and internally diverse than the archaeological litera-

ture would lead one to believe. Born out of tremendous effort, they also required a substantial effort to hold together. Their constituent provinces were always more stable than the larger polities of which they were part. In virtually every region of the world, provinces kept escaping and having to be reclaimed. Given the number of attempts at consolidation that failed, one can only marvel at the states that lasted for half a millennium or more.

DIRECTIONS FOR FUTURE RESEARCH

Seminar participants concurred that archaic states can only be understood if we study them at a number of scales: the household, the site, the region, and the macroscale. In many of the regions discussed here, we are just beginning to achieve the outlines of such a multiscalar perspective that has taken as much as 50 years of prior research. Clearly, the research goals and questions defined here are long term and multigenerational in nature. Meeting and resolving those aims provides a key challenge for students in the present and the future.

Almost everyone at the seminar was struck by how much more we know about those ancient states for which extensive ethnohistoric or historic texts are available. There are things Yoffee can say about Babylonian states that simply remain unknown for the Uruk state. There are things Morris can say about the Inka state that remain unknown for the Moche and Wari states. In such situations, there is a real temptation to push the institutions of third- and fourth-generation states back in time to earlier states that may not have shared them. We all agreed that we need refined archaeological tools, both conceptual and methodological, for getting at the sociopolitical institutions of the very first states. Flannery makes a start at this in chapter 2, but it is only the first step of a long journey. The fact that neither Possehl (this volume) nor Webster (this volume) believes he has sufficient evidence to apply the term "state" to the impressive society he is studying indicates how badly we need refined archaeological tools. One of our future tasks should be to craft them.

NOTE

1. See, for example, R. E. W. Adams 1977; Claessen and Skalník, eds. 1978, 1981; Claessen and van de Velde 1987; Claessen, van de Velde, and Smith 1985; Cohen and Service 1978; Cohen and Toland 1988; Culbert 1973; Ehrenreich, Crumley, and Levy 1995; Friedman 1979; Friedman and Rowlands, eds. 1977; Gledhill, Bender, and Larsen 1988; Kautz and Jones 1981; Larsen 1978; Patterson and Gailey 1987; Yoffee and Cowgill 1988.

2

The Ground Plans of Archaic States

KENT V. FLANNERY

M ost of the world's primary states arose at times when writing was either absent or limited in subject matter. By the time texts become richly informative, we are often dealing with second- or third-generation states. And in regions like the Andes, even such later states had no texts.

For this reason there has long been a need for a set of clues by which archaic states can be identified on the basis of archaeological data. I use the term "clue" deliberately, since archaeological evidence is circumstantial rather than eyewitness. None of us was there to see Mesopotamia's Uruk state, Peru's Moche state, Mexico's Monte Albán II state, or Egypt's Dynasty 0. Those early states, however, left the archaeological equivalent of fingerprints, hair and fiber samples, and blood drops with recognizable DNA. They left settlement patterns and buildings whose ground plans reflect the social, political, and religious institutions of the archaic state (Flannery and Marcus 1976).

In this essay I look at the settlement hierarchies of early states, their governmental and residential palaces, their temples and priests' residences, and their royal tombs. Had I no page limit, I would add fortifications, military and political expansion, state-sponsored craft production, and many other clues to the list. Since I have elsewhere given my agreements and disagreements with Childe's ten criteria for urban civilization (Flannery 1994), I will not repeat them here.

Note that I am not proposing an archaeological *definition* for the state; its definition must remain in the realm of anthropology and political science.

What I am working toward is a set of archaeological clues for identifying an anthropological and political phenomenon. Mammals were originally defined by zoologists, but paleontologists can now identify their bones. States were originally defined by anthropologists and political scientists, but archaeologists can now identify the skeletons of their institutions.

SETTLEMENT HIERARCHIES

At the peak of their power, archaic states were centralized systems with an administrative hierarchy in which commands traveled downward while tribute and information on output traveled upward (Flannery 1972, 1995). Early states tended to have more levels of administrators and settlements than the chiefdoms that preceded them, and these differences can sometimes be detected from survey data.

In the Near East, Wright and Johnson (1975) have suggested that chiefdoms tended to have only two or three levels (or tiers) of settlements, whereas states tended to have a hierarchy with at least four levels: cities, towns, large villages, and small villages. While not a hard-and-fast "law"— of which archaeology has few—this rule of thumb has proved useful in other world regions, such as the Valley of Oaxaca (Marcus and Flannery 1996), the Maya Lowlands (Marcus 1983a, 1993a), and the north coast of Peru (Wilson 1995).

It should be noted that "administrative hierarchy" and "settlement hierarchy" are not synonyms. The former refers to the number of tiers of administrators in the system, which may not be archaeologically detectable in societies without written texts. The latter refers to the number of tiers of community sizes (which may be detectable through the use of histograms like those shown in fig. 2.1) and to the administrative institutions present in each tier (only some of which may be detectable through the excavation of public buildings and residences).

For example, the earliest clearly identifiable state in the Zapotec region of Mexico (100 BC–AD 100) seems to have had a site-size hierarchy of at least four tiers. Its heartland, the Valley of Oaxaca, had an estimated 41,000 inhabitants distributed through 518 sites (Kowalewski et al. 1989). Tier 1 of the settlement hierarchy was a capital city covering 416 ha, with an estimated population of 14,500. Tier 2 of the hierarchy consisted of six "towns" with populations estimated at 970 to 1,950 persons, all located within 14 to 28 km of the capital. Tier 3 consisted of at least 30 "large villages" in the 5–10 ha range, with populations estimated at 200 to 700 persons. Tier 4 consisted of more than 400 "small villages" with estimated populations below 200 persons.

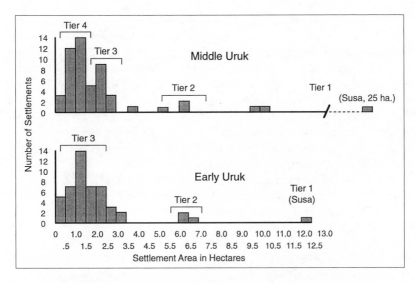

Figure 2.1. The emergence of a four-tiered hierarchy of settlements on the Susiana Plain, southwest Iran. As Susa grew to be the 25-ha capital of an archaic state during Middle Uruk times, peaks in site sizes appeared at 5–7 ha ("towns"), 2–3 ha ("large villages"), and 0.5–1 ha ("small villages") (redrawn from Johnson 1973).

At least where excavation data are available, these settlement tiers are also characterized by the presence or absence of buildings related to the administrative hierarchy (Marcus and Flannery 1996:111–12). In the Zapotec case, the capital city had a large "governmental palace," a ceremonial plaza, multiple residential palaces and princely tombs, multiple standardized temples, more than one I-shaped ball court, and a building with hieroglyphic records of subject provinces. Tier 2 sites sometimes had smaller versions of the "governmental palace," fewer temples, fewer residential palaces and tombs, and only one ball court. Tier 3 sites usually had only one temple, no palace, no ceremonial plaza, and no ball court. Tier 4 sites had no evidence of public structures at all.

A four-tiered hierarchy of settlements may therefore have administrators only at its upper three tiers. This does *not* mean that there are only three levels of administrators in the society. It means only that state administrators (number of existing levels notwithstanding) are usually not present at small villages.

In the Maya Lowlands, where hieroglyphic inscriptions are available, textual information can be added to site-size data. For example, more than two decades ago Marcus (1973) argued that the Maya city of Calakmul was at the head of a "central-place hierarchy." This is a term for an administrative hierarchy so well integrated that Tier 2 towns encircle the Tier 1 city at very regular distances; in turn, Tier 3 settlements encircle Tier 2 settlements at regular (and shorter) distances (fig. 2.2a). In the Calakmul case, not only were Tier 2 centers like Oxpemul, Sasilhá, Naachtún, and Uxul spaced regularly, 34 km from each other and from Calakmul, but also many subordinate centers mentioned Calakmul's "emblem glyph" in their inscriptions. This was part of a widespread pattern in which Tier 3 centers mentioned the Tier 2 centers to which they were affiliated, while Tier 2 centers mentioned the Tier 1 capital for their region (Marcus 1976a). Recently, Folan, Marcus, and Miller (1995) have discovered that a series of raised roads connected Calakmul to its Tier 2 settlements.

Four-tiered settlement hierarchies are extremely widespread among archaic states, a pattern that has escaped many Mayanists. There may be several reasons for their failure to recognize hierarchies. For instance, some Maya archaeologists are reluctant to see "their" Tier 2 or Tier 3 site as subordinate to any other center, apparently resenting it if their site is considered anything less than a capital. Some Maya epigraphers, in addition, assume that if a site possessed its own emblem glyph it could not be hierarchically below any other site. Some have, as a result, proposed that the Maya area had as many as 80(!) autonomous "capitals," each ruling a minuscule territory (Mathews 1985). I know of no archaic state that had such a nonhierarchical structure.

It is instructive, in this regard, to look at the situation in Mesopotamia. Like the Maya region, Early Dynastic Mesopotamia was composed of distinct polities, some of which maintained their integrity over centuries. Some Near Eastern scholars (e.g., Diakonoff 1974) have compared these polities to the *hesps* or nomes of ancient Egypt, and the analogy is apt: both regions had periods when polities were unified under powerful rulers and periods when centralized control broke down.

Consider the polity of Lagash in southeastern Mesopotamia. It contained at least three cities, more than 20 towns, and at least 40 villages (Adams 1966:101). Diakonoff (1974) has estimated its population of "free citizens" as greater than 100,000, a figure that Henry Wright (personal communication 1997) considers conservative. Its two largest cities, Lagash and Girsu, had populations estimated at 36,000 and 19,000, respectively. Though archaeological surveys have not yet determined the total area of the polity, its irrigated fields alone are calculated to have exceeded 2000 km^2. It had a 45-km-long frontier with the polity of Umma to the north, and a frontier of unknown length with Ur to the south.

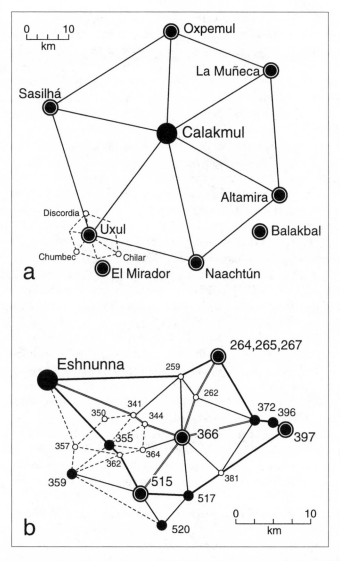

Figure 2.2. Central-place lattices around ancient cities: a, *the lattice around the Maya city of Calakmul in the seventh century* AD *(redrawn from Marcus 1973);* b, *the lattice around the Early Dynastic Sumerian city of Eshnunna, showing one city (Eshnunna), four Tier 2 towns (e.g., 515), six Tier 3 large villages (e.g., 517), and a number of Tier 4 small villages (e.g., 381) (redrawn from Johnson 1972).*

Each of the polity's largest cities—Lagash, Girsu, and Nina—was run by an *ensí,* or ruler drawn from a family of high status. At various times, these rulers appointed their eldest sons to the office of *sanga,* or manager, in the estate of their city's largest temple—a position the sons held until they acceded to the throne (Tyumenev 1969). Lagash's cuneiform texts are therefore full of city names, town names, rulers' names, rulers' titles, and their relatives' names and titles. None of this implies autonomy for *any* of the cities or rulers involved; in fact, there were times when all of the polity of Lagash was under the control of rulers at Kish, Akkad, or Ur.

The lesson for Maya epigraphers is clear: the mere fact that a city has its own name, and its ruler his own title, does not mean that either was autonomous. Some Early Dynastic kings took the title *lugal* to emphasize their hegemony over the various *ensís,* or city rulers, within their realms. The Maya had a comparable hierarchy of *ahauob, sahalob,* and *batabob.* All were hereditary lords, but some were above others, and some Maya lords used *all* these titles, as well as others (Marcus 1993a).

In the case of Lagash, its history shows a cyclic "rise and fall" like that proposed by Marcus (1992a, 1993a) in her Dynamic Model. During Early Dynastic II, Lagash was for a time subordinate to Mesalim of Kish, a ruler who "exercised hegemony far beyond the walls of his own city" (Cooper 1983:7). During Early Dynastic III, Lagash rose to greater prominence under a ruler named Eanatum, who assumed the kingship of both Lagash and Kish. When Sargon of Akkad unified all of Mesopotamia, Lagash came under his hegemony. With the fall of the Akkad dynasty, a ruler named Gudea brought Lagash briefly to prominence again—only to have it later come under the control of the Third Dynasty of Ur.

In other words, the history of Lagash is that of a polity subordinate for a time, then powerful and independent, then subordinate again. I have no doubt that most Maya polities went through the same cycles of hegemony and breakdown, since virtually all archaic states behaved this way (see Marcus, this volume).

Another instructive case is that of the Sumerian city of Eshnunna. Using the raw data of Robert McC. Adams's (1965) survey of the Diyala region, Johnson (1972) has shown that during Early Dynastic I the settlements east of Eshnunna formed a central-place lattice (fig. 2.2b).

Does the fact that Eshnunna lay at the head of a four-tiered settlement hierarchy imply that it was "the capital of a state," or at least "an autonomous city"? Actually, there were periods when it was surely not autonomous. During the reign of Gimil-Sin (or Shusin), a king of the Third Dynasty of Ur (2037–2029 BC), Eshnunna was under the hegemony of Ur. The ruler of Eshnunna, whose name was Ituria, dedicated an important temple there to Gimil-Sin. The dedication text refers to Gimil-Sin as "divine," a "mighty king" of Ur, and to Ituria as "his servant" (Frankfort, Lloyd, and Jacobsen 1940:134–35). With the fall of the Ur III Dynasty, however, Eshnunna gained its autonomy; its ruler Ilushuilia, emphasizing his independence, built his palace next to the Gimil-Sin temple. Ilushuilia's inscriptions portray him as a "mighty king," beloved by a whole series of goddesses, and territorially expansionist for a time (Frankfort, Lloyd, and Jacobsen 1940:196).

To summarize, the discovery of a four-tiered settlement hierarchy, especially if it forms a central-place lattice around a major city, can be a clue to the presence of a state. It cannot, however, always be assumed that the city at the head of that hierarchy is wholly autonomous. Regions like Mesopotamia and the Maya Lowlands were, to borrow Diakonoff's (1974) phrase, "oligarchies in which large numbers of rulers and nobles struggled constantly for the upper hand." In such a system, even cities as powerful as Eshnunna, Lagash, Umma, Uaxactún, Quiriguá, Naranjo, and Naachtún came under the control of other cities at one time or another. Treating all cities as independent capitals at all times oversimplifies the ancient rulers' constant struggles to extend their hegemony.

THE PALACES OF ARCHAIC STATES

In an extensive cross-cultural study of chiefdoms and states, Sanders (1974) discovered an interesting difference. Although chiefs could organize corvée labor to build temples and other public buildings, they usually could not have their residences built for them. Kings, on the other hand, could use corvée labor to build their palaces.

The reasons for this difference are not hard to imagine. Chiefdoms are rank societies; all but the most elaborate had a continuum of statuses without a division into social classes. In a village of 1,000 persons, one might expect to find as many as 10 to 15 chiefly families, all with relatively elite residences. It is rarely possible for an archaeologist to specify one residence in such a village as "the house of the chief," especially since brothers, half-brothers, cousins, and nephews from highly ranked families competed continuously for the post. Many archaic states, on the other hand, were stratified societies that built monumental palaces for their royal families.

Like the principle of the four-tiered hierarchy, however, this should be considered a rule of thumb rather than a hard-and-fast "law." In some parts of the ancient world, unmistakable palaces appear with primary states, while in others they appear only with second-generation states. Mesopotamia had standardized temples before it had clear palaces; the Aegean had unambiguous palaces before it had standardized temples.

There are, moreover, several *types* of palaces. Some palatial buildings seem largely administrative, suggesting places of governmental assembly rather than residences. Others, like the Royal Villa of Knossos or the Zapotec palaces of Mexico, seem largely residential. Among the most interesting are multifunctional structures like the Labyrinth of Knossos and the *ciudadelas* of Peru's Chimú state, in which large areas were devoted to craft production, lower-level administration, or other nonresidential activities. Let us look at a sample of palaces, in roughly descending order of complexity.

The Labyrinth of Knossos, Crete

A classic example of multifunctional complexity—combining royal residences with artisans' quarters—is the Minoan palace at Knossos on Crete (Evans 1921–36; Graham 1987; Michailidou 1989). The remains visible today are Evans's reconstruction of the second palace, built during the seventeenth century BC. It had at least two stories, of which only the ground floor survives; it is at least 150 m on a side and covers 20,000 m^2 (fig. 2.3).

The heart of the palace is its huge Central Court (50 × 25 m). All movement to and from the various sectors of the palace originated in this court; traffic was controlled by narrow corridors that combined privacy with a system of multiple routes from one sector to another. Small wonder that the building's name—Labyrinth, or "House of the Double Axe"—has come to be synonymous with "maze."

In the southeast quadrant of the palace lay the royal residential quarters, separated from the artisans' workshops by a thick wall. According to Michailidou, the Hall of Double Axes belonged to the king, while the queen had her own hall, featuring a private bathroom. The five different routes to the queen's apartment were so indirect that she could maintain her privacy. Stairways for royal family members and servants indicate that the rulers' quarters continued on the floor above.

To the north and east of the thick wall separating them from the royal quarters were workshops filled with raw materials and unfinished products of potters, lapidaries, and metalworkers. Surrounding them were storerooms of various sizes, filling much of the northeast quadrant of the palace. Almost the entire western margin of the complex was devoted to storage rooms. As in all major Cretan palaces, there were monumental storage facilities for grain, wine, oil, and other commodities. For example, more than 400 *pithoi* (huge clay jars probably used for olive oil) were found, representing a storage capacity of 246,000 liters.

Off the west side of the Central Court was a throne room, with the king's chair carved from gypsum. Not far to the south lay a room believed to be a shrine; numerous other rooms throughout the palace seem to have had religious functions, but there was no formal temple.

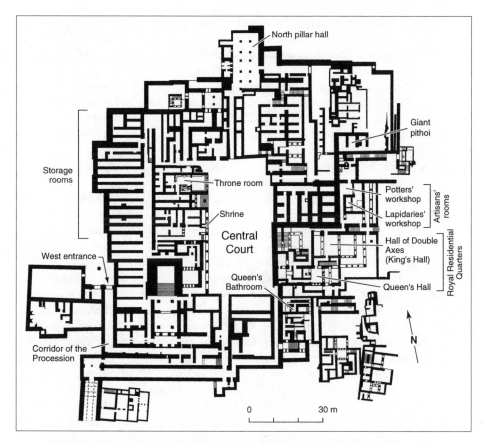

Figure 2.3. The Minoan palace of Knossos on Crete, a large multifunctional palace complex (redrawn from Michailidou 1989).

The Royal Compounds of Chan Chan, Peru

Among the New World's best examples of large multifunctional palace complexes are the *ciudadelas* or "great enclosures" of Chan Chan, a Chimú city on the north coast of Peru. Built between AD 1000 and 1400, each of the ten great enclosures is thought to have been the work of a single Chimú ruler (Day 1982; Moseley 1992).

The *ciudadelas* of Chan Chan range in size from 87,900 m^2 (the Rivero Compound) to 221,000 m^2 (the Gran Chimú Compound), making them many times larger than the Labyrinth of Knossos. Each is enclosed by adobe or *tapia* (pressed earth) walls up to 9 m in height, which separate it from the smaller compounds of the lesser nobles and the *kincha* (wattle-and-daub) houses of the commoners. The Rivero Compound, which can serve as an example, contained royal residential quarters, an elite burial platform, kitchens, walk-in wells, servants' quarters, "offices" for administrators, and abundant storerooms (fig. 2.4).

Traffic was rigorously controlled, and access to a *ciudadela* was often through a narrow, single-file entrance on the north side. (In the case of the Rivero Compound, access was made even more indirect by the presence of an annex north of the Main Compound.) Once inside the north sector of the *ciudadela,* the visitor reached a large "entry court" flanked by a kitchen, possible residential areas for administrators, a series of "offices," and standardized 2–4 m² storage units. These storage facilities could not be reached without passing through the "offices," each with its own U-shaped *audiencia* where an administrator is believed to have sat. Each *audiencia* was 5–6 m², had walls a meter thick, and was roofed (in contrast to most rooms on the virtually rainless desert coast).

This northern sector of the complex was separated from the more private central sector by a thick wall; one entered the central sector through a narrow doorway to a second entry court. In the case of the Rivero Compound, this court was flanked by a kitchen with a walk-in well and a series of storage units. The central sector, which housed the royal family, had more storerooms and fewer *audiencias* than the northern sector. It also had a huge burial platform with a ritual forecourt, built not only for the ruler's tomb but also for his relatives and sacrificial victims.

Finally, the southern sector of each *ciudadela* consisted of a *canchón* or huge, rectangular, walled courtyard accessible through a small doorway and a long, narrow corridor. Such walled courtyards are believed to have housed a large resident population of servants or retainers, living in wattle-and-daub structures that have since disintegrated. These commoners were probably considered part of the royal household.

Although the *ciudadelas* of Chan Chan have not yielded evidence of artisans' quarters like those of the Labyrinth of Knossos, there are suggestions of barrios of such artisans just outside (and associated with) most of the large compounds. Called "small irregularly agglutinated room complexes" by John Topic (1982), these commoners' barrios had grinding stones set in benches, storage vessels, copper ingots, copper scrap, hammers, beads, tweezers, spun and unspun cotton, yarn, loom parts, spindles, woodworking tools, and other signs of craft activity (Topic 1982:151).

An Early Dynastic Palace at Kish, Mesopotamia
In the ancient Near East, recognizable temple plans antedate recognizable palace plans by several millennia. The situation is thus analogous to Mesoamerica, where clear public buildings had already been built by the

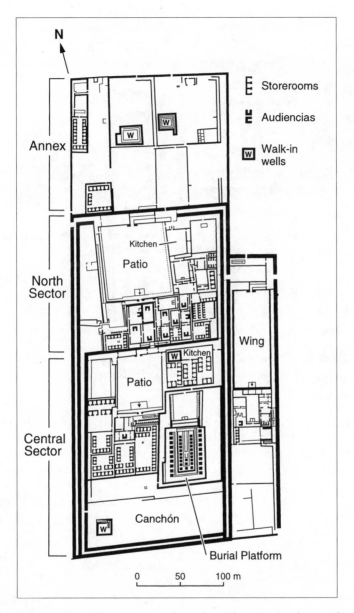

N

Annex

North
Sector

Central
Sector

Storerooms

Audiencias

Walk-in
wells

Kitchen

Patio

Wing

Kitchen

Patio

Canchón

Burial Platform

0   50   100 m

Figure 2.4. The Rivero Compound at Chan Chan, Peru, a large multi-functional palace complex (redrawn from Day 1982).

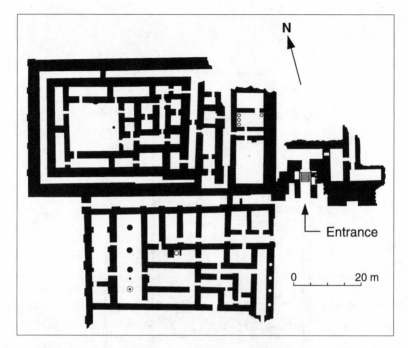

Figure 2.5. Ruins of Palace A at Kish in Mesopotamia, a complex and possibly multifunctional building (redrawn from Moorey 1978).

rank societies of the Formative period but indisputable palaces did not become common until the state had formed (Marcus and Flannery 1996).

There are hints of possible Uruk palaces at Uruk and Eridu, and by Early Dynastic times (third millennium BC) there is unmistakable evidence of palaces in the archaeological record. It is perhaps significant that two of the earliest examples are from Kish (Moorey 1978), since the ruler Mesalim of Kish (c. 2550 BC) is thought to have "exercised hegemony far beyond the walls of his own city." According to Diakonoff (1974:10), some Early Dynastic rulers of Kish called themselves "*lugal* [king] of the universe" and had supreme control over the rulers of other provinces, who were only allowed to use titles like *ensí* or *ensí-gar* (governor).

Palace A at Kish, built at no great distance from the city's temples, consists of at least two architectural units covering an area of perhaps 90 × 60 m (fig. 2.5). The larger of the two units was surrounded by a massive, buttressed defensive wall, which helped protect the royal residential quarters deep in the western portion of the building. The monumental entrance was on the southeast and led to offices and archives that had only indirect access to the royal apartments. The smaller of the two units was separated from the first by a narrow corridor and almost has the appearance of an annex. Deep in its interior was a decorated reception hall with large columns.

Governmental vs. Residential Palaces at Teotihuacán, Basin of Mexico

Building plans at Teotihuacán provide further support for the typology of palaces mentioned above: some large complexes appear to be administrative or governmental; others appear largely residential. It should be noted that many scholars have worked at Teotihuacán over the years, and not all agree on the functions of each building.

George Cowgill (1983) believes that the seat of government at Teotihuacán may have shifted over time. Early in the city's history it may have been near the Pyramid of the Sun; later it may have shifted to the Ciudadela (see below); still later it may have moved to the Avenue of the Dead Complex. I will restrict myself here to discussion of the Ciudadela, which includes a pair of structures referred to as the North and South Palaces (Millon 1973).

The Ciudadela is a walled enclosure 400 m on a side, east of the Avenue of the Dead. At least 15 minor temples frame the Ciudadela, whose interior is a vast sunken court. At the eastern limit of this court is a stepped pyramid called the Temple of Quetzalcoatl, "the Plumed Serpent." This building (actually the pyramidal platform for a now-vanished temple) is one of the best-known and most extensively explored religious complexes at Teotihuacán. Its oldest building stage dates to AD 150–200 (Cabrera Castro 1991). Recent excavations by Cabrera Castro, Sugiyama, and Cowgill (1991) show that more than 200 individuals, many with military paraphernalia, had been sacrificed during the pyramid's dedication.

Already at this period there were residential structures to either side of the pyramid. No plans are available for them, however, since they were later covered by the residential complexes known today as the North and South Palaces (fig. 2.6). These large twin palaces were built around AD 200–350, when the Temple of Quetzalcoatl had a second stage attached to its west face (enlarging it but covering its old façade).

Each of the twin palaces measures 80 m on a side and has an interior courtyard that probably served as a light-well. Around each courtyard are arranged five or six complexes of rooms with varying degrees of privacy. The need for space seems to have increased over time, since an annex (known as "Building 1C-prime") was later added in front of the North Palace.

Since Millon (1992) and Cowgill (1983) see the Ciudadela as the seat of government at Teotihuacán, they interpret these buildings as related to the administration of the city. If so, I believe these structures would qualify as

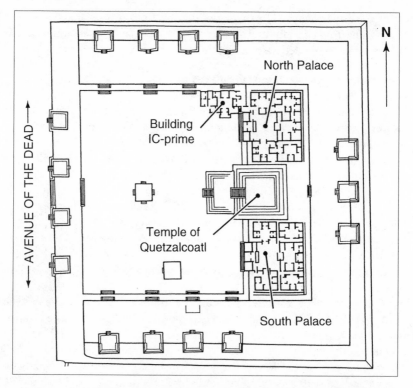

Figure 2.6. The Ciudadela at Teotihuacán, showing the Temple of Quetzalcoatl flanked by the North and South Palaces (redrawn from Cabrera Castro 1991). The Ciudadela is 400 m on a side. The "north" arrow actually points 15° 30' east of true north (the orientation of the city's major buildings), sometimes called "Teotihuacán north."

"governmental" rather than "residential" palaces. Other Basin of Mexico specialists, including William T. Sanders (personal communication 1994), have raised the possibility that the North and South Palaces housed the priestly staff associated with the Temple of Quetzalcoatl. This would imply a considerable temple staff, since both palaces are larger than the *gipar* of Ur (see below).

Such differences of interpretation are to be expected when dealing with early civilizations that had minimal separation of church and state. For example, the building at Uruk once called "Temple C" (Perkins 1949:fig. 16) is now believed by many to be an elite residence, if not an actual palace. As the anachronistic view of Teotihuacán as a theocracy gradually fades, it is likely that more structures will be seen as governmental rather than religious.

Let us turn now to residential palaces, or at least "palatial residences." Once again there are disagreements among Basin of Mexico scholars, and I am not sure that any of their interpretations will closely match mine.

Millon (1976) has made the point that everyone (or nearly everyone) at Teotihuacán lived in large, multiroomed residential complexes. These buildings usually presented heavy, rubble-cored masonry walls to the outside world, and Millon describes them as "multi-apartment" compounds because so many are divided into noninterconnecting units. Both Millon (1976) and Manzanilla (1993) emphasize that these compounds differ greatly in size, layout, and elegance. Oztoyahualco (Manzanilla, ed. 1993) and Tlajinga 33 (Widmer and Storey 1993) could probably be described as housing "commoners." Tlamimilolpa (Linné 1942), large and clearly divided into multiple apartments, probably housed artisans and their families.

At the more elegant end of the continuum, however, are compounds that I regard as housing extended families of the hereditary nobility. These structures seem to include royal or noble apartments (access to which was controlled), one or more private temple complexes, and numerous rooms that could be for servants, retainers, and other staff. Often the walls of important rooms in these complexes were decorated with polychrome murals of mythological scenes, thematically and stylistically consistent throughout a unit of rooms. I believe that such elegant complexes were essentially residential rather than administrative. Thus they would be more analogous to the Palace of Nestor at Pylos (see below) than to the Labyrinth of Knossos.

Most palatial compounds date to AD 200–600. Techinantitla, the largest so far excavated, may once have measured 100 × 105 m, or more than 10,000 m^2. It also has the largest temple of any such compound, 12 × 20 m in extent. So spectacular were the murals associated with this palace that many were stolen within days of their having been discovered; a substantial number wound up in a museum in California (Millon 1988; Millon and Sugiyama 1991). Some of the best-known (and most completely reconstructed) palaces, such as Tetitla, Xolalpan, Yayahuala, and Zacuala, measure 1,300–3,600 m^2 and have temples that are 10–15 m on a side (Manzanilla 1993). Some of the largest palatial compounds lie very close to the Avenue of the Dead—the city's main north-south axis—while smaller compounds often lie thousands of meters away. There are hints that some compounds housed royalty; others, major nobility; and still others, minor nobility, although we still have no reliable way of drawing lines between such categories at Teotihuacán.

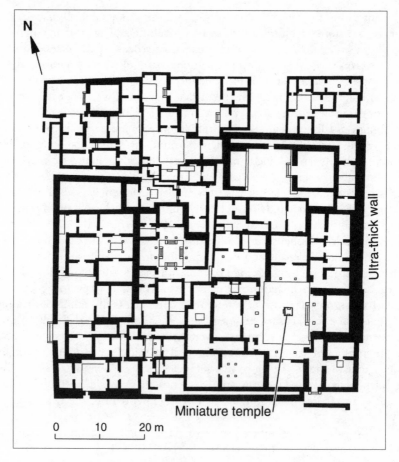

Figure 2.7. Tetitla, a palatial residential complex at Teotihuacán (redrawn from Manzanilla 1993). The arrow points to true north.

Figure 2.7 shows Tetitla, a palatial compound published by Séjourné (1966). The thickest walls enclose an area of 30 × 45 m on the east side, probably the apartments of the highest-ranking residents. In the center of the largest patio in this area sits a miniature temple on a miniature pyramid. This patio could be reached only by indirect routes, either from the center of the complex or by an L-shaped corridor that passes what may be (by analogy with Old World palaces) a guard room.

Near the center of Tetitla is a second, smaller patio surrounded by four rooms with columned entrances. Annexed to the north side of the building are smaller room complexes that could have accommodated a large number of servants or retainers. Since one could not enter the main compound directly from these northern room complexes, it is likely that they were for staff members who only needed access to the interior during the day.

As mentioned above, the royal compounds at Chan Chan were surrounded by relatively ephemeral structures that housed artisans. Recent discoveries in the La Ventilla district of Teotihuacán suggest that a similar patron/client relationship may have existed between noble families and commoner artisans there. La Ventilla lies not far west of the Ciudadela and consists of a "neighborhood" in which several compounds are separated only by narrow alleys. At least one compound, unstuccoed and less elegant, seems to have been occupied by commoner craftsmen working with a wide variety of raw materials. Their higher-status patrons may have lived in a more elegant, stuccoed, red-and-white painted compound just across the alley. I look forward to the eventual publication of La Ventilla by Rubén Cabrera Castro, Sergio Gómez, and Nestor Paredes.

The Palace of Nestor at Pylos, Greece

During the late second millennium BC, Pylos in southwestern Greece was the capital city of the Mycenaean king Nestor. Nestor's well-preserved palace, measuring roughly 54 × 30 m, appears to be a royal household without the complexities of the earlier Labyrinth (Taylour 1983:87–97).

Entry was from the southeast by means of the *propylon*, an entrance with an inner and outer porch, each supported by a single column. On the right was a guard room. To the left of the *propylon* was an archive where the taxes due the royal household, and the manpower and materials allotted by the government, were all recorded (fig. 2.8).

From the *propylon* one reached a large court that gave access to other parts of the palace: left to a waiting room, straight ahead to what the excavator considers the king's *megaron*, right to the queen's apartments. The waiting room, which was just to the left of the columned porch leading to the king's *megaron*, was designed to allow the visitor to wash and have a little wine before meeting the king. There were large storage jars (*pithoi*) in the waiting room, and thousands of drinking cups (*kylikes*) stored in the pantries just beyond.

A vestibule with wall frescoes gave access to the king's *megaron*, a great audience hall with four tall, fluted columns set around a "great hearth" on a raised circular bench; Nestor's throne was set against the northeast wall of this room. It is likely that the king's private apartments were on the now-destroyed second floor of the palace, reached by a stairway to the right of the vestibule. Flanking the *megaron* were corridors that gave access to storage rooms and pantries in the rear and sides of the palace. The double

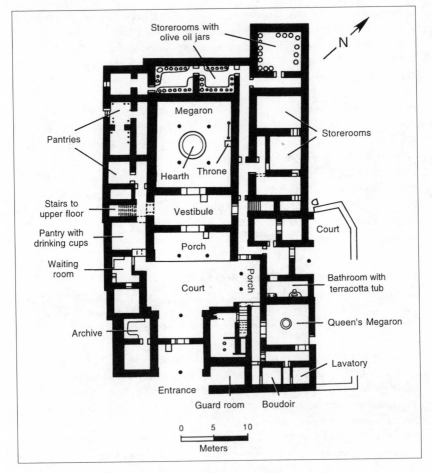

Figure 2.8. The palace of Nestor at Pylos, a Mycenaean royal residence (redrawn from Taylour 1983).

storage room in the rear had vast supplies of olive oil in heavy *pithoi* sunk in the ground; one of the pantries on the southwest had the broken stems of 2,853 drinking cups. We can assume a staff of household servants, but there is no evidence of artisans' quarters within the palace.

The supposed queen's apartments, occupying the eastern corner of the building, were reached by a columned porch and a narrow corridor that limited traffic. The queen apparently had her own *megaron*, a boudoir, and a lavatory. A larger bathroom with a terracotta bathtub, not directly accessible from the queen's apartments, seems to have been for more general use by the residents of the palace.

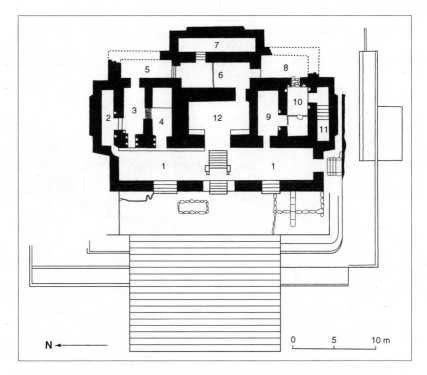

Figure 2.9. Structure III at Calakmul, Mexico, an Early Classic Maya palace (redrawn from Folan et al. 1995).

A Maya Palace from Calakmul, Mexico

It is not known precisely when the palace first appeared in the Maya Lowlands (Marcus 1995a:13). Ongoing research at Copán, Honduras, by Loa Traxler (1996) suggests that some early Maya palaces may have been built of adobe, which does not preserve well in the rainy lowlands.

One of the earliest stone masonry palaces from the Lowland Maya area is Structure III at Calakmul, a major center of the Early Classic (Folan, Marcus, Pincemin et al. 1995). This bilaterally symmetrical building measures 17 × 26 m and is divided into a dozen rooms. It sits on a 5-m-high platform with an impressive stairway, and in its original state it had elaborate roof combs, vaulted ceilings, and small, windowlike ventilators that promoted the circulation of air. The doorways of some rooms were provided with cordholders for draperies that afforded privacy (Marcus 1987a:29–33).

Structure III is shown in figure 2.9. Tentatively, we can suggest that Rooms 2–5 and 8–11 might have been residential, while Room 12 was a main entrance hall of some kind. Room 7, at the rear of the palace, occupied a position not unlike that of the throne room of the Royal Villa of

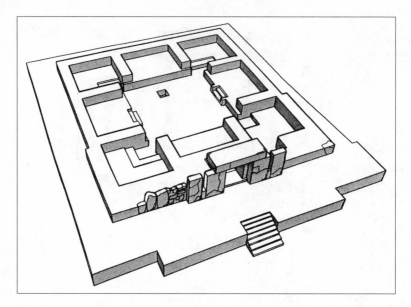

Figure 2.10. A small residential palace at the Zapotec city of Monte Albán, Oaxaca, Mexico (redrawn from Marcus and Flannery 1996).

Knossos (below). This Lowland Maya palace, like the Zapotec palaces of Monte Albán, appears to be a royal residence largely unaccompanied by servants' and artisans' quarters.

The Zapotec Palaces of Oaxaca, Mexico

The Zapotec of Oaxaca, Mexico, apparently had several kinds of palatial structures. The largest seem to have been "governmental" palaces, designed for elite assembly and the affairs of state rather than residential quarters (Marcus and Flannery 1996:179). Such governmental structures had colonnaded porticos and large sunken patios, reached after ascending grand staircases.

More clearly residential are the smaller palaces of Monte Albán, which generally consist of a dozen or so rooms on a low rectangular platform. Often measuring 20–25 m on a side, these residential palaces have an interior courtyard that served as a light-well. They were afforded privacy by a "curtain wall" that obstructed an outsider's view of the interior and made entry into the palace indirect. Often built of adobes above a stone foundation, they could have an elaborate façade with huge stones weighing several tons forming the jambs and lintel of the doorway. In many cases there was also a royal tomb beneath the floor (fig. 2.10).

While such residential palaces may have had space for a small number of servants, unlike some Old World palaces they do not seem to have room for

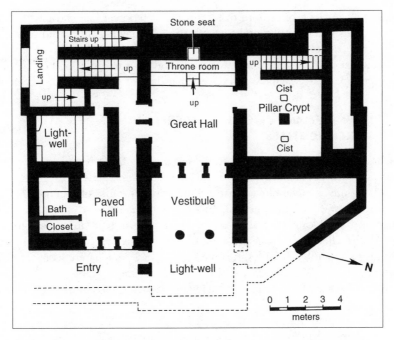

Figure 2.11. The Royal Villa at Knossos, a small Minoan residential palace (redrawn from Michailidou 1989).

resident craft specialists. Rather, these Zapotec palaces seem to have been more like the Royal Villa of Knossos (below).

The Royal Villa of Knossos
A short distance northeast of the labyrinthine Palace of Knossos lies the Royal Villa (fig. 2.11). This smaller structure, like the Zapotec palaces of southern Mexico, appears to be purely residential; it lacks the craft quarters and extensive storage areas of the "House of the Double Axes."

Measuring roughly 18 × 10 m, the villa originally had three stories. Entry was from the east via the large, unroofed light-well. This room, which provided sunlight for the building's interior, was the first in a line of four rooms forming the east-west axis of the villa. From here the visitor stepped between columns into the vestibule, passed through one of three doors into the *megaron* or great hall, and climbed three steps to the throne room with its formal stone seat.

Residential quarters of the Royal Villa were mostly on the upper two floors, each reached by its own stairway. The ground floor of these quarters, lying south of the great hall, had a paved hall, a closet, a bath, and another light-well. At least one room to the north of the great hall was devoted to ritual. This was the pillar crypt or cult room, its ceiling supported by huge split tree trunks laid horizontally and resting partly on a centrally placed rectangular pillar. There were two cists in the floor to either side of the pillar, presumably receptacles for poured libations.

TEMPLES AND PRIESTS' RESIDENCES IN ARCHAIC STATES

Shrines and temples were present long before the rise of the state—indeed, from the beginnings of sedentary life in some parts of the world. In some regions, temples already had a standardized ground plan centuries before states and palaces appeared. In Mesopotamia, that ground plan took the form of a long central room with an altar and podium, flanked by rows of smaller rooms. On the coast of Peru, many early temples took the form of a block U. Temples in some regions had an apparent astronomical orientation: in Mesoamerica it was the *sides* of the temple that faced the cardinal points, whereas in Mesopotamia it was the *corners* of the temple (see below).

While chiefdoms might use corvée labor to build their temples, only the most complex had full-time priests supported by tithes or tribute. Many archaic states had not only full-time priests, but also special residences for them; the existence of such priestly residential quarters may signal the presence of a state. For example, in Mesoamerica one-room temples gave way to two-room temples by the first century BC. Although worshipers could come to the outer room, priests sometimes lived in the inner room and often had their own entrance or stairway, separate from that of the public (Marcus and Flannery 1996:181–94). In other regions, such as Mesopotamia, there were separate priests' residences (like the *gipar* of Ur) not far from the temple.

Some state religions had a hierarchy in which high priests (or priestesses) were members of the nobility, while minor priests were trained commoners. In no archaic state have we discovered the full range of residences lived in by major and minor priests. All we can say is that convincing "priests' residences" are more likely to occur in states than in chiefdoms.

Once again, the presence of standardized temples and priests' residences in states should be considered only a rule of thumb. Some possible archaic states, like those of the Aegean, even lack standardized temples. They relied instead on features called "shrines," "shrine rooms," or "cult centers" by Aegean archaeologists.

Let us now look at a sample of temples and priests' residences from archaic states, beginning with those having the most formal ground plans.

The Temples of Mesopotamia's First State

In Mesopotamia, as in Mesoamerica and the Andes, temples with a consistent orientation and recognizable ground plan appeared long before the first state. By 4000 BC, their builders had developed a standardized tripartite plan (fig. 2.12a). The main axis of the temple was a long central sanctuary with an altar at one end and a podium or "offering table" near the other, anticipating the *cella* of later temples. To either side of this central axis were rows of smaller rooms. External decoration took the form of buttresses and recesses in the mud-brick walls; internal decoration took the form of plaster and paint. Ritual artifacts suggest that libations were poured from special vessels, and that incense was burned in terracotta censers with pierced openings.

When the city of Uruk emerged as the capital of Mesopotamia's first state around 3500 BC (see Wright, this volume), we begin to see multiple temple precincts within the same urban area. The White Temple in the Anu precinct at Uruk, so-called because of its repeated layers of gypsum whitewash, was built on a high platform of mud bricks held together with bitumen or natural asphalt. Measuring 22 × 18 m, it had the standard orientation of most early Mesopotamian temples: its corners faced the cardinal points (fig. 2.12b).

The diversity of temples and temple precincts at Uruk—too numerous to be described in an essay of this length—strongly suggests that we are dealing with a familiar Sumerian pattern: the dedication of multiple temples to a variety of deities, with the city's "patron deity" having the grandest temple. Our data from Uruk, however, are insufficient to identify the deities involved.

Priests' Residences in Mesopotamian States

Just as it is difficult to pin down the emergence of the first Mesopotamian palace, it is hard to identify the first residences of full-time priests. Safar et al. (1981) have reported a series of plastered and painted residences near the Uruk-period temples at Eridu, thought to be associated with the latter (Crawford 1991:78). These structures have the same orientation as the temple, with their corners facing the cardinal points. To some, they are priest's residences. To others, they may be parts of an early palace, though whether "governmental" or "residential" is unknown.

One of the most interesting "priest's residences" of the Early Dynastic II period (c. 2700 BC) is House D, inside the Temple Oval at Khafajah (ancient Tutub). Here the occupants of the Diyala River region enclosed their temple with concentric walls, tucking House D into the northern corner between the inner and outer walls (Delougaz 1940). Its association with the temple is so close that, during House D's original construction phase, it could only have been reached by someone who had already entered the outer entry court of the walled oval. (Significantly, during the house's second construction

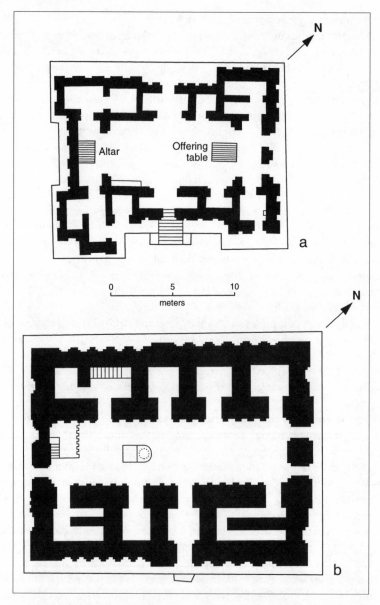

Figure 2.12. Early Mesopotamian temples: a, *Temple VII at Eridu, a prestate temple of the ʿUbaid period (c. 4000 BC) that already has the tripartite plan of later Mesopotamian temples (redrawn from Safar, Mustafa, and Lloyd 1981);* b, *the White Temple in the Anu precinct at Uruk, capital of an early Mesopotamian state (redrawn from Perkins 1949).*

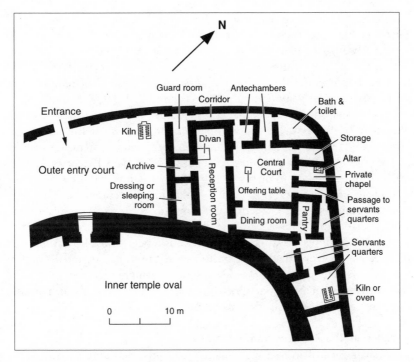

Figure 2.13. The plan of House D, a possible "high priest's residence" within the walls of the Early Dynastic Temple Oval at Khafajah (ancient Tutub), Iraq. Room functions are those suggested by Delougaz (1940).

stage, access to the outer entry court was blocked, and a new entrance was cut through the wall of the oval to the street outside.)

Figure 2.13 shows the initial layout of House D. Roughly 30 × 40 m in extent (but fitted into the irregular space between the oval's walls), the house was entered by a small door that led the visitor past a guard room to a narrow access corridor. Off this corridor were two antechambers; one was flanked by a bath and toilet where visitors could refresh (or, more likely, purify) themselves. This done, they could enter the building's central court, perhaps pouring libations at its offering table.

The central court was a major hub for traffic within House D. To its south lay the priest's reception room, complete with a divan on which he could receive visitors. Behind the reception room were his archive and dressing/sleeping room. East of the court was a dining room, and behind it a pantry with access to the servants' quarters. To the north of the central court lay a storage room, the priest's private chapel, and an L-shaped passage leading to the servants' quarters. The latter consisted of three rooms east of the pantry, one of which contained a kiln or oven.

House D looks so much like a miniature palace that it must have been for a very high priest, possibly drawn from a family of some importance. In some Early Dynastic states there were strong ties between the civil and religious hierarchies, and as we have seen, city rulers sometimes appointed their heirs apparent to the position of *sanga,* or manager of the temple estate of the city's patron deity (Cooper 1983; Tyumenev 1969:9).

In later periods Mesopotamia had very large priestly residences, like the *gipar* of Ur, which was set aside for the high priestess of the moon god Nanna. The temple to Nanna lay atop a huge ziggurat, or stepped pyramid, and the *gipar* built by the ruler Amar-Sin of the Ur III dynasty (2046–2038 BC) measured 75 m on a side. The *gipar* contained a temple dedicated to Ningal—female consort of Nanna—plus an elite residence for the high priestess, complete with kitchens, bathrooms, storerooms, ceremonial rooms, and a burial crypt (Oates 1986; Postgate 1992; Woolley and Moorey 1982). High priestess of Nanna was a very prestigious office, whose holder received the title *en*—a word that, since Protoliterate times, had denoted nobility. Sargon of Akkad (2334–2279 BC) sent his own daughter Enheduanna to be the *en*-priestess of Nanna at Ur, beginning a tradition of royal nepotism there that continued for half a millennium (Oates 1986:39).

Temples of the Zapotec and Maya States

In Mesoamerica, as in Mesopotamia, temples preceded both the rise of the state and the first clear palaces (Marcus 1978, 1983b; Marcus and Flannery 1996). Most prestate temples, however, had only one room. With the rise of the state in the Valley of Oaxaca, the Basin of Mexico, and the Maya Lowlands, it became common to see two-room temples built to a relatively standard plan. Such temples, in which a state religion was carried out, had a more sacred inner room in which the priests performed their rites, and a less sacred outer room to which worshipers could come.

Figure 2.14a shows an early Zapotec temple from Monte Albán, Oaxaca, dating to the first century AD. Measuring 8 × 10 m, this temple stood on an elevated platform and had two rooms whose doorways were flanked by columns. As is typical of the Zapotec, the inner room was 15 cm higher and had a narrower doorway. Stone models of Zapotec temples show that some had their outer doorways closed with draperies or feather curtains (Marcus and Flannery 1996: fig. 267).

Lowland Maya temples, like the one from Chichén Itzá shown in figure 2.14b, were similar to their Zapotec counterparts. A few, however, like the Temple of the Cross at Palenque, might have three enclosed spaces, each room smaller and more private than the one outside it (fig. 2.14c). Such temples were often set on tall, steep-sided pyramids, further reducing accessibility to those who were not priests or members of the nobility.

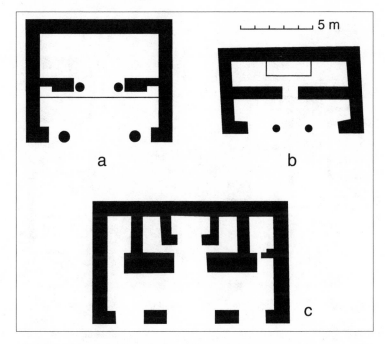

Figure 2.14. Plans of temples from Mesoamerican states: a, Zapotec temple on Mound X at Monte Albán, Oaxaca, Mexico, discovered by Caso (1935); b, Maya temple at Chichén Itzá, Yucatán, Mexico (redrawn from Marcus 1978); c, the Temple of the Cross at Palenque, Chiapas, Mexico (redrawn from Marcus 1978).

Temples and Possible Priests' Residences at Teotihuacán

At the city of Teotihuacán in the Basin of Mexico, typical Mesoamerican two-room temples were present by the thousands, suggesting that every unit of society may have had its own set. Some of the most important temples—those crowning the great Pyramids of the Sun and Moon—have unfortunately been lost to erosion or nineteenth-century excavation. Still surviving around the bases of those pyramids are room complexes, presumably occupied by the priests who maintained the temples.

The relationship between temples and priests' residences is relatively clear in the Conjunto Plaza Oeste (Morelos García 1991), a small temple group that formed part of the larger "Avenue of the Dead Complex" (fig. 2.15). Reached by a stairway leading west from the avenue, the Conjunto Plaza Oeste consisted of a stuccoed patio with an adoratory (similar to the feature that Mesopotamian archaeologists call an "offering table"); a columned entry between twin residential units; pyramidal mounds on the

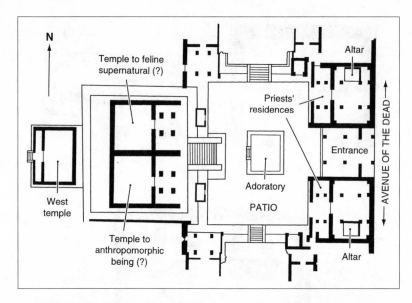

Figure 2.15. The Conjunto Plaza Oeste at Teotihuacán, Mexico, which contains both temples and priests' residences (redrawn from Morelos García 1991; no scale in original). The "north" arrow actually points 15° 30' east of true north (the orientation of the city's major buildings), sometimes called "Teotihuacán north."

north and south; and a large pyramid on the west, thought originally to have borne twin temples. The main building stages of the pyramid are thought to run from AD 100–200 to 500.

Privacy was achieved by having the interior patio serve as the point of entry for all buildings. The twin residential units, presumably for the temple staff, were mirror images of each other; both had prominent altars and traces of paint on their walls. The one on the north contained a stone sculpture of a jaguar or puma, whereas the one on the south had anthropomorphic sculptures. Collapsed stucco friezes elsewhere in the complex reinforce this dichotomy, suggesting to Morelos García that the temples had complementary roles. If Teotihuacán's temples (like those of some Old World states) were dedicated to different deities, different rituals, or different dates in the sacred calendar, it could explain why the city had so many.

The Temples of Peruvian Coastal States
Just as Mesopotamia had a long tradition of tripartite temples with a central *cella* and rows of flanking rooms, the Peruvian coast had a long tradition of

temples in the form of a block U. Such temples were already present in the preceramic era (Donnan 1985), and by the time of the earliest coastal states their location had been raised to the summit of stepped pyramids. Often the temple staff occupied a residential compound behind the *huaca*, or sacred pyramid.

During Peru's Middle Horizon (AD 600–900), the site of Pacatnamú is believed to have been a temple center for the north coast, both the site of an oracle and a destination for religious pilgrimages (Donnan and Cock 1986: 19; Keatinge 1982). More than 35 truncated pyramids cover an area of 1 km^2 overlooking the sea. The largest pyramids (Type A) are up to 13 m high and have multiple terraces with access ramps, altars, associated plazas, and side platforms. Other pyramids (Type B) are smaller but still have platforms, plazas, ramps, and accessory room complexes. Finally, there are more than 65 smaller structures (Type C) with U-shaped temples that can be approached at ground level. The great differences in size and complexity among the temples and shrines at Pacatnamú recall those of some Mesopotamian cities, where the temple of the city's patron deity was the largest, the temple of his female consort was smaller, and the temples of other deities were smaller still (Diakonoff 1969, 1974).

Figure 2.16 gives the layout of one of the larger (Type A) temples at Pacatnamú, with its forecourt, side platform, altar, and stepped pyramid. Behind the pyramid was the probable residential compound of the temple staff. One such compound—whose inner court could be reached only after a circuitous trip down narrow corridors, and through doorways shielded by curtain walls—had two U-shaped *audiencias* like those of the *ciudadelas* at Chan Chan. The floor of one of those *audiencias* was covered with crushed *Spondylus* shell. This suggests that it had been used by a hereditary lord, since crushed seashell dust was used to prepare surfaces for Andean lords to walk upon (Keatinge 1982:216; Rowe 1946:47).

Minoan and Mycenaean "Shrines"

Not every culture with large, elaborate palaces also had formal standardized temples. In contrast to their neighbors in Egypt and Mesopotamia, the Minoans and Mycenaeans of the eastern Mediterranean region "built no great temples and carved no large statues of their deities" (Graham 1987:19). That is not to say, however, that they did not produce recognizable and fairly standardized ritual spaces. According to Graham (1987:18),

> we seem scarcely able to move in the Palace of Minos . . . without running into small shrines or small representations of deities or their symbols: lustral chambers, pillar crypts, columnar shrines, temple repositories, incurved altars, sacral horns, double axes, libation tables . . .

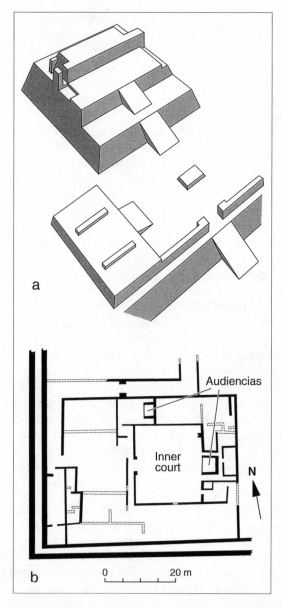

Figure 2.16. Temple and "priests' residence" from Pacatnamú, Peru: a, Type A temple with its forecourt, side platform, altar, and stepped pyramid; b, "priest's residence" with its private inner court and audiencias (redrawn from Keatinge 1982).

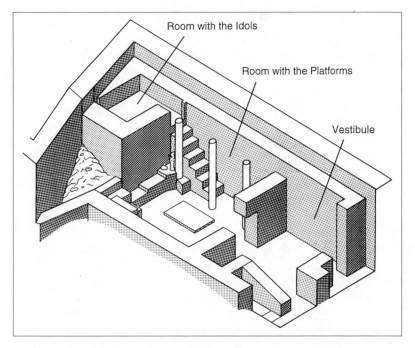

Room with the Idols

Room with the Platforms

Vestibule

Figure 2.17. "Cult Area" from the foot of the acropolis at Mycenae in Greece (redrawn from Taylour 1983).

The later Mycenaeans also seem to have set aside certain rooms within their palaces as sacred places and built recognizable but unstandardized shrines, "cult centers," and sanctuaries (see for example Renfrew 1985). There are hints that these features might lack standardization because each was a shrine to a different member of a pantheon, since—as pointed out by Taylour (1983)—some of the later Greek deities are already detectable in Mycenaean art.

Two "cult areas" were found at the foot of the acropolis of Mycenae itself, just within the cyclopean walls of the citadel. One of these (somewhat optimistically called a "temple" by Taylour 1983:51), consists of three stone masonry rooms: the Vestibule, the Room with the Platforms (5.1 × 4.3 m), and the Room with the Idols (1.8 × 1.8 m) (fig. 2.17). On one of the platforms that gave the second room its name lay a female idol 60 cm high. In the Room with the Idols, reached by a small stairway, were found more than 20 additional idols (both male and female), as well as snake effigies, libation bowls, and drinking cups.

ROYAL TOMBS IN ARCHAIC STATES

One of the most frequently used clues to the existence of kings and queens is the presence of royal tombs. Unfortunately, tombs are somewhat slippery clues because there is no clear-cut distinction between the burial of a king and the burial of a paramount chief. Some paramount chiefs in Panama, for example, were buried atop a layer of 20 or more sacrificed retainers, accompanied by gold jewelry (Lothrop 1937).

Most chiefly societies have a continuum of statuses without a clear division into class-endogamous social strata, and hence no true "commoners." In some highly advanced chiefdoms, however, such as protohistoric Hawai'i, a commoner class was created by severing kin ties to the lower-ranking families (Kirch 1984:258). In states, the gap between noble and commoner is larger; indeed, in some kingdoms the difference between the tomb of the king and the tombs of the minor nobles below him can become so great that the latter appear "middle class" by comparison (Marcus 1992b:221).

Taken alone, spectacular tombs are usually insufficient evidence for a state. However, when they occur beneath the floor of a palace in a society with a four-tiered hierarchy, they can represent an additional line of evidence—especially when their construction involves considerable corvée labor and the offerings represent a quantum leap in elegance beyond those of previous chiefdoms in the same region. We will look now at a sample of tombs that might qualify.

Mesopotamian Royal Tombs

The earliest possible "royal tombs" in Mesopotamia come from Level X of Tepe Gawra in northern Iraq (Tobler 1950). They belong to the Gawran phrase, roughly equivalent in time to the Uruk period in southern Mesopotamia. Unfortunately, these tombs present many of the same problems as the spectacular interments of the "lords of Sipán" on the north coast of Peru (see below). That is, although they clearly reflect a society with enormous differences in hereditary status, we still have a lot to learn about the details of that society. Once we know more about the size of the largest relevant sites, the number of levels in the settlement hierarchy, and the nature of elite residences and public buildings, we will be able to speak more confidently about whether Gawran society was an archaic state or a maximal chiefdom.

The Gawran tombs, built of mud brick with wooden roofs, had spectacular sumptuary goods of gold, electrum, copper, turquoise, lapis lazuli, jadeite, hematite, carnelian, obsidian, marble, steatite, and ivory. One tomb had more than 25,000 beads, and many skeletons had ornaments on the head, neck, hands, wrists, waist, knees, or ankles. There were ivory combs and hairpins, possible gold handles for fans, gold rosettes with lapis lazuli centers, and vessels of marble, serpentine, and obsidian.

By the time of the Royal Tombs of Ur—thought to contain the remains of rulers of the Early Dynastic period—there is no longer any doubt that we are dealing with an archaic state. The most often cited tombs are those of a king possibly named A-bar-gi(?) and his queen, variously called Shub-ad or Pu-abi(?). His tomb had been plundered, but her body lay on a wooden bier or litter in a vaulted chamber (Woolley 1934). In a "Death Pit" associated with the royal pair were more than 60 attendants, who are thought to have willingly accompanied them in death. Included were two wagons drawn by three oxen each and attended by drivers and grooms; all the animals, drivers, and grooms had been sacrificed in place. Although most of the sacrificed attendants were women, there also were six men in military helmets laid to rest on the entry ramp to the Death Pit. Gold, silver, copper, and shell artifacts accompanied the queen's corpse, and at least a few of the attendants were musicians accompanied by harps (fig. 2.18).

These royal burials at Ur may be contrasted with those of "minor nobles" or "well-to-do commoners" at the same site. Such individuals were wrapped in matting or given a coffin of basketwork, wood, or clay, accompanied by personal belongings that (in the case of some bureaucrats) included their administrative seals (Woolley 1934).

Andean Royal Tombs

Andeanists currently believe that the pristine state for their region was Moche society, which from the first to the eighth centuries AD held sway over an estimated 550 km of the Peruvian coast. They are probably right, but except for Wilson's (1995) analysis of Casma Valley settlement patterns, little has been done to confirm the existence of a four-tiered hierarchy in Moche times, nor do we as yet have the ground plans of palaces for Moche "kings."

With the excavation of the "Royal Tombs of Sipán" by Alva and Donnan (1993) in Peru's Lambayeque Valley, we now have Moche interments as spectacular as the Royal Tombs of Ur. Tomb 2 of Sipán, buried deep within a mud-brick pyramid, can serve as an example (fig. 2.19).

The principal figure in the tomb chamber, a 35- to 45-year-old male, was buried fully extended in a plank coffin. Wearing nose and ear ornaments of gold, silver, and turquoise, he was accompanied by hundreds of copper discs, thousands of shell beads, copper bells, copper slippers, gilded copper necklaces of human-head beads, and a massive "owl headdress" of gilded copper.

The tomb also included possible members of the ruler's family. To his far left, in a cane coffin, was a male 14 to 17 years old buried with two large copper discs. Lying at the ruler's feet was a smaller cane coffin with a child of 8 to 10 years buried with a copper headdress; sharing his coffin were a sacrificed dog and snake. To the ruler's immediate left, apparently buried

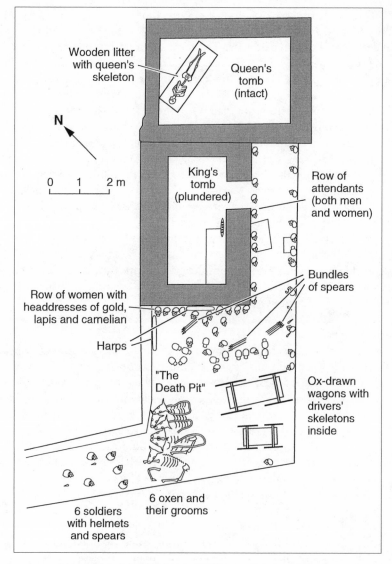

Figure 2.18. The royal tombs of King A-bar-gi(?) and Queen Shub-ad or Pu-abi(?) at Ur, southern Mesopotamia (redrawn from Woolley 1934).

without a coffin, was a 19- to 25-year-old woman wrapped in a textile with discs of gilded copper sewn to it. She also had a large copper headdress.

A number of additional humans and animals had been sacrificed at the ruler's death. To his right lay an 18- to 22-year-old woman sprawled face

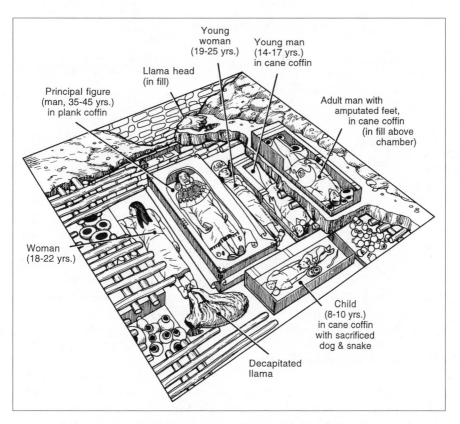

Figure 2.19. Tomb 2 at Sipán, Peru, the burial of a Moche lord with possible family members and/or retainers (redrawn from Alva and Donnan 1993).

down with no grave goods, perhaps a servant or retainer. Near her feet was a decapitated llama with its feet tied together. A llama head (which might have come from the decapitated animal) was found in the fill above the tomb roof. Also in this fill was a cane coffin containing an adult male whose feet had been cut off at the ankles; he was accompanied by a feather headdress with a large copper shaft, a copper crown, and numerous gourd containers, all preserved by the aridity of the Peruvian coast.

Surrounding the tomb chamber were hundreds of ceramic vessels plus offerings that included human hands and feet, "quite possibly the trophies taken from sacrificed prisoners whose bodies were dismembered, exactly as shown in Moche art" (Alva and Donnan 1993:165). Thus, while the Early Dynastic citizens of Ur thought it appropriate to sacrifice the rulers' servants and bodyguards, the Moche included in their royal tombs the body parts of sacrificed enemies.

While we are only beginning to glimpse the splendor of Moche tombs, we have abundant data on the royal burials of the later Chimú. One of the standard features of the *ciudadelas* or palatial complexes at Chan Chan on the northern Peruvian coast were massive burial platforms (Conrad 1982). Each was a truncated pyramidal mound of adobe or pressed earth, ranging in size from 52 X 34 m to 190 X 90 m and in height from 3.5 m to more than 12 m. Walls enclosed (and reduced access to) each burial mound, and the summit was reached by a series of earthen ramps whose entry point was a nearby forecourt (fig. 2.20).

All the Chan Chan platforms contained a series of burial or offering cells, the number varying from 15 to more than 100. The principal cell, usually T-shaped and centrally located, was probably the resting place of the Chimú ruler (unfortunately, many of these had been looted). The surrounding cells, usually smaller and rectangular, may have contained noble relatives of the king, as well as sacrificial victims. The majority of the latter were women, believed on ethnohistoric grounds to include numerous "virgins of the sun," like those documented at the time of the Spanish Conquest. Crushed shells of *Spondylus,* or spiny oyster, were placed on the floors of many cells. As at the temples at Pacatnámu (see p. 43, this volume), such cells were probably destined for members of royal or noble families.

Because some cells contained more than a dozen skeletons, Conrad (1982:99) estimates that the burial platform of one *ciudadela,* the Laberinto Compound, may have had 200 to 300 burials before it was looted. The areas least affected by looting had high concentrations of prestige goods, including fine textiles and pottery, carved wood, metal, and *Spondylus* shell; there were also sacrificed llamas below some cell floors.

Because of the high numbers of possible relatives, servants, retainers, and sacrificial victims included in the Chan Chan burial platforms, they probably provide our best New World analogy for the Royal Tombs of Ur. They were among the last features in a Chimú compound to be built, but virtually every compound seems to have space set aside for one.

Royal Tombs of the Zapotec and Maya

In both the Zapotec and Maya regions of Mesoamerica, rulers were laid to rest in stone masonry tombs. Some of the more elaborate tombs had mural paintings, were closed with carved door stones, and could be reached only by subterranean stairways. In both areas, royal tombs have been found beneath buildings with a palace ground plan as well as buildings with a temple ground plan.

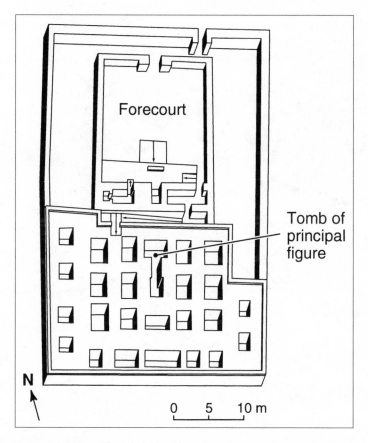

Figure 2.20. Royal burial platform from the Laberinto Compound at Chan Chan, Peru (redrawn from Conrad 1982).

One of the most famous Zapotec interments was Monte Albán's Tomb 104, dating to roughly AD 500–600. Here archaeologists found a single, fully extended skeleton with a funerary urn and four "companion figures" laid at its feet. The tomb was closed by a door stone carved on both sides with hieroglyphic text; a large funerary sculpture occupied a niche in the tomb's façade. The main chamber had been equipped with five wall niches for offerings; dozens of pottery vessels occupied the niches and overflowed onto the floor. The left, rear, and right walls of the tomb were covered with polychrome murals referring to royal ancestors of the deceased (Marcus 1983c:140–43; Marcus and Flannery 1996:212–16).

At Calakmul in the Lowland Maya region, a masonry tomb was

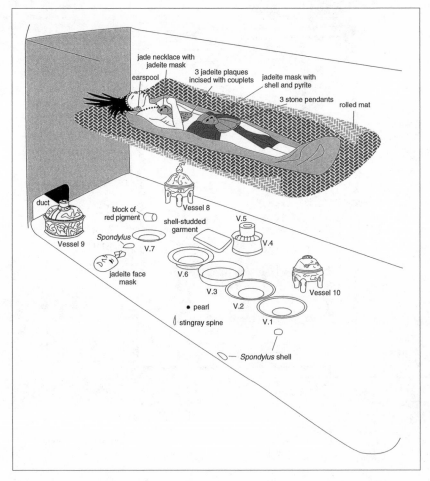

Figure 2.21. Tomb 1 from Structure III, Calakmul, Mexico, the burial of a Maya lord (redrawn from Folan et al. 1995). Vertical distances have been exaggerated to show the offerings.

intrusive through the floor of Room 6 of Structure III, the palace already described above. Called Tomb 1, it contained the skeleton of a man at least 30 years of age, lying fully extended in a rolled mat (fig. 2.21). His wrapped body had been placed on five dishes that elevated him above the floor; more elaborate vessels had been set around the skeleton. The most spectacular offerings were three jade mosaic masks—one originally made for his face, one for his chest, and a third for his belt. Spiny oyster shell, a stingray spine, and a pearl were included as offerings. The tomb also had been equipped with a

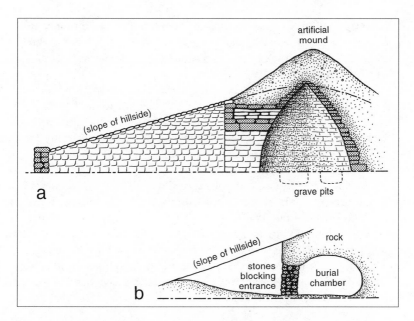

Figure 2.22. Mycenaean tombs: a, *ashlar masonry* tholos *appropriate for a royal family;* b, *cavern excavated in bedrock, appropriate for a noble or wealthy commoner (redrawn from Taylour 1983).*

"psychoduct" through which the spirit of the deceased ruler could leave and return (Folan et al. 1995).

Mycenaean Royal Tombs

Aegean archaeologists are not in agreement as to whether Mycenaean society was a large state or something less (see discussion in Marcus, this volume); nevertheless, Mycenaean rulers clearly lived in impressive palaces, like that of King Nestor at Pylos. And in their burials we see a dichotomy between ashlar masonry tombs (which could belong to kings) and bedrock chamber tombs (which could belong to lesser nobles). The masonry tombs were found not beneath the floors of palaces but dug into the sides of natural hills. The most spectacular (and most convincingly "royal") are the *tholos* tombs, at least nine of which were constructed at Mycenae between 1500 and 1250 BC (fig. 2.22a).

Each tomb consists of a conically roofed circular chamber or *tholos,* up to 13.7 m high and 14.9 m in diameter, done in ashlar masonry (a construction style shared with the Inka). This chamber, deeply buried in a hillside and marked with an artificial mound of earth, was reached by a corridor

ST CHARLES COMMUNITY COLLEGE
LIBRARY
WITHDRAWN

or *dromos* up to 40 m long, also dug into the hill slope. The entrance to the chamber was a monumental doorway up to 5.5 m high, closed with bronze doors. After burial had taken place, the mouth of the *dromos* was blocked with a stone wall (Taylour 1983:65–81).

Mycenaean nobles (and perhaps some of the wealthiest commoners) imitated royal *tholoi* by digging less spectacular "chamber tombs" (fig. 2.22b). These irregular caverns were dug into bedrock, given a small entry corridor, and closed with stone walls. Such chamber tombs were apparently family burial vaults, opened over and over again for additional burials. Drinking cups broken in the *dromos* show that libations were poured for the dead (Taylour 1983:83). These rock-cut tombs lacked the labor-intensive ashlar masonry and bronze doors of their royal counterparts. They were, however, noticeably more elaborate than the simple grave of the average commoner.

Note that this typology of *tholoi*, chamber tombs, and simple graves does not imply that the Mycenaeans had a third social stratum or "middle class." It is likely that all members of the hereditary nobility ended up in a chamber tomb of some kind. Perhaps only those nobles who ascended to the rank of king received a *tholos* with ashlar masonry and bronze doors.

SUMMARY AND CONCLUSIONS

We cannot rely on textual information to identify the earliest archaic states, since most had no writing (e.g., Moche) or only limited writing (e.g., Uruk). By studying the archaeological ground plans of the better-known second- and third-generation archaic states, however, we can establish a set of clues by which states can be identified in the absence of textual information. Bear in mind that all such clues are simply rules of thumb. The more clues we have, the more confident we can be; one clue is not usually enough.

Because archaic states were stratified societies with kings and queens, they often featured palaces. As we have seen, however, palaces can be as large and multifunctional as the Labyrinth of Knossos and the *ciudadelas* of Chan Chan, or as small and residential as those of Mexico's Zapotec. It is also the case that, in many regions, there was a time lag between the first evidence of statehood and the first unmistakable palace.

Royal tombs can be a clue to kingship, especially if they were part of the construction of the palace, as they often were among the Zapotec and Maya. In some places, like Sipán on the north coast of Peru, we have burials that look "royal" but date to a period for which no clear palaces have yet been excavated. In other places, like Teotihuacán in Mexico, we have the palatial residences of the city's rulers, but so far no spectacular royal tombs to go with

ST. CHARLES COMMUNITY COLLEGE
LIBRARY

them. With time and patient excavation, however, these missing data can be discovered.

Archaic states often had an official religion, one featuring standardized temples and full-time priests. We have seen archaeological evidence not only for such temples, but for the residential quarters of the priests. Depending on the region involved, the latter may be incorporated into the temple itself, or situated nearby. Modest in first-generation states, the priestly residence grew more spectacular in second- or third-generation states, as exemplified by the *gipar* of Ur (Woolley and Moorey 1982) or the high priest's residence at Mitla in Mexico (Marcus and Flannery 1996:figs. 6, 7).

All states were hierarchical societies. As Marcus (1989, 1992a, 1993a) has suggested, however, there were stages of development during which states were larger and more centralized, and stages during which they broke down into their constituent provinces. During these periods of breakdown, the constituent provinces of a state might gain some degree of autonomy, but this autonomy was often short-lived.

A four-tiered site hierarchy is one clue to this process, so long as one can show administrative functions at the three upper tiers. Almost all pristine or first-generation states, such as the Uruk state in Mesopotamia or the Monte Albán II state in southern Mexico, show such a structure. However, when such states broke down, it was their various provinces that emerged as the largest stable units. Some of these individual polities might only have three-tiered hierarchies (the Mixtec *cacicazgos* of Postclassic Mexico would be an example). That does not mean that such provinces had reverted to being "chiefdoms." Their societies remained stratified, their rulers still lived in palaces and expected to be treated like kings, and many such polities kept trying to subdue (or ally themselves with) neighboring provinces to reestablish a large regional state.

By using large-scale "total coverage" settlement pattern surveys (Fish and Kowalewski 1990) we can document the appearance of pristine states with four-tiered hierarchies, their breakdown into provinces with three-tiered hierarchies, and their reintegration into a second-generation state with four tiers. I would stress, however, that site size alone is not sufficient information: *we must also excavate sites at the upper three tiers of the hierarchy to recover the buildings that reflect state institutions.*

An Application of the Approach

As a way of demonstrating the utility of a "ground plan" approach to the archaic state, let us now apply it to a society about which there has been considerable controversy: the Olmec of Mexico's Gulf Coast (1150–300 BC). In their site report on the Olmec site of San Lorenzo, Michael Coe and

Richard Diehl (1980) reveal that they are not in agreement as to whether the Olmec constituted a chiefdom or a state.

> Coe is convinced that the Olmec had . . . a state-level organization and so-cial stratification analogous to those of later Mesoamerican societies, while Diehl maintains that they were organized along chiefdom lines with ranking of individuals and kin groups but no socioeconomic classes. (Coe and Diehl 1980, vol. II:147)

Applying the rules of thumb described in this chapter, we have no choice but to side with Diehl. San Lorenzo—a site so far without stone masonry, adobes, or lime plaster—has produced nothing resembling a real Meso-american palace, nor is it likely to. It also has none of the standardized two-room temples so typical of Mesoamerican states. There is no sign of res-idences for full-time priests, either in temples or nearby. And since Coe and Diehl found no burials at all, we can hardly debate whether the most ele-gant tombs look "chiefly" or "royal." (A basalt column tomb from the later site of La Venta looks "chiefly.")

As far as an administrative hierarchy goes, the evidence is inconclusive. Since Coe and Diehl's work, there has been a determined survey of the San Lorenzo region under the direction of Ann Cyphers (Symonds and Luna-gómez 1994). At this writing, however, the survey treats the entire Forma-tive period (1500 BC–AD 200) as a single block of time, not breaking it down into the cultural phases defined by Coe and Diehl. The Formative settle-ment pattern is one in which numerous smaller sites cluster within 4 km of San Lorenzo, then drop off dramatically beyond that point (Symonds and Lunagómez 1994 : fig. 8). This looks very much like the pattern of smaller sites clustered around San José Mogote in the northern Valley of Oaxaca (Marcus and Flannery 1996 : fig. 128) or around Chalcatzingo in the Valley of Morelos (Hirth 1987 : fig. 21.3). Both those sites are considered to be the paramount centers of chiefdoms, not the capitals of states.

Because of the tropical forest and savanna vegetation in the San Lorenzo area, it is difficult to calculate site sizes accurately. In fact, the categories of sites defined by Symonds and Lunagómez do not represent a site hierarchy, but rather a site typology, based on variables such as presence or absence of visible mounds and surface sherd densities in 3 × 3 m sample areas. Until we have a histogram of actual site sizes, comparable to those available for southwest Iran (see fig. 2.1) or the Valley of Oaxaca (Kowalewski et al. 1989), it will not be clear how many site-size modes the continuum can be divided into. Then will come the task of demonstrating administrative func-tions at sites in the larger modes.

I suspect that when this is done, Olmec-period San Lorenzo will prove to be the paramount center of a maximal chiefdom, rather than an archaic state on the order of Period II Monte Albán, Early Classic Teotihuacán, or Early Classic Tikal and Calakmul. We do not yet know when the state formed on Mexico's Gulf Coast; when we finally do, we will likely find that it displays a much more convincing set of clues than do the Olmec of San Lorenzo.

NOTE

A great many colleagues working in the New and Old Worlds provided me with insights and information for this essay. I am particularly indebted to Henry T. Wright and George L. Cowgill for extensive constructive criticism.

3

The Peaks and Valleys of Ancient States
An Extension of the Dynamic Model
JOYCE MARCUS

I n 1989 I presented a model for the formation, expansion, and breakdown of Maya states (Marcus 1993a). Drawing on data from excavation, settlement pattern survey, and epigraphy, I argued that ancient Maya states were not static entities whose structures remained constant over time. Two of the earliest states arose in the fourth century AD when two powerful chiefdoms—Tikal and Calakmul—managed to subjugate their respective neighbors.

Tikal used a combination of military force, royal marriage alliance, and diplomacy to dominate preexisting polities like Uaxactún, Río Azul, and Yaxchilán, and to found new polities like Dos Pilas, until its expansionist state covered approximately 30,000 km^2 of noncontiguous territory (Marcus 1976a:56–74, 1992a:406–7). Not long after this maximum territorial expansion had been reached, Tikal's territory began to shrink. Some subject provinces (such as Naranjo) were lured away by Calakmul, Tikal's principal rival. Still other provinces (such as Dos Pilas) broke away on their own and achieved independence. Eventually, some of these newly independent provinces went on to assemble their own expansionist states, beginning the whole cycle over again.

At the peak of each cycle, Maya states were territorially extensive and had a settlement hierarchy of at least four tiers, the upper three of which had administrative functions and were ruled by hereditary lords (Marcus 1976a: 24–25, 46–47). At the low point of each cycle, formerly extensive states had broken down into loosely allied or semiautonomous provinces that sometimes had settlement hierarchies with only three tiers. These provinces were run by hereditary lords who continued to call themselves *batabob* or *ch'ul ahauob,* even though the territories they controlled were now much smaller. Because of its repetitive cycles of consolidation, expansion, and dissolution, I referred to this framework as the Dynamic Model.

WIDER APPLICATIONS OF THE DYNAMIC MODEL

Shortly after I first presented the Dynamic Model, colleagues from other parts of Mesoamerica began to tell me that the model fit their regions as well. I therefore prepared a second paper in which I extended the Dynamic Model to central and southern Mexico (Marcus 1992a). In particular, it seemed to fit both the Zapotec and Mixtec regions, where the first states were large polities whose capitals were mountaintop cities like Monte Albán (Blanton 1978; Kowalewski et al. 1989; Marcus and Flannery 1996) and Yucuñudahui (Caso 1938; Spores 1983a).

The breakdown of these early states converted their former provinces into a series of autonomous polities, much smaller in territory than the early states to which they had belonged. As in the case of the Maya, these *cacicazgos* or principalities were managed by rulers who still referred to themselves as "kings" in spite of their much smaller realms. Occasionally these *cacicazgos* were reunited into larger territorial states, as happened under the Mixtec ruler 8 Deer "Tiger Claw" (AD 1063–1115).

Central Mexico, too, seems to have gone through similar dynamic cycles. Its first state, centered at Teotihuacán, had colonies or enclaves of some kind at Chingú in the state of Hidalgo, Matacapan in Veracruz, Mirador and Los Horcones in Chiapas, and Kaminaljuyú in the Guatemalan Highlands. There are hints that some of Teotihuacán's contemporaries, cities like Cantona in eastern Puebla (García Cook 1994), may have fortified themselves to resist incorporation by Teotihuacán. With the dissolution of the Teotihuacán state, Central Mexican polities like Xochicalco, Cacaxtla, and eventually Tula began to flourish, expanding into provinces formerly controlled by Teotihuacán.

No sooner had I published this extension of the Dynamic Model than colleagues from other regions of the world wrote me to say that it fit their areas as well. Mesopotamia's first major state, with its urban capital at Uruk, resembled Teotihuacán's in some ways. Although its total area of direct control is uncertain, Uruk had fortified "colonies" as far up the Euphrates as Syria, and enclaves in towns in eastern Turkey (Algaze 1993a). Its collapse was followed by almost seven centuries of competition among rival cities (which Yoffee would call "city-states") until the region was firmly reunified by Sargon of Akkad. Mesopotamia then broke down again into rival cities for a century, until unified by Ur—a region that had once been but a province of Sargon's realm.

Colleagues working in the Andes wrote me of similar cycles there. The Moche state, 550 km from north to south—so territorially extensive that some Andeanists consider it an empire—broke down into its constituent provinces, only to see Wari take control in the south. With the collapse of the Wari state came the Chimú, who controlled perhaps 1000 km of Peru's coast until they were overcome by the Inka. In many cases, the region that rose to prominence had once been a subject province of a previous state.

Encouraged by all those colleagues who see parallels in their regions, I will extend the Dynamic Model still further in this chapter. I do not expect that the model will be applicable to every archaic state in the ancient world, but it seems to be applicable to quite a few. I will begin in Mesoamerica and extend outward to include the Andes, Mesopotamia, Egypt, and the Aegean.

THE MAYA CASE

During the Late Preclassic in the Maya region (300 BC–AD 250) we have evidence for societies with hereditary differences in rank, settlement hierarchies of two or three tiers, and sufficient interpolity raiding so that some sites have ditches, ramparts, palisades, and other defensive earthworks (Marcus 1995a, 1995b; Webster 1976a, 1976b). It is after this period of chiefly competition that first-generation states started to make their appearance—for example, in the Tikal and Calakmul regions (Coe 1990; Folan, Marcus, and Miller 1995; Folan et al. 1995; Marcus 1976a, 1983a, 1988, 1995a). The Early Classic (AD 250–500) was characterized by states with palaces, standardized two-room temples arranged on platforms in groups of three, royal tombs, and a four-tiered settlement hierarchy, but not all states were stable. A partial political breakdown (known as "the hiatus") characterized some, but not all, Petén sites during the Middle Classic, AD 534–593 (Proskouriakoff 1950; Willey 1974).

The Late Classic (AD 600–900) witnessed a surge in population, accompanied by the formation of second-generation states such as Quiriguá, Dos Pilas, Palenque, and Piedras Negras. Often the regions central to these Late Classic states had been subject provinces of Early Classic states. This second cycle of state formation was followed by a second collapse at many Petén cities during the Terminal Classic/Early Postclassic (AD 800–1000). This moment is widely—and inaccurately—known as "the Maya Collapse." I say "inaccurately" because we now know that this collapse was only one of many, and that it did not signal an end to Maya civilization—simply the abandonment of some cities and the political transformation of others

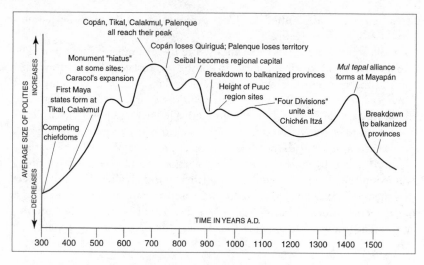

Figure 3.1. The Dynamic Model as originally applied to the Maya Lowlands (redrawn, with modifications, from Marcus 1993a:fig. 26).

(Marcus 1994; Sharer 1991:196). At the very moment that cities like Tikal were collapsing, others in Belize (such as Lamanai) and in the Puuc region of the Yucatán Peninsula were ascending to their greatest heights (Chase and Rice 1985; Pendergast 1985, 1986; Sabloff and Andrews 1986; Sabloff and Tourtellot 1991). And when some cities in Belize and the Puuc began to decline, there was a new surge in state formation and expansion, particularly in northern Yucatán—first at Chichén Itzá (AD 800–1000) and later at Mayapán (AD 1250–1450). Our notion that Maya civilization had totally collapsed is due to the fact that when the Spaniards arrived in the 1530s, the Mayapán state had fragmented into 16 autonomous provinces (Quezada 1993; Roys 1957), and many areas of the Petén had dispersed rural populations. Much of the Postclassic population had relocated to the coasts and lakes.

My graph of these cycles (fig. 3.1) emphasizes the cyclic buildup and breakdown of Maya polities, but the real pattern is too complex to be conveyed by one graph. It would require a series of graphs to show, for example, that as the chiefdom at Nakbe decreased in importance around AD 100, El Mirador reached new heights. When El Mirador collapsed around AD 200, Calakmul—its principal rival—rose to greater prominence. After AD 378, Tikal rose at the expense of Uaxactún. During this same period Kinal, a city subordinate to Tikal, rose at the expense of Río Azul, another of Tikal's subordinates (Adams 1990). Just as Calakmul's rise came at El Mirador's expense, so later did Tikal's rise come at the expense of other sites (Folan et al. 1995; Marcus 1976a, 1988, 1992a, 1993a).

Recently, it has become fashionable to refer to the highest peaks in figure 3.1 as "superstates" (Martin and Grube 1995). This term is unnecessarily hyperbolic, since the polities involved are merely typical states. We have long known that, at their peaks, cities like Tikal and Calakmul were the capitals of large regional states (Marcus 1973, 1976a). The point here is that the smaller units into which they occasionally fragmented were not usually states at all. Like the Postclassic Mixtec *cacicazgos,* these former subject provinces should be considered no more than principalities or petty kingdoms. (Some Mayanists refer to them as "city-states," but as we shall see below, this term has little to recommend it.)

Cycles in the Calakmul Region

During the period 300 BC–AD 200 in the northern Petén, two large chiefly centers arose only 38 km from each other. Calakmul and El Mirador commanded sufficiently large labor forces to construct huge pyramids and build a major causeway linking their two towns (Folan, Marcus, and Miller 1995). Although all the details of their interaction are not known, it appears that El Mirador collapsed before AD 300–400, precisely the period during which Calakmul went on to become a capital of an early state.

As is so often the case with newly formed states, one of Calakmul's periods of major expansion came early in its history. Calakmul was able to incorporate various provinces into its realm during the fifth and sixth centuries AD. Nevertheless, its territory was a mosaic since some intervening provinces were not incorporated. Just before the beginning of the fifth century, a royal tomb was placed beneath the floor of a palace on Calakmul's Main Plaza (Folan et al. 1995; Pincemin 1994). The earliest dated Calakmul stela (at AD 431) depicts a lord who was a contemporary of Tikal's ruler Stormy Sky and Copán's "first" ruler Yax K'uk Mo' (Marcus and Folan 1994:22).

Calakmul formed so many alliances and incorporated so many provinces that it became the Maya capital most frequently mentioned on monuments outside its region. Part of Calakmul's early success was undoubtedly due to its having been one of the earliest polities of the Maya Lowlands to achieve statehood; it was expanding against neighbors still organized on a chiefdom level.

Calakmul reached new heights during the reign of Jaguar Paw, who ascended to the throne in AD 686. Jaguar Paw led Calakmul on a new expansionist campaign based on two strategies: threatening attack and establishing political and military alliances with neighbors who shared an antipathy toward Tikal (Folan et al. 1995; Marcus 1988; Marcus and Folan 1994; Schele and Freidel 1990). Such alliances, aimed at keeping a major rival at bay, were typical of archaic states in many parts of the world (Marcus 1983a, 1989, 1992c, 1995b). Calakmul's political clout was supposed to have ended at AD 695, when Jaguar Paw was reportedly taken captive by Tikal. Although a battle with Jaguar Paw is claimed by the ruler of Tikal (as expected, this event is not mentioned at Calakmul), the person shown as prisoner is not Jaguar Paw, but a Calakmul lord with a different name (Marcus 1976a:52, 1988:5; Marcus and Folan 1994:23; Schele and Freidel 1990:206–7).

Were it not for this claim by Tikal, we would have interpreted the period from AD 600 to 810 as an uninterrupted, nonviolent time for Calakmul's rulers. Even after Jaguar Paw's battle with Tikal, Calakmul continued to erect buildings and carve more than 30 stelae. But around AD 850, Calakmul's government failed and the city lost substantial population. In addition to its political and economic problems, Calakmul may have faced a severe drought at this time (Gunn, Folan, and Robichaux 1995). Many cities that continued to flourish were near the rivers and lakes of the Petén or the coasts of Yucatán, and some were nucleated and quite unlike the sprawling, dispersed cities of the Classic period.

Cycles in the Tikal Region

Tikal's transition from a chiefly center to the capital of an archaic state apparently gained momentum with its subjugation of Uaxactún in AD 378. Its collapse as a regional state occurred after AD 800. During the course of its history, Tikal displayed two types of dynamic cycles that can be detected archaeologically.

The first cycle is a clear, but incompletely documented, jockeying for power by the sites in Tikal's regional hierarchy. As the result of this jockeying, certain sites rose or fell in the settlement hierarchy. For example, Dos Pilas was founded as a subject polity by a relative of Tikal's ruling dynasty; later, it became a secondary center and succeeded in breaking away to achieve independence from Tikal. Still later, Dos Pilas became an expansionist capital itself.

Another example of this jockeying would be Río Azul, which apparently began as an autonomous polity but was conquered by Tikal around AD 380. Río Azul was for a time a tertiary site in Tikal's realm; later, after the imposition of a Tikal lord at Río Azul, the latter site rose to become a secondary administrative center in the Tikal state (Adams 1990). Such cycles within Tikal's realm will, however, remain poorly known until its huge hinterland has been systematically surveyed. Obviously this kind of survey will take considerable effort, since Tikal's state may have covered more than 20,000 km^2 at AD 500, and more than 10,000 km^2 at AD 700 (Adams 1990; Adams and Jones 1981; Culbert et al. 1990; Marcus 1992a:407).

Better known than the political cycles within its realm are the cycles of monumental construction at Tikal itself, which indirectly reveal the fortunes of the capital. Chris Jones (1991:121) has noted that large-scale construction projects were completed at Tikal on the order of every 200 years, and that at least three were associated with the burials of rulers. Two of seven projects were related to breaks in the dynastic sequence, and in both cases the former rulers had successors who "took pains to re-establish their connections with the broken dynastic line while also honoring the intruder" (Jones 1991:122).

The first major construction project at Tikal—the initial stage of the North Acropolis—took place around 400 BC when a platform was built on top of a natural hill (Coe 1965:7–8); it was rebuilt around 200 BC. Shortly after AD 1, the Great Plaza was paved for the first time. By AD 75, the center of Tikal had developed its characteristic pattern—an acropolis (containing the burials of important leaders) that supported a large temple on the north, a multiroom structure on the south, and one or more flanking pyramids. In AD 200 a broad stairway was built to allow direct access from the North Terrace to the top of the acropolis for the first time.

Hieroglyphic inscriptions personalize the history of Tikal, indicating that 29 rulers reigned there. The first of these, possibly inaugurated in AD 170, may have been known as Jaguar Paw (Jones 1991:109). Excavations by Laporte and Fialko (1990) in the Mundo Perdido complex have yielded Stela 39, dated to AD 376, bearing the name of Tikal's ninth ruler, also named Jaguar Paw. We know little about Tikal's first eight rulers, owing to a lack of contemporaneous texts; however, inscriptions at subordinate sites like Uaxactún suggest that Tikal's rulers occasionally used force to subjugate other centers (Marcus 1976a, 1992a; Mathews 1985; Schele and Freidel 1990; Valdés and Fahsen 1995).

The ninth Tikal ruler, who might have taken the name Jaguar Paw in order to link himself to the dynasty's founder, may have been the first to construct a recognizable palace at the site. A text found on a vessel in an Early Classic palace on the North Acropolis states that the palace was "his house, Jaguar Paw, Ruler of Tikal, 9th ruler" (Jones 1991:111). This is a significant event in light of the importance of the palace for identifying archaic states (see Flannery, this volume).

Around AD 400, a ball court and the antecedent stages of Temples I and II were built. Tikal's prosperity (and its royal dynasty) seems to have continued, even though Lord Water in his inscriptions at the rival city of Caracol claims to have had battles with Tikal in AD 556 and 562 (Chase and Chase 1987). The ruler of Tikal at this time was named Double Bird (21st ruler in the sequence), and his fate is unknown in spite of claims that he died in the battle with Caracol. Haviland (1991:5–6) suggests that Double Bird survived his battles with Lord Water, to die a natural death at Tikal years later.

Animal Skull, the 22nd ruler, was responsible for massive remodeling in downtown Tikal, including a new paving of the Great Plaza. Opinions differ on whether this building program reflects a peaceful transition from

Double Bird or the response to a disruption by Caracol. Haviland (1991:9) interprets the continued building as "an *absence* of evident Caracol influence at Tikal precisely when Lord Water is supposed to have 'conquered' the city." Jones, on the other hand, believes that Animal Skull was an intruder or, at the least, a person not in direct line to rule. Jones (1991:116–17) links the purposeful destruction of several Tikal stelae from AD 557–682 to a raid by Caracol, believing that this disruption was followed by a restoration of "the old Tikal [dynastic] line."

The next big construction program at Tikal, around AD 600, coincides with Burial 195 (possibly the tomb of Animal Skull himself). We then see a succession of rulers to which letters of the alphabet have been assigned (Rulers A, B, and C). The climactic stage of Temple I was contributed by Ruler A (Hasaw Kaan Kawil) prior to AD 734, the date when Ruler B acceded to the throne. Ruler B (AD 734–768) went on to add huge buildings; a later phase of massive construction is attributed to Ruler C. Finally, the last ruler of Tikal—depicted on Stela 11 at AD 869—seems to have lacked the manpower or political clout for large construction projects.

Tikal thus presents us with a number of cyclic processes that should be familiar to Mesopotamian archaeologists: (1) Early in its history its territory exceeded 20,000 km^2; later it shrank to 10,000 km^2, and still later to nothing. (2) At least part of this shrinkage may be the result of battles with some of its former dependencies (such as Dos Pilas and Naranjo), many of which became strong enough to break away to become rivals. (3) Its dynastic history may have been interrupted by intruders from outside the royal line; these "new" rulers outdid themselves in public construction, using hieroglyphic texts to link themselves to respected earlier rulers. (4) Over time, many of Tikal's dependencies moved down or up in the hierarchy, with those moving upward occasionally becoming rivals of the capital. All four processes also are detectable in archaic Mesopotamian states (see below).

Cycles in the Copán Region

The Copán Valley of western Honduras has one of the longest occupation sequences within the Maya area. As far back as 1000 BC, it had village cultures whose burial ceramics show ties with the Mexican Highlands (Fash 1982, 1991; Marcus 1993b, 1995a). Between 300 BC and AD 200 the valley went through a period with little or no population growth (Fash 1991). This was only one of the "fits and starts" the region seems to have experienced over a 2000-year period (Sharer 1995).

From AD 200–400, the city of Copán witnessed a surge in population and the establishment of strong ties to both the highlands and lowlands of Guatemala. I suspect, on the basis of incomplete data, that Copán's initial state formation took place in the Early Classic around AD 400, followed by a lull or even a trough of decentralization (Marcus 1976a). Shortly after AD 400, monumental construction began 100 m west of the Copán River, and by AD 540 three architectural groups—connected by shared floors— had been completed. One of these groups, the Northeast Court Group beneath the East Court, appears to have been the palace of Copán's earliest "kings" (Traxler 1996).

The alleged founder of the first Copán dynasty, Yax K'uk Mo', ruled around AD 426. The earliest contemporary date (AD 435) associated with him appears on Stela 63 (Fash 1991). Other texts at Copán, however, refer to still earlier rulers—retrospective mentionings of individuals who ruled as far back as AD 159.

The record is incomplete because we are missing contemporaneous texts for the second, third, fifth, sixth, eighth, and ninth rulers in Yax K'uk Mo's line, although their names are included in later retrospective lists of past rulers (Fash 1991; Marcus 1976a, 1995c; Morley 1920; Schele and Freidel 1990). Sharer et al.'s (1994) deepest excavations beneath the Copán acropolis have yielded evidence for residential platforms of the period AD 240–400, but we still lack a clear-cut monumental palace that could have housed rulers of that period.

Middle Classic times (AD 400–700) saw Copán still linked to the Guatemalan Highlands as well as to Teotihuacán (Kidder, Jennings, and Shook 1946; Longyear 1952). At this period, some sites in the Guatemalan Lowlands were experiencing a "hiatus" (a period of decentralization or breakdown); but Copán was not, and neither were the Guatemalan Highlands. In fact, Copán seems to have undergone considerable population growth during the Middle Classic, revealing further evidence of state formation (Fash 1983). I would interpret this as a *second* cycle of state formation, following the aforementioned lull.

The emergence of this Middle Classic Copán state took place around AD 630–659 under a ruler named Smoke Imix. Smoke Imix had expansionist goals and employed the strategy of setting up boundary stelae to delimit the frontiers of his "realm" (Fash 1991; Morley 1920). In addition to Stelae 10, 12, 13, 19, and 23, which served this function, Smoke Imix commissioned at least 14 other monuments to glorify himself. In all those actions he reminds us of the Early Dynastic Mesopotamian ruler Mesalim of Kish (2550 BC), who put up stelae as far away as the Lagash-Umma boundary (Cooper 1983).

Fash (1983:225) has suggested that Smoke Imix's boundary stelae served defensive purposes, discouraging rival states from crossing the frontier. On the other hand, Smoke Imix did not hesitate to cross others' frontiers, claiming Quiriguá in Guatemala's Motagua Valley as a subject province. As our research proceeds, it will be interesting to see if Smoke Imix was merely

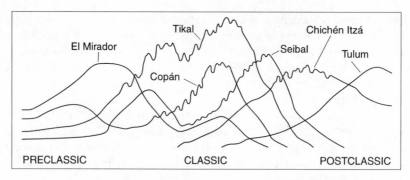

Figure 3.2. *Robert Sharer's view of consolidation and breakdown in the Maya Lowlands emphasizes the "sawtooth" nature of each major center's rise and fall (redrawn from Sharer 1991:fig. 8.1c).*

reconquering a province that had once been annexed by earlier Copán rulers (Marcus 1974, 1976a).

Whatever the case, Copán's domination of Quiriguá was not permanent. The Quiriguá ruler named Cauac Sky claims in his texts to have defeated 18 Jog, Smoke Imix's successor at Copán, liberating Quiriguá in AD 738. Cauac Sky recorded his victory on five huge monuments at Quiriguá; the latter site then experienced a flurry of growth and monumental construction (Sharer 1978, 1990, 1991). This alleged defeat of its ruler did not lead to a collapse at Copán, but the two cities did follow separate paths until AD 850. At this point their populations shrank, and both governments collapsed.

The Copán data remind us that, as Robert Carneiro once said, the rise to statehood is a "sawtooth ascent" rather than a straight line (Carneiro 1969:1015). States might form initially in the Early Classic, collapse, form anew in the Middle Classic, collapse, then form again in the Late Classic (fig. 3.2). Subject territories might be conquered but later win their autonomy, only to be reconquered. Rulers like Copán's Smoke Imix and Kish's Mesalim might erect boundary stelae, only to see them later trampled by people they had considered their vassals.

THE ZAPOTEC CASE

The Valley of Oaxaca, cradle of Zapotec civilization, covers more than 2,000 km^2 in the Southern Highlands of Mexico. Between 700 and 500 BC, during the Middle Preclassic, there were 75–85 communities in the valley (Kowalewski et al. 1989). These communities form three groups, perhaps representing three chiefdoms of unequal size. Separating them was an 80 km^2 buffer zone in which no settlements of this period have been found. The

buffer zone—combined with evidence for raiding, burning of public buildings, sacrifice of enemies, and one possible fortification wall—suggests a
high level of competition among several chiefdoms (Marcus and Flannery
1996:123–24).

During the next stage of the Middle Preclassic (500–300 BC), a number
of striking demographic changes took place. A large number of villages in
the northern part of the valley (including the largest community of the previous period) were abandoned, and their populations apparently moved to
the top of a defensible mountain in the former buffer zone. The initial population of this first Zapotec city has been estimated at 5,000 persons, and between 300 and 100 BC it rose to an estimated 17,000 (Blanton 1978). During
this period Monte Albán, as the city is called today, built 3 km of defensive
walls and surrounded itself with 154 valley-floor communities (Kowalewski
1983). It appears that this dense ring of satellite communities was a deliberate concentration of farmers and warriors needed not only to support
Monte Albán with food (Nicholas 1989), but also to give it the necessary
demographic advantage to subdue rival chiefdoms in the southern and eastern parts of the valley (Marcus and Flannery 1996:155–71).

Rival chiefly centers in the southern and eastern valley (one of which is
currently undergoing excavation by Elsa Redmond and Charles Spencer)
grew larger during 300–100 BC, and in some cases sought higher and more
defensible locations. Eventually, however, they fell to Monte Albán, as did
some areas 50 to 60 km outside the valley. As early as 500–300 BC, Monte
Albán had erected a gallery of more than 300 carved stones, each displaying
a slain prisoner. By 100 BC–AD 200, the city had carved another 40 stones
naming subject provinces up to 150 km distant from Monte Albán (Marcus
1976b, 1980, 1984, 1992c; Marcus and Flannery 1996:figs. 234–36).

Taking advantage of the fact that it was now organized as a state—
while most of its neighbors were not—Monte Albán expanded to control
20,000 km² of southern Mexico by AD 200 (fig. 3.3). Its ultimate goal seems
to have been to establish a "corridor of influence" between Cuicatlán in the
north (the gateway to Central Mexico) and Tututepec and Chiltepec in
the south (the gateway to the tropics). Some subject areas, like the Valleys
of Miahuatlán and Ejutla, may have been taken over by political and economic persuasion (Feinman and Nicholas 1990, 1993). Other areas, like the
Cuicatlán Cañada, were clearly kept in line by military force (Redmond
1983; Spencer 1982).

As so often happens in the cases I examine in this chapter, the Zapotec
state was most territorially extensive early in its history. It reached its limits
in the Protoclassic and by the Early Classic (AD 200–500) had already begun to shrink. One by one its outer provinces grew strong enough to break
away, just as Quiriguá had broken away from Copán (see above). During the

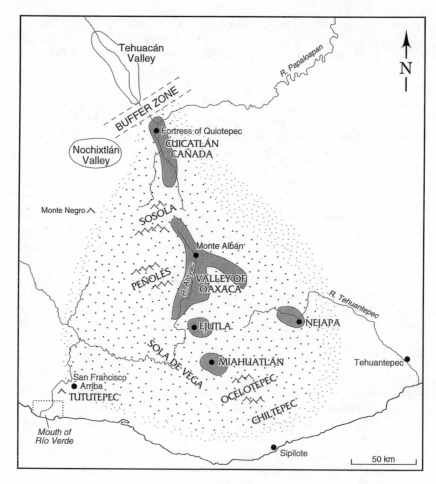

Figure 3.3. At its peak in the first or second century AD, the Zapotec state may have covered 20,000 km² (redrawn from Marcus and Flannery 1996:ill. 242).

Early Classic there were 1,075 occupied places in the Valley of Oaxaca, but almost two-thirds of the valley's estimated 115,000 persons lived at 38 communities in fortified or defensible localities (Kowalewski et al. 1989). No longer the expansionist aggressors, the Zapotec were now busily defending themselves against hostile neighbors. After reaching its peak size of 24,000 persons between AD 500 and 700, Monte Albán began to lose population and importance. By AD 900, Jalieza, a mountaintop city in the southern valley, was the region's largest community (Finsten 1995).

During the Terminal Classic and Postclassic, the Zapotec state underwent a period of decentralization not unlike that seen during the "troughs of dissolution" in the Maya Lowlands. Centers like Zaachila, Cuilapan, Macuilxochitl, Lambityeco, Yagul, and Mitla arose to control certain sectors of the valley, but no city ever again dominated the entire region the way Monte Albán had during its heyday (Flannery and Marcus 1983b:184). The carved stone monuments of AD 600–900 do not feature military conquests; rather they seek to establish the genealogical credentials of each town's rulers (Marcus 1976b, 1983d, 1992c). The Postclassic seems to have been a period during which small principalities jockeyed for position, not unlike the situation revealed in the Mixtec codices (Smith 1983, 1994). Some Zapotec princes sought to build power by marrying princesses from the Mixteca, even going so far as to provide land for the *tay situndayu,* or agricultural workers, who labored on the estates of Mixtec rulers (Marcus and Flannery 1983:220).

In summary, the Zapotec show us one more case of a state that (1) formed when one chiefdom succeeded in subduing its rivals; (2) took advantage of its superior political and military organization to expand against less-developed neighbors; (3) reached its maximal territorial size early in its history; and (4) later lost its outer provinces and began to contract, even as its capital city continued to gain population.

THE CENTRAL MEXICAN CASE

As in the case of many pristine states, the first state in the Basin of Mexico arose in the context of competing chiefdoms. Between 600 and 300 BC only a few hamlets existed in the area that would become the city of Teotihuacán. Indeed, prior to the second century BC, that arm of the Basin of Mexico is considered a "backwater" (Millon 1992:385). The most impressive chiefly center in the region was Cuicuilco in the southern Basin of Mexico, which may have had 10,000 occupants (Sanders, Parsons, and Santley 1979).

While Cuicuilco's population had doubled by 100 BC, a sizable community at Teotihuacán was emerging as a rival. Almost certainly taking advantage of the irrigation potential of its springs, Teotihuacán grew to the point where it virtually rivaled Cuicuilco; the two centers are seen as "balanced powers in the early first century" (Evans and Berlo 1992:7). Mother Nature then played her hand; the eruption of a volcano named Xitle buried Cuicuilco and its immediate sustaining area with lava. Some scholars believe that this natural disaster gave Teotihuacán the advantage it needed to grow rapidly to a position of political supremacy, siphoning off most of the manpower formerly under the control of Cuicuilco. Other scholars are reluctant to see political evolution attributed to a natural accident.

The first state at Teotihuacán is believed to have emerged around the first century AD. The evidence is largely based on settlement pattern survey and intensive surface pickup of the emerging urban area; at present we have little evidence for palaces or standardized temple plans for this early period (Marcus 1983b). Teotihuacán administered a noncontiguous territory estimated by René Millon at 25,000 km^2; George Cowgill's estimate is 50,000 km^2 (personal communication 1996). Teotihuacán seems to have done this not only by suppressing the development of competing centers nearby, but also by deliberately bringing in rural populations to create an immense urban center. One of Teotihuacán's strategies was to extend its principal streets, particularly the East Avenue, several kilometers beyond the limits of the early city, suggesting that it intended to bring in thousands of new farmers, artisans, and urban laborers (Charlton 1972, 1991; Drewitt 1967; Sanders 1965). Sanders (1965:121) and Charlton (1991:fig. 15.2) note that Teotihuacán's suburbs and rural towns were aligned with the city's avenues, including sites 5 km to the south and as far away as 11 km to the east. As early as AD 200, the city covered at least 20 km^2. Its maximum population is estimated at 125,000 (Millon 1992:341).

Like Monte Albán, Teotihuacán expanded its influence into provinces beyond its immediate physiographic region. It established a secondary center at Chingú, 50 km away in the state of Hidalgo; a "military colony" at Matacapan in Veracruz; enclaves of some kind at Mirador and Los Horcones in Chiapas; and perhaps an elite enclave at Kaminaljuyú in the Guatemalan Highlands more than 1,000 km away. Teotihuacán controlled the nearby Otumba obsidian source; virtually monopolized the Sierra de las Navajas obsidian source near Pachuca, Hidalgo; and may have had access to the El Chayal obsidian source near Guatemala City through its enclave at Kaminaljuyú (Sanders 1974). Any designs it may have had on the Guadalupe Hidalgo obsidian source near the Puebla/Veracruz border, however, may have been thwarted by Cantona, a non-Teotihuacán-style city on a fortified lava flow near Guadalupe Hidalgo (García Cook 1994).

Teotihuacán's area of "direct control" was irregular (Millon 1993:fig. 7), circumventing areas powerful enough to resist. There can be little doubt, however, that part of Teotihuacán's expansion was by force; under one of its principal temple pyramids, more than 200 sacrificed individuals (most wearing military gear) have been found (Cabrera Castro, Sugiyama, and Cowgill 1991; Sugiyama 1989).

Like many early states examined in this chapter, Teotihuacán's greatest expansion was early in its history. As time went on, it lost more and more of its distant colonies, and by AD 600 the city itself was declining. With its collapse by AD 650, its downtown area was burned, followed by a 200-year period of decentralization. Between AD 750 and 1100 cities like Tula in Hidalgo, Xochicalco in Morelos, and Cacaxtla in Tlaxcala rose to prominence.

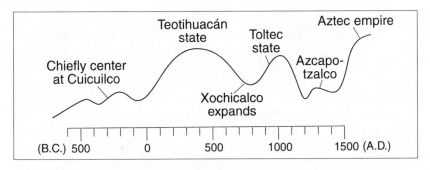

Figure 3.4. Consolidation and breakdown of states in Central Mexico.

All these cities lay close enough to the Basin of Mexico to have had their growth suppressed by Teotihuacán during its heyday. Now, with Teotihuacán reduced by two-thirds, they became major urban centers in their own right (fig. 3.4).

One of the most interesting of these second-generation states was the one centered at Tula in Hidalgo. With Teotihuacán's collapse, the administrative center at Chingú had ceased to be important and Tula began to grow between AD 800 and 1000 (Healan 1989). Tula became the capital of the Toltec state, the most powerful polity in Central Mexico in its day. By AD 1168, however, it too had collapsed, with many of its noble families emigrating to the Basin of Mexico.

After a period of decentralization and considerable jockeying for power, a third-generation state arose at Azcapotzalco in the Basin of Mexico. This was the Tepanec state, which by AD 1300 controlled a number of less powerful centers such as Texcoco. The hierarchy of settlements below Azcapotzalco consisted of at least three tiers, with tribute passing from Teotihuacán (now only a modest town) to the larger town of Huexotla, from there to Texcoco, and then up the line to Azcapotzalco (Gibson 1964; Hodge 1984).

Among the ethnic groups serving as vassals to Azcapotzalco were the Mexica, the people we call the Aztec. In AD 1427 the Mexica lord Itzcoatl allied himself with other disgruntled tribute-paying groups, such as the Texcocans and the Acolhua, and succeeded in overthrowing Azcapotzalco. The Mexica then formed a political and military alliance with Texcoco and Tlacopan to create what might be considered a fourth-generation state that dominated Central Mexico at the time of the Spanish Conquest (Berdan 1982; Bray 1968; Davies 1973; Hodge 1984; van Zantwijk 1985). This state, like others before it, expanded rapidly during its first 90 years; but because of the arrival of Europeans in AD 1519, its development was abruptly truncated, and it never went through the usual phase of breakdown.

While many Aztec cities have been referred to as "city-states" in the literature, they did not closely resemble the Greek poleis from which that term is taken. Nor do they resemble the modern Vatican "city-state" in which the city and state are isomorphic. Aztec cities were in fact closely tied together by royal marriage alliances, military alliances, the sharing of tribute, and various types of economic interdependence (Barlow 1949; Carrasco 1971, 1974, 1984; Davies 1973). In the future it might be better to use *altepetl,* the indigenous Náhuatl word for such polities, rather than the term "city-state," because they are not like the autonomous Greek poleis (Charlton and Nichols 1997; Hodge 1984; Marcus 1983b).

THE ANDEAN CASE

The Andes is another region where periods of breakdown alternated with periods of territorially expansionist states. At first glance, this situation would seem to be fully covered by the long-established Andean chronological scheme of "horizons" (periods of widespread styles) and "intermediates" (periods of multiple localized styles). The situation is a bit more complicated than that, however, since periods of highly centralized states do not correlate perfectly with stylistic "horizons."

Our current Andean chronology had its origins around the turn of the century, when Max Uhle (1902, 1903, 1913) organized his Peruvian and Bolivian materials into six periods. (For example, his second period was the "horizon of the culture of Tiahuanaco," and his sixth was the "horizon of the Inca.") Uhle had been influenced by the division of Egyptian chronology into "kingdoms" and "intermediate periods" by Sir Flinders Petrie (1900, 1901). Following the lead of Petrie and Uhle, John Rowe (1960, 1962) proposed the scheme of six periods we use today: Initial period (1800–800 BC), Early Horizon (800–200 BC), Early Intermediate period (200 BC–AD 600), Middle Horizon (AD 600–1000), Late Intermediate period (AD 1000–1470), and Late Horizon (AD 1470–1540).

Rowe made it clear that these periods were temporal, not developmental, stages. In spite of his warnings, the rough association between Middle Horizon and Tiwanaku (Tiahuanaco), and between Late Horizon and Inka, led to unintended developmental overtones. Much attention has been focused on the Andean horizons, with the intermediate periods sometimes treated as the "leftovers" between them (Conklin and Moseley 1988:145; Willey 1991). As time has passed, three possibilities have become increasingly likely: (1) that the earliest Andean state appeared during the Early Intermediate period, rather than during a horizon; (2) that the horizons display more diversity than expected; and (3) that some intermediate periods have more unity than expected.

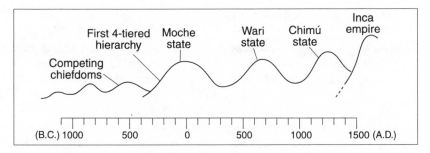

Figure 3.5. Consolidation and breakdown of states in the Andes.

There are still enormous lacunae in our understanding of just how the first Andean state formed. On the basis of available data, it appears that the Early Horizon was a period of competition among powerful chiefdoms, such as those centered at Chavín de Huántar (Burger 1992) and Cerro Sechín (Samaniego, Vergara, and Bischof 1985). During the Early Intermediate period the first Andean state, called Moche or Mochica, emerged on the north coast (Hastings and Moseley 1975; Moseley 1983:222; Shimada 1994; Wilson 1988:332–42).

Our first hint of a statelike, four-tiered settlement hierarchy comes from David Wilson's survey of the Casma Valley (Wilson 1995). This hierarchy is based both on modal site sizes and differentiated functions, and it dates somewhere between 350 BC and AD 1. Below the largest site in Casma are five rather evenly distributed secondary centers, then a number of tertiary centers, and finally a still larger number of villages forming the fourth tier. A series of fortresses were built at this time, suggesting that we are dealing with a state forged from competing polities, just as happened in Oaxaca (Marcus and Flannery 1996:155–58), Hawai'i (Service 1975), and among the Zulu of South Africa (Gluckman 1940). Wilson's estimate of the Casma Valley population at this time is greater than 50,000.

Casma was one of 14 valleys in a 550 km stretch of the Peruvian coast incorporated by the Moche state (Alva and Donnan 1993; Conklin and Moseley 1988:151). Moche ceramics and textiles show battle scenes with the victors taking prisoners, and important rituals involving human sacrifice and the offering of valuable objects.

Moche would seem to be another example of an early state that expanded at the expense of less-developed neighbors, reaching its peak early, then collapsing (fig. 3.5). We know something of its pyramids and flamboyant tombs (Alva and Donnan 1993) but lack data on whether or not its rulers had palaces. I expect Christopher Donnan's current excavations at Dos Cabezas, and Carol Mackey and Luis Jaime Castillo's work at San José de Moro, will fill these gaps in our knowledge.

Second-generation Andean states continued the expansionist legacy of the Moche. During the Middle Horizon, Wari (in the Ayacucho highlands of Peru) and Tiwanaku (near Lake Titicaca in Bolivia) both rose to power (Bermann 1994; Isbell and McEwan 1991). The capital city of Wari covered several square kilometers. The Wari state built provincial centers as far away as Pikillacta near Cuzco (McEwan 1985, 1991; Sanders 1973; Schreiber 1992) and Cajamarquilla on the central coast (Stumer 1954).

The Andes' best-known third-generation state was that of the Chimú, which rose to power during Late Intermediate times (Moseley and Day 1982). Its capital, Chan Chan, reached 20 km^2 between AD 1100 and 1400. The Chimú state covered perhaps 1,000 km of the Pacific coast, from Tumbes in the north to the Chillón River in the south (fig. 3.6). The Chimú were eventually conquered by the Inka, Peru's fourth-generation state, who came to control an empire that stretched 4,000 km from Ecuador to Chile and Argentina (D'Altroy 1992; Hyslop 1984; Morris 1982 and this volume; Morris and Thompson 1985).

The Andes is yet another area where the term "city-state" is inappropriate. All the Andean states mentioned above were large and expansionist, and when they did break down into constituent provinces, the latter often took the form of *curacazgos*—a hybrid Quechua-Spanish term for the territory ruled by a *curaca,* or native hereditary lord. An example of a Late Intermediate *curacazgo* on the central coast of Peru would be the Kingdom of Warku, which included the archaeological sites of Cerro Azul and Ungará (Marcus 1987b, 1987c; Rostworowski 1978–80).

THE MESOPOTAMIAN CASE

The alternation of strong centralized political control with periods of turmoil is so characteristic of Mesopotamian history that the events recorded in royal inscriptions cannot be simply ignored: documentary and archaeological sources cluster in the periods of peace, and the recurrent effects on the social institutions we are describing are too evident to be missed. Changes may be the direct consequence of political acts, or more indirectly of economic conditions or of the expansion or contraction of geographical horizons. Even the more subtle changes, such as the apparent shift towards private from institutional enterprise, or the gradual separation of cities from their hinterland, can be related more convincingly to particular political situations than to some long-term yeast. It would be dangerous to deny that some underlying trends may have been at work within the Mesopotamian urban society independently of, or indeed in spite of, the potent extraneous influences imposed by dynastic ambitions and disasters, but they are hard to detect behind these much more dramatic oscillations. The similarities between one period of prosperity and another, one "Dark Age" or *Zwischenzeit* and another, seem more than their differences. (Postgate 1992:22–23)

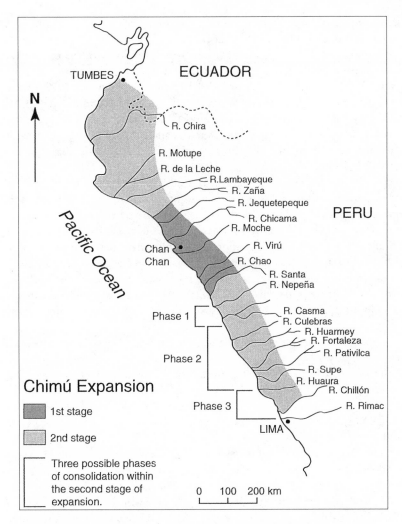

Figure 3.6. The expansion of the Chimú state involved at least two major stages, with possibly three phases of consolidation during the second stage of expansion (redrawn from Mackey and Klymyshyn 1990:fig. 1).

The Near East is yet another region where primary states formed after a long period of competition among chiefly societies. As far back as the Samarran phase (5500–5300 BC [uncalibrated]), competition between large villages was so intense that some featured ditches and defensive walls, watchtowers, and piles of sling missiles (El-Wailly and Abu al-Soof 1965; Oates 1969). During Late 'Ubaid, sometime around 4000 BC, the archaeological record has examples of raided villages, with elite residences burned and unburied corpses left behind (Tobler 1950:26).

While the details of their formation are still not known, the first archaic states in Mesopotamia (Iraq) and Susiana (Iran) seem to have flourished between 3700 and 3200 BC (Adams 1981; Adams and Nissen 1972; Algaze 1993a; Johnson 1972, 1987; Wright, this volume; Wright and Johnson 1975). By Early Uruk times in southern Mesopotamia, and by Middle Uruk times in Susiana, settlement pattern surveys and site-size histograms reveal a four-tiered hierarchy of cities, towns, large villages, and small villages (Johnson 1973, 1980).

The early state centered on Susa in southwestern Iran seems to have had a particularly turbulent history. Collapse of one or more chiefdoms at the end of the 'Ubaid period (c. 4000 BC) seems to have been followed by a period of economic and political reorganization during Early Uruk times. By Middle Uruk (c. 3700 BC), Wright and Johnson have detected the presence of an early state with centralized craft production, administered local exchange, administered labor, and a four-tiered settlement hierarchy (Johnson 1987:107). At its peak, this early Susiana state seems to have had outposts like Godin Tepe, situated 250 km away in the Zagros Mountains (Young 1969).

During the Late Uruk (c. 3400 BC), the early Susiana state fractured into two physically autonomous and hostile entities, one centered at Susa and the other at its former subject community, Chogha Mish. Johnson (1987:124) suggests that Chogha Mish broke away from Susa in order to retain sole use of the land, water, and labor in its region. This split may have been similar to Quiriguá's "battle for independence" from Copán in the Maya Lowlands.

The early state centered on the city of Uruk (Warka) in southern Mesopotamia was even larger and more territorially extensive than the one centered on Susa (fig. 3.7). The city of Uruk may have reached 200 ha by Late Uruk, and 400 ha before the end of Early Dynastic I (Adams and Nissen 1972). After this point (c. 2700 BC), however, Uruk suffered a fate similar to that of Susa in the Late Uruk period; its ascendancy was "increasingly challenged by the growth of a number of rival cities like Umma, Shuruppak, Zabalam, Bad-Tibira, and others" (Adams and Nissen 1972:19). Possibly these rival cities contributed to the collapse of the Uruk state by appropriating much of its former land, water, and labor.

At its peak, some believe, the Uruk state controlled an area stretching from Ur to Abu Salabikh; increasing evidence shows that its "influence" extended far beyond. "Colonies," "outposts," or "enclaves" with ceramics, tablets, administrative seals, and/or architecture in Uruk style have been found as far up the Euphrates and Tigris Rivers as eastern Turkey (Algaze

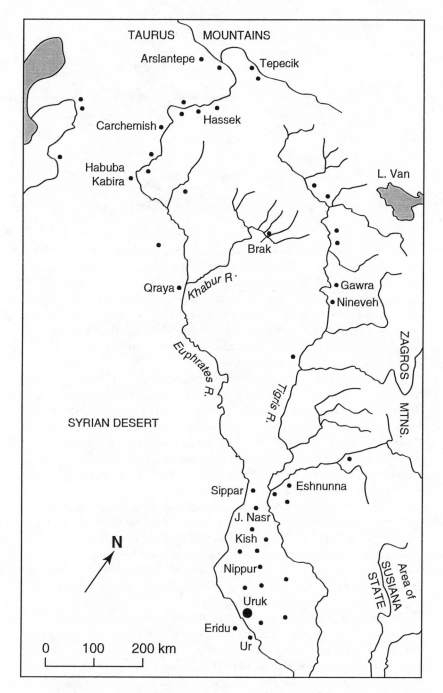

Figure 3.7. The total area directly controlled by Mesopotamia's Uruk state has not been determined, but its "outposts" or "colonies" extended as far as eastern Turkey (data from Algaze 1993a; Oates 1993).

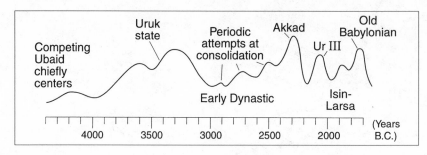

Figure 3.8. Consolidation and breakdown of states in Mesopotamia.

1989, 1993a). Some "colonies," like Habuba Kabira South, are heavily for-tified (Strommenger 1980). More distant "enclaves," as at Haçinebi, are not (Stein et al. 1996). The parallels with Teotihuacán are clear: a "hyperurban" capital, direct control of an irregular and noncontiguous territory, and dis-tant "colonies" or "enclaves," some of which were peacefully integrated into the surrounding region, while others were not (for a range of such sites, see Boese 1989–90; Frangipane and Palmieri 1988; Oates 1993; Stein et al. 1996; van Driel 1983; Wattenmaker 1990).

There are divergent interpretations of these Uruk "colonies" or "out-posts" on the upper Tigris and Euphrates. Oates (1993) believes that they reflect a short Late Uruk presence (100–150 years at most), and that their main purpose was to acquire resources that were unavailable in southern Mesopotamia. Johnson (1988–89), on the other hand, suggests that at least some Uruk "colonies" or "outposts" may have been founded by the refugee elites of losing factions in Middle or Late Uruk power struggles, accompa-nied by their political followers.

Whatever the case—and it will probably take decades to resolve the de-tails of the Uruk expansion—it is clear that Mesopotamia's first state had a demographic and political impact on an area roughly 1,000 km from north-west to southeast. This is approximately the distance between Teotihuacán and its "elite enclave" at Kaminaljuyú. Like the Monte Albán, Copán, and Teotihuacán states, the Uruk state first lost its more distant outposts, then lost its grip on more nearby areas (fig. 3.8).

As this first-generation state collapsed, southern Mesopotamia entered a 650-year period of decentralization known as the Early Dynastic (3000– 2350 BC). This period was characterized by smaller polities, autonomous or semiautonomous, to which a number of terms have been applied. Diakonoff (1974) refers to them as "nomes," using the word the Greeks applied to the districts comprising the Egyptian state; Adams (1981) refers to them as "en-claves." Yoffee (this volume) and others refer to them as "city-states."

The appropriateness of using the term "city-state" could be challenged by data from the Kingdom of Lagash, one of the best documented of southern Mesopotamia's Early Dynastic polities. It contained at least three cities, more than 20 towns, and at least 40 villages (Adams 1965:101). Diakonoff (1974) has estimated its population of "free citizens" as more than 100,000. Its two largest cities, Lagash and Girsu, had populations conservatively estimated at 36,000 and 19,000, respectively; since Lagash alone covers 600 ha, the figure could be twice as high. Although the total area controlled by the Kingdom of Lagash has not been determined, its irrigated fields alone are thought to have exceeded 2,000 km^2, and it had a 45 km frontier with the rival Kingdom of Umma. This sounds like something beyond a "city-state."

Around 2350 BC, the ruler Sargon of Akkad succeeded for a time in unifying all of southern Mesopotamia (fig. 3.9). Because of earlier rulers' attempts to extend their hegemony (see below), Sargon's state must be considered "third generation." At their peak, Sargon and the later members of his dynasty exerted control over a large area, from Tell Brak and Chagar Bazar in Syria to Ur and Lagash in southern Iraq (Postgate 1992:fig. 2:11a).

Around 2250 BC, the Akkadian dynasty lost control of Mesopotamia. Nomadic Gutians from the Zagros Mountains took advantage of the Akkadian collapse to loot unprotected cities. Not long after this, however, the rulers of the Third Dynasty of Ur managed to step into the power vacuum and establish their own hegemony over the area (fig. 3.10). Ur had spent much of the previous 200 years as a subject province of Akkad and other polities; between 2222 and 2118 BC, it became the capital of a fourth-generation regional state. The territory controlled by Ur, however, was only about half that claimed earlier by the Akkadian dynasty; for example, it fell hundreds of kilometers short of reaching the areas of Brak and Chagar Bazar (Postgate 1992:fig. 2:11b).

In other words, Mesopotamia shows the same dynamic cycles of consolidation and collapse seen in Central Mexico and the Maya region, and the same tendency for subject provinces to become the core provinces of later states. When the Third Dynasty of Ur lost power, it was followed by a 260-year phase of decentralization known as the Isin-Larsa period (fig. 3.11). From 1760 BC, a fifth-generation regional state had arisen under Hammurabi with its capital at Babylon (Oates 1986; Postgate 1992:fig. 2:11d).

Yoffee's analysis provides a detailed explanation for the eventual collapse of this fourth-generation Mesopotamian state (Yoffee 1977). It would appear that one of Hammurabi's mistakes was the continual bypassing of lower-level administrators in the hierarchy, a process that archaeologists with an interest in systems theory have called *meddling* (Flannery 1972). Following Hammurabi's unification of Mesopotamia by conquest, local administrators were bypassed and higher-level state administrators were assigned the duties of policing agriculture and fishing. Taxes were collected and most land was entailed to the Babylonian state. The Babylonian state's policy of co-opting

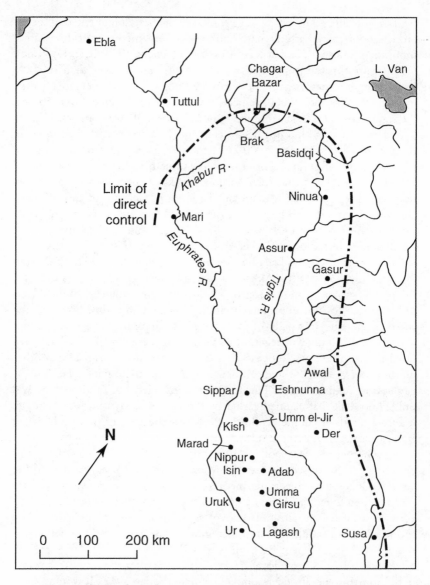

Figure 3.9. The area controlled by the Akkad dynasty, a moment of peak consolidation in Mesopotamia (redrawn from Postgate 1992: fig. 2:11a).

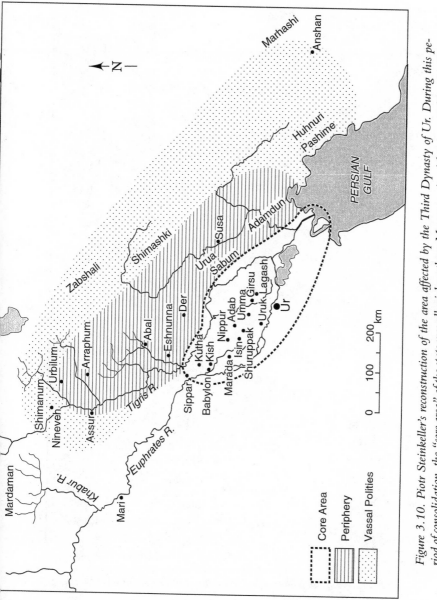

Figure 3.10. Piotr Steinkeller's reconstruction of the area affected by the Third Dynasty of Ur. During this period of consolidation, the "core area" of the state was alluvial southern Mesopotamia. A larger area, from the plains of Nineveh to the plains of Susa, was incorporated as the "periphery" of the Ur III state. Beyond that was an even larger region of "vassal polities" in the mountains of Iraq and Iran (redrawn, with modifications, from Steinkeller 1987: figs. 1 and 6).

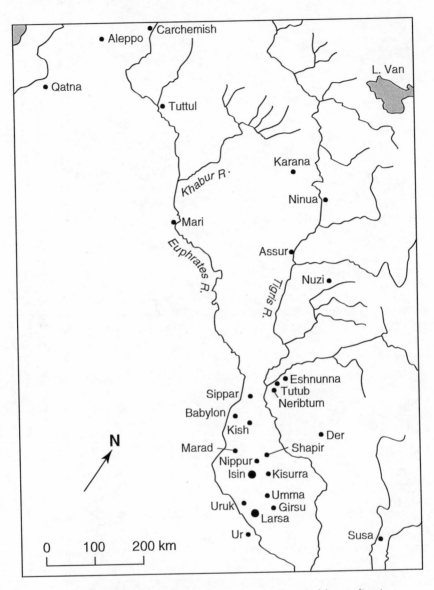

Figure 3.11. Mesopotamia during the Isin-Larsa period of decentralization (redrawn from Postgate 1992: fig. 2:11c).

local authority in newly conquered territory served to sow the seeds of its own destruction (Yoffee 1977:148). In the Old Babylonian period this highly centralized state was administered from the capital of Babylon; because it proved to be highly oppressive to its subjects, conquered territory quickly decomposed into its constituent elements, each of which reestablished its local autonomy (Yoffee 1977:143). The empire built by Hammurabi experienced a long decline, not through the personal inefficiency of succeeding rulers but because Hammurabi's system was too rigid and oppressive to adapt.

The highly centralized state had initially become prosperous from the tribute and taxes exacted from far-flung provinces. The Babylonian state then undertook massive building and waterworks projects. When the southern, western, and eastern provinces were able to break away, however, the resources needed by the state to maintain its ambitious building projects were severely reduced.

As the late Babylonian period progressed, bureaucrats not directly controlled by the state tended to emphasize loyalties to the groups from which they had been recruited. The state was overthrown by a Hittite king, and the bureaucracy reverted to the position of a locally based aristocracy, while the institutional framework of the political system collapsed. The ruling house in Babylon fell victim to its long-standing oppressive policies and the resulting internal instability (Yoffee 1977:149).

Whereas most Mesoamerican field archaeologists think of the "peaks" of state consolidation as normal, and the "troughs" of dissolution as temporary aberrations, the situation in Mesopotamia is somewhat different. There, most epigraphers think of the periods of decentralization and provincial autonomy as normal, and the peaks of unification as rare events. The reason, I believe, is that written documents first become abundant and decipherable during the Early Dynastic, a 650-year period of decentralization. It stands to reason that epigraphers—not focusing on the fact that Early Dynastic decentralization followed the breakdown of an earlier, influential Uruk state—might come to think of small autonomous polities as the normal situation.

What is often unappreciated, however, is the fact that the Early Dynastic witnessed countless attempts by the rulers of various enclaves to subjugate their neighbors. Some of these attempts temporarily succeeded in reunifying parts of Mesopotamia. For example, the Early Dynastic ruler Mesalim of Kish "exercised hegemony far beyond the walls of his own city" (Cooper 1983:7). Calling himself "*lugal* [king] of the universe," Mesalim left royal inscriptions as far away as Girsu in the Kingdom of Lagash; in fact, he is credited with erecting a monument that established the border between the provinces of Lagash and Umma. In this act he reminds us of the Maya ruler Smoke Imix of Copán, who also set up boundary stelae to delimit his "realm."

During Early Dynastic III, Lagash itself rose to prominence under a ruler named Eanatum, who assumed the kingship of both Lagash and Kish (Cooper 1983:42). A later ruler of Lagash, Enshakushana (2432–2403 BC) "apparently exercised hegemony over most of Sumer for a short period of time," conquering Kish and Akshak and dedicating his booty to the temple of the god Enlil at Nippur (Cooper 1983:42). In fact, the epigraphic literature of Early Dynastic Mesopotamia provides dozens of examples of rulers who temporarily united two, three, or even more small polities into a larger unit.

My point here is that even periods of relative decentralization in Mesopotamia cannot be sweepingly characterized as consisting only of independent "city-states." Strong rulers fought incessantly to incorporate their neighbors into a larger polity; weak rulers did whatever they could to retain their autonomy. It might be more accurate to describe such periods as consisting of *relentless attempts to create larger polities by alliance or conquest,* even though none succeeded on the scale achieved by Sargon or Hammurabi. I suspect that when we know more about the Maya Lowlands, we will find that their periods of decentralization look much the same. I therefore conclude that Mesopotamia fits the Dynamic Model, just as some of my Near Eastern colleagues had suggested.

THE EGYPTIAN CASE

As is the case with many pristine states, the first Egyptian state resulted from the amalgamation of chiefdoms, allegedly by force. While the details are not known, most believe that prior to 3200 BC there were two maximal chiefdoms involved (Emery 1961; cf. Kemp 1989). One lay in Lower Egypt, with its paramount center at Buto in the Nile Delta. The other was in Upper Egypt, with its paramount center at Hierakonpolis (Hoffman 1970). Different headgear distinguished the political leaders of each chiefdom, with the leader of Lower Egypt wearing a red crown while his Upper Egyptian counterpart wore a white crown.

Scenes and texts on artifacts from the Main Deposit at Hierakonpolis (such as the Narmer Palette, and the maceheads of Narmer and Rosette Scorpion) suggest that the unification of Egypt occurred around 3100 BC when Upper Egypt conquered Lower Egypt. (Unfortunately, we lack relevant contemporaneous records from Lower Egypt, whose version might have been quite different.) This unification resulted in a single state whose ruler wore a "double crown," combining the red crown of Lower Egypt with the white crown of Upper Egypt (fig. 3.12). A new capital for all of

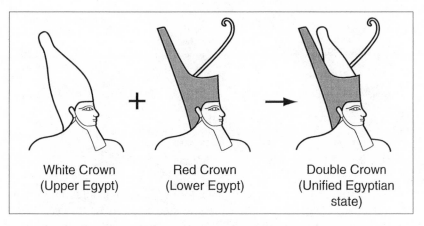

| White Crown | Red Crown | Double Crown |
| (Upper Egypt) | (Lower Egypt) | (Unified Egyptian state) |

Figure 3.12. When the Upper Egyptian chiefdom conquered the Lower Egyptian chiefdom, the ruler of the newly unified Egyptian state wore a "double crown" combining the white crown of Upper Egypt with the red crown of Lower Egypt (redrawn from Emery 1961:fig. 68).

Egypt was then established at Memphis, strategically located near the former border between the two chiefdoms (Kees 1961). Memphis was fortified, and it is probably there that we see the first Egyptian palaces (although Emery [1961:178] has argued that the palace might predate the founding of Memphis since a *serekh,* or palace façade, is present on the Narmer Palette).

The early Egyptian state was divided into districts, known as *hesps* in Egyptian and nomes in Greek. Each nome had its own specific customs, traditions, and patron deity (*njwty,* "city or local god"). Greek historians refer to the rulers of each nome as *nomarchs* and make it clear that these provincial lords had considerable power. We might see this situation as analogous to that of the Lowland Maya, where the capital was run by an *ahau* but his subject provinces were run by *batabob* (Marcus 1993a:119–20).

By 2400 BC there were 22 nomes in Upper Egypt. The number of nomes in Lower Egypt varied over time, but eventually there were 20 (Silverman 1991:38). The nomarch of each province had important administrative and decision-making powers, and nomarchs sometimes formed alliances with one another, thereby becoming powerful rivals of the pharaoh. Indeed, the history of the early Egyptian state shows periods of strong centralized rule alternating with periods of pharaonic weakness; during the latter, the nomes had a great deal of autonomy. So similar is this Egyptian pattern to that in Mesopotamia that Diakonoff (1974) applies the term "nome" to Sumerian provinces like Umma, Lagash, Ur, and Kish.

Egyptologists have recognized this cyclic pattern of consolidation versus

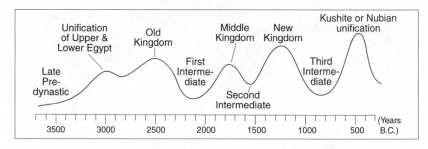

Figure 3.13. Consolidation and breakdown of states in ancient Egypt.

provincial autonomy in their use of the terms "kingdom" and "intermediate." They see Egypt unified into a pristine state between 3100 and 2600 BC, during Dynasties 0–3 of the Early Dynastic period. A subsequent period of strong centralized control by the pharaohs during Dynasties 4–8 is known as the Old Kingdom (2600–2150 BC). Dynasties 9–11, on the other hand, are seen as belonging to a period of relative decentralization and provincial autonomy known as the First Intermediate (2150–1950 BC) (fig. 3.13).

Egypt was reunified during Middle Kingdom times (1950–1650 BC). This second-generation state might be compared to Sargon's reunification of Mesopotamia (see above). It broke down during Dynasties 15–17, a period of decentralization known as the Second Intermediate (1650–1550 BC). The rulers of Dynasties 18–20 succeeded in reunifying Egypt into a third-generation state during the New Kingdom (1550–1050 BC). That unified state eventually broke down during Dynasties 21–24, known as the Third Intermediate (1050–712 BC). Finally, the Nubians conquered Egypt during Dynasty 25, assembling an even larger state that unified Egypt and Nubia during the Late Period (712–343 BC).

I conclude that Egypt shows cycles of unification and breakdown similar to those of Central Mexico and Mesopotamia, providing another case for the Dynamic Model. I would argue, however, that Egypt's cycles are less fully understood because so much of our information comes from royal inscriptions at capitals. Obviously, royal inscriptions are unlikely to call our attention to periods of weakness, during which some of the stronger nomes were able to set their own agendas. More attention should be paid to such "intermediate" periods to evaluate the impact of provincial nomarchs on the political system. Available data suggest that the duration of most "intermediate" periods in Egypt was shorter than "intermediates" in Mesopotamia; however, such periods in Mesopotamia may not be as long or decentralized as we have imagined, because we have downplayed the lines of evidence that indicate various rulers attempted and partially succeeded in unifying Mesopotamia's polities.

THE AEGEAN CASE

I have included the Aegean in my sample in spite of the lack of consensus on whether the Minoan, Mycenaean, and Archaic Greek societies were actually states. One reason for including them is that they show the same pattern of cyclic consolidation and dissolution seen in the rest of my cases. A second reason is that the Greek case supports my suspicion that societies called "city-states" are often *not* states.

Sometime around 1900 BC there was a major transformation of the political organization of Bronze Age Crete. The population of the island had reached 75,000 persons when construction began on four very clear palaces at Knossos, Phaistos, Malia, and Zakros. Each palace is alleged to have been associated with a king, and "that of Knossos is the largest and most important, and so the king of Knossos may perhaps have enjoyed some sort of suzerainty over the kings of the other palaces" (Michailidou 1989:29). At their peak between 1800 and 1500 BC, the Minoan kings built palaces with extensive storerooms and artisans' quarters (see Flannery, this volume), as well as royal villas, country mansions, and tombs in *tholos* style. Surviving two periods of partial destruction and rebuilding in 1600 BC and 1500 BC, the palaces were totally destroyed by 1400 BC, when Minoan civilization came to an end.

The destruction of Minoan Knossos is at least partly credited to the Mycenaeans, an expansionist, militaristic society that had been developing on the Greek mainland during late Minoan times. The Mycenaeans, by taking over the palace of Knossos and rebuilding it, became a potential second-generation state in our terms (fig. 3.14).

Aegean scholars have conflicting views as to whether or not Mycenaean society was organized as a state. Renfrew (1972:369) sees the Mycenaeans as consisting of several groups that were "something more than chiefdoms, something less than states," a description close to the one Flannery and I have applied to the Monte Albán I period in Oaxaca (Marcus and Flannery 1996:171). Both Renfrew and Ferguson find the term "palace principalities" appropriate (Ferguson 1991:173). Others, such as Desborough (1964: 218), consider Mycenaean conquests sufficiently extensive to designate them an "empire."

One could make a case for the Mycenaeans as an archaic state. Their society was stratified, and they were ruled by a monarch who lived in a palace inside a fortified citadel at Mycenae on the Peleponnesus; the commoners lived outside the walls. Hierarchically below the capital were smaller towns and villages. The Mycenaeans had an extensive road network, armed forces, a writing system, well-developed craft specialization, an elaborate system of land ownership, and a system of taxation (Snodgrass 1980:15). Their rulers

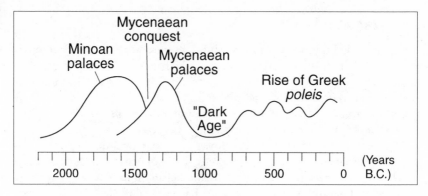

Figure 3.14. Periods of consolidation and breakdown in the ancient Aegean. Whether the periods of peak consolidation resulted in states or principalities is still under debate.

were buried in ashlar masonry *tholoi* closed with heavy brass doors (see Flannery, this volume).

Sometime between 1200 and 1100 BC, allegedly because of warfare and intense economic competition, Mycenaean society collapsed. There was a complete cessation in temple construction and the use of writing. No urban centers (or even sizable towns) are known from this so-called Dark Age. Snodgrass (1971, 1977, 1980) characterizes the Greeks of this period as having broken down to a pastoral society in which family, clan, and tribe were the important units. The *ethnos,* or local group, had no centralized authority; when a military leader was needed, he was elected (Champion et al. 1984:259, 261).

After 800 BC, Greece witnessed a dramatic increase in population and the appearance of new urban centers. Although the *ethnos* typical of the Greek Dark Age persisted in many areas, other regions saw the emergence of a new type of government, the polis. Since it is this ancient Greek political unit for which the term "city-state" was coined, it is worth looking at in some detail.

The polis was a self-sufficient unit in which secular and religious administration was joined; indeed, the construction of a monumental temple to a recognized patron deity is taken as proof that a polis had come into being (Snodgrass 1977:24). The polis differed in many ways from the Mycenaean kingdoms that had preceded it. For example, the towns and villages within each polis had a high degree of autonomy and exerted very little economic control over their citizens. When fortifications were present, they protected all members of a community, not just the ruler; the major focus of each community was its temple, rather than its palace (Snodgrass 1977:7–8).

Fine (1983) stresses the small size of the polis; most averaged no more than 5,000 free male citizens. Conflict and competition among poleis were commonplace, reflecting a degree of decentralization. However, larger units could be created through mechanisms such as marriage alliances between the elites of several poleis, political confederacies, and military confederacies in which two or more poleis joined forces in order to subjugate other peoples, temporarily expanding the territory from which they received tribute.

Two large units established in this way belonged to Sparta (which at one point controlled 8,300 km^2 after absorbing Laconia and Messenia) and Athens (which at one point controlled 2,800 km^2 after absorbing Attica and Salamis). It should be stressed that these territories were made possible only by alliance building and conquest; other poleis usually controlled as little as 80 km^2 to 1,300 km^2 and had relatively low population densities. Such territories are as small as those controlled by the *cacicazgos* of Mexico's Postclassic Mixteca (Spores 1967), and it is probably inappropriate to consider them "states."

During the fifth century BC, most Greek poleis belonged either to the Peleponnesian League under Spartan hegemony or the Delian League/ Athenian Confederacy under the control of Athens. During the third century BC, some confederacies of poleis (such as the Achaean League) had attracted as many as 60 cities into their orbit (Snodgrass 1980). Such moments of widespread unity, however, were "transient" (Hammond 1986); they required alliances among normally autonomous small units whose only hope of overcoming their small population sizes was through confederacy. Like the aforementioned *cacicazgos* of Mexico's Mixteca, the *curacazgos* of Late Intermediate Peru, or the *señoríos* that existed in the Postclassic Basin of Mexico before Azcapotzalco's hegemony, the Greek poleis represent a social form that is unlikely to represent a first-generation state for its region.

CONCLUSIONS

We have now looked at seven series of archaic states—the Maya, Zapotec, Central Mexican, Andean, Mesopotamian, Egyptian, and Aegean. A number of common patterns emerge, one of which is the cyclic unification and dissolution predicted by the Dynamic Model. It should be stressed that my seven cases do not include all archaic states, only a subset for which archaeological data are available; there is no guarantee that the patterns seen in those seven cases are universal. I also realize that I have not distinguished between states involving only one ethnic group (such as the Maya) and "empires" that involved the conquest of foreign peoples (such as the Aztec or Inka). I have not done this here because the differences between "state" and "empire" could fill a chapter of equal length.

Bruce Trigger (1993:8) has recently contrasted large, unitary "territorial" states with the clusters of smaller polities sometimes referred to as "city-states." I agree with the distinction that Trigger is making, but I suggest that these two categories were often *different stages in the dynamic cycles of the same states*, rather than just contrasting sociopolitical types. Central Mexico, for example, gave rise to both of Trigger's types, but the clusters of "city-states" were always the breakdown product of an earlier unitary state. I join many colleagues in believing that we should avoid the term "city-state" whenever possible, substituting instead a more appropriate regional or indigenous term such as *cuchcabal, ahaulel, altepetl, hesp, nome, cacicazgo, curacazgo,* or *señorío.*

I find it significant that in every case I have examined, the first state to form in a region was unitary in Trigger's terms. I suspect that it could happen no other way. In a recent review of social evolution, Flannery (1995) has examined two non-Western states whose origins are known in detail: the Hawaiian and Zulu states. In neither case did a group of chiefdoms grow into a group of "city-states." Rather, the state formed in the context of a group of competing chiefdoms when one of those chiefdoms succeeded in subjugating its neighbors, turning them into the provinces of a larger, unitary state. Elsewhere Flannery and I have presented evidence that the Zapotec state formed in a similar way, when one member of a group of chiefdoms succeeded in subduing the others (Marcus and Flannery 1996:155).

I cannot, therefore, agree with Yoffee's sweeping statement that "all the earliest states (Mesopotamia, Indus Valley, China, Andes, Maya, Teotihuacán: the exception is Egypt, which is a regional state) are not states at all, they are city-states" (Yoffee 1995a:546). In fact, all the pristine states we have examined—Tikal, Monte Albán, Teotihuacán, Moche, Uruk, Egypt, and so on—were unitary in Trigger's terms, with their capital cities sometimes placing enclaves as much as 1,000 km away. Nothing resembling a group of "city-states" appeared in those regions until after the early unitary states collapsed. Often, it is the newly autonomous former provinces of those collapsed states that look like a group of "city-states" (Marcus 1989). And the second-generation states in each region frequently formed when one of those provinces succeeded in subjugating the others.

I consider it very unlikely that a pristine state could emerge as a group of "city-states," because I see no mechanism by which a group of chiefdoms can evolve into a group of tiny statelets. A state is not just a chiefdom that has received an injection of growth hormones. It is a large polity, each of whose provinces was a former chiefdom, forged together by deliberate political and territorial reorganization rather than simple growth.

As for the multiple autonomous polities called "city-states," we should not be seduced into considering all of them *states* simply because their rulers drew heavily on the ideology and symbolism of their more powerful predecessors. Both Egyptian and Maya rulers did this extensively, linking themselves to the lords of an earlier age of large states and making it appear that there had been no "troughs" in their history. As archaeologists we know there were many consolidations and collapses, but many royal Egyptian and Maya inscriptions do their best to convince us otherwise (Marcus 1995c; Rhodes 1986).

Although I am convinced that the Dynamic Model fits these seven cases, there are interesting differences in the lengths of the dynamic cycles involved. In my review of the cycles of various Mesoamerican states (Marcus 1992a), I pointed out that most unitary states lasted only about 200 years. The seven cases examined here suggest a much greater range of variation. Some strong, territorially extensive states, such as that controlled by the Third Dynasty of Ur, may have lasted only a century. Others, like that of Old Kingdom Egypt, may have lasted as much as 500 years. Cowgill (1988:266) has suggested that the longevity of states may have something to do with whether they were put together by "subjugation" or "incorporation," with the former being more "decomposable."

A similar range of variation characterizes the troughs of dissolution and decentralization. Some periods of breakdown, such as that between the dynasty of Akkad and the Ur III state, may have lasted only a century. The relative decentralization of Early Dynastic Mesopotamia, in contrast, may have lasted 650 years. However, as we have seen, this decentralization was interrupted by periods of consolidation under rulers like Mesalim of Kish and Eanatum of Lagash; thus the Early Dynastic may represent a series of shorter troughs, rather than a single long one. I think that a similar pattern of short troughs, rather than one "apocalyptic collapse," followed the breakdown of the Maya states centered at Calakmul and Tikal (Marcus 1993a).

Finally, it is worth noting that epigraphers and field archaeologists seem forever destined to view the rhythmic cycles of states differently. In monumental public buildings and rapidly expanding pottery styles, archaeologists see the rise of the earliest states in their regions. For them the peaks in the Dynamic Model are the normal state of affairs, and the troughs of dissolution are enigmatic collapses. For epigraphers it is the corpus of texts that count, whether they come from a peak or a trough in the dynamic cycle. Mesopotamian epigraphers, for whom the Early Dynastic and Old Babylonian periods are important sources of texts, see decentralization as the normal state of affairs. Forgetting how extensive the impact of Uruk states was in Mesopotamia and southwest Iran, they sometimes treat Sargon's hegemony as if it were a first-generation state, rather than a third-generation phenomenon.

In much the same way, some Maya epigraphers take decentralized moments of the Late Classic to be the normal state of affairs, since relatively few subject lords admit to subordinate status in the inscriptions they commissioned. The result is that when some epigraphers find evidence for the hegemonies that we archaeologists described long ago, they declare such polities not merely states, but "superstates." I remain convinced that the Dynamic Model can reconcile those contrasting positions by reminding us that we are simply looking at different stages in the evolution of states.

As for why the peaks of consolidation inevitably gave way to valleys of dissolution, I suspect it had something to do with the difficulty of maintaining large-scale inegalitarian structures for long periods of time. Large-scale, asymmetrical, and inegalitarian structures were more fragile and unstable than commonly assumed, even though most scholars who work exclusively on states consider such large-scale structures durable.

NOTE

I wish to thank Henry Wright, who gave me extensive comments on this essay, particularly on Mesopotamia; George Cowgill, who supplied insightful and detailed comments on Teotihuacán and other sites; Gary Feinman, who not only helped me edit all the chapters in this volume but also did the thankless task of reformatting every paper many times; and all the conference participants who ensured that the week was so successful. Most participants arrived in Santa Fe loaded down with slides to accompany their excellent oral presentations, and from those talks I gained new insights into comparative states. Last, but not least, I thank Doug Schwartz and all the staff of the School of American Research, because they always create a marvelous environment for open discussions.

4

Scale and Social Organization
Perspectives on the Archaic State
GARY M. FEINMAN

> Many analysts are prisoners of ideal types. In their view, there are
> "chiefdoms" and there are "states"—and never the twain shall
> meet: however much variation exists *within* these categories.
> —*Yale H. Ferguson, "Chiefdoms to City-States"*

> Larger, highly centralized and urbanized states, while more vis-
> ible, are not necessarily the most durable and adaptable of com-
> plex political systems.
> —*Ronald Spores, "Marital Alliance in the Political Integration of Mixtec
> Kingdoms"*

When I first conceptualized the topic of scale, settlement pattern, and the
archaic state, I envisioned a rather straightforward comparative discussion of the territorial extent and population size of different preindustrial polities that are generally considered to have sociopolitical organizations
more hierarchical, differentiated, and stratified than middle-range societies
or chiefdoms (Feinman and Neitzel 1984). Now I recognize that such preliminary thoughts were rather optimistic. For the periods prior to written
histories in most geographic regions, few archaeologists have ventured to estimate the exact size or full geographic scope of bounded political domains.
Rough estimates have been attempted for regional and continental populations during these eras; however, little agreement has been reached regarding these postulations, and even less consensus has been achieved concerning
the political configurations and subdivisions of these geographic landscapes.
One can only concur with Elvin (1973:17), who noted that "the question
of the size of political units seems never to attract among historians and so-
ciologists the attention which it deserves."

Various evolutionary overviews have offered general dimensions for the
demographic size and territorial extent of early states, yet the scarcity of

quantitative information on these topics is both frustrating and, in some senses, informative. Although my analysis cannot immediately remedy the empirical gap, general observations drawn from a comparative literature review can serve to highlight key issues and debates that revolve around scale, organization, and archaic states. Concentrating on states, several oft-cited arguments that propose a direct correlation between scale and complexity are considered. Preliminary estimates and postulated thresholds for the size of preindustrial states are reviewed. The oft-cited notion that state size somehow increases in regular or predictable increments also is examined. Although the long-recognized, basic correlation between societal size and organizational complexity is acknowledged, more precise definition of this relationship is found to be hindered by the general dearth of attention given to other key societal features (boundedness, temporal cycling, and strategies for integration) (Blanton et al. 1993:13–18). Several of these theoretical considerations provide the analytical framework for the examination of a single historical case of long-term change and the cycling of prehispanic polities in the Southern Highlands of Mexico.

The remainder of this chapter proceeds from broad theoretical comparisons to the brief examination of a single ancient Mesoamerican region. In the next two sections, general statements and debates concerning the spatial and demographic parameters of preindustrial states are assessed. Simple linear notions are challenged. This review is followed by a broad-ranging comparative discussion that emphasizes (despite our empirical biases toward the study of large core states; Stein 1994a:10) that some ancient states tended to be small, rather modular components of multipolity networks. These state systems were characterized by cyclical fluctuations and periodic instability. Large political entities did form, but they often were relatively short-lived, with rather dynamic linkages between the component segments of these great polities. In more spatially extensive, centralized polities, the kinds of integrative strategies and the implementation of power relations often varied markedly over space and time. Variation and change in integrative strategies (see Blanton, this volume) are suggested to have had important organizational and spatial implications for early polities. These theoretical observations in conjunction with the illustrative case analysis focused on prehispanic Oaxaca (Mexico) serve to challenge a number of broadly held views concerning the size, developmental trajectories, and breakdowns of archaic states. By raising and reassessing these issues, the aim is to aid the eventual closure of the aforementioned intellectual lacuna decried by Elvin (1973:17).

GENERAL PARAMETERS AND CONTRADICTIONS

Less agreement than one might expect exists in the scholarly literature concerning the size and scale of the archaic state. Demography has often been advanced as a prime mover of organizational change, and population size is viewed as an implicit indicator of different levels of organizational complexity (e.g., Carneiro 1967; Upham 1987). Nevertheless, no agreement on the demographic threshold between chiefdoms and states has been reached. For the ancient Americas, both Sanders and Price (1968:85) and Upham (1987:355–56) propose a population cutoff around 10,000 people. Yet, to their credit, neither views this figure in a rigid manner, as the former recognize that certain chiefdoms may range up to ten times that threshold value in size, while the latter views population density, as well as size, as a key correlate of organizational complexity. The 10,000 figure also is used implicitly by Friedman and Rowlands (1977:220), who see early "Asiatic states" as roughly that size. Yet Renfrew (1982) views some small states as having had as few as 2,000 to 3,000 people. Other authors place a chiefdom/state threshold at a somewhat larger population. Baker and Sanders (1972:163) argue that chiefdoms become unstable above 48,000 people. This figure corresponds roughly with the findings from a sample of 70 middle-range societies from the Americas in which the maximal estimates for societal population all fall below 31,000 people, except in a single case (Hispaniola Arawak) where estimates from 100,000 to 6,000,000 have been proposed.

In contrast, Johnson and Earle's (1987:314) examples of complex chiefdoms (Hawai'i) range up to 100,000, while their selected examples of archaic states begin at 14,000,000 (Inka). Flannery (1972), like Lenski (1966:145–46), describes archaic states as having hundreds of thousands of people. Although each of these authors may take a slightly different emphasis in their definitions of the state, the intellectual bases of these theoretical positions stem from closely related scholarly traditions. All refer to the state as a societal mode more complex than chiefdoms or middle-range societies, and characterized by a multitiered hierarchy of decision making and a degree of social stratification.

Quantitative estimates of the size of state populations are rare in the comparative literature. No specific figures are offered in the valuable synthesis by Claessen (1978a:586), who concludes that states have more than 500 people, "a sufficient population to make social categorization, stratification, and specialization possible." Cross-cultural overviews by Naroll (1956), Ember (1963), and Carneiro (1967) use maximal community size as a substitute for other societal demographic parameters. Although Carneiro (1967:236) hoped to examine societal populations, "considerable difficulty was encountered" in attempting to ascertain this variable. Likewise, for later historical times, data have been accumulated for ancient cities (e.g., Chandler and Fox 1974; Russell 1958), but little synthesis has been published concerning polity sizes.

Another perspective on scale and the archaic state has focused on the territorial extent of these early polities. Renfrew (1975, 1986) argues that early state modules should be roughly 1,500 km². Although there is no simple, uncontroversial way to convert this figure to a demographic estimate, it is interesting to note that one minimal population density (4 people/km²) associated with "civilizations" (Sanders and Price 1968:85) would yield an estimate of 6,000 inhabitants. At the opposite extreme, Taagepera (1978a) estimates that the Old World's largest empires were 100,000 km² in 3000 BC, and an order of magnitude larger several millennia later.

The point of the prior discussion has not been to reinforce or resume a rather sterile taxonomic exercise. My views (Blanton et al. 1981:23; Feinman and Neitzel 1984) on that issue are clear. Rather, this brief review reveals the dearth of cross-cultural demographic figures, the absence of consensus on the question, and the enormous range of size estimates used for the archaic state.

Another commonly held belief concerning the scale of political systems is that polity size has increased regularly and continuously since the Neolithic. Carneiro (1978) views this trend as so regular that it is "a general principle of human development." This process is assumed to be continuous and inevitable, so few questions are directed toward the mechanisms of integration. As a result, Carneiro places the root cause of this presumed linear trend on the principle of competitive exclusion, an almost innate urge to expand and outcompete neighbors (see also Kosse 1994; Sanders 1984). The inevitability of the process is asserted and assumed, so Carneiro (1978:216–19) and others (e.g., Naroll 1967) confidently predict the date on which a unified world government would emerge.

In part, Carneiro's observations follow Hart (1948), who modeled the areal size of the world's largest empires. Yet a more systematic, recent analysis (Taagepera 1968, 1978a, 1978b, 1979) calls into question both the postulated linearity of this territorial growth and its presumed regularity through time. Taagepera's study of the largest Old World empires since the third millennium BC found major upswings or jumps in polity size, which were associated with significant shifts in the technologies of power and communication. These cyclical growth spikes were punctuated by periods of relative stasis and even declines in the extent of global empires. Rises and falls in polity size were even more dramatic when Taagepera (1978b, 1979) examined his findings at the smaller scale of continents (as opposed to the global scale). In fact, polity sizes at various times in the past were larger in

the Mediterranean world and in western Asia than found in those areas today. For prehispanic Mesoamerica, Marcus (1992a) proposes that some later
states (investing in infrastructure) were smaller than earlier states in the same
region.

Although Carneiro (1978:211) has always been aware of this continen-
tal-scale cycling in polity size, he prefers to emphasize the larger global trend
toward unification. This logic is somewhat analogous to the common mis-
conception that there has been steady or uniform growth in mammalian
brain sizes because the largest mammalian brains have increased over time.
In actuality, these cranial changes are accounted for almost entirely by evolutionary transitions in select lineages (e.g., primates) of brainy mammals,
which have become brainier. Within many groups of mammals, the most
common brain size has remained unchanged over millions of years since the
lineage was established. The range of mammalian brain sizes has increased
over evolutionary time (as brain size in select lineages has increased), yet no
intrinsic force has pushed for larger brains across the entire taxonomic class
(see Gould 1985). Rather, one must examine the specific set of factors that
affected each lineage. Thus, returning to sizes of preindustrial empires, the
scale of the world's largest polities does increase over time. Yet that does not
imply a constant or necessary increase in the size of every state or in the size
of the largest states on each continent. As with the mammalian lineages, the
specific set of factors that influenced the preindustrial polities on each continent or in a specific ancient world would seem to be key.

Although a general worldwide trend toward growth in polity size does
seem apparent, the actual trend is more jagged (with peaks and valleys).
Fluctuations are amplified when the process is examined in specific continents and regions. From Carneiro's (1978) vantage, this inevitable global
progression requires little explication (and so is assigned to innate first principles). Yet if this process is recognized as cyclical and variable (in space and
time), it would seem to require further investigation and explanation focused at the continental and regional scales (see also Chase-Dunn 1990;
Taagepera 1978a). Such investigation should include greater attention to the
constraints, thresholds, mechanisms, and strategies associated with political
integration, expansion, and contraction (see also Marcus, this volume).

CYCLING IN ARCHAIC STATE SYSTEMS

At the continental scale, variations and cycles in the size and extent of preindustrial polities have long been recognized. In that sense, Taagepera's findings are not surprising. Decades ago, Steward (1955) included a "dark age"
in his now-classic, comparative trajectory for complex societies. Yet like
many other pioneers in the neoevolutionary research on early civilizations,

Steward's synthesis gave relatively little attention to this postulated stage of fragmentation; instead, he chose to focus on episodes of growth, development, and continuous expansion. In part, this ongoing emphasis owes much to both anthropology's long-standing concern with origins (e.g., states, cities) and the "archaeological loot" often associated with the concentration of wealth, power, and labor in the capitals of expanding states. We like to study "golden ages" rather than "dark ages." However, the developmental focus of our theorizing also may be a partial product of the progressivist intellectual climate in which our discipline was born and has flourished. Until the fragmentation of state control in eastern Europe (i.e., balkanization), the former Soviet Union, and elsewhere during this decade, the past several centuries have witnessed an unprecedented expansion of nation-state power and territorial spread, often suppressing local/ethnic diversity and economic/political autonomy in the process. Perhaps it is not surprising that archaeology has tended to direct so much attention to earlier episodes that feature the centralization of power, territorial expansion, and the extension of political control.

More recent studies of complex societies have broadened the spatial and temporal perspectives of investigation (e.g., Knapp 1992). The accumulation of archaeological and historical data now permits an examination of variability within continental regions in a manner that was not possible in Steward's time. Settlement pattern surveys draw attention away from great centers and force consideration of regional sequences that include alternating oscillations/fluctuations of nucleation and fragmentation (e.g., Adams 1978; Fish and Kowalewski 1990; Marcus 1992a, 1993a). No longer is it sensible to isolate specific cases of rise and collapse, or to treat societies or cultures as closed entities that go through a predetermined life cycle of florescence, maturity, decadence, and collapse (see important discussions in Yoffee and Cowgill 1988).

Taagepera's (1978a, 1978b) measurement of empires has recognized cyclical changes in the sizes of the largest political entities. Even more dynamic oscillations in polity size, political centralization, and population agglomeration have been recognized by subcontinental and regional studies synthesizing long trajectories of history in the Eastern (Maya) Lowlands of Mesoamerica (Marcus 1993a), Central Mexico (Smith 1992), the Valley of Oaxaca (Kowalewski et al. 1983), Mesopotamia (Adams 1978; Yoffee 1988b), and Southeast Asia (Bentley 1986). Collectively, these findings should direct our thinking away from the simple taxonomic dichotomies that have been drawn between weak or segmental states and bureaucracies, and toward more continuous models (e.g., de Montmollin 1989; Easton 1959; Wallace 1971) that recognize preindustrial organizations as dynamic formations that may oscillate in scale, integration, and complexity. Recent culture-historical syntheses (e.g., Willey 1991) that have focused on material culture variation over large regions also indicate oscillations in integration and communication at the subcontinental scale, with cycles of unified horizons interspersed with intermediate periods marked by greater stylistic diversity and regional fragmentation.

In a sense, these findings complement Price's (1977; see also Chase-Dunn 1990; Wesson 1978) suggestion that the study of the state should be extended beyond the single polity to larger landscapes in which clusters of such entities interact. Consequently, for a given social field, episodes of relative multipolity decentralization, when the landscape was occupied by many autonomous or semiautonomous states, might alternate with periods of centralization, when a single polity or center dominated or extended its boundaries to incorporate others. Yet in contrast to the implicit expectations of Carneiro's model, there is no reason to assume that cultural or economic boundaries should necessarily conform with the political boundaries of the state (see also Blanton 1976; Blanton and Feinman 1984). Yoffee (1991; see also Marcus 1983a) has illustrated this disjunction for the prehispanic Maya and ancient Mesopotamia, where shared cultural networks generally exceeded the political boundaries dominated or administered by any single polity. In other words, in a dynamic state system, the size of the sociocultural network of interaction might remain more or less comparable, while the power relations and boundaries of individual component polities ebbed and flowed (see Kowalewski 1990). As Eisenstadt (1988:236) has aptly noted, "the construction of boundaries of social groups, collectivities, and institutions is a continuing aspect in the life of human societies and not an anomalous response to some sort of irregular or periodic stress." The nested, multiscalar, and dynamic nature of these systems of states might in part account for the enormous range in the recorded sizes (see above) of archaic states, and for some of the difficulty that researchers have had in reporting size/scale estimates.

Although the notion of state or peer-polity systems has a significant presence in the archaeological literature (e.g., Renfrew 1972, 1975, 1986; Renfrew and Cherry 1986), the concept generally has been applied to networks in which most component entities remain largely autonomous (or semiautonomous) for an extended period. As a consequence, such landscapes at times have been contrasted with those in which single centers or states (or a temporal sequence of them) have dominated for an extended sequence. Yet the point here is that such dichotomies should not be drawn too sharply, since over time a single landscape may oscillate between episodes of relative centralization and "balkanization" (see Leach 1954; Marcus 1993a).

Significantly, there does not seem to be a single unilinear trajectory of change when it comes to these oscillations. Many cultural regions, including the Maya Lowlands and Mixtec Highlands of prehispanic Mesoamerica (Marcus 1989; Spores 1974), long were occupied by networks of multiple polities. Although the relative power and size of these component polities varied through time, the cultural region remained, to a degree, politically fragmented prior to Spanish Conquest. Yet in other regions, such as Central Mexico, single polities or "petty states" (Tenochtitlán) emerged and subsequently dominated the entire regional network (e.g., Brumfiel 1983; Smith and Berdan 1992). A similar process has occurred on the Italian Peninsula with Rome (Potter 1980). Episodes in which large dominant core states fragment into landscapes of small polities have long been described by archaeologists and historians alike (e.g., Bowersock 1988; Marcus 1989; Yoffee 1988a, 1988b).

SIZE AND THE ARCHAIC STATE

To this point I have argued that archaic states varied greatly in size and were often part of larger networks of interconnected states. Furthermore, I have noted that at times these networks were combined (fully or partially) into larger polities dominated by one or a few powerful centers. This latter circumstance has been described by Marcus (1993a; see also Martin and Grube 1995) for the Late Classic Maya, when a few regional states appear to have held sway over large segments of Mesoamerica's Southern Lowlands. In this section, I suggest that despite our long-standing focus on larger bureaucratic or imperial states, several observations indicate that many preindustrial states were rather small. Although the specific sizes vary in accordance with geography and time, many were roughly comparable in scale to the smaller or middle range of estimates presented above.

Given the absence of solid quantitative estimates for polity size and political boundaries, the aforementioned argument (for generally small preindustrial states) is not easy to make. However, several (largely indirect) inferences would at least seem to give it a degree of plausibility. For one, if we return to the culture-historical cycles discussed by Willey (1991), it is interesting to observe that in both Mesoamerica (see Price 1976) and Andean South America (e.g., Moseley 1992), the episodes of supposed imperially dominated horizons and larger states (the Middle and Late Horizons) comprise a relatively short proportion of the sequences during which systems of states were found in these regions. While this is not to deny the existence of specific large polities during other times in the ancient Andes, these powerful states only dominated relatively small parts of the prehispanic world. In prehispanic Mesoamerica, no single polity ever came close to controlling the entire culture area (Blanton and Feinman 1984), yet, even so, the two Mesoamerican episodes of relative political centralization were short (encompassing a total of roughly 750 years). In contrast, the two intermediate periods together endured for twice that duration (Price 1976). In the Andes, a similar pattern is found, as the two horizons are thought to last less than half a millennium, while the two intermediate periods cover 1,250 years.

This pattern corresponds with Adams's (1978) findings for Mesopotamia, where episodes of political unification were short and regularly succeeded by much longer periods characterized by greater local political autonomy. For the same region, Yoffee (1988b:59) notes that the ideal of governmental unity expressed in the native historiographic tradition does not appear to correspond to political reality. Tambiah (1977:84) has observed a similar pattern for Southeast Asia, where large, powerful, centralized states were rare and short-lived. Even the Old World's largest empires generally lasted no more than several centuries (Taagepera 1979). As the historian Elvin (1973:17; see also Hartwell 1982; Skinner 1985) has written, "the Chinese Empire is the major exception in the pre-modern world to what would appear to be the rule that units of territorial and demographic extent comparable to that of China are not stable entities over long periods of time." Yet even in the case of China, the degree and extent of political unification may have been smaller than certain traditional documentary accounts have suggested (Falkenhausen 1993; Keightley 1983; Rudolph 1987).

Braudel (1973:660) has suggested that some times are favorable for small states and others for large states, but that the period beginning in the fifteenth century in the Mediterranean was propitious for the latter. Although that seems to be so, the conditions and circumstances present earlier in much of Europe appear often to have fostered smaller polities. In part, we have not adequately recognized this pattern of small-state networks because of the taxonomic muddle that we have long been in. Although archaeologists and historians have had few difficulties recognizing and categorizing large preindustrial states, the smaller components of state systems (Wesson 1978), interstate systems (Chase-Dunn 1990), or peer-polity networks (Renfrew and Cherry 1986) are more difficult to classify. Perhaps that is why we have such a plethora of terms for such societies (see Houston 1992), including peer-polities, early state modules (Renfrew 1972), palatial territories (Bennet 1990), city-states (Bray 1972; Burke 1986; Calnek 1978; Ferguson 1991; Marcus 1989; Pounds 1969), feudal states (Mann 1987), segmentary states (Fox 1987; Southall 1956), galactic polities (Tambiah 1977), theater states (Geertz 1980), inchoate early states, typical early states, transitional early states (all from Claessen and Skalník 1978a:23), stratified societies (Fried 1967), Asiatic states (Friedman and Rowlands 1977), *cacicazgos*

(Redmond and Spencer 1994; Spores 1969), and petty kingdoms (Kowalewski et al. 1989).

Certainly, many of these small polities (characterized in the citations given above) overlap in scale and political complexity with "complex chiefdoms" (e.g., Kirch 1984). Yet it seems somewhat of a conceptual stretch to describe many of the aforementioned polities as "chiefdoms." (1) Many of these polities were composed of economically stratified classes (often with slaves); (2) their rulers or kings lived in palace structures; (3) the regional population densities were greater than is sometimes found in the same area when that region was unified under more centralized states; (4) writing systems often were employed; (5) in certain instances market systems were in place; and (6) at least three (often more) decision-making levels were present (although this was frequently not uniform for the individual polities that composed a single network; e.g., Hodge 1984; Pounds 1969). Perhaps more significantly, these component polities often were linked through marriage, conquest, political alliance, and other ties into multitiered confederations of greater vertical complexity (albeit ones that tended to be relatively unstable and shifting with variable degrees of integration). Nevertheless, sometimes the ties and connections that articulated these small states into larger confederations became more bureaucratic and centralized (as Smith 1992 describes for the concentration of power at Aztec Tenochtitlán). Finally, it is worth stressing that the above list is not intended to suggest or promote any simple analogies or parallels between these enumerated cases beyond the small sizes of the component polities. In fact, from case to case, the integrative strategies and mechanisms that bound leaders to followers (and leaders to leaders) often were distinct (e.g., Blanton et al. 1996; Lewis 1974a; see also Blanton, this volume).

INTEGRATION, SCALE, COMPLEXITY, AND THE ARCHAIC STATE

Social scientists (e.g., Spencer 1885:449–50) have long been aware that a relationship exists between societal size and complexity. A number of synchronic studies (e.g., Carneiro 1967; Ember 1963) have noted that when a large number of populations are examined (encompassing a diversity of environments), a strong relationship is found between increases in societal scale and more hierarchical organizational forms (vertical complexity). Carneiro (1967:239) has characterized this relationship: "If a society does increase significantly in size, and if at the same time it remains unified and integrated, it must elaborate its organization." Curiously, despite a long-standing interest in the formation and elaboration of human groups and groupings (see Johnson 1982), most anthropologists, archaeologists, and historians have tended to sidestep a direct examination of the size/organization relationship. Despite great environmental and technological diversity in these crosscultural samples, most theorists have evoked population pressure on food supply as the source of stress to which organizational change is a response (e.g., Carneiro 1970a; Sanders, Parsons, and Santley 1979).

This emphasis on population pressure as an explanation reflects several problems that we have in trying to understand general processes that govern the formation and evolution of human groups. As Flannery (1972) warned 25 years ago, it is not enough to examine only the socioeconomic stresses (e.g., demographic growth, population pressure, technological innovation, environmental change) and the specific sequences of societal transition; attention must be given to the decisions of individual actors as well as institutional structures and responses. In other words, it is difficult to model or compare systemic or evolutionary change if there is little understanding of the preexisting and potentially diverse structure (including the component segments, integrative mechanisms, constraints, and thresholds) of the system under investigation. This dual attention to the prior conditions as well as perturbative forces is what Gould (1986) means when he says "history matters," as it does for understanding archaic states as well as biological evolution (see also Feinman 1997; Schreiber 1987:267).

In the study of long-term social change there continues to be little in the way of "social physics" (Bernard and Killworth 1979). Although notable exceptions do exist (e.g., Johnson 1978, 1982; Kosse 1990; Wright 1977), the models and concepts that have been developed remain largely untested. This is not an argument for the construction of general laws (see Drennan 1996). In fact, I would comfortably substitute "social change studies" for "biology" in Mayr's (1982:37–38) statement that "there is only one universal law in biology . . . all biological laws have exceptions." Yet the time is ripe for greater systemization, comparative application, and careful consideration of what we do know about human organizations—their scale, integration, and complexity.

Bringing Integration into the Scale/Complexity Equation

Johnson's (1982) reanalysis of Ember's (1963) earlier study noted that the strong relationship between societal scale and complexity weakened greatly when narrower size ranges were examined in more discrete segments. The restudy goes on to outline three general conceptual directions (cycling, nested structures, integration) that should be examined to unravel the weaker fit found between sociopolitical complexity and scale (Carneiro 1967; see Feinman and Neitzel 1984 for the recognition of similar patterns in crosscultural data). Although Johnson's (1982) primary focus is not states, the conceptual directions that he elaborates provide promising avenues to probe

the significant variation in the sizes and organizational poses of complex societies. Although each of these directions has long tap roots in anthropology, the implications have not been incorporated sufficiently in most prior
presentations of neoevolutionary thought.

Drawing an example from the !Kung San, Johnson (1982:396–403)
illustrates how household organization (basal unit size) shifts to preserve
an egalitarian organization as camp size increases seasonally. Curiously,
Carneiro (1967:241–42) aptly described similar seasonal changes in Plains
Indian organization with tribal aggregations for buffalo hunts. However,
unlike the !Kung San case, the cyclical shifts on the Plains involved the temporary institution of both vertical and horizontal decision-making structures, with an overarching chief, a council, men's societies, and a police
force. One can see how these cyclical transformations might complicate the
relationship between scale and complexity based on cross-cultural samples
of static "snapshots" (Bernard and Killworth 1979:36).

Such seasonal fluctuations may not be a key consideration for archaic
states, yet complex preindustrial formations do show more organizational
fluidity than we generally associate with contemporary Euro-American institutions and bureaucracies (e.g., Wallace 1971). Recent studies of the late
prehispanic Inka (e.g., D'Altroy 1992) and Aztec (Hodge 1984; Rounds
1979; Smith and Berdan 1992; van Zantwijk 1985) polities emphasize both
marked temporal fluidity in their strategies of political integration (along
with the associated ideologies of incorporation) as well as significant synchronic spatial variation in strategies of administrative organization (for an
African example, see Kopytoff 1987; for China, see Hartwell 1982).

The accommodation of this short-term temporal and synchronic spatial
variability in preindustrial organization requires us to move beyond the
simple polar or taxonomic divisions (e.g., kinship/territorial, city-state/im-
perial bureaucracy) to more flexible analytical paradigms that examine core
features (Blanton et al. 1981; Kowalewski et al. 1983) and bundled continua
of variation (de Montmollin 1989; Easton 1959). By so doing, the Aztec
tributary domain (large in scale with a centralized settlement pattern, but
limited administrative bureaucracy) may not have to be seen as "anomalous"
or "transitional" between ideal forms (e.g., small polity vs. large bureaucratic
state). Rather, like the Aztec state, many large preindustrial states functioned
without formal, entrenched bureaucratic institutions, but their more fluid
organizational structures had ramifications for exaction, control, and stability (e.g., Hassig 1985; for African states, see also Lloyd 1965:71). To be
more explicit, our taxonomies ought not conflate large scale with imperial
bureaucratization, for in the preindustrial world it may have been easier for a small state than a very large one to centralize (see Kowalewski et al.
1983; Southall 1988:81). We should not be reductionist nor view states as
monolithic.

In reanalyzing Ember's (1963) findings, Johnson (1982:413–14; see Blau 1970:201) also made an important observation concerning the inverse relationship between system size and proportion of the population involved in administration. In a sense, Carneiro (1967:240) recognized the same pattern when he wrote that "unit for unit, . . . a society's structural complexity increases more slowly than its population." Yet Johnson (1982:413) saw that "these data contain what would appear to be a basic contradiction. If scalar stress increases as a function of size, how can an increment in the apparent response to stress decrease with increments of size?" He answers his query by noting that human groups have horizontally (sequential) as well as vertically (simultaneous) linked segments, and that the formation of more egalitarian horizontal subcomponents (e.g., larger household groupings, nonhierarchical social groupings) often can diminish scalar stresses on vertical decision-making structures. That is, since the individuals in a population generally belong to an array of nested social groups and arrangements, the nature and number of those groupings have implications when it comes to organizing or integrating the whole population.

This basic principle has been applied to all complex systems (Simon 1973:7), and certainly may be one explanatory factor behind the inability to find a simple numerical correlation between population size and vertical political complexity. In other words, new vertical decision-making levels may be sustainable in populations above a certain size, but when other populations (situated in other historical circumstances) reach that same size, these evolutionary changes may not occur owing to horizontal linkages, larger basal units, the presence of different organizational strategies, or other factors that may diminish scalar stress. Thus, on this "social grammar" alone, one might find that (in a comparative sample) some groups with two decision-making levels are somewhat larger (demographically) than others with three, and groups with three may be found to be more populous than some with four vertical levels. While no simple size/complexity threshold (to segregate chiefdoms from states) may be discernible, the basic pattern across the entire sample of preindustrial societies could still show the strong overall positive empirical correlation that we see between scale and vertical complexity. The above observation also would not contradict the notion that, at some still higher population threshold, scalar stress might become sufficiently great that additional vertical complexity would be required to maintain integration (and suppress tendencies toward fission).

Sizes of States

The range of estimates for archaic state sizes should now be reconsidered. The lower values (e.g., less than 10,000) may approximate the sizes at which marked structures of inequality, the stratification of wealth and power, and the integrative formations generally associated with states (Carneiro 1981:69) may be sustained by politically autonomous polities under certain conditions (economic, interpolity) (Claessen 1978a). Such polities are most common as the component parts of larger social/cultural networks, linked through interaction and elite marriage alliances. Conversely, the middle-to-higher population estimates (100,000 or more) may be closer to the demographic group sizes that cannot be politically assembled and integrated without the vertically tiered decision-making complexity generally associated with states (Wright 1977, 1986a).

The importance of intersocietal interaction and intrasocietal integration to the size/complexity relationship can be illustrated by briefly stepping away from the archaic state and examining the "magic number" 2,500 ± 500 (Kosse 1990). Bernard and Killworth (1973, 1979) calculate that the size of the maximum group where information can still reach everyone (albeit with some time lag) is roughly 2,500. This figure corresponds with the maximum sizes of folk taxonomies (where oral histories supplement short-term recall) and estimates for long-term human memory capabilities (Kosse 1990), notwithstanding the intensive efforts that can raise these limits further.

Empirically, in a study of the maximal community sizes found in 45 non-industrial societies (Lekson 1985), a rather sharp cutoff was recognized around 2,500. Although societies with communities of fewer than 2,500 people had a broad range of organizational structures, from stateless to state, all societies with communities greater than that size had at least two levels of decision making. In a sample (Feinman and Neitzel 1984) of 21 middle-range societies in the Americas, a similar pattern was observed, with maximal community sizes larger than 2,500 noted in only two cases. As in the Lekson study, each of these cases had two or more decision-making tiers, while the smaller communities were associated with one to three tiers of decision makers. None of the 46 "single-community societies" studied by Carneiro (1967) or the 37 New Guinea societies compared by Forge (1972a) included communities larger than 2,000. Likewise, only one of 17 New Guinea populations had organized political groupings larger than 2,500 (Brown and Podolefsky 1976), although some of these tribal/linguistic populations were considerably larger in total size. The majority of the New World "middle-range" societies also were greater than 2,500 in total population (Feinman and Neitzel 1984).

Based on these findings (see also Ember 1963), it seems apparent that, whereas communities (or politically integrated groups) larger than 2,500 ± 500 do seem to require significant organizational infrastructure (two or more decision-making levels), more dispersed populations or societies that may be much greater in total size do not. These cases, from diverse environmental and economic settings, indicate that the nature of the interaction between group members (and the kinds of integrative tasks that they must perform) have critical implications for the size/complexity relationship. Clearly, for groups of equivalent size, the levels of interaction and cooperation necessary to avoid fission are greater per capita at the community scale than at the societal scale (Feinman 1995). Therefore (not surprisingly), size thresholds and scalar stress points would be expected to be lower and the administrative load greater (all other things being equal) for settlements as compared to societies (see Kasarda 1974). Perhaps this pattern was recognized by Carneiro (1967:238) when he found that "as they grow more populous, multi-community societies appear to elaborate their social structure more slowly than do single-community societies."

Minimal estimates for politically autonomous states also range around 2,500 (Renfrew 1982), thereby strengthening the possibility that the population necessary to sustain a second- or third-generation state is smaller than the higher demographic levels above which states may develop under "pristine" conditions (see Marcus 1992a, this volume). Preexisting stratification, extant ideologies that sanctify and legitimize inequality (Marcus 1989), intense competition between elites of different polities of comparable size and power, and the absence of political competition (see Kosse 1994) are some of the conditions that could foster the maintenance or persistence of states at markedly lower demographic levels than those at which they might evolve initially. Although most scholars would recognize few, if any, societies with only 2,500 people as states, later preindustrial states in many regions were small. Further documentation of small second- and third-generation states would provide a strong counter to Carneiro's (1967) expectation that polity size necessarily increases in a linear and continuous fashion over time.

Integration and the Archaic State

Although the prior discussion is fairly general, there are implications for the study of the archaic state. At the macroscale, integrative differences lie at the core of the conceptual continuum between territorial and hegemonic empires (D'Altroy 1992; Hassig 1985, 1988; Luttwak 1976). From the perspective of the core, the territorial strategy entails more intensive occupation and direct governmental control of the periphery, with greater transport and supply costs. Generally, this strategy also returns greater tribute/tax exactions (often from agricultural production) from the periphery. In hegemonic organizations, peripheral elite have much greater autonomy, and the mechanisms for resource exaction are less formal and standardized. Other things being equal, the hegemonic integrative strategies (e.g., co-opting peripheral elite through exchange and intermarriage, military threat, frontier garrisons, occasional campaigns) involve lower costs for core elite than the construction and supply of a full-fledged governmental infrastructure in peripheral realms.

In the Late Imperial Chinese empire, where communication and transportation, as well as agricultural production, were relatively well developed, provinces on the frontier were smaller than those close to the capital (Skinner 1977a). According to Skinner (1977a; see also Johnson 1982), these outlying provinces were smaller because the duties of peripheral administrators were more demanding. These officials were responsible for both resource exaction and boundary relations (the latter being a more significant concern than in the core). To maintain a more-or-less comparable level of integration throughout the empire and to minimize potential threats to the core from peripheral regions, provincial administrators (with greater costs and broader duties) generally monitored smaller domains. Conversely, in the Aztec polity (with less developed transport, communication, and agricultural technologies), peripheral provinces generally were larger than those closer to the core (often they were not even territorially demarcated) (Berdan 1987; Smith 1987). At the same time, political integration and tribute collection were much less frequent on the periphery than they were close to Tenochtitlán. Clearly the degree of integration was less in outlying provinces as a concession to time and the friction of distance. This contrasts with the Chinese case, where size was diminished at the edge to maintain (or even intensify) political integration. In other words, for empires (see also Doyle 1986), one cannot really understand the size/organization relationship without considering the nature of integration as well as scale and complexity.

At a still broader theoretical level, a related pattern has been recognized by Friedman (1977; see also D'Altroy and Earle 1985), who finds that (holding other factors more or less constant) nations dependent on trade as their primary basis for support tend to be spatially more extensive than those dependent on agriculture. Exaction of agricultural resources would seem to require greater politico-economic integration, and thus more infrastructural support. In the preindustrial world, late Old World territorial empires may be somewhat of an exception to this pattern, but these formations were expensive to maintain and rather unstable (see Taagepera 1978b). If we employ Friedman's expectations synchronically, it is interesting to note that both the Aztec and Inka polities practiced more territorial-like integration and exaction strategies near their capitals, while they implemented more hegemonic rule and had a greater focus on tribute and trade at the limits of their political spheres (e.g., Berdan 1975; Blanton 1985; D'Altroy 1992). Yet the causal link between organizational capabilities and economic strategies is far from simple or unidirectional. Likewise, in both of these cases, much of the exchange at the peripheries was merchant driven, and not really a total expression of state administration.

At smaller scales, different integrative strategies also have transport and

administrative costs and requirements, which therefore entail spatial implications and limitations. We currently know much less about these than we
do about the movement of goods and armies (e.g., D'Altroy 1992; Drennan
1984; Engels 1978; Hassig 1988), although some similar constraints would
seem to apply. Yet in discussions of different integrative strategies and the
likelihood of fission, the "cost-benefit" ratios cannot measure just energy or
time, since all societal bonds and interactions do not promote or diminish
the possibilities for fission in the same manner; we must go beyond an examination of economic relations, political complexity, and scale to understand this variation.

As noted above, greater attention must be given to the diverse strategies
by which human populations are articulated (see Blanton, this volume;
Blanton et al. 1996; Feinman 1995). Some integrative strategies, like kinship, tend to have lifelong durability (Barnes 1972); others require much
more constant inputs. At the same time, certain integrative strategies (kinship, fictive kinship, ritual) are more constrained by physiological limits and
distance costs. Diverse integrative strategies also have different implications
for recruitment. Sahlins (1972) systematically evaluated some of the economic ramifications for kinship relations across space; however, an expansion of this work to consider alternative integrative strategies (beyond
kinship) and other kinds of costs/benefits is in order (see Drennan 1991;
Renfrew 1974).

Spatial variation in integrative strategies also may help explain and compare the "near-decomposability" (Simon 1969) of large social systems. Applying general systems principles, Simon (1969; cf. Yoffee 1988a) argued
that empires often collapsed or decomposed into the same smaller segments
that existed when the higher-level linkages were first forged. The basis of his
argument lies in the greater durability given to the horizontal linkages that
are present in the smaller component segments as compared to the more
ephemeral vertical connections hypothesized to bind these segments.

Yet despite some empirical validity, Simon's expectations (or a general
consideration of structure alone) cannot explain why some large states de-
compose into their prior component pieces and others break up into new
subunits, while, in rare instances, some fragment entirely. Part of that understanding goes beyond structural considerations and is a function of how
the component segments were integrated (internally), and how much these
specific mechanisms of integration were transformed during the episode
of amalgamation. For example, a lesser degree of "near-decomposability"
might be expected following early episodes of state development. During
such growth episodes, kinship and fictive kinship often were supplemented
or replaced (as the key mechanisms that bound followers to leaders) by new
economic, ideological, political, and military strategies. If the early state

endured, the original bonds, which integrated the preexisting components, would have had relatively little remaining importance centuries later at the time of collapse. Consequently, with collapse, decomposition would presumably be into rather different segments than composed the original, unified state (e.g., Schreiber 1987:282).

Simon's expectations may better conform to those instances where small states were bound into mechanically organized (in the Durkheimian sense) large states or hegemonic empires of short duration. In these cases, the internal integration of the preexisting components may have undergone less transformation as preexisting ruling elite lineages retained a considerable degree of power despite the presence of a loosely overarching central authority. When these larger polities eventually collapsed, fragmentation likely would have occurred, reverting to a number of the preexisting modular segments (cf. Eisenstadt 1988; Marcus 1989). In these cases, the leader/follower bonds would not have been restructured significantly during incorporation. Thus, following collapse, the degree of "near-decomposability" may depend on the nature of the integrative strategies employed (before and after the specific expansion episode) as well as system duration.

THEORETICAL SYNTHESIS

The prior analysis critically evaluates key issues and conceptions concerning the size of the archaic state. Some points of conventional wisdom have been challenged, and directions and questions for future research have been advanced. Before proceeding to a brief examination of empirical findings from the highlands of southern Mexico, some central themes from the above discussion are reviewed and synthesized.

Although the general increase in polity sizes since the Neolithic is recognized, this general trend was not unilineal, inevitable, innate, or constant in tempo. At the continental scale (compared to a global one), shifts in polity size were even more dramatic and cyclical. Growth in the size of specific polities can be neither presumed nor seen as a universal lawlike consequence of evolutionary forces. Consequently, changes in the scale of political entities are seen as explicable (though historically contingent), and future investigations should focus on transport, communication, and administrative technologies to understand historical and political trajectories. We should systematize what we already know about the relative effectiveness of different integrative mechanisms and strategies, and how they worked (or did not work) at varying spatial scales (e.g., Blanton, this volume; Kohr 1957).

Archaic states were extremely variable in size, with no clear threshold separating all states from all chiefdoms (see discussion in Voorhies 1989). Significantly, secondary states that formed in the context of preexisting

systems of legitimation and stratification may be much smaller and less populous than the first primary states that arose in the same region. As a consequence, preindustrial states (in toto) were most likely to be small and part of
wide-ranging, interlocking state systems. These networks were dynamic,
with the similarly sized polities having variable degrees of political and economic autonomy at different times. Individual polity size alone will never
be an adequate guide for understanding either the nature of these states or
the larger networks that they formed. More broadly, and in sharp contrast
to Wallerstein (1979), the precapitalist world clearly was not composed exclusively of tribal societies, minisystems (aggregations of small autonomous
chiefdoms and states), and empires. Rather, preindustrial worlds also com-
prised a diverse array of complex interlocking state systems. In such networks, the political, cultural, and economic limits of specific polities were
neither always coterminous nor closed. The advent of multipolity "world"
systems long precedes the advent of capitalism (see Peregrine and Feinman
1996).

The study of long-term change requires simultaneous consideration of
at least three analytical dimensions: specific trajectories of change, socioenvironmental stresses, and the social properties of human groups and
groupings. The latter (still the dimension least considered by archaeologists
and historians) involves the reassessment of the size/complexity relationship
(see Johnson 1982), with greater attention placed on spatiotemporal cycling,
the nested interplay between horizontally and vertically organized groups,
and a broad consideration of the diverse means and strategies of integration.
Significantly, if secondary states were frequently smaller than primary states,
cross-national, ethnographic comparisons (based on secondary cases) may
signal relevant directional relationships but will provide little specific guid-
ance for understanding primary states. The empirical picture for the size of
early states can only emerge from field and regional studies in archaeology.

On a more specific level, preindustrial polities were seemingly more dynamic and cyclical in scale (e.g., Fry 1990; Marcus 1993a), integration, and
even complexity (e.g., Kowalewski 1990) than our theories generally have
envisioned them. This should not be entirely surprising since their transport
and production technologies were frequently more similar to those of ancient chiefdoms (on cyclical change in chiefdoms, see Anderson 1990;
Stemper 1989) than to those of postindustrial states. At least for prehispanic
Mesoamerica, whenever historical records are available (to supplement the
archaeology and provide an additional perspective on interpolity relations),
the picture of political relations appears particularly fluid and dynamic (e.g.,
Culbert, ed. 1991; Marcus 1976a, 1993a; Martin and Grube 1995; Smith
and Berdan 1992; Spores 1974). Yet it is important to remember that, as with
the indigenous southeastern U.S. and Ecuadorian chiefdoms, dynamism and

flux at the polity scale may translate to relative persistence at more macro-scopic levels of analysis (see also Appel 1982:145; Marcus 1992a).

In general, archaic states were characterized by marked spatial variation in the strategies of interconnection/integration. These spatial differences were not simple, direct consequences of travel time. But they do reflect the friction of distance (the nature and degree of integration varied with space) as modified by specific polity-to-polity (ruler-to-ruler) histories, strategies, and interactions. A consideration of integrative mechanisms, and how they shifted (or did not) with polity expansion, should help refine expectations concerning "near-decomposability." The replacement of largely mechanical integrative mechanisms by more bureaucratic, organic strategies would diminish the likelihood that a large polity would simply break down into the segments that were joined to compose it initially.

SCALE, INTEGRATION, AND PREHISPANIC STATES IN OAXACA

The remainder of this chapter turns to the Southern Highlands of Mexico during the prehispanic era. The primary focus is the more than 2,500 km² contiguous area that has been surveyed by two settlement pattern projects: the Valley of Oaxaca project (Blanton 1978; Blanton et al. 1982; Kowalewski et al. 1989) and the Ejutla Valley project (Feinman and Nicholas 1990). Some findings also are drawn from regional studies conducted in the smaller, neighboring valleys (fig. 4.1) of Nochixtlán (Spores 1972, 1983b, 1983c), Tamazulapan (Byland 1980), and Cuicatlán (Redmond 1983).

This discussion is not an explicit test of any of the research positions expressed above, nor does it attempt a major recasting or synthesis of Oaxacan prehistory (see Blanton et al. 1981; Flannery and Marcus, eds. 1983; Marcus and Flannery 1996). Rather, regional-scale settlement information from Oaxaca is examined using a slightly different analytical lens than has been used before. This lens adjusts for a more dynamic, fluid, and spatially diverse vision of archaic states, and this selective examination provides initial support for several of the concepts discussed above. My brief survey here conjoins the regional-scale findings from Oaxaca and Ejutla more completely than I have in previous publications. Rather than give a full phase-by-phase analysis, I consider only five temporal segments: the Rosario phase (c. 600–500 BC), Monte Albán Late I (c. 300–200 BC), Monte Albán IIIA (c. AD 200–500), Monte Albán IV (c. AD 700–900), and Monte Albán V (c. AD 900–1520). The order of this discussion is rather unorthodox. I begin with the last prehispanic epoch (Monte Albán V) and then trace the emergence of the region's small Late Postclassic polities back to Monte Albán IV. To examine "near-decomposability," the focus then shifts to the Rosario phase,

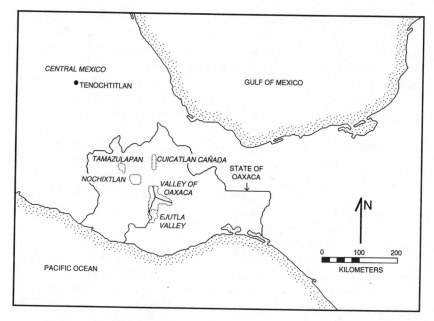

Figure 4.1. The state of Oaxaca in southern Mexico, showing the location of regional settlement pattern surveys.

which predates the foundation of the key valley center of Monte Albán. Subsequently, the Monte Albán polity is examined during Monte Albán Late I and IIIA.

Late Postclassic (Monte Albán V)

I start with the Late Postclassic period at the end of the prehispanic era, for this phase allows for the evaluation of both written and archaeological sources (e.g., Appel 1982; Flannery and Marcus, eds. 1983; Kowalewski et al. 1989; Paddock 1983; Whitecotton 1992). The Southern Highlands were fragmented politically at this time into a network of small, semiautonomous polities that stretched from the highlands of the Mixteca Alta to the Valley of Oaxaca and, perhaps, south to the Pacific. At the macroscale, population densities were greater than at any time in the past. Less scholarly consensus exists concerning the degree of polity autonomy, the relative importance of the specific integrative mechanisms (e.g., warfare, elite marriage, marketing), and the place of these small states in the larger tributary domain established by Aztec Tenochtitlán at the close of this phase.

Specifically, this discussion examines political geography in the valleys of Oaxaca and Ejutla from several scales. Population estimates for the area's political segments are presented. The estimated values for central Oaxaca are compared with those for the three smaller regions (Nochixtlán, Tamazulapan, and Cuicatlán). In general, population size estimates are based directly on the distributions of artifact scatters (sites) (see Blanton et al. 1982; Feinman et al. 1985; Kowalewski et al. 1989; Parsons 1971). When precontact population values were not presented for specific sites in the three smaller regions, estimates were calculated from the settlement area using procedures equivalent to those employed in Oaxaca/Ejutla.

The first reconstruction (fig. 4.2) divides the Oaxaca/Ejutla region into 24 settlement clusters. This figure is an extension of the map drawn previously for the Valley of Oaxaca (Kowalewski et al. 1989:345) and uses "shatter zones" to subdivide the regional population. This method identifies uninhabited zones between clusters of settlements on the assumption that the boundaries between polities would be sparsely settled. This map may represent the smallest Postclassic "petty kingdoms." A second map (fig. 4.3), with 13 components, gives greater attention to the size and locations of the region's largest centers as well as ethnohistoric findings (see Kowalewski et al. 1989:344–48). This reconstruction seems to reflect the regional political geography toward the end of the Postclassic period, following a degree of political consolidation.

A final reconstruction uses basic nearest-neighbor principles (see Haggett 1966:231–33) to define site clusters. Sites within 1,500 m of their neighbors generally were placed in the same cluster. This procedure segments the region into only five clusters (three small peripheral polities and two major ones) (fig. 4.4). The latter two are centered around the two valley communities that were known to be most powerful at Spanish contact (Sa'a Yucu/Cuilapan and Macuilxochitl). The sixteenth-century documents suggest competition and shifting alliances (military and marriage) between late prehispanic Oaxaca polities, with some trending toward centralization around these latter two sites (see Paddock 1983). The three alternative archaeological reconstructions seem to reflect the fluid, nested, and mechanical (in the Durkheimian sense, as opposed to organic) political integration of Postclassic Oaxaca, which corresponds closely to the dynamism described in the ethnohistoric accounts.

The assignment of population estimates to these bounded units must be viewed as approximate. Besides the general archaeological problems of chronological control and converting sherd scatters to people, this exercise also is problematic because the bounds of the Oaxaca polities certainly were not coterminous with the settlement pattern survey region. Not surprisingly, this was evident after the Ejutla survey, when some of the Valley of Oaxaca settlement clusters (defined previously) were shown to extend south to encompass neighboring settlements in the Ejutla region. Prior to the Ejutla

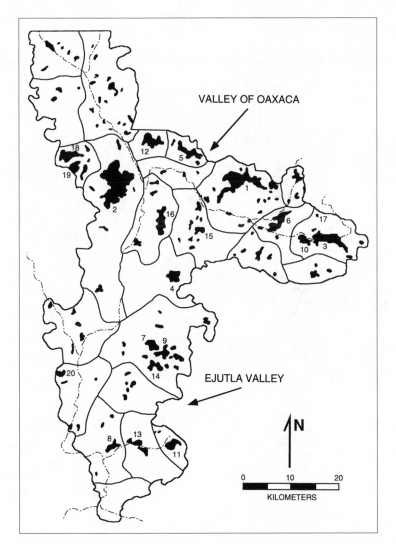

Figure 4.2. Boundaries of Monte Albán V petty kingdoms, based on shatter zones (only sites with estimated populations of 200 or more are shown; the largest sites are numbered 1–20).

survey, the size of these clusters was underestimated. Since little archaeological information is available concerning the mountains which surround the valleys of Oaxaca and Ejutla, the estimates presented here also probably underestimate polity extent and population. In a few cases, some frontier settlements may have been included in the estimates for valley polities when

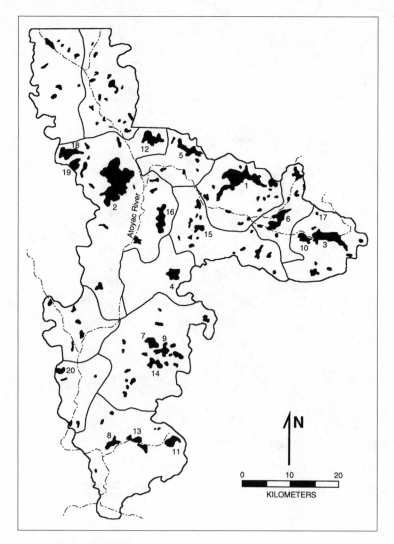

Figure 4.3. Boundaries of Monte Albán V petty kingdoms, based on location of large centers and ethnohistoric accounts.

these sites actually were subject to head towns in the mountains that lie outside the study region. In these cases, the population values may be too large.

Based on the shatter-zone reconstruction (see fig. 4.2), the Oaxaca/ Ejutla polities ranged in estimated size between 2,100 and 23,400 people, with some of the smallest entities on the region's edge (table 4.1). In this reconstruction, mean polity size was close to 5,000 people in the Valley of Oaxaca. Settlement clusters in Nochixtlán, Tamazulapan, and Cuicatlán con-

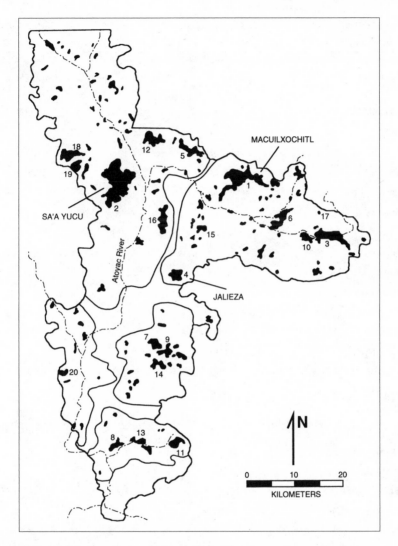

Figure 4.4. Boundaries of Monte Albán V settlement clusters (the clusters are separated by 1500 m or more of unoccupied space).

form to the same range (table 4.2). These estimates for the Southern Highlands are roughly comparable to the ranges of population size presented for small states elsewhere (e.g., Pounds 1969; Renfrew 1982), and to the sizes of the smallest political districts in the Basin of Mexico in AD 1568 (Sanders et al. 1970:443−62). At contact, these Central Mexican districts were amalgamated into larger political jurisdictions. Many, if not most, of these larger units are thought to have been politically autonomous or semiautonomous

TABLE 4.1. *Population of Late Postclassic Polities in the Central Valleys of Oaxaca*

Polity/Area	Shatter Zone	Centers/Ethnohistory	Large Clusters
Macuilxochitl	23,400	23,400	81,000
Mitla	19,500	21,600	
Sa'a Yucu	18,800	32,400	60,000
San Pedro Mártir	16,600	20,800	20,500
Eastern Etla	9,900	9,900	
Teitipac	9,300	15,000	
Tlalixtac	9,200	11,700	
Jalieza	8,800	8,800	
Yagul/Tlacolula	8,300	12,500	
Ixtlahuaca	5,900		
Quialana	5,700		
Taniche	5,000		
Coyotepec	4,600		
Ejutla	4,300	12,900	12,900
San Miguel del Valle	4,200		
El Choco	4,200	4,200	7,500
El Vergel	4,100		
Huitzo	3,500	5,900	
Coatecas	3,500		
Tlapacoyan	3,300	3,300	
San Luis Beltrán	3,000		
Tule	2,500		
Zautla/Tejalapan	2,400		
Matatlán	2,100		
Yogana[a]	250		
Median size	4,800	12,500	20,500

[a]Part of polity extends into Miahuatlán.

TABLE 4.2. Population of Other Late Postclassic Polities in Oaxaca

Polity/Area	Population
Cuicatlán	
Cuicatlán	4,300
Dominguillo	2,300
Quiotepec[a]	400
Tamazulapan	
Tejupan	10,900
Tamazulapan	6,600
Teposcolula[b]	2,300
Nochixtlán	
Yanhuitlán	20,500
Chachoapan	8,500
Nochixtlán	10,750
Etlatongo	9,500
Jaltepec[c]	700
Median size	10,125

[a]Part of polity extends north to Tecomavaca and Tehuacán.
[b]Part of polity extends south toward Nochixtlán.
[c]Part of polity extends beyond surveyed area.

until the last two centuries before Cortés, although the nature of the external linkages are thought to have been dynamic and cyclical. Interestingly, the range of demographic estimates for these larger Basin of Mexico jurisdictions (generally between 10,000 and 30,000, excluding Tenochtitlán) prior to contact (Bray 1972; Sanders et al. 1970) overlap the population figures for Oaxaca / Ejutla that were derived with closest attention to ethnohistoric accounts (see table 4.1; fig. 4.3). These larger units may reflect the smallest late prehispanic Oaxacan political entities with considerable autonomy.

Early Postclassic (Monte Albán IV)
In the remainder of this chapter, the same basic site clustering procedures that were employed for Monte Albán V are applied to earlier phases. Given the absence of historical information, clusters were formed considering both

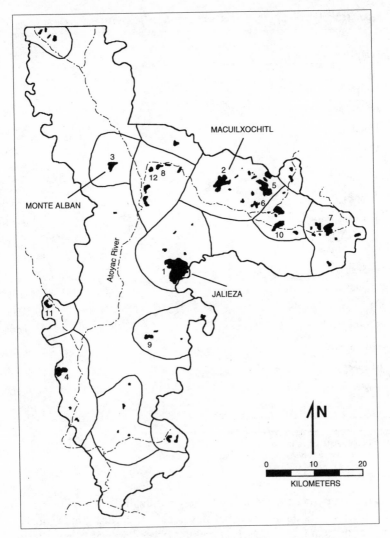

Figure 4.5. Boundaries of Monte Albán IV settlement clusters, based on shatter zones and the location of large sites (only sites with estimated populations of 100 or more are shown; the largest sites are numbered 1–12).

site spacing and the distribution of the region's largest settlements. There was no single nearest-neighbor delimiter for the definition of clusters, although these boundaries were always drawn through sparsely occupied areas. Clusters always were defined to include at least one major center. The cluster map (fig. 4.5) for Monte Albán IV indicates both key differences with the subsequent era as well as some significant continuity.

By Monte Albán IV, the monumental hilltop center of Monte Albán (so important in the immediately prior Classic period) had lost much of its population. Monumental building at the site ceased. In contrast to Monte Albán V, settlement during this earlier period was much more nucleated, and there were sizable open areas between substantial occupations. Because of these "shatter zones," the definition of site clusters was fairly straightforward in most instances. This spatial separation of population clusters, several of which were positioned in defensible hilltop locales, may reflect tension and reorganization following the collapse of the Monte Albán–centered polity that dominated the region for more than a millennium (Finsten 1983; Kowalewski et al. 1989). Intraregional integration appears to have been lower at this time than it was in either Monte Albán V or during the previous (Classic) period.

Significantly, the spatial distribution of most of the Monte Albán IV settlement clusters seems to correspond closely to the small polities of the next epoch (see figs. 4.2, 4.3). The most consistent difference between the two phases is that additional Monte Albán V polities emerged in areas that had been Early Postclassic (Monte Albán IV) shatter zones. As in Monte Albán V, Macuilxochitl (see fig. 4.5) was one of the region's two most populous polities; however, the largest Monte Albán IV cluster (Jalieza) lost most of its population by the end of the prehispanic era. Jalieza was occupied in Monte Albán V, but it is not mentioned in ethnohistoric accounts, so its significance may have been minimal by the time the Spaniards arrived (Kowalewski et al. 1989).

In terms of population, two Monte Albán IV clusters were much larger than any others. Nevertheless, despite this marked bipolarity, the estimated median polity size for period IV was similar to that found for the Monte Albán V clusters (table 4.3; see table 4.1). The overall size range in Monte Albán IV also was comparable, but the small size of some of these units may indicate that the period IV polities stretched into the mountains. If this pattern holds, it would conform with the poor valley integration and centrifugal trends that followed the political demise of Monte Albán. Greater valleywide integration (although not political centralization) was achieved in the Late Postclassic (Monte Albán V) with population growth and filling-in, and the replacement of Jalieza as a key center by Sa'a Yucu/Cuilapan, situated near the centrally located former valley capital of Monte Albán.

Middle Formative (Rosario Phase)

The above analysis noted continuity in the settlement distributions of the Postclassic period. This discussion now leaps back more than a millennium in the Oaxaca sequence to the Rosario phase, the time prior to Monte Albán's foundation (fig. 4.6). By so doing, the regional settlement pattern for the Rosario phase is contrasted with the Monte Albán IV pattern, which

TABLE 4.3. *Period IV Population Clusters in the Central Valleys of Oaxaca*

Polity/Area	Population
Jalieza	19,300
Macuilxochitl	17,200
Animas Trujano	6,000
Mitla	5,900
El Choco	5,000
Monte Albán	4,300
San Pedro Mártir	3,900
Yagul	3,700
San Miguel del Valle	2,000
Mixtepec	1,600
Ejutla	1,400
Tlalixtac	1,100
Coatecas	1,000
Huitzo	750
Median size	3,800

coincides with Monte Albán's decline. A comparison of these two phases (see figs. 4.5, 4.6) finds little support for Simon's "near-decomposability" argument; beyond some general separations, which follow the three arms of the valley, and a sparseness of occupation at the regional hub, settlement clustering during these two phases was rather different. The area that was most densely inhabited in Monte Albán IV (around Jalieza between the eastern and southern arms) was relatively sparsely settled in the Rosario phase. There really was only one dense Rosario phase population cluster, that in the north around the pre–Monte Albán head town, San José Mogote. In contrast, the northern arm was not densely populated in Monte Albán IV. Furthermore, the estimated population for the entire Oaxaca/Ejutla region was smaller in the Rosario phase than the size of the median Monte Albán IV settlement cluster (e.g., Feinman 1991).

These findings do not prompt an outright rejection of Simon's model. Rather, as discussed above in the theoretical section, they suggest that the

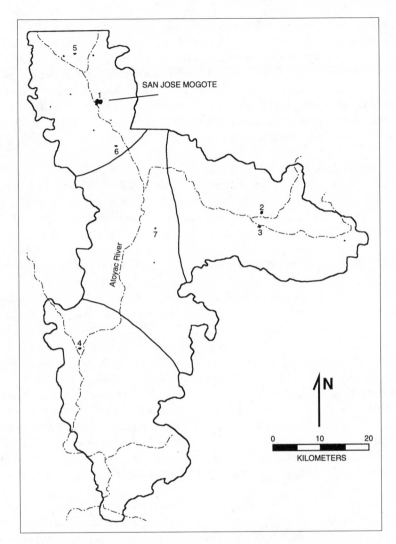

Figure 4.6. Boundaries of Rosario phase settlement clusters, based on shat-ter zones and the location of large sites (only sites with estimated popula-tions of 20 or more are shown; the largest sites are numbered 1–7).

degree of "near-decomposability" must be evaluated in relation to duration of the episode of amalgamation and the extent of the changes in the mech-anisms of integration that bound societal segments. Monte Albán was not only a powerful polity (judging from its size and architectural monumentality), but during its long hegemony the population within its immediate vicinity underwent dramatic transformations in scale, integration, and complexity (e.g., Feinman and Nicholas 1987; Kowalewski et al. 1983, 1989). The formation and relatively long duration of Monte Albán appears to have led to a marked restructuring of pre–Monte Albán patterns of socioeconomic integration. The Monte Albán polity was not simply a weak amalgamation of pre–Monte Albán political entities or population segments. Rather, after generations in power, the organizational effects of Monte Albán on the Valley of Oaxaca would seem to have been much more radical.

Late Formative (Monte Albán Late I)

By Late I, Monte Albán was established as the regional capital at the hub of the three arms of the Valley of Oaxaca. Four to five tiers of civic-ceremonial architecture and an equal number of settlement size classes were present in the region (Kowalewski et al. 1989). The Oaxaca/Ejutla population is estimated to have been more than 25 times what it was during the Rosario phase. No site in the study region (or for many kilometers beyond) approached the size or architectural complexity of Late I Monte Albán.

This discussion is not focused on what led to Monte Albán's foundation, nor does it evaluate or draw inferences concerning the nature of Monte Albán's influence or control outside of the valleys of Oaxaca and Ejutla. Rather, subregional differences in the nature and degree of political/economic articulation are proposed and examined. Results of the clustering analysis (fig. 4.7) support earlier findings (Kowalewski et al. 1989:121, 145–52) that the core of the Monte Albán state was Etla (northern arm), the central area (around Monte Albán), and the northern Valle Grande (southern arm). Alternatively, most of the Tlacolula (eastern) arm and the far south (including Ejutla) appear to have been linked less tightly to Monte Albán. I am not implying that these latter areas were completely independent of Monte Albán, only that the nature of their linkages was less direct than is indicated for the core.

Several features separate the core zone from the rest of the study region. A number have been reported previously (Kowalewski et al. 1989), although with slightly different emphases. Most of the region's largest settlements and the sites with the most elaborate architecture were situated in the core cluster. To the east, north, and south, the core area's largest sites form two rings around Monte Albán. Blanton's (1989) architectural analysis found that the sites in the ring closest to Monte Albán lacked formal architectural groupings, while those further from the capital had unusually large amounts of construction with formal and closed plazas. Perhaps these latter sites replicated civic-ceremonial activities enacted at Monte Albán (e.g., Morris and Thompson 1985). A comparative analysis of site size and the volume of architectural construction also noted that sites with large volumes of public

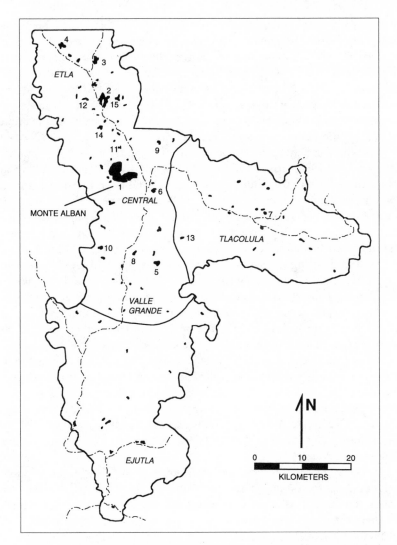

Figure 4.7. Boundaries of Monte Albán Late I settlement clusters, based on shatter zones and the location of large sites (only sites with estimated populations of 100 or more are shown; the largest sites are numbered 1–15).

building (civic-ceremonial importance) relative to their size generally were situated in the core area (Kowalewski et al. 1989:145).

Land-use models (e.g., Feinman and Nicholas 1987, 1992; Nicholas 1989) indicate that inhabitants of Monte Albán could have been fed regularly from surplus exacted from the core zone alone. Although the most energy/

transport-efficient models (Nicholas 1989:490) predict that a negligible proportion of this agrarian surplus would have been drawn from the edge of western Tlacolula (outside the core cluster), this small amount of agricultural produce also could have been exacted from areas in Etla (included in the core cluster) that are 12 to 20 km from the hilltop center. Most of the new piedmont settlement at this time, areas that my colleagues and I (Kowalewski et al. 1989:145) associate with agricultural intensification ("the piedmont strategy"), also lie inside this core cluster.

Elsewhere it has been argued (Blanton et al. 1981:71–72; Feinman 1986; Winter 1984) that the advent of the *comal* (tortilla griddle) in Monte Albán I may signal a key shift in labor/agricultural intensification strategies away from strict household subsistence. That is, if people were working away from home (perhaps in communal or centrally supported work groups), tortillas would constitute an excellent portable food source (just as they do for such workers today). Significantly, 95 percent (774 of 814) of the *comales* found during the Valley of Oaxaca survey were collected in the core cluster, where intensification is suggested. Furthermore, period I *comales* are scarce in the collections from the more peripheral Ejutla survey region.

There is only a single large center (with significant public building) in Tlacolula, and no such place in Ejutla or the extreme southern arm. These more peripheral areas were less densely occupied. During Monte Albán I, a number of sites were positioned in defensible locations. Excluding Monte Albán, all defensible localities occupied in Late I were either situated outside the core cluster (in either Tlacolula or the southern Valle Grande) or at the extreme western and northwestern edges of the Etla region (in places where passes to the Mixteca Alta could have been monitored) (Elam 1989:404; see also Feinman and Nicholas 1996). There were no defensible Late I settlements in Ejutla.

Based on the differences in settlement pattern, the distribution of public buildings, and the findings from man/land studies, I propose that the central cluster around Monte Albán was more closely linked to (and directly integrated with) Monte Albán than was the rest of the study region. This area is the most likely agricultural supply zone for the hilltop center. In contrast, Tlacolula and the southern Valle Grande may have been incorporated more for defense and perhaps long-distance exchange, while Ejutla was even more of a frontier. During Monte Albán I, new economic, political, and ideological mechanisms of integration were introduced in Oaxaca with the advent of new funerary treatment (tombs), effigy vessels depicting lightning and other supernatural forces, new public buildings, changes in storage technology, and, perhaps, distinct modes of exchange (Feinman, Blanton, and Kowalewski 1984; Flannery and Marcus, eds. 1983; Kowalewski et al. 1989). Further study is necessary to evaluate how these strategies of

interconnection may have varied in conjunction with the distinctions discussed here.

Early Classic (Monte Albán IIIA)

Monte Albán IIIA generally is recognized as the time when Monte Albán
integrated its immediate hinterland (the Valley of Oaxaca) to the greatest degree (e.g., Appel 1986). The central cluster surrounding Monte Albán was
larger in extent (fig. 4.8) than during any other phase. Once again, this core
zone was composed primarily of the central area, Etla, and now most of the
region's southern arm (see fig. 4.7). Ejutla remained outside this core zone,
although it was no longer a sparsely settled frontier. The eastern arm of the
Valley of Oaxaca was still outside the core cluster but was more closely
linked to it than the spacing of settlements indicated for Late I (Kowalewski
et al. 1989:211). Interestingly, Tlacolula (the eastern arm) may have been
linked to the core through the region's second-largest settlement (Jalieza),
rather than directly to Monte Albán. Thus, some decentralization of functions may have been linked to scalar expansion of the hinterland over which
Monte Albán had greatest interaction and control.

It is not surprising then that settlement pattern, architecture, and land use
(as well as ceramic and carved stone styles) appear not to have been as spatially different (e.g., core cluster vs. outside core) in the Valley of Oaxaca as
they had been earlier. Population also was distributed more evenly. Yet, as
might be expected (given the cluster map), the lattice of centers was more
intricate and multitiered in the Valle Grande than Tlacolula. Nevertheless, a
multilevel network of centers was more evident in the latter region than it
had been in Late I. In Monte Albán IIIA Ejutla, the distribution of centers
was more similar to Tlacolula. Compared with the core zone, Tlacolula and
Ejutla also were dominated to a greater degree by a single center or cluster
of centers, so that the linkages between these regions and Monte Albán may
still have been somewhat different than for the IIIA core zone. Likewise, the
most efficient agricultural support zone for Monte Albán and Jalieza lies almost entirely inside the core cluster (Nicholas 1989:490). But piedmont
agriculture was more intensive in the eastern arm than for Late I.

Despite the greater integration of the Oaxaca/Ejutla region as a whole,
the settlement clusters do seem to indicate differences in regional organization (as compared to the core cluster) that may signal cracks or tension zones
that emerged later in the Classic period. A network of defensible hilltop terrace sites ringed roughly half of the study region in Monte Albán IIIA (Elam
1989:389; Feinman and Nicholas 1991:265, 1996). Most of these sites were
situated around the edge of Tlacolula, and along the eastern and western
sides of the study region's southern extension. For the most part, these sites
faced outside, shielding Tlacolula, Ejutla, and the southern part of the core

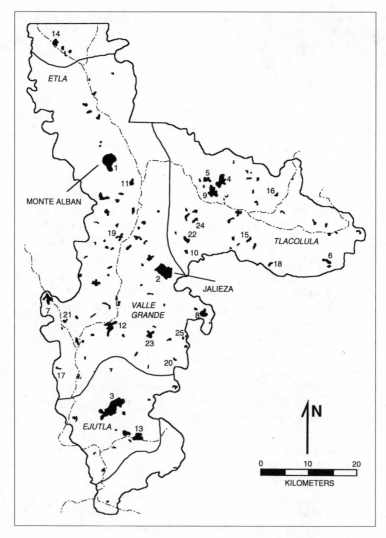

Figure 4.8. Boundaries of Monte Albán IIIA settlement clusters, based on shatter zones and the location of large sites (only sites with estimated populations of 100 or more are shown; the largest sites are numbered 1–25).

cluster. Yet, two lines of defensible sites were located *inside* the valley. One of them subdivides Tlacolula from the eastern Valle Grande (Elam 1989: 406). The other separates Ejutla from the southern edge of the Valle Grande core. Both of these lines of defensible sites are almost coterminous with (and parallel) the divisions drawn between settlement clusters.

Given the spatial (core zone vs. Tlacolula/Ejutla) differences in integration and organization, it also is interesting that funerary urns, closely associated with death ritual (Marcus 1983e) at Monte Albán, were found (in survey collections) to be proportionately well represented in the Valle Grande core and at the largest sites in Tlacolula and Ejutla. But otherwise these artifacts were underrepresented in the latter two regions. In general, Monte Albán as well as Valle Grande and Etla centers also had greater access than did Tlacolula and Ejutla centers to the wide assortment of ceramic goods available in the region (Kowalewski et al. 1989:240). Since Monte Albán had just about the full range of ceramic variability, this pattern may be another indicator of lower interconnection between these latter areas (Tlacolula and Ejutla) and Monte Albán than existed for the core cluster. These findings would seem to foreshadow the spatial patterning of Monte Albán's collapse by the end of the Classic period. In this balkanization process (that culminated in the fragmented political landscape of Monte Albán IV), Monte Albán was separated politically from both Tlacolula and Ejutla (see fig. 4.5).

CONCLUSION

This examination of Monte Albán's immediate hinterland provides a clue as to why empirical measures of archaic state size are so difficult to find. What were the limits of the Monte Albán polity in Late I and IIIA? Was it the core zone, the entire region, or some still much larger area in which the outer-valley segment was less integrated (and probably somewhat more autonomous) than Tlacolula or even Ejutla? Regardless, even the core clusters of these early Monte Albán polities were more populous than most, if not all, of the polities of Monte Albán IV and V.

A brief consideration of prehispanic Oaxaca has illustrated a number of the theoretical arguments advanced above. (1) No linear increase in Oaxaca state size was evident in the prehispanic period. (2) Spatial differences in polity integration have been described, although the exact nature of the linkages was not constant over time. (3) Nevertheless, in both Monte Albán Late I and IIIA, the core zone was most responsible for the center's agricultural support, while the less integrated areas had important defensive functions. Diverse integrative strategies appear to have been employed in these zones. (4) Modifications in Simon's "near-decomposability" argument that consider the nature and duration of integration have been proposed, and (5) short- and long-term cycles in the prehispanic Oaxacan state system have been described.

These findings correspond to the more general arguments regarding scale that were presented at the outset of this chapter. Ancient states were generally small. Often, but not always, these small states were the break-down products of larger, earlier states (as in Monte Albán IV in the Valley of Oaxaca; Marcus, this volume). In a given region, the size of states did not necessarily increase linearly over time. There is no simple numerical threshold that demarcates all states from all chiefdoms. The ways in which ancient states were integrated and interconnected often varied markedly over space, and differences in organization and integration have profound implications on state size.

It is evident that the theoretical issues investigated here require regional-scale data. The kinds of broad-scale and diachronic information considered for the valleys of Oaxaca and Ejutla are unfortunately rare in archaeology and history. Yet it is just this kind of information that is necessary to dissect the complex relationships between polity size and organization. We will not really understand the complicated linkages between human demography and organization until archaeologists, historians, and geographers more regularly extend their investigatory perspective away from ancient capitals and monumental centers. At the same time, and as noted above, more work on the different kinds of integratory connections that joined followers to leaders and hinterlands to capitals is needed.

No effort has been made here to advance a new theory of the state. As North (1986:248) aptly has written, "the long path of historical research is (already) strewn with the bones of theories of the state." Likewise, no new "magic" thresholds have been proposed. Archaic states were diverse in scale and integration, and past considerations of the scale/complexity relationship require greater examination of variation in strategies of integration. This work has challenged several simplistic positions, linear principles, and taxonomic schema. An understanding of societal change and preindustrial states requires much more than a single theory, evolutionary scenario, or set of prime movers. Rather, this discussion has offered several complex considerations and long-term research directions for modeling and studying the size and organization of ancient states. By endeavoring to offer bridges between history and process, this essay hopefully nudges us a small step along a long and complex road. For as Wallerstein (1992:6) has noted, "History and universalizing social sciences are the identical activity. The object is not to reduce complex reality to simple generalizations, either middle-range or large-scale. The object is to construct an interpretation of complex reality by surpassing simple generalizations, interweaving them, and defining the degree of their relevance."

NOTE

I am deeply grateful to the School of American Research and its president, Douglas W. Schwartz, for the opportunity to exchange ideas with such an exceptional and stimulating group of colleagues. Our stay in Santa Fe was magnificent and much appreciated.

Thanks are due all of my collaborators on the Valley of Oaxaca and Ejutla Valley Settlement Pattern Projects. A special debt of gratitude is owed Richard E. Blanton and Stephen A. Kowalewski, who directed the Oaxaca research, and Linda M. Nicholas, who has been instrumental in the Ejutla investigations. Linda generously prepared the figures that are presented here, while Lane Fargher assisted. I appreciate the essential support of the National Science Foundation and the important assistance of the Instituto Nacional de Antropología e Historia and the Centro Regional de Oaxaca. I wish to thank all the seminar participants for their camaraderie and the free exchange of ideas that occurred during our week in Santa Fe. Joyce Marcus, Richard E. Blanton, George L. Cowgill, and an anonymous reviewer are especially acknowledged for the extremely helpful comments that they offered on early drafts of this work.

5

Beyond Centralization
Steps Toward a Theory of Egalitarian Behavior in Archaic States
RICHARD E. BLANTON

In their proposal for a School of American Research symposium on the archaic state, Joyce Marcus and Gary Feinman asked participants to accomplish a number of tasks, two of which I thought would be particularly apropos of certain contemporary theoretical issues in anthropological archaeology and adjacent fields. Participants were asked to make use of a comparative approach to explain variation between archaic states, and we were asked to rethink and critique the typological evolutionary approaches like those of Fried, Service, and Polanyi. In this chapter, I tackle the assignments by elaborating on a topic only infrequently addressed in the literature on archaic states, which I refer to as "corporate political economy." I take a first step in the direction of comparative analysis by describing the varied forms of corporate political economy in selected examples from several world areas. I believe the results of this preliminary comparative effort constitute a useful starting point for future research.

In applying this approach, I found it possible to clarify a number of issues that previously had clouded my thinking about archaic states. Most importantly, I found the approach useful in its ability to summarize many of the major conclusions about archaic states made by previous researchers, while at the same time pointing to several topics that require a fresh look, as well as new concepts, theory, and analysis. To take this new direction I had to deviate considerably from theories currently in favor among anthropological archaeologists, including those inspired by Marxist thought and systems analysis. The springboard for my discussion is a critique of the systems approach.

CRITIQUE OF A SYSTEMS APPROACH TO THE
ARCHAIC STATE

The origin and evolution of the archaic state has been regarded as a central question for processually oriented anthropological archaeology since the rebirth of cultural evolutionist theory some 50 years ago (e.g., Steward 1949). One of the most widely utilized neoevolutionist theories in recent decades is a systems analysis (described below) that analyzes the growth of archaic states in terms of political centralization, in general, and as the development of specialized hierarchical decision-making control mechanisms, in particular (e.g., Flannery 1972; Wright and Johnson 1975). This theory has many useful insights, some of which I describe below, but I begin with a critique of certain elements that I find theoretically limiting and anthropologically sparse.

Perhaps the most disappointing aspect of systems analysis is that its narrow focus on control mechanisms and centralization diminishes our ability to comprehend archaic states as they have developed within their broader social and cultural settings. Hence, systems theory connects poorly with the traditional sociocultural evolutionary concern with the growth of *civitas* (civil-based society that incorporates elements of private property, entrepreneurial economic activity, and related features, in addition to state government itself) out of *societas* (small-scale, kin-based, communal society). Viewpoints more holistic than systems analysis have been proposed in our time, including, prominently, V. Gordon Childe's concept of an "urban revolution" (e.g., 1952). But Childe's approach, and others that bring into play factors such as political competition, economy, technology, household behavior, and the growth of cities (for example, as found in Adams 1966, 1981; Blanton et al. 1993; and Wheatley 1971), have had less saliency in recent neoevolutionist inquiry. In this chapter, I develop an approach that makes use of some of the concepts of systems analysis but avoids its overly narrow focus on the process of administrative centralization.

The definitive statement of systems analysis is found in a provocative article by Kent Flannery (1972), "The Cultural Evolution of Civilizations." Although Flannery's own thinking (Marcus and Flannery 1996) has gone beyond this 1972 piece, it remains an oft-cited and generative statement in the archaeological study of states. In the 1972 article, Flannery points to twin evolutionary processes in the growth of complex societies, segregation ("the amount of internal differentiation and specialization of subsystems") and centralization ("the degree of linkage between the various subsystems and the highest-order controls in society") (p. 409), although most of his ensuing discussion pertains to the evolutionary process of centralization alone. In this theory, a "human ecosystem" is made up of subsystems and their control mechanisms, arranged hierarchically. Control mechanisms assess the output of their respective subsystems, comparing them with "goal values" that indicate acceptable levels of functioning. Goal values include "ideological values," which are the human population's "cognized model of the way the world is put together" (1972:409). Government is a higher-order control system able to assess the functioning of lower-order (i.e., less inclusive) subsystems. By assessing the output of subsystems in relation to output goals and ideological values, governmental institutions are able to assess deviant values in subsystem output, and then respond to them adaptively so as to preserve overall system functioning (Flannery 1972:409; cf. Rappaport 1977:53–58).

According to this adaptationist approach, governmental controls are strengthened (centralization) when socioenvironmental stresses such as warfare or population pressure provide an adaptive milieu in which evolutionary mechanisms are triggered. The basic mechanisms resulting in centralization are "promotion," in which a subsystem is raised to a higher, more inclusive position in the control hierarchy, and "linearization," in which control of lower-order subsystems is captured by higher-order subsystems (Flannery 1972:412). These adaptive responses to socioenvironmental stresses preserve system functioning, but system collapse, fission, or decentralization (devolution) may result from an inability to respond appropriately to deviant subsystems states. In addition, excessively high levels of centralization may eventually result in "hypercoherence," a systems pathology that may lead to collapse or devolution owing to excessive integration (1972:420–21; Rappaport 1977:60).

An important element of systems analysis is the idea that an increased quantity of information is generated within and between subsystems as society becomes more complex. Therefore, a main trend in cultural evolution is the elaboration of institutions that process, store, and analyze information (Flannery 1972:411). Gregory Johnson and Henry Wright have elaborated on this latter point in several papers, showing, in particular, the advantages of an increased hierarchical structure of control systems under conditions of increased demands on information-processing institutions (Johnson 1978, 1982, 1983; Wright and Johnson 1975). From their information-processing perspective, the state is defined as having minimally three levels of administrative hierarchy (e.g., Flannery 1972:418; Wright 1969; Wright and Johnson 1975).

Systems analysis contains within its theoretical position a useful strategy for integrating cognitive and ecological (or cultural materialist) theories, since, as stated by Flannery (1972:400), "In an ecosystem approach to the analysis of human societies, everything which transmits information is within the province of ecology" (e.g., as discussed in Wilson 1992). This admirably integrative theoretical position is considerably weakened, in my opinion, by the fact that in its strongly adaptive systems/homeostasis perspective (e.g., Vincent 1986:104), the obviously important political element, the competition for power in complex society, is never adequately addressed (e.g., Brumfiel 1992). Systems theory's tendency to see the state as an information-processing control mechanism results from its extensive adoption of ideas from contemporary hierarchy theory and management science (e.g., as stated by Johnson 1982:392, 417), and adaptive systems theory (Rappaport 1977), while barely making any use of the more apposite, rich, and abundant literature on political processes in archaic states found in sources discussed below. As Adams (1981:77) reminds us: "Nothing we know of the historic records of any society . . . would allow even the full battery of administrative routines . . . to stand as surrogate for its political system as a whole. The routines not only constitute a gross over-simplification of politics but also provide a misleading picture—one lacking in the pervasive but volatile and usually unexpressed elements of contingency, calculation, and coercion" (cf. Adams 1984:88–89). Gregory Johnson (1987:127) himself notes, following his systems analysis of the Susiana Uruk, "We can probably expect that this complex society was in fact complex: that it was composed of a variety of noncoterminous groups of administrators of different grades, elites of different status, specialized craftsmen, simple laborers, agriculturalists, and so forth, all pursuing noncoterminous ends. The naiveté of models like that presented [in his administrative flow diagram] becomes ever more obvious."

By emphasizing change in the decision-making functions of government, other important dimensions of sociocultural change that impinge on governing institutions are inadequately addressed in systems analysis. It barely acknowledges the evolution of commercial institutions and their potentially important political implications (Blanton 1996; Eisenstadt 1969: 47). Domestic institutions are largely excluded from analytical consideration, even though aspects of social change relating to fertility, migration, gender relations, production, and consumption, among others, are to a great degree situated in the behavior of households. Urbanism is treated largely as an epiphenomenal outcome of state formation (e.g., Wright 1977). I also view as problematic the assumption that political centralization is the central process in the evolution of states. And this commonly accepted assertion of systems analysis can be found elsewhere in the literature on states (e.g., Roscoe 1993) (for example, in a recent work comparing early states [Claessen and Skalník, eds. 1978], only centralized, sovereign-centered cases were included in a sample that ignored more decentralized states such as Classical Greece [van der Vliet 1987]). Long-term trends in the evolution of civilizations manifesting a pattern of political decentralization, or patterns of cycling between periods of relative centralization and decentralization, are only minimally addressed in most contemporary theory, including systems analysis. System collapse, or devolution, is simplistically viewed by systems analysts as a consequence of maladaptive response to socioenvironmental stresses, as described above, or as a result of an inability to respond to an increased communications workload (Johnson 1982:416, 1983:177).

The simplistic approach of systems analysis ignores the fact that long-term decentralization of complex societies, involving more than just maladaptive collapse or devolution of the state, is a central issue for neoevolutionist inquiry. Decentralization is a highly significant outcome of system-shaping social processes in the long-term evolution of states (e.g., Adams 1992; Blanton et al. 1982:134−37; Kowalewski et al. 1989:513−18; McGuire 1983:110−14). For example, Skinner (1977b:23−25) notes a general trend of decline in state control in China from AD 200 to Late Imperial times (cf. Hall 1989), and Rathje (1975:421−22, 437−38) describes a process of decentralization from Old to Middle Kingdom Egypt and in the Classic to Late Postclassic transition in the Lowland Maya area. A comprehensive understanding of archaic states will demand that we develop conceptual tools that make it possible to understand both centralization and decentralization, and their interactions and relationships, in the long-term evolution of the state. Below I elaborate on the idea that decentralization, rather than reflecting an adaptive failure, is instead the result of the development of specific cultural practices put into place to constrain or limit the unregulated exercise of state power. Before I can address this issue, I summarize a processual analytical approach for the comparative study of the archaic state.

A BEHAVIORAL APPROACH TO TEMPORAL AND CROSS-CULTURAL VARIATION IN ARCHAIC STATES

As will become clear in the following pages, my intent in this chapter is to follow up on the communications emphasis found in the writings of Flannery, Rappaport, Wright, and Johnson, but I reorder and amplify it to better incorporate the important dimension of political behavior. This reordering of systems analysis can be done by addressing, as a first order of business, the issue of competition for power and its outcomes in complex societies. My political-behavioral approach builds on a well-established literature in political economy and political sociology, stemming from the writings of Marx, Weber, and their predecessors, and elaborated on by many researchers influenced by them, especially the sociologist Eisenstadt (1969). I also have been influenced by the growing processual orientation in political anthropology (Vincent 1990), and by the discursive theories of Bourdieu (1977:72−95), Giddens (1984:1−40), and Sewell (1992). A discursive approach points to the fact that social life consists of a discursive interaction of social structure, carried intergenerationally, and social actors pursuing varied goals. Political actors are influenced by the prevailing social structure, and make use of it, but do not always accept the prevailing system; they may struggle against it, or even elaborate on it, in accordance with their political aims. Detailed knowledge of a social system and its culture is thus a political resource, not simply a determinant of behavior.

In the approach developed here, I start from the position that a state is the major governing institution within a particular geographic territory (e.g., Collins 1981:71; Mann 1984; Weber 1978:54). While we may define a state (as opposed to a chiefdom) by reference to the presence of an administrative hierarchy of minimally three levels, the direction I take does not view the state primarily as a hierarchically structured control mechanism. Rather, my behavioral approach views the state, wherever it is found, as the major social arena within which the competition for power is played out in society. This approach leads the researcher to focus on political process, in other words, the competition among various individuals and groups attempting to exert power in such a way as to shape or control the state (cf. Bright and Harding 1984:3–4). Thus I concur with Sewell (1992:22) when he writes that states are "consciously established, maintained, fought over, and argued about rather than taken for granted" (compare the comments in Hindess 1982:500–501; S. F. Moore 1993; M. Estellie Smith 1985). Political actors with varying aims, such as secondary elites (e.g., local patrimonial nobility or middle-level bureaucrats) versus central elites (who control the central institutions of the state), often employ diverse, often conflictive, political strategies, frequently making use of differing material and symbolic resources to further their aims (see below). In this framework, the state is not necessarily the kind of highly integrated information-processing subsystem the systems theorists would have us believe. Instead, the formal, functional, and dynamic properties of the state are outcomes of the often conflictive interaction of social actors with separate agendas, both within and outside the official structure of the decision-making institution. These social actors attempt to exert power in order to influence the state, its form, policies, and activities.

My expansion of a systems approach to incorporate political behavior does not deny a simultaneous administrative role of the state as a functional control mechanism. But I would maintain that to understand both cross-cultural variation and temporal change in states, a politically based theory will be far more productive and realistic than systems and adaptational analyses alone, because it goes directly to the issue of human behavior rather than basing its analysis on an abstract, idealized, reificationist analysis of system functioning that suffers from many of the epistemological difficulties of functionalist theory (Vincent 1986). In the next section I outline an approach to a behavioral theory of archaic state politics that can substitute for a management-inspired systems analysis.

TYPES AND SOURCES OF POWER IN ARCHAIC STATES

Political processes are analyzed here by reference to the relationships found among types of power, on the one hand, and sources of power, on the other, an approach I will call "political economy." I illustrate some of the major kinds of relationships found among types and sources of power, with selected examples, in the conceptual scheme detailed in tables 5.1 to 5.4 and discussed below. Each table lists several categories of political economy and selected examples illustrating a type of power (see below), subdivided into upper and lower cells to illustrate the dual dimension of material (or objective) versus cognitive-symbolic sources of power. I refer to each of the categories listed in the table's cells as a political-economic strategy (e.g., debt peonage in table 5.1).

These tables were constructed to illustrate the basic elements of political economy found in archaic states; they do not contain exhaustive lists of even the major types of political-economic strategizing that conceivably could be identified. To enumerate that list would be a far larger project than I have attempted here. In developing the tables, I included those types and sources of power that have been discussed at length in the political economy literature, but I add several categories, relevant to my particular interest in corporate political economy, that require additional commentary. The tables are arranged so that those political-economic strategies that have been subject to wide treatment in the literature are found in the upper part of each cell, while those that are less well understood, or less frequently discussed, are placed lower in the cell spaces. Owing to space limitations, most of the frequently discussed political-economic strategies are not addressed in this chapter beyond their citation in the tables. Several political-economic strategies requiring extensive commentary are followed by numbers in brackets that are keyed to numbered paragraphs found below. In the next section, I discuss the logic of the four tables by explaining the system used here to categorize types and sources of power.

Sources of Power
Sources of power (or "funds of power" in Wolf 1982:97 and Brumfiel 1992:554–55) are those resources that can be mobilized by political actors as they pursue their political agendas. I divide those political-economic strategies found in tables 5.1 to 5.4 into two categories to illuminate one

TABLE 5.1. *The Most Commonly Occurring Expressions of Intermember Exclusionary Domination, Subdivided by Objective and Cognitive-Symbolic Bases of Power, with Selected Examples*

Objective Base of Power

Politically charged reciprocal exchange transactions, i.e., political gifting in building a client following (e.g., Gregory 1980; Veyne 1990:70) [2]1

Utilitarian basis of patron/client relationships (Campbell 1964:259)

Benefit and fief in feudal Europe (Bloch 1961:chap. 12)

Prestige-goods systems in kinship-based societies (e.g., Meillassoux 1978)

Debt peonage (e.g., Wolf and Hansen 1972:145–47)

Cognitive-Symbolic Base of Power

Patrimonial domination ("personal loyalty" in Weber 1978:chap. 12; cf. Eisenstadt 1969:22–24); political control in "traditional" and "ascriptive" domains (Eisenstadt 1969:27)

Moral basis of patron/client relationships (Campbell 1964:259)

Senior-generation control of knowledge in kinship-based society (Meillassoux 1978:138)

Aristocratic descent reckoning and ancestor worship, e.g., in Shang period China (Chang 1983:chap. 1)

---

[1]Numbers in brackets refer to numbered sections of the text.

important dimension of variation in sources of power, following Lehman's (1969:454–55) discussion. I distinguish between a primarily objective base of power, in which material resources are utilized to achieve political ends (including physical threats based on control of coercive resources), and a primarily cognitive-symbolic base of power, where shared symbols or other forms of what Lehman calls "normative resources" constitute the base of power (cf. Weber 1946:280, 1978:943; similar dichotomous schemes are summarized in Blanton et al. 1996:table 1).

TABLE 5.2. Major Strategies in the Development of Systemic Power, Subdivided by Objective and Cognitive-Symbolic Bases of Power

Objective Base of Power

Bureaucratic administration (Weber 1978:chap. 11) supported by "free-floating" resources not tied to traditional ascriptive domains (Eisenstadt 1969:47, 1980:850)

Development of commercial systems in which "broad markets cut across ascriptive units" (Eisenstadt 1969:47, 1980:850)

Free peasantry and mobility of labor weakens traditional/ascriptive domains (Eisenstadt 1969:34, 136)

Cognitive-Symbolic Base of Power

Codification of law limits autonomy of secondary elite (e.g., Eisenstadt 1969:138)

Curtailment of traditional/ascriptive domains through the development of a transcendent cognitive code emphasizing mechanical integration of society at large and group representations; social groups defined in "universalistic terms" (Eisenstadt 1986:9)

Structurally integrative classification of social statuses (D. Miller 1989:70)

By subdividing power sources into their material and cognitive-symbolic dimensions, I do not mean to imply that any political actor is likely to employ only one or the other kind of source. Both are likely to be mobilized simultaneously, and almost every political-economic strategy has both material and symbolic dimensions (e.g., Campbell's [1964:259] discussion of patron/client relationships in Greece). But the dichotomization helps to illustrate several major trends in the evolution of archaic states, viewed broadly, that will become evident in the course of this chapter. In this regard, I point to a notable elaboration evident in the cognitive-symbolic power sources in the corporate states I discuss below. At a more basic level, I hope that the manner of construction of the tables provides evidence that our often excessively materialist discipline should devote more of its efforts to integrating both cognitive and materialist factors in analyses of political evolution (Cowgill 1993; Roscoe 1993:111).

TABLE 5.3. *Major Strategies of Systemic Exclusionary Domination, with Selected Examples, Subdivided by Objective and Cognitive-Symbolic Sources of Power*

Objective Base of Power

State control of distribution of prestige goods ("wealth distribution" in D'Altroy and Earle 1985); state monopoly of production of goods symbolizing official offices, e.g., Shang period bronze metallurgy (Chang 1983) ("Exclusionary Metal Age") [2][a]

Attached craft specialists (Brumfiel and Earle 1987), e.g., state subordination of the artist-specialist in ancient Egypt (Davis 1989)

State control of exotic instruments of war (Goody 1971)

Cognitive-Symbolic Base of Power

Whole society considered the patrimony of a ruler, e.g., ancient Egypt (Eisenstadt 1969:23)

Subordination of the bureaucracy by the ruler (Eisenstadt 1969:278–79, 285–86; 1980:864), similar to "pseudodecentralization" (Blau 1968:465; Fesler 1968:373)

Hierocracy, theocracy, and caesaropapism as types of hierocratic organization in which "spiritual domination" enforces monopoly control of religious benefits (Weber 1978:54, chap. 15)

Ritual sanctification of authority (e.g., in Bloch 1974, 1980)

Imperial ideology (Veyne 1990:377); promulgation of interest ideology (Carlton 1977: 158–65); hierarchical solidarity supported by heroic history idealizing rulers (Sahlins 1983); hegemonic ideology (Hoare and Nowell-Smith 1971)

[a]Numbers in brackets refer to numbered sections of the text.

Types of Power

Viewed cross-sectionally and diachronically, archaic states exhibit a wide range of political-economic strategies. The main patterns of variation can be illustrated using a scheme that groups strategies by what I call types of power. A principal dimension of variation captured by the resulting typology is the distinction between person-centered networks of power, on the one hand, and the varied expressions of what I will refer to as "systemic" power, on

TABLE 5.4. Major Elements of Corporate Power Strategy, with Selected Examples, Subdivided by Objective and Cognitive-Symbolic Bases of Power

Objective Base of Power

Redistributive integration (Polanyi 1957:253–54) [2]^a

Liturgies and *euergetism* ("civic gifting") in the Greek polis (Veyne 1990:72–77; Millett 1989) [2]^a

Decentralization of prestige-goods systems ("Distributive Metal Age") [2]^a

Cognitive-Symbolic Base of Power

Legitimate authority based on social contract; accountability of ruler (e.g., Eisenstadt 1986:8; Veyne 1990:301)

Commonwealth government [1]^a

Decentralization of sources of power, including status determination through moral/ritual exemplarity [2]^a

Reflexive communication [3]^a

Ritual sanctification of corporate cognitive code and ritualization of political communication [4]^a

Semiautonomous functioning of lower-order subsystems [5]^a

^aNumbers in brackets refer to numbered sections of the text.

the other. The tables break into two parts when viewed in these terms, consisting of the "intermember" power type (see table 5.1) and the various systemic power types (see tables 5.2–5.4). This dichotomy makes use of Lehman's (1969:455–56) terminology identifying intermember power as the form of superordination found within individual-centered social networks developed on the basis of personal social ties. European feudal society and similar social formations dominated by varieties of patron/client relations ("noncorporate groups" in Schneider, Schneider, and Hansen 1972) are built around intermember political-economic strategizing. I include in the intermember category clan systems and similar social structures in which deference to power wielders is bound up in kinship rhetoric emphasizing concepts of shared ancestry. Power sources mobilized in the pursuit of inter-member power are varied, ranging from client-building wealth distributions to claims of direct descent from the distinguished ancestors of a traditional or "ascriptive domain" (in the phraseology of Eisenstadt [1969:27]) (see table 5.1).

While intermember power is structured around person-centered net-works, it is obviously not irrelevant to political competition as it is found in archaic or modern states. Chang (1983) details the important role played by clanship in Early Dynastic China. Eisenstadt (1969) discusses at length the various political-economic strategies put into place to limit intermember power, in the terminology used here, through the development of systemic power strategies (see below). But even where systemic power prevails, po-litical actors may build intermember networks to realize political goals. "Influence," in Parsons's (1967) terms, is the process whereby intermember power can be translated into political prominence in the larger arena of the state.

In what Lehman (1969:455–56) calls "systemic power," in contrast to intermember power, institutions are established that are capable of preclud-ing, or at least limiting, the exercise of intermember power strategies. Sys-temic power is basic to the establishment of politically unified states that can transcend the scale limits inherent in personalized power networks (Eisen-stadt 1969:chap. 2). And, as in the case of ancient Greece, discussed below, systemic power can serve to reduce the social disruption resulting from com-petition between person-centered factions. As indicated in table 5.2, the major political-economic strategies employed in the struggle to control intermember power are bureaucratic management structures and codes of law, both of which help ensure that power wielders will conform to formally established standards of conduct. Although a struggle between intermember and systemic interests is found in all complex societies (Lehman 1969:461; see Yang 1989 for a modern example), this aspect of the competition for power is one of the key aspects of the political process in the evolution of archaic states. It is discussed at length in sources that follow up on Max Weber's discussions, especially Eisenstadt (1969), whose conclusions are summarized in table 5.2.

In Lehman's (1969) scheme, systemic power permits the implementation of what he calls "collective goals." In my scheme, I maintain the essence of Lehman's terminology while further subdividing his category of systemic power to better reflect the realities of political processes found in certain highly centralized states that illustrate kinds of political processes he does not discuss. I do this by subdividing Lehman's systemic power into "exclusion-ary" and "corporate" power (see tables 5.3 and 5.4, respectively). Exclusionary power implies that power wielders have few or no restrictions on their exercise of power (like "integral power," following Wrong 1979:11, and Weber's *Herrschaft,* translated as "domination"; Parsons 1960:752). Intermember power, centered around individuals who dominate networks of subordinates, illustrates one dimension of exclusionary power. But systemic power strategies also may be exclusionary, as table 5.3 indicates. In systemic exclusionary power, the bureaucracy, law codes, and so on, are constituted so as to ensure that the policies and directives of the ruler or ruling group are followed without challenge or negotiation. Ancient Egypt (excepting its intermediate periods, which were more decentralized) is one of the foremost examples of this form of hypercentralized systemic domination. Here, the whole society was conceived of as a ruler-centered patrimonial domain writ large (Eisenstadt 1969:23; Weber 1947:350). Systemic exclusionary power is accomplished primarily through a ruler-centered subordination of the bureaucracy, but other monopolistic strategies are employed, including control of access to the supernatural and the promulgation of an ideological cognitive code and its accompanying rituals that mystify the underlying political inequality (see table 5.3). These features are discussed below.

The presence of exclusionary domination in some archaic states forces me to depart from Lehman's scheme. In cases like Egypt's, the systemic structure of the bureaucracy limits the free play of intermember power, but it is not likely that the goals of the pharaohs could be described as "collective goals" in the corporate sense implied by Lehman. In what I refer to as the corporate form of systemic power, on the other hand, there is a more egalitarian, legitimated political structure constituted so that a power wielder's ability to exercise power unilaterally is constrained by the countervailing efforts of what Mann (1984:185) refers to as "civil society groups" (see table 5.4). This is Weber's *legitime Herrschaft,* or "legal authority" (Weber 1978:212–16, 217–26, passim), which serves the "integration of the collectivity" (Parsons 1960:752). Corporate political-economic strategies emphasize, variously, (1) restrictions on the exercise of power; (2) reduced potential to monopolize sources of power; (3) a greater degree of openness in access to positions of power; (4) communications channels that allow an assessment of conformance to codes of accepted political behavior; and (5) what I refer to as the "semiautonomy" of lower-order subsystems. I discuss these topics below.

The evolution of the corporate power type is a complex issue that refers to the degree of expression of what I will call egalitarian behavior in complex society, or what Wrong (1979:11–12) refers to as "measures that limit integral power." In the corporate power type, the free play of intermember power is constrained, primarily through the development of bureaucracy, as in the systemic exclusionary power, but in corporate situations the bureaucracy is not entirely subordinated by the ruler and, instead, is constituted so as to ensure that persons in power, including the ruler, conform to established political practices. In addition, the particular practices utilized for recruitment into the state's administrative apparatus may be designed to level social differences in society (Weber 1946:224–28), as I discuss below. For example, in contrast to the pattern of aristocratic dominance of the Shang dynasty, by the first century BC, Chinese government officials were drawn from a wide range of social strata (Creel 1970:7). I mention these examples preliminarily here to make the point that in a behavioral theory of the state the importance of the bureaucracy is not to be found only in its information-processing efficiency, as systems analysts would emphasize, but also in its potential role in political processes whereby intermember power is constrained by systemic power, and whereby corporate political strategies constrain exclusionary power.

Having laid out my conceptual scheme of political economy, I next turn to the main focus of this chapter, which is a discussion of the elements of corporate power, presented in a conceptual framework that facilitates comparative discussion. First, though, I wish to reiterate several points regarding my scheme and the contents of tables 5.1 to 5.4. The purpose of the tables is to facilitate a comparative analysis of political processes in archaic states by pointing to the highly variable nature of political-economic strategies found in them. In part this variation reflects cross-cultural and diachronic variation between and within states, but it also may describe the variant strategies of political actors who compete for power within a social formation at a single point in time (e.g., Rowlands 1985). Given the possibility of coexisting but distinct political-economic strategies (e.g., Barth 1959), the tables aim at the elucidation of the nature of political process and cannot be expected to produce a neat political-economic classification in all cases. M. Estellie Smith (1985:98) is correct in her estimation that the political anthropology literature has too many typologies of states, and certainly tables 5.1 to 5.4 are not meant as one more typological scheme.

Social actors with conflictive aims make use of various power sources and types to those ends, so tidy categorization of political systems often may elude the researcher. Further, while a given social formation at a particular time may represent a preponderance of some particular dimension of political-economic strategizing and thus, perhaps, be construed as a particular political type, such arrangements are always contingent and subject to change, shifting, in essence, that society's major form of political action from one area of my tables to another. Cycling between types of power may be a common historical pattern, as my colleagues and I point out for prehispanic Mesoamerica (Blanton et al. 1996).

PROLOGUE TO A DISCUSSION OF CORPORATE
POLITICAL-ECONOMIC STRATEGIES

In the numbered paragraphs below, keyed to sections in tables 5.1 to 5.4, I address several issues inadequately discussed in the contemporary neoevolutionist literature on archaic states. Of these topics, those found in table 5.4 illustrating corporate political economy present the most challenges for analysis, owing to both conceptual difficulties and a deficiency of information. In my opinion, systems analysis and other approaches that have devoted excessive attention to centralization have limited our ability to figure corporate political economy into our sociocultural evolutionary theory (cf. Cowgill 1993; Crumley 1987:160–63). Some of the discussion during our Santa Fe seminar centered around states lacking the kind of ruler-centered political hierarchy that we often associate with archaic states, and which may be outcomes of corporate political strategies. Teotihuacán (beginning during the Tlamimilolpa phase, AD 200–400) and Indus civilization, especially, were discussed as prominent examples lacking the usual material indicators of centralized controls (see Possehl, this volume; on Teotihuacán, I am following Cabrera Castro, Sugiyama, and Cowgill 1991; Cowgill 1983, 1992a, 1992b, 1993, 1997; Millon 1988, 1992; Pasztory 1992, 1997). In these cases, we find an absence of royal tombs; few or no figural representations of, or textual references to, specific rulers; and no named ruling dynasties. "Heroic histories" (in Sahlins's [1983] terminology), which glorify rulers in publicly displayed written narratives and in art, are also not found in these and similar cases. During the course of our seminar deliberations in Santa Fe, we came to designate such societies as "faceless polities." How were they governed?

In a recent paper, my colleagues and I (Blanton et al. 1996) proposed that Mesoamerican researchers incorporate into their considerations of sociocultural evolutionary processes the evolution of corporate political strategy. This proposal was stimulated by Renfrew's (1974) suggestion that one form of European chiefdoms was, as he called it, "group-oriented." The group-oriented social formations he described are characterized by the presence of impressive public works, including large architectural spaces suitable for communal ritual, but a notable degree of egalitarianism. In them, individuals are "faceless and anonymous" (1974:79). His other category, "individualizing chiefdoms," manifests a greater emphasis on features related to the expression of personal wealth and status, including the consumption of elaborate prestige goods as found in "princely burials" (1974:82).

In our discussion of ancient Mesoamerican corporate political economy and culture, we emphasize the key role played by the establishment and cultural legitimation of cognitive codes that, as we put it, "emphasize a corporate solidarity of society as an integrated whole, based on a natural, fixed, and immutable interdependence between subgroups" (Blanton et al. 1996: 6). Further, we point out, the ecumenical viewpoint of the corporate orientation supplants or replaces the ancestral ritual that legitimated the control of society by a few high-ranking individuals or households and replaces it with collective representations and the accompanying ritual emphasizing universalistic themes of fertility and renewal in society and cosmos (cf. Pasztory 1992). Corporate strategy thus transcends the scale limitations and narrower scope of kinship rhetoric, which exclusionarily empowers particular individuals or groups based on gender, generation, and primacy of descent from common ancestors. In addition, corporate social formations constrain the exercise of power by subsuming it within hierarchically graded sets of roles and statuses, what D. Miller (1989:70) refers to as "structurally integrative classifications."

In our conceptualization, corporate power is like Mann's (1986:22–23) concept of "ideological power," a "transcendent sacred authority" (p. 22) (note that in what follows in this chapter, unlike Mann, I use the term "ideology" to refer specifically to cognitive codes that mystify exclusionary domination; where Mann uses the phrase "ideological power," I would substitute "corporate cognitive code," as I discuss below). Ideological power, according to Mann, is based on the promulgation of norms that are "shared understandings of how people should act morally in their relations with each other" (p. 22). Thus it is similar to Durkheim's concept of mechanical integration, but operationalized for the governance of complex society. Further, and related, I would argue, to Renfrew's observation that the group-oriented chiefdoms include large architectural spaces suitable for group ritual, Mann's ideological power is supported through the institution of what he calls "aesthetic/ritual practices." I discuss the importance of ritual integration in corporate political strategies below.

By pointing to the integrative importance of group ritual and mechanical integration based on a corporate cognitive code, I do not mean to imply that corporate political economy is necessarily a "primitive" social form, well suited only to small-scale social formations but unsuited to larger-scale societies where only centralized administration would suffice as a control mechanism (see below). Nor would I regard corporate organization as simply a transitional evolutionary stage of the archaic state preceding larger and more complex societies integrated through the centralized power of rulership. Over a period of 3,000 years, for example, regions of Mesoamerican civilization displayed a complex pattern of cycling between more corporate and more overt ruler-centered social formations, rather than a simple evolutionary stage sequence (Blanton et al. 1996) (a similar interpretation of long cycles in South Asian civilization is proposed in Miller 1985:62–63).

An additional point requires clarification in connection with a discussion of corporate systems. As I argued, corporate need not imply "primitive" in my conceptualization. Although corporate systems may lack the kind of centralized political structure often regarded as characteristic of archaic states (e.g., in Claessen and Skalník, eds. 1978), I also would argue that corporate governance need not imply an absence of power in society. This point can be clarified in part by reference to Mann's (1984:188–89) distinction between "despotic power" and "infrastructural power." In despotic power, a ruler is able to take actions ("off with his head") without, as Mann puts it, "routine, institutionalized negotiation with civil society groups" (p. 188). In the case of infrastructural power, the governing institution is able to "actually penetrate civil society, and to implement logistically political decisions throughout the realm" (p. 189). Mann makes the important point that the two forms of power may vary independently. The centralized focus of power in a despotic regime may not imply much actual power in society, in the sense that despotic power does not always imply a great deal of infrastructural power (1984:189). On the other hand, I would argue that a more corporate system, such as those discussed below, although lacking the centralized focus of despotic power, might still develop and maintain a high degree of infrastructural power.

EGALITARIAN BEHAVIOR AND CORPORATE POLITICAL ECONOMY

One of my main goals in this chapter is the development of concepts and definitions that will facilitate a comparative discussion of corporate political economy, a discussion that has been largely absent from the recent neoevolutionist literature on archaic states. I start by suggesting a redefinition of an often-used anthropological concept—egalitarian—that will allow me to employ it productively in the context of complex societies including archaic states. "Egalitarian," as used here, does not imply an absence of hierarchical control, or perfect political or economic equality; complex societies governed by states always have varying degrees of all three. I define as egalitarian any behavior that aims to establish and uphold restrictions on the exercise of exclusionary power, whatever its social setting in simpler or more complex societies. The position taken here follows the logic of those who argue that nonhierarchical, egalitarian societies should not be perceived as having failed to develop centralized government or economic inequality. Rather, these societies have in place specific cultural practices that prevent unacceptable degrees of accumulation of power or wealth in the hands of specific persons or groups (e.g., Boehm 1993; Cashdan 1980; Clastres 1977; Kent 1993; Mann 1986:68–69; Miller 1955; Poyer 1993; Woodburn 1982). In my discussion below, however, I depart from Clastres's assertion that egalitarian behavior represents a "radical rejection of authority" (Clastres 1977:34).

By contrast, in corporately constructed archaic states, an authority structure is a salient social factor, but it is constructed along corporate lines, and its structure and function reflect the outcomes of egalitarian behavior. Thus, following Boehm (1993:228), I make a distinction between egalitarian society, a descriptive concept, and egalitarian behavior, a type of political action that aims at preventing the exercise of exclusionary power strategies. Corporate power strategies in archaic state societies are expressions of egalitarian behavior viewed in this way. In corporate strategy, specific cultural practices are put into place, a corporate cognitive code that serves to limit the exercise of power.

The study of corporate political economy in the archaic states presents many difficulties. Owing to the previous overemphasis on centralized states in the neoevolutionist literature, few researchers have addressed egalitarian behavior as it is expressed in corporately structured archaic states. In addition, the subject of egalitarian behavior in general is one in which the anthropological researcher finds primarily scattered ideas and examples, and a lack of conceptual synthesis or extensive comparative research. Only a limited number of sources are available that can serve as background to the discussion of corporate political behavior presented below, and these are often regionally specific and descriptive rather than comparative or theoretically informed. For sub-Saharan Africa, a well-developed literature describes rituals of rebellion and other checks on the abuse of power by rulers (Beattie 1967; Bohannan 1958; Gluckman 1959, 1963; Norbeck 1963; cf. Sahlins 1972:145–48 on rituals of rebellion in Polynesia), and Lewis (1974b) describes an African case of assembly government. Egalitarian behavior is evident in the evolution of the Asante state during Osei Tutu's reign (Chazan 1988), where power was shared between the ruler and an advisory council (cf. Bradbury 1969 on Benin political culture). The nature of "communal society" in small-scale social formations is discussed in Saitta and Keene (1990; cf. McGuire and Saitta 1996; Saitta 1994); Iroquois strategies for maintaining economic and political egalitarianism are outlined in Trigger (1990). The destruction of kingship in Europe and elsewhere is discussed in Feeley-Harnik (1985). The processes of political decentralization and federalism in modern states are summarized in B. Smith (1985). Other relevant topics include considerations of revolutionary cognitive orders (e.g., Carlton 1977:33), peasant resistance and class consciousness (e.g., Kahn 1985; Scott 1985, 1990), popular collective action (B. Moore 1978; Tilly and Tilly 1981), and other aspects of resistance to elite hegemony (Castells 1983) and male dominance (e.g., Maher 1984).

The ritual expression of egalitarian behavior is found in rites of reversal and symbolic inversion (summarized in Miller 1989:67–68; cf. Kertzer 1988:131, 145; Scott 1985:331), and in other aspects of the role of ritual in political competition (Kertzer 1988). The roles of witchcraft and sorcery in social leveling are discussed in Besnier (1993), Rodman (1993), Rosaldo (1968:534), and Rowlands and Warnier (1988). Forge (1972b:533–34) reminds us that reciprocal gift exchanges do not necessarily result in social equality among exchanging parties. Instead, in reciprocal gift exchanges, "to be equal and stay equal is an extremely onerous task requiring continued vigilance and effort"—in other words, egalitarian behavior.

Few sources directly address the evolution of corporate political economy in archaic states. Haas (1982:112), for example, mentions the paucity of studies of resistance to authority that can be found in the archaeological literature. One possible reason for this lack of interest is the persistent idea that the European enlightenment's social contract theory is largely a recent and culturally specific phenomenon, with little relevance to non-Western states. Lamberg-Karlovsky (1985:23), for example, argues that

> The "moral obligations" imposed on rulers for constituting freedom, equity and justice are as old as the ancient palaces and temples of the Near East. Such "moral" concepts continued to receive affirmation whether in the Acropolis of democratic Athens, the Magna Carta of King John, or the principles of Liberté, Egalité, and Fraternité of the French Revolution. As certain as these concepts are pivotal to Western Civilization, they are foreign to the political ideology of ancient Egypt, China, and India.

My understanding of the nature of egalitarian behavior leads me to propose that Lamberg-Karlovsky's contrast of Western and others is overdrawn, although one of the societies he mentions, ancient Egypt, did not, in fact, develop corporate political economy (e.g., see Humphreys 1978).

The form of egalitarian behavior developed in the stream of Western civilization, extending in time from the ancient Near East to the modern democracies, is unique in some important ways, a point discussed below. A less sharp distinction between the Western pattern and others is evident, however, when the researcher adopts a more broadly conceived notion of egalitarian behavior in archaic and modern societies governed by states (e.g., Scott 1990:81). In the following, I discuss several of the elements making up such an expanded conceptualization, but it should be kept in mind that this subject matter is exceedingly complex and involves a highly varied domain of human experience. The suggestions I put forward constitute only a small step toward a lengthier discussion of this seminal topic that I hope will develop in the neoevolutionist literature in the coming decades.

THE ELEMENTS OF CORPORATE POLITICAL ECONOMY IN ARCHAIC STATES

I propose five main elements constituting corporate political economy in archaic states (not all of which will necessarily be found in any one case): (1) assembly (or commonwealth) government, (2) corporate regulation of sources of power, (3) "reflexive communication," (4) ritual sanctification of corporate cognitive code and ritualization of political communication, and (5) "semiautonomy" of lower-order subsystems (table 5.4). Each category will require extensive consideration as we expand our knowledge of archaic states. Here I am only able to characterize each category briefly, illustrating them by reference to selected examples.

1. Assembly or Commonwealth Government

M. Estellie Smith's (1985:106–8) discussion is a useful starting point for a consideration of commonwealth government (cf. Richards and Kuper 1971). Of the variety of commonwealths discussed by Smith, the form addressed here is assembly government. Commonwealth (including assembly government) is defined in the Oxford English Dictionary as "a body in which the whole people have a voice or an interest; a body or a number of persons united by the same common interest." This form of political decision making is similar to that described by Johnson (1983) as "sequential hierarchy," where nonranked representatives of domestic or other groups consult together as needed to make decisions regarding the group as a whole, as in the example of gerontocracy described by Weber (1947:346) (cf. Bargatzky 1988). In the sense that the participating representatives are unranked with respect to each other, assembly government is an example of the process Crumley (1987:158) refers to as heterarchy (Ehrenreich, Crumley, and Levy 1995). Although Johnson's discussion is limited to sequential hierarchy among hunter-gatherers and nomadic herders, his concept can be extended to cases of assembly government in archaic states. In these cases, political decision making occurs in assemblies representing a society's constituent groups. Decisions arrived at are implemented by a specialized administrative organization (Bailey 1965:14) that, expanding on M. Estellie Smith's (1985:107) phraseology, is staffed by persons who hold nondurative positions for which they are selected at random or according to personal qualities germane to the problem at hand (e.g., Weber 1978:289–90).

Classical Athenian democracy (the polis state) is the best known example of assembly government in an archaic state society (Humphreys 1978). Evidently, owing to this example's direct historical connection to the rise of democracy in western Europe, the United States, and elsewhere, it is thought to be uniquely Western and hence has not figured importantly into the broader neoevolutionist literature on early state evolution until recently (Ferguson 1991; I. Morris 1987, 1994:43; Runciman 1982; Small 1994; Snodgrass 1986). But the Athenian experience is only the best-known example of a more general type of political structure found in other eastern Mediterranean polities that included representative assemblies, such as the Syria/Palestinian region in the second millennium BC, early Israel, Phoenician city-states, and Carthage (summarized in Humphreys 1978:181−82; cf. Snodgrass 1980:32). As Humphreys (1978:181) points out, the presence of assemblies in these cases can be traced historically to the governing assemblies of pre−Early Dynastic Mesopotamia, as first described by Jacobsen (1943, 1957; cf. Lamberg-Karlovsky 1985).

It should be, but unfortunately has not been, of considerable theoretical interest to anthropological archaeology that Mesopotamian social formations appear to have emphasized corporate forms of government from an early period, including forms of assembly government that evidently had developed by the Uruk period (3800−3100 BC) (Jacobsen 1943, 1957). Even for the preceding ʿUbaid period (5500−3800 BC), Stein (1994b) found it necessary to develop what he called a "revised chiefdom model" because the usual attributes of chiefdoms as described in the neoevolutionist literature are absent. As he points out, ʿUbaid lacks elite burials (p. 39), iconographic evidence of chiefs (p. 39), as well as "exotic, rare, or high-status trade goods," or elite craft goods (p. 40). Instead, the ʿUbaid people developed "an egalitarian ethic of shared group membership and ideology" based on an elaboration of temple ritual (1994b:43; cf. Oates 1977:475). Although the evidence indicates state formation during the subsequent Uruk period (3800−3100 BC) (Johnson 1973), there is considerable agreement, following Jacobsen, that assembly government existed during this period and that rulership and palace institutions developed only later in the Early Dynastic periods of the third millennium BC (Adams 1966:138−41; Oates 1977:475−76; Postgate 1992:80−81, 137). The contrast of Uruk with the Predynastic and Archaic periods of Egypt, given the abundant evidence in ancient Egypt of elaborate elite tomb burials and early forms of pharaonic and palace symbolism, is striking (Kemp 1989:chap. 1; see Baines and Yoffee, this volume). Two highly distinct patterns of sociocultural evolutionary change leading to early state formation are suggested for these two regions, with Egypt's built principally around exclusionary political economy while Mesopotamia's was more corporate.

2. Corporate Regulation of Sources of Power

Corporate regulation inhibits the potential for exclusionary control of objective and symbolic sources of power. There are many aspects of this domain of corporate power, and I am able to address only a few key topics here. In table 5.4, following Polanyi (1957:253–54), I include redistributive economic integration as a possible expression of corporate behavior. This is potentially a problematic usage since, as developed by Polanyi, the idea does not adequately distinguish between a distributive economy benefiting the collectivity and a centralized control of the economy for purposes of exclusionary mobilization of resources for state use (e.g., Earle 1977). An avenue of inquiry more productive than the concept of redistribution is found in Veyne's (1990) stimulating analysis of the democratic Greek polis state and Roman society. Veyne investigates the distinction between the "political gift," or "largess" (e.g., pp. 70, 72), made by wealthy patrons for the purposes of building networks of clients, and the "civic gift" (*euergesai*), in which the giving of wealthy individuals benefited instead the collectivity, transcending tribe and clients. The development of the concept of *euergesai* served to reduce the power-enhancing potential of politically motivated gifting, weakening the intermember power strategy. Thus, the growth of Athenian democracy and its *euergesai* "took shape outside these networks of clientage and . . . in opposition to them" (Veyne 1990:75; cf. Humphreys 1978:69–70, 201; Millett 1989).

The example of social changes that occurred in the development of the Greek polis state serves to illustrate the importance of one dimension of exclusionary political-economic strategy, namely, the manipulation of prestige-goods systems. In one expression of prestige-goods political strategy, individuals or groups who monopolistically control valuable "politically charged" goods (Brumfiel and Earle 1987:5) are able to build networks of followers through political gifting. Alternately, political actors strive to control goods used as symbols of political office (what might be called the "Golden Fleece Effect"), or used militarily (Appadurai 1986:24–25; Douglas 1967; Ekholm 1972; Frankenstein and Rowlands 1978; Friedman and Rowlands 1977:214; Goody 1971:52; Peregrine 1991, 1992; Weber 1978:1092). Chang (1983), for example, describes the role of bronze metallurgy in Shang dynasty politics. Corporate political economy must develop strategies, such as the Greek *euergesai*, to counter politically charged gift exchange and prestige-goods systems because they are consistent with the establishment and maintenance of exclusionary power. Market systems are consistent with corporate political economy viewed this way. An elaboration of systems of commercial exchange reduces the potential for monopolization of goods distribution found in patron/client and similar systems

(Eisenstadt 1969:47; Weber 1978:1092). Following the phraseology of Gregory (1980, 1982), this is a process whereby "gift" exchange is transformed into "commodity" exchange.

I propose that to more fully comprehend those political strategies antithetical to exclusionary control of goods, we investigate the social patterns of production and distribution of goods involving advanced technologies, particularly metallurgy (Blanton et al. 1996). In this connection, I suggest we make the terminological distinction between "distributive" metal ages, where metal tools and other valuable objects are widely available and in ordinary household use, and "exclusionary" metal ages, where society's most advanced technological production is controlled for use as a source of exclusionary political power. Several of the prominent cases discussed in this chapter, illustrating features of corporate behavior, also were characterized by a widespread distribution of metal tools in society—in other words, they illustrate distributive metal ages. I include the Greek later Iron Age after the eighth century BC (during the preceding Dark Age, 1000–750 BC, iron clearly served as a prestige good; I. Morris 1989), the Chalcolithic (Copper Age) periods of pre–Early Dynastic Mesopotamia (4500–3300 BC; Moorey 1985), and Indus civilization (Possehl 1990:279). Costin and Earle (1989) discuss the Inka strategy of widely distributing bronze tools for ordinary household use, which may constitute a parallel example of a distributive metal age. Ehrenreich (1995) contrasts the broad distribution of ironworking with the centralized production of bronze in the Iron and Bronze Ages of Wessex.

Much contemporary theory takes the position that technological change is a reflection of social change (e.g., Bender 1990), an approach that avoids what is rightly regarded as the naive technological determinism of earlier materialist theory. Childe (1942:191), for example, argued that the development of inexpensive iron production technology abolished commoner dependence on state monopolies of metal. His technological determinist argument begs the question, however, of why iron would have been any less subject to monopolization by a political elite than bronze had been; iron metallurgy appears to be consistent with either exclusionary or distributive use, as is indicated by its changing role in Greece during the first millennium BC. However, we lack an adequate social theory of what I am calling a distributive metal age that would overcome the difficulties of a technological determinist approach. As we might expect, given anthropology's analytical bias toward social behaviors that permit the reproduction of exclusionary political control, prestige-goods systems and their monopolies of exotic technology and other rarer categories of goods have been subject to much recent theoretical and empirical treatment. Morris (1989), for example, convincingly demonstrates iron's role as a prestige good in the early Iron Age of central Greece (1000–750 BC), but he simply mentions in passing that iron came into much more widespread household use after the eighth century BC, coincident with the rise of the corporate Greek polis state.

I suggest that a social theory of distributive metal ages and analogous "democratizations" of other technologies is required as a counterpart to the theories of prestige-goods systems. I do not attempt the full development of such a theory here, but I propose that distributive metal ages are an outcome of egalitarian behavior in the construction of corporate political economy. The widespread distribution of society's most advanced technologies would have the result of reducing their potential roles in exclusionary political economy (cf. Blanton et al. 1996, regarding prehispanic Mesoamerica). In this connection, it is of interest to trace the situation of Chalcolithic Mesopotamia mentioned previously. Prior to the development of ruler-centered polities of the mid-third millennium BC, tools and simple personal ornaments of cast copper were widely used in domestic contexts, but exotic metals were infrequently used (Moorey 1985:23–26, 1994:235–36, 252). By the mid-third millennium, a notable increase occurred in the frequency of luxury goods in copper, bronze, gold, and silver, among other materials, for example, in the royal cemetery at Ur (Moorey 1985:27–29, 1994:221, 236). The comparative infrequency of such exotics in earlier Mesopotamian periods may have been a result of a social process regulating goods distribution there, insofar as this can be inferred from the frequent presence of silver in the nearby regions of Egypt, the Levant, and Anatolia in sites dating to the fourth millennium (Moorey 1985:114, 1994:235–36). These data suggest an evolutionary sequence in Mesopotamia from a distributive metal age to a prestige-goods system coincident with the rise of the palace institutions of the third millennium.

A probable example of corporate-based technological change is the Chinese Iron Age of the Zhou dynasty (1022–256 BC). Pokora (1978:208–9) takes the Childean technological-determinist position when he attributes the revolutionary social changes of the Zhou period to the "advent, in the middle of the [first] millennium, of the Iron Age" (cf. Chang 1983:8). By contrast, C.-Y. Hsu (1965:130–31) proposes that the Chinese Iron Age will be understood by reference to social changes that occurred during the Zhou dynasty and later. I would hypothesize, following up on Hsu's suggestion, that the Chinese Iron Age was an example of a distributive metal age and was one dimension of a complex of social changes that brought about a more corporate Chinese society, breaking down the old aristocratic system and its exclusionary use of metallurgy. Evidently, the process of technological democratization began even before the widespread use of iron. Hsu and

Linduff (1988:317–37) note that during the Western Zhou period (1100–770 BC), a bronze technology developed that was in wider use, displayed a greater secularization of design motifs, and was more commercialized, by comparison with the bronze-based prestige-goods system of the preceding Shang dynasty. A debate between state authorities and Confucians during the reign of Chao Ti of the Han dynasty (in 81 BC), reported in the "Discourses on Salt and Iron" (Esson 1931), affords a glimpse into the social contexts of early Chinese iron production. During this debate, the Lord Grand Secretary notes several reasons for maintaining the state monopoly of iron production: (1) to increase the productive efficiency of agriculture (e.g., p. 7); (2) to generate revenues for the state (e.g., p. 41); and (3) to facilitate an equitable distribution of goods (pp. 6–8). The latter is threatened, he argued, when powerful producer families and "vassal houses" (the aristocracy) gain control over industries such as iron (pp. 54, 87).

In addition to the materialist factors discussed to this point, cognitive codes also facilitate corporate regulation of sources of power. One important strategy is giving persons of a wide range of social statuses access to positions of power—what Weber called "democratic administration" (1978: 948). In this and similar situations, a cognitive code is developed in which a prime determinant of access to positions of political power is exemplary moral and/or ritual behavior (similar to Kelly's [1993:14] "prestige-stigma hierarchy"). As expressed by Dumont (1980:56), in these cases, the "distinction of purity is the foundation of status." Cognitive codes of this type reflect egalitarian behavior in that positions of power in society may be opened up to persons of a wider range of social ranks, rather than being ascribed or restricted to those who control material resources.

Moralistic and ritualistic determination of social status is an outcome of egalitarian behavior also in cases where the system of moral rules applies to all persons in society, including rulers and other power wielders (e.g., see Norbeck 1977:73). In Eisenstadt's formulation (1980:851, 1981:157), such moralistic cognitive codes are predicated on the development of a "symbolic problematization." Here, what I am calling the corporate cognitive code envisions a "basic tension between the transcendental and mundane orders" in which "political order is conceived of as lower than the transcendental one and . . . had to be structured according to the precepts of the latter" (1981:159). Moral orders so constructed are corporate in that political actors, including rulers, can be called to judgment and deposed for failure to comply with the dictates of the moral code. For example, according to the Confucian system, the Chinese ruler's behavior was "open to official reprimand" (Weber 1951:31–32; cf. C.-Y. Hsu 1988:180–81; Wei-Ming 1986). According to C.-Y. Hsu (1986:308), the significance of the Chou conquest was the emergence of the Mandate of Heaven which endowed the supreme being with an authority as well as the responsibility of ensuring the people to be governed by pious and righteous rulers. I think such a transformation of characteristics of supreme being in ancient China should be regarded as an important breakthrough.

Such corporately inspired mandates, whereby the ruler is the upholder of the "purity of the collectivity" (Eisenstadt 1981:175), are distinct from cases of "spiritual domination" (Weber 1978:54–56), where divine kingship (e.g., in ancient Egypt) is an exclusionary political strategy predicated on control of access to the supernatural. Ancient Egypt is an example of Weber's (1978:54–56) "hierocratic organization," where there is monopoly control of what he terms "religious benefits." The Classic period Maya concept of kingship (ahau) provides an additional example of spiritual domination. This concept placed rulers at the center of the temporal cycles of history, shamanistic prophecy, curing, and divine ancestor worship (Freidel and Schele 1988; Schele and Miller 1986).

Although it is not my purpose here to elaborate on the varied material manifestations of corporate political economy, note that the form of the major Egyptian temples, with their sequence of hallways, passages, and rooms arranged hierarchically along a central axis (e.g., Badawy 1968:chap. III; Kemp 1989:94), places the image of the temple's deity in a secluded back space accessible only to the pharaoh and a few high-ranking priests or temple officials. This placement is consistent with exclusionary control of supernatural forces. Such exclusionary architectural strategies date to the earliest periods of Egyptian temple construction (Kemp 1989:66–83). These architectural forms can be contrasted with the plan for the Islamic temple of Kufa, on the east bank of the Euphrates, built in AD 636. Its more corporate aim was to band "together disparate groups through a collective variety of worship that knew no priestly hierarchy, mysteries, or hidden sanctuary within the precincts of worship itself" (Campo 1991:60).

In addition to architectural layout of the temple, the potential for monopoly control of supernatural forces also can be limited by extending important ritual practices to households of all social statuses. A decentralization of ritual emphasizes the commonality of all of society's constituent elements and the mutual interdependencies of varied social sectors in the reproduction of nature and society (Miller 1985:61). The gradual evolution of the pattern of ancestor worship in China is a case in point. Earlier forms of ancestor worship revolved around images of the prominent ancestor gods of clan groups; their use in sacrificial rituals was a "prerogative of the aristocracy" (Laufer 1965:449). In the Confucian reforms, by contrast, clan structure was de-emphasized and an elaborated code of household behavior substituted for it, informed by a concept of filial piety that extended to family ancestor worship. Accordingly, clan ancestral images were replaced by conventionalized tablets used in the ancestral rituals of ordinary households. As a result, "ancestor worship developed into a thoroughly democratic institution, and the effect was that ancestors sank in value and became at a discount" (Laufer 1965:449). In this case, the cultural efficacy of ancestor worship in Chinese culture was maintained, but it was reconceptualized so as to weaken aristocratic control, while at the same time serving to bolster the functional integrity of households, a process I discuss further below.

Research into the evolution of writing, I suggest, would benefit from use of the concept of corporate political strategy. Given the considerable potential of writing for furthering the aims of centralized states through textual glorification of rulers' exploits and the documentation of aristocratic genealogies, it is often employed in exclusionary political strategy, as Marcus (1992c) recently demonstrated for prehispanic Mesoamerica (cf. Larsen 1988). Presumably, competing corporate strategies would attempt to counter the use of writing in furthering the aims of exclusionary political interests, but how this might happen has not been adequately addressed in the literature on writing in archaic states. One topic along these lines that requires consideration in the context of archaic states is the role of literacy. It is widely recognized that the political reforms of the Reformation in Europe were aided by widespread literacy and the printing press (e.g., Corcoran 1979:68–69; Febvre and Martin 1976:chap. 8). Similarly, Laufer (1965: 449) notes a relationship between the development of writing in China and the transition from aristocratic ancestral images to the conventionalized ancestral tablets used in the household rites mentioned above. Also in China, the official Gazette figured into the theory and practice of accountability of rulers. In the Gazette system, "the whole administration . . . took place before the broadest public . . . [it] was a sort of running account of the Emperor before Heaven and before his subjects" (Weber 1946:437–38). Writing in this case exemplifies a type of political communication I will refer to in the next section as "reflexive communication."

Printing presses, ancestral tablets, and official Gazettes imply at least a reasonably widespread degree of literacy in society. I would propose that a corporate strategy found in some archaic states aims, instead, to restrict writing and literacy (in a manner perhaps behaviorally analogous to the shamanic rejection of writing and codification described in Hamayon 1994:88). In two of the cases I have used to illustrate elements of corporate behavior, namely Teotihuacán and Indus civilization, the potential of writing to further the aims of individual power wielders may have been diminished by severely restricting its forms and usages. Pasztory (1988) suggests that, rather than making use of hieroglyphic texts (as used by Teotihuacán's Maya contemporaries), writing at Teotihuacán was restricted to an iconographic form seen primarily in mural scenes to integrate a heterogeneous population speaking multiple languages. Also of interest in Teotihuacán writing, beginning during the Tlamimilolpa phase, is its use primarily in domestic contexts, as opposed to widely visible public venues, and its nearly complete avoidance of genealogical accounting or glorification of the exploits of named ruling dynasties (Millon 1988:112–13; Pasztory 1992:303–4). While not one Teotihuacán ruler can be definitely identified, many are named in the contemporaneous and highly exclusionary political economy of the Classic period Maya (e.g., Schele and Miller 1986). Millon (1988: 112) asks:

> Why, over a span of five hundred years or more, did not some rulers set up their images, glorifying their exploits, as the Maya and other contemporary and earlier Mesoamerican rulers did? Is it perhaps because powerful ideological and institutional checks on the glorification of personal power had been established early in Teotihuacán's history?

In this connection, writing was in use in protoliterate Mesopotamia (3800–3000 BC), but was restricted primarily to economic accounting and similar nonpolitical contexts. It was not harnessed to serve the glorification of kings in royal inscriptions and literary texts until the rise of the rulers and palaces of the Early Dynastic period (Postgate 1992:fig. 3:13; Baines and Yoffee, this volume). A thesis for future consideration to explain this interesting situation (and the perhaps analogously limited role of writing in Indus civilization) is that writing in the context of some corporate systems was restricted to apolitical uses in order to minimize its application to exclusionary political strategy. By contrast, texts demonstrating the exploits of named rulers, and making use of palace symbolism, constitute the earliest writing in ancient Egypt (Kemp 1989:84).

3. Reflexive Communication

In Flannery's (1972:411) systems perspective, high-order institutions monitor those of lower order, allowing the controlling institutions to respond adaptively to "deviant" variable states in the system. A growth in the quantity of information passing through these channels requires institutional change to increase information-processing capacity. The institution of corporate political strategy is also an information-intensive process because it brings with it a need for increased means for processing, storing, and analyzing information, but of a type I refer to as reflexive communication. Corporate cognitive codes requiring exemplary behavior of rulers and others in positions of power are meaningless in the absence of specific communication channels that provide information concerning power-wielders' compliance with the expected behavior, such as the official Gazette system of China mentioned above. Below I describe several of the variety of reflexive communicative channels that developed in archaic states. But in archaic states, generally, this kind of behavioral monitoring is problematic. Institutions capable of correctly identifying breaches of norm-governed political behavior, and of communicating information about it that makes possible an appropriate redressive action, are typically not well developed. One of the major differences between the archaic states and modern democratic states is to be found in the complexity and effectiveness of the instrumentalities for reflexive communication (Apter 1965:456; Wirsing 1973:163). Typically, in archaic states, mechanisms of enforcement of the cognitive code are only weakly developed (Eisenstadt 1980:847).

In the Axial Age civilizations, reflexive communication was vested primarily in a cultural elite who served as carriers of the moral order, such as Jewish prophets, Greek philosophers, Chinese literati, Hindu Brahmins, and Islamic Ulema (e.g., Eisenstadt 1980). The role of the vizier, minister, or similar high-ranking administrator or advisory council (e.g., in Benin; Bradbury 1969) is often pivotal in the reflexive communicational capacity of archaic states. Persons in these roles maintained considerable political autonomy, were highly versed in society's moral precepts, and were able to observe the ruler's behavior in specific political and ritual situations closely. Thus, they could authoritatively detect and report deviations from accepted practice. (By contrast, in ancient Egypt's highly centralized political system, the vizier was little more than an administrative assistant to the pharaoh; Eisenstadt 1969:279.) Moral evaluation of those who govern also may occur more broadly in society, for example, when Roman emperors were judged by their demeanor in public venues such as the Circus, or by reference to the "sobriety of their private lives" (Veyne 1990:304). Roman imperial edicts, Veyne (1990:300) points out, often evinced a concern "not so much to be obeyed as to prove to his people that he shared the principles and sufferings of his subjects; as if the law was not essentially imperative but aimed also at bearing witness." In the next section, on ritual sanctification of egalitarian cognitive codes, I discuss additional elements of reflexive communication as it is manifest in the ritualization of political communication.

4. Ritual Sanctification of the Corporate Cognitive Code and Ritualization of Political Communication

Ritual may serve as a kind of "primitive government" by making its underlying propositions appear "powerful and holy" (Bloch 1974:57). According to Bloch, it is "precisely through the process of making a power situation appear a fact in the nature of the world that traditional authority works" (1974:79; cf. Bloch 1977a; Rappaport 1979:197). This view is like the commonly held assumption of Marxist critical theorists who see various aspects of culture, including ritual and religion, as expressions of a dominating ideology serving to reproduce an order of inequality through the mystification of power relations and inequality (cf. Althusser 1971:149–51; Bourdieu 1978–79; Claessen 1978a, 1978b; Godelier 1978; A. Knapp 1988: 137; Shanks and Tilley 1982:133; Wolf 1982:83; cf. Scott 1990:chap. 4). But unlike Rappaport (1971), Bloch (1974, 1977a), and the Marxists, I do not make the assumption that ritual is always a primitive form of government that serves only the interests of exclusionary political strategy. Where corporate political strategies are found in archaic states, ritual may serve in part to sanctify and culturally reinforce, through numinous experience (see Rappaport 1971), the propositions of the egalitarian cognitive code. In my opinion, the social analyst should make no a priori assumptions about the role of ritual or religion in politics and should remain aware of its possible role in corporate political economy, even though this will mean parting company at times with the prevailing "politically correct" critical theory.

In archaic states in particular, the propositions of corporate cognitive codes are reinforced through systems of ritual. Through their participation in such ritual events, persons in positions that allow them to control symbolic and material resources, who thus potentially are able to subvert the limitations imposed on the corporate political order, experience the emotional force upholding the sanctity of the egalitarian cognitive code. Ritual also may serve to reinforce their roles in society as functional parts of an integrated social system (similar arguments are made by Abercrombie, Hill, and Turner 1980:158; cf. Bender 1990:259). I return to the well-documented case of China to provide an example of the role of ritual in reinforcing corporate cognitive code. As C.-Y. Hsu (1986:309) notes, Confucius was one of a number of social philosophers in China writing during approximately the middle of the first millennium BC who understood the importance of ritual not simply as an expression of religious belief, but as a mechanism of social integration (as Hsu points out, some 2,500 years prior to the rise of anthropological functionalism in the West). Under the influence of these writers, the Chinese pattern of rulership after the Shang dynasty combined the forces of ritualism and ethics found in the doctrines of the literati. These moral codes and the obligation to express them ritually were applied as forcefully to rulers as to others, and they were bound up in the requirements of pacifism and ancestral piety (Mote 1968:398; Pokora 1978:203; Weber 1951:31–32, 169, 216; Wei-Ming 1986).

There also is a metacommunicative dimension to rituals of this type, which places them within systems of reflexive communication. This is true in the sense that, through correct performance of the rituals, the power-wielder's acceptance of limitations on power expressed in the moral code is publicly proclaimed. Thus ritual expression may carry with it what Rappaport (1979:196) calls the "notion of obligation." For example, oaths of office in Classical Athens "marked the assumption of political roles and reiterated the norms governing behavior in political contexts, particularly the obligation to leave aside all personal interests" (Humphreys 1977:348). As Rappaport puts it (1979:196), "the formal and public nature of liturgical performance makes it very clear that an act of acceptance is taking place, that the acceptance is serious, and what it is that is being accepted."

This argument can be further elaborated by recasting Maurice Bloch's (1974, 1975) interpretation of "political language." Political language is a particular kind of formalized language that includes elements such as the extensive use of homilies, patterned timing and emotive levels, and separation of the speaker from invariant text that has been "handed down from ancestors" (Bloch 1975:8). Bloch argues that this formal communicative mode enforces a hierarchy of social statuses by placing speaker and hearers in a "highly structured situation" (p. 9) that provokes acceptance, what he calls "illocutionary force" (1975:22; cf. Bloch 1974, 1977a, 1980). From the perspective of corporate strategy, however, I see political language serving as a channel of reflexive communication. Its precise form and often lengthy, complex ritualization require skill acquired through extensive training and rehearsal (Bloch 1975:22; cf. Geertz 1980:130). As such, it is metacommunicative; even though political language may not transmit much actual information (see below), its demanding requirements allow viewers and hearers to assess the degree to which an act of acceptance of the cognitive code underlies the formalized behavior. It is reflexive communication because it allows, as Bloch himself notes (1975:23–24), an evaluation not so much of the message, but of the speaker (as illustrated in the case of Confucian China, see Creel 1970:96; Elvin 1986:328–31; Weber 1951:31–32). In addition, ritualization of political communication, as Bloch (1977b) puts it, disconnects power from rank in the sense that "If the ruler totally adopts the mode of communication of ritual for carrying out his will he at the same time loses his ability to affect events for his own *personal* ends as opposed to the ends of his office" (p. 331).

Metacommunicative ritual and political language are important dimensions of communication between those who rule and their subjects in all societies governed by corporate codes, but they are particularly prominent in archaic states. Certainly not all political communication relates to adaptive control functions, as the systems analysts would have us believe, nor would it necessarily consist of heroic history or other interest ideology that is expressed in narrative form. In political language, the message may not be expressed in ordinary language, and thus is not capable of communicating much information of any kind. The communication taking place is, as Bloch

(1975:13–15) puts it, "impoverished." Owing to its formalization, the ritualized communication of political language is what Bernstein (1965, 1971) calls a "restricted code" (cf. Humphreys 1977:360–67, 1978:262–75). It is a type of language whose connection to reality is more tenuous than that found in ordinary language.

Applying the concepts of metacommunicative ritual, political language, and restricted code may help us to understand the enigmatic mode of expression of the masked and elaborately costumed figures in murals and other artistic media at Teotihuacán. Although writing is minimally used, the portrayed figures often show elaborate, largely undecipherable speech scrolls. As Pasztory (1992:305) notes: "At Teotihuacán, writing exists, but it is speech that is glorified in art. This speech is entirely local in character; it is among members of the group who know what they are saying, and it is not clarified for an outsider. One can decipher Maya hieroglyphic writing, but one cannot decipher most speech scrolls."

The pervasiveness of ritual and ritualized political communication in such societies, however, entails a significant dilemma. According to Bloch (1980:94), "Formalized-ritualized communication . . . does not bear direct relation to events; new experience neither modifies nor contradicts its content directly because its form rules out such modification and contradiction." The dilemma that arises in the context of many archaic states results from the time and resources that officials of a state—if they are to maintain their legitimate hold on power—must devote to forms of communication not involving ordinary language. Particularly in cases where political metacommunication and ritual sanctification are greatly elaborated, such as in nineteenth-century Bali, the demanding requirements of exemplary ritual behavior "imprisoned" the king in the ceremony of rule (Geertz 1980:133). The inefficiency and costliness of this is apparent, especially near the top of the governmental hierarchy, "where the 'far beaming blaze of majesty' consumed so much more fuel, the necessity to demonstrate status warred with the necessity to assemble the support to make the demonstration possible" (Geertz 1980:133). In a similar vein, Kilson (1983:421) notes that Ga ceremonial kingship "consumes energy, time, and money but it does not produce solutions to poverty, urban congestion and disease. Ceremonial kingship recreates a heroic tradition, but fails to create new worlds."

5. Semiautonomy of Lower-Order Subsystems

In the previous two sections, I argued that the implementation of corporate political economy is predicated on the development of additional communication channels that allow an assessment of the degree of compliance of power holders to the expectations of the corporate cognitive code. The strategy I refer to as semiautonomy also requires alterations in communications channels, but along other lines. In this strategy, lower-order subsystems are reconfigured so as to operate more autonomously. This allows a reduction in the amount of information flow between lower-order subsystems and central control systems. The sociocultural evolutionary outcome of semiautonomy is a reduced degree of centralized control in society, the opposite of Flannery's (1972:413) process of linearization, in which lower-order subsystems lose autonomy. Although not all governing functions will be vested in such low-order institutions, the greater degree of control situated at lower hierarchical levels necessarily reduces the scope of centralized administrative action in society. From the systems-analysis perspective (e.g., Rappaport 1977:54, 61), gains from decentralization include information-processing efficiency and adaptive advantage, but in my perspective, semiautonomy may reflect the outcome of political processes as well.

Semiautonomy is predicated on the development and promulgation of a cognitive code that provides a detailed program for the conduct of everyday life that can make subsystems, such as households, more self-governing; Islam and Confucianism (discussed below) are two major examples. However, not all such codes are corporate in nature. Blau (1968:465) describes a strategy, similar to Fesler's (1968:373) "pseudodecentralization," in which there is the promulgation of "impersonal control mechanisms that constrain operations to follow automatically the policies and programs specified by top executives" (Blau 1968:465). Control mechanisms of this latter type are egalitarian only if the prescribed code applies equally to the behavior of rulers and other officials as it does to ordinary households or other social entities and individuals, and if the intent of the code is to decentralize political controls. Blau's pseudodecentralizing codes are, in contrast, strategies for the "subordination of the bureaucracy," as indicated in table 5.3, and are manifestations of exclusionary systemic domination. In corporate systems, it is not likely that new codes will be developed and promoted by "top executives," as Blau indicates, since the aim of these codes is to constrain central authority, not augment it.

The devising of new social codes to promote semiautonomy in lower-order institutions need not imply a decomposition of society into completely autonomous local systems; in fact, no net decline in integration need occur. Corporate society may be highly integrated, but the modalities of social integration, control, and communication are changed. Some aspects of central control are kept in place, owing to needs such as external offense-defense management. But as an outcome of semiautonomy, higher-order controls have fewer functions and will be less able to exercise centralized power in at least some domains of societal governance. In addition, semiautonomy is not complete social decomposition in the sense that the code and its accompanying ritual expressions often are found in the practices of rulers and ordinary households alike. Thus, administrative control linkages are likely to be replaced by a form of cultural mechanical integration based on ritual expression shared societywide.

The loci of institution building in strategies of semiautonomy may be quite variable cross-culturally. Change in household form and function is often an outcome of semiautonomy strategies in archaic states, as it is among many fundamentalist movements today (Hardacre 1993). The Teotihuacán masonry apartment compound is one example (Pasztory 1992:285–88). As Millon (1992:400) points out, beginning during the Tlamimilolpa phase, an

> obvious agent for cohesion and integration is the apartment compound, instituted in the third century, that eventually provided permanent housing for most of the city's population. The advantage to the state in having relatively large, structured populations in apartment compounds forming the basic building blocks of Teotihuacán society has been clear since their distinctive attributes were first set forth more than twenty years ago.

Semiautonomy was an important dimension of political evolution in China, beginning in the reforms of the Zhou period and in the promulgation of the Confucian code. In one aspect of this process, like the institutional enhancement of Teotihuacán's apartment compounds, semiautonomy bolstered the functional independence of extended patrilineal households. Creel (1970:380) notes the increasing emphasis placed on what he calls "nuclear families" (technically, extended households or lineage segments) at the expense of clan structures, beginning in the Western Zhou period (1122–771 BC). According to the Confucian ideal of domestic structure, the wife, children, and junior married couples of the extended household should accept the centralized control of household production, consumption, marriage, and ritual, which are vested primarily in its senior-generation male manager (e.g., F. Hsu 1949:109) (in southeastern China, lineages were analogous units of semiautonomous functioning; Freedman 1958:138; Pasternak 1976:123). The sanctity of the centralized kinship group and its multigenerational solidarity are reinforced through a house form first adopted extensively during the Han dynasty (R. Knapp 1986:13–14). This house form as "habitus" (Bourdieu 1977:118) uses strategies of "axial symmetry based on directional symbolism, number symbolism, cosmological considerations in orientation and location (geomancy), shrines as liminal spaces manifesting household social solidarity, and a hierarchy of space-use related to generational (and sometimes gender-based) distinctions in status" (Blanton 1994:81).

Ancestor worship served not so much to establish household status through the demonstration of primacy of descent from clan ancestors as to reaffirm household solidarity and its multigenerational continuity (e.g.,

F. Hsu 1949:109). Above all, in relationships to ancestors, family members, and others, the Confucian code speaks to the overriding importance of maintaining a sense of decorum and civility in social interactions. In Weber's (1951:156) words, "The conventionally educated man will participate in the old ceremonies with due and edifying respect. He controls all his activities, physical gestures, and movements as well with politeness and with grace in accordance with the status mores and the commands of propriety, a basic concept (!) of Confucianism."

At this juncture in my discussion of the Confucian cognitive code, a caveat will serve to reinforce a point made in my introductory comments, namely, that political strategies must be viewed in processual terms, not in terms of political types or enduring structural arrangements. Corporately oriented codes like those of China elaborated by Confucius and others should not be viewed as static systems of perfect functioning, above challenge, or entirely resistant to change. Elements of society favoring a more centralized state promoted exclusionary political strategies and were successful to varying degrees in some periods. Proponents of the legalist schools of thought, along with Taoists and the palace eunuchs, pushed for a more powerful rulership with less accountability (e.g., Creel 1970:442–43; C.-Y. Hsu 1986:313, 1988:187). In addition, the Confucian system itself, in which officials were selected and advanced based on meritorious behavior (e.g., Hsu 1986:319), was perverted from within in some periods through favoritism and nepotism, creating a new kind of "aristocracy" (C.-Y. Hsu 1986:322, 1988:185). Some wealthy Chinese regions came to dominate the ranks of the literati (Ho 1962:chap. VI). And, over time, revisionist neo-Confucian thought, especially during the Ming period (AD 1368–1644), allowed for a greater degree of political centralization (Mote 1968:405–7; Nivison 1959).

Nonetheless, I suggest that corporate strategies, including semiautonomy, have been important system-shaping social processes in the evolution of many archaic states and are deserving of more analytical attention than they have received. For example, semiautonomy may provide one clue as to how some large, complex systems were governed without a highly centralized state. And, owing to the partially self-governing nature of the constituent building blocks of society, the process of semiautonomy may be associated with substantial growth in the scale of society with minimal growth in the central administrative apparatus. Growth through replication of highly self-sufficient social entities implies few additional administrative costs per added unit; thus some of the scale limitations to growth inherent in more pervasively administered systems (Blanton et al. 1993:14–16; Boulding 1956; Kasarda 1974:26) will not apply so forcefully where features of semiautonomy have been developed.

The importance of a semiautonomy strategy is indicated, I suggest, by the enigmatic Indus civilization, which extended over 1,000,000 km² but lacked any obvious centralized state (Fairservis 1967:42, 1971:299; see Possehl, this volume). The basic units of semiautonomous functioning in this extensive system evidently were communities. Each community was structured by a dualistic civic code that spatially separated a zone of public buildings and ritual spaces (a "citadel") from a carefully gridded residential zone; this basic community plan evidently informed the layout of village and city alike (Fairservis 1967:14, 1971:263–67; Miller 1985:44).

How civic governing institutions functioned is difficult to understand in the absence of narrative texts, heroic histories of rulers (no named rulers are known), identifiable palaces, or temple institutions (Fairservis 1971:301). Instead, an elaborate cultural code embodying egalitarian elements was reinforced ritualistically. What are likely to have been rituals of purification, involving fire altars and baths or similar bathing facilities, were replicated across society from the "grand ritualized level" (Miller 1985:61) of the citadel areas down to the everyday purificatory rites of ordinary households. The famous sewer systems facilitated the management of polluting waste. In this system, as interpreted by Miller (1985:63), "power resided in those organizational forms which ensured the reproduction of order." Social integration was achieved through the widespread acceptance of a broadly shared cognitive code that resulted in a surprising degree of similarity in architecture and artifacts (despite decentralized production) over the 1,000,000 km² area. The code evidently included a marked egalitarian ethic in material standard of living and public display of wealth (e.g., Sarcina 1979, on houses; Rissman 1988, on the absence of public displays of costly goods; cf. Miller 1985:48, 53). Miller (1985:59) describes this ethic as a "standardization of and around the mundane."

CONCLUSION

My comments in this chapter represent a limited effort in light of both the complexity and the significance of corporate political strategy in the sociocultural evolution of archaic states. In these brief comments, I have tried to argue convincingly that our discipline needs to move away from the excessive emphasis on political centralization that has grown out of its use of Marxist and systems approaches. I have also tried to illustrate the difficulties inherent in seeing the accountability of rulers as solely a product of Near Eastern and Western political evolution (based on the "significant breakout" of the ancient Near East). Corporate behavior is found outside the Near East and the West, and it takes many forms; the accountability of rulers is only one dimension of a far more complex political process that at this time is not well understood or very much studied.

Rather than sharply contrasting "the West and the rest," a productive avenue of comparative inquiry will be to trace the evolution of corporate systems in all of their considerably varied cross-cultural and temporal forms, and to compare them with situations in which exclusionary political strategies dominated. Why do some centralized social formations, like ancient Egypt, evolve with little corporate structure? Why are some corporate strategies emphasized and not others? China's "significant breakout," beginning before the middle of the first millennium BC, was built around an elaborate theory relating a system of ethics to ritual. In my conceptualization, this brought with it a cognitive code emphasizing ritual sanctification and ritualization of political communication, reflexive communication, status determination through moral/ritual exemplarity, and semiautonomy, as well as a distributive Iron Age. An older Mesopotamian pattern, probably dating to the Uruk period and perhaps with antecedents in the comparatively egalitarian 'Ubaid period, was carried forward into the eastern Mediterranean and beyond. In it, by contrast with China and many other archaic states, modalities of assembly government were central to the evolution of corporate strategy.

These specific cases require explanation with corporate strategy kept in mind, but general trends in sociocultural evolution also need to be addressed by comparative research. When viewed in the most general evolutionary sense, a trend is evident in the evolution of archaic states, and in the evolution from archaic states to modern states, from intermember to systemic power types, from material to symbolic bases of power, and from exclusionary to corporate power, but these broad trends have not been simple unilinear changes or simple evolutionary stages. Such broad patterns of political change cannot be explained by an anthropological archaeology that only builds rigid evolutionary stage typologies and that sees cultural evolution primarily in terms of one political process—centralization.

At present we have few theories to explain the rise of corporate government or the cross-cultural variation therein, since most of our discipline's attention has been paid to identifying the socioenvironmental stresses that bring about centralization (Flannery 1972). Which socioenvironmental stresses brought about the evolution of corporate strategies in the archaic states? Discontent with the outcomes of exclusionary power may prompt change, but we need to know more about the specific sources of stress and how discontent is articulated, so as to reconstruct the social order (Eisenstadt 1977). A growing wealth inequality may have fueled the prevailing clientalism in Attica prior to the revolutionary rise of the assembly-governed polis state about the middle of the fifth century BC (I. Morris 1987:202–5; van der Vliet 1987). Powerful tyrants accumulated fortunes in part through their control of the silver trade, and silver also was used by them as a prestige good in politically charged exchange (van der Vliet 1987:73, 75).

A central aim of the polis system was the regulation of the political-gifting and client-based intermember politics. Millon's view of the revolutionary rise of the Teotihuacán system, beginning in the Tlamimilolpa phase, sees behind it an established, highly centralized state rather than a tyranny of clientship based on wealth inequality. In Teotihuacán, he (1992: 400) hypothesizes, "Effective means were institutionalized by a collective leadership to prevent rulers from transforming executive authority into personal rule. The rejection of personal rule was so thorough and so lasting, and the checks on rulers so effective, that it placed its stamp on Teotihuacán's history for another 500 years, profoundly affecting its political system, its religion, and its art." From Stein's (1994b) discussion of the highly egalitarian and evidently not politically centralized 'Ubaid period, it seems unlikely that either of these two situations—wealth inequality or a powerful state—could have prompted the development of corporate political economy in early Mesopotamia. I hope that Near Eastern archaeologists will address this perhaps unique and important sequence from the perspective of the evolution of egalitarian behavior, but anthropological archaeologists working in other areas should devote increased attention to corporate political economy in the many forms it has taken.

NOTE

I am grateful to Doug Schwartz and the staff of the School of American Research, who provided a comfortable and stimulating environment during our weeklong meeting. Comments I received from the other session participants helped me think more carefully about some of my topics and issues; I also acknowledge the helpful comments on an early draft of this essay made by Stephen Kowalewski, Peter Peregrine, and two anonymous reviewers. My wife, Cindy Bedell, helped me solve several terminological problems. I particularly thank Gary Feinman and Joyce Marcus, who carefully and patiently read through and edited several earlier versions of this chapter; however, all errors are my own.

6

Uruk States in Southwestern Iran

HENRY T. WRIGHT

nthropology developed within the institutions of state polities. The perceptions and theoretical perspectives of anthropologists have been forged
by the contradictory demands of our research disciplines and of the
peoples, living and dead, whom we have come to represent. It is therefore
not surprising that we want to know as much as possible about the kinds of
entities that give contexts for our work, including how states came to be and
how they came to differ from the diversity of other kinds of polities. Such
interests lead to a focus on the earliest states. There is, however, much disagreement among scholars about the characterization of early states. Are
they theater polities, mere symbolic games in the minds of self-appointed
princes? Or are they apparatuses that controlled the material resources and
lives of their participants? Such disagreements benefit from consideration of
the evidence of past states.

Primary states, those that arose from interaction between prestate societies (Wright 1977), rarely had the capacity to record discursive accounts of
their genesis and operation. The task of understanding how such polities
worked is largely the responsibility of archaeologists, who must proceed by
evaluating the consequences of different ideas about the past with material
evidence, criticizing the assumptions of proposals that fail, generating new
ideas, and evaluating these yet again. The process is tedious, but it has enabled archaeologists to go beyond idealist and racist conceptions of cultural
formation, beyond elementary material/energetic theories of change, to the

more complex systemic and existential conceptions that are the focus of research today.

The application of such approaches during the past few decades in widely separated parts of the world by the small cadre of anthropological archaeologists has generated far more insight into operation than genesis. The reasons for this disparity are various. On the one hand, the periods in which primary states originated were times of conflict, characterized by the movement of communities and by general human misery. The relevant archaeological layers are often ephemeral, badly eroded, or deeply buried by the debris of later, more prosperous periods; the modest discarded material remains have attracted less interest than they merit. On the other hand, even if we could obtain the archaeological record needed, we would still lack the theoretical structures essential for talking about the complex social, symbolic, and material transformations that seem to have been important in the origins of states. It may be useful to consider the better-known operation of developed primary states, where in some cases we do have rich archaeological records of material remains and even documentary records of individuals' actions, beliefs, or ideological claims. In this essay, I take a systematic perspective to discuss the operation of one of the regional states of the mid-fourth millennium BC in Southwest Asia.

Scholars' assessments of mid-fourth-millennium polities are evolving rapidly. Four decades ago, when I first read about this period, it was viewed as a time of urban growth. Each developing town was centered on its temple, whose priests and dependent craftsmen were among the few specialists in a largely egalitarian world of farmers. The most developed governmental institutions were thought to be assemblies of prominent citizens (cf. Frankfort 1956:52–78). Rulers, dynasties, and state administration were thought not to have arisen until the middle of the third millennium BC. This assessment was based upon a concordance of three classes of evidence, each of which is open to question.

First, the earliest known written records of rulers and dynasties were of the mid-third millennium BC. However, such political statements are only possible with writing systems able to represent language. Mesopotamian writing prior to this time appears to have been graphic systems for representing numbers and objects, not language; it could have conveyed only indirect economic information about politics.

Second, the earliest architectural evidence of palatial residences separate from temples also dates to the mid-third millennium. This seemingly late appearance, however, results from the erosion at many southern Mesopotamian town sites that has exposed third-millennium layers. Early in the twentieth century excavators were able to expose a number of mid-third-millennium towns and to identify temples and palaces. Since temples tend to be rebuilt in the same location, archaeologists could reveal progressively earlier temples. Palatial residences, in contrast, were built in new locations. It is only recently that extensive exposures of fourth-millennium towns have documented such buildings.

Third, elaborate burials of political figures—marked by weapons, carts, and sacrificed animals or people—are attested from this same period. In fact, for whatever reason, few burial areas of the preceding periods have been excavated; the absence of a particular funerary procedure is meaningless given the general absence of funerary evidence.

Today, polities of the mid-third millennium are generally viewed as second- or third-generation states, the products of several successive phases of state development and collapse. Few who know the evidence of settlement scale and structure, economic activity, administrative activity, and iconography think that the cultural entities of the mid- to late-fourth millennium had theocratic political organization or egalitarian ideologies. Before turning to the current evidence for state organization in one part of the fourth-millennium world, however, some methodological remarks are appropriate.

If we are to evaluate processes in larger cultural entities and over long spans of time, archaeologists have to monitor individual decision making and action. Critics may argue that this is unattainable or at least impractical. It is sometimes said—I myself have said it (Wright 1980)—that archaeological records and documentary records are incommensurate, that archaeological garbage samples represent aggregate community action over long periods of time, and that only written texts represent the statements of specific actors about perceptions and decisions over short periods of time. I have come to believe that such statements result from archaeologists' failure to use both their imaginations and adequate archaeological methods, specifically excavation controls and dating approaches. If we take advantage of existing means of time control—microstratigraphy, microseriation, dendrochronology, and so on—and devise new ones using untapped biorhythms in shells, tusks, teeth, or unutilized isotopes, we can deal in short periods of time. Once lenses of garbage can be precisely recovered and dated, then we are at liberty to use them to evaluate propositions about actions and decisions at the level of individuals. This is what I try to exemplify in the following presentation.

My focus is on what I (and the colleagues with whom I was privileged to work in southwestern Iran in the 1960s and 1970s) termed the "Middle Uruk" and "Late Uruk" periods. This continuous period of cultural development dates between about 3800 and 3150 BC. My spatial focus is the Susiana Plain, or the Plain of Shush, and the regions dominated by the ancient town of Shushun (Vallat 1993), which English speakers know as Susa during this time (fig. 6.1). The polities that existed on the Susiana Plain are identified as states, albeit of an elemental form, because there is evidence of

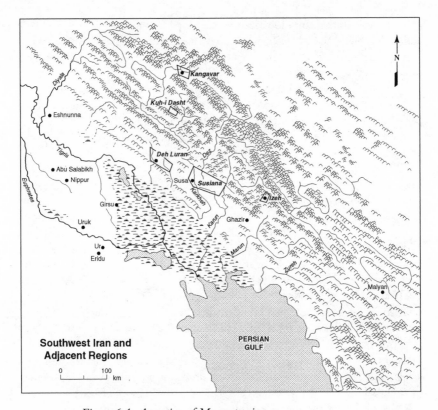

Figure 6.1. A portion of Mesopotamia.

the operation of control hierarchies with contrastive specialization in the control process—specifically, specialization between aggregation of goods, information summary, information transport, information checking, adjudication, and probably policy making. Such contrastive specialization allows the maintenance of hierarchies with four or more levels of control and spans of control able to integrate hundreds of communities and tens of thousands of people (Wright and Johnson 1975:270–72).

I first discuss the real and cognized environments, followed by aspects of cultural structure and process on the rural Susiana Plain. I then discuss parallel aspects of the towns that dominated the plain. Finally, I deal with aspects of structure and process in the marginal regions of southwestern Iran. That our evidence relevant to these issues is episodic rather than comprehensive, and that our conclusions are limited, is a result of the cessation of research in this troubled region. We can only hope for a better future.

ENVIRONMENT AND COSMOGRAPHY
IN THE FOURTH MILLENNIUM

The enduring geographical structure of what is today southwestern Iran (Adams 1962) is dictated by the uplifted folds and thrusts of the Zagros Mountains arcing around the northern and western edge of the lowlands. The foothills of these ranges are chaotic karstic areas interspersed with alluvial fans laid down by the Zagros streams (Oberlander 1965). Three rivers converging on the center of the region—the Karun from the east, Dez from the north, and Karkheh from the northwest—bring the waters of much of the central Zagros to a limited central area, where they have formed the Susiana Plain (fig. 6.2). Their fans coalesce and join with the vast Mesopotamian plain to the southwest. These geological structures are perhaps the only remaining elements of this region that would seem relatively familiar to peoples of the fourth millennium before our era. Much else has changed. In lowland Southwest Asia, the time span from at least 5500 until 3200 BC seems to have been wetter than the present (Larsen 1983; Rosen 1989), which would have had an impact on the natural vegetation and the possibilities for farming. The one published lake core from southwestern Iran, from Lake Mirabad at 950 m above sea level, 60 km north of Susa, does indeed show increased oak relative to grasses in the pollen rain, suggesting that forests flourished in the mountains at the expense of grassy pastures (van Zeist and Bottema 1977). We expect that mountain goat, red deer, bear, leopard, and other animals also flourished. In the lower elevations, the original diverse cover of shrubs and leguminous herbs had long since been replaced by a limited suite of grasses able to survive constant grazing (Helbaek 1969), but these grasslands would have flourished well to the south of the Susa area, their southern limit today. Though in direct competition with domestic stock, wild gazelles, sheep, pigs, and onagers were still common enough to be regularly hunted during the Uruk period (Hole, Flannery, and Neely 1969; Redding 1981).

In their representations on ceramics and on seals, however, pre-Uruk and Uruk peoples chose to focus on certain natural features, providing some indication of the assumptions they made about their world. The ordinary stamp seals of the pre-Uruk period (Amiet 1972:pls. 39–54) emphasized the wild goat or sheep, and only infrequently gazelle, deer, onager, pig, or other wild animals of the hills and plains. These animals usually occur singly. Cormorants and other wild fowl appear as minor elements. Those stamp and cylinder seals of the Middle and Late Uruk periods with representations of animals show changes in emphasis and structure. Domestic sheep and cow, and wild lion, pig, deer, and fish, are the most frequent recognizable

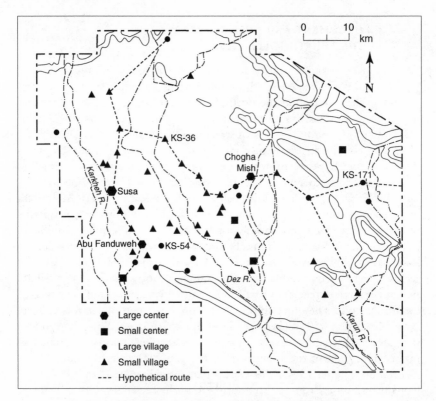

Figure 6.2. Mid-fourth-millennium southwest Iran (adapted from Johnson 1973:fig. 26).

vertebrates on the seals; the representations occur in banks and rows (Amiet 1972:pls. 56–77). Nature was shown as more domesticated and ordered, and this order could be represented repeatedly by rolling the cylinder seals (Le Brun 1985). The more elaborate stamp seals of pre-Uruk elite figures have either a central anthropomorphic figure holding opposed animals or a symmetrical quadripartite cosmic figure (Amiet 1972:pls. 48–50; Wright 1994). In contrast, the more elaborate Middle and Late Uruk cylinder seals had representations of human activity, perhaps thematically related to the activities of the seal bearer (Brandes 1979). Sometimes several figures were shown in reciprocal relations; sometimes one figure was dominant over the others (Amiet 1972:pls. 78–90). The people who commissioned these more elaborate seals seem to have chosen images of reciprocity or overt dominance, in contrast to the centrality and symmetry preferred by their predecessors. These representations indicate that actors in mid-fourth-millennium Susiana cultural systems made decisions in a world ordered in space and time, with expectations of reciprocity from others, whether in nonhierarchical or hierarchical relations.

PRODUCTION AND CONTROL
IN THE SUSIANA COUNTRYSIDE

During the Middle Uruk period, the most prosperous time during the fourth millennium BC, about 25,000 people lived in the settlements on the Susiana Plain (Schacht 1980). Scattered across the agriculturally more productive 1,400 km² of the plain were almost 60 communities, represented today by *tappehs,* mounds of mud-brick debris and garbage. Many of these settlements were previously occupied in the poorly known Early Uruk period, and Middle Uruk ceramics show a development from local Early Uruk types (Wright 1985). Sites on the plain developed evidence of a four-level settlement hierarchy by Middle Uruk times. On grounds of surface area, Johnson categorized 46 of these sites as "small villages" (covering up to 1.5 ha) and "large villages" (covering from 1.5 to 3.0 ha), contrasting with a few larger settlements, discussed below (Johnson 1973:101–43, fig. 10). Excavations have been conducted at two of the small Middle to Late Uruk communities, one a small village and the other a large village. Though both have evidence of grain cultivation and the exploitation of sheep, goats, and cows—patterns of production developed over the preceding two millennia in the region (Hole, Flannery, and Neely 1969)—the two communities were organized in very different ways.

The small village site of Tepe Sharafabad (KS-36) is located near the northern edge of the Susiana Plain, on the east side of the alluvial fan of the Dez River (see fig. 6.2). It was situated on a traditional route between the eastern and western portions of the plain, and not far from paths that cross the foothills in the direction of the higher pastures used by nomads since early Holocene times. During the Middle Uruk period, the occupied area covered about half a hectare, and Tepe Sharafabad is estimated to have had a population of about 100 inhabitants. Fragmentary architecture shows that people lived in modest, unplanned mud-brick houses, but the occurrence of the clay cones used to decorate special buildings in this period indicates that there also was some kind of elaborate building in the settlement. The domestic remains included few special goods, such as stone vessels, and the beads and amulets are of such modest materials as limestone, ceramic, and carnelian. These few items of social display indicate that rural elite residing in this small settlement had a lifestyle little different than that of other inhabitants.

Most of our evidence of Middle Uruk village life comes from a large pit filled with seasonally stratified garbage (Wright, Miller, and Redding 1980; Wright, Redding, and Pollock 1989). Miller's analysis of the plant remains from this pit indicates that the people of Sharafabad cultivated fields of barley, wheat, and lentils and had access to irrigated flax. However, we cannot estimate proportions grown or eaten, since barley may enter the record in the form of carbonized seeds through the burning of animal dung as well as the accidental burning of food, whereas wheat is evidenced primarily by the burned by-products of grain winnowing and cleaning. There is no evidence of other plant foods such as orchard crops or wild foods. Redding's analysis of the animal bones has shown that the inhabitants culled local herds of sheep and goats, primarily the former, killing lambs and kids in late summer and older female animals in late winter. In the first agriculturally successful year represented by the pit, animals of all types and ages were culled, following a strategy that optimized the reproductive capacity of the herd. In the following year of agricultural crisis, the number of sheep and goat killed dropped to 26 percent of its former level, and there was a focus on the killing of younger animals, even of females that would normally be saved for future breeding stock. The villagers also butchered an occasional cow or pig, hunted waterfowl, and fished.

Sharafabad, however, did not have a self-contained village economy. Many of the things people used came from outside, and some of their activities were coordinated by outside authorities. Most of their durable goods—pots, chert cores, grinding stones, and so on—probably came from elsewhere. There is evidence that most jars and bowls came from one or the other of the larger towns (Johnson 1973:113–29; Wright and Johnson 1975:279–82), perhaps depending on market opportunity. The other goods could have come from specialists elsewhere or been obtained by the villagers themselves. For the most part, vessels were discarded at similar rates, regardless of season or of whether or not the year was prosperous. A cylinder sealing of nonlocal clay on a jar rim shows that at least some of the pots came with goods sealed in them (James Blackman, personal communication 1980). Some sealings on bales and baskets, particularly several with impressions of a cylinder seal with a beer-drinking or "symposium" scene, may represent the closure of goods by officials at another place and their subsequent dispatch to Sharafabad. Other seals—stamp seals with iconically similar representations of a canid and a person, stamped on both bale seals and on the seals of storage room door locks—are those of an official or several officials who either were residents or visited the site to authorize closure of its storerooms. Regardless of whether the year was agriculturally good or bad, the same number of bales and jars seemed to have been opened at Sharafabad.

It is notable that storehouse doors were opened on the site, most often in winter or early summer. While few discarded door sealings were found in debris of the first prosperous year, many were found in debris of the second year, that of agricultural crisis, when we might expect institutional storehouses to have been opened as domestic food supplies ran out. Conversely, in the good year, there is more evidence of involvement by Sharafabad people in institutional labor. The crude bevel-rim bowls, probably made for the issuing of institutional rations or meals (Johnson 1973: 129–39; Le Brun 1980; Nissen 1970:137), were recycled in domestic tasks and discarded at least twice as frequently in the prosperous first year as during the second year, indicating either that local people participated in more institutional labor or that more outside laborers came in when times were good. Also, what are believed to be fragments of unfinished clay envelopes—"pherical bullae" wrapped around clay tokens indicating quantities of items (Amiet 1972; Schmandt-Bessarat 1992) and probably recording goods leaving the site—were discarded twice as frequently during the prosperous first year, suggesting double the rate of transport from the site that year. Sharafabad people seem to have profited from their labor in the good year, discarding four times as many sheep and goat bones as well as more bones of pig, cow, and wild animals. During the bad year they lived less well but received some supplementary help from institutional storehouses in jars and bales, as noted above.

The large village site of KS-54, the second rural site for which we have a range of information, covered up to 2.5 ha during the Middle and Late Uruk periods and perhaps had as many as 500 inhabitants. It is located in a dense settlement concentration on the long-occupied, but more arid, southern edge of the Susiana Plain, west of the Dez River. Unfortunately, two-thirds of the site was leveled before investigation could take place. Our evidence comes from a variety of contexts, mostly of the Late Uruk period, from a series of small excavations along bulldozer-cut faces transecting the settlement (Johnson 1976). These soundings revealed social differences in architecture, including the remains of a large domestic building with massive mud-brick walls in the center of the settlement and more modest structures elsewhere. Differences in possessions discarded around these two types of architecture indicate marked social differences. Stone vessels, decorative plaques, and beads of gold and lapis lazuli were associated with the elaborate building, but no such embellishments were found around modest buildings.

Subsistence patterns at KS-54 were broadly similar to that at earlier Sharafabad. Naomi Miller (personal communication 1974) examined the plant remains from samples taken along this section at the time of initial survey and found carbonized grains of domestic barley, glumes of wheat, and lentils. Detailed quantitative study of the fauna from Johnson's excavation by Karen Mudar (1988) shows that sheep and goat provided most of the meat consumed, but there was more use of domestic cow and pig than at Sharafabad. Few wild resources were consumed at KS-54. Comparison of equivalent types of depositional contexts around an elaborate higher-status dwelling and a modest lower-status dwelling shows more discarded remains of birds and fish and meatier cuts of mutton, goat, and beef around the higher-status buildings. The overall density of bone, however, was lower in the higher-status building, perhaps a result of maintenance by servants.

KS-54 was no more a self-contained village than Sharafabad, but the available evidence shows that its relations with the broader area were quite different. Although we do not have information from a deep stratified pit like that at Sharafabad, we can nonetheless argue for some broad differences between the two sites. First, most of the durable goods at KS-54 probably came from other settlements. There is little evidence of pottery production, and the site was much farther from sources of chert and grinding slabs than Sharafabad. Detailed study of the stylistic attributes of the pottery indicates that it came from one production center, rather than several (Wright and Johnson 1985:28). Second, even though ashy deposits that might preserve sealings, counters, and envelope fragments were carefully searched, no such administrative items were found. This could be a result of limited samples, but it suggests that goods were rarely shipped into KS-54 in sealed bales and bottles and were rarely shipped out to institutional warehouses elsewhere. It seems likely that the surpluses extracted from the farmers of KS-54 were consumed locally, with the more desirable resources being consumed by local elite families.

In sum, country people of the Susiana Plain derived most of their durable consumer goods from other types of settlements, while producing foods for themselves and other settlements. We have evidence that at least one small rural settlement from the end of the Middle Uruk period (KS-36, Tepe Sharafabad) gave up some of its foodstuffs, but it received goods from institutional storehouses both elsewhere and on site. Another rural settlement from the beginning of the Late Uruk period (KS-54) produced no evidence of the shipping out of its products; many of its producers may have been in the service of a resident local elite. With a sample of only two settlements, we cannot say whether there was a shift through time toward greater exploitation of rural workers, but we can certainly propose marked differences in institutional relations from settlement to settlement. Let us now turn to the larger settlements on which these varying relationships seem to have been centered.

CONTROL AND CONSUMPTION
IN THE SUSIANA TOWNS

Johnson (1973:73, fig. 10) classified four of the larger settlements on the Susiana Plain as small centers from 4 ha up to 8 ha. None of these sites has been excavated; we can only note that three of these interesting settlements are on the margins of the cluster of settlements and may have been involved in frontier activities.

The larger centers or towns (settlements larger than 8 ha) on the plain seem to have been organizationally similar in their spatial structure, the production activities pursued in them, and their span of control, as indicated by seals and sealings. All show a distinct separation between a smaller, upper town situated on the mounded remains of an earlier settlement and a larger, newly founded or refounded lower town. All have discarded sickle blades, indicating participation of townspeople in the harvest, when ripened crops must be brought in as quickly as possible. All have evidence of the production of pottery and stone tools. All have indications of the administrative technology that in Mesopotamia implies control of the storage of goods. However, the three known larger towns differ in their historical trajectories, in the maximum size they reached, and in the particulars of their economic and political organization.

Susa, on the west edge of the plain, was by far the largest; its 9-ha upper town was established during the Early Uruk period on the remains of the great ritual platform of the late fifth millennium after a brief abandonment. At the beginning of the Middle Uruk period, the lower town extended several hundred meters to the north and covered at least 25 ha. Evidence of larger buildings (Dyson 1966; Stéve and Gasche 1973) and administrative activities comes from the upper town (as detailed below). However, evidence of a large pottery kiln is well reported from the lower town (Miroschedji 1986), and there may have been larger buildings there as well (Stéve and Gasche 1990). There is little evidence this lower town was occupied during the Late Uruk period.

Abu Fanduweh (KS-59), on the south edge of the plain, was much smaller. Its 4 ha upper town was established during the Early Uruk period on the remains of a platform of the late fifth millennium; its lower town extended to the north during Middle and Late Uruk times to cover an additional 6 ha or more. Excavation was limited prior to the cessation of fieldwork in 1978; the only evidence of administrative activity is a door sealing from the surface of the upper town. On the northern periphery of the lower town, however, a large series of small pottery kilns has been recorded (Johnson 1973:107–8).

Chogha Mish, on the northeast periphery of the plain, was intermediate in size. It was refounded late in the Middle Uruk period, when its upper town occupied the remains of a small late-fifth-millennium citadel of little more than a hectare, and its lower town spread south over the low ruins of the major regional center of the early fifth millennium. During Late Uruk times, when Chogha Mish seems to have been independent of Susa (Johnson 1973:142–47, 1987), the lower town grew to cover at least 17 ha. Larger buildings in the small upper town are not yet reported. However, there is evidence from the lower town, in the form of sealed spherical bullae and numerical tablets, that Late Uruk administration in the larger settlement utilized parts of the lower town. Also in the lower town, individual pottery kilns were found in the rooms or courts of modest domestic units (Delougaz and Kantor 1996).

Due to the limited nature of excavation on all three towns, we cannot be sure that large pottery firing areas like that at Abu Fanduweh did not exist on the edges of Susa or Chogha Mish, or that administrative areas similar to that at Chogha Mish did not exist in the lower towns of Susa or Abu Fanduweh. Taken at face value, however, the extant evidence indicates some variability in the spatial organization of activities at the three major towns. Recognizing that its history and great size may render it atypical, let us take a close look at the evidence of varying activities at Susa, where the information is somewhat more detailed.

Our best perspective on the daily lives of townspeople comes from Alain Le Brun's superb excavations of domestic structures on the Southern Acropolis of Susa. These "Acropole I" structures date primarily to the Late Uruk period, when the town seems to have diminished in size to encompass primarily the old upper town. The people consumed wheat and lentils but also had access to grapes and nuts such as almonds (Naomi Miller, personal communication 1996). They used chert blades, small rough bowls, medium-sized finer bowls, jars, and bottles, and large jars not very different from those found at contemporary villages. Layer 17B2 in the Acropole I sounding (Le Brun 1978) can be considered in detail (fig. 6.3).

Two discrete architectural units are present, connected by a door. One is rectangular. It is laid out in approximately 12 x 9 units of linear measure of 65 m and has three rooms, all with exterior access. The largest room, with a sunken oval fireplace at one end and a small platform at the other, was kept clean (see fig. 6.3, Locus 770). This unit also has a small room with a dense concentration of items (Locus 757). There are domestic artifacts such as a tall jar, a few small cups, bowls, and jars, grinding stones, and a spindle whorl. Administrative artifacts include two tokens, a stamp seal, a cylinder seal, and three numerical tablets. Items of social display, including a stone vessel, a metal pin, beads, and pendants, were made from materials available

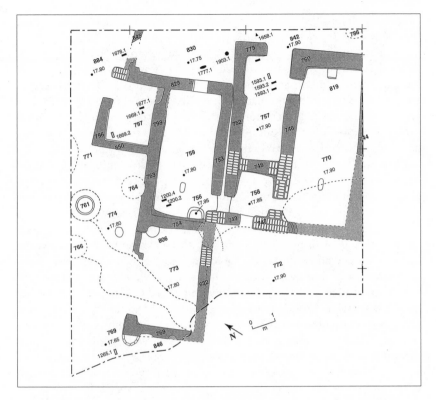

Figure 6.3. Susa Acropole I, Layer 17B2 (adapted from Le Brun 1978).

in the region, such as alabaster, calcite, or bitumen. Just outside the door of this small room was a possible kitchen area (Locus 830) with a single spherical bulla and an oblong bulla with several impressions of a single cylinder seal, which could be used either for verification of other sealings or validation of a messenger.

The other unit is L-shaped and somewhat smaller. Its three rooms have exterior access but no access to each other. The largest room has a sunken oval fireplace and a raised fireplace, but only a few sherds and a toothed mandible of a sawfish on its floor (Locus 759). Another room with an oven and mortars may have been a kitchen (Locus 773). The L-shaped unit also has a small room with dense concentrations of discarded material on its floor (Locus 797). There are domestic artifacts such as a bottle and bottle sealing, many cups, bowls, and grinding stones, and a spindle whorl. Administrative artifacts such as a cylinder seal and a numerical tablet were recovered. There also are four alabaster and calcite maceheads of a type fixed onto a handle with straps, some finished and some unfinished, perhaps for social coercion or display. Oblong pecking stones may have been used to manufacture these maceheads and other stone items.

The assemblages on the floors of these units are probably items not deemed worthy of systematic disposal or recycling when the buildings were leveled. Scattered items are difficult to interpret, but the concentrations in small rooms are stored items that either spoiled or were broken in place. The regular occurrence in both storerooms of bottles or tall jars and cups or small bowls probably indicates routine serving of liquids in each unit. The seals and numerical tablets probably indicate the general involvement of the occupants in record keeping. It is notable that both of the cylinder seals in these two units are small and share spiderlike motifs, but they were not used to impress any of the other items found. The numerical tablets in these units had impressions of large cylinders with files of animals, or with scenes in which human figures manipulate jars, or with both. The numbers recorded are small, ranging from 3 to 22, but we do not know what commodities were monitored and whether the tablets record past deposits, promised future transactions, or both (Le Brun and Vallat 1978). The concentration of macehead production debris in one unit and social display items in another indicates individual specializations just before rebuilding of the complex. But similar concentrations occur on floors of the succeeding Layer 17B1, albeit in different rooms, so these specializations were enduring and not merely a result of unique circumstances. The debris pattern suggests these special activities—presumably in support of social rituals—were performed only episodically by the inhabitants of this residential area.

From bullae found long ago at Susa (Amiet 1972), we know that during the Middle and Late Uruk periods summary documents reached Susa, were assessed by a higher authority, and then were stored or discarded there. However, we have very few well-excavated contexts that can be informative about the organization of the Middle Uruk control apparatus. Nevertheless, still-incomplete excavations on the Northern Acropolis, the "Acropole III" excavation, provide useful details of office life (Wright 1985). The building in question, that of Layer 2, seems to have faced north within a rectangular space between a vacant area (fig. 6.4, Locus 157) and the court of another building. One crossed a courtyard (Locus 163), entering the building though a vestibule on the left (Locus 160), and turned right into a large room (Loci 131/154) with only a simple surface hearth in the center (Locus 159). From this room one could enter a corridor (Locus 106) which gave access to several small rooms at the rear of the building, now largely eroded away. The single surviving nearly complete rear room (Locus 102) had very small hearths, one deep and one shallow. This building had been carefully cleaned prior to its final leveling; only a small stone vessel in a niche by the

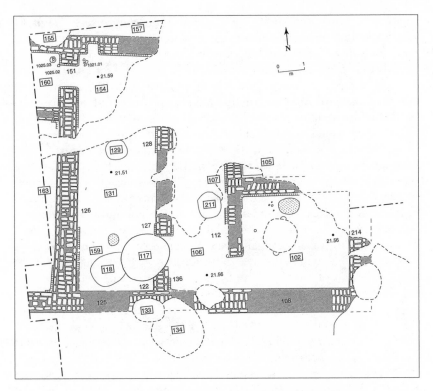

Figure 6.4. Susa Acropole III, Layer 2 (adapted from Wright 1985).

door (1021.01), a bevel-rim bowl sherd, and a cup sherd remained on its floors.

Excavation revealed a pit containing debris probably discarded by workers in the immediate predecessor of this building, which was very similar to the building described here. This pit contained many nearly complete bevel-rim bowls and some small jars, sheep/goat bones, charred debris, and various artifacts resulting from administrative activity. Among these were bale and basket sealings with the impressions of perhaps eight different seals, most frequently of two small cylinder seals, one representing a spider and one with rows of small figures, presumably removed from incoming packages. There also was a sealing from the opening of a storeroom. In contrast were items probably indicating outgoing summary information, both unfinished bulla coverings and tokens representing various quantities of items. Although we can presume no necessary relation between the opening of the packages or storerooms and the preparation of the summaries—the packages might have been incidental to the central activities of what we might term an "office"—numerical records were prepared here. Whether these records were summaries of prior transactions, as argued for Sharafabad, or agreements for future transactions, as may have been case for the Late Uruk Southern Acropolis, their preparation indicates the recording of precise numerical information for future reference.

We learn almost as much about the organization of the Middle Uruk control apparatus from the way this public building was constructed and repaired as we do from the evidence of activities within it. It was laid out as a rectangle of 18 by 15 units (each measuring .65 m), similar to the larger unit in Acropole I, 17B2. The use of similar units of measure indicates that masons had strict standards, as did other crafts such as potting and stone working, but this need not imply centralized control of these crafts. The walls of the Acropole III, Layer 2 building were not laid precisely upon the footings of the earlier buildings in the area, so the footings settled irregularly into the softer sediments of former room fills. To remedy this, the mud-brick walls were cut down almost to floor level and relaid with a brick of slightly different size, suggesting that a different work crew was called in to deal with the problem. Finally, thick mud-plaster floors had to be put in place to cover additional irregularities. Thus, the building hierarchy was able to correct for the errors of imposed architectural design.

After some period of use, the building required minor replastering and reflooring. A pit was dug inside the building, blocking a key doorway (see fig. 6.4, Locus 117), and presumably used to make mud plaster. Later, slabs of old plaster were dumped into the pit. Then a set of complete bevel-rim bowls (in which rations or institutional meals of stew or bread could have been served, as noted above), a few small jars and their jar stoppers, and some sheep/goat bones—the durable remains of a meal for a number of people very similar to meals consumed by the building's normal occupants (as represented by the external pit)—were thrown into the internal pit. A large mass of evidently unneeded still-wet mud plaster was dumped in, followed by a load of miscellaneous stone and battered sherds. Finally, its purpose as a source of mud and as a receptacle for the debris of the repair operation finished, the pit was sealed beneath a new mud flooring. Thus, when the building needed repair, it was evacuated, a work crew subsidized by an institutional kitchen was called in, and the work was finished in a brief period of time. In sum, when maintenance was needed, a higher-level organization, whether the same organization that built the building or not, could see to its repair with dispatch. At least one modest urban organization was able to deal routinely both with its basic operations over time and with errors in the construction and operation of its material infrastructure.

We know only a few of the basic elements of the network of control at Middle and Late Uruk Susa and even less about the higher-order context of control. Only limited excavations have been attempted at buildings that could have been the residences or offices of controlling figures. The sealings and seals themselves, however, have important implications for higher-order control. If there was a disagreement between parties over a transaction, a sealed bulla could be broken open and its counters could be checked. This implies an adjudicating authority. Adjudication implies a system of precedents or regulations. Although human societies can handle adjudication and policy formation in diffuse and ad hoc ways, there are indications of a higher-order structure of offices at Susa and Chogha Mish, offices that were probably concerned with issues of policy and ultimate control.

Different levels of control should have different seal iconographies. As noted above, the majority of cylinder sealings portray activities. Many are directly related to production—herding, the filling of storehouses, or craft activities—whereas others seem to portray daily life, such as drinking parties. These latter occur on both commodity sealings and information-bearing bullae (Amiet 1972; Charvat 1988). They are probably the seals of low-level overseers. Some seals portray scribes taking records of activities (Pittman 1993); where the item being sealed can be determined, these occur on information-bearing bullae and tablets (Amiet 1972:pls. 79–81). The seals showing scribes probably pertained to activities concerned with the receipt of information. A few sealings portray distinctively dressed figures holding audiences, involved in conflict, or performing rituals (Amiet 1972:pls. 18, 85, 87; Schmandt-Besserat 1993), but exactly what such seals were used on is unclear. They may represent the highest offices with ultimate control of Susiana political policy, ritual, and warfare.

SETTLEMENTS IN THE HINTERLANDS OF SOUTHWESTERN IRAN

In the six or more centuries during which Susa reached a peak of prosperity, declined as Chogha Mish grew to become a competing center, and finally was abandoned, the peoples of the marginal valleys developed varying relations with larger centers. The Deh Luran Plain is centered 110 km, or three to four days' travel time, to the northwest of Susa in the foothills of the Pusht-i Kuh, the front range of the central Zagros (see fig. 6.1). The plain is a relatively large foothill valley, covering about 940 km², watered by the perennial Mehmeh and Dawairij (or Ab Danan) Rivers. Most of its rolling surface is difficult to irrigate, though well suited to grazing and dry farming. Deh Luranis had direct access to oak forests on the flanks of Kabir Kuh to the north, bitumen seeps, and gravel beds rich in cherts and other useful stones. There was easy access not only to the Susiana Plain, but to the Mesopotamian plain to the southwest; it is not surprising that the small communities of the Deh Luran area were often dominated by other areas. We know of fourth millennium events on this plain through detailed archaeological survey (Neely and Wright 1994) and through excavations at the small center of Farukhabad (Wright 1981).

The Deh Luran Plain was resettled during the Early Uruk period after several centuries of near abandonment. In Middle Uruk times there were about 770 people on the plain, only a third of the population maximum reached a millennium earlier. Settlement hierarchy had only two tiers—the little center at Farukhabad and four or five small villages (Neely and Wright 1994:208, table VI.16). Small excavations in the center revealed fragments of modest mud-brick houses, ovens, and the familiar technology of blades, sickles, grinding stones, bowls, and jars. The striking feature of this assemblage is that the pottery is not a development of the local Susiana traditions but is in the "chaff-faced" tradition that became established during the late fifth millennium in the mountain and foothill valleys of the Zagros, anti-Taurus, and Amanus Mountains.

Our small soundings did not reveal evidence of elaborate Middle Uruk buildings, but the presence of mother-of-pearl furniture inlay (Wright 1981:156, fig. 75j, pl. 19a) hints at such buildings elsewhere. The occurrence of a sealed spherical bulla made of clay probably from elsewhere on the Deh Luran Plain (James Blackman, personal communication 1980) indicates the receipt of messages by administrators in the little center (Wright 1981:156, fig. 75d, pl. 16e). About a quarter of the animals consumed around modest housing in this center were hunted gazelles and onagers. Sheep and, to a lesser degree, goats provided the bulk of the meat in the Deh Luran diet; cows were rare and pigs were absent. About half the sheep and goats, probably the males, were butchered between the ages of one and three, a prudent strategy for herders interested in the reproduction of their flocks.

The preponderance of barley in the preserved Middle Uruk plant remains, a reversal of the fifth millennium pattern, may indicate increasing salinization (Helbaek 1969) but may equally result from an increased focus on herding and increased use of dung as fuel (Miller 1984). There also is much evidence of spinning and weaving technology, suggesting that cloth production, presumably from animal fiber, was a local industry. Other industries are the preparation of bitumen and large coarse-grained chert blade cores, apparently for export (Wright 1981:266–70, 275–77). Imported durable goods include copper, fine-grained cherts, and marine shell for ornaments (Wright 1981:272–75). In sum, Middle Uruk Deh Luran had a small, prosperous population involved in craft production and export of animal products, bitumen, and chipped stone. From the broader Uruk world, they received modest supplies of exotic commodities.

During Late Uruk times, the organization of the Deh Luran Plain changed, even though the basic two-tier settlement hierarchy was maintained. There were about 400 people, most in the center at Farukhabad, the rest scattered among two or three small hamlets. The distribution of settlements was similar to that during Middle Uruk times, but there seem to have been fewer people—less than a tenth the number that would occupy the plain at the beginning of the Early Dynastic period, three centuries later (Neely and Wright 1994:208, table VI.16).

Our excavations in the center revealed an area with fragments of modest mud-brick houses (fig. 6.5a) with the usual blades, sickles, grinding stones, bowls, and jars. A notable feature of this assemblage is that the local chaff-faced wares were used only for some of the cooking jars; the serving and storage vessels were made with the sand-tempered, often wheel-thrown, Uruk Wares typical of the larger centers of Mesopotamia, such as Nippur, Uruk, and Susa. In the trash around these modest residences, the density of the bones of hunted animals drops off and that of domestic animals increases in comparison to that of Middle Uruk times (Redding 1981:table 69). Goats appear to predominate over sheep. One-third of the kids and lambs were killed before reaching the age of one year, a less-than-optimal butchering pattern that may be a result of restricted access to summer pasturage (Redding, personal communication 1996). As during the Middle Uruk, barley predominates in the seed samples. There is evidence of pottery firing and spinning and weaving around these simple structures, and a lightly baked sealing, probably from a bale of skins, was discarded near them (Wright 1981:156, pl. 16a).

Our excavations also documented an area of nonresidential activities and elaborate buildings with massive walls of miniature mud bricks (fig. 6.5b), circular platforms (fig. 6.5c), and ceramic drains. There are high proportions of bevel-rim bowls around all of these features, and a high proportion of cups and spouted bottles around the platforms. A concentration of bitumen and chert-processing debris was found around these buildings. Whether these were residences or institutional buildings, the occupants apparently were involved in mass labor and in the preparation of items for export. The discard of waste products relative to the actual local use of these materials increases greatly, indicating increased production for export. In spite of a continued emphasis on herding, evidence of spinning and weaving decreases, suggesting that animals on the hoof or unprocessed fibers, rather than cloth, were exported (Wright 1981:266–72). Notwithstanding the evidence of

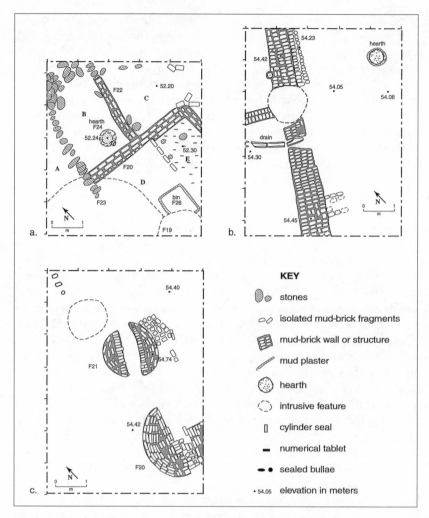

Figure 6.5. Late Uruk features at Farukhabad (adapted from Wright, ed. 1981): a, *Excavation A, Layer 21;* b, *Excavation B, Layer 30;* c, *Excavation B, Layer 29.*

increased production for export, import of durable goods such as fine-grained cherts, copper, carnelian, and other material for ornaments decreased (Wright 1981:272–75).

In sum, Late Uruk Deh Luran had a small population involved in the production and export of quantities of unfinished animal products, bitumen, and chipped stone, perhaps under the control of a central institution. From the broader Uruk world, they received modest supplies of consumer goods but few exotic commodities. It seems likely that an outside polity, whether Susa or some other, took direct control of Deh Luran and its strategic route and exploited local sources of stone, bitumen, and perhaps wood, as well as the pasturage of the area.

On the Plain of Izeh or Malamir, 155 km east-southeast, or five to six days' travel from Shush (see fig. 6.1), a very different situation developed. The Izeh Plain is a basin in the midst of the central Zagros, only 750 m above sea level, though surrounded by peaks reaching as high as 3,100 m. It covers only about 135 km², including two seasonal lakes on its floor. It receives ample rainfall throughout the winter and has excellent land for grazing and dry farming but only a few springs that provide water during the dry summer. Oak forests cover the mountain slopes and may have spread onto the plain in the past, but there are few mineral resources. We know of events on this plain through detailed archaeological survey and through soundings at the small Uruk center of Tepe Zabarjad (Wright 1979, 1986b).

The Izeh Plain seems to have been settled continuously from the early fifth millennium into the Early Uruk period, when a small center and a large village indicate that the maximum population of the plain was about 2,400 people (Wright 1979:59, fig. 26). Neither settlement was close to a permanent water source, suggesting they may not have been fully inhabited during the summer. The absence of smaller settlements, which are common in several earlier and later periods, suggests that Early Uruk settlements were not secure. We have few excavated samples from Early Uruk layers, but the ceramics from the surfaces of sites are similar to the earlier Uruk ceramics that developed on the Susiana Plain. This contrasts to those of Deh Luran, which are in a northern tradition.

Only the small center at Tepe Zabarjad survived into the earlier Middle Uruk period, and it diminished in size, with at most 500 inhabitants (Wright 1979:59). Small excavations in the center revealed the familiar technology of sickles, grinding stones, bowls, and jars. The pottery is identical to ceramics from contemporary sites on the Susiana Plain (Wright 1979:69–81). Our small soundings revealed only a remnant of the stone footing of a small wall. However, a mass of partially burned mud brick and a group of smashed bevel-rim bowls in a pit indicate that mud-brick buildings had been built and repaired. The lack of evidence of administrative technology such as sealings or counters may be a result of the intensive weathering of the upper layers of the site.

At least a quarter of the animals consumed around modest housing in the center were hunted pigs and gazelles. Domestic sheep and goat bone were the most common bones. Although we lack sufficient samples to construct age curves and sex ratios and assess exploitation, all elements of both old and young animals are present, suggesting local herding. Cow bone, however, constituted 12 percent of the discarded material, the largest proportion known from any southwestern Iranian Uruk site (Redding 1979). The restricted Izeh Plain, with its bitter winters, is not an ideal area for cattle. This raises the possibility that the Middle Uruk outpost at Zabarjad received supplies of cattle from elsewhere, perhaps from the Susa area. Even though the sickle blades suggest plants were locally harvested, we have no evidence regarding plant use. Imported durable goods include a few ceramic vessels, copper, and small quantities of finished blade tools of both coarse- and fine-grained cherts (Wright 1979:81–82). In sum, earlier Middle Uruk Izeh had one small settlement with no evidence of durable exports. From the broader Uruk world, however, the occupants received modest supplies of cattle, consumer goods, and exotic commodities.

In succeeding later Middle Uruk times, the Izeh Plain was abandoned; the only outpost in the area was on the high rock of Qaleh Tul, 20 km to the south. This is the time when Chogha Mish was reestablished on the vacant northeastern portion of the Susiana Plain (Johnson 1973:109–11). By Late Uruk times, all the mountain valleys of the central Zagros seem to have been abandoned; the nearest settlement was the outpost of Qaleh-i Rodeni (KS-171), on the eastern margin of the Susiana Plain (Johnson 1973:143–47). At this time or not long after, a major center and series of large villages related to the "Proto-Elamite" Banesh phase of Tal-i Malyan on the southern Iranian Plateau (see fig. 6.1) were founded on the Izeh Plain (Sajjidi 1979). It is reasonable to relate the withdrawal of communities with close relations to Middle Uruk Susa from the mountains, the founding of Chogha Mish and nearby settlements, and the emplacement of Banesh-related communities in Izeh as facets of a prolonged period of conflict in the mountains. In this context, the sustaining of the outpost at Zabarjad, in a region that had no exceptional resources, can be seen as a tactic used by the rulers of Shush to protect a difficult frontier, a tactic that was ultimately unsuccessful.

There are indications of yet other strategies by which the larger polities dealt with or exploited marginal peoples. Some formerly populated plains seem to have had no sedentary communities, for example the Kuh-i Dasht Plain in the mountains of inner Luristan to the north of Susa (Goff 1971; Wright 1986b:146–47). Other mountain plains that maintained prosperous local populations have evidence of small numbers of Uruk residents, whose presence could only result from some kind of negotiated diplomatic agreement. The Godin V fortified oval compound in the largest local center on the Kangavar Plain, with its sealings, tablets, and pottery locally made but in Late Uruk style (Weiss and Young 1975; Young 1986), may be evidence of such a relationship.

In addition to the sedentary peoples of the smaller peripheral valleys, the leaders of larger polities had to deal with transhumant and nomadic com-

munities whose archaeological traces are poorly known. While the campsites and cemeteries of such people seem rare and show none of the evidence
of hierarchical organization notable after 3000 BC (Wright 1986b:147–49),
they do exist. Smaller interstitial mountain valleys, for example the Hulailan
Plain just southeast of Kuh-i Dasht (Mortensen 1976; Wright 1986b:146–
47), have campsites probably of Middle or Late Uruk times. Similar campsites have been found on the arid lowland plains elsewhere in Mesopotamia
(Bernbeck 1993); it seems likely that future survey in the arid foothills will
reveal similar evidence in southwestern Iran. Although nomadic people may
not have posed a military threat to larger polities, they probably sought
goods from farmers and townspeople in return for animal products.

SOUTHWEST IRAN AS AN ELEMENT
IN GREATER MESOPOTAMIA

It is not my purpose in this essay to outline the nexus of early societies that
developed throughout Southwest Asia during the fourth millennium, but a
few comments on the broader relations of the Late and Middle Uruk Susiana polities may help us understand their organization. Not much is known
of the broader relations of Early Uruk communities in general, or on the Susiana Plain in particular, but there is little reason to believe that anything
other than a development of local communities in interaction with their
neighbors occurred. Early and Middle Uruk ceramics from the Susiana Plain
show local features related to earlier assemblages and provide no evidence of
massive immigration (contra Algaze 1993a:11–18), though the movement
of smaller groups—traders, craft specialists, herders, soldiers, or refugees—
seems likely to have occurred at various points in the long period under discussion (cf. Johnson 1988–89).

By Middle Uruk times, there is evidence that bitumen, alabaster, and
chert from hinterland valleys was moved to settlements on the Susiana Plain.
As noted above, animal products appear to have been exported from the Deh
Luran Plain and imported into the Izeh Plain. Items from distant regions,
such as marine shell from the Persian Gulf, copper and carnelian probably
from the Iranian Plateau, and obsidian from the Anatolian Plateau, also
reached southwestern Iran, albeit in small quantities. Whether such materials moved as a result of direct visits to distant sources, social gifts, or systems
of trade, we cannot yet say. However, larger quantities of some materials
were moved between regions. Half of the chert artifacts in predominantly
Middle Uruk samples from Abu Salabikh, a town on a former course of the
Euphrates, 200 km west of Farukhabad, result from medium gray chert
blade cores of the sort procured from sources between the Deh Luran and
Susiana Plains (Pope and Pollock 1995; Wright 1981:262–72). Other cherts

common at Abu Salabikh may have been brought down the Euphrates from Syria, and the quantities of bitumen found at the site could have come either from southwestern Iran or the middle Euphrates.

With such mass movement of materials, however it was organized, it is not surprising that some larger Late Uruk polity reached out to control sources of chert, bitumen, goat hair products, and woods on or near the Deh Luran Plain. The evidence does not indicate whether this polity was centered at Susa or at a center on the Euphrates (Wright 1981:187–88). The presence of a major Middle Uruk trading partner on the Euphrates and the evidence of conflict within the Susiana Plain, discussed below, suggest that the center of control was on the Euphrates. This economic takeover may not have involved overt conflict; given Deh Luran's tiny settled population, mere threat may have been enough to bring it under the control of stronger neighbors.

It is clear that Middle Uruk Susiana had a direct interest in areas of the Zagros to the east. As discussed above, while the little settlement cluster in Deh Luran to the west maintained its own local ceramic style, those in Izeh and other valleys to the east used ceramics identical to those of Susa. There is no evidence that relations between southwestern Iran and areas to the east involved the mass movement of materials. It is possible that Susa was interested in low volumes of high-value goods such as copper. It is also possible that its interests were not economic at all but simply involved securing its frontier against expanding plateau communities. In any event, the abandonment of mountain valleys and the settling of Chogha Mish on the eastern Susiana Plain at about the same time is difficult to understand unless external force was being exerted.

Given the pressures from both the east and the west, it is not surprising that problems within the Susiana polity were exacerbated. Johnson (1973: 143–56, 1987, 1988–89) has argued cogently that Late Uruk settlement patterns and iconography indicate conflict between the western plain under Susa and the eastern plain under Chogha Mish. Chogha Mish was abandoned before the end of the Late Uruk period, and Susa itself was abandoned near its end. Their populations could have moved as refugees to other parts of Southwest Asia, leaving the rich Susiana Plain with few inhabitants (Alden 1987).

LESSONS LEARNED

The diverse, if far from comprehensive, evidence assembled here allows a qualitative evaluation of the operation of the first states in southwestern Iran and their impact on the lives of their inhabitants. It is clear that goods and labor were extracted from rural producers, probably to support rural elites, and both elite and ordinary town dwellers. Figures with complementary hierarchical roles in a system of control acted to control the movement of labor or the flow of goods, as well as to keep records of transactions. They also acted to maintain their own institutional apparatus, building and maintaining installations, manufacturing appropriate paraphernalia, and no doubt using it in the impressive rituals portrayed in some of the cylinder seals. In bad years, some ordinary producers did receive assistance from central institutions, but an ordered life of reciprocal relations may have benefited only some of the participants in the state and for only limited periods of time. At other times conflict broke out, polities were shattered, and people became refugees. A more measured assessment of the relations within these states and of how these relations developed over the several centuries of the Uruk period in Mesopotamia will be possible only after future cycles of fieldwork have been completed.

7

Order, Legitimacy, and Wealth in Ancient Egypt and Mesopotamia

JOHN BAINES AND NORMAN YOFFEE

By around 3100 BC in ancient Western Asia and the northeastern corner of Africa, the two earliest states/civilizations in the world are believed to have emerged. (In this chapter we define "states" as the specialized political system of the larger cultural entities that we denominate "civilizations." We explain and defend this distinction in our conclusion.)

In Mesopotamia (fig. 7.1), early political development is most clearly evident from archaeological surveys (Adams 1981) and from excavations at the urban site of Warka (ancient Uruk), with its massive temple complexes (including a possible palace), monumental art, cylinder seals, ration system, presumed central place in its hinterland, surplus production, and writing system (Boehmer 1991; Pollock 1992). Warka was probably one among a number of such city-states. The urban implosion, in which city-states carved up the countryside while the population of smaller sites shifted into the new cities (thus creating a depopulated, "ruralized" countryside), also produced—it has been argued—an explosion outward (Algaze 1989; Schwartz 1988; Yoffee 1995b). Mobilizing unprecedented numbers of dependent personnel, the leaders of these city-states established far-flung colonies (and/or immigrants from the south settled in northern villages) up the Euphrates into Syria and Anatolia, and onto the Iranian Plain (Algaze 1989, 1993a, 1993b; Sürenhagen 1986; cf. Johnson 1988–89; Stein 1993; Yoffee 1995b); the colonies proved easier to found than to maintain.

In Egypt (fig. 7.2), the signs of unification and civilization are less archaeologically conventional, encompassing the rapid development of large

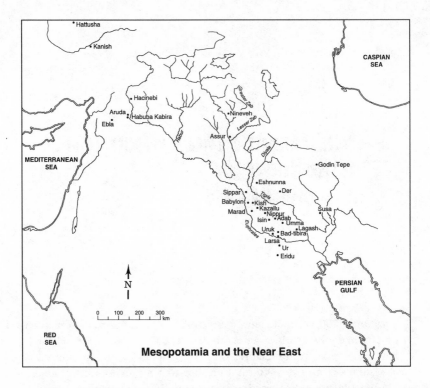

*Figure 7.1. Mesopotamia (after Postgate 1992; Edzard, Farber, and Soll-
berger 1977).*

cemeteries and standardization of the material culture of the late Naqada II
and Naqada III phases throughout the country toward the end of the fourth
millennium BC. In the wake of these changes came political centralization of
the Nile Valley and Delta (from the First Cataract at Aswan to the Mediterranean), polarization of wealth, the decline of regional centers, and the development of mortuary architecture, luxury goods, characteristic art forms,
and writing. The centralized polity reached out briefly to the south to dev-
astate, but not occupy, Lower Nubia, and to the north to assert hegemony
over southern Palestine.

Thus, at around the same date the two regions evolved highly differentiated and stratified societies (table 7.1). Both societies exhibited specialized
political systems with bureaucratic administrations (or what soon became
such—the earliest evidence does not permit a definite statement) based on

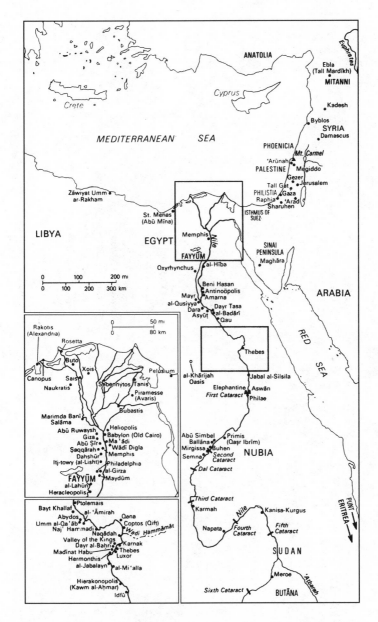

Figure 7.2. Egypt and Syria-Palestine. From "Egypt" (author and map consultant John Baines) in Encyclopaedia Britannica; *reproduced with permission from* Encyclopaedia Britannica, 15th *edition,* ©1988 *by Encyclopaedia Britannica, Inc.*

TABLE 7.1. *Prehistoric Periods, Historic Periods, and Dynasties: Egypt and Mesopotamia*

Egypt		Mesopotamia	
Merimda (Delta)	5000	'Ubaid	5000–4000
Badari (Nile Valley)	4500		
Naqada I (Nile Valley)	4000	Uruk	4000–3100
Ma'adi (Delta)	3800		
Naqada II (Nile Valley, later all Egypt)	3500		
Naqada III (late predynastic/Dynasty 0)	3100	Jemdet Nasr	3100–2900
Early Dynastic (1st–3rd Dynasty)	2950–2575	Early Dynastic II	2700–2600
		Early Dynastic III	2600–2300
Old Kingdom (4th–8th Dynasty)	2575–2150	Akkadian (Dynasty of Sargon of Akkade)	2350–2150
		Third Dynasty of Ur	2100–2000
First Intermediate period (9th–11th Dynasty)	2150–1980		
Middle Kingdom (11th–13th Dynasty)	1980–1630	Old Babylonian period	2000–1600
		Old Assyrian period	2000–1750
Second Intermediate period (14th–17th Dynasty)	1630–1520	Kassite Babylonia	–1150
New Kingdom (18th–20th Dynasty)	1540–1070	Middle Assyrian period	1400–950
		Various dynasties in Babylonia	1150–730
Third Intermediate period (21st–25th Dynasty)	1070–715	Neo-Assyrian period	1000–610
Late Period (25th–30th Dynasty)	715–332	Neo-Babylonian period/Chaldean dynasty	625–539
		Persian period	539–330
Macedonian–Ptolemaic period	332–30	Seleucid dynasty	330–164
Roman period	30–AD 395	Parthians and Sasanians	238–AD 651
Byzantine period	AD 395–640		

Note: All dates before 715 BC are approximate. Dates are BC unless otherwise noted.

a written recording system, surplus production, and a managed system of distribution. They also displayed symbols of rulership, specialized elite ritual forms (although priests are not clearly visible in Egypt), and the demarcation of a "core–periphery" structure with the external world.

In this essay we compare some aspects of these two ancient civilizations, proceeding from one or the other according to the topic at hand. Most striking to Egyptologists and Mesopotamianists are the many salient differences between these two civilizations, which developed at roughly the same time in nearby regions, probably with some indirect contact (e.g., Kantor 1992; the mode of contact is still disputed), and with a comparable reliance on irrigation/floodplain agriculture as the subsistence base upon which all social institutions depended (although the river regimes differed, and the organization in Egypt was simpler). Yet, so far as we know, there has never been a comparative examination of the two most ancient states and civilizations, although particular institutions have been studied (e.g., Engnell 1943; Frankfort 1948). Indeed, the specialized training needed to master the primary written and archaeological sources for either area virtually precludes any one person from attempting such comparisons.

Egyptian or Mesopotamian scholars rarely have attempted any overall historical and cultural assessment of the character of either civilization (exceptions include Kemp 1989; Oppenheim 1977; Postgate 1992), because both civilizations persisted for millennia and underwent major social and cultural change, while the nature of the nonwritten sources, scripts, and languages changed as well. Few Egyptologists and Assyriologists have the skills to assess all the periods in their particular culture, let alone two cultures. Moreover, few scholars of these civilizations are inclined to be comparativists, and many even regard the principle of comparison as violating the "conceptual autonomy" (*Eigenbegrifflichkeit*, a term coined by the Assyriologist Benno Landsberger 1976[1926]; see Yoffee 1992) of their area of study—its unique developmental trajectory and historical character. All too often, comparison seems to be sampled principally either to reaffirm uniqueness or to claim that a particular culture offers the quintessential example of some cross-culturally attested phenomenon (for the former, see Kraus 1973; for the latter, see Assmann 1991).

We therefore present this essay with some diffidence, not because we suspect the astonishment of some ancient Near East colleagues; we take that for granted. Rather, we are concerned that a theoretically oriented account of social and cultural life of the two areas cannot easily be presented in a brief survey, using nonparochial terms, and navigating through (but not disregarding) problems of interpretation. Because the subject matter is so vast, we fall back to an uncomfortable extent on studies the two of us happen to have made. We justify the comparison precisely because, by specifying in which dimensions and for what reasons institutions—and what may presumptuously be termed the spirits of both civilizations—differ, we learn more about their structure and character.

We do not, then, compare the two civilizations to enumerate similar traits or to establish the core principles of an abstraction, the "archaic state." Rather, through this controlled comparison in time, place, and historical contact, we seek to identify major axes of variation and to advance an important anthropological principle: by knowing what is institutionally and structurally dissimilar in one society judiciously compared with another, we can begin fresh investigations of the principles of organization and change in either society, or in both. Our larger intention is to contribute to the set of comparisons of archaic states or early civilizations in general, to see what organizational principles are widely shared, what, if anything, is truly unique, and what general societal and transactional models can address data from a wide range of societies (cf. Trigger 1993).

SOME PRINCIPAL DIFFERENCES BETWEEN ANCIENT EGYPT AND MESOPOTAMIA

We review differences between Egypt and Mesopotamia in terms of the relation between political and cultural systems, kingship, and urbanization. Egypt exhibits nearly total convergence of polity and culture. The establishment of the unified and centralized polity was characterized far more by territorial extent than by urbanization, although settlement sites, which might round out the picture, are almost inaccessible. From ancient Egyptian civilization into modern times, there has been a clear definition of the extent of the country. The principal change has been that, whereas in antiquity the Nile Valley and Nile Delta made up the area ruled, lines have recently been drawn on a map and used to justify a geographical claim to rule adjacent deserts with their transit routes, as well as resources of a few oases, a very small number of nomads, and significant mineral deposits. In antiquity, these regions (except for the nearer oases), although exploited, were treated as being "abroad." In some periods Egypt conquered large sectors of the Middle Nile and of Palestine and Syria, but these were never held permanently. Attempts to integrate the southern domains into a larger conception of "Egypt" did not succeed in the very long term.

This congruence of country and region also was cultural: Egyptian civilization extended to its southern border at the First Cataract of the Nile. At times, Egypt had great influence farther south, but generally less in Syria-Palestine.

The most apparent of all differences between Mesopotamia and Egypt is that there never was any enduring political unification in Mesopotamia until the Persian conquest in the mid-first millennium BC; if there must be a political definition of the state, then there was no "Mesopotamian" state. In a wider comparative perspective, however, it is Egypt that is exceptional in displaying convergence between a polity and a more abstract civilizational boundary. Mesopotamia consisted politically of a congeries of city-states and culturally of an overarching cultural tradition.

In later periods, after 1600 BC, there were trends toward the formation of Assyrian and Babylonian regions, which in the south were especially loose fitting. Although Assyria did conquer Babylonia in the seventh century BC, absorbing it into its "empire," that unification diverted military authority and resources from other imperial ventures. Ultimately, Assyrian rule over Babylonia was successfully resisted, and this led to, or was combined with, other missions toward independence by former Assyrian subjects. These struggles were followed in rapid order by military defeat and the demise of Assyria (Dalley 1993; Postgate 1993; Yoffee 1988b).

Kingship and Other Forms of Rule

Among forms of political structure, kingship can be defined, rather inexactly, as rulership by a single individual holding a supreme office in a lifelong tenure, most often succeeding on a hereditary principle and wielding—or not, as the case may be—great personal power. As such, it may be the single most frequent form of state government, but it is by no means the only one. It occurs typically both in states and in nonstate entities such as chiefdoms: there is no easy distinction between "chief" and "king." Conversely, city-states (Yoffee 1997), while belonging firmly with state forms in which administration is at least partly disembedded from kinship rules, generally display a range of types of government and often do not focus on kingship (compare speculations on the nature of rule at Teotihuacán [Cowgill 1992b] and at Mohenjo-daro [Kenoyer 1991; Possehl, this volume]). These contrasting options are exemplified by the ancient Near East. Egypt offers a type case of the kingship-dominated non–city state; in the more diverse city-state forms of Mesopotamia, kings were at their most salient during periods of centralization, and then during the Neo-Assyrian and Neo-Babylonian empires of the mid-first millennium.

A form of leadership whose symbols developed directly into those of kingship can be identified in Egypt by the early fourth millennium BC, before social complexity had developed to a significant extent. Kingship emerged before unification, and, probably through internal assimilation and conquest in the formative period of the late fourth millennium, kings created the unified polity whose ideology set the trajectory for all later times (Baines 1995a). During Dynasties 0–3 (c. 3100–2600 BC) the king acquired a complex titulary that proclaimed he manifested aspects of various deities on earth. Official forms displaying his qualities related him to the gods, but he was not the same order of being as they—more central and salient for human society, but of lesser status and potential.

The two basic terms for "king," *njswt* and *bjtj*, related to hierarchically ranked aspects of kingship and, in dynastic times, were connected with Upper and Lower Egypt (roughly equivalent to the Nile Valley and the Nile Delta). This characteristically Egyptian dualism held that only entities formed from dualities were meaningful (e.g., Hornung 1982:240); by implication, the unity of the country—typically known as the "Two Lands" and long lacking an overall proper name—was vested in king and kingship. Neither the country of Egypt nor full rulership could be imagined without kingship, because the king was the sole formal intermediary with the gods. Only around 750 BC, toward the end of several centuries of the Third Intermediate period, did significant numbers of regional leaders emerge who did not claim the title of king.

The king's role in relation to and in combination with the gods perpetuated the fragile order of the cosmos, offering a central legitimation that overrode the "moral economies" of smaller social organizations (Baines 1995b). This principal ritual requirement remained in force into Roman times, when the emperor, who could have known little of what he was subscribing to, was represented in temples in forms that conveyed essentially the same message as the key originating works of the late Predynastic period (Derchain 1962).

The ritual and cosmological aspects of kingship are embodied in much of the country's vast monumental legacy, but also in royal action and in foreign relations. Missions abroad were undertaken to bring back materials needed for king, cult, and the dead. Conquest was an "extension of the boundaries" that built upon the idea of maintaining the cosmos. The basis of kingship was not, however, strongly military, and for much of the third millennium the country seems to have lacked a standing army.

Within Egypt, royal authority was underpinned by the king's theoretically absolute ownership of the land and rights over his subjects. Even in Greco-Roman times, streets running past private houses were termed "the street of Pharaoh" (e.g., Smith 1972:711). Kings appear to have asserted these rights in early periods by redefining landholding patterns on principles defined at the center and by constructing many new settlements, imprinting their requirements on the fabric of the land (Helck 1974:49–53; Janssen's reservations [1978:226] seem excessive—such phenomena are known elsewhere).

The king's most powerful influence was probably on the elite. Their status and wealth depended on him—often on his personal favor and caprice. The palace was the central institution that mobilized the country's resources, although in most periods there also were significant "secular" and temple administrations. The term "pharaoh," regularly used for kings of Egypt by foreigners at least since the first millennium BC and by Egyptians from around the time of Akhenaten (c. 1350 BC), derives from the ancient "Great Estate (*pr-ʿ3*)" that focused on the institutional and economic aspects of kingship.

Mesopotamian kingship contrasts strongly with that of Egypt. Without an overarching political state, its forms of kingship were markedly different. Kingship acquired its character in the endemic struggle among the Sumerian city-states in the time before Sargon of Akkade (c. 2350 BC; Cooper 1983). It seems that kings were at first elite landowners, perhaps important figures in community assemblies, who progressively assumed more power as war leaders and who bought land from corporate landholding groups (Diakonoff 1969; Gelb 1979; Jacobsen 1957). In pre-Sargonic land-sale documents (Gelb, Steinkeller, and Whiting 1991), the buyer of the land is often a ruler or high official; the seller is denoted both in the body of the document and by the list of his relatives who are recorded as the witnesses and who receive gifts. While the texts do not indicate what happened to these newly landless people, it is assumed that they did not actually move from their land, but acknowledged its new owner and paid him both taxes and obligations of service (Yoffee 1995b). These documents show the strong difference from Egypt in how early Mesopotamian kings were able to gain power, labor, and resources. The Mesopotamian king was a local lord whose acquisition of power was internal and unrelated to conquest outside his own state.

Rulers of pre-Sargonic city-states were variously called *en, ensí,* or *lugal.* Although these titles have different etymological meanings, and some have tried to see a progression from priestly to secular kingship as reflected in their evolution, they can all be translated as "ruler" for pre-Sargonic times. With the conquest of Sargon, however, *lugal* (Akkadian *šarrum*) became the accepted title for "king" and *ensí* was reserved for the governors of city-states (and *en,* originally "lord," became a title of the priesthood). In the Old Babylonian period *ensí* became further devalued, meaning "manager of an agricultural field."

Early Mesopotamian city-states were arenas for a normative and constant struggle between the burgeoning royal authority and the power of the temple estate. The so-called reforms of Urukagina of Lagash (c. 2400 BC) in southern Mesopotamia indicate that there the temple was able to stage a coup d'état against the kings who were seizing its land and privileges, but that the coup was only a minor interruption in the trend toward increasingly centralized power vested in the royal government (Nissen 1982).

In the succeeding Akkadian period, Sargon and his grandson Naram-Sin reorganized administration, founded a new site as capital of a regional state, and established new titles in order to imply that the House of Akkade was not just another powerful dynasty: it was the legitimate political center ruling over all Mesopotamia (see Liverani, ed. 1993). Naram-Sin himself became deified, thus reinforcing his imperial status over the Mesopotamian city-states (Glassner 1986). When the Akkadian dynasty fell, city-states reemerged, as they did also after the short-lived regional state of the Third Dynasty of Ur. The kings of these newly independent city-states once again began the struggle with their neighbors, just as had their predecessors in the days before Akkade.

In sum, while Mesopotamian kings were powerful leaders in war and in civil administration, they never achieved the same position as the foci of ideology, economy, and social life as the kings of Egypt did. In some periods the Mesopotamian king shared power with temple estates and local assemblies. Furthermore, the palace often contracted with, and sometimes depended upon, private entrepreneurs to supply its local subsistence needs, as well as its desire for distant luxury goods (see section on "Economy"; Yoffee 1995b).

Urbanization

Mesopotamia and Egypt contrast strongly in the vital area of urbanization. City-states were the major arenas for the interplay of characteristic Mesopotamian institutions. This statement can be defended, even against the charge that written sources and archaeological investigations are utterly biased toward urban places (a bias that intensive field surveys seek to correct, e.g., Adams 1981). It is not that villages, nomadic, seminomadic, or cryptonomadic pastoralists, and de-urbanized bandits were not integral to the Mesopotamian scene. However, it is in the comparison with Egypt that one can see the significance of city wards (Gelb 1968; Yoffee 1992), local assemblies, resistance to urban rulers, a temple-versus-palace struggle, an urban prejudice against the countryside, and the superior ability of nonurban people to use their extensive ties to seize political power (Kamp and Yoffee 1980). All of these features of Mesopotamian civilization are conspicuous by their absence in Egypt, or are extremely attenuated in the context of the central symbols of Egyptian civilization.

The urban implosion of late-fourth- and early-third-millennium Mesopotamia resulted in a massive population shift into large sites (Nissen 1988). These new city-states, consisting of one or more large sites, such as Lagash and Girsu of the city-state of Lagash, Uruk and Kullaba of Uruk, Kish and Hursagkalama of Kish, and attendant towns and villages (for third-millennium Lagash, see Grégoire 1962), set the pattern for Mesopotamia as "the heartland of cities" (Adams 1981). For as long as Mesopotamian civilization remained independent, with multiple polities, it retained not only the configuration of city-states and countryside, but also the ideology of the city-state (Postgate 1992). Rulers were mainly defined in connection with the city-state from which they ruled; even those associated with extensive conquests focused their domains on a core city (e.g., Hammurabi of Babylon, 1792–1750). Major reorganizations of empire, however, from Sargon of Akkade and notably including Tukulti-Ninurta of Assyria (fourteenth century) and various Neo-Assyrian rulers in the first millennium BC, were often accompanied by the establishment of new capitals. These new cities served to dislocate and disenfranchise old elites and bureaucratic networks, and they also were monumentally emblematic of changes in administrative power and purpose. From the end of the Uruk period to the conquest of Cyrus the Great of Persia (539 BC), city-states were an irreducibly essential quality of Mesopotamian civilization. In the Sumerian King List, a historiographic text relating the birth of Mesopotamian political systems (Michalowski 1983), kinship descended from heaven to *cities:* without autonomous cities, a Mesopotamian way of life was unthinkable.

For Egypt, central places were important on a number of levels; the idea of a walled, nucleated settlement goes back into prehistory. Certain crucial towns, such as Buto in the Nile Delta, Hierakonpolis in the south, and Elephantine at the First Cataract, played key roles in defining the extent of Egypt during the period of state formation. Nonetheless, only scholars who appear to feel that urbanism is a sine qua non of civilization (e.g., Kemp 1977) are prone to maintain that the city was a primary motor of development or strongly characteristic of Egypt. In early times the Egyptians seem to have been almost more interested in their frontiers than in their center (e.g., Seidlmayer 1996); government policy toward regions and settlement patterns appears to have disfavored cities in certain respects, notably by using an estate-based system of redistribution. The elite's ideology had a rural tinge—rather like that of the English country gentleman—despite the pattern of land tenure, which was theoretically insecure because rights to land were based upon holding administrative office.

These biases changed in periods of insecurity and decentralization, and more profoundly in the New Kingdom (c. 1520–1070 BC) and later, when the ideal of the city was well established along with the notion of city as cosmos (Kozloff, Bryan, and Berman 1992:103–4; O'Connor 1998). From early Islamic times to the present day, the country's common name, Misr, has been the same as that of the capital city; this congruence also can be observed for the first millennium BC. The city was the country.

Moreover, when the Assyrian king Assurbanipal described Egypt around 660 BC, he did so in terms of cities and their rulers, most of whom he designated with the Akkadian word for "king" (*šarrum/lugal*). This was a period when the Delta in particular had moved toward something like city-state forms, but one wonders whether his approach owed more to his background and that of his recording officials in a city-state civilization than to what was observed on the ground.

Nature of the Sources

Cuneiform tablets, the main source for our understanding of Mesopotamian history and culture, preserve decently in general and wonderfully well after a good sacking and burning; they record not only myths and epics but also private letters, bureaucratic notes, private contracts, records of smuggling, and so on. It is important to take into account the systematic bias of the documents from the various periods. For example, it is not easy to reconstruct anything like a comprehensive history of a period or place from archives, however rich, that deal mainly with long-distance trade (e.g., Larsen 1976). Consider the following characterization of the major tablet finds in early Mesopotamia: for pre-Sargonic Lagash, the archives come mainly from temple estates (Diakonoff 1969; Maekawa 1987); for the Ur III period, they are almost entirely from the royal bureaucracy (Civil 1987; Steinkeller 1989); for the Old Babylonian period, although there are temple and palace archives, many tablets come from private houses and record business transactions, family law, and private correspondence (see Kohler et al. 1904–23; Kraus 1964). This distribution could depend on chances of recovery, but most scholars believe that it reflects the cultural and organizational emphases of distinct periods and important differences between them.

For one example, we can rightly infer that the absence of textual documentation in the time after the collapse of the Old Babylonian and Old Assyrian states in the middle of the second millennium BC reflects the absence of centralized states and the written products of bureaucracies. In another case, for the last days of Mesopotamian civilization, most literary and economic documents come from temple precincts, since temples clung to the vestiges of Mesopotamian belief systems and also maintained control of dwindling land and resources.

Inscribed texts are part of the archaeological record and need to be appraised alongside settlement patterns, architecture, and artifactual finds. It is only in recent years, however, that texts and other materials have regularly been utilized together (Charpin 1986; Postgate 1992; Stone 1981, 1987; van de Mieroop 1992). Most studies of Mesopotamian art and artifacts have been concerned with styles as chronological markers or as powerful statements of royal actions. In contrast to these few studies (but see Winter 1981, 1983, 1991, 1992, 1995; M. Marcus 1995), the understanding of Egyptian culture is enriched by much work on visual media.

Comparison of this skeletal list of Mesopotamian source categories with material from Egypt throws into relief the fact that many aspects of life are represented little or not at all in Egyptian written and pictorial evidence, which is mainly monumental and centered on the ruling group, on religion, and on the symbols of Egypt as a single polity—much of it filtered through the characteristic requirement of tomb building. This focus reflects, above all, the disappearance of administrative records, which were written on papyrus and other perishable media that were used in the floodplain and not the desert (it also reflects earlier excavators' interest in the "treasures" to be found in tombs). Nonetheless, the role of the centralized Egyptian state, the relation of royal government to the temples and the civil administration, and the character of private (nonroyal, nontemple) activities appears different from that in Mesopotamia—for example, in most periods there was less mercantile activity and less opportunity for political struggle. What it does not reflect is a reticence in using writing in state administration. In his classic work, Adolf Erman rightly wrote of a "mania for writing" (*Schreibwut;* Erman 1923:125) as pervading documents of state administration from the Ramessid period (thirteenth century BC).

This contrast with Mesopotamia should not be overdrawn. Thus, we find evidence of Egyptian trade and foreign expeditions in reliefs and inscriptions of kings and nonroyal officials; the archaeological record indicates that trade was substantial already in Predynastic times—even though such products as gold, linen, papyrus, and cereals, which are likely to have been important Egyptian exports, are more or less untraceable archaeologically. Despite these indications of substantial movement of goods and associated foreign contacts, the relative absence in Egypt of individual or local enterprises that conducted exchange reveals a significant difference with Mesopotamia. In pursuing such questions, it would be desirable to examine the nature of trade in the two areas and their respective degrees of dependence on imports and exports, as well as differences in the organization of foreign contacts; such investigations are beyond the scope of this essay.

On another level, Egyptian sources, many of them iconographic rather than written, may take us closer to understanding ideals of daily life than we can get in Mesopotamia, even if the ideals were those of a small fraction of the population who mostly prettified the life of the rest in the depictions they commissioned.

Despite this reservation, Egyptian art gives forceful impressions of the nature of labor, as do observations and calculations in relation to large monuments; in Mesopotamia the analogous evidence is mainly in large lists of laborers and their rations. But in Mesopotamia the many documents from "upper-middle-class" land sales, contracts, family law, and litigation provide glimpses of activity only rarely attested in Egypt, principally for the Ramessid and Greco-Roman periods (c. 1300–1075 BC; third century BC–AD fourth century).

Terms of Comparison: Order, Legitimacy, and Wealth

Differences in the sources for Mesopotamia and Egypt tend to focus research along distinct paths in the two regions—toward somewhat more material issues for Mesopotamia and more ideological ones for Egypt. Whether or not this bias reflects genuine differences, the material from both regions amply supports the view that a balanced and fruitful comparison must integrate the material and the ideological, the pragmatic and the spiritual. Scholars of the ancient Near East have long argued against the "Oriental Despotism" picture of their societies' evolution that would reduce much interpretation to ecological determinism; environmental factors are now mostly seen as enabling rather that dictating social forms. But within this more sociocentric perspective there is little consensus over the vital stimuli in the trajectory toward civilizations, or over the critical foci of civilizations once they formed. Here we comment briefly on the terms and foci we have chosen to chart through the material; we hope this terminological discussion is also useful to others.

In a temporal comparison with preceding epochs, what stands out about early civilizations is their rapidity of formation and relative instability. In view of the much greater instability of later societies and civilizations, this assessment may seem perverse, especially when applied to an Egypt that was characterized by Plato (*Laws*, 656) as seeing no change for "literally" ten thousand years. But here we fall too easily victims to an overly synoptic vision of our regions as single entities. The different, archaeologically distinctive periods of historic Egypt and Mesopotamia succeeded one another far more rapidly than the major subperiods of the Neolithic. The evolutionary course seems to be one of gradual change in the Neolithic, followed by an explosive period of political, economic, and architectural restructuring.

In this context of instability, and perhaps especially of the rapid process of state formation and consolidation, the issue of *order* is fundamental. Order is an insistent preoccupation of Mesopotamian literature and is consistently expressed in so-called law codes and (self-survivingly) in royal inscriptions. In Egypt this focus is still more evident, both in the largely visual complex we discuss in the section on "high culture" and particularly in the central concept of *ma'at*, a notion that is so fundamental to Egyptian ideology that a wide-ranging study of it was long lacking (Assmann 1990). In both cases, this centripetal "rage for order" (to quote Wallace Stevens's poem "The Idea of Order at Key West") stands against a pessimistic background that was overt in the Mesopotamian case and largely dissimulated in the

Egyptian. The terms of order, the negotiation of order, and its appropriation by elites are defining activities of civilizations. Order cannot be taken for granted.

The elite appropriation of order is one of many legitimations of inequality, which was perhaps most extreme in Egypt. It was far from natural or necessarily easy for ancient elites to achieve *legitimacy* in the eyes of others and of themselves. Elites sustain their self-image and transmit it down the generations both through their pragmatic actions in maintaining inequality and through their understanding of their own position and mission. These legitimizing activities and attitudes encompass the mission, one that the elite take upon themselves, to achieve and maintain order in their societies. Legitimacy, however, is most strongly expressed in the "dialogue" between the ruler and his superiors or peers, the gods. Ancient Near Eastern rulers or elites did not have exclusive access to religious life, but they did have access to more grandiose varieties of it and to more of its profound meanings, while others were excluded from some of its domains. A major thrust of religion, on which so much of society's resources were expended, was legitimation.

In complex societies, *wealth,* especially conservable wealth, is a vital feature that sets elites apart from others. The division and administration of society enhance enormously the potential of wealth to be produced, differentiated, stored, and negotiated, while the organizational capacities of the new social forms allow great distances to be exploited in order to move goods and people so as to generate and mobilize wealth. All this is administered by the elite or their employees; so far as our sources allow us to gauge, these activities seem principally to benefit the elite. Yet wealth is probably not the prime motive force in the development and maintenance of complex social forms; rather, it is an enabling factor, one that has an extraordinarily powerful communicative and persuasive potential. Wealth and legitimacy are almost inextricably linked. Wealth, controlled and channeled, can sustain order. Destitution of wealth spells disorder or a reversal of order.

Thus, the three interrelated aspects—*order, legitimacy,* and *wealth*—cover much ground in the study and comparison of features distinctive of early (and other) civilizations, of their emergence, persistence, and eventual collapse. Below we survey the evidence according to more traditional subject divisions instead of these rather abstract ones, but in singling them out we emphasize the active role of the elite in constituting and, especially, transmitting the characteristics of a civilization. Our longest case study, of high culture, addresses most directly the nexus between these factors.

Finally, these three terms have the advantage of bridging analysts' and actors' categories. Although such terms and topics as politics and economics have no counterparts in the ancient evidence (which is not to say that they are invalid as fields and methods of study), order is a central ancient idea, wealth is much mentioned in the texts and displayed in the record, and the theme of legitimacy has manifold and close correspondences in verbal and iconographic sources.

DEVELOPMENT OF THE STATES

Mesopotamia

We begin a brief consideration of state development in Mesopotamia with the ʿUbaid (c. fifth millennium BC; Oates 1983, 1987), since this is the period to which significant elements in the character of later state development in Mesopotamia can be traced. It was once thought that the south of Mesopotamia was unoccupied in early prehistoric (Neolithic) times (e.g., Redman 1978, 1991), the land itself being the product of alluviation and progradation into the Persian Gulf (Sanlaville 1989). However, the site of ʿOueili near the ancient city of Larsa, which antedates the ʿUbaid, shows that southern Mesopotamia was occupied before the ʿUbaid (Adams 1981; Calvet 1987). Presumably, small sites in the south are alluviated and/or deflated. If there has been progradation into the Gulf, the amount of new land created in this way does not justify the traditional "unoccupied-niche" model of development.

The ʿUbaid has long been characterized as a "unified" culture (e.g., Perkins 1949; Porada 1965), mainly on the basis of similarities in temple plans, distinctive pottery, and certain artifacts that are found at the northern type site of Gawra and the southern one of Eridu (see also Henrickson and Thuesen 1989). After the ʿUbaid, and continuously into historic periods, the northern and southern regions of Mesopotamia (that is, Assyria and Babylonia) differ in aspects of their material cultures, form independent arenas of political struggle, and develop distinctive belief systems—in particular the "national" religion of the god Assur, which had no counterpart in the south. Nevertheless, overarching the two regions was a larger cultural sphere that one calls "Mesopotamia" (see section below on high culture); it is this regional Mesopotamian culture that can be traced back to the ʿUbaid (Stein 1991, 1994b; Yoffee 1993a).

In the fourth millennium BC, the Uruk period is marked at the beginning with a change in pottery from the ʿUbaid (Oates 1960) and ends (conventionally) in the decades after written tablets appeared. While the ʿUbaid, which is characterized by few and relatively small sites and by modest degrees of social and economic differentiation, represents a gradual development of Neolithic trends, the later Uruk period, known best from the city-state of Warka, constitutes a major "punctuated" change. The enormous size of the city-state at the end of the Uruk period and the appearance of such features as cylinder seals, monumental art and architecture, and writing are hardly prefigured by the ʿUbaid.

The origins of writing are a good case in point for the dazzling innovations that accompanied the rise of the Uruk (and other) city-state(s). Although Schmandt-Besserat (e.g., 1992) has assiduously shown that a system of "tokens" preceded writing by millennia, many have criticized her argument that the tokens evolved directly into writing (Friberg 1994; Le Brun and Vallat 1978; Lieberman 1980; Michalowski 1990, 1993b; Zimansky 1993). The shapes of most tokens bear no relation to later cuneiform signs; the tokens are distributed over a much wider area than that in which writing later developed. In Elam, where some of the tokens and bullae enclosing them were found, the form of the writing and language were not the same as in Mesopotamia. And at Tell ʿAbada, one of the few archaeological contexts from which we have tokens, the small clay objects were found in children's graves, not a likely locus for trade and business records, which Schmandt-Besserat has argued was their primary function.

Michalowski (1990, 1993b, 1994) has emphasized that the earliest preserved written signs are extremely complex and abstract, bearing little resemblance to the tokens. Tokens are part of a long process of signification that includes glyptic arts, pottery decoration, and potters' marks, but they cannot explain the nature or form of the writing system. Indeed, writing seems to have originated through invention (see Boltz 1986 and 1994 for similar views on the ancient Chinese script), perhaps the product of a single individual's work (Powell 1981:419–24). In Warka, the reasons (or at least the context) for the appearance of writing are reasonably clear. Upon the formation of a city-state with a central core of around 300 ha and a suggested population of more than 20,000 (Nissen 1988)—Warka was only one of a number of city-states in southern Mesopotamia—the ability to manage a burgeoning economy was greatly facilitated by a new system of record keeping and communication that could name names, specify obligations, and count resources. While most early tablets consist of such economic accounts, a significant percentage (c. 15%) are lists of professions and other matters that were aids for teaching the new scribal arts; these demonstrate the institutionalization and cultural import of this new technology. Writing is, however, only one of a series of rapid and dramatic innovations that occurred at the end of the Uruk period.

As noted, the nucleation of settlements at this time represents a demographic implosion in which the countryside was progressively depopulated over about 500 years while large urban sites grew. This process of implosion also led to a significant explosion, since, it is argued, the southern city-states sent forth expeditions to establish colonies up the Euphrates into Syria and Turkey, and also into Iran (see Yoffee 1995b). Although these colonies, whose purpose was to serve as access and transshipment points, were easy to found in a countryside of relatively low political centralization or organized resistance, they were impossible to maintain in the medium term, and many disappeared within 50 years or less.

Since no political unity was present in southern Mesopotamia and neighboring Khuzestan, Algaze (1993a: 115–18) suggests that each independent city-state established its own colonies, as in the case of early Greek colonial expansion (Schwartz 1988). We know little about other city-states in the Late Uruk period. Furthermore, according to some (e.g., Stein et al. 1996), "Uruk colonies" may date to the Middle Uruk period. Stylistic criteria have been inferred to show that sealing motifs from these colonies resemble those from Susa as well as, or rather than, those from Uruk (Pittman in Stein et al. 1996). Although it is hard at present to test the hypothesis that individual city-states in middle- and late-fourth-millennium Mesopotamia and Khuzestan established distant colonies, it is clear that, aside from ephemeral conquests and alliances, no political unity existed in Mesopotamia before the imperial successes of Sargon (c. 2350 BC), despite the region's self-image as belonging to a single civilization. If third-millennium city-states, thus, are the logical outcomes of rapid social evolutionary trends at the end of the fourth millennium, their destiny was to compete unceasingly for the best agricultural lands and for access to trade routes. Although political unification was a likely result of such endemic conflict among city-states, it was equally improbable that the independent traditions of city-states could be overcome and that they could be easily integrated into a regional polity.

Egypt

A quite different evolutionary story can be seen in Egypt. Around 4000 BC, the material culture and social forms of sedentary groups in different regions of Egypt and the Middle Nile was of a fairly uniform Neolithic/Chalcolithic character (Wetterstrom 1993); few signs of social complexity are to be found (Midant-Reynes 1992). Nonetheless, some material and ideological elements of inequality typical of later periods can be seen in the southern Nile Valley, in the Naqada I culture (e.g., Bard 1994:68–75). Notable among them is the emphasis on elaborate burials and the realm of the dead. While the apparent prominence of this sphere owes much to the siting of cemeteries in the desert, where they could be excavated, the expenditure of resources is striking. Moreover, the crucial site of Hierakonpolis contains a small group of Naqada I tombs that are distinctively larger than anything else of that date, suggesting the prominence of a single leader and providing a topographical marker that was significant for the later, Naqada II inhabitants of the area (Hoffman et al. 1982:38–60).

The Naqada II culture (from c. 3500 BC), which originated in Upper

Egypt, is a more important watershed (cf. Baines 1995a; Kaiser 1990). Naqada II was culturally distinct from the A-Group of Lower Nubia, as well as being no doubt politically separate, while the Ma'adi culture, which covered the region north from the Fayyum, disappeared in the middle of the period. Ma'adi had strong links with Palestine, which may have been a focus of southern interest in expanding northward. In a process whose political ramifications cannot yet be charted, Naqada II material culture, which probably encompassed several polities in Upper Egypt, spread throughout the northern part of the country, and all of Egypt had a single material culture by the final subphase of Naqada II or the beginning of Naqada III (c. 3200 BC). Around the same time there was significant contact with Mesopotamia, attested most tangibly at Buto in the Nile Delta and probably routed through the Uruk colonies in Syria. It is a moot question how crucial this contact was for Egypt. Since the chief stimulus to political and cultural development came from the south, which was farthest from Mesopotamian influence, it is not likely to have been decisive.

On the low desert bordering the Nile Valley, the sites of Hierakonpolis (in the far south), Naqada, and Abydos show the greatest expansion and differentiation. All have small separate cemeteries of rich tombs; Hierakonpolis Tomb 100 (mid-Naqada II) has wall paintings with royal content. At the end of Naqada II, an outlier of the culture appeared in the northeastern delta at Minshat Abu Omar (Kaiser 1987; Kroeper and Wildung 1994). Sometime around this date, the whole country probably was united under a single king buried at Abydos in central Upper Egypt, while the previously largest site of Naqada was in sharp decline (some scholars argue for Hierakonpolis as the unifying polity and others for a slower pace of unification).

Tomb U-j in the elite cemetery at Abydos shows a range of royal symbols, as well as the earliest use of writing in a secure context, on small ivory tags that the excavator suggests were attached to bales of cloth among the grave goods (Dreyer 1993; Kaiser 1990). This royal tomb is some generations earlier than those nearby in Cemetery B, which form a rough sequence, generally termed Dynasty 0, ending with the well-known Narmer. The phases before and after Tomb U-j could have lasted up to 250 years. Symbols of kingship from Dynasty 0 are found all over Egypt, and their motifs supply the principal evidence of a developing centralizing ideology. The archaeological phase Naqada III corresponds to this time and the early First Dynasty.

In this development, the strongest evidence of social complexity dates to the time after the country's material culture had become uniform, and much of it after the territorial polity had formed; but since the amount of evidence increases sharply with unification, this appearance may be rather misleading. There are indications of walled settlements and elaborate brick architecture.

Much else is beyond recovery; settlement sites are virtually inaccessible beneath the floodplain silt, whereas cemeteries were sited for preference on the low desert. Cemeteries evince massive consumption of luxury goods, involving the mounting of expeditions into the deserts for minerals; long-distance transport of goods, including many Palestinian imports and probably delivery of basic foodstuffs; and the presence of specialized artists and craftsmen alongside the nascent scribal group. The inner elite was integrated into a small group of administrative officeholders near the king. These people, who were almost certainly literate, were bound to the king both by office and perhaps by membership in a distinct group (the $p^c t$) that would have consisted of notional or real kin and who were qualified for the highest office. Even if this group once existed as a distinct entity, it quickly became a retrospective fiction (Baines 1995a:133).

Elite and other cemeteries became numerous in the Memphite/Cairo region—which has been the focus of population ever since—and also are scattered through the country. These cemeteries demonstrate that in Dynasties 0–2 resources were by no means so narrowly concentrated on the king and inner elite as in the following period, and they probably attest to a gradual erosion of elite privileges that existed before and during unification and centralization. They set the stage for the foundation of the city of Memphis at the start of the First Dynasty, when administration and the requisite people were focused there, while royal burials and perhaps the ceremonial center remained at Abydos. In this period, burial and the realm of the dead consolidated their position as a principal mode of display and signification, as well as a consumer of resources. Burial sites were basic to Egyptian society, and especially to the elite who could aspire to a privileged afterlife denied to those who had no proper burial.

The Egyptian state's characteristic territoriality is evident at the frontiers. The First Cataract region was annexed during Naqada II and was henceforth the southern boundary. In the north, Egypt asserted a brief hegemony in southern Palestine, probably founding some small colonies there, but withdrew during a recession or consolidation in the mid-First Dynasty. In Lower Nubia, the royal cemetery of an A-Group polity around Qustul that imitated the style and iconography of Egypt was thoroughly vandalized (Williams [1986] sees Nubia as the source rather than the recipient of these styles), and the A-Group itself disappeared, leaving an archaeological vacuum—but probably not a complete habitation blank—spanning more than 500 years. It seems that Egypt wished either to incorporate and exploit a politically weaker culture in the surrounding area or to set up a cordon sanitaire, within which its unitary civilization long stood in isolation (for a Nubian-centered view, see W. Y. Adams 1977; O'Connor 1993). These features contrast strongly with Mesopotamia's treatment of its neighboring cultures.

The Pace of State Evolution

Although the Neolithic progression from the first sedentary agricultural villages in which sites and social institutions became progressively differentiated and stratified was protracted, political centralization emerged rapidly in both Egypt and Mesopotamia. Apparently, the various aspects of rivaling and cooperating groups, both occupationally specialized and socially distinct; the complex routes of circulation of goods, services, and information from both local and long-distance ventures; and conflict with neighboring cities and regions all built up a head of sociopolitical and ideological steam manifested in the emergence of new leaders, new forms and symbols of centralized authority, and new demographic shifts. In detail these processes look very different in the two areas, and their phasing was complex. In Egypt, a cultural and political development with the elaborate forms of state and kingship emerged toward the end of the process; in Mesopotamia, forms of social and political struggle were never quite resolved by kings, and regional states were atypical and unstable.

POLITICS AND ECONOMY

The earliest political system in third-millennium Mesopotamia was the network of city-states that endemically vied for arable land and access to trade routes. Before the unification of Sargon of Akkade (c. 2350 BC) some ephemeral hegemonies were achieved by successful city-state rulers. Thus, it is not in Sargon's conquest but in his administrative and ideological innovations that a territorial Mesopotamian state was created (see below in the section on high culture as a vehicle for political and cultural change). The early Mesopotamian city-states, however, were also later the normative products of imperial breakdown and were the loci of political struggle, especially between the royal and temple estates (see earlier section on "kingship and other forms of rule"). In this section we delineate the contrast between the politics of early Mesopotamian city-states and the Egyptian tendency toward territorial centralization. Apart from temple and royal estates, community assemblies are prominent integrative institutions in Mesopotamia. Furthermore, the diversity of ethnic groups in Mesopotamia profoundly affected the modalities of social organizations and social and political struggle.

The centralized Egyptian state left much less evidence of how its political life and its regions were organized than can be gleaned for many periods in Mesopotamia. Internal conflict and disorder were largely suppressed from the record of all but decentralized periods, and signs of dissent that can be identified relate most often to personal antagonisms among the elite and to the disgrace kings inflicted on people or on their memories. But the monumental record is very uneven. Given the favorable conditions for preservation of the chosen style of display in tombs, its variations must attest, even if indirectly, to fluctuations in royal power. The play of central and regional forces and the tendency of the country to divide in periods of weakness exemplify the fact that strong centralization, while more easily achieved in Egypt than in many countries, exacted a price from all but the inner elite. The way in which this price was claimed from most people in the form of production and the curtailment of freedom can be modeled to some extent. What is striking is the relatively small proportion of history during which the country was not united and centralized.

Local Power

Mesopotamia has produced important but controversial evidence for the organization of local power, in terms of controlling both institutions and social groups. In one of the classic articles on early Mesopotamian history, Jacobsen (1957) considered that secular kingship arose not from sacral auspices, but from community assemblies. His argument was that incessant warfare in the earlier third millennium, as documented especially from the Lagash archives, required the election or appointment of a war leader. Other sources used for his argument were epic compositions (especially the tale of "Gilgamesh and Akka" [Katz 1993; for further notes on Enmebaragesi of Kish, see Katz 1995; Shaffer 1983]) and myths (especially *Enūma eliš*, the "Epic of Creation"; Foster 1993), in which assemblies (or councils) are mentioned. Critics (e.g., Evans 1958) rejoined that these poetic works composed in the second and first millennia were too late to refer specifically to third-millennium events, and furthermore, that it was naive to think that what happened in heaven reflected what was happening on earth. In the "Epic of Creation," moreover, it is at a banquet assembly of the gods that Marduk performs the magic trick of making a constellation vanish and then reappear, thereby convincing the drunken deities to choose him as their war leader. Whereas Jacobsen (1943) viewed Mesopotamian assemblies as a form of "primitive democracy," others thought that they were residual institutions of tribal, nomadic groups that were being progressively assimilated in urban Mesopotamia.

Jacobsen's argument received support from those studying land-sale documents (see earlier section on "kingship and other forms of rule"), in which the sellers of property were thought, especially by Diakonoff (1969), to be the "elders" of inferred third-millennium assemblies (see also Westenholz 1984, who discusses *ab-ba uru,* "elders of the city"). In Late Uruk and Early Dynastic lexical texts, the term "leader of the assembly" appears, and the sign for "assembly" occurs in economic texts from Uruk, Jamdat Nasr, and

Ur (Englund, Nissen, and Damerow 1993; Green and Nissen 1987. According to Englund, however, the sign conventionally assumed to be "assembly" is no more than the representation of a pot!).

Although references to assemblies are otherwise rare in third-millennium texts (Wilcke 1973), which mainly come from temple and palace archives, a term in the Ebla vocabulary texts has been interpreted as referring to an assembly (Durand 1989). In the early second millennium, from which there are many private documents, references in the texts to assemblies, elders, mayors, and judges are legion. Local authorities decide cases of family law and other matters not requiring royal intervention; headmen notarize the hiring of community laborers on palace estates; and it has been suggested (Yoffee 1988b) that the *babtum,* interpreted as a "city ward" by the *Chicago Assyrian Dictionary* (University of Chicago 1992), might be a patrilineage. In a brief essay on the *kārum,* Kraus (1982), like others before him (Walther 1917), noted that the term was not simply a collectivity of merchants, as it was in the Old Assyrian texts, but functioned as a judicial assembly. In the Old Assyrian texts, it is clear that there were "assemblies/councils of big men and small men" and a "city hall" in the city-state of Assur (Larsen 1976), and that the council shared power with the king, at least until the time of Shamshi-Adad's seizure of the kingship in the eighteenth century BC.

In sum, we may infer that political integration in Mesopotamia was not solely encompassed by the formation of centralized governmental institutions. Indeed, the evolution of the state government in Mesopotamia, which came to hold ultimate jurisdiction in matters of dispute among existing corporate groups, did not mean that the political functions of these groups ceased to exist. Such local organs of power typically represented both opportunities for the centralized state to channel local resources to its own advantage as well as arenas of resistance to the goals of the state—and thus were an essential locus of political struggle.

In Mesopotamia, the role of ethnic groups and their ability to mobilize personnel across the boundaries of city-states was one of the most important factors promoting political change (Kamp and Yoffee 1980). Thus, after Sargon's coup in Kish and his foundation of the new city-state of Akkade as his capital of a united Mesopotamia, the Akkadian language was employed in place of Sumerian as the primary language of administration. This linguistic switch, formerly interpreted as evidence of a new group of people—Akkadian speakers—entering Mesopotamia, is now seen as a mechanism to privilege scribes who could write in Akkadian and who were trained in the new royal court. Akkadian had been spoken in Mesopotamia for hundreds of years before Sargon's conquests, as is seen, for example, in the Akkadian names of scribes who copied Sumerian texts (Biggs 1967). In the Ur III period, when the imperial bureaucracy was swollen to unprecedented numbers, scribes conversely were trained in Sumerian and owed their positions to the new royal system in Ur (Michalowski 1987).

In the second millennium, with the political ascendancy of various Amorite groups in Mesopotamian cities, the inference is again no longer that there was an Amorite invasion: "Akkadeians" were in "Sumer" well before Sargon, and Amorites were in Mesopotamia before 2000 BC, interacting in a multilingual, multiethnic population. Amorites made alliances with—and against—other Amorites, mobilizing kinsmen across the countryside in the struggle for power within various city-states (Whiting 1987). Down to the middle of the second millennium, civil order in Mesopotamia was fragile, and it was negotiated both within city-states and among them. During periods of extreme political decentralization, "solidarity" within ethnic groups could be the decisive force in the struggle for regional power. In this instance, language change did not accompany dynastic political change: no document was ever written in Amorite, and Amorite rulers were careful to present themselves as reproducing venerable Mesopotamian cultural traditions in order to legitimize their rule.

In Egypt, the center aimed to control local offices in a way that was hardly attempted in Mesopotamia. During most periods down to the Greco-Roman, the goal of government administration in Egypt was generally to take as much power and as many resources as desired for the personnel and projects of the center. But the long, thin form of the country, with significant concentrations of specific resources scattered over its length, required much transport of goods, as well as organizational structures that could handle both local and central affairs (Fischer 1977; Helck 1974, 1977). How far the concerns of the provinces or of provincials mattered to the center no doubt varied, but the lack of a developed urban ideology at the center in earlier periods may have militated against extremes of neglect of the countryside and its inhabitants. The frequent presence of a southern national center at Abydos or Thebes, in addition to the political and economic center in the Memphite area, may have had a similar effect. Suggestive of the opposite possibility (neglect of the provinces) is that in Egypt today—a country whose basic orientation is toward the north (in antiquity it was toward the south)—few venture away from the dominant direction and travel south of Cairo.

A local administrative structure of nomes (provinces), of which there were nearly 40, was set up in the first few dynasties. This system appears to have respected traditional settlement patterns and loyalties to some extent, but it was a centralizing creation. Most nomes were similar to one another in size, arable extent, or population, and in many periods they were not favored as major administrative or political units, except for the densely populated Greco-Roman period. Some nomes therefore acquired significant roles while others are like ciphers. In several periods nome organization seems to have been passed over in favor of larger, more centralized groupings.

Two tendencies could disturb the efficacy of a centralizing administration: regional dissolution of the country, as in the First Intermediate period, and an overproliferation of central bureaucracy that stifled activity, as in the late Middle Kingdom. These two factors came together at times, but also could be distinct.

The state's essential strategy in creating the economic basis for administration was to found estates that were attached to central institutions or offices but geographically scattered (Jacquet-Gordon 1962). This pattern had the advantage, perceived by medieval centralizing rulers, of avoiding a concentration of landholdings controlled by a single beneficiary in a single place. It also probably brought economic and ecological benefits by exposing only small holdings to local risks of failure and diversifying forms of exploitation across regions. Important offices in the central administration (Strudwick 1985) were concerned with gathering and redistributing harvests and controlling animal wealth (less significant economically than in Mesopotamia). High officials held large numbers of titles, all of them providing sources of income or, as "ranking titles," marking positions in the elite hierarchy that were no doubt at least as important in the eyes of some holders as were substantive offices.

In addition to functions concerned with products of the land or of workshops and specialized production, important central officials had purely administrative duties, for example, running royal bureaus. There was much ceremonial and some seeming caprice, as during the mid-Fifth Dynasty, when a whole hierarchy of titles of "palace manicurists" briefly became prominent (Moussa and Altenmüller 1977:25–30). These functions or ceremonies centered on the person of the king and fostered contacts and networks that he may have exploited to shortcut elaborate administrative structures. In the later Old Kingdom there were frequent rearrangements of the hierarchy of rank (Baer 1960); the introduction of these no doubt helped the king maintain his dominance.

During the earlier Old Kingdom (c. 2600–2350 BC), this central, redistributive administration, one of whose principal concerns was to organize enormous building projects, was supported by a provincial administration (Martin-Pardey 1976), but the principal officials seem to have resided, when possible, near the capital—or at least built their tombs there. Little survives from the nomes themselves. This changed around the end of the Fifth Dynasty, when some officials began to be buried near nome capitals; toward the end of the Old Kingdom they increasingly displayed local loyalties. Unified rule collapsed around 2150 BC. Although the semblance of a single kingship was maintained, regional centers competed until rival dynasties (the Ninth / Tenth and Eleventh) were set up at Memphis (deriving from Herakleopolis) and Thebes; this development is known as the First Intermediate period.

The consequences of late Old Kingdom decentralization seem clear in retrospect, but the processes leading to it are disputed. Earlier writers argued that there was a positive weakening and loss of control, whereas some recent scholars have seen the innovations as a deliberate central response to changing conditions (e.g., Kanawati 1980). These approaches have contrasting weaknesses, the older one in working largely from hunch and the newer one in keeping close to the inscriptions and probably taking too much at face value their assertion that all was well. It is uncertain whether the nascent regionalism of the late Old Kingdom derived from a politically motivated identification by members of the central elite with local areas, or whether the leaders genuinely originated from the areas they came to champion and use as power bases. Two such strategies could have coexisted.

Although the dissolution of the Old Kingdom must be ascribed to some extent to regionalism, that of the Middle Kingdom (c. 1980–1640 BC) seems to relate more to bureaucratic proliferation and stasis at the center. The Twelfth Dynasty kings gradually suppressed nome organization and nomarchs in favor of a division of the country into four large units. Mid-ranking administrative offices began to multiply vastly, and a few leading officials acquired great power. Under the Thirteenth Dynasty, about 60 kings ruled for an average of around two years each, while officials held office for much longer. Prosperity was maintained initially, but there followed a political decline that led finally to the division of the country between ethnic Asiatics (the Hyksos) in the north and a local dynasty (the Seventeenth) based in Thebes.

These intermediate periods exemplify local regionalism and the breakdown of the country into two units (cf. Franke 1990). Later periods show other patterns of struggle for power more clearly. In the New Kingdom (c. 1520–1070 BC), the priesthood and the military emerged as distinct forces. The military acquired their position through imperial conquest, and subsequently through a response to invasion and immigration that ultimately brought ethnic Libyan groups to political prominence (Baines 1996; Leahy 1985). The priesthood derived their influence from enormous royal dedications to the temples of the fruits of conquest in the form of sacred buildings, goods, and land for endowment.

These more recent foci of power acquired a dominant role in the first millennium BC, when political life was more fragmented than that of earlier times. By the late eighth century the country was divided into numerous domains, only some of them ruled by kings. Yet Late Period (664–332 BC) and Greco-Roman (332 BC–AD 395) rulers were able to revive centralization and the nome structures, the latter perhaps through study of old records rather than through experience on the ground. Here, the maintenance of high-cultural and "scientific" traditions may have aided pragmatic government. The history of Greco-Roman Egypt, although known principally from the rural provinces of the Nile Valley and Fayyum, illustrates most strongly the ability of the center to dominate the country in its own interest (Bagnall 1993; Bowman 1996); in Roman times that center was Rome rather than Alexandria.

Economy

In the earlier Mesopotamian states (until c. 1600 BC, roughly the end of the Old Assyrian and Old Babylonian periods), the major economic units were palace estates and temple estates. For all periods, however, there is evidence of "community" and/or "private" organizations and families that owned land, the chief form of enduring wealth; mercantile associations and entrepreneurial traders contracted with temples and palaces to supply distant goods and to manage facets of their economies. The economic history of Mesopotamia must be written in terms of the dynamic forces of struggle among these economic sectors, and of degrees of intersection and cooperation among them.

Both the palace estates and the temple estates were, in essence, households. They consisted of large tracts of land, numbers of laborers and managers of labor, residential and ceremonial structures, and facilities for the storage and manufacture of goods. Older interpretations held that the early third-millennium temple estate was the primary focus of economic, social, and political activity—the so-called Tempelstadt theory (Falkenstein 1974 (originally published in 1951, refuted by Diakonoff 1969; Gelb 1969)—and gave way to totalitarian control of the economy by the state under the Third Dynasty of Ur; recent studies find the nature of economic activity to be far more complex.

In the early third millennium, for example, the physical structures of palaces and temples were separate, as were the units of land and personnel managed by them; there also were endemic antagonisms over the wealth of these estates. The trend through the third millennium was the familiar encroachment by the royal sector on sacral property (an opposite tendency to that observed in New Kingdom and later Egypt). This struggle, however, was a subtle one: kings required ideological support from the clergy and were important players in religious ceremonies (although the evidence for this comes from much later documents, such as the New Year ceremony texts preserved from the later first millennium BC [Black 1981; Thureau-Dangin

1921]). Kings recorded their dutiful activities in building and refurbishing temples; Early Dynastic kings were nurtured by goddesses and, in the Akkadian period (beginning with Naram-Sin, grandson of Sargon) and Ur III, were themselves deified. A temple to the deified Shu-Sin (fourth king of the Third Dynasty of Ur), which was constructed in Eshnunna by the local governor during that king's reign, shows that worship of the royal figures must be taken seriously.

There is an ecological reason for the development of the great estates of temples and palaces in southern Mesopotamia, a trend that is thought to run counter to the general evolutionary logic of the breakup of estates owned corporately by lineages into nuclear family units (Netting 1990). With the need to leave irrigated and potentially saline land fallow every other year whenever possible, ownership of large amounts of land enabled the great estates to minimize environmental risk and to shift personnel across the countryside while housing them in central locations in cities. Thus, the nature of the soil and the exigencies of irrigation agriculture promoted both corporate ownership of large landholdings and also nucleation and urbanization. As already noted, if cities were in part the result of centralizing agricultural activities, the phenomenon of urbanization is simultaneously one of ruralization. Furthermore, the trend toward "enclavization" of the southern Mesopotamian landscape in the early third millennium resulted in regions dominated by the city-states. Each region was composed of an urban complex, along with its productive hinterland. This arrangement led to warfare among the city-states for control of the countryside, which progressively increased the central powers of the royal estate over the temples.

Land-sale documents show that in the third millennium there also were large and wealthy "community" estates, while the existence of assemblies demonstrates that there were forms of community self-government. Even under the extreme control of the Ur III state, private economic transactions occurred (Steinkeller 1989), although Diakonoff, for example, has supposed that the Ur III kings sought to limit such activities, perhaps under some right of eminent domain they had instituted.

In the collapse of the Ur III state and subsequent absence of tight political authority, the economy of southern Mesopotamia was, as it were, let off the leash. Large private estates were formed, and new ways of circumventing partible inheritance practices were employed to keep the estates intact in succeeding generations. The most interesting of these was the assignment of daughters to "convents," preventing their marriage and the alienation of property that was part of their dowries (Harris 1964, 1975; Janssen 1991; Renger 1967). These "nuns" (*nadītum*), however, also enriched by movable property they were given in the form of "ring money," bought, sold, and leased property and loaned silver to such an extent that they became great real-estate entrepreneurs of the Old Babylonian period. Freed from the authority of husbands and fathers, they presumably led richer and more interesting lives than other women in Mesopotamian antiquity.

The increasingly wealthy "private sector" was further drawn into the economic activities of the royal and temple estates. Although no full picture of these interactions has yet been drawn, a number of detailed studies have appeared (Charpin 1980, 1986; Diakonoff 1985, 1990; Renger 1989; Stol 1982 [reinterpreting Koschaker 1942]; Stone 1987; van de Mieroop 1992; Yoffee 1977, 1982). While there were strong differences between north and south Babylonia (which cannot be enumerated here), an important similarity is that the great estates employed large numbers of outside people in addition to their own staff of dependents. These private contractors, members of the "community" rather than of the temple estate or the royal estate, supplied the estates with food (from fish to meat and wool products) and notarized the hire of laborers on the estates' fields. In times of political centralization during the reigns of Hammurabi and Rim-Sin in the eighteenth century BC, the state naturally tried to control this independent sector, but in the time of weakness towards the end of the Old Babylonian period, the power of these private contractors grew enormously.

In the Old Babylonian period, the economic resources of the great estates were not small. On the basis of van de Mieroop's study (1992) of the texts from Ur, dating to c. 1984–1864 BC, some figures can be cited to illustrate this point. Tablets from the warehouses attached to the Ningal temple complex record (mostly annual) deliveries (from various years) of 140,000 liters of grain, 50 tons of dates, a group of 31 shepherds managing about 20,000 sheep, 16,803 cattle inspected, 18,710 liters of ghee, 16,200 liters of cheese, and 1,498 kg of wool. The temple storehouse also purchased 9,600 liters of bitumen from a private businessman for 1 kg of silver. In one text a group of merchants delivers 4,123 kg of copper to the palace. During the same early Old Babylonian period, the royal estate controlled some 23 km^2 of land.

Such enormous quantities of goods were produced not only in the "redistributive" sectors of the temple and palace estates. In Ur, private entrepreneurs organized the fishing industry, engaged in long-distance trade, supplied bread to the palace, and functioned as money lenders. One individual loaned 1.03 kg of silver to a colleague at 20 percent interest that was due in one month! An individual sent 14,700 liters of bread or barley to the palace. Another businessman rented a boat with a capacity of 9,000 liters for a business trip.

It is not necessary here to repeat the importance of the private sector to the Assyrian economy in the Old Assyrian period. As numerous studies have shown (e.g., Larsen 1976, 1977, 1982, 1987a; Veenhof 1972, 1980), private merchants transported tons of tin and textiles to central Anatolia and made huge profits on the silver and gold markets there. The Assyrians did not control access to any resources, but they were expert in moving goods from where they were plentiful to where they were scarce, transacting business, forming joint banking partnerships to accumulate capital, and taking advantage of the lack of political centralization in the areas they exploited. Finally, it is worth repeating Larsen's (1976) judgment that the merchants were important players in the Old Assyrian state, members of councils in Assur, and provided reasons for state military intervention in foreign lands.

We have unavoidably drawn a superficial and too coherent picture of economic behavior in earlier Mesopotamia. Research on the relations among the various sectors of the economy, especially the private economy; how these relations changed through time; and how economic activities were restrained and/or facilitated by political processes has changed our understanding not only of the production and distribution of goods and services in Mesopotamia, but of the structure of Mesopotamian society itself.

The Egyptian economy is neither as well documented nor as well understood as that of Mesopotamia. The best known periods are the late New Kingdom (c. 1300–1100 BC) and the Greco-Roman period, but the monetization and "colonial" character of the latter differs from the situation of earlier times. The general picture is an extreme one of a centralized, command-driven economy (e.g., Janssen 1975b), but one that, contrary to today's wisdom, worked acceptably for long periods (see Kemp 1989 for a contrasting interpretation). Much interpretation has been in the shadow of Karl Polanyi, but there is no consensus as to how viable his approach is. Both the overall context and the detail of its operation are poorly known (see, e.g., Helck 1975). In particular, the proportion of economic life that is covered by the sources cannot be well estimated—as is true also for today's command economies—and this unknown leaves the picture of subsistence strategies and private enterprise uncertain. Because of these difficulties, discussion tends to focus as much on issues of social organization and administration as on economics more narrowly defined.

There was no "money," although various units of account and exchange were used. The highly administered sector of the economy may have touched the lives of most people relatively little, except to the extent that they had to pay rents or taxes. The fact that most organization was in terms of goods and the appropriation of labor, rather than of credit and such abstractions, may have restricted what the center and, in particular, what entrepreneurs could do. (This is not to say that the Egyptians could not work with abstractions: legal documents often record regularizing fictions [e.g., Eyre 1992; Lacau 1949], while grain was lent at interest in a local context [e.g., Baer 1962:45].)

The state's basic economic interest was in ensuring that the land was cultivated and in exacting taxation or rents from the produce. The state was then responsible for storage and redistribution, notably of grain, in particular to those who did not produce for themselves. The state and temples made many craft goods in their own workshops. Specialized workers were paid essentially in emmer wheat for bread and barley for beer, the two staples of the Egyptian diet. Much production was channeled through state institutions (e.g., Posener-Kriéger 1976). The elite appear to have received their remuneration primarily in the form of land, from which they could derive an income, and of other productive elements such as herds. The Old Kingdom elite presented itself in tomb decoration as enjoying vast estates that produced most of the necessities of life and many luxuries (e.g., Harpur 1987). This picture is idealized, but it is one pointer to how the monolithic character of the command economy might be tempered by a more complex reality.

Apart from securing what was needed for the daily life of the center and of specialists, major building projects, with their attendant requirements for expeditions into the desert to extract raw materials (including gold), were an important part of economic life and often of international relations. There is a clear correlation between monuments and centralization; hardly any major monuments were constructed in decentralized periods, but when the country was centralized the amount of construction varied in both the short and the long term. This pattern is anything but economically "rational" and clearly obeyed other dictates (e.g., Morenz 1969). Two periods when the resources invested in construction were at their greatest were the Fourth Dynasty, with the building of the largest pyramids, and the late Eighteenth and early Nineteenth Dynasties (c. 1400–1225 BC), with vast temple and tomb building by Amenhotep III, Akhenaten, Sety I, and Ramesses II (as well as major private monuments). Even during these periods, there were significant interludes without major construction. (Theories that the great pyramids, and the ziggurats of Mesopotamia, were constructed as some sort of unifying project for the country—e.g., Engelbach 1943; Mendelssohn 1974—founder on this difficulty.)

Land was held on a use-value rather than an absolute basis of tenure, although parcels might remain in the same nonroyal hands for centuries. Generally, the cultivator was not the owner/tenant; most land belonged to large institutions, including royalty, high officials, or perhaps wealthy individuals. Cultivators were not free to leave their land. If land, whoever controlled it, fell out of cultivation, the state assigned it to a new responsible tenant and collected revenues from that institution or person (e.g., Gardiner 1951). Those who fled and left their land uncultivated seem to have become vagrants who were then organized for labor by a state works department (e.g.,

Quirke 1988) and put to essentially the same tasks as those they had abandoned. In Greco-Roman times, it was temples that performed this resettlement function (Posener 1975). The reason for this regime—which is perhaps characteristic of command economies while having obvious analogies with feudal patterns—was probably that people were in shorter supply than land (see Baer 1962); such evidence as can be gathered suggests generally low levels of population density and life expectancy (Bagnall and Frier 1994; Baines and Eyre 1983:65–74).

Salient questions raised by this rather bleak picture include how major institutions meshed their economic activities together, how far the command economy could provide the requisite range of goods, and the extent to which there was an independent "private sector"; the latter two are closely related.

Relations between institutions have been discussed primarily for the New Kingdom (e.g., Janssen 1975b), from which numerous economic documents are preserved (Gardiner 1941–52; Gasse 1988). These sources suggest that the principal crown and temple institutions were not economically distinct, and that temples, in particular, could provide storage and supplies for state concerns and interests. The state also could use temples as administrators or as intermediaries in the transmission and import of goods. Nonetheless, the basis of temple power, which was in landholdings, allowed the high priest of Amun in Thebes to become politically autonomous at the end of the New Kingdom (c. 1070 BC; Jansen-Winkeln 1992; Kitchen 1986:248–54). The region in which the temple of Amun was the principal landowner, which stretched from the First Cataract to about 150 km south of Memphis, with its northern border fortress at el-Hiba, became effectively independent during the Third Intermediate period.

Representations of marketplaces, where small numbers of perishable goods were sold, are found in Old and New Kingdom reliefs and paintings (e.g., Altenmüller 1980; Hodjash and Berlev 1980). A late New Kingdom administrative papyrus records the voyage of a ship belonging to a temple along the river. The ship dispenses clothing and honey, probably from the temple's estates and workshops, to women on the river bank; in return the women give these and other goods, the latter presumably ones the temple did not produce itself (Janssen 1980). This is one of the few clear cases of an interaction of "state" institutions and the private economy (on transport, see Castle 1992).

More detailed material, which shows the privileged artisans who built the New Kingdom royal tombs trading among themselves and selling their services, derives from papyri and ostraca (inscribed flakes of limestone and sherds) from their desert settlement of Deir el-Medina (Janssen 1975a). Among the most revealing aspects of their lives is that some of the artisans, who were amply salaried state employees, owned land in addition and farmed it or employed people to farm it (McDowell 1992a). They were thus also small-scale entrepreneurs with diverse interests. Such a finding does not, however, warrant the more generalized assumption of Kemp (e.g., 1972, 1981, 1989) that the major institutions and principal officials of the land were "trading for profit" on the basis of the incomes they derived from cereals and more specialized produce. Evidence Kemp (1981, 1989) has cited from the size of storage installations at the short-lived city of el-ʿAmarna may not support his case in the way he suggests (see Janssen 1983 for one alternative); more probably it relates to the vast numbers of dependents for whom such people were responsible, to conspicuous display of material resources, to the need to maintain massive stocks against crop failure and other contingencies, and perhaps to control of seed stocks issued in the form of loans (known from the Ptolemaic period; e.g., Crawford 1971:26).

Other aspects of individual enterprise fit more characteristically within the command-economy structure. People tried, notably in the Old and Middle Kingdoms, to set up endowments that would secure their mortuary cult in perpetuity (Goedicke 1970). This mechanism, which both king and elite members employed, created exemptions from general patterns of tenure and obligation; but the longevity of such foundations is uncertain, because the cults themselves seldom survived more than a couple of generations in anything like their original form.

Administrative and priestly offices were bought, sold, and made into family inheritances, at least from the Middle Kingdom, attesting to the success of officeholders in appropriating as personal property something to which they were appointed by the crown. In a grandiose example from the Second Intermediate period (c. 1620 BC), a high official "sold" to a kinsman the office of mayor of Elkab, a major town south of Thebes, for the equivalent in accounting terms of 5.5 kg of gold (Lacau 1949). The transaction was registered in Thebes, the capital of the day, and ratified by being set up on a stela in the city's principal temple. The transfer itself was a fiction, devised to honor a debt that the vendor was otherwise unable to repay to the purchaser. The debt in itself has economic significance, as does the prevalent activity of tomb robbery, because both exemplify what one might expect, that substantial amounts of wealth were dispersed, in ways that are invisible to us, through what cannot have been official, command-driven channels. Nor can the materials derived from such activities have been secret: they must have formed part of the conspicuous display of the wealthy, as well as being recycled again and again in tombs. Such evidence illustrates that a high proportion of economic activity is not accessible to study; these gaps must be drawn into any overall model.

The best illustration of how little the Egyptian economy was oriented toward major private activity may be given by the intermediate periods, from which there is little evidence for significant entrepreneurship and much for such local grandees as nomarchs taking over traditional royal functions of administration, military action, storage, and largesse. One also can contrast dynastic times with the progressively monetized Greco-Roman economy, from which there are attested such features as banking, forward sale of standing crops (Pierce 1972:81–93), and elaborate internal accounting on great estates (Rathbone 1991). Nonetheless, the essential thrust of the Ptolemaic economy, like its predecessors, was state control, which extended through taxation, ownership, or regulation to the most minor activities (e.g., Bowman 1996:56–121).

Insufficiencies of Political and Economic Analysis

Perhaps most clearly for Egypt, we have encountered areas where the data resist analysis in primarily political and economic terms. In a socioeconomic perspective, the essential difficulty is created by the scale of inequality in the ancient social systems and by the vast expenditure of human and material resources on such projects as pyramids and major temples, or simply the burial equipment of a minor king like Tutankhamun. In Mesopotamia, where the economy was more diversified and contested than in Egypt, the relation between politics and economy was itself very complex. Political goals were shaped through the forces of production, consumption, and distribution; rulers alone did not dominate these economic spheres. Also, while the economic activities of members of local groups were affected by policy goals of the state, one still needs to ask to what extent these political goals were motivated by economic factors.

Inequality, such as existed in both civilizations, created a large surplus for a small elite—the ruling group of high officials in Old Kingdom Egypt numbered perhaps 500 people (Baines and Eyre 1983:66); this required legitimation to the people from whom the surpluses were exacted, or so modern analysts tend to suppose. Although state formation created great economic potential, its consequences may have left those below the elite, after the exactions required of them, in an economic condition similar to that of their prestate forebears. Throughout the history of the early state, the majority of people hardly had alternatives or points of comparison beyond their own societal environment; this limited perspective would have reduced the requirements of legitimation, in comparison with those the outsider may feel to be necessary. Data on "lower-class" residential areas, nonelite burials, and the material inventory of people who are absent or depersonalized in writing (all of this more accessible for Mesopotamia than for Egypt) provide some evidence for the status of such people and of their social groups and the way in which they were integrated into society as a whole.

While traditional forms of local social organization and their "moral economies" may have retained some validity for the nonelite, precisely because the state (and/or large manorial estates) removed from them the means of storage and provision against misfortune, the state appropriated the salient discourse on the constitution of social order. Although we should not assume that those outside the elite always accepted the rhetoric of their superiors, state legitimations were generally designed so that elites could exploit rather freely the resources available to them. Elites were able to be profoundly separate from the rest of their societies. This separateness extended to the system of values, which was hardly accessible to those outside an inner social layer.

Despite the residual survival of the moral economy on which their inferiors relied for a legitimation of their dependence, elites had little regard for the human lives of those whose efforts they were eager to utilize for their own grand plans, taking huge disparities of circumstances between groups for granted. Only rarely and mainly in the later stages of these two ancient states did the moral economy appear to a significant extent in the texts. Since much of society was involved in the execution of the grand plans, additional values and interests must have held societies together both in these goals and more generally. But the analysis of those plans needs to focus principally on the elite groups and on the ways in which they created and sustained among themselves the mechanisms for supporting and ensuring the success of specific types of goals. These elite values were not only political; economics were a means more than an end. Political and economic analysis only partly addresses elite motivations. In the next section we outline a different approach to these issues, which are common to the study of many civilizations.

HIGH CULTURE

Context and Definition

The inner elite controlling ancient Near Eastern (and presumably all other) states and civilizations were few; during early postformative periods their numbers became further reduced. In Egypt, this process culminated in the Fourth Dynasty (c. 2500 BC), when a high proportion of the country's resources was devoted to the king's funerary monument. The number of the surrounding, less grandiose tombs of the inner elite suggests that this group consisted of no more than a few dozen male officeholders, in a population of perhaps 1–2 million for the entire country. These men formed the central decision-making group, who together with their families controlled and enjoyed the fruits of the country's labors. The group was larger in other periods, but it can never have numbered far into the thousands.

The more populous and numerous city-states in Mesopotamia did not gather resources to a single center in the same way, but in Mesopotamian civilization, too, wealth and status were highly concentrated. The urban implosion that began in the late fourth and reached its apogee in the mid-third millennium accentuated the formation of an urban inner elite that is reflected in extravagant practices, such as the mid-third-millennium royal tombs of Ur and other cities. The lexical "list of professions" shows that many bureaucratic titles already existed in the late fourth millennium, as well as names of occupational specialists and community officials (Civil et al. 1969; Englund, Nissen, and Damerow 1993; Green and Nissen 1987). Few of these, however, can be described as privileged elites. In all periods, these Mesopotamian elites, which included high temple officials, private land-owners, community elders, and wealthy traders as well as high military and administrative officials, however numerous they may have been, formed a minuscule percentage of the population, as can be seen by comparing lists of officeholders in later third-millennium texts with the vastly greater numbers of people who received rations during that period.

The formation and maintenance of elites, and then of elites within elites, lie at the heart of civilizations: inequality is fundamental. For these two ancient civilizations, the option of equality or of a serious search for an integrating "moral economy" hardly existed (contrast with Classical Greece; Morris 1997). Cosmological elaborations and "political economies" are among the features that can distinguish civilizations from noncivilizations. The formation and entrenchment of such inequalities set the evolutionary trajectory toward civilization apart from trajectories that led to less differentiated and stratified societies.

In the most ancient civilizations, elites controlled material and symbolic resources but were scarcely subject to cultural requirements to disburse them in fulfillment of social obligations. The distinctive achievement of archaic civilizations is as much to transform the meaning of wealth as to create more wealth. Elites control symbolic resources in such a way as to make them meaningful only when it is they who exploit them. This appropriation of meaning is complementary to, and at least as important as, other legitimations available to controlling individuals or groups. There is also the "religious" affirmation that cosmic order is maintained only by the activities of leaders, typically of the king and the central priestly officiants or, if religious imperatives are acted out in the wider world, of the military.

These elite activities are characterized by the massive appropriation of material resources, which are put to use in the enduring forms characteristic of ancient states. Such resources are due to the ruler and elite because they are the carriers of exclusive and expensive cultural meanings that require such exactions for their maintenance and development. Elites, as the principal human protagonists and prime communicants to the deities who are the supreme members of the total society, require the highest products of culture (cf. Chang 1983). High culture, therefore, is one of the essential loci, even the essential locus, in which order exploits wealth for legitimacy. Here, high culture becomes self-motivating and self-sustaining, while its meaning-bearing acquires a measure of autonomy through the expertise and internal discourse of the specialists who maintain it.

These points are not new. As is widely accepted, if not in precisely these terms, high culture is a central phenomenon of most civilizations from the ancient Near East until today. Large-scale democracies and social movements, among others, redefine high culture in terms different than those of the ancient civilizations we are considering; few dispense with it. Cultural pluralism, however, turns the question of what constitutes high culture into an issue that appears to have been largely absent in our cases. This point will become salient for Mesopotamia, where the existence of many ethno-linguistic groups tended to promote rather than fragment high culture.

Despite the significance and centrality of high culture, it often does not receive its share of attention as a factor in the creation and maintenance of elites and civilizations. It is ironic that, while archaeologists acknowledge the importance of high culture when they recover elements of it in the physical record, they tend, for understandable reasons, to place more value on evidence for less exclusive social phenomena. The general public, with its interest in "treasures," may here be closer to the ethos of ancient elites than are socially aware archaeologists.

We take high culture to be characteristic of civilizations rather than simply of states, and we see the boundary between one form of high culture subscribed to by local elites and another as the boundary between one civilization and another. We define high culture as *the production and consumption of aesthetic items under the control, and for the benefit, of the inner elite of a civilization, including the ruler and the gods.* The phrase "aesthetic items," rather than "works of art," is intended to encompass a wide range of domains including visual art, visual, verbal, and musical performance, garments, perfumes, and the most highly prized food and drink. The phenomenon also extends to such extravagant forms of "traditional" practice as big-game hunting, the keeping of exotic animals, and the breeding of highly specialized ones. At the extreme, the whole lives of the ruler and elites are aestheticized, as well as strongly ritualized—the two aspects being mutually supportive. The range of high culture is such that it can accommodate a diversity of interests and aptitudes among rulers and inner elite.

The aesthetic character of high culture does not imply that works of art are ends in themselves. Many scholars object to the term "art" as applied to non-Western cultures, and we do not wish to engage this issue here (see

Baines 1994; Hardin 1993). Works and practices of high culture are strongly aesthetic, but the aesthetic element is mostly integrated into some broad context, such as the conduct of royal and elite life, religion, festivals, or provision for the dead.

Communication, Expertise, and Restriction

High culture is a communicative complex: it enacts, celebrates, and transmits meaning and experience. It incorporates writing systems as well as artistic production, and in doing so, it may mark a distinction between writing as a specialized medium of expression and as a broad instrument of social control. The spiritual, moral, and intellectual content communicated in high culture may be realized in visual art and architecture, in which case it can be largely independent of verbal form, although in Egypt the verbal and the visual are very closely integrated (e.g., Baines 1989b; Fischer 1986). We discuss some issues relating to writing below, while noting here that because of writing's verbal character, the content of its less materially extravagant manifestations is in theory available through language to anyone and is more difficult to control and integrate into the high-cultural complex than is visual art. Literature, initially no doubt in its oral forms and integrated with other elements of performing art, contains the most complex and multivalent responses to the exclusive character of high culture (Parkinson 1998). Literature may, on occasion, be subversive of the high-cultural order, but in our two cases such tendencies were mostly kept in check (Vogelzang and Vanstiphout 1992). Even what is superficially subversive can be incorporated into a richer pattern that confronts the complexities of human experience and reaffirms the established order, as we illustrate in our discussion of each area.

Yet the communication of high culture appears as if subverted. It addresses itself to very few. Many richly communicative objects are deposited in places where no one could ever apprehend their communication. In this regard, past, future, and the world of the gods are as important as producers or recipients of the communication as is the present world. Part of the extravagance of high culture is that its message should be fully received by few or none.

The exclusiveness of high culture requires formalization, probably because simple wealth is always too crude a criterion for access to elite activities and concerns. Thus, access to high culture is controlled not just by wealth but also by social hierarchy, rank, initiation or the holding of specific offices, kinship or other group adherence, or a mixture of these. Moreover, the forms that are crystallized in high culture are vital to the institution as a whole. We consider formalization and access under the categories of knowledge, style, and the maintenance of tradition.

Knowledge is a vital element in the control of cultural resources. Crucial parts of high culture itself, or of the meanings that sustain and motivate them (Baines 1990), may be secret. Such restriction of knowledge is common to all societies, but it has special ramifications for inner elites. Much of what is involved may be recondite without being secret, as may be true notably of conditions surrounding works of art. Obvious aspects are the amount of learning involved in becoming a provider of high culture, either as a specialized artist/craftsman or as a performer, and the special and restricted settings in which such activities take place.

There is a corresponding, if less onerous, investment in being a full consumer. Only those who have the time and inclination are in a position to appreciate the products of high culture, and even they may not do so, being "philistines" who are wealthy enough to consume without appreciating. These possibilities vary with social forms and, no doubt, with individuals. Thus, the professional, literate elite of Egypt may have been more directly involved in the production and the meaning of works of art than were nonliterate elites in Mesopotamia (where literacy was restricted to scribes who were not necessarily members of the controlling elites), or other semi-independent and landholding elites in such places as medieval Europe. But because of the great significance of high-cultural items, the elite almost always exercise some control over them, even if its members lack relevant expertise. Members of elites use high culture and access to it in mutual competition for status.

Style is produced within the broader elite and consumed principally by the inner elite. Style is vital to a civilization's definition and to its demarcation against what lies outside. High culture has specific carriers and a particular status as a tradition, and it is integrated in particular ways into a civilizational, cultural, and stylistic context. Typically, the visual forms of a civilization are so distinctive that an informed onlooker can identify them at a glance. While this applies especially strongly in Egypt, one easily discerns "Mesopotamian" styles from "Syrian," "Iranian," or "Anatolian" ones.

In most cases, a civilization's style (which is different and more encompassing than pottery types or lithic types as "styles") is more or less coterminous with its extent in space and time. The style is created in a high-cultural context, is sustained by an elite that commissions and consumes the works that transmit the stylistic tradition, and incorporates fundamental values. In the case of Egypt, this fusion of style and values is central to a system of decorum circumscribing and sustaining high-cultural artifacts and activities (Baines 1985:277–305, 1990:17–21). The values may often be submerged or tacit, but they are no less powerful for not being expressed in verbal form. This value-laden stylistic complex is crucial to the transmission of the civilization's essence through time (Assmann 1992).

The aesthetic character of high culture is a powerful legitimizing force, because works of art and architecture involve great material outlays, and often or mostly require activities that can neither be expected of the consumers nor provide directly for more than a small proportion of society. Both in the dedication of high-cultural products to deities and to the ruler, and in the consumption of those products by the elite, there is little questioning of the view that it is impossible to do things in a less extravagant way and that the necessary labor is provided by a dependent workforce.

The transmission and interpretation of high culture is a significant preoccupation of the elite, reinforcing their status as a community of discourse. This community, with its many shared interests, diverts attention from the effects of the attendant inequality on the rest of society. To the members of the group commissioning, consuming, and creating the works, those outside are hardly of account.

As indicated, the producers and the consumers of high culture are normally not identical. Despite the importance and scale of artistic and high-cultural production, the executant mostly has the status of, at best, a privileged member of the broader, as against the inner, elite. The existence of specialized craftsmen among this larger elite, and the privileged position of the overlapping group of the literate, create subgroups who share concerns both with the inner elite and with the rest of society, partially bridging the gap between the two poles. This limited involvement of producers with elite concerns strengthens the position of high culture, because several interest groups are involved directly in its propagation. No doubt even the broader exploited society—which is itself not a homogeneous whole—has an interest in the maintenance of the high-cultural complex because it is seen as a stabilizing institution and, ultimately, as an almost unalterable given.

But these mitigations of the divisions introduced by high culture do not alter the fact that the phenomenon itself necessarily encompasses only a small proportion of society, and that its prime intent is to remain restricted. Moreover, in the absence of advanced technology or gross exploitation of outsiders, the production of elite high culture adversely affects the material culture and living standards of the rest. Thus, high culture contains an inner dynamic and a paradox: it seeks to legitimize the whole order of society, along with the role of the elite, as cosmologically just. If it is to do so without simply imposing authority from above, it must offer real or perceived benefits to the rest of society, but those who count most in perceiving the benefits are once again the elite.

Civilizations must *maintain their traditions* if they are to persist for long periods. These traditions form complex entities. The complex of high culture, whose full extent can be modeled from the archaeological and historical record, is ideally perceived as an entity but tends not to be transmitted as one. Its precise range, the style of its components, and their development and potential all change, but either at a slow pace—which may seem faster to the intense and informed interest of the actors—or in a "punctuated" phase of innovation or reform, the latter often being presented as a revival of the past. Revivals, too, may not seem to the outsider to be such, because what is done appears sufficiently new for the notion of revival to appear out of place. In Western art, phases of renewal have often gone under the banner of return to antiquity, and calls for such returns are often more artistically genuine than a nonartist may accept. Their essential aim is to distance the artist from immediate predecessors, for which purpose a good point of reference is the more remote past, with the degree of remoteness depending on various factors (Baines 1989a: 135–40; such uses of the past are generally the opposite of the modern ones described by Lowenthal [1985]). What is less conceivable for the ancient context is the creation of an altogether different style, or still less a different representational rendering of nature (see next section).

Some writers on Egypt who do not use art-historical methods or are concerned more with a theoretical abstraction from the works than with specific analysis take the slow pace of artistic change as indicating that the purpose of the art forms—and hence for our purposes of the high-cultural complex—was to stifle change (e.g., Assmann 1992:169–74; Davis 1989). Such a view is difficult to reconcile with phases of significant change, as seen in Egypt with the new literary and artistic forms in the Twelfth Dynasty (c. 1900 BC) or in Mesopotamia with the production of "wisdom literature" (Lambert 1960; see conclusion) and the development of relief carving in the first millennium BC (e.g., Winter 1983), and with the ample high-cultural evidence for interest in novelty and its display. High culture persists in a fruitful tension between maintenance of the status quo and renewal or change, and readily incorporates both. The notion that its aim is stasis may be influenced by its suppression of radically different alternatives, which is integral to the identification of civilizations with their high-cultural styles. Only when that link is broken, as it was in the eastern Mediterranean with the civilizationally heterogeneous Persian Empire and its successors, does a more rapid rate of change come to seem normal or desirable.

One way in which the high-cultural complex does have restrictive tendencies is in the primacy of visual forms. In our cases, this primacy should be connected with the tendency to anchor cultural forms and central values in symbols that are more readily recalled and more stable than are verbal modes. The complexity of the artifacts carrying these meanings in a high-cultural tradition is one factor that favors the elite and the executants most strongly in their role as guardians of a tradition. Here, we see no need for a particular explanation of Egyptian civilization as striving especially after permanence and opposing change and competition (e.g., Assmann 1991:5–92); for Mesopotamia, Irene J. Winter (e.g., 1983) has elegantly developed a case for the existence of intraelite competition.

The Persistence of High Culture: "Two Cultures"?

The division between elite and the rest leaves open the question of whether the rest have a different culture or values from those of the elite (not the same as Assmann's [1991:16–31] "two cultures"). So far as archaeological and epigraphic evidence in Egypt and Mesopotamia goes, that does not seem to be the case. Rather, elite high culture appears to stand in contrast to a poverty or an absence of distinctive materialized ideology for others (DeMarrais, Castillo, and Earle 1996). Of course, our sources are desperately biased in the attempt by ancient elites to assert and propound just such a state of affairs, since both the cohesiveness and potency of high culture are compromised if it is divorced from the culture of the rest of society.

Nonetheless, the social conditions in which ancient states and civilizations formed appear partly comparable to more modern ones in which social historians have seen a drawing apart of elite and other culture (e.g., Sharpe 1987:122–23; Thomas 1978:3–24; Wrightson 1982:220–21). Enormous disparities in wealth create ample opportunities for difference and legitimize the need for cultural elaboration among the elite. At the same time, major disruptive social movements and changes in settlement patterns result in the extensive displacement of older social forms and their moral economies (cf. Scott 1985). These changes all could and did lead to the self-conscious formation of rival ideologies in some ancient states—and in the modern world. But this evolution did not happen in ancient Egypt or Mesopotamia; "Axial Age" cultures (after Jaspers, see Eisenstadt, ed. 1986) were a later development.

Essential factors favoring the persistence of high culture in Egypt and Mesopotamia seem to lie in the lack of available effective alternatives within the same culture and, until the first millennium BC, even in neighboring cultures. The assumption that only the native culture had validity appears to have applied in both Egypt and Mesopotamia, where the civilizations persisted for many centuries after foreign rule had become the norm (Yoffee 1988b). The view that one's own polity constituted the cosmos existed in both large and small states (Liverani 1990).

The Formation and Exploitation of the High-Culture Complex

Since the main focus of our work is not on origins, here we need only to recall the speed with which high cultures appeared in Mesopotamia and Egypt. Although the changes of the late fourth millennium built on what came before, the transformation of art, the introduction of writing, and the centralization of symbolic structures all suggest that new meanings and values were arising from the cauldron of state formation. We further infer that the evolution of centralized government and an inner elite was seen as having the mission of enhancing the new order through its exploitation of the wealth it created. In the new social and cultural hierarchy, the invention and elaboration of high culture become self-legitimizing. We explore below how this happens and how the high culture is maintained.

This legitimation also relates to the issue of change versus stability, since both are goals of elites. Egyptian and Mesopotamian civilization endured for longer than any of their successors and achieved great consistency and stability of primarily high-cultural style. This style was adhered to by ruling groups, and it was maintained and transmitted by them and by specialists on the edge of the elite. In considering Egypt one can set aside short-term political instability, which often affected only the inner elites. The pace of change in any period could have been almost imperceptible to the actors (whose generally short lifespans render change more difficult to perceive than it is for us); this imperceptibility was no doubt deliberately sought, for it reinforces the image of the high-cultural order as given and immutable. In Mesopotamia, the high culture was maintained in the face of numerous episodes of political and other change, and it was reproduced to render such changes orderly and legitimate.

An illustration of the value of restricted transmission incorporated in works of art is the early Egyptian complex of representation and writing (Baines 1988a, 1989b). Egyptian writing divided from the beginning into a cursive variant used for administration and the "monumental," hieroglyphic form used in works of art. In early times neither encoded full syntactic forms of the language, yet the limited forms endured for some centuries. Writing was an adequate and valuable tool of administration, even with little expression of syntax; in art it essentially supplied captions and was not needed for continuous text. Captions were integrated with figural representation to form a genre of record and display of such things as royal exploits; in combination with the power of the visual image, this created a form that was probably more effective for being laconic. Moreover, the visual qualities of the hieroglyphs, and their interaction with fully representational images and with an intermediate emblematic mode of representation (Baines 1985:41–63, 277–86), created an enormously powerful complex; the best parallels may be in Mesoamerican artistic practices (e.g., Marcus 1976c, 1992c; Reents-Budet 1994). These features were embedded in the system of decorum already mentioned.

Most of the surviving early objects that bear hieroglyphs and pictorial representation are quite small (e.g., Adams 1974), many of them dedicated in temples that were accessible only to those qualified by office and by induction into the cult. The larger pieces, such as royal mortuary stelae, were set up in the desert, far from settlements, where only mortuary priests would see them. Their communication cannot have been addressed to people at large, or even to a large proportion of the elite. Rather, they addressed society in the widest sense, which included the gods and the dead; their creation was a focus of elite interest and discourse; and they related to a broader past and future. The cultural complex of which they formed a central part became self-sustaining and value laden.

The centrality of artistic forms was reinforced by the way in which they defined the cosmos and implied its maintenance, celebrating the world's order and arranging it into hierarchies in which god and king were central. Somewhat paradoxically, even the elite play a relatively modest role in early works. This reticence may have a legitimizing force: what are most significant are the gods, the cosmos, and the king. These essential components can be seen as important for all of society and not just the elite, even though the rest could not have had access to the objects that codified these conceptions. Probably few of them were aware of much of what the artistic hierarchies and system of decorum implied.

The domains of early Egyptian art had a specific configuration that reinforced their high-cultural character. The most characteristic surviving products from around the beginning of the dynastic period are small-scale relief carvings, decorated ivory objects (e.g., Quibell 1900:pls. 5−17), and stone vases (e.g., el-Khouli 1978), some of which almost constituted sculpture in the round. All have precursors, even though there are gaps in the inventory among types of objects that might be expected to survive, notably high-quality, three-dimensional stone sculpture. Stone vases were complemented by copper and possibly precious metal containers, of which few survive (for copper, see Emery 1949−58[I]:18−58, pls. 4−7).

Already in Predynastic times, stone vases, most of whose raw materials had to be fetched by expeditions into the Eastern Desert, were vehicles of conspicuous consumption, finished to a high level through great expenditures of labor. The First Dynasty brought a vast increase in production that must have required huge numbers of craftsmen. The sculptural qualities of the vases (e.g., Fischer 1972) are superior to anything in other media from the period. By the late Second Dynasty, major royal stone statuary appeared. Apparently at a stroke, the Third Dynasty innovator Djoser buried tens of thousands of vases from the First/Second Dynasties under his Step Pyramid, the first such monument to be constructed; not all these deposits have even been surveyed (Lacau and Lauer 1961−65). Stone vases never again had the same importance as prestige products.

The vases have been found in temples and in nonroyal and, especially, royal tombs. The most significant indications of their function come from inscribed examples from Djoser's monument. It is uncertain whether their uses were also typical of the uninscribed vases, but the inscriptions show that they were used in temple rituals. A number were inscribed with names of phyles, elite social groups evidently involved in major rituals (Roth 1991: 145–95). They seem to have been significant artistic furnishings of structures that might otherwise appear to be culturally less important than the mortuary monuments (but see O'Connor 1992). Some vases also could have been destined for royal or elite ceremonial use.

Two points emerge from this example. First, genres of high-cultural materials were pervasive in all attested contexts of elite action. It is not clear whether any of these actions involved public display of the objects, or whether the objects were accessible only to their immediate users; temple and tomb contexts were in any case semisecret. Such large numbers of people participated in the manufacture of the vases, however, that their status in the high-cultural sphere must have been well known. Second, high-cultural genres could belong in any domain: the emphases among them cannot be taken for granted. This genre, to which a rather wider elite probably had access in the late Predynastic period, was annexed by the small central group. Emblematic stone vessels, whose meaning could only be comprehended by those who knew some writing, point to the completely high-cultural character of the whole genre; they were not marginal, and the significance of their Predynastic precursors was transformed.

The best-known early relief sculpture is on palettes and maceheads from the late Predynastic period and Dynasty 0 (c. 3200–3000 BC; Asselberghs 1961). The latest exemplars, the Cities and Narmer palettes and the Scorpion and Narmer maceheads, convey normative values that endured through dynastic and Greco-Roman times. Their principal organizing features are strict register composition and the hierarchical system of decorum, whose crucial aspect here is that it centered on representations in human form of king and gods (often with animal heads) interacting equally, without other human participation. Such scenes characterize temple relief, which is not attested until the late Second Dynasty although it very probably existed earlier, as is suggested by parallels in the partially pictorial year tags of the First Dynasty. The palettes and maceheads ceased to be made at the beginning of the First Dynasty, leaving a gap in the range of "monumental" genres. The finest First Dynasty stone reliefs are carvings of royal names on royal mortuary stelae from Abydos (e.g., Lange and Hirmer 1968:pl. 6). Rather more informative nonroyal stelae, which ranked far below royal reliefs, appeared by the late First Dynasty but are artistically inferior (e.g., Emery 1949–58[III]:pls. 23b, 39).

Thus, stone relief carving, which was vital in the artistic development of central ideology, seems to have disappeared from public contexts in the First Dynasty. The general absence of high-quality work, in contrast with the representational mastery exhibited in stone vases, cannot be due to lack of competence; it must relate to production in lost contexts—perhaps small-scale temple reliefs within the floodplain—or to the transfer of skills into other media and genres. Whichever was the case, these genres were appropriated to the largely invisible context of decoration within temples, and they focused on scenes of king and deities that continued to form the core of the system but did not become publicly visible for 1,500 years. Artistic skills were divided into the more public, but still high-cultural, component of stone vases and the largely secret one of temple relief, so that hierarchies within the supernatural and the elite were reinforced artistically, with the gods and the king as the ultimate authority that provided the core of meaning. State formation, legitimation, and hierarchization were thus played out in art, to the shorter-term detriment of its availability even to the inner elite. Although the communicative core of high-cultural forms remained, negotiation with them was thus essentially through restriction of access.

This restriction can be exemplified in writing, the most ostensibly expansive domain of high culture. Developments in writing, architecture, and artistic style exemplify ways in which the high-cultural complex is elaborated. It is typically Egyptian that the first known major changes in the writing system, in the late Second and early Third Dynasties (c. 2700 BC), extended its use to speeches of deities to the king, as well as being used to proclaim the king's receipt of a favor from a god on a seal inscription, and thus do not focus on general human utility or display. Nonroyal use of continuous writing in prestige contexts did not develop significantly until the Fourth / Fifth Dynasties (c. 2550 BC), during and after the period of maximum centralization and construction of the grandest monuments. Until then, visual forms of very limited currency, rather than verbal ones, remained the most important expressions of cultural values.

These developments share with wider historical processes the characteristic of being "punctuated" changes identifiable in subtle high-cultural shifts such as the status of stone vases, as well as in grosser features. In the complex of high culture, superficially minor changes or innovations can be profoundly important. Limitations we may discern in the initial complex, such as the absence of continuous written language or of topographical rendering in pictorial representation, may not then have appeared as such. The complex as it was must have been adequate for the demands placed upon it, since it received the enormous material and cultural investment required for its maintenance (arguments in Cooper 1989 and Michalowski 1994 touch on this point for Mesopotamia).

The way in which developments appear to mirror change in power relations, and to document the maneuvers of different interest groups, is probably too neat, because the integrated artistic system acquired its own momentum and detailed execution was in the hands of subelites rather than central elites.

Nonetheless, the high-cultural complex was so important that the main elite must have participated in changes.

The general development of the First–Fourth Dynasties was toward ever more extravagant and elaborate monuments for the king and for a diminishing proportion of the inner elite. There is a striking contrast between the extensive and widespread cemeteries of the First/Second Dynasties and the central Fourth Dynasty, when almost all major tombs were at Giza, surrounding the king's massive pyramid (for a provincial exception see Garstang 1904).

The Giza tombs were broadly separated into two groups. The highest-ranking tombs were sited between the Nile Valley, on the east, and the Great Pyramid, while the slightly less prestigious were sited to the west of the pyramid (e.g., Dunham and Simpson 1974–80). All were massive and, for the first time, constructed in stone, and they partook in a grandiose undertaking that projected elite hierarchies into the next world. The secondary, western group lacked public decoration and, thus, marked a step back from the finest tombs of the previous generation. The concealed stelae and sculptured heads found in the tombs (e.g., Smith 1949:pls. 5–9, 32) show that art of the highest quality was available to these people (see also Russmann 1995:118). Even though relief decoration may not have been carved in earlier tombs of the same status—which belonged to extremely few people—its absence in these Giza tombs constituted a severe restriction of choice in the context of a generally increased potential of writing and an existing decorative repertory. This restriction conveyed in high-cultural terms the appropriation of all major symbolic means to the king and his immediate group, most of whom were members of his family. It also may have related to a wider use of such media in lost temple contexts. An aesthetic aspect of the development is visible in the contrast between the full decoration of the temple of Snofru at Dahshur (Fakhry 1961) and the remarkably austere and abstract style of the Second Pyramid complex of Re'kha'ef (Khephren) at Giza (e.g., Arnold 1992:198–202; Baines 1994:77–78).

This development was reversed by the end of the Fourth Dynasty, and more clearly in the early Fifth, when both royal and nonroyal monuments became smaller but richly decorated, and the beginnings of a nonroyal "literature" appeared in the form of inscriptions in elite tombs containing extended titularies and brief narrative passages (Baines 1998). This change was political as well as cultural. A narrative preserved in a literary work from a millennium later implies that the transition from the Fourth to the Fifth Dynasty had the sanction of the sun god Re', the principal deity, and was in some sense subversive (Lichtheim 1973:217–22). Yet both dynasties accorded Re' great prominence, and an explanation in such terms does not appear evident. Rather, there may have been struggles between elite groups that mildly disfavored the kingship, which never again had quite the same control of symbolic and material resources, and favored a strongly entrenched elite that was not closely bound to the king by kinship. This development restricted the role of the royal family, while probably enlarging the general ruling group. A crucial point of contention appears thus to have been the restriction of display and high-cultural resources. Those associated with the Fifth Dynasty spread these resources a little more widely, at least in semipublic display on the monuments.

The broader society did not participate to any great extent in such transitions; rather, high-cultural resources were exploited both for their own sake and for their political potential. The nature of the material at issue is also significant: the eventual development toward a more widespread literate high culture was very difficult to reverse. No later reversal comparable with the progressive restriction of the far less literate First–Fourth Dynasties is known, although there was much variation; the indigenous temple culture of the Greco-Roman period, which was significant in many ways for the whole country, was accessible only to tiny numbers.

As before, those outside the inner elite appear not to have had a significant historical role. What becomes visible is the existence of different factions within the elite; one of these factions evidently offered benefits to somewhat more people than did the tiny central group of the Fourth Dynasty. Later in the Old Kingdom people exploited their old and secret religious knowledge in the play of status (Baines 1988b), again indicating a diversity in the inner elite, which was then probably larger, if not wealthier. Such displays, which rely upon shared high-cultural values, are part of the currency of status competition in all ancient states.

In Mesopotamia, writing lies perhaps still more at the heart of high culture than it does in Egypt. Mesopotamian high culture crystallized at about the time of the formation of the first city-states, but its raison d'être cannot be explained simply as part of the political and social transformations of the Uruk period (Yoffee 1993b:64–68, 1995). Writing was from the start concerned not only with economic recording but also with the re-creation and standardization of Mesopotamian cultural "encyclopedism"—the description and systematization of titles of people and things that became part of the high-cultural complex. Although writing as a semiotic system was invented in the late Uruk period (Boltz 1994; Michalowski 1990, 1993b), and "lexical lists" appear among the first tablets (Englund, Nissen, and Damerow 1993) and were used as part of the scribal curriculum, Sumerian writing did not achieve much standardization until the mid-third millennium BC. It is remarkable that such standardization owed little to political developments, since the early third millennium was a time of endemic warfare among city-states. It was in a multilingual environment of independent city-states that systems of measurement and mathematical notation became regularized

(Friberg 1978–79; Powell 1989–90); indeed, it was because of the need to write Akkadian names that the Sumerian script became increasingly phoneticized.

Emblematic of the formalization of systems of communication and education across independent polities is a particular corpus of cylinder seals (mainly attested in the form of sealings), called "city seals." Their decoration, which consists mainly of the names of city-states, has been interpreted in various ways. Jacobsen (1957) thought the names implied an early Sumerian "amphictyony" (Hallo 1960), a league of cities bound together as a community of worshipers. Wright (1969), Nissen (1988), Matthews (1993), and Michalowski (1993c) consider the cities listed to document trade routes— the seals to have been applied to vessels whose movement and storage were thus charted. Another view holds that the names on the seals do not reflect either a political grouping or an economic purpose, but are signs whose playful combinations were charged with symbolic meaning (Yoffee 1993c, 1995b). It is suggested that the names of cities are written not with some functional goal in mind but as a metalinguistic reflection of the cultural interaction that also included the process of linguistic standardization that was occurring in the Early Dynastic period.

For Mesopotamianists, more emphasis has always been placed on the linguistic than the artistic in the preserved Mesopotamian record. This apparent dominance may depend to a considerable extent on the media used in ancient art, many of which are poorly preserved in tells; nevertheless, the "limited" character of Mesopotamian art (Porada 1979) is easily contrasted with the far more extensive artistic record from Egypt. Egyptian highcultural forms that found material expression were primarily mixed visual–verbal. In contrast, Mesopotamian ones were more strongly verbal. Although even this weak generalization breaks down if one reviews evidence for, and scholarship of, the first-millennium states, we concentrate on the highcultural complex as it can be read in the cuneiform sources.

Whereas some Mesopotamian texts—for example, private letters—relate to informal speech, most tablets are administrative or private records or school texts. Indeed, the formal education required for scribal proficiency (Civil 1992; Sjöberg 1975) included belletristic compositions, lexical lists (lists of gods, official titles, vocabularies), ritual texts, and other compendia (Civil 1975) that Oppenheim (1977) and Machinist (1986) have called the "stream of tradition." While the nature of the "canon" (a term perhaps misappropriated from biblical studies but in wide use) changed over time, it is significant that such texts were consciously collected, edited, commented upon, and copied to the end of Mesopotamian civilization (Falkenstein 1951, 1953; Hallo 1962, 1963; Lambert 1957; Michalowski 1993c).

As the context of the scribal schools themselves changed from the Old Babylonian period (early second millennium), when "school texts" are found in private houses (Charpin 1986), to the first millennium, when private libraries were owned by priests (Parpola 1983) and schools were affiliated with temples, so the context of the texts themselves changed. For example, epic compositions of the early second millennium such as "Atrahasis," which contains a creation story, were part of a ritual in the first millennium, when the text was used to cure barren women (Lambert and Millard 1969). Although social and economic records and certain correspondence (especially in the Old Assyrian and Old Babylonian periods, when the writing system was the simplest; Larsen 1987b:219–20) were written at the behest of elites, the art of writing was inaccessible to the population at large. Written texts spoke to other written texts, and a high-cultural corpus of written matter reinforced the separateness of the inner elite and scribal class. Although scribes themselves did not often achieve the status of elites, they were themselves not independent of the institutions of palaces and temples and never became semiautonomous guilds of literati, as Hsu (1988) describes for Han China. As in Egypt, some written texts faced walls or were placed in mountain aeries: these impediments to sight, however, mattered little to the intended divine readership.

Again as in Egypt, high culture was mobilized in, and formed a leading part of, major political and cultural changes. It is a commonplace in Mesopotamian scholarship to note that Sumerian texts were learned well after the time when Sumerian was actually spoken (c. 2000 BC), and indeed until the end of Mesopotamian civilization. This continuity of an aspect of high culture illustrates well the power of the textually denoted Mesopotamian discourse community (Cooper 1993). By this term, at least for Mesopotamia, we obviously do not mean the vast majority of Mesopotamians, who could neither write nor understand the arcane language of belles lettres, religious texts, or royal pronouncements. Rather, it was the inner elite (and their scribal dependents) who sponsored and reproduced the texts that delineated the hierarchies composing the world and defined the critical roles of rulers and gods. There were, however, enormous changes in political systems throughout Mesopotamian history, and it was the role of high culture to be flexible enough to legitimize and naturalize those changes.

In the middle and late third millennium, official writing systems changed at least twice. With the conquest of the House of Akkade, Akkadian became the normal language of the administration, and scribes/bureaucrats were trained in new ways in Akkadian as well as Sumerian. In the Ur III period, Sumerian was again the language of the bureaucracy, and scribal schools were reoriented in the new imperial structure (Cooper 1973; Michalowski 1987). Ur III rulers, however, sought to depict themselves as descendants from the heroic past, avowing their kinship with Gilgamesh and other kings of legend from the city of Uruk. In scribal schools, as well as in the inculcation of new administrative language, tales of these kings were copied and/or composed. High culture was thus manipulated in order to legitimize new kings, a new bureaucracy, and new imperial rule.

In the second millennium BC, after the fall of the Third Dynasty of Ur, the governments of city-states in Mesopotamia were progressively seized by Amorite leaders, and the number of Amorite personal names in the texts also increased. By the end of the seventeenth century BC, one royal edict describes the population of Babylonia as "Amorites and Akkadeians" (Kraus 1984). Naturally, scholars (beginning with Clay 1909) have sought to identify Amorite social institutions and systems of beliefs that ought to accompany these political and demographic changes. However, ascriptions of new levels of private enterprise as a reflection of the business mentality of Semites (Pettinato 1971)—whatever that might be—or new marriage customs deriving from a tribal past (Falkenstein 1956–57) are oddly juxtaposed against the absence of any texts written in Amorite. Indeed, it is the lack of large-scale culture change in early second-millennium Mesopotamia, other than those economic and social changes that can be accounted for as internal historical developments (Yoffee 1995b), that can be explained as a conscious policy of the new rulers of Mesopotamian city-states.

Seizing political power in city-states, Amorite leaders contested not only with local elites but also with other Amorite elites. One mechanism that advantaged Amorite leaders was their ability to mobilize support across the countryside, that is, beyond the borders of the autonomous city-states. In a letter from the king of Uruk to the king of Babylon, the former appeals for help against enemies because the kings of Uruk and Babylon are of "one house" (Falkenstein 1963:56), presumably of one particular Amorite group (the Amnanum Amorites). These Amorite rulers, having successfully gained power in Mesopotamian city-states, made sure that Mesopotamian high culture was reproduced faithfully. The Akkadian language of Hammurabi of Babylon (descendant of the same Amorite ruler of Babylon mentioned in the letter cited above from a king of Uruk), as embodied in his "Law Code," is regarded to this day as a classical text to be assigned to first-year Akkadian students; most of the Sumerian poetic compositions that were presumably composed in the late third millennium are known from schoolboy copies discarded in Nippur and Ur in the Old Babylonian period.

After the collapse of the Old Babylonian order in the mid-second millennium, the Kassites, who spoke a non-Semitic language (an isolate, possibly evolved in remote valleys in the Zagros Mountains), established a new dynasty in Babylonia. Their family structure, composed of landholding lineages (Brinkman 1980), seems distinctive in this period. The *kudurrus* (boundary stones) of the Kassite period are similarly distinctive, and the Kassites were endogamous (Maidman 1984). Yet the literary and high-cultural corpus of the period is traditionally Mesopotamian. Inscriptions on cylinder seals are written in Sumerian (Limet 1971), and the great scribal guilds of the first millennium traced their origins back to the Kassite period rather than to earlier times (Lambert 1957). The "author" of the late version of the Gilgamesh epic lived and worked under the patronage of Kassite kings.

In the last days of the Neo-Assyrian period (late eighth century BC), when the population of Assyria included many thousands of subjects who had been forcibly resettled, especially from the Levant (Oded 1979), and the language of the Assyrian empire was becoming progressively Aramaicized, the Assyrian warrior kings appealed increasingly to venerable Mesopotamian cultural traditions. In a famous example, Assurbanipal, the last great Assyrian king, was obsessed with collecting all possible texts from Babylonia, including those arcane ritual texts that were incomprehensible to Assyrian kings, citizens, and subjects alike (Machinist 1984/85). Similarly, in the sixth-century-BC Neo-Babylonian empire, kings like Nebuchadnezzar and Nabonidus faithfully emulated the styles of Babylonian kings who ruled more than a millennium earlier and launched "archaeological" expeditions to recover their Mesopotamian past (Beaulieu 1989).

The composition of the *Enūma eliš*, the "Babylonian Epic of Creation," represents a major change in Mesopotamian religion. Although one still finds arguments that the work was written in the Old Babylonian period (e.g., Dalley 1989:228–30), none of the manuscripts dates before about 1000 BC. Lambert's argument (1964) that it was the return of the statue of Marduk to Babylon at that time from Elamite captivity that provided the inspiration for the text remains plausible. The text's major point is, of course, not the creation of the world, but the accession of Marduk as paramount among the gods. Threatened by primordial monsters, the fearful gods give a tremendous banquet, become drunk, and, after witnessing the performance of a magic trick, sign over to Marduk the supremacy of the universe. Other texts imply that the personalities and powers of all the gods are now simply parts of the ineffable nature of Marduk (Sommerfeld 1987–90).

Through this movement toward henotheism (or perhaps monotheism), Marduk (Bel) became the most important divinity in the Babylonian pantheon. This religious change, however, was cast in the most conservative possible terms, squarely within the high culture of Mesopotamia. The *Enūma eliš* borrowed its motif of a god competing with monsters from much older Sumerian compositions, especially the contests of the dragon-fighter Ninurta (Lambert 1986; Machinist 1992). Whereas a former generation (Kramer 1944) thought that all Mesopotamian literary compositions ultimately went back to Sumerian prototypes, the reason why such older motifs were used in the *Enūma eliš* was precisely to cast religious change within the idiom of high-cultural conservatism. The very unoriginality of the poem's structure, and its ultimate mid-first-millennium raison d'être as part of the New Year ceremonies, suggest that those who composed it were trying to achieve the maximum Mesopotamian orthodoxy for their new theological doctrines.

Ethnic groups in Mesopotamia, far from fractionalizing Mesopotamian high culture, served to promote it and safeguard it (Yoffee 1988b). Precisely by appealing to high culture, new political elites could legitimize their participation and leadership in Mesopotamian society. Even large-scale theological change represented no challenge to the high culture, but could be molded as part of it.

Examples of the significance of high culture, of the concept's analytic utility, and of its application to various contexts could be multiplied. Those we have chosen are intended to illuminate comparisons and differences between Mesopotamia and Egypt, especially by marking differences in the manipulation and reproduction of a textual "canon" in the former and the salience of visual modes in the latter. It is worth citing one further case that exemplifies points we have been arguing.

In Middle Kingdom Egypt (early second millennium) belles lettres were introduced and a retrospective golden age of civilization was created and sited in the Old Kingdom (e.g. Baines 1989a:135–38). The late Old Kingdom was the artistic point of departure, whereas belles lettres looked to the reign of Snofru, its first great king, and to famous names of the period as wise men (Helck 1972). Perhaps a little later, works that fictionalized more recent times were composed. None of this literature was "popular"; it was written within the elite for the elite (see McDowell 1992b for a later, slightly more "popular" local perspective on the past).

In Mesopotamia, too, Ur III kings looked back to Early Dynastic heroes, and Old Babylonian scribes copied panegyrics to the Ur III kings. For Mesopotamia the existence of a "popular" literature is also debatable. While "wisdom texts" (Gadd 1963; Lambert 1960) presumably reflect aspects of daily life and occasional street language, most of the texts use rare words, arcane grammar, and difficult signs that were accessible only to scribes.

Summary: High Culture

In brief, several distinctive features of change in high culture have been noted here. First, novelty legitimized itself not as something new but by its creative negotiation of an older, putatively timeless tradition (the "revolution" of Akhenaten in Egypt is the major exception; Baines 1997b). Invented traditions are archaeologically recoverable because they are sustained through visual forms that afford, among other things, the periodization and objectification that archaeologists mark in the material record. Such traditions are made feasible by writing and material high culture, which recursively enhance their meaning and which can be shaped by inner elites. In the cases we have chosen, then, change is particularly warranted in times when new political leadership requires stabilization and legitimation.

Major innovations in high culture were fundamentally important for the self-image of Egyptian civilization; later times looked to the Middle Kingdom as the "classical" epoch. Despite the continuing significance of the visual arts, the clearest later focus of this classicism was language and literature, so that the Middle Kingdom reforms of written language and genre acquired a retrospective conservatism that protected the continuity of Egyptian self-definition. In Mesopotamia, scribes in Hellenistic and later times were doggedly half-learning languages and textual traditions that were of little meaning or importance to anyone but themselves. Singing the praises of antediluvian sages (Klochkov 1982; Reiner 1961), they appealed to a tradition that now was totally divorced from any inner elite or high culture and was soon to disappear even from that marginal condition.

CONCLUSION: COMPARISONS, CONTRASTS, COLLAPSES

Order, Legitimacy, and Wealth: Coda

In this comparison of Egypt and Mesopotamia, we have attempted to delineate some critical institutions of these civilizations and to investigate what made these civilizations distinctive and what allows them to be compared. We have devoted little space to origins. In conclusion, we review our findings and consider still more briefly the collapse of the civilizations.

In the rapid crystallization of states in both regions, we see the rise of a new kind of order that reformulated the cosmos so that a new form of leadership and the principle of hierarchization were proper to the continuance of that cosmos. In all aspects, from the material and economic to the religious, the institutionalization, continuance, and, on occasion, expansion of the new order are the essential tasks of the leaders.

Although this ideological principle of order evolves or is invented in both civilizations, in Egypt the cosmos is firmly connected to one head of state and one organized system of values and beliefs; office and values are inextricably linked. Even the much discussed diversity of such conceptions as creation myths proves to apply principally to later periods (Bickel 1994). The manifestations of values and beliefs, which in the archaeological record begin with artistic forms, spread very slowly to extensive verbal forms and to texts of the type known from many civilizations (but are hardly preserved, for example, from Mesoamerica) as transmitting central concerns; the artistic forms are maintained for as long as the civilization.

In Mesopotamia there was no single political system, but a strong cultural sense of unity was manifest in the material culture and in standardized language and school curriculum. In part, this order was originally imposed because of the necessity to keep track of people and commodities, which is the logical outcome of trajectories toward differentiated societies that result in centralized administrative institutions. Nevertheless, the early trends toward standardization of written expression across separate and independent city-states and the counterfactual conception (especially vivid in the Sumerian King List) that there should be political unity in the land bespeak the existence of an overarching cultural sphere of interaction (Yoffee 1993a) that cannot be reduced to economics.

Order is more than a political necessity. It is the logic of a new way of thinking about society and about the cosmos, one that justifies the association of people who are not kin, especially those in the service of the inner elite, and establishes the principle of stratification and of limited access to wealth. Insofar as order itself creates a "natural" progression toward increased order, complexity, and hierarchy, especially in its high-cultural manifestations, it must exploit wealth for this self-enhancement; it cannot be generalized to everyone.

Wealth, together with its restriction to certain groups, is one of the most obvious facts of civilization. The acceptance of agreed measures of wealth and the creation of storable and to some extent convertible forms of it transform its social potential. The move toward imperishable forms is especially significant, even if fashion may bring an opposite effect by devaluing the wealth of the recent past. Wealth is displayed, and such displays require further stratification because it is obtained through the labor of others, from networks in which the negotiants are not kin, or from organizing the procurement of materials, some of them from remote regions, on a scale not feasible for kin groups alone. Wealth therefore requires new codes of communication that establish the ability to trade with foreigners and connect these distant people in a community of interests. Such activities assume a scale and importance hardly seen outside complex societies. "Interaction spheres" in the archaeological literature usually denote such elements of elite negotiation that interconnect people and regions above any commonality in ethnicity, language, or politics. Alternatively, wealth may involve "raiding" on a scale that is feasible only if highly unequal relations can be imposed on surrounding groups. In either case, civilizations contend in their search for wealth with other groups whose values and organization may be quite different from their own. In doing so, they must achieve more than a simple material domination; in ambivalent fashion, they must moderate and enhance their comprehension of those with whom they deal, assigning negative values to the world defined as outside and thus further limiting access to their own values.

The internal elaboration of order and its exploitation of and expression through wealth involve significant legitimation. The ruling elite must return benefits to the rest and to posterity. This return is made in matters of war and defense, economic security, and legal procedures, but above all in perpetuating the cultural patterns that establish and maintain order. These patterns include sacred rites, which may sometimes be the irreducible focus of elite activities, but they also extend to the entire high-cultural complex within which the rites have meaning. Kings and rulers must show their concern with the whole population by promulgating "laws" and edicts that present such concerns and by staging events in which spectacle and ceremony define the state's role. Through the common definition and labor of ruler and ruled, the arenas of temple, palace, city, and country in which the ruling elite act out their role, their concerns, and their privileges are constructed as interlocking representations and enactments of the cosmos and its maintenance. All these activities emphasize the dispersive ties between ruler and ruled, interweaving order, wealth, and legitimacy into the civilization's fabric. What they do not do is enact any legitimizing requirement that the elite redistribute the wealth created by order throughout society.

State and Civilization

We have insisted on the utility of employing the term "state" in the sense it took on in the European Renaissance: as the central, governing institution and social form in a differentiated, stratified society in which rank and status are only partly determined through kinship. We use "civilization" to denote the overarching social order in which state governance exists and is legitimized. As such, civilization includes the possibility of social resistance from groups both apart from and within the elite, since all participate in a community of interests within the civilization. Cohesive tendencies, disruptive tensions, and enduring continuities were played out in different ways in our two cases.

Although we have hardly discussed nonurban folk, peasants, and the nature of dependency, or kinship and how it is affected through time (Adams 1978), we have attempted to assess both centripetal tendencies and modes of local authority through assemblies and provincial and supraprovincial groupings. If we have dwelt less on the differential access to agricultural property than on the power that accrues through control of knowledge and values, that is because there has been far more study of obvious matters of political control and economic differentiation in ancient states than of what mattered most to those who led and motivated those states: cosmologies. It is a relief that some colleagues who study New World civilizations also have come to this conclusion (e.g., Demarest and Conrad 1992).

Mesopotamian states, which used to be considered centralized and stable or totalitarian monarchies (depending on the politics of the observer), are now regarded as inherently decomposable, incapable of instituting a region-wide form of administration. They sowed the seeds of dynastic destruction in the very act of conquest. It is suspected that ideals of Mesopotamian political unity and claims to control foreign territory are mainly attempts to justify ephemeral conquest and political rhetoric (e.g., Liverani 1993; Michalowski 1993a). The cultural ideals of a single civilization (as opposed to state), while easily incorporating diverse ethnic groups, languages, and social strata, could not be converted effectively to political ends. Separating political ideologies from cultural ones may at times seem odd to an onlooker from a large nation-state, but that seems precisely to have been the case in Mesopotamia. It would probably seem more natural to an inhabitant of pre-1870 Italy or Germany.

The Egyptian case differs from the Mesopotamian. Egyptian ideology focused on one or two centers, the administrative and religious capitals that were sometimes the same and sometimes not, and strongly on the frontier, especially to the south, which was in Egyptian terms the "front" (Posener 1965). The ultimate defining concern was with the dualities of Egypt and with what was within the Egyptian world and what was not. This interest in demarcations and boundaries that responded to the Egyptian environment was elevated into a general principle, powerfully visible in the architecture and iconography of temples (e.g., Arnold 1992:40–44; Baines 1997a; Winter 1968). Temples formed microcosms, enacting and symbolically encapsulating in nested layers a model of the order they defended and celebrated. The city around them could give that model enormous extra resonance (Kozloff, Bryan, and Berman 1992; O'Connor 1998). Each major temple, while following a similar architectural and cosmological model, was dedicated to a different group of deities, so that gods encompassed the land. Yet, just as the model of the temple dominated the diversity of gods, so the centralizing impetus dominated tendencies to regional variety (see Seidlmayer 1996 for administration, Bickel 1994 for ideas). As we have noted, Mesopotamian civilization, with its lack of sharp, permanent, internal boundaries and manifold interactions and interdependencies with the surrounding regions, was vastly influential as a totality throughout the ancient Near East, whereas Egyptian civilization, like Egyptian script and language, was far less disseminated except farther up the Nile.

The Collapse of Egyptian and Mesopotamian Civilizations

While the difference between the convergence of state and civilization in Egypt and their extreme divergence in Mesopotamia is enormous, it is the commonality of an active inner elite that defines these civilizations (perhaps all civilizations) as such. Another way of shedding light on their role is to look to periods of dissolution.

We suggest that political and economic change are not the decisive forces that determine dissolution and collapse. Here, we restrict our discussion to a single fundamental point: as we hope to show, it is the eclipse of the Egyptian and Mesopotamian cosmologies, and especially the subscription to them by elites, that defines collapse.

If alternative value systems were present in these civilizations, they were so weak that they neither had a major effect nor are visible archaeologically. In Mesopotamia even the most radical changes, in ruling groups and in religious orientations, did not take the form of systematic challenges to the core values of venerable traditions, but instead used such traditions to cloak and to legitimize change. However, after the conquest of Cyrus the Great in 539 BC, when new rulers accepted all possible belief systems as legitimate and deprivileged the Mesopotamian tradition from its connection with government and especially the bureaucracy and those contracting with it, Mesopotamian culture became progressively attenuated. Ultimately, only a few temples maintained it, and finally none. Mesopotamian civilization thus collapsed hundreds of years after the Mesopotamian state (see Yoffee 1988b).

Some reasons for the withering of Mesopotamian high culture and decomposition of the inner elite may have had less to do with political conquest by others. As Larsen (1992) has discussed, in a number of first-millennium-BC "wisdom literature" texts (Lambert 1960), it is the very orderliness of the universe that is in jeopardy. In a world in which any action or feature of the universe can and must be interpreted for the ruling elite, especially through the skill of the divination priests, uncertainty and even nihilism now became evident (Jacobsen 1976:226–39). Although it is unclear how much these learned texts reflect public feeling, it would require undue skepticism to propose that such emotions were felt only by scribes. No breakthrough to moral systems that would replace ceremonial ones, rationality that would supplant magic, or transcendental philosophies appearing next to state religions occurred (Garelli 1975; Machinist 1986; Oppenheim 1975; Tadmor 1986). The world had changed and Mesopotamian high culture, which had endured for minimally 3,000 years, could not.

The Egyptian case offers a clear ancient outsider's perspective on what mattered to a civilization (e.g., Bowman 1996). The Macedonian and Ptolemaic dynasties (332–30 BC) were culturally alien to Egypt, and in some respects lacked cultural self-assurance. They sought such assurance principally in the Hellenic world, but within Egypt the kings worked through the traditional elites, temples, and general cultural forms. The Greco-Roman period saw the greatest expansion of high culture in the numerous large and small temples constructed throughout Egypt and Lower Nubia (e.g., Arnold 1992), and for Ptolemaic times in widespread artistic and literary production. This cultural provincialization—since native culture was not strongly represented in the capital Alexandria, and Hellenistic culture was in second position outside it—had a partially leveling effect, because the entire native population could be set as provincials against the Greek incomers. There also was broad religious participation of a kind poorly attested from earlier times. Yet the main temples were even more elite products than their predecessors, with inscriptions carved in an arcane elaboration of the script that few could read. In relation to central patronage, it is characteristic of this development that the peak of temple construction in the south—financed by the ruler, not the local population—was around the time of the Roman conqueror Augustus (30 BC–AD 14). The Ptolemies and the Roman emperors made Greek the official language, and the Romans suppressed the traditional elite politically, but they had to use the core symbolic forms of the ancient civilization (it is said that only Cleopatra VII [51–30 BC] ever learned Egyptian, but also that she learned a host of other languages).

If we are not to follow Voltaire's Brahman interlocutor (see Müller-Wollermann 1986:1) and say that Egyptian civilization died because it had lived, it is difficult to explain its demise and inappropriate to attribute this to any single cause. So far as one can speak of demise, the notion that a civilization is an interconnected entity remains valid. While the world within the temples never accepted the Ptolemies as fully as it had accepted native kings (Quaegebeur 1989; Winter 1976), the changes imposed by the new rulers were not irreversible and are insufficient to have set the scene for dissolution. What seem more serious are the disappearance of a wealthy native elite in early Roman times, reduced integration of the temple high culture into local communities (Baines 1997a), and the difficulties of the Roman Empire in the late second and third centuries AD, which led to a worsening of general conditions (Bagnall 1993). This was when Christianity began to spread, being taken up in Egypt by both the elite and others (Frankfurter 1998). At this point, a reversal of interests is very suggestive. Although traditional Egyptian religion maintained a hold in the extreme south into the mid-sixth century, when pagan cults had already been suppressed in the empire, Christianity gained ground by accompanying a revival of the Egyptian language written in Greek letters (now known as Coptic) and was thus both a religious and a cultural rallying point for Egypt against the foreign rule that was now almost a millennium old. Thus, Egyptian civilization was long able to maintain itself in the face of foreign rule through its focus on the high-cultural concerns of religion. It was a new religion that provided some renewal, but in the idiom of a successor civilization.

These continuities and transformations—which focus on high culture even though Christianity aimed to reach more widely than its predecessor religion—appear far more significant in the long term than the vagaries of political and economic life. Egyptian high-cultural evidence also supports this view. In the religious ferment of late antiquity, numerous Gnostic, Hermetic, and related texts were composed in Egypt (mainly in Greek). Some of them eloquently formulated the connection between the maintenance of traditional culture and of what they saw as Egypt, turning to apocalypticism in presenting what would happen when the cult ceased to be observed (Fowden 1986). These developments were influential even among elites in very remote communities, as is documented by new finds in Dakhla Oasis. Some of these ideas can be traced in Ptolemaic Egyptian texts (Derchain 1990:25–28). Here again, the same preoccupations of ancient elites are at the fore.

Civilizations of the Ancient Near East and Ancient Civilizations

Finally, it is worth emphasizing that these two civilizations, emerging at roughly the same time and with some mutual contact at crucial stages, offer no justification for any concept of a unitary "civilization of the ancient Near East" (cf. the title of Sasson 1995). The two civilizations are profoundly different in mode of emergence, shape, nature of kingship, and avenues of resistance and change. In these differences we have found certain analytical concepts useful, notably that of an "inner elite" that provides an "order" to the civilizations, exploiting wealth and aspiring to be self-legitimizing through its role as the carrier of the civilization.

Even though our approach derives from thinking about the ancient Near East, we have formulated our initial statements on this point in an abstract, quasi-axiomatic form. This is deliberate, not because we can claim to have established patterns for, or still less studied, the whole possibly relevant range of civilizations, but because the enterprise of comparison may be served by a model that can, we hope, be assessed against other material, among which early China offers an obvious possibility (e.g., Schwartz 1985:1–55). We have alluded to modern civilizations that could not be described adequately in such terms; Classical Greece is another society with a different orientation, as probably are most major empires. Yet even in such cases, the positions of elites and the role they allot to high culture and to wealth may offer important elements of comparison.

In view of the central significance we give to cosmologies, an obvious point should be made, even though its role in distinguishing our cases from others is uncertain. In civilizations with autochthonous character that looked to no outside influence for their formation (whether such influence played a part or not), the ideologies of Egypt and Mesopotamia did not need to come to terms with a cosmology that would relativize their own presence as one society among many that could not claim global centrality. Many other states and civilizations—not just those that are often seen, following Karl Jaspers, as being on the other side of an "Axial Age" divide (e.g., Assmann 1990; Eisenstadt, ed. 1986)—are secondary in that they relate to an older civilization of the same general type and region. Yet the lesson of other examples seems to be that in this area elites and whole cultures can incorporate an overarching ideology and still have a local focus or a "galactic," regional one; the Buddhist and Hindu polities of India and Southeast Asia studied by Tambiah (1976; see also Geertz 1980) illustrate this phenomenon (for the ancient Near East see Liverani 1990:33–78). Universalism may be valuable for aspiring world empires, but otherwise it is something states and civilizations find uncomfortable, not least, perhaps, because it sits uneasily with the high culture of a particular civilization.

The principles we have outlined are not recipes for analysis, but they do allow certain kinds of comparisons to be pursued beyond the cases we have studied. We would ask, for example, what Mayanists may think is comparable to Egypt in the realm of an encompassing royal ideology that orders the universe. In Maya civilization, despite the prominence of the role of rulers, one finds no overall political state like that of Egypt; rather, in the political dimension, the Maya city-states (large and small, hegemonic and resisting hegemony) resemble the Mesopotamian ones—independent and fated to military and other rivalry under the belief that there should be one order that binds them all.

While we conclude that Egypt and Mesopotamia differed profoundly in their political and cultural organization, we wish to reaffirm strongly the value of the act of comparison. Through comparison we see exemplified what is unique in a civilization, why what works in one state does not work in another, and what is the more general shape of a civilization. We believe that "shape" and "style," although nebulous and hard to define, are vital to the actors, operating at deep levels and in the focused concerns of elites. We, too, apprehend them in our objects of study and wish to render them accessible. Contrasts allow such characteristics to emerge for analysis. Finding contrasts among ancient states and civilizations, therefore, is an enterprise that suggests more comparison is warranted, not less.

NOTES

We are grateful to Jeremy Black, Marianne Eaton-Krauss, Geoff Emberling, and Andrea McDowell for commenting on drafts, and to Alan Bowman, John Davis, and, especially, Geoff Emberling, for patching holes. John Baines's initial formulation of the ideas on high culture was presented in a lecture to the School of American Research, Santa Fe, in April 1992. Norman Yoffee wishes to acknowledge the NEH fellowship that enabled him to be a resident scholar at the School of American Research, 1991–92, when this essay first took shape.

This essay is argued principally on a theoretical level. In the frequent absence of syntheses, the argument could not be supported with references without extending the bibliography beyond reasonable bounds. Citations are selective; where possible, we have chosen items that lead to additional material. Our text was composed in 1992 for the seminar at the School of American Research and revised for publication in 1993. Since then we have not extended the number of citations significantly.

8

Sociocultural Complexity Without the State
The Indus Civilization
GREGORY L. POSSEHL

The Mature phase of the Indus, or Harappan, civilization flourished from circa 2500 to 1900 BC on the plains and in the mountains of the greater Indus Valley (Possehl 1993; Possehl and Rissman 1992; Shaffer 1992) (fig. 8.1). This civilization covered about 1,000,000 km^2, including southern Baluchistan, Gujarat, Sindh, the Punjab, Haryana, northern Rajasthan, and western Uttar Pradesh. There are 1,022 Mature Harappan sites. Ninety-five have been excavated, but the civilization is probably known best from the research at the two great urban centers of Mohenjo-daro and Harappa (Mackay 1937–38; Marshall 1931; Meadow 1991; Vats 1940; Wheeler 1947) (fig. 8.2).

From the first day that Sir John Marshall announced the discoveries at Mohenjo-daro and Harappa (September 20, 1924), archaeologists have spoken of these cities as part of a civilization. The term "civilization" is somewhat ambiguous and has a long, rather complicated history. In choosing to use the term, Marshall and his colleagues in the Archaeological Survey of India were attempting to convey a sense that they were dealing with "high culture"—people who knew the art of writing, had developed technologies, and lived in cities.

It is often proposed that the Harappan civilization was one of the early or archaic states of Asia, along with Mesopotamia, Dynastic Egypt, and Shang China. The conclusion that they were all sociocultural systems that could be called states has promoted the use of the comparative method as an analytical tool to understand their internal dynamics. However, recent

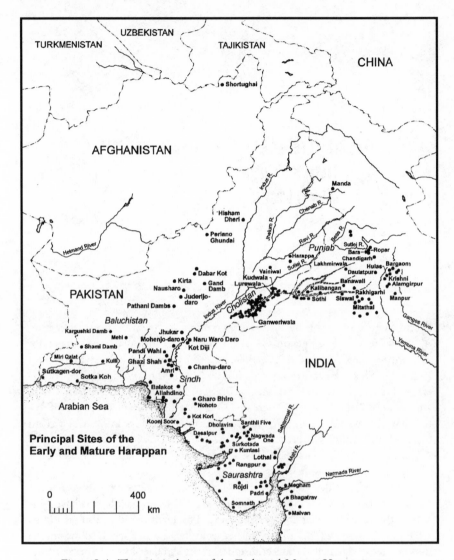

Figure 8.1. The principal sites of the Early and Mature Harappan stages.

research has led a number of scholars to question the proposition that the Indus civilization was the kind of complex sociocultural system that is usually associated with the archaic state. If this is the case, it suggests that the internal workings of the Harappan civilization were significantly different than those found in Mesopotamia and Egypt at a comparable time. This essay examines this critical question.

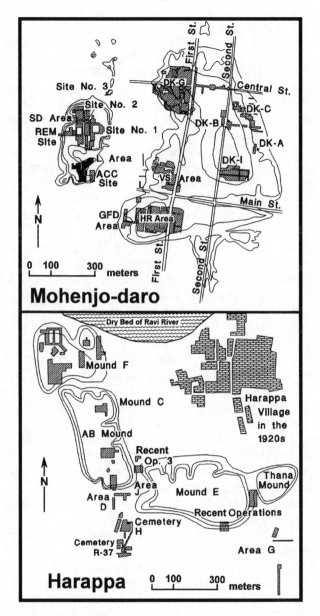

Figure 8.2. *The great urban centers of Mohenjo-daro and Harappa.*

WHAT IS A STATE?

My own thoughts on the nature and definition of the state are found throughout this chapter. No claim is made that there is a consensus among archaeologists who study early sociocultural complexity on the definition of the archaic state, although there seems to be some agreement on a few points. The state is a form of political organization. It developed among peoples with large-scale economies, having considerable specialization in craft and career tracks. The administration of the state is a prominent feature of this form of political organization, and some portion of the career specialists formed a bureaucracy. The craft and career specialists, and the other peoples of their society, were arranged in a hierarchy of classes. The state monopolizes the legitimate use of force as a means of social control and an agency to protect, if not expand, the sovereignty of the people it encompasses. The state form of organization places the management of diplomacy and warfare in the domain of a strong, forceful leader. There is an imperative among states to focus on individual leaders, usually called "kings," which reflects the presence of unequivocal political leadership.

Kings can be seen as the symbolic embodiment of the people and their sociocultural system. They are often deified, or allowed to flirt with notions of human deification. From the point of view of the citizenry, the deification of one's king might be thought of as the deification of oneself. Such matters of ideology and self-identification mean that the ties between the state political apparatus and state ideology are intimate and involved with the idea of political legitimization. These ties may lead to considerable tension between the state as a political form and religion as an institution of ideology, unless, as was often the case in ancient Egypt, the "king" (pharaoh) was also the chief religious personage. The economy of the archaic state is partly shaped by the political form to protect and expand its sovereignty. The king, as the leader in war, even cold wars, was in constant need of resources to serve his political ends. He strove for an economy that was responsive and productive in a quantitatively superior way. Historically this is accomplished best through centralization, and all that the centralization of a political economy implies in terms of a bureaucracy.

The political form we have come to call the archaic state has a strong focus on kingship, or centralized leadership, that is in all likelihood given to the aggrandizement of the individuals who rise to this office. The economies of states tend to be centralized, heavily (not exclusively) controlled from the office of the king, so that it can effectively serve the diplomatic and military needs of the political apparatus. This implies a staff of functionaries (a bureaucracy) to implement and monitor the economic decision making, as well as to collect revenue and produce for the use of the center.

There are many conceptual and definitional problems with the archaic state (e.g., Cohen 1978), and there is still no sound definition useful in archaeological terms (Crumley 1976). It is often suggested that states are composed of people whose allegiance is determined territorially, rather than by their kinship. Those who have perused the ethnographic record know that this view is not well-founded; many people in very small, simply organized societies use territoriality to define group membership, such as the Punan of Borneo. The records of disputes among Native Americans are filled with evidence for this point.

For classical unilineal evolutionists, the state is a level of sociocultural integration where the means of integration is "that special control, the use of force and constant threat of force from an institutionalized body of persons who wield the force. A state constitutes itself *legally:* it makes explicit the manner and circumstances of its use of force, and it outlaws all other use of force as it intervenes in disputes between individuals and groups" (Service 1963:xxvi). An archaic "state differs from a chiefdom most strikingly because it is integrated by a special mechanism involving a legalized monopoly of force" (Service 1963:xxviii).

Other thoughts on the nature of the state suggest that it is "the organization for the regulation of social relations in a society that is divided into two emergent social classes, the rulers and the ruled" (Skalník 1978:597). In strict terms this definition is as appropriate for tribes and chiefdoms as it is for the state; it is a good example of some of the fuzzy thinking that emerges from many discussions of the archaic state.

The state is held in opposition to the chiefdom, which is seen as a step lower on the evolutionary scale.

> The rise of centralized leadership involves a rise in the prestige of the person holding the office of chief. This prestige attaches to relatives of the chief, depending on genealogical nearness; and as the status becomes more permanent: hereditary. Thus, we find not only that unlike *parts* have arisen in society but also unlike *persons.* That is to say that chiefdoms are typically nonegalitarian, that they are characterized by differences in the hereditary rank, higher and lower status of persons and their families, in addition to the universally human age-sex status differentiation. (Service 1963:xxiv–xxv)

The economics of chiefdoms involve delayed reciprocity and large-scale exchange systems. Population size is increased through the power of integration, specialized labor, and exchange. Chiefdoms are often militaristic and can be economically integrated through warfare. They are said to be familial and hierarchical, with some sense of central direction and authority. They do not have a government, although government is difficult to define in these contexts. The social hierarchy is based on unequal control over goods and production, but with no true private property. Social stratification is present, but true socioeconomic classes are not.

Robert Carneiro, a unilineal evolutionist who published an important paper on the origins of the state, emphasized that states are able to "draft men for work, levy and collect taxes, and decree and enforce laws" (Carneiro 1981:69). The problem with the words used in this kind of definition is that, in developmental terms, they lack precision. When does the force of persuasion in interpersonal relationships give way to being able to "draft men for work"? How does a "tax" differ from the kind of tribute that "big men," sometimes only "charismatic men," are able to coerce out of their followers? What is a "law" in developmental terms, and how can we differentiate it from a pronouncement? Moreover, true law codes appear many centuries after hypothesized states appeared. Some hold that laws are made by states, and lesser organizations on the continuum of sociocultural development do not formulate them. But laws define the state and are not simply an attribute of them.

In reviewing the nature of states, especially from the point of view of Mesopotamia, Charles Redman (1978:280) suggests that they (1) hold a concentration of economic power; (2) are organized along political and territorial lines; (3) are hierarchical in terms of differential access of resources; and (4) hold a monopoly of force. One might wonder how "concentrated" is a "concentration of economic power"? Try to find a society that is not organized in some way and to some degree along "political and territorial lines." Social hierarchies are found in many societies that are not states. What is a monopoly of force, when perfectly legitimate states are *forced to admit* (do not merely allow) that every citizen has the right to bear arms, and turn a blind eye to physical combat between urban gangs and citizens?

The state is seen as functioning with an administration headed by a sovereign—a form of administration that involves what is generally called a "bureaucracy," with full-time administrative specialists who are on a permanent career track different from other specialists. The bureaucracy is arranged hierarchically and charged with the functioning of government according to accepted norms and with ensuring that the wishes and desires of the ruler are carried out, down to the lowest levels of society. Because bureaucracies handle the collection, processing, and dispersal of information, and the organization of settlement patterns, from urban centers to village and hamlet outliers, they are thought to be a proxy through which the growth or evolutionary stage of a sociocultural system can be measured (Wright and Johnson 1975).

In Claessen and Skalník (1978b) we learn that the following four factors, regardless of their historical sequence, had a relatively direct influence on the formation of the early state: (1) population growth and/or population pressure; (2) war, the threat of war, conquest, or raids; (3) conquest; and (4) the influence of previously existing states.

> Regardless which of these factors actually triggered off the development, the ultimate result was always very much the same, namely the early state. The above four factors promoting the rise of the early state do not replace the essential conditions of a producing economy with a surplus and the consequent conditions of social inequality and the beginnings of social stratification, without which the early state would be inconceivable. (Claessen and Skalník 1978b:642)

These causal factors are in line with the well-developed theory of state formation put forth by Robert Carneiro (1970a). Other general findings by Claessen and Skalník (1978b) on formative processes for the early state can be summarized as follows. (1) Historically, social stratification began much earlier than the emergence of the state; however, the early state took this social differentiation and expanded and codified it (Claessen and Skalník 1978b:642–43). (2) Conquest can lead to the formation of the early state, although this was not well represented in their sample (Claessen and Skalník 1978b:643). (3) Population growth and/or pressure was found to lead to more complex political organizations (Claessen and Skalník 1978b:644). And (4) urbanization was found to play a decisive role in the formation of the early state (Claessen and Skalník 1978b:644).

Unfortunately, the role of trade and commerce, especially in the formative contexts of early states, was poorly handled by Claessen and Skalník (1978b). However, an independent review of the individual studies in their book shows that trade and commerce act as stimulants to the growth of more complex management and governmental institutions. They can be accompanied by raids, warfare, even outright conquest, which also are stimulants to the differentiation of sociocultural systems.

An aside seems to be in order here. In a very useful review of the chiefdom, Earle and his colleagues (Earle, ed. 1991) investigated those factors that seem to lead to the emergence and integration of this form of sociocultural organization. They found that neither ecological factors nor population pressure were useful explanatory concepts (Earle 1991a:5). In contrast to Claessen and Skalník, Earle and his colleagues focused more on issues of production (debt, creating infrastructure, means for powerful people to cause others to work), political configuration (circumscription, power, force, forging external ties), and ideology (seizing and/or creating means and signs of legitimacy). The importance and utility of ideology emerged as a powerful force in culture change and the stability or collapse of chiefdoms.

The state is a highly successful form of sociocultural organization. In spite of bureaucratic inefficiencies and sometimes wasteful competition between institutions, especially those of government and ideology, its success as a form of human organization is so well documented that it cannot be questioned. It is a proven, probably generalized organizational form that is effective at governing large numbers of people, funding its needs, handling divisive forces of cultural and ethnic diversity, and, perhaps most important, protecting its own interests against those of others. Peoples organized as states are often able to expand through conquest; this political form can be seen as aggressive, even predatory. No matter how complex a sociocultural system might be, or has been, the case can be made that, if it does not form along the lines of a state, or an archaic state, it will not survive over long periods of time because of the "strategic" edge that the state form of organization seems to possess.

If this perspective is admitted as a possibility, it might explain why history and the ethnographic record are replete with examples of the state. Other forms of sociocultural complexity simply fell prey to state forms of organization or their own internal failings in organization. There may have been comparatively few of these forms to begin with. The nonstate type of complex society may not have developed in many places, or lasted for long periods of time, since the organization for survival was the state.

THE BEGINNINGS OF INDUS URBANIZATION

There is no well-developed body of theory on the beginnings of the Harappan civilization. As survey and excavation data have accumulated, a number of observations can be made on this problem.

Population Growth

The compilation of a reasonably comprehensive gazetteer of sites dating from the beginnings of village farming communities and pastoral camps through the Early Iron Age provides insight into the growth of settlement in the greater Indus region. The outlines of the trends from the beginnings of food production through the Post-Urban Harappan are seen in table 8.1.

Some parts of the greater Indus are reasonably well explored, some parts less so. The archaeological periods used here are very long, which probably leads to an inflation of the total settled area. But there is reasonable documentation for population growth reflected in a steady increase in sites and settled area. The key time in this sequence seems to be the Togau and Kechi Beg/Hakra Wares periods, when there was a fourfold increase in population. The growth between the Early and Mature Harappan would not seem to be sufficiently large to be considered one of the elements in the birth of civilization.

TABLE 8.1. *Site Counts, Total Settled Area, and Average Site Size for Some of the Indus Age*

	Site Counts	Settled Area in Hectares	Average Size
Post-Urban Harappan c. 1900–1400 BC	1281	1837	3.50
Mature Harappan c. 2500–1900 BC	1022	3846	7.16
Early Harappan c. 3200–2600 BC	477	2113	4.50
Kechi Beg/Hakra Wares c. 3800–3200 BC	256	1336	5.21
Togau c. 4300–3800 BC	84	295	3.51
Burj Basket-marked c. 5000–4300 BC	33	85	2.58
Kili Ghul Mohammad c. 7000–5000 BC	20	53	2.65

Notes: The Early/Mature Harappan transition, which occurs c. 2600–2500 BC, is not included in this table. Many sites are not measured; therefore average size cannot be computed by dividing the settled area listed in the table by site counts.

Evidence for Warfare

There is no direct evidence for warfare during the Mature Harappan. There are no murals picturing warriors, prisoners, or battle; no settlements can be shown to have been attacked, with defenders who died on the spot, their bones scarred by blows, or arrow points sticking in the fire-blackened walls of destroyed buildings.

This does not mean that all of the peoples of the greater Indus region were peaceful, always eager to please and do the bidding of their neighbors. There were surely confrontations between the diverse peoples of the Mature Harappan civilization. What is not known is the form these confrontations took, how pervasive it was as a social and political force, and what effect it had, if any, on forming and maintaining the Harappan civilization.

Some observations in the archaeological record at a number of sites in the Indus Valley and surrounding areas suggest the transitional phase between the Early and Mature Harappan (c. 2650–2550 BC) may have been a time of trouble. Periods of disruption are seen from the archaeological record at Balakot, Kot Diji, Gumla, Kalibangan, Amri, and Nausharo. Radiocarbon dates for Period II Mature Harappan occupation at Balakot are solidly within the second half of the third millennium and suggest "a hiatus of several centuries between the Balakotian and the Harappan periods at Balakot" (Dales 1979:247).

The stratigraphy of Kot Diji is complex and not yet completely understood. There are obvious signs of massive burning over the entire site, including the lower habitation area and the high mound. As F. A. Khan has observed, "A thick deposit of burned and charred material, on top of layer (4), spreading over the entire site, completely sealed the lower levels (Kot Diji) from the upper ones (Mature Harappans). This prominent and clearly marked burnt layer strongly suggests that the last occupation level of the early settlers (that is the Kot Diji) was violently disturbed, and probably totally burnt and destroyed" (Khan 1965:22).

Period III at Gumla, the Kot Diji occupation, also seems to have come to a fiery end. "The end of their period appears to be violent. There is a thick layer of ash, charcoal, bones, pot-sherds, etc. which all belong to Period III. This thick ashy layer separates the structure of Period III from that of Period IV. But there does not seem to be any gap between Periods III and IV. The reoccupation of the site must have started soon after destruction" (Dani 1970–71:39–40).

There is an abandonment of Kalibangan between Periods I (Early Harappan) and II (Mature Harappan). The excavators detected signs of cleavage and displacement of strata in the Early Harappan levels, which might have been caused by an earthquake (Lal 1979:75). B. K. Thapar has noted: "This occupation continued through five structural phases, rising to a height of some 1.6 m, when it was brought to a close by a catastrophe (perhaps seismic), as evidenced by the occurrence of displaced (faulted?) deposits and subsided walls in different parts of the excavated area. Thereafter the site seems to have been abandoned, though only temporarily and a thin layer of sand, largely infertile, accumulated over the ruins" (Thapar 1973:87).

There is no evidence for human violence at Kalibangan, but it is interesting that the site was abandoned at the end of the Early Harappan. Even a catastrophic earthquake would not have caused this complete abandonment if Kalibangan had been an important settlement functioning within a healthy political and economic system. The abandonment of this settlement, whatever the cause, is in keeping with the notion that the end of the Early Harappan was a time of disruption in the greater Indus region.

Period II at Amri, the transitional phase between the Early and Mature Harappan, ended with signs of a significant amount of burning. The excavator has observed: "The upper levels are blackish and ashy, but they are mostly so near the surface that it is difficult to say whether this occurrence should be interpreted as evidence of some sort of violence or of fire" (Casal 1964:7). A large fire was also evident in Period ID, associated with a building that Casal believes was a *godown,* or storage facility. The walls of this structure had been reddened by fire, and parts of the superstructure had fallen to foundation level.

The excavations at Nausharo have not yet been completed, but the excavation team, under the direction of Dr. Jean-François Jarrige, has found evidence of extensive burning associated with Period ID, a transitional-phase occupation at the site. He has noted: "The two architectural complexes of Period ID in sector NS.G and NS.L have been heavily burnt and the walls have turned red due to heat. At Kot Diji, too, the final phase of the pre-Indus period has been destroyed by fire. This could support the romantic hypothesis of the Harappans destroying by fire the pre-Harappan settlements. But fires can be as well accidental" (Jarrige 1989:64–65).

Renewed work at Harappa has uncovered a settlement of the transitional phase of some 24 ha, covering most of what is called Mound E; however, there are no signs of disruption or burning (R. H. Meadow, personal communication 1993).

An Evaluation of the Burning at the End of the Early Harappan

It is difficult to evaluate this kind of archaeological evidence. Jarrige's caution that fires have many causes is true. Attributing burning to warfare or raiding is out of fashion in archaeological explanation, no matter how prevalent these activities were in the lives of people during historical times in the Near East and South Asia. These disruptions also have been noted by S. P. Gupta (1978:142), who tends to think of them in terms of natural calamities, which might well be true for Kalibangan (Raikes 1968). Nonetheless, there is a conspicuous amount of evidence for burning at the historical junction where the Early and Mature Harappan meet. This is in contrast to earlier times when there is little evidence for large-scale burning in the greater Indus region. For example, there is little, if any, evidence for large-scale fires in levels at Amri, Gumla, or Nausharo preceding the transitional period. The same is true at Kalibangan, Balakot, and other sites in the greater Indus region.

If fires are only accidental domestic events, one would expect a random, or haphazard, pattern to their occurrence, an occasional "blip" in the archaeological record resulting from the careless handling of a lamp, or a child's play getting out of hand, or a cow knocking over a lamp and the milk stool. The scarcity of evidence for this kind of day-to-day tragedy in the lives of the ancient inhabitants of the region is, therefore, significant. It leads one to think that much of the evidence for the little fires, the kind that destroy one or two buildings and are the unhappy grist of daily life, is erased by the process of cleaning up the mess and rebuilding. Some evidence is probably still there, but it is a detail of the archaeological record; it does not jump out at the excavator as a catastrophe and become a significant observation in the site report. When signs of large-scale burning are noted in an excavation, as at Kot Diji, Gumla, and Nausharo, and to some degree Amri, it is likely to denote a large conflagration, the damage from which is so massive that it cannot be diffused by cleanup and rebuilding.

There is a pattern in these conflagrations. First, they seem to have been relatively large-scale—not little domestic fires, but events that consumed a significant portion of a settlement, if not all of it. Second, they are associated with the Early/Mature Harappan conjunction. Such fires are rarely documented at sites prior to this time. Still other observations relating to the conjunction of the Early/Mature Harappan have a bearing on the development of the Harappan civilization.

Further Suggestions of Disruption

Archaeological exploration has proceeded to a point where we can see that many Mature Harappan sites were founded on virgin soil, and many Early Harappan sites were abandoned and not reoccupied during the Mature Harappan. This is well documented in the deep settlement histories of Sindh and Cholistan (see fig. 8.1). Table 8.2 presents site counts from Sindh and Cholistan (Mughal 1982, 1997) to illustrate the abandonment of Early Harappan sites and the founding of Mature Harappan settlements.

The numbers are striking. In Cholistan, 33 of the 37 Early Harappan (Kot Dijian) sites were abandoned by the end of this period. For the Mature Harappan, 132 of 136 sites were established as new settlements on virgin soil. A similar, if less dramatic, pattern is evident in Sindh. The peoples of the Mature Harappan clearly preferred to find new places to live, cutting their historical ties with the older Early Harappan settlements. This is another significant disjunction between the Early and Mature Harappan. It complements the signs of burning and strengthens the notion that important changes took place at this junction, which emerges as a period of both disruption and of renewal—a time when the peoples of the Harappan civilization seem to have severed ties with older places and sought fresh, new places to establish themselves and their new way of life. While the burning could represent one of the consequences of war, or raiding, it also could result from an act of renewal.

TABLE 8.2. *Occupation Changes in Settlement: Sindh and Cholistan*

	Sindh			Cholistan		
	Site Count	Total Hectares	Average Site Size	Site Count	Total Hectares	Average Site Size
Early Harappan	54	79	2.85	40	256	6.40
Mature Harappan	86	436	7.95	176	877	5.62
Early and Mature Harappan	23	42	3.48	2	12	6.25
Early Harappan sites abandoned	27	37	2.48	38	244	6.42
Mature Harappan sites on virgin soil	63	415	9.43	170	947	5.64

Note: Many sites are not measured; therefore average size cannot be computed by dividing the settled area listed in the table by site counts.

The Early/Mature Harappan Transition

These observations on disruptions and possible conflict are important for understanding the transition between the Early and Mature Harappan, since it appears to have been a period of relatively rapid culture change during which the majority of the distinctly urban features of the Harappan civilization came into being (Possehl 1986:96–98, 1990). The transitional period is thought to have been three or four generations long, anything but "instantaneous."

Jim Shaffer and Diane Lichtenstein have suggested that the Harappan civilization is a fusion of "ethnic groups" in the Ghaggar/Hakra Valley on the borders of India and Pakistan. They also have spoken of the rapidity of the rise of the Mature Harappan.

> [This] fusion appears to have been very rapid, reinforced no doubt by its own success. The earliest set of Harappan dates are from Kalibangan, in the northern Ghaggar/Hakra Valley at ca. 2600 BC; while dates from Allahdino, Balakot and sites in Saurashtra indicate Harappan settlements were established in the southern Indus Valley by ca. 2400 BC. Possehl (1986:96–98;

Possehl and Rissman 1992) suggests a rapid origin of 150 years for the Harappan. We suggest it was even less, or 100 years, ca. 2600–2500 BC. Within the next 100 years, the Harappan became the largest ethnic group within the Indus Valley. This rapid distribution rate was matched only by Harappan abandonment of large sections in the Indus Valley which was under way by ca. 2000 BC, a process intensified by later hydrological changes. Whatever the Harappan group's organizational complexity, it was a cultural system promoting rapid territorial expansion. (Shaffer and Lichtenstein 1989:123)

This short period of rapid, paroxytic change seems to occupy the century from about 2600 to 2500 BC. Such precision probably goes beyond the discriminating powers of radiocarbon dating. The transitional stage is a good example of a time when a major acceleration in the rate of culture change led to the development of a new level of sociocultural complexity.

Some Observations on the Nature of the Mature Harappan

What the ancient Indians called this new civilization still eludes us, but the Sumerian place name "Meluhha" would seem to have been their gloss for it (Possehl 1996). Excavation and survey have detected signs of Mature Harappan social stratification, craft and career specialization, and sophisticated engineering and technology. This civilization was extensive; it covered about 1,000,000 km^2. Contemporary approaches to the cultural geography of the Mature Harappan give clear indications that the civilization should not be characterized by the boring sameness that Sir Mortimer Wheeler and Stuart Piggott proposed. Wheeler pursued this issue best in *Five Thousand Years of Pakistan:* "All is orderly and regulated . . . dull, a trifle lacking in the stimulus of individuality," characterized by an "absence or suppression of personality in its details from street to street" and giving a "sense of regimentation" (Wheeler 1950:28). In another place he refers to the "astonishing sameness of the civilization" and says that "Another quality of it is its *isolation*" (Wheeler 1950:29, original emphasis).

Rather than emphasizing "sameness" and "isolation," recent research on the Harappan civilization has defined regional "polities" and interaction and has sought to understand the long-distance relationship between ancient India, the Horn of Africa, the Arabian Gulf, Central Asia, the Iranian Plateau, and Mesopotamia. The regional mosaic of Early and Mature Harappan remains is taken as a proxy for ethnic diversity (fig. 8.3). We do not know the languages spoken by these people, or much about their social life and organization, but there is a very strong sense that the Early and Mature Harappan represent many kinds of people.

There also are Mature Harappan cities. The two best known are Mohenjo-daro and Harappa, but a third Mature Harappan city known as Ganweriwala (see fig. 8.1) has been found in Cholistan (Mughal 1997:49–50).

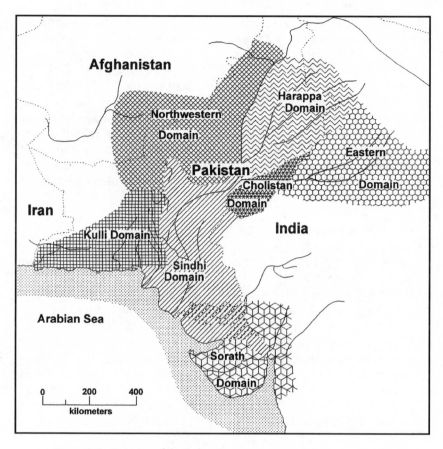

Figure 8.3. Domains of the Indus Age.

Mohenjo-daro and Harappa are known to have been large (100 ha) multi-functional settlements set within a grid of other contemporary, if smaller, settlements. It is in these cities, and there may be others in the Bhatinda district of the Indian Punjab (Joshi 1986), where the Mature Harappan is most clearly and fully expressed and where the class structure and ethnic diversity of the Harappan social order seem to have been played out in the clearest way.

It would be a mistake to think of cities as a primary variable in the ongoing life of a complex sociocultural system. Cities emerge and are maintained through the interaction of a complex set of social, cultural, and historical variables. Nevertheless, the Mature Harappan cities are the most visible, and in some ways clearly defining, characteristic of this civilization.

In this sense, urbanization is a hallmark, a symbol of the internal differentiation and structural specialization of Harappan life. It is these sociocultural variables, and the sociocultural processes they engender, that allow us to define and differentiate complex societies from others.

This new way of life involved urbanization—the building of large, multifunctional, internally differentiated settlements where many of the various classes and occupational categories of people lived and worked. Many smaller settlements were integrated into the whole as well; they preserve signs of their own level of sociocultural complexity. Two of the most prominent institutions of the archaic state—temples and palaces (Flannery, this volume)—seem to find little or no expression in the archaeological record of the Harappan civilization.

There Are No Harappan Temples or Palaces
There is no monumental religious architecture associated with the Mature Harappan: none, for example, at Mohenjo-daro (Mackay 1937–38; Marshall 1931), Harappa (Vats 1940), Chanhu-daro (Mackay 1943), Lothal (Rao 1979, 1985), or Surkotada (Joshi 1990). The pyramids of Dynastic Egypt and the ziggurats of Mesopotamia have no parallel in the Indus Valley.

A succinct definition of the Harappan religious institution or institutions is elusive, but it is clear that these were peoples with strong religious beliefs on several dimensions, which they expressed in a totally different way than their neighbors to the west. The construction of huge, physical monuments to the Mature Harappan gods and goddesses was apparently inappropriate. The capability in terms of engineering skills and the ability to mobilize a work force are apparent in the archaeological record of the large urban centers, but no such tasks were undertaken.

Another contrast between Egypt, Mesopotamia, and the Harappan civilization is the absence of palaces—the large abodes of heads of government and their powerful associates charged with managing the fortunes of the Harappan political apparatus. Perhaps the Harappan political system did not focus on a single personage, like a king or a pharaoh. But whatever role the powerful may have played in Mature Harappan life, the manner in which the sociocultural system expressed it is significantly different from that of the archaic state.

The tension and competition between the religious and political institutions of Egypt and Mesopotamia were a source of some creativity. The construction of ever larger temples and ziggurats, funerary monuments, palaces, and city walls was fueled by this rivalry. Competition was not the only source of inspiration for the construction of such monuments, but it was an important factor. Their absence in the Harappan civilization suggests that the fundamental organizing and operational principles of the Harappan civilization were different than those of Egypt and Mesopotamia. It does not necessarily mean that the Harappan civilization was any less complex or developed in a sociocultural sense. The refined nature of Harappan city life and management, the mastery of complex technologies, the writing system, and the ability to mobilize resources from distant lands all argue for a very high level of sociocultural development.

Some structures at Mohenjo-daro are proposed to have been used by the Harappan religious establishment. Marshall lists several such structures, none of which, on detailed examination, turns out to be a good candidate for a temple or place of worship (1931:22–23; see also Wheeler 1968:51–53). The best candidates for buildings with religious functions include three buildings on the Mound of the Great Bath (fig. 8.4): the Great Bath itself, the so-called College of Priests, and an "Assembly Hall," in L Area. In the lower town, Structure 10 in HR-A Area and two buildings in DK-G Area have also been discussed in this context (Wheeler 1968:51–53). There are structures that have been called "fire altars" at both Lothal and Kalibangan, along with the "ritual structure" at the latter site, but the city of Harappa is conspicuous by the absence of architectural remains associated with religious activities. None of these buildings, except possibly the Great Bath, seems to fulfill the expectations of a religious or ritual structure; this possible exception does not seem sufficient to invalidate the hypothesis advanced here concerning the absence of monumental expression for the Mature Harappan religious institution.

The Indus Civilization Is a Faceless Culture

Almost certainly related to the absence of monumental architecture expressing the Mature Harappan political and religious institutions is the lack of representations of individuals in Mature Harappan life. There are many human figurines in terracotta and other materials. They offer some insights into daily life and the diverse dress of men and women, but there is very little that could be called portraiture. The bronze dancing girl from HR Area of Mohenjo-daro could be a portrait (fig. 8.5). On a slightly larger scale is the famous "priest-king" from DK-B Area of the same site (fig 8.6). Although it is not certain that he was either a "priest" or a "king," let alone someone who held dual offices, it does seem that this artwork could be the portrait of an upper-class Harappan, and that he might have held an important office, or offices, in the political and/or religious institutions. Three or four other pieces of sculpture from Mohenjo-daro might fit the same description. None is inscribed or identified in any way, nor are there representations in other forms of art that would seem to identify or single out the individual in Mature Harappan life, whether of the upper classes or lower down on the social scale. Moreover, it cannot be confirmed that any of them are portraits

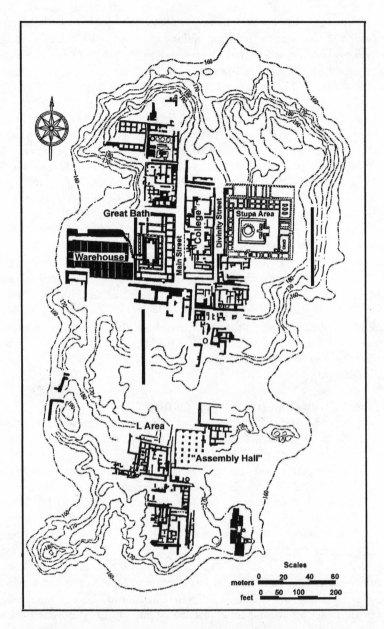

Figure 8.4. *The Mound of the Great Bath at Mohenjo-daro.*

Figure 8.5. Bronze dancing girl from Mohenjo-daro,
15 cm high (courtesy of Michael Jansen).

or representations of actual people. This is only my surmise. In the end, the Mature Harappan is a faceless culture, without the kind of aggrandizement of the individual that we associate with archaic states, with their "cults of personality" surrounding the king and other upper-class functionaries.

WAS THE HARAPPAN CIVILIZATION A STATE?

There is growing dissatisfaction among some archaeologists working on the Indus civilization with the thought that it can be understood to result from a simple unilineal path of human development, which places the archaic state above a level generally called the chiefdom. The reasons for this dissatisfaction have been expressed best by W. A. Fairservis (1961, 1967, 1971: 299), S. C. Malik (1968), and J. Shaffer (1982). Their critique comes down to one point: there is an increasingly poor fit between the "facts" as we know them and traditional evolutionary constructs. This position also is reflected in the archaeology of other regions of the world with a general concern about the idea of the "chiefdom" as a necessary precursor to the archaic state, or the kind of sociocultural complexity reflected in the Harappan civilization (see, for example, Drennan and Uribe 1987; Earle 1991a; Earle, ed.

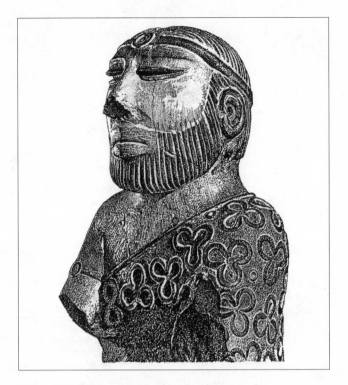

Figure 8.6. Harappan "priest-king" sculpture.

1991). The diversity that is being found in the form, adaptive capacities, and evolutionary position of the "chiefdom" suggests that more than one socio-cultural and evolutionary form is represented.

Not much of the Harappan civilization appears to fit the definition of the state as developed by Claessen, Skalník, or Service. Nor do the archaeo-logical markers of the archaic state as outlined by Flannery (this volume) seem to fit the Mature Harappan. Where is the evidence for a prime sover-eign and the bureaucracy that supports this kind of administration? There are no accounting records; there is no evidence, even a hint, of a series of specialized administrative positions, carrying out orders from the capitals via the nested hierarchies of officials that characterize state-level administration. Where is the evidence for a state religion, high priests, or royal graves? Where is the face of the individual, the highest of the elite, revealed to us as the supreme authority, or self-proclaimed hero of Harappan life? Many early states have these features, but not the Harappan civilization. Therefore, I am inclined to think that it had a different form of organization.

Dealing with this form of question concerning the peoples of the ancient Indus region has not always been seen as important. For the early investigators of the Harappan civilization, the case was clear.

Marshall, Mackay, Wheeler, Piggott
For Sir John Marshall and those who followed him in the interpretation of the Harappan civilization—Ernest J. H. Mackay, Stuart Piggott, and Sir Mortimer Wheeler—the level of development of this culture was not in question, or at least was never specifically addressed. They were dealing with a civilization, and that was enough for them. The Wheeler/Piggott position on the Harappan sees an especially strong government with "rigorously authoritarian rule" (Piggott 1950:140) and a "rigid and highly evolved bureaucratic machine capable of organizing and distributing surplus wealth and defending it" (Piggott 1950:154, quoting Wheeler).

The Allchins
Bridget and Raymond Allchin (1968, 1982) have written two syntheses of South Asian archaeology that attempt to place the Harappan civilization in a broader context of prehistoric life in the subcontinent. They found little, if any, support for "twin capitals," an Indus "empire," or "priest-kings" (Allchin and Allchin 1968:129, 1982:169). They do not, however, directly address the question of the level of development for this civilization: "Even if the political and economic unity is admitted, there remain profound and tantalizing problems of how it came about and how it was maintained." Many of these issues have yet to be tackled successfully (Allchin and Allchin 1982:169).

The Indus Civilization Was Not a State: Recent Views
More recently, several scholars have presented evidence that the Harappan civilization was not a state. They have challenged the "traditional" view of the level of sociocultural differentiation of the Harappan civilization. The first serious questions came from Walter A. Fairservis, Jr., in two seminal papers published in 1961 and 1967 (reprinted in Possehl 1979:49–65 and 66–89). In a reexamination of the evidence, Fairservis begins to erode the testimony supporting the infrastructure of the Indus civilization as seen by Wheeler and Piggott.

> I submit that Mohenjo-daro was almost purely a ceremonial center and that its functional intent was similar to the Old Kingdom Egyptians and the Mayans. Consequently, I think there are grave doubts that trade had much influence on its location or its upkeep. I suspect that the political or military orientation involved in the term "empire" is unwarranted by the present evidence. (Fairservis 1961:18)

Fairservis offers a cautionary view, suggesting that the Mesopotamian model for an ancient civilization would not promote an understanding of the Harappan civilization.

> The centralization of administrative control obviously required to build large structures, and to cultivate acreage, harvest and store is not beyond the powers of an elaborated village administration, though certainly adjustments were necessary, for example, in recording storage quantities and noting flood levels. But there is no good evidence for priest-kings, slaves, courts of officials, and standing armies. (Fairservis 1967:42)

Fairservis echoes the thoughts of Robert Redfield (1953; Redfield and Singer 1954).

> On these terms the evidence we have indicates that a "great tradition" marked by both urban and rural elements evolved out of hybrid "little communities," characteristic of the pre-Harappan Indus Valley. These were not isolated elements but were interrelated; in the Mature Harappan stage of development they had been transformed into an indigenous or "primary" civilization in which village and city alike shared a common culture. (Fairservis 1967:43)

> The impression one gains from the study of the Harappan civilization is that it is a civilization still emerging out of an essentially village ethos. It is paradoxically a civilization more village-like than city-like in the Western sense. (Fairservis 1971:299)

> My interpretation of the texts indicates that Harappan society consisted of groups bound together by ties of kinship and ideology. The paramount leader or leaders, the chiefs, would have been entitled to regular tribute, even from far-off settlements. Such chiefs probably resided in larger, more elaborate settlements such as Mohenjo-daro or Harappa. (Fairservis 1986:49)

In his recent book on the Indus script, Fairservis elaborates this position with the proposition that the "civilization" was a hegemony of chiefdoms with paramount chiefs and subsidiary chiefs who were responsible to them. The latter's responsibilities included administration as called for by the paramount chiefs and providing leadership in Harappan settlements or settlement areas (Fairservis 1992:133).

Fairservis constructs an image of the Harappan civilization as a chiefdom, an evolutionary step below the state, and yet he retains the idea of a civilization. He advocates a political structure lacking strong central rule, either secular or sacred. There was no bureaucracy. The writing system was, by and large, used to identify the holder of a seal. While he admits to the possibility of written records, direct evidence for an accounting system is not known. The cities—like Mohenjo-daro, Harappa, and Ganweriwala—were the seats of the chiefs but had the character of supervillages, more complex than villages but not like Ur, Uruk, or Nippur, which were centers of vast political power with large temples dedicated to their civic deity.

This proposal that the Harappan civilization was neither sufficiently internally differentiated nor structurally specialized enough to be considered a state is shared by S. C. Malik (1968), who wrote a thorough review of what he called the "Formative period" of Indian civilization. Malik (1968:99) approaches the level of integration of Harappan culture from the standpoint of *societas* (kinship society) and *civitas* (civil state society) and concludes that, from the point of view of unilineal evolution (he cites the work of Elman Service), the Indus civilization was at a level of "specialization, redistribution, and the related centralization of authority which can integrate still more complex societies" (Malik 1968:103). This is just below the "state" and, while he does not use the word, would be the equivalent of a chiefdom. Malik reiterated his position in 1979.

While there is an appreciation here of many of the points raised by Fairservis and Malik, their view of the level of complexity of the Harappan civilization is not the one I hold. Nor is it the position taken by J. Shaffer. In 1982 Shaffer published a broad review of the nature of the Harappan civilization, intended to revitalize our examination of it:

> For too long one has let preconceived notions about the nature of Harappan Culture dictate what the archaeological data will reveal. It is time to view the archaeological data for what it is, and not what one thinks it is. Recent studies are just beginning to indicate the real importance of Harappan studies, showing that in South Asia a unique experiment in the development of urban, literate culture, was under way. Such a culture was highly attuned to local conditions and not a mirror image of Mesopotamia's urban experiment or, for that matter, any other region which witnessed the development of comparable cultural achievements. (Shaffer 1982:49)

Shaffer is a severe critic of the current study of Harappan civilization, questioning the grandiose notions generated from modest excavations, most of which were conducted at the two principal cities (Shaffer 1982:43). The so-called cultural unity of the Indus civilization is seen to have been overstated and misunderstood. Rather than being an artifact of regimentation, according to Shaffer it reflects the integration of the economy and internal trade of the Harappans (Shaffer 1982:44–45). The "state granaries" are dismissed as misinterpretations (Shaffer 1982:45; see also Fentress 1976:133–83). He advises that there is little evidence for an elite population based on the study of artifacts and their distribution (Shaffer 1982:46–47) and makes one final, extraordinary point. The small (1.4 ha) site of Allahdino, on the Malir River east of Karachi, has nearly all of the features of the Harappan civilization as found at Mohenjo-daro, except for its size. Shaffer's view is that the Harappan civilization was not a state and could have been a unique form of organization in the sense that there is no close parallel in the archaeological, historical, or ethnographic record.

The Indus Civilization Was a State

Three recent reviews of the Harappan civilization attempt to sustain the proposition that the civilization does represent an archaic state. Jerome Jacobson, whose primary interests are in Palaeolithic archaeology (Jacobson 1986, see also Jacobson 1979:487–88), considers 12 sociocultural features of the Harappan civilization: (1) urbanization; (2) writing; (3) population size and geographic range; (4) social stratification; (5) full-time centralized government or bureaucracy; (6) police power; (7) communication, market system, trade, and commerce; (8) taxes; (9) sovereignty; (10) religion; (11) militarism; and (12) expansion and colonization.

The discussion of social stratification is critical. His first index for this variable is architecture (Jacobson 1986:146–47). He notes the presence of very large structures at Mohenjo-daro and Harappa (citing Allchin and Allchin 1968:242 and Dales 1982:199) and the alleged presence of residential units on the "citadel" of Kalibangan (Lal 1979:85–86). The presence of small houses next to larger buildings at Lothal also is noted (Rao 1973). His point is linked in a theoretical way to Claessen and Skalník (1978b:639), who state: "There is a tendency on the part of the emergent class of rulers or the ruling stratum to live more or less apart from the other citizens of the state." However, the data from Lothal compare domestic structures with other kinds of buildings that are thought to have served public, nonresidential functions. Moreover, the large buildings at Mohenjo-daro are integrated into the lower town and not isolated on the Mound of the Great Bath. Thus, at least a portion of the elite population of this city was not living "more or less apart from the other citizens."

In his extended discussion of government and bureaucracy, Jacobson brings in the issue of settlement hierarchies and differentiation in the Harappan civilization (Jacobson 1986:152–53). In discussing "artifacts" (Jacobson 1986:149), he agrees with Shaffer's (1982:47) analysis of the distribution of luxury items at Harappan sites, which concludes that there is no evidence for social differentiation based on this criterion. But this is moot since he also notes that according to Skalník (1978:614) there is little economic differentiation within any archaic state; the Mature Harappan pattern is what would be expected.

Attention also is drawn to physical anthropology (Jacobson 1986:149–50). It is widely known that Harappan skeletal remains are remarkably free of trauma and differences in terms of nourishment and general health. This lack of difference might indicate a bias in the archaeological record; perhaps only elites were buried in the cemeteries that have been excavated, and the poorer classes were disposed of by other methods (Kennedy 1981:24). In his discussion of "disposal of the dead," Jacobson also notes another widely recognized feature of Harappan interments: they rarely contain artifacts of significant value. If there were wealthy people at Harappan sites, it was not appropriate for them to take artifacts with them to the grave. His discussion of why this might be is useful (Jacobson 1986:315), but he concludes that it makes little difference because of Skalník's (1978:614) dictum that there is generally little economic differentiation among the citizens of archaic states.

Jacobson (1986:150) deals with writing and social stratification as "documentation." No one doubts the presence of writing, but its role in the life of Harappans is not well understood.

The final proxy for social stratification is "art" (Jacobson 1986:151). The Indus seals are discussed in terms of their possible use as identifiers for elites. Terracotta female figurines and the well-known bronze dancing girl from Mohenjo-daro (fig. 8.5) are noted as possibly indicative of a class of performers as opposed to the fully clothed "mother goddesses." These observations are all interesting and worth noting, although Jacobson correctly recognizes that there is no overwhelming case here.

Overall, Jacobson presents a strong case for his position, but he does not deal with the key issues of centralized leadership—bureaucracy and central government. In the end we need to know, "Where are the Harappan kings and the rest of the state apparatus?" Jacobson does not answer this question.

J. Mark Kenoyer (1992, 1994) has written two articles that relate directly to this topic. The first is a well-reasoned review of craft specialization and social segregation that is the best statement on this important feature of Mature Harappan life. The second deals directly with the question of whether the Mature Harappan political system was a state (Kenoyer 1994).

The position Kenoyer takes on the issue of whether the Mature Harappan was a state revolves around what he terms the "state-level" of a society (1994:71, 73, 75). He correctly assesses Fairservis's position that the Mature Harappan was a step below the complexity we would generally associate with a state. Kenoyer (1994:75) observes that "In a similar vein, Shaffer argues that the urban centers of the Indus region were a unique feature of an equally unique form of pre-state society (Shaffer 1982, 1993; Shaffer and Lichtenstein 1989)." This does correctly represent Shaffer's work (personal communication 1997). Shaffer's position is that the Harappan civilization is not "prestate" in its form because he does not hold stock in evolutionary theory of this type. Since the Harappan civilization is sufficiently different in sociocultural form that it does not compare well with Mesopotamia or Dynastic Egypt, which are by convention called "states," Shaffer is reluctant to use this term to describe Mature Harappan organization. Shaffer is somewhat reserved in his assessment of the level of sociocultural complexity witnessed in the Mature Harappan, but he does see a society based on class coupled to craft and career specialization. The level of urbanization and the size of the Harappan civilization also are indicators of considerable complexity for him. Although Shaffer does not know how the Harappan civilization was organized, he is willing to say that it was as complex as Mesopotamia.

Shaffer's position is in some ways the one held here. The Harappan civilization is sufficiently different from Mesopotamia and Dynastic Egypt that it should be separated from these "states" of the archaic world. The issue is not evolutionary in the sense of being "prestate" or even "poststate." The Harappan civilization was a "nonstate."

In the end, whether or not we call the Harappan civilization a state is of less importance than the central issue of recognizing the diversity of organization and form among the sociocultural systems that are associated with this term. All societies are unique, and yet they share some set of features that allows us to call them "societies." On the other hand, terminology has its practical utility. When one begins to understand a complex sociocultural system like the Harappan civilization and finds that using models from other places has a dismal record of failure—witness Wheeler's priest-kings, granaries, and implications of Mesopotamian origins—one may wish to set the Harappan civilization apart, conceptually and terminologically, from other complex societies called "archaic states." It is at least an act of intellectual renewal and a candid admission that the "state" paradigm does not work; it could be time to attempt to understand the Harappan civilization by using another conceptual framework.

Shereen Ratnagar is a historian of ancient India at Jawaharlal Nehru University whose first work (1981) on the Harappan civilization dealt with the third-millennium maritime commerce between the Indus Valley and Mesopotamia. Her interests have since turned to the political organization of the Indus civilization (Ratnagar 1991). Ratnagar proposes that the Harappan civilization was a state. Her position poses an interesting, not fully resolved question. Are "urbanism" and the "state" linked in a causal way? If they are, she makes her case by definition, because no one seriously questions the status of Mohenjo-daro and Harappa as "urban." But if urbanism and the state are not necessarily linked, if historically documented cities exist outside the structure of a state, she may be on the wrong track. In spite of her opinion on the differences between chiefdoms and states (1991:16–18), this point is never resolved; the contention that "urbanism is not viable in the context of chiefdoms" is never demonstrated.

In fact, it is widely believed in anthropological archaeology that the city or urbanization is impossible without the state. Bruce Trigger says that: "The state is a necessary condition for the development of urbanism" (1972: 592). Nothing in the archaeological or ethnographic record would lead one to believe that this contention is a demonstrated fact. There are examples of cities and urbanism existing in the absence of states. Pre-Islamic Mecca seems to present one such case of "stateless" urbanization in a historical era (Wolf 1951). Anthropologist Robert Foster has noted that the modern nation of Papua New Guinea is not a state, if one considers a monopoly of the legitimate use of force as a critical part of its definition (Foster, personal communication 1977). Other examples of this level of sociocultural complexity in the absence of a state may be seen in the mosaic of polities that Maurizio Tosi (1977, 1979a, 1979b, 1986) has brought together under the rubric of the "Turanian civilization." Although Tosi refers to these polities as "states," the archaeological signatures that the "Turanian civilization" carries do not compare well with those developed by Flannery in this volume for a state form of organization. The Harappan civilization appears to have been another case.

WHAT MIGHT THE HARAPPAN POLITY HAVE BEEN LIKE?

The evidence, as it is perceived here, suggests that the Harappan civilization was as internally differentiated and structurally specialized as archaic states like Mesopotamia and Egypt. In these latter two areas, there is abundant archaeological evidence for highly developed, competitive societies backed by their own versions of state ideology. In terms of levels of sociocultural differentiation, the Indus, Mesopotamia, and Egypt compare well with one another.

The principal evidence for sociocultural complexity in the case of the Indus is the existence of three Mature Harappan cities: Harappa, Mohenjo-daro, and the unexcavated Ganweriwala in Cholistan. Dholavira, currently under excavation in Kutch (Bisht 1991), may be another urban settlement. There is literacy in the form of the yet to be deciphered Indus script (Possehl 1996), used mostly on stamp seals made from soft stone. Long-distance trade and culture contact, some signs of architectural differentiation, and the size of the civilization, which implies powerful mechanisms to hold the whole together, also are important. The presence of class and social stratification in the Indus is evident in the range of houses at Mohenjo-daro and the other large, excavated sites. These dwellings can be graded by size and elaborateness, and by the evidence for the lodgings of domestic servants and other workers. Contrasts between city dwellers and farmers and herders documented from smaller sites also suggest well-developed social stratification.

Indus burial customs are not well understood, but the use of cemetery interment is consistent with the notion that a single class of Harappan citizens may have been disposed of in this manner. It appears unlikely that burial in cemeteries was the norm for the whole of the Harappan population. Class also emerges from an examination of craft specialization in the Indus civilization, which is sophisticated and well represented at many sites. The absence of palaces and temples, and the faceless quality of the Harappan civilization, are the contrasts that emphasize my point on the kind (not level) of development in the political and religious institutions of Indus civilization.

The image of the Indus civilization that appears as a result of this study places little emphasis on political and/or economic centralization, which seems to have been at a minimum. There is no evidence for kingship; the ideology does not express itself through the centralization of resources and the construction of monuments. The faceless nature of these peoples is in keeping with this position. Centralization is also one of the hallmarks of the archaic state. Lacking evidence for strong, centralized institutions of the type characterized by the archaic state, one might logically begin to look for an understanding through a model using strong, decentralized institutions.

The "nonstate" model has to include the notion that Mature Harappan institutions were strong, since there is evidence for strength in Harappan culture. There is a suite of artifacts and an associated style that covered about 1,000,000 km^2 for a period of about 600 years. It includes such things as the writing system, the system of weights and measures, and a host of artifact categories like ceramics, beads, figurines, and metal objects. Architectural standards are apparent, as well as the ability to build and maintain a city like Mohenjo-daro with its grid town plan and a hydraulic system, the *Wasserluxus* of Michael Jansen (1993). The control and manipulation of water within settlements is a notable feature of many Mature Harappan sites. These peoples were also adventurous seafarers and overland explorers, venturing into the Arabian Gulf and to the mouth of the Red Sea. They knew eastern Iran, Afghanistan, Central Asia, and the western Ganges, as well as central India. Some of them also lived and worked in Mesopotamia. Strong institutions were needed to create and maintain this sociocultural system. Therefore, one has to eschew the notion that centralized is automatically "strong" and that decentralized is therefore "weak."

The political strength of the Mature Harappan, or the emerging Mature Harappan, can also be seen in the Early/Mature Harappan transition. This might have been a period of political unrest involving some level of combat, raiding, and conquest, with the ancestors of the peoples we see documented at a place like Mohenjo-daro and other Mature Harappan sites being the winners. The absence of centralized leadership and a proposal of multi-regional political success may seem contradictory, but it is possible to imagine strong temporary alliances among a number of groups. Political issues may then have been resolved through decentralized councils and negotiation. The sense that the defining quality of the Mature Harappan was a distinct, new ideology leads one to suggest that these beliefs may have been used as the force that bound these decentralized units together, giving them a powerful common ground.

The same kind of decentralization also might be true for the religious institution. Worship or devotion seems to have been a personal matter, carried out in the home for the most part. The Great Bath at Mohenjo-daro suggests that there was a civic level of worship, but this is not the predominant theme, and other prominent sites (e.g., Harappa, Kalibangan, Nausharo, Chanhu-daro, Dholavira) do not seem to have comparable religious architecture. One of the emerging themes within the study of Indus civilization is that it represents an ideology, a way of life in a holistic sense, much like Islam. This ideology was more than a simple religion; it is better understood as a *genre de vie* (Sorre 1962). Michael Jansen has come to believe that Mohenjo-daro was a physical manifestation intended to symbolize the Harappan ideology and way of life (Jansen 1983, 1985, 1987, 1989, 1992). This line of thinking is relatively new and immensely interesting. Jansen also has proposed that Mohenjo-daro was a founder city, established by the peoples of the Mature Harappan as their premier urban environment.

Whatever the ideological life of the Harappans may have been, there is reason to believe that their political system was segmented and decentralized, lacking a "king." Considering what is known of the Harappan civilization, the system might have looked something like the following. (1) There is no evidence for a central government, or bureaucracy, implying that older "tribal" organizations wielded political power within regional contexts. (2) Territorial sovereignty for the Harappan civilization, as a whole, would have been weakly developed compared with that of the regional centers. Lacking a strong center, this system would be vulnerable to collapse without the presence of powerful integrating forces. The whole was held in place through a strong Harappan ideology, which crossed the segmented, regional political boundaries, reaching into every Harappan family (Possehl 1990). Other forms of solidarity, such as trade, ecological interdependence, and intermarriage, would have augmented the ideological basis of Harappan civilization. (3) There were few, if any, bureaucrats and public administrators. Crafts and trades were highly developed. Private administration by merchants, traders, "money" managers, religious practitioners, bards, and others could be admitted as possible career specialists, given the level of sociocultural development and the absence of a strong central government. (4) The monopoly of force, so often associated with states, was weakly developed at both the civilization level and that of the regional polities as well. It would not be surprising to find that it was a subject of controversy and contest within regional contexts. (5) There seem to be two levels of allegiance built into this kind of system, one for the region and another for the civilization as a whole. To some degree, the foundations for this allegiance are different;

one is a kind of "national" ideology, and the other is related to lineage, territory, and history. (6) Given this duality, the system would have been in a constant battle against fissiparous forces: on one side, ideology, trade, ecological integration, and marriage; on the other, lineage, brotherhood, territory, history, one's occupational locus, and pride in one's social group and the memory of ancestors who helped to make it great. This seems to have been a lopsided battle, and over the long term the forces of division and disintegration had the upper hand. From the point of view of cultural ecology, it was not a satisfactory form of adaptation. It succeeded for a while, probably because the ideology was new and strong, and the manner of socializing young people to the norms of the civilization as a whole was undertaken effectively. But sooner or later this too failed.

The actual form of organization for the Mature Harappan is obviously not well understood. In fact, there may be considerable debate about certain key points presented here: ruling councils during the transitional period, settling disputes through decentralized debate, the lack of strong central government, diffused territorial sovereignty, control over force, and the like. This all sounds rather different than the usual thoughts on the organization and operation of a civilization, but then this one failed; the Harappan civilization was a fleeting moment of Bronze Age urbanization. As such, the proposal that the founding principles of its organization were "different," flawed from the standpoint of an ecological or adaptive perspective, makes perfectly good sense.

CONCLUDING REMARKS

It is not possible in a short essay to develop adequately a number of important themes characterizing the Indus civilization as an example of ancient sociocultural complexity without the archaic state form of political organization. Nor has the case been proved, in the sense of logical finality, leaving much to be done on this issue. But one thing is clear. The Harappan civilization has been the subject of an immense amount of thought, most of which has been couched in conventional comparative terms. One of the most important themes has been an assumption that it was a state, which has led to a host of comparative assumptions and no small amount of interpretation of this civilization in terms of its contemporary neighbors to the west, in Mesopotamia. There are many examples of this practice, some not to be taken seriously (Pran Nath 1931, 1932; Sankarananda 1962; Waddell 1925). But there also are serious, even eminent, scholars who have failed to understand the Harappans on their own terms and relied too much on what we know, or think we know, of ancient Mesopotamian life. One of these is Sir Mortimer Wheeler:

If . . . we now review the comparison between the two civilizations as a whole, it is fair to recognize a general affinity with recurring and important differences in detail which are at least sufficient to set aside any likelihood of immediate or wholesale colonization of the Indus region from Sumer. For the physical structure of the Indus civilization we must look to more local sources and causes. But this is not to rob Mesopotamia of a close responsibility in the matter. Mesopotamia, and none other, retains her world-priority, not to the "invention" of town life (in which at present Jericho in Jordan is far in the lead), but to the production of a mature and literate civilization, with organized accounts and archives: in other words, to the essential *idea* of civilization. Thanks to Mesopotamia, by the end of the 4th millennium the idea of civilization was in the air of the Middle East. Ideas have wings, and from Mesopotamia, the mature idea of civilization, always including that of writing, later reached the Indian coast and the Indus Valley by an easy sea route and perhaps by land, to be adapted there to local taste and circumstances. (Wheeler 1959:104)

If such a line of thought remains the prevailing mode to understand the ancient peoples of the Indus, is there any wonder that so little is known for sure? With so much evidence against it, is there any reason to continue to see the Harappan political system as a copy of the Mesopotamian archaic state and, in so doing, miss one of the truly important aspects of the ancient Indian experiment with urbanization?

What we have learned from the new studies of the Harappan civilization is that ancient civilizations, or complex societies, are far more variable in their form and organization than the typological schemes of traditional, unilineal evolution can accommodate. Concisely stated, well-conceived definitions have an important role to play in archaeology, along with typological schemes. For the most part these tools can assist us in reaching our ends, but they are not ends in themselves. Whether we call the Indus civilization an archaic state or something else is of less importance than recognizing the variability inherent in the experiment with the level of sociocultural complexity that it represents. Much work is left to be done in terms of describing and defining this diversity of complexity. But we already know something about the diversity; the time has come to phrase our analytical questions in a way that tries to understand it. Why, for example, did Mesopotamia and the Indus take such different courses to civilization? Why are these sociocultural systems so different in so many ways and yet seem to share a level of sociocultural integration that brings them together on other important terms? Such a research agenda is entirely different from the one that is now in place. Its implementation would represent a significant step forward in the study of Harappan civilization as well as sociocultural complexity in general.

9

Inka Strategies of Incorporation and Governance
CRAIG MORRIS

T he most important features of the growth of early state societies are (1) the centralization of the decision-making mechanisms in the hands of a small elite, (2) the expansion of this centralized power so that it plays an ever larger role in controlling the behavior of the people and the natural resources they exploit, (3) the differentiation of the centralized power structure so that it can manage an increasingly complex social and economic order, and (4) the elaboration of ideologies and symbolic forms by which the multiplicity of subunits can communicate and be articulated into the complex political and economic structure. The primary questions as we look at the evidence for the growth of sociopolitical complexity involve, on the one hand, how power is centralized and increased, and, on the other, how the mechanisms are constructed through which that increasingly centralized power is effectively exercised and administered (Flannery 1972; Wright 1977, 1986a).

As we examine the growth of political complexity for the central Andes, where the archaeological evidence is still very incomplete, I believe it is profitable to look first in some detail at the best known of the archaic Andean states, the Inka (fig. 9.1), even though many centuries had elapsed between the Inka and the earliest states in the region. In spite of the enormous success of the Inka in extending their control to become ultimately the New World's largest native empire, they did not have writing, and their economy functioned without major marketplaces. Political and economic processes were extremely dynamic, and the changes that the evolving empire was

Figure 9.1. Map of the Inka empire in western South America, showing principal sites and places mentioned in the text.

undergoing can therefore be instructive in understanding sociopolitical growth in the Andes in general, including those processes that centuries before might have led to pristine Andean states. Indeed, if we could trace the entire prehistory of the Inka as they evolved from a small regional polity (probably at the level that some would call a *macroetnía* and others a chiefdom), we would be able to see the relatively uncontaminated birth of a state, though obviously not a pristine state (Rostworowski 1988).

Reliable data on the initial stages of Inka prehistory are still virtually nonexistent. My strategy for evaluating the Inka expansion is to look briefly at a few of the better understood examples of the regions and kingdoms they incorporated. In these cases we can see markedly different strategies of incorporation and governance. These differing strategies were shaped mainly by the different circumstances of the local regions at the time they were added to Tawantinsuyu, but they also probably reflect that the annexed regions were added at different phases in the process of Inka political development. The results of this examination reveal, I believe, a need to shift the focus somewhat from military coercion and administrative bureaucracy to an increasing stress on the mechanisms whereby new levels of sociocultural identity, political collaboration, and economic growth were attained. Both military force and a very complicated administrative bureaucracy were indeed involved, but many analysts have tended to view these in terms of a European model (D'Altroy 1992; Patterson 1991). Although the Inka may have taken some steps toward such a model in their final decades, at the time of the Spanish invasion they can still be best understood in terms of some of the principles of traditional, small-scale societies—in spite of the vast size and enormous complexity that had been achieved.

Three features or tactics characterized the Inka's rapid march to empire: first, an ideology of rule communicated and instilled through a set of elaborate ceremonial activities and visual symbols; second, the provision of notable economic rewards; and only third (and probably late in the process), the use of coercive military force. These features or tactics were used in varying degrees and with great flexibility, depending on the local circumstances the Inka encountered.

VARYING STRATEGIES OF INKA EXPANSION

The hallmark of Inka rule was the flexibility and variability with which Inka rulers governed their provinces. These variations were related to several factors, including the specific resources they sought to exploit, the extent to which incorporation into the empire was resisted by local peoples, and the densities of population in the various regions. One of the key conditions that the Inka faced was marked differences in sociopolitical scale and degree of centralization of authority in the areas they ultimately ruled. Those regions populated by small-scale societies are especially instructive in considering the initial rise of state societies in the Andes at least a millennium earlier. Some of the strategies used by the Inka state to build larger sociopolitical scale—especially in areas of small, frequently confrontational, political units—can be useful in constructing models and hypotheses for looking at earlier cases in the emergence of Andean sociopolitical complexity.

On the desert coast of Peru, the richest part of the Andean region because of the great concentrations of irrigated agricultural and maritime resources, Inka strategies of incorporation and domination seem to have depended in part on the degree to which the Cuzco rulers were able to achieve a degree of peaceful collaboration or were forced to deal with resistance and confrontation. One strategy involved the utilization and enhancement of the extant structure of authority. This classic strategy of indirect rule through the existing power structure appears to have been followed only rarely by the Inka, in large part because few really large centralized states existed in the Andes at the time of the Inka expansion. In part it also was the result of strong resistance to Inka rule by some large kingdoms, such as the Chimú on the Peruvian north coast. A prominent case of the peaceful incorporation of a centralized polity was the Chincha kingdom on the south-central coast of Peru. There, our current research is beginning to provide a picture of how the Inka inserted themselves into an important state and manipulated its internal workings.

María Rostworowski's (1970) studies of the written sources on Chincha suggest a gradual incorporation in which Chincha was permitted to retain its rich trade—apparently including metals, textiles and, especially, *Spondylus* shell—by sea with the coast of what is now Ecuador and overland with the altiplano regions in the south. Incorporation was initiated by the Inka with the exchange of gifts and women. As the relationship proceeded, Chincha gave lands that were cultivated for the Inka, and women for making cloth and beer, two of the state's most essential products. They also agreed to an Inka request to construct a palace in the Chincha capital, now the archaeological site of La Centinela (Morris 1988b).

La Centinela is a group of massive compounds that were the focus of public activities of the groups, perhaps based on economic specialization and descent, that constituted the Chincha kingdom. In their midst, the Inka palace compound was constructed of adobe bricks, in contrast to the earlier Chincha construction of *tapia* (walls of pressed earth). The Inka compound used the trapezoidal niches and doorways characteristic of Inka architecture. But alongside the buildings that appear to have served as a typical Inka palace was a truncated pyramidal platform reminiscent of Chincha architecture. It was constructed of adobe bricks and was a formal part of the Inka compound. Yet its shape almost seems to mimic the central features of the Chincha compounds. It is almost as if the Inka had recognized and legitimized local patterns within the compound from which people closely identified with Cuzco-controlled Chincha.

As revealing of Inka tactics for controlling the Chincha capital as their own administrative compound were the modifications—at the same time subtle and powerful—they carried out in the existing Chincha architecture. Several of the *tapia* compounds built in Chincha times were altered by the Inka. Adobes were added to *tapia* construction; niches were incorporated into some public spaces; traffic flow of at least one compound was altered to align it with the Inka compound. However, the evidence suggests that activities were not drastically modified by the Inka overlords. They changed the façade but not the functions. The *tapia* compounds with their pyramid-like architecture were clearly public and ceremonial in nature, but they seem to have been related to relatively small and probably fairly tightly structured groups. It may be speculated that these compounds were the backdrops for rites of political legitimation and social reproduction, such as initiation and marriage, of the groups that composed the Chincha kingdom. If this interpretation is correct, the Inka essentially used the compounds to promote individuals of their choosing within the local Chincha hierarchy. Their administration was based on selecting and manipulating administrative personnel while leaving the existing structure of positions and statuses basically intact.

The Chincha model of Inka "conquest," which brought a wealthy group into the empire peacefully and then ruled it through a well-established local power structure that could be controlled, and perhaps enhanced, by Cuzco from the top, was perhaps ideal for the Inka. It gave them great economic and political advantage with relatively little investment. However, the opportunity for this kind of expansion was rare. Most of the area the Inka came to dominate did not have Chincha's strong centralized political structure. Much more common were the small and relatively unstable groups we can see in the ethnohistoric and archaeological records for the highlands. We may attribute some of the statements in the chronicles that credit the Inka with the pacification of a region characterized by almost constant conflict to exaggerations by Inka officials glorifying the accomplishments of their state to Europeans. However, the archaeological records from areas such as the upper Yanamarca Valley (D'Altroy 1992; Earle et al. 1987), the upper Huallaga Valley (Morris and Thompson 1985; Murra 1962b), and part of the Lake Titicaca region (Hyslop 1976; Julien 1983) suggest an immediately pre-Inka pattern of small polities with little public architecture built frequently in defensible positions—a pattern that suggests uncentralized polities in frequent conflict.

These areas are particularly interesting from the point of view of political growth. Changes in settlement pattern and other aspects of the archaeological evidence imply an Inka attempt to reduce conflict and increase control by establishing a hierarchical political structure. They were interested in controlling the key personnel in a multitiered structure of administration, as was the case in Chincha. In these cases, however, the intermediate administrative tiers were either nonexistent or extremely unstable and had to be established or stabilized by the Inka. The sixteenth-century inspection by Garci Diez de San Miguel shows part of the region of Lake Titicaca to have been the relatively centralized Lupaca kingdom under the dual leadership of Cari and Cusi. Based on the written source alone, it is reasonable to conclude that the Lupaca was a pre-Inka entity (Murra 1964), not unlike Chincha in scale and centralization. But my reading of the still limited archaeological evidence leads me to suspect that the Lupaca kingdom may at least in part have been the result of successful Inka efforts at local-level centralization. Hyslop's (1977:170) emphasis on the great elaboration of burial towers (*chulpas*) for the local leaders during Inka times is a case in point. According to his analysis, the power of certain cooperative local leaders was enhanced as a system of indirect rule was put into place. In the Yanamarca region of the central highlands, the Wanka also seem to have been moving toward some degree of organizational complexity, though not necessarily loyalty to the Inka rulers. The peoples of that region promptly allied themselves with the Spaniards in the aftermath of Cajamarca (D'Altroy 1992: 47, 186).

In the three regions mentioned, the Inka had built major provincial administrative centers: the Yanamarca area was under the settlement of Hatun Xauxa; the Lupaca part of the Lake Titicaca area was under Chucuito; and the upper Huallaga Valley was under Huánuco Pampa. One of our best avenues to understanding Inka rule is to examine the functioning of these provincial capitals. However, both Xauxa and Chucuito are now largely covered by modern towns; only Huánuco Pampa has received extensive archaeological study.

HUÁNUCO PAMPA

Huánuco Pampa probably had a relatively small permanent population; its nearly 4,000 structures served instead to house many thousands of people who came periodically for state festivals and to work for the state as part of their *mita* labor tax. The buildings also provided various kinds of public space, housed production of certain arts and crafts, and served as warehousing for the supplies that made the other activities possible.

Our research in the 1970s (Morris 1972, 1982; Morris and Thompson 1985) has shown that the great central plaza and the buildings around it witnessed public ceremonies, probably including the festivals of the elaborate Inka ritual calendar and possibly also ritual battles, such as those known for Cuzco (Cobo 1990[1653]:135, 215, 245), which helped define relations among groups in the region. Royal dwellings and temples formed a compound at the city's eastern edge. The thousands of corn beer jars and plates found in buildings around smaller plazas between the royal compound and the central plaza suggest that public feasts were prominent in these areas.

More than 500 warehouses held food and other supplies. A compound of 50 houses provided work and living space to a group of weavers and brewers who turned out the cloth and maize beer that were such fundamental parts of the Inka's gifts to their subjects, on the one hand, and their hospitality obligations on the other (Morris 1974, 1982; Murra 1962a, 1980; Rostworowski 1988). Most of the activities identified archaeologically through excavations at Huánuco Pampa fit with the picture of a regional capital where the Inka could fulfill obligations of asymmetrical reciprocity. It was a provincial administrative center, but one that fit into a system of reciprocal administration rather than being based on bureaucratic and military mechanisms. These patterns of royal hospitality based in asymmetrical reciprocity functioned through a structure of dual divisions that offered the building blocks of a hierarchical political and economic organization.

A second set of evidence from Huánuco Pampa that is pertinent to Inka political processes is somewhat more abstract. It comes from an analysis of architecture and the way space was organized in the administrative center's architectural plan (C. Morris 1987). Huánuco Pampa is divided into two main divisions by the Cuzco-Quito road that runs through it from northeast to southwest. One of these divisions contains more elaborate and finely made buildings and can probably be considered *Hanan,* or the "upper" half, in Inka principles of organization as expressed at Cuzco. The two main divisions are clearly subdivided, creating a quadripartite pattern around the large rectangular plaza (fig. 9.2). The four divisions may have been further subdivided into three divisions each, creating twelve zones.

It seems likely that the city plan of Huánuco Pampa reflected basic Inka organizational principles that permeate several aspects of Inka ideology and practice. The best documented expression of these principles is in the organization of the shrines around Cuzco (Cobo 1990[1653]:47–84; Rowe 1979; Zuidema 1964). There is no written evidence as to the meaning of the complex set of divisions at Huánuco Pampa; however, the similarity to the patterning of the Cuzco shrines and the way they were worshiped seems too close to be coincidental. Similar principles of division and combination pervade other aspects of Inka organization and ideology, such as the calendar.

The elaborate set of divisions expressed in the plan is probably related to Huánuco Pampa's role as an administrative center. For Inka rule to function effectively, it would have been more efficient to establish a hierarchical order among the small local groups comprising that region, so that the state would have to deal with fewer local leaders. It is intriguing to speculate that the city plan might have been used not just as an abstract expression of important ideological principles, but actually to place groups of people in a physical relationship to each other that mirrored the hierarchical relationships

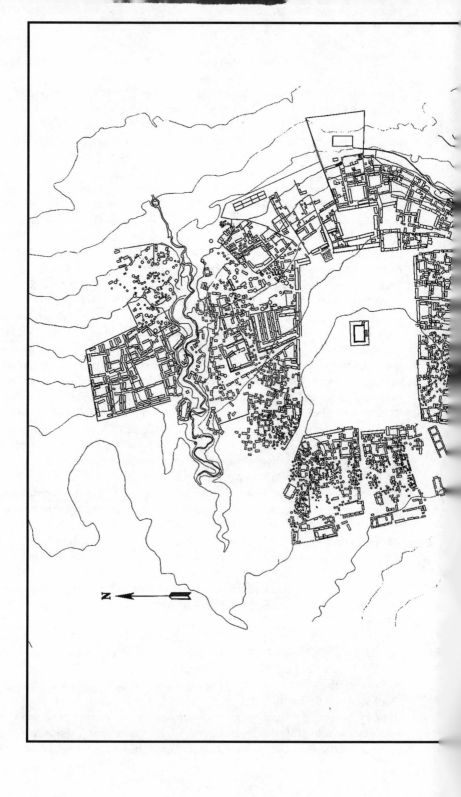

N

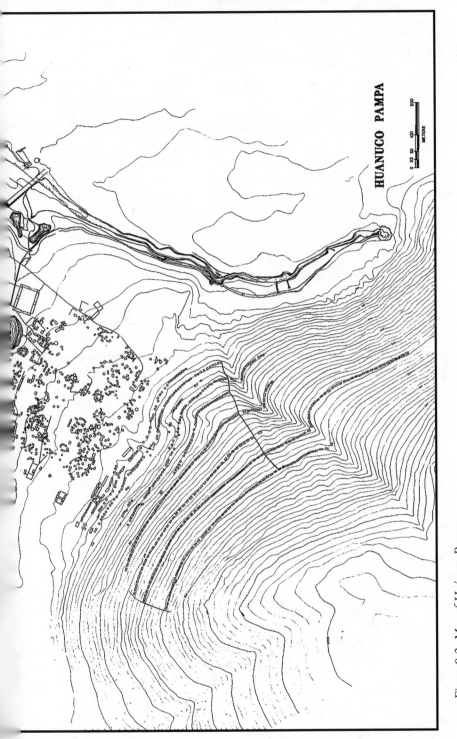

Figure 9.2. Map of Huánuco Pampa.

the Inka state wanted them to assume. These positions could then have been reinforced (and occasionally rearranged) through participation in the ceremonies prescribed in the ritual calendar. Seen in this way, the city plan becomes a diagram of sociopolitical ideology and a template for the creation of actual social, political, and economic organization. It is a way of defining, maintaining, and, if the need arises, sometimes restructuring the social segments that are the building blocks of state society. Relationships among and between the various divisions were probably mediated and manipulated through reciprocity; in this way the various small polities could be converted into a coherent hierarchical local organization by creating new levels of sociopolitical scale that the Inka manipulated.

From the Huánuco Pampa example we can begin to formulate an idea of an Inka strategy for converting groups of relatively noncentralized polities into small kingdomlike units that they could administer through indirect rule—by manipulating personnel within a hierarchical and centralized system, similar to the way they controlled Chincha. Even though we are still far from confirming the identities or intergroup activities of the peoples who used the various sectors of Huánuco Pampa, it is reasonable to suggest that public architecture was used as a means of encoding and teaching an overall political structure. In a society that lacked writing, architecture and other media carried an especially heavy burden in facilitating communication and assisting the inculcation of new beliefs and behaviors.

POLITICAL GROWTH PROCESSES IN THE INKA STATE

I mentioned at the outset that the fundamental processes in the creation of Tawantinsuyu were political. They involved the inculcation of a complex ideology of rule instilled through elaborate ritual, as outlined for Huánuco Pampa, and communicated with visual symbols. They also were economic, involving the provision of important sumptuary and subsistence goods through the redistributive economy. These two processes were intertwined by the important social and ideological symbols carried by the sumptuary goods that the emerging complex economy produced and utilized in highly visible and ritually important ways (see Morris 1991 for fuller presentation). These goods—along with the symbols encoded in architecture and site planning and the *khipu*—formed a technology of communication that enabled a highly differentiated political and administrative structure to function, even without writing.

The examination above of cases of the Inka incorporation of hinterland regions suggests some of the ways the economic and political processes worked in actual strategies of annexation and governance. The flexible nature of Inka rule put great emphasis on the adjustment of state policy to the details of local realities. But overlaying this flexibility was an insistence on the actual physical presence of governmental installations and personnel in the hinterlands. This took the form of the well-documented system of state installations linked by roads (e.g., Hyslop 1984; Morris 1972, 1981). The ceremonies and the symbolic paraphernalia of the central authority were carried to the outlying "capitals" of the state in places like Huánuco Pampa, La Centinela, and dozens of other administrative centers. In this way reciprocal administration could be dispersed and differentiated but would still function almost as if the highest level of the Inka elite (perhaps even the ruler himself) was everywhere present. This same system redistributed the key sumptuary and subsistence goods, thereby conferring prestige, assigning roles and positions, building support for state authority, and generating state revenues. Huánuco Pampa and La Centinela, each in its very different way, fulfilled these primary ceremonial and economic functions that were the foundation of the state.

This brief examination of Inka governing processes allows a somewhat different perspective on some of the features that we have often thought to be essential defining characteristics of state societies. The Inka certainly possessed most of these characteristics, including control over a very extensive territory and a well-developed structure of centralized authority. While the centralized rulership was not strictly hereditary, there were well-established mechanisms for selecting the new ruler from among a limited number of potential successors in the event of the death or deposing of the sitting ruler. Rulership was an institutionalized and permanent position.

There was also a well-established ruling elite, even though this elite group was probably viewed more in ethnic terms (i.e., Inka vs. the various non-Inka groups) than in terms of social class in a strict sense. Many of the members of this elite were organized into an impressive and apparently highly effective administrative bureaucracy. There were certainly record keepers (*khipu kamayuq*) and other administrative officials, as we would expect in any bureaucracy. But just as much of governance was based in an administration of reciprocity and ceremony, the bureaucracy, too, was a bureaucracy of reciprocity that managed the feasts of an elaborate ritual calendar and saw to it that the goods and people were in the right place at the right time throughout a vast administrative network. The more we begin to grasp the details of what was accomplished, the more impossible it seems given the communication technology then available.

The Inka also managed the economy to an unusual degree. This mainly consisted of the large-scale mobilization of labor to produce goods to support the redistributive economy and the elite. As we have seen, the functions of goods produced in this redistributive economy went well beyond

the economic, being critical to communication as well. The vast labor resources were also used for enormous capital projects. On the one hand, they
built the elaborate system of state cities, way stations, and roads that constituted the infrastructure of administration; on the other, they were used for
investments in irrigation and terracing systems to increase production and
for warehousing systems to even out seasonal and annual variations in the
availability of goods.

A complex hierarchy of settlements, taken by archaeologists to be essential material indicators of state-level organization, is easy to discern in the
Inka case: there is a hierarchy of administrative centers within the installations built by the state (Guaman Poma 1980[1613]:1000–1007; Hyslop
1990; Morris 1993). In addition, there is the superimposition of Inka over
non-Inka settlements (Morris 1972); in some of the cases where preexisting
complex societies were incorporated by the Inka into Tawantinsuyu, the
pre-Inka settlement hierarchies may have continued to function. This seems
to have been the case in Chincha. The settlement system was thus extremely
complex, both in terms of hierarchy and in terms of horizontal functional
specificity.

From all this evidence there is no doubt that Tawantinsuyu was one of
the most vast and important of ancient states. There are, nevertheless, some
incongruities that our picture of the Inka raises for our traditional conception of ancient states. I briefly emphasize two. The first is that principles of
economic reciprocity remained central to the nature of authority and to the
functioning and growth of the state, even at its impressive scale. This emphasis on bringing the ruler and the elite, with all the attendant hospitality
and generosity, into direct contact with large numbers of people mim-
ics simpler levels of political organization (Morris 1982; Murra 1960:400;
Rostworowski 1988). The second incongruity has to do with the kinds of
conflict and warfare that were part of the political process. The topic of Inka
warfare is far more complex than the studies of it have implied. The comments below raise questions that will hopefully encourage more research
aimed at producing new information and a greater understanding of the
issue.

While there is no question that elements of force were involved in Inka
rule (Murra 1986), I suspect that we have tended to exaggerate its coercive
role (D'Altroy 1992; Hyslop 1990; Morris 1982). Much of this exaggeration
derives from the early Spanish sources, which tended to assume that the Inka
expansion had been based on imperial conquests not unlike the one in
which they were engaged (see Webster, this volume, for an alternative perspective). They also assumed that most of the elaborate royal retinue of the
Inka were soldiers. Most important, they did not grasp the distinction between ritual battles and battles of coercion. Although ritual battles were

planned events, usually tied to the ceremonial calendar, they usually produced injuries, and even fatalities. Hartmann (1972) has noted their possible ritual role; blood was spilled, in a kind of substitute for sacrifice, to ensure the fertility of the earth. Victories in ritual battle conferred prestige (Gorbak, Lischetti, and Muñoz 1962; Hartmann 1972) and helped establish relationships of dominance and subjugation resulting in a political hierarchy, but they were not intended to inflict real military defeat leading to coercive control supported by a continuing military presence.

My evidence for altering the role we have traditionally assigned to warfare is almost entirely archaeological. It is, in addition, heavily influenced by personal research. In the 3,000 or so provenience units excavated in imperial Inka contexts at several sites by projects I have directed, such as those mentioned in the cases summarized above, we have recovered fewer than 50 artifacts that can be classified as weapons. Furthermore, all of these could just as well be attributed to ritual warfare as to coercive warfare. I emphasize that the sites we have studied have been basically administrative in nature, and none was located in a defensive position. Nevertheless, we fully expected to find military remains at Huánuco Pampa; the first excavations we conducted there were in an area I suspected to be military barracks (Morris and Thompson 1985:70). In the past I have offered elaborate rationalizations for the rarity of weapons in the city (Morris 1982:158, 160); many of them were made of perishable materials (Rowe 1946:274–78), and they were probably not the kind of artifacts abandoned, except on the battlefield (Morris 1982:160). I also argued that military activities were probably focused on the frontiers, and that they would have been reduced at sites like Huánuco Pampa as such sites became increasingly devoted to administrative matters as the frontier moved far away. Some of the same factors may have accounted for the absence of weapons in the warehouses (Morris 1967), yet some Spanish writers insist that weapons storage was one of the functions of the warehousing system (Cieza 1959[1553]).

The excavated archaeological evidence for Inka weapons elsewhere is not much greater. In his assessment of Inka military sites, John Hyslop (1990: 154) noted: "The identification of military settlements is compounded by a curious lack of evidence of arms in the few sites that have been excavated or where extensive surface collections have been made." But he went on to observe that no sites thought to be of a primarily military function have been thoroughly excavated. Small excavations in the Quitaloma section of the enormous walled hilltop site of Pambamarca, about 30 km from Quito, have yielded sling stones (Oberem 1968:338–42). Pambamarca is one of a number of heavily fortified sites near the part of the Inka frontier that was still expanding in 1532.

Most of the archaeological attribution of military functions is based on architecture and site location, as Hyslop's (1990) summary indicates. There is virtually no archaeological evidence of facilities for the regular stationing of garrisons. One of the few major Inka sites that is stated in reliable written sources to have had explicitly military and conquest functions is now known as Inkawasi in the Cañete Valley. According to Cieza (1959[1553]: 338–39), the installation was built specifically for the purpose of subduing the recalcitrant Cañete region, and when that had been accomplished the site was abandoned.

Although incorporation of a new region into the realm was clearly the objective, and military tactics were among those employed, Inkawasi was not a simple garrison site. Cieza (1959[1553]:339) refers to it as a city, called New Cuzco by the ruler (Thupa Yupanki) who built it and ordered that the "districts of the city and hills should have the same names of Cuzco." These implications that Inkawasi supported a variety of functions are amplified by Hyslop's (1985) archaeological work. The architecture and the site plan have heavy ceremonial connotations, with the most concrete suggestion of military importance being the extensive storage areas. "The evidence for housing is limited, and certainly not sufficient to indicate that an army could be housed within the site. Possibly, armies camped on the side of the installation, which was used more for storage, food preparation, lodging officials, and ceremonial activities" (Hyslop 1990:174–75). These data suggest that the Inka employed their full arsenal of strategies for gaining control of the Cañete region; military coercion was only part of the picture.

If these arguments are correct, military coercion became a significant feature only late in the evolution of Tawantinusyu, as part of the series of changes toward more bureaucratic efficiency and effectiveness that Murra (1986) has outlined. If this is the case, further research will find its expression in the archaeological sites near the empire's last frontiers in what are now Ecuador, Bolivia, Chile, and Argentina. Pambamarca, mentioned above, would be such a site, as would Pucará de Andagalá in the province of Catamarca, Argentina, and Inkallakta, near Pocona, Bolivia, all covered in Hyslop's (1990:164–90) survey of large military installations. Indeed, except for Inkawasi, all of the sites included in his summary of supposedly military sites are late and located far from the heartland of the empire.

If we assume that this limited archaeological evidence for large-scale armed conflict is more reliable than the suppositions of the Spanish sources, none of which actually had the opportunity to observe a battle between indigenous Andean groups (Hyslop 1990:147), we still must determine how more limited kinds of conflict were incorporated into the overall pattern of Inka governance and expansion. Just as there are dangers in assuming that Inka warfare was aimed at coercive conquest and rule, there are equal dangers in simply minimizing its importance.

One of the most insightful observations on Inka warfare comes from Murra (1986:52): "Rapid incorporation into Tawantinsuyu is recorded as frequently as the urgent need to reconquer, to defeat again and again ethnic groups listed as already inside the porous frontier. Recent restudies of the ninety-year history of the Inka convince us that rebellion and rapid expansion were both facets of the same process." This indicates that conflict, if not actual warfare in the fully coercive sense, was part of the process of governance. While this may seem to contradict the peaceful look of Inka centers like Huánuco Pampa, it does not do so if we suppose that many of the battles occurred as highly ritualized warfare that was nevertheless a symptom of true conflict. I (Morris 1988a:47) have speculated elsewhere, based on the slender evidence of a few probable sling stones, that the great central plaza at Huánuco Pampa was a scene of ritual battles. Ritual battles would be one use of the big open area (550 × 350 m) and are consistent with the other functions of the administrative city outlined above, especially those related to establishing hierarchies. References to such battles in ethnographic and ethnohistoric contexts suggest that they were usually staged in large open pampas or plazas, and the victor was sometimes referred to as "winning the plaza" (Hartmann 1972:129).

Although the role of battles, whether ritual or coercive, in establishing domination and hierarchies is relatively obvious, other results of conflict would seem to be nonadaptive. For example, the relatively constant, but inconclusive, conflict during the period preceding the Inka expansion would seem to have hindered the effective utilization of dispersed resources and economic growth that came with *Pax Incaica*. But there may be subtle advantages to conflict, especially in regions of high resource diversity. The creation of political, cultural, and, particularly, technological homogeneity is not the most effective way to deal with markedly different ecosystems. Also, from an administrative point of view, the segmentation of authority is an important feature of the state form of organization, as Wright (1977:383) has argued. In the Inka case, the realm was simply too large to control directly without mechanisms of administration and military suppression that I believe had not yet developed. Given this, a fragmented state within which the Inka could manage conflicts, balancing one group against another, was perhaps preferable to a strategy of unification. While such a strategy might produce a structure that would seemingly be easier to administer, it also could provide a base from which more unified discontent could topple a ruler.

The maintenance of some level of managed conflict, therefore, can be seen to be an important ingredient in the preservation of a state level of organization. It also may be that one of the features in which a state level is created involves the control, hierarchization, and ritualization of conflict—not its elimination. Gluckman (1954) brought up some of these issues on the role of internal conflict in his work on African states. Although there are interesting parallels with the Inka example, those states were smaller and less diverse, and Gluckman's analysis led him in a somewhat different direction.

In the Inka case, conflict seems to have become a process in which there is an ever present threat of coercion (maintained as much by myth and ritual as by actual military force) from the top along with frequent battles, ritual and sometimes real, which provide segmentation and shifts in the hierarchy that prevent lower units in the structure of authority from gaining too much power. This kind and level of conflict provides for segmentation and hierarchy without the negative economic implications of military coercion. It enabled the Cuzco rulers to establish a certain level of local centralization, but the centralization was a delicate and shifting balance that allowed local polities to compete as well as to collaborate in the coordination of different ecologies and economies. It allowed the rulers to participate directly in a way that suggested the governing patterns of prestate societies at the same time that diversity and segmentation were fostered. There is neither sufficient time nor available evidence to trace the evolution of this delicate balance of conflict, control, and cooperation in the Andes, but clearly most of its elements already had a long history by Inka times.

CONCLUDING THOUGHTS

At the outset I stressed the importance of economic factors in understanding the expansion and functioning of the Inka state. In conclusion I return to these factors and their relationship to the political and military factors just sketched. It has frequently been observed that societies are best viewed as a set of intricately intertwined subsystems in which changes in one subsystem trigger changes in others in ways that are extremely complex and difficult to measure and analyze (Flannery 1972). The systems that relate to political authority (including those that manage conflict and war), those that relate to communication, and those that relate to the economy (including production, exchange, technology, land and resource management, and labor management) all changed very rapidly during the period of Inka expansion, although the rates of change in the many subsystems varied enormously.

It is the rapid growth in the subsystems that relate to authority that is most impressive. The powerful centralized authority could quickly drive changes in communication, implement more effective technologies of production, and mobilize the economy in general (in the Inka case through the mobilization of labor that was under rather direct political control). This resulted in a kind of mobilization economy in which goods were produced for the state's use (Smelser 1959)—not strictly because of war in this case, but

because of the obligations of reciprocal administration and the need to produce symbols of prestige and markers of social position and status. The state
was the primary beneficiary of overall increases in production, but the economy as a whole probably benefited from the increases as well as from im-
proved redistribution. The motivations for the workers' contributions, thus,
came in part from economic benefits, in part from increased prestige, and
probably in smaller measures from threats of governmental or supernatural
punishment. The rapidity of these changes perhaps resulted from the society's sudden capacity to move to a new level and scope of resource management in dealing with the multiple ecologies that formed its environment.

The mechanisms of Inka rule were based in the redistribution of economic goods, of power and prestige, and of the potential of supernatural favors with their incumbent feelings of security. They were backed up by the
threat, implied and real, of both physical and supernatural punishment.
These mechanisms of Inka expansion and rule were based in strategies and
innovations that had begun centuries earlier. The underlying economic and
adaptive benefits of a coordinating central authority that built an umbrella
over extreme diversity also had been known for centuries and probably
made people, whether consciously or not, more willing to accept a central
authority that was at times distant and benign, and at times direct and even
oppressive (see also Marcus 1987c). The advantages of access to a wider variety and greater quantity of goods outweighed alienation of certain lands
and the displacement of large amounts of labor from the community economy to maintenance of an elite and a bureaucracy, as well as the substantial
program of investment in infrastructure and in capital improvements.

Research on the Inka state is still in its infancy. Recent work has shown
that the situation was extremely complex and that real understanding can
come only from detailed information. It also has shown that our two primary sources of evidence are not always in agreement. The written record
and the archaeological record can give quite different perspectives; interpretation based only on written sources can lead to overly simple, Europeanized
models. A fuller body of archaeological information is urgently needed to
give a more complete and reliable picture of how the Inka state grew and
governed. With its juxtaposition of characteristics associated with simpler
societies and those associated with more modern ones, and the concomitant
suggestion that the various subsystems of archaic polities may evolve at different rates, the Inka case can help move us toward a better general understanding of archaic states and their growth.

10

Warfare and Status Rivalry
Lowland Maya and Polynesian Comparisons
DAVID WEBSTER

Warfare was associated with the origins of virtually all preindustrial civilizations. My original assignment for the School of American Research seminar was to make a detailed comparison between Maya warfare and that of one other ancient archaic state. This approach turned out to be unsatisfactory because, despite its ubiquity, early warfare is poorly understood. Fortunately, the "archaic state" concept also logically includes more recent and better-documented examples of state formation, and another opportunity suggested itself while I was reading about Polynesia. I found the Polynesian data opened up stimulating comparative perspectives, and since I recently lamented the lack of comparative studies of Maya war (Webster 1993), it seemed only fair that I should undertake one.

Of particular comparative significance are patterns of status–rivalry warfare that both Marcus (1993a) and I (Webster 1993) have inferred for the Maya (see also Houston 1993:130). Status-rivalry war is accordingly the subject of the last and most important part of this essay. I emphasize it in an attempt to show that Mayanists do not have to envision a dichotomy, as much of the literature seems to suggest, between ritual conflict on the one hand and conflict motivated by population pressure on the other. Rather, ritual war and territorial aggrandizement complement one another in a syndrome of competition that was widespread in many cultures, including those of Polynesia.

Polynesia may seem an inappropriate choice. The knee-jerk anthropological reaction envisions a region characterized by chiefdoms or rank

societies when first encountered by Europeans. Indeed, our classical conceptions of these societal "types" derive strongly from Polynesia. Behind the
widely shared façade of ranking, however, was an enormous range of sociopolitical complexity, from the essentially egalitarian Maoris of New Zealand
to the stratified systems of Tonga, Tahiti, and Hawai'i.[1] The most complex
Polynesian societies have, in fact, been characterized as or compared with
"archaic" or "incipient" states or civilizations by many anthropologists (e.g.,
Bellwood 1979; Cordy 1981; Goldman 1970; Hommon 1986; Oliver 1974;
Suggs 1960). Others, such as Earle (1978) and Kirch (1984), retain the term
"chiefdom" while describing sociopolitical patterns that are in many respects
"statelike." General comparative treatments (e.g., Claessen and Skalník, eds.
1978) of early state formation commonly include complex Polynesian societies such as Tahiti (Claessen 1978c) and Hawai'i (Seaton 1978), emphasizing their "stratified" organization.

Such confusion of terminology itself is revealing, since it signals the existence of complex sociopolitical forms for which our comparative or evolutionary terminology is inadequate. No issue discussed during the seminar
generated more heated and diverse opinion than the utility of such labels and
their associated evolutionary models. Whatever our personal views on this
controversy, I think we would all agree that the concept of archaic state, the
theme of the seminar, includes the evolutionary processes by which the basic institutions and attendant "great traditions" of the earliest states emerged
from preexisting forms. This very transformational dimension is what makes
the concept so interesting.

One fruitful perspective is that of Fried (1967), who envisioned the state
as a set of institutions that uphold an order of stratification. Incipient states,
and probably some archaic states, as I understand these terms, should exhibit
some forms of stratification. But the institutions and great traditions that
support these systems of stratification may be only incompletely evolved.
The most complex Polynesian societies certainly accord with this definition.
Gailey's (1987) very detailed analysis of Tonga, for example, concludes that
processes of class formation began long before European contact, although
kinship modes of organization were not replaced by mature state institutions.

My intention is not to suggest a Polynesian model for the Maya, nor that
the Maya were in detail "like" any particular Polynesian society. Emphasis is
instead on Polynesian warfare in its wider sociocultural contexts and the insights that it can provide about Maya war in its own distinctive sociocultural
setting. In particular, I use Polynesian data to discuss three hotly debated issues: (1) how were Maya wars conducted? (2) who fought Maya wars? and
(3) what were the purposes and functions of Maya war? Of these, the last is
most important and relates to the subject of status-rivalry war. As we shall
see, Polynesia offers Mayanists not only interesting insights about these issues, but also some cautionary tales as well.

War was a conspicuous feature of Polynesian society: "Warfare—ranging from simple raiding aimed at restoring the honor of the insulted party to major wars of territorial or inter-island conquest—was ubiquitous in Polynesia" (Kirch 1984:195). Evidence concerning war is abundant, since it was featured in Polynesian oral histories, observed and participated in by Europeans, and represented in the archaeological record. Although only occasionally treated as a specialized topic in the Polynesian literature, references to war pervade more general accounts. Perhaps for no other region are conflict and competition so consistently emphasized as essential for understanding how societies were structured and how they changed. As we shall see shortly, one of the more elegant and sensible general anthropological models of warfare is partly based on Polynesian data.

Although I have been erroneously characterized as an advocate of warfare as a "prime mover" in cultural evolution (Sharer and Ashmore 1987: 539), I have in fact taken pains to emphasize war as only *one* variable in much more complex evolutionary processes (Webster 1975). The following discussion reflects this perspective, which also is consistent with general analyses of Polynesian war by scholars such as Earle (1978) and Kirch (1984). Most of my comparisons involve complex Polynesian societies, but important lessons can be learned from simpler ones as well.

WARFARE

Although warfare is much discussed by anthropologists, it is difficult to define because of the many forms that conflict can take. Hassig (1992), for example, offers no general discussion of the concept in his recent synthesis of Mesoamerican warfare (which includes the most up-to-date and exhaustive compilation of source material on Maya war). Below is a brief overview, partly abstracted from another publication of my own (Webster 1993).

Definitions of War

Following Otterbein (1973) and Berndt (1964), warfare consists of planned confrontations between groups of people who conceive of themselves as members of separate political communities. Political communities are composed of individuals who possess and recognize a high level of common interest, have the organizational capacity to cooperate effectively, and are prepared to defend or augment their collective interests through the use of violence. Such groups are often, but not always, territorially defined. Complex polities may consist of multiple, differently constituted political communities that might be better characterized as factions. Members of factions may not share equally in the conduct, risks, or rewards of war.

Warfare is organized and sanctioned group violence that involves armed conflict, including confrontations that combatants recognize may result in deliberate killing. Conflicts are organized and carried out by at least one of the factions with the intent of maintaining the status quo or bringing about a shift of power relations, usually the latter.

Finally, Otterbein (1968) makes the distinction between *internal* war, which consists of conflicts between culturally similar groups, and *external* war between culturally dissimilar groups. This distinction is important because some treatments of Maya warfare (Demarest 1978; Freidel 1986) assert that Maya internal war was usually limited in its political, social, and economic consequences because of shared ethics or charters of permissible behavior.

War as a Process

Vayda (1976), partly basing his ideas on Maori warfare, has avoided the strict definitional problem by emphasizing war as a long-term, graded process with a series of distinct but related phases. The simplest phases might be confrontations between individuals (who inevitably represent factions), which then escalate into larger-scale conflicts, eventually resulting in all-out, deadly competition between political communities. It is these most intense phases that we generally recognize as warfare, but Vayda's point is that this process of escalation is not inevitable. Each phase generates information in cultural systems concerning the efficacy of escalation as opposed to other behaviors. Another implication is that some phases of warfare may not be highly organized and planned by combatants, or even highly lethal. Confusion results if we focus too specifically on one particular phase of the warfare process—something we are very prone to do since some phases are much more visible in the archaeological record than others.

These definitions of warfare cover a wide range of behavior that includes individual acts of mayhem, small groups independently raiding a neighboring community, and full-scale engagements between large, highly organized armies. They also incorporate intrapolity conflicts, such as struggles over succession or civil wars. Finally, they include acts of violent treachery with overtly political ends.

Analyzing Warfare

Any effective analysis of warfare must take into account the following factors, which partly serve to structure my comparative discussion:

Scale refers to the number of combatants and support personnel and the energetic components of the defensive and offensive facilities at their disposal.

Arena is the natural and sociocultural landscape on which the process of warfare is played out.

Entities are firstly the antagonistic political communities or factions in whose interests warfare occurs, and secondly their organized representatives who actually take part in fighting.

Intensity means the duration and frequency of the phases and operations associated with the warfare process.

Organization refers to the means by which those members of a political community who participate in the warfare process cooperate in decision-making, logistical, and combat operations and share the consequences of success or failure. It has two dimensions—general organization and battlefield organization.

Strategy/Tactics: Strategy is the means whereby personnel and other resources are brought to bear to accomplish the goals of warfare. Tactics refer to the actual deployment and maneuver of personnel essential to any phase of the warfare process, with attendant use of appropriate instruments and facilities. Armament is subsumed under this factor.

Phase refers to the level of conflict (à la Vayda) and its systemic purposes and functions.

Purpose/Motivation means the emic goals or policies in the pursuit of which combatants organize themselves and devise strategies and tactics.

Function refers to all the anticipated and unanticipated effects of the warfare process (political, social, demographic, economic, territorial, etc.) on the sociocultural systems of which it is a part. This etic factor may or may not directly correspond to the emic factor of purpose/motivation.

Although any thorough understanding of warfare involves all of these factors, some (e.g., function) are more important than others. Some are also easier to reconstruct than others using the archaeological record. Potentially useful archaeological evidence includes written records, iconography, weapons, fortifications, paleopathology, incidents of violent destruction, and sudden disruption of cultural pattern. Disruption includes shifts in settlement systems, sudden intrusions of new pottery styles or art forms, and so on. A very important distinction is made between evidence that specifies historical events (writing and art) and that which is "event-free"—in other words, cannot be associated with written dates, names, titles, or places.

Despite all these lines of evidence, warfare is not very visible in the archaeological remains of early archaic states, even including those that left us comprehensible "historical" records. As Postgate (1992:241) remarks for Mesopotamia, where the oldest archaic states emerged,

> Unfortunately, though, we have little to go on: with war, perhaps more than any other subject, we are prisoners of what the Mesopotamian rulers wanted us to know: both their royal inscriptions and the public art are essentially propaganda, and we must be more cautious than ever about reading between

the lines. There is the danger of allowing a single triumphant event to colour our perception of an entire disastrous, or essentially peaceful, reign. The situation is made worse because there is little in the way of compensating documentation of an archival kind: the obsessive bureaucracy of the Meso-potamian palaces did not up sticks and tag along on campaign; and we don't have archives of any military quarter-master. Hence we are unable to gauge the extent of the communal investment in offensive and military measures, or the impact of organized campaigns or civil disorder on the lives of the bulk of the population.

Much of this dismal prognosis derives not from our inability to investi-gate war using archaeological methods, but from the fact that these methods have not been effectively applied on the necessary scale. On the level of cul-ture history or particular events, such application still has much to tell us. To continue the Mesopotamian example, whether or not the city of Uruk was walled before Early Dynastic times is surely a resolvable issue. So, too, are the effects of war on a settlement system, although this issue presents much greater practical problems. Diachronic processes and functions of war are much more difficult to understand, particularly through the lens of what passes for history in most archaic states. Postgate's apt comments have gen-eral relevance and should be borne in mind as we consider the Maya and Polynesian records.

Lowland Maya Archaic State Warfare

The Lowland Maya, paradoxically, offer significant insights into the role of warfare in the comparative process of archaic state formation. I say para-doxically because most Mayanists have emphasized the unique aspects of Maya culture at the expense of comparison. Also, until very recently, the Classic Maya were envisioned as peaceful theocrats who lacked not only warfare but also the general political institutions characteristic of early states. They have accordingly often been omitted from comprehensive surveys of early state formation (e.g., Claessen and Skalník, eds. 1978), though almost invariably being included in comparative discussions of the decline of civi-lizations (Tainter 1988; Yoffee and Cowgill 1988). Particularly prescient among those who recognized early on the importance of warfare among the Maya was Robert Rands (1952), although his work has not been widely cited or appreciated.

Our perception of Maya warfare has been revolutionized during the past 20 years by the presence of historical information preserved on Classic (and sometimes Postclassic) monuments, along with associated iconographic depictions (fig. 10.1). It is largely due to our increased understanding of in-scriptions that many Mayanists have abandoned their long-cherished no-tions of the "peaceful Maya" and swung around to an almost polar opinion

*Figure 10.1. This lintel from the Classic Maya center of Yaxchilán shows
the capture of enemies by the ruler Bird Jaguar (right) and an associated elite
warrior (drawing by John Klausmeyer, courtesy of Joyce Marcus).*

that emphasizes the Maya as compulsively warlike (in my opinion an equally
unlikely idea). Inscriptions have revealed the dates, participants, and at least
some of the claims of victory resulting from many military confrontations.
These typically are found at the centers of putative victors, but in at least one
case a monument of the victor (Caracol) was set up at the defeated site
(Naranjo).

Most current debates among Mayanists about the nature of Maya society in general, and warfare in particular, stem from different interpretations
of inscriptions. These interpretations in turn often reflect divergent opinions
about the degree to which inscriptions represent reliable historical accounts,
myth, or self-serving elite propaganda (e.g., Coe 1992; Marcus 1992c).
What is clear is that the epigraphic record is extremely spotty in time and
space; limited in content, given current knowledge, to essentially elite/royal

concerns; and still imperfectly understood. This is especially true for warfare (D. Stuart 1993). On the one hand, I agree with Norman Hammond that Maya inscriptions have "brought the Maya from the margins of prehistory into merely liminal history"(1991:256). On the other, the enormous importance of emic epigraphic data is apparent.

To date (interpretational difficulties aside), the epigraphic record has primarily provided culture-historical information about Maya war (see Stuart 1995 for the most useful and up-to-date overview). As archaeologists have long insisted, culture history is not explanation, but rather what needs to be explained. Combining epigraphic data and robust archaeological approaches is the effective road to explanation (Webster 1989:1–4).

My discussion of Maya warfare focuses heavily on the Late Classic, a period (AD 600–900) for which dates, inscriptions, and art are most abundant, but clearly such a view distorts evolutionary perspectives. The Classic period was preceded by at least 1,000 years of complex sociocultural development during which there is evidence for war. There are Preclassic and Early Classic fortifications, and the iconography of the latter period (AD 250–600) is "replete with martial imagery" (Houston 1993:138). Unfortunately, associated inscriptions referring to warfare are virtually absent. Only after about AD 650 did such inscriptions become numerous, especially proliferating in the eighth century (Marcus 1976a; D. Stuart 1993, 1995). After AD 800, dated inscriptions fell off markedly but warfare continued. Our effective historical window on Classic Maya war is thus a scant 150 years long.

Archaeology apart, our understanding of Postclassic Maya war (AD 900–1520) derives mainly from a few native books written shortly before or just after the arrival of Europeans, from the accounts of Spanish explorers and soldiers (Cortés 1986; Díaz 1963), and from reconstructions of preconquest Yucatán (e.g., Landa 1941; Roys 1943, 1957). In many respects the Maya Lowlands and Polynesia present us with mirror-image data sets concerning warfare—heavily archaeological and epigraphic for the Maya, and heavily ethnohistoric for Polynesia.

GENERAL COMPARATIVE FRAMEWORK

The Maya Lowlands and Polynesia share many sociocultural features that make comparisons fruitful, but there also are important differences. I will return to some of these in detail later, but a brief discussion is necessary here. To avoid implication-laden language, I use the word "polity" to refer to the most complex independent political systems, rather than "chiefdom" or "state," and "paramount," "ruler," or "elite" rather than "chief" or "king" for various leadership statuses. My general sources for Polynesia are Bellwood (1979), Buck (1934), Cordy (1981), Earle (1978, 1991b), Gailey (1987),

Goldman (1970), Hommon (1986), Kirch (1984, 1991), Kirch and Sahlins (1992), Oliver (1974), Spriggs (1988), Suggs (1960), and Vayda (1960, 1976). Kirch (1984:195–216) provides the best condensed overview of Polynesian war.

Most important from the perspective of the archaic state, in the largest and most complex Polynesian societies (Tonga, Tahiti, Hawai'i) dimensions of kinship ranking remained significant even as elements of stratification and, in some cases, class structure emerged. At European contact there was considerable political centralization around powerful, sacrosanct paramounts representing exalted hereditary lineages. Hereditary claims to office often were ambiguous and could be manipulated to reflect the realities of political power, resulting in frequent internal discord over succession.

Rulers and associated elites were supported by goods and labor appropriated from commoners. Local kin/territorial segments were highly independent in economic terms, so secession by breakaway territorial factions was common. Large archipelagos or even single large islands had multiple sovereign polities. Status rivalry was rampant both within and between polities. Interpolity interactions among paramounts and their constituent elites included temporary alliances, visitations, gift exchanges, politically advantageous marriages, and war on several levels, including outright territorial conquest. Populations were ethnically very homogeneous, and elites shared common great traditions. Much of this should sound very familiar to anyone who has read recent syntheses of Classic Maya political history (e.g., Culbert, ed. 1991; Houston 1993; Sabloff and Henderson 1993).

Both Polynesian and Maya Lowland economies were based on human labor, with no animals available for burden or traction in either region. Tropical plant agriculture supplemented by some gathering of wild plants was fundamental to both subsistence systems, but the root crops and arboriculture of Polynesia contrast sharply with the seed-crop systems (which also were supplemented to an unknown degree by arboriculture) of the Maya. Animal protein was much more abundant in Polynesia, where fishing was supplemented by domesticated animals (dog, pig, and fowl). Local productive variation existed in the agricultural landscapes of both regions but was more marked in much of Polynesia, with its leeward/windward rainfall contrasts, frequent drought, and steep slopes. In both regions pioneer populations utilized extensive systems of shifting rainfall agriculture that became more intensive as populations increased, reflecting in part population growth and environmental degradation. Terracing and water-control systems were present in Polynesia and the Maya Lowlands, but they appear to be much more significant to the political economies of some Polynesian societies, especially Hawai'i. Producer populations of both regions generally lived in dispersed settlements.

Both Maya and Polynesians had generally similar nonmetal technologies. Terrestrial transport, especially of bulk goods, was difficult in both regions, but probably more so in the rugged topography of Polynesian high islands. Sophisticated sailing craft facilitated water transport in Polynesia. Although some exchange occurred, there was comparatively high resource redundancy in both subsistence and nonsubsistence commodities in both regions, and full-time, nonsubsistence occupational specialization was poorly developed.

Polynesian islands were highly circumscribed both geographically and socially, with social circumscription much more important in the Maya Lowlands. In parts of the latter region, such as the northeast Petén, large independent or quasi-independent centers were much more numerous and closely "packed" than anywhere in Polynesia, so the political landscape was physically larger, contiguous, and much more complicated. Population densities per overall unit of arable land in the largest island systems were on the order of 80 to 120 per km^2 (Kirch 1984:98), with local densities on the most productive land considerably higher (Earle 1978:75). These figures are roughly comparable to those reconstructed for the Maya (Culbert and Rice 1990). Maximum populations of the largest precontact independent Polynesian polities ranged from 9,000 to 40,000 (Kirch 1984:98), with territories in the several hundred to several thousand square kilometer range. The biggest individual Maya centers, such as Tikal, probably had somewhat larger dependent populations on the order of 60,000 people (e.g., Culbert 1991; Marcus 1992c). Effective conquest warfare in Hawai'i during the several decades after European contact resulted in a single polity of at least 250,000 people, roughly comparable in order of magnitude to the large polities postulated for the Maya.

Although both Polynesian and Maya societies were nonurban, the Maya had throughout their history well-developed central places that were essentially royal households, sometimes immediately surrounded by establishments of lesser elites and commoners (Sanders and Webster 1988). With a few exceptions, such as Tonga, Polynesia lacked central places of comparable size, durability, diversity of function, and fixed location, although it did have traditions of large stone architecture and certainly local elite establishments in which considerable energy was invested. Maya central places included durable monumental constructions on a scale unmatched in Polynesia, devoted both to private elite functions and to public political/ritual display. A related Maya development, as we have already seen, was a complex set of numerical, epigraphic, and iconographic conventions that recorded royal/elite themes in both durable (e.g., stone monuments) and nondurable forms (e.g., paper or hide books). While lacking such innovations, Polynesians possessed elaborate oral traditions that recorded events (including wars), genealogies, and myths extending back in time many generations.

Finally, an important difference is relative isolation. Polynesian islands or island groups were often separated by hundreds or thousands of kilometers from their nearest neighbors. The Lowland Maya, by contrast, participated in cultural exchanges with many distant Mesoamerican societies over a very large land mass, including people who were ethnically and culturally distinct from them.

MAYA WARFARE: COMPARISONS WITH POLYNESIA

Because of the combination of archaeological and epigraphic data at our disposal, we have more detailed and abundant information about Lowland Maya warfare than are available for other ancient archaic states. Maya warfare was quite variable in time and space. Even during the conflict-ridden Late Classic, there must have been, for example, striking differences in warfare in the northeastern Petén, where many large sites were densely packed, and on the southeastern frontier, where major centers such as Quiriguá and Copán existed in comparative isolation (fig. 10.2 shows locations of centers mentioned in the text).

Mayanists disagree on several fundamental issues concerning warfare that, along with the factors previously listed, structure the following discussion. For each issue I summarize what we know or reasonably infer, the basic unresolved questions, and appropriate Polynesian comparisons that may help to clarify them. My concern lies not with the origins of either war or social complexity, but rather with how these factors interacted during Classic and Postclassic times.

How Were Maya Wars Conducted?
This issue mainly relates to the factors of armament, strategy, tactics, battlefield organization, intensity, arena, and duration, and is the least controversial. The factors of phase, scale, and general organization, which also relate to the conduct of war, are also addressed.

ARMAMENT. Archaeology, iconography, and ethnohistoric accounts provide a clear picture of Maya armament. According to Spanish descriptions, Maya weaponry was quite simple (Hassig 1992 provides an exhaustive review of the evidence). Weapons were made primarily from wood and stone. Close-quarter weapons included various sorts of clubs and swordlike implements, as well as knives and axes. Short thrusting spears were also carried, and some spears may have been thrown. Long-distance weapons included slings, atlatls, and bows and arrows. At least elite warriors were protected by elaborate headgear, and they also carried shields and wore cotton body armor. These weapons, except the bow and arrow and possibly cotton armor, were widely used prior to the Postclassic. Except for the bow, there seem to have

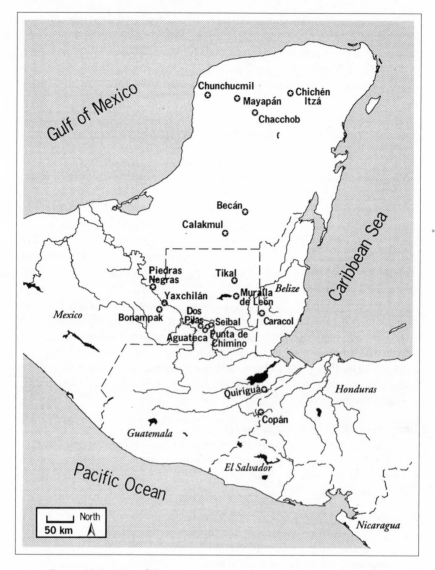

Figure 10.2. Map of the Maya Lowlands showing locations of sites mentioned in the text.

been virtually no important innovations in the technology of weaponry throughout Maya culture history.

Polynesian arms were remarkably similar. Wood was the primary tool for weapons of all sorts, but points and cutting edges were more often made from organic materials such as shark's teeth rather than chipped stone.

Close-quarter weapons such as clubs, thrusting spears, polished stone axes, and daggers were most fundamental. Distance weapons were slings and javelins, and thrown darts were used on some islands. The bow was known but seems to have been rarely if ever used in war. Various kinds of body protection were employed, mainly made from vegetable fibers such as coconut, but shields were absent. One major Polynesian innovation was the war canoe, which could be in excess of 30 m in length, with special elevated fighting platforms. Although smaller canoes were used by Maya warriors on rivers and along the coast, none seems to compare in size and strategic importance with Polynesian examples.

In neither the Maya Lowlands nor Polynesia could groups of elite warriors dominate lesser people through privileged access to weapons that were more effective than those widely available, such as the bronze swords, shields, helmets, armor, chariots, and horses (considering the horse as a weapon) characteristic of some Old World archaic states. Any manually dexterous Maya or Polynesian commoner could have cobbled together, from immediately available materials, weapons reasonably equivalent to those used by elites, with the possible exception of some forms of cotton armor. Moreover, most accounts suggest that warriors of all statuses personally possessed weapons and kept them in their houses. An exception was the war canoe, which could be incredibly costly to build. In complex Polynesian polities construction and use of such canoes were the prerogatives of elites. Canoes apart, privileged access to expensive or specialized weaponry was not a factor in elite dominance. Parity of access to weaponry was, however, a vital factor in status-rivalry war, since no factions were notably inferior in armament.

This shared repertoire of predominantly close-quarter weapons heavily influenced phase, strategy, tactics, and intensity, along with battlefield organization, to which we turn next.

PHASE, STRATEGY, TACTICS, AND BATTLEFIELD ORGANIZATION. Ethnohistoric accounts, epigraphy, art, and archaeological evidence indicate that Maya warfare was characterized by raids, pitched battles, sieges, and individual combats, with occasional acts of treacherous political violence. (I believe an example of the latter is the "axe event" perpetrated by Cauac Sky of Quiriguá on XVIII Jog of Copán in AD 738; Marcus 1976a:130–40; Stuart 1992:175–76.) Of these, individual combats, though prominent in Maya art, were probably merely parts of larger confrontations. Unfortunately, historical records do not allow us to detect all phases of warfare, or to assemble them into larger sequences of escalating conflict.

Raids were necessarily conducted by small forces moving as quickly and inconspicuously as possible. Maya pitched battles, like those of other, more militarily sophisticated Mesoamerican peoples, such as the Aztec (Hassig

1988), probably began with fairly organized formations and then after an exchange of missiles degenerated quickly into general melees, including single combat between prestigious warriors. Both raids and pitched battles could include ambushes, feints, false retreats, and other stratagems to confuse and disorganize the enemy.

Maya rulers fought personally in some battles, obviously supported by lesser warrior elites, but there is little unambiguous evidence of battlefield organization or command. Notable warriors (*holcans*) were important in Postclassic conflicts, but there is no strong evidence for the existence of elite military orders such as are found among the Aztec. My own guess is that most Maya war parties had minimal organizational structure and that a ruler, a few elite captains, and a stiffening of experienced warriors sufficed for directing combat, especially once battle was joined.

The same basic range of conflicts is found in Polynesia, although here again the relationships among the various phases is generally not clear. Pitched battles were conducted in much the same fashion as among the Maya. Maori chiefs typically participated personally in combat, leading by exhortation and example but not giving orders (Vayda 1960). In more complex Polynesian polities the highest-ranking leaders were present at battles but sometimes remained aloof. Special Tahitian "battle shapers" and "exhorters," often attired in gorgeously cumbersome military costumes reminiscent of those worn by Maya elites, helped direct battles but apparently with more psychological than organizational effect (Oliver 1974:390–95). Apart from special bodies of slingers, the only other distinctive participants were the *aito,* described by Oliver as especially prominent and experienced warriors; similar high-status warriors existed elsewhere as well, such as the *toa* of the Marquesas (Kirch 1991:126).

Polynesian war canoes seem to have been used most often to disembark warriors on enemy beaches, where conflicts then occurred. According to some accounts, naval battles required considerable discipline and concerted maneuvering. None was ever witnessed by Europeans, although Captain Cook observed an enormous muster of Tahitian warcraft and associated mock engagements.

FORTIFICATIONS. One form of conflict—sieges—leads us to the subject of fortifications. Although prominent during the Late Postclassic, only in the past 25 years have Preclassic, Classic, and Terminal Classic Maya fortifications been recognized (see Webster 1976a for a summary, now slightly out of date). Functionally speaking, the Maya built several kinds of durable fortifications. A few defensive systems, such as that at Tikal (Puleston and Callender 1967) and possibly Los Naranjos (Baudez and Becquelin 1973), protected very large areas of settlement and functioned as distant defensive

*Figure 10.3. Plan of the Becán fortifications; the inner parapet of earth is
not shown (drawing courtesy of Joyce Marcus).*

screens. More commonly, various sorts of walls, ditches, and embankments
were situationally erected immediately around preexisting royal/elite centers, protecting the central ruling apparatus of the polity, as at Becán (figs. 10.3,
10.4; Webster 1976b). Occasionally, some centers seem to have been established with fortifications as integral parts of their plans (as at Chacchob and
possibly Muralla de León; Rice and Rice 1981), but only at Postclassic
Mayapán and Chunchucmil did wall systems protect large numbers of residences. The Petexbatún project has recently identified emergency
fortifications apparently erected to protect cores of larger centers, such as at
Dos Pilas, or specially sited refuges in defensible situations, such as Aguateca
and Punta de Chimino (Demarest 1993).

Several kinds of Polynesian fortifications (summarized in Kirch 1984:
206–16) broadly correspond to those of the Maya and were built or arranged using similar construction or siting techniques. The most impressive,

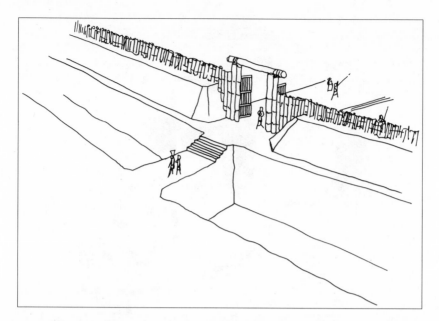

Figure 10.4. Hypothetical reconstruction showing how palisades and gates might have augmented the causeway, ditch, and parapet system.

homeland defenses, protected settlements where people resided permanently, or were vacant neighborhood forts to which people living in dispersed households could retire to defend themselves. Less common were *strategic defenses,* designed to deny access to larger territories. Finally, *refuges* were established in distant, isolated places that were hidden and/or naturally defensible, to which losers in larger conflicts could flee. We have no ethnohistoric accounts of how large fortifications were built or used by the Maya, but fortunately these exist for parts of Polynesia.

Surprisingly, the most abundant and sophisticated fortifications were built by the Maori, who had the least complex sociopolitical organization. Some 4,000 to 5,000 are known, reflecting both incessant pre-European warfare and that of the nineteenth century, which often involved Europeans. Maori warfare is generally most comparable with early patterns of Maya war that existed long before any lowland archaic states emerged, but it can nevertheless provide valuable insights, especially involving sieges and fortifications.

Maori forts, or *pas,* consisted of systems of terraces, embankments, ditches, and associated palisades, usually erected on defensible eminences but also on flat ground (fig. 10.5; Bellwood 1971; Brailsford 1981; Fox 1976; Vayda 1960). Sometimes they permanently sheltered whole communities, but more often they were vacant strongholds surrounded by dispersed

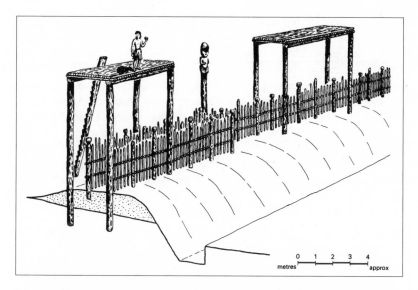

Figure 10.5. Reconstruction of earthworks, palisades, and fighting plat-forms associated with a Maori pa *(from Fox 1976:14). Reprinted with permission of Penguin Books (NZ) Ltd.*

populations. Chiefs might have their houses permanently within the *pa,* but the most important nonmilitary constructions were storage facilities for staple foodstuffs of the community at large. Well-established Maori *pas* often had multiple lines of defense, tricky entrances, and elevated fighting stages that gave advantage to the defenders' missiles. Apart from *pas* themselves, outlying scattered residences were protected by light stockades (Vayda 1960: 10–11) that would probably be archaeologically invisible.

Once effectively manned, *pas* were difficult for enemies to take by storm, since attacking war parties generally had no significant numerical advantage over the defenders and usually could not even invade the defensive perimeters adequately. This is one reason why Maori warfare depended so much on surprise raids; major damage could only be done if victims were caught unprepared outside the *pas,* or the *pas* themselves were seized quickly. Although sieges sometimes occurred, defenders had the advantage of stored food supplies. Only when attackers could live off the land (warfare tended to be scheduled during seasons when foraging was possible), or when undefended stores could be seized, were prolonged sieges possible. A related factor was the vulnerability of the attackers' own communities if warriors were absent for too long.

Maori forts have several implications for Maya war, given generally similar weaponry and logistical capabilities (see below) of the two cultures. One is that even small-scale raids could have important political consequences if enemy defenses could be taken by surprise. Also, the integration of durable earthworks and perishable barriers is a reminder that the surviving ditches and walls around Maya centers were only parts of more formidable defenses. Another lesson is that defensive systems could be quite small and simple and still be very effective barriers. In fact, many Maya systems were puny compared with some built by the Maori, and the most sophisticated Maori defenses are much more complicated than any the Maya are known to have erected.

Also surprising is how quickly *pas* could be built by small groups of essentially egalitarian people. During the colonial wars of the nineteenth century, quite serviceable *pas* were thrown together by tiny war bands in as little as two days, and one of the most impressive, built to withstand artillery, was built by 600 men in only ten weeks (Holt 1962:144, 254). Muriel Porter Weaver finds the labor required to build the Maya fortifications at Becán "staggering to contemplate" (1993:138). Quite the opposite, these earthworks required far less per-capita energy (given the much larger labor pool available) than expended on many Maori *pas,* and certainly no more specialized design or centralized leadership.

These comparisons are made not to denigrate Maya defensive efforts, but rather to emphasize how quickly and cheaply effective fortifications could be erected. In all likelihood the Maya used them much more often than current archaeological evidence indicates. In particular, light palisades integrated with the monumental architectural cores of many major Maya centers would have served the same functions as Maori *pas.*

Although we normally think of fortifications as having defensive functions, they may also, as Hassig (1988) points out, be used to project power, as when fortified garrisons or even walled cities are built by expanding empires. Neither the Maya nor Polynesians used fortifications this way.

Finally, a larger lesson emerges from the Polynesian data. As I have continually argued (Webster 1976a, 1976b, 1993), archaeologists cannot make assumptions about warfare based on the absence of fortifications or the presence of dispersed settlement. Fortifications were weakly developed and played little part in warfare in precisely those societies, notably Tahiti and Hawai'i, where warfare was carried out on the largest scale and with the greatest lethal and political effect. In both these island systems, as well as in most of the rest of Polynesia, settlement was remarkably dispersed given the intensity and frequency of war.

INTENSITY. How intense was Maya war? For any given Maya polity, especially during the eighth century, a general atmosphere of hostility might have been constant, as it seems to have been during the Late Postclassic. At the very least there were long episodes of general military confrontation, probably involving many phases, punctuated by more peaceful intervals. We must infer such long episodes from specific conflicts recorded by the inscriptions. Data are not very good, but events recorded at some centers supply clues. According to 17 dates associated with apparent military events (Hassig 1992: 219–21), Yaxchilán seems to have been engaged in some sorts of conflicts at average intervals of about 13 years, over a period of two and a half centuries. This is a minimal estimate since I have not listed the occurrences of multiple commemorations in a single year; also, many Yaxchilán inscriptions probably remain unknown, and many conflicts might have been too insignificant to record. Yaxchilán might be an extreme case, but at least some centers seem to have experienced repeated episodes of war that became more frequent toward the end of the Classic period. Unfortunately, monuments at many centers record no information about warfare events, so the overall picture is inconclusive.

Polynesian oral traditions are replete with accounts of one or another sort of warfare recurring at generational or subgenerational levels (Cordy 1981:44). This is to be expected because, in addition to interpolity war, there were frequent intrapolity conflicts over succession and secession. As an example, Oliver (1974:387–88) lists 15 large-scale wars involving polities in Tahiti and Mo'orea over a period of 47 years, with many more raids and skirmishes.

DURATION. Maya campaigns, defined as the intervals during which military forces operated away from their home bases, were necessarily very short, in part for logistical reasons. The Maya seem to have generally deployed fairly small numbers of warriors with rather minimal organization. These operated, usually on foot, over comparatively short distances and intervals, except perhaps where water transport was feasible. Small military efforts would have required little time and effort to set in motion, hence heightening the frequency of war.

Warfare must have been very seasonal, both because of the difficulty of movement during the rainy season in a tropical environment and because of scheduling conflicts. Roys (1943:67) states that the period between October and January was the warfare season in the comparatively dry parts of the northern Yucatán Peninsula. Marcus (1992c:table 11.1) discerns in dated events a later dry-season campaign interval for the wetter heartland of the Classic Maya. In any case, only a few months would have been convenient for campaigns. It would have been very costly to draft large numbers of commoners for offensive operations far from home during the agricultural season, although the same restriction would not have affected elite warriors or situational defense. In this seasonal aspect of warfare, the Maya resembled all other agrarian states; the Polynesian data on interpolity war suggest the same broad picture. On the other hand, intrapolity conflict would not have been similarly constrained by the seasons.

What Hassig (1988) calls the "friction of distance" severely limited Aztec campaigns, and would also have constrained Maya war. Except where water transport was available, all food and other supplies were carried on human backs. Even if parties of warriors were accompanied by noncombatant porters, food supplies would have been extremely limited. Stephen Houston has pointed out to me an apparent war-preparation scene on a polychrome vessel (Reents-Budet 1994: fig. 1.8) that seems to show elite warriors picking up their burdens to set off on a campaign. In Polynesia the friction of distance was to some extent overcome by the use of canoes, which could quickly deliver warriors to the beaches where raids or battles took place and also cheaply carry sizable amounts of supplies.

Given the dispersed nature of rural settlement, offensive Maya forces would even have found it difficult to requisition food from their own populace as they moved through their own rural hinterlands. Once in enemy territory, their ability to live off the land would have been extremely limited, especially during the end of the dry season when there were no crops in the fields and household stocks that could be looted were low. This is one reason why duration of conflict must have been short and why operation of large forces must have been the exception rather than the rule. Protracted sieges of fortified towns probably were impossible.

Dispersed rural settlements around centers undoubtedly affected Maya military tactics. Although much of the current literature emphasizes the small-scale raid as a basic tactic (consistent with elite warfare), such raids would have been highly dangerous, except when carried out by very small groups moving over very short distances. Roys (1943:67) says that the Postclassic Maya posted guards near polity boundaries to give early warning of attack; a dispersed agricultural population would have served the same function. The deeper the penetration into enemy territory, the greater the danger of early detection. Major political capitals of large regional states (if these existed), surrounded by subsidiary centers and far-flung rural populations, would have been virtually invulnerable to surprise or to attack by small raiding parties of elite warriors. This may be one reason why defenses were typically light.

ARENA. Approximately 20 known Maya centers/polities are recorded as having engaged in wars or conquests, or in their ritual (usually sacrificial) aftermaths (Hassig 1992:219–21; Schele and Mathews 1991). The named centers themselves (leaving aside the extents of their territories) range from huge and venerable ones like Tikal down to small centers that emerged late and had comparatively short dynastic histories, such as Dos Pilas. Some of the other centers referred to in the inscriptions remain archaeologically unidentified. Large centers predictably defeated small ones, but small centers also claimed to have defeated, or broken away from, larger ones.

Using a sample of 16 paired real or putative antagonist centers, I calculated straight-line distances between protagonist centers. The range is from 19 to 109.5 km; the mean distance is 57.5 km. Assuming that attackers actually traveled from their own centers to those of their enemies, the spatial arenas of Maya wars were often surprisingly large. In some cases (e.g., Tikal-Yaxhá, Dos Pilas–Seibal), however, Maya wars were very localized. But these distances are generally minimal ones, since Maya war parties would have had to negotiate both terrestrial and aquatic obstacles (e.g., hills and swamps), even on their comparatively low-relief landscape. Only on the western margins of the lowlands and in Belize would river transport have facilitated travel (e.g., in the Dos Pilas / Yaxchilán and Piedras Negras conflicts). War parties also could have utilized the long chain of lakes across the central Petén, although some portages would have been necessary.

In all but two or three of the cases, combatants moving on a relatively straight line between opposed centers would probably not have had to trespass on the territory of an independent third center. If opposing centers each possessed large contiguous territories, preparation and staging for attacks might have taken place at subsidiary places near territorial boundaries, thus overcoming some logistical constraints.

Unfortunately, these figures are not very useful because we generally have no idea where Maya battles were fought. Only where fortifications exist can we be certain that conflicts occurred or at least were anticipated. According to Roys (1943:67), contact-period Maya armies often met on the roads or trails *between* warring provinces. If Classic period combatants met at or near the midpoints between their centers, then travel would be effectively halved, to an average of about 28 km. Hassig estimates that sizable bodies of men with weapons, perhaps accompanied by porters carrying provisions, could travel overland about 19 km per day (1992:44). The exceptional maximal distances would thus necessitate round-trip journeys of ten to twelve days, and the shorter distances three to four days, if only the straight-line distances are calculated. Time must be added for additional distance, but we cannot know how much. At the outside, any recorded Maya campaign (assuming battles themselves were short) could have been accomplished in two weeks or less; most probably lasted only a few days.

Arenas of Polynesian war were quite different. Except in New Zealand, enemies on any particular island were closely juxtaposed because of the small sizes of terrestrial environments. For example, Hawai'i, the largest of the Polynesian islands after New Zealand, has an area equivalent to a zone with a 58-km radius around Tikal. High island environments often were much more rugged than the Maya landscape, but both small, sharp raids and major engagements were facilitated by rapid water transport. Distance was of little relevance both in intra- and interisland warfare, and canoe transport also lessened logistical constraints as already mentioned. Enemies approaching by sea were much more difficult to detect, and both attack and withdrawal were more rapid. Such mobility allowed effective interisland conflict over comparatively short distances (e.g., between the main islands of the Hawai'ian archipelago) and sometimes expansive conquest warfare over distances of 800 to 1,000 km (e.g., Tongan conquests of parts of Fiji and Samoa).

Another difference is the comparative lack of fixed elite places. Households of paramounts were often shifted around dependent territories, in part to take more efficient advantage of local subsistence resources. Protagonists in Polynesian wars, like the Maya, probably always knew where the establishments of enemy paramounts were located, but the ease of relocating such places in much of Polynesia must have created more complex and dynamic political arenas.

Mobility of warriors rendered the arenas of Polynesian war spatially larger than those of the Maya, with associated differences in strategies and tactics, but in another sense they created similarities as well. At least in the large archipelagos, mobility allowed war to extend over complex political landscapes and involve multiple polities, as it did among the Maya.

Who Fought Maya Wars?

Warfare in all archaic states was an elite enterprise in the sense that it was initiated by elites; commanded, and at least partially fought, by elite contingents; and served elite interests most directly. The only exceptions were when outsiders with forms of nonhierarchical political organization intruded on archaic state territories, or when nonelite political factions rebelled. Neither the Maya nor the Polynesians were much affected by either, with the possible exception of the peasant rebellions that J. E. S. Thompson (1954) believed responsible for the Classic Maya "collapse" of the eighth and ninth centuries AD.

Mayanists agree that Classic rulers and elites initiated warfare, organized campaigns, and participated in battles and their ritual aftermaths, but there consensus ends. Freidel (1986:107), summarizing a view held by many, asserts that Maya war was "a prerogative of the elite and fought primarily by the elite, [and] the bulk of the population was neither affected by, nor participated in, violent conflict"; he offers no evidence for this conclusion. I personally (Webster 1993) advocate more general and pervasive dimensions for Maya war, as we shall shortly see.

ENTITIES AND GENERAL MILITARY ORGANIZATION. Maya wars could involve several kinds of entities, all of which represented elite factions. First, independent polities of equal or unequal rank engaged in warfare on behalf of their sovereign rulers and associated elites. Such confrontations also might include temporary allies. Second, factions internal to a polity fought for control of its offices and titles. Finally, territorial segments of a larger polity fought to break away under strong local elite factions and assert their independence. All these sorts of warfare probably occurred among the Late Classic and Postclassic Maya (Marcus 1992c, 1993a).

There were many forms of archaic-state elite warfare in terms of the recruitment and organization of combatants. Probably none (except the Eastern Zhou, a Chinese state, 770–256 BC) had a professional army in the European sense of the word—in other words, a body of strategically stationed, trained men of different ranks, permanently mobilized and with its own command structure, whose members identified themselves as full-time military specialists, used special weaponry, and were recompensed for their services to the state or ruler. On the other hand, elite males in some archaic states were highly trained as warriors, and participation in combat was essential to their status and role. In some cases, warfare seems to have involved fairly small numbers of elite warriors, perhaps supported by lower-ranking servants (e.g., Bronze Age Greece, early Japan, early feudal Europe), whereas in others there appears to have been situational conscription of commoners to fill out the ranks (Sumer and probably Egypt).

Though Maya inscriptions and monumental public art predominantly feature rulers and their defeated opponents, there also are many group depictions of Maya warriors, usually on wall murals, ceramic vessels, figurines, lintels, and wall panels (most portray war-related rituals rather than combat) that refer to other individuals. The latter are usually unidentified by title or name but are typically shown armed and costumed in elaborate fashion, including what may be emblematic or heraldic devices (e.g., the Bonampak murals; see Miller 1986). Most of these supporting personages seem to be elites, judging both from their accouterments and their close association with impressive rituals.

Apart from rulers themselves, there is only the sparsest evidence for any kind of specialized military leadership before the Postclassic. David Stuart (1993:330–31) notes that the *sahals,* subordinate lords who figure prominently on monuments in some regions, often have overtly military roles. Schele's (1991) reconstruction of what she believes is the first historically documented Maya war includes a personage, Smoking Frog, brother of the Tikal ruler, who possibly functioned as the Tikal war chief. If her interpretation is correct (and it is disputed by many archaeologists, e.g., D. Stuart 1993:334), there were specialized Classic elite military roles in some sense analogous to that of the contact period war chief, or *nacom.* Also present during the Late Postclassic were "braves" or notable warriors called *holcans* (Landa 1941; Roys 1943). The next generation of decipherment will probably provide more detail on Classic military roles and offices.

Was Classic Maya warfare restricted to elites, or did it involve large numbers of commoner soldiers? Unfortunately, the Maya generally avoided producing large-scale narrative scenes that might help answer this question. To my knowledge, there is no depiction of a battle or other war–related event that clearly shows elite warriors leading large contingents of commoner soldiers. Exceptions might be the large figural compositions at Terminal Classic/Early Postclassic Chichén Itzá, although by this time the organization of warfare might have been rather different than in the Classic period Maya heartland to the south. The iconographic/epigraphic data can thus be used to promote a view of warfare that involved only elites. This view is conspicuous in much of the current literature, and it inevitably leads to considerations of military scale and entities.

SCALE. If Classic Maya polities recruited their combatants only from those segments of society who were hereditary elites, the forces involved must have been tiny. Hassig, who thinks Maya warfare was mainly conducted by elites, calculates that, out of a core population of 49,000, Tikal could have fielded an offensive force of only 619 to 1,055 combatants (1992:77), perhaps supported by additional noncombatant burden bearers. At Copán, the highest elite segment of the population probably represented no more than 10 percent of the total of about 28,000 (Webster 1992; Webster, Sanders, and van Rossum 1992). If one-fifth of these were adult males of military age, Copán's "army" would have numbered between 500 and 600 men. Many Maya polities were smaller than Tikal and Copán, with correspondingly low elite military potential. Regardless of the imprecision of these numbers, it is obvious that if a strict "elite warfare" model is adhered to, the forces involved from any particular center were minuscule. In fact, the scale of Maya war would be almost that of the essentially egalitarian Maori. If, on the other hand, larger regional states consisting of multiple centers were the entities and mobilized their collective elites, forces several times this size could have been mustered. The same is true if there were military alliances among several independent centers (e.g., between Calakmul and Caracol, or Calakmul and Dos Pilas).

Alternatively, Maya rulers may situationally have drafted much larger contingents of commoners into their military forces. A Copán king under these circumstances might in a dire emergency have scraped together an army of 3,000 to 4,000 men just from his own kingdom, but this would have been an all-out effort. Large regional states or alliances might have mustered 20,000 or more, although assembling them would have been much more difficult; forces of this size were more feasible for defensive than offensive operations.

There are reasons for supposing that the Classic Maya did in fact sometimes assemble sizable armies. First, we know that the contact-period Maya did so. Roys (1957:6), summarizing the early colonial evidence, notes that rulers could summon all adult males of their provinces for war. Such mobilization is consistent with eyewitness Spanish accounts (e.g., Cortés 1986; Díaz 1963) suggesting that, even allowing for customary exaggeration, very sizable Maya forces, probably numbering at least in the several thousands, could be assembled quickly from the local populace. Not all participants could have been elites; Roys (1943) clearly identifies low-ranking and high-ranking warriors. When advance warning of the Spanish approach occurred, Cortés claimed not only that many thousands of warriors were arrayed against him, but that they were assembled from eight provinces and even had written lists of their contingents (Cortés 1986:22). Unless there are extremely serious discontinuities between Postclassic and earlier military traditions, Classic (and perhaps Late Preclassic) Maya warfare was at least sometimes fought on a scale beyond that of elite contingents. The implication is that Maya males of all statuses were prepared to fight and probably possessed weapons.

Also, some fortifications are much larger than would be necessary to repel small elite forces. The most obvious cases are Becán, fortified at the very end of the Preclassic period, and the somewhat later boundary defenses of Tikal (Puleston and Callender 1967; Webster 1976b). Advocates of large Maya conquest states involving numerous large centers seldom discuss military organization in detail, but the clear implication is that forces must have been at least situationally large ones.

In suggesting that Maya warfare involved sizable armies, I am not implying that it always did so, nor that only large conflicts had important consequences. Maya war probably had many phases or dimensions, as suggested by Vayda's model. The problem is that only *some* of these are represented in Maya art and epigraphy, and even then they are unclear. Only a very intense phase of warfare could have necessitated defenses like those at Becán. But what phase is represented by depictions of kings shown dispatching royal captives? It could be anything from a Becán-scale engagement to a much more restricted ritual/royal duel.

We have already seen that warfare in complex Polynesian polities involved paramounts and lesser elites, including some with special roles and military experience, and thus was reasonably similar to that of the Maya. Some paramounts appear to have maintained entourages of experienced warriors as parts of their households (Oliver 1974:878); Cordy (1981:20) refers to the outright hiring of warriors by elites in Hawai'i. Crucial in understanding recruitment for war is the relative proportion of elite and nonelite segments of the society as a whole. Unfortunately, I found no such numerical estimates for Polynesian societies. Unexpectedly, Mayanists seem to have better information in this regard from archaeological studies than is available in the Polynesian ethnohistoric accounts.

Virtually all accounts of Polynesian warfare indicate that commoner males routinely participated alongside elites. Quite possibly in Hawai'i or Tahiti only elites or specially chosen warriors took part in some phases of war, such as raiding, but there is no question that very large contingents were raised for major battles. The Tahitian naval muster observed by Captain Cook, for example, consisted of 160 war canoes, accompanied by a similar number of auxiliary vessels (Cobb 1979; Oliver 1974:30-31). Although estimates of eyewitnesses differ, the total force manning this fleet was on the order of 6,000 to 7,000 men (whether all were prepared to fight, as opposed to paddle, is another question). Armies of similar size or larger were certainly fielded by the great conquering rulers of Hawai'i just before and after European contact. Kamehameha resettled no fewer than 7,000 warriors on O'ahu after its conquest (Kirch and Sahlins 1992). To the extent that large numbers of commoners were drafted into battles, the entities or political factions involved were entire polities headed by a sovereign ruler.

Contingents of local warriors were apparently raised by local high-ranking men as parts of their obligations to even higher-ranking paramounts and seem to have fought as units. Women sometimes followed their husbands to Tahitian battles, occasionally fighting as well, and some upper class women actually led warriors (Oliver 1974:387). Even the most powerful Tahitian rulers consulted their principal supporters at formal councils before going to war (Oliver 1974:383–84). Orations and deliberations were lengthy, and priests simultaneously scrutinized signs and omens. All this occurred publicly, witnessed by common people. Even powerful leaders seem to have been limited in their ability to initiate war unilaterally, and lesser notables sometimes publicly discouraged proposed campaigns. The implication is that war was not decided on lightly by rulers, who had to take account of wider sentiments, even commoner ones. Although Polynesian warfare was initiated from the top down by elite personages for elite purposes, lesser members of society were involved both in decision making and in the conflict itself. There is no necessary equivocation between elite war and such wider participation in Polynesia, nor is there for the Maya.

What Were the Purposes and Functions of Maya War?

No issues raise more disagreement than those of the purposes and functions of war, partly because of limitations of glyphic evidence: "Unfortunately, the inscriptions that we can read are not at all explicit about the motives for warfare, nor its character" (D. Stuart 1993:333). I have recently summarized much of the varied opinion on these issues (Webster 1993) and do not repeat the details here. Briefly, one pole of opinion is that Classic Maya war consisted primarily of highly choreographed, ritualized conflicts between rulers and elites, with few territorial, economic, political, or social purposes or functions apart from maintaining boundaries and the political status quo. Only when the ethics or charters that maintained equilibrium broke down did unlimited, destructive war occur (Demarest 1978; Freidel 1986). My own opposing perspective is that, in addition to its ritual dimensions, war in all periods had larger political and economic purposes and consequences, especially related to status rivalry.

Epigraphers and iconographers continue to identify new dimensions of Maya war that relate to material concerns. Stuart (1995), for example, summarizes new information that identifies exaction of tribute and the presentations of status objects apparently made by rulers to their victorious noble warriors. I think much more fine-grained information of this sort will emerge in the near future, and that Classic Maya warfare will increasingly be seen to resemble Aztec war on some levels, particularly in its meritocratic dimensions.

WAR AS RITUAL. Everyone agrees that Maya war was heavily ritualized, not only on the battlefield but also during its preparation and aftermath. This much is conspicuous from artistic depictions alone, in which military themes are extremely frequent. Such depictions, along with associated inscriptions, allow us to reasonably infer some of the major emic purposes or motivations for war.

First, Maya rulers sought to project the image of powerful and successful warriors both to other elites and to commoners. Participation in war was part of the royal role and one way in which the efficacy of ruling personages was made manifest, particularly at critical junctures in their lives, such as accession and heir designation. Second, war provided victims in the form of illustrious warrior captives (most desirably, rival rulers) for sacrifice in post-battle rituals, which might include ballgame contests. One obvious purpose of such sacrifices and contests was to publicly demonstrate the captor's prowess and the humiliation of the victim. Stephen Houston (personal communication 1995) notes that the long hair on a figure shown on a Toniná monument probably indicates a noble female captive (Villar 1996:71).

Because Maya rulers were ideologically and ritually responsible for the well-being of their subjects and the harmony of the Maya cosmos, it is possible that war-related sacrifices were seen as essential to cosmological order, as they were elsewhere in the Mesoamerican great tradition (although the Maya seem to lack a major deity specifically identified with war). Heads and other body parts of sacrificial victims or slain enemies were apparently kept as trophies, and these, or facsimiles thereof, formed parts of elite ritual costume and regalia. Much of the imagery of Classic period rulership, including warfare roles, was borrowed from non-Mayan Mesoamerican societies, particularly Teotihuacán. Resorting to such "foreign" symbolism was obviously impossible for Polynesian rulers. Interestingly, contact-period Maya rulers seem to have been much less fixated on public display of military roles than their Classic counterparts.

Presumably some phases of war were highly choreographed and ritualized, perhaps even prearranged with an eye to auspicious dates and convenient places. Classic and Postclassic ritual warfare seems to have been particularly identified with Tlaloc / Venus imagery (Schele 1991) and may have been to some degree regulated by the cycle of that planet. Unfortunately, the only direct evidence we have for ritualized battlefield behavior is the gorgeous and distinctive attire of participants.

Although most overviews of Maya war pay lip service to multiple levels or functions, by far the most conspicuous dimension emphasized is war as royal ritual. For example, Schele and Miller (1986:220) say that "while the Maya made war as a ritual of intrinsic interest, and one that was necessary for the functioning of their world, they also fought to achieve the material ends that mankind has always sought in war." Yet these "material ends" scarcely figure in their preceding discussion of Maya war, so heavily does it focus on the dramatic depictions and events of royal victory and defeat, torture, and sacrifice. To the extent that Maya warfare was motivated by ritual / religious purposes, it was about irresolvable and nonnegotiable issues. The extreme view that Maya war was mainly ritual but occurred in a landscape of political fragmentation characterized by constant war is a far cry from the "peaceful Maya" perspective.

Polynesian warfare also was highly ritualized. One of the more detailed summaries is given for Tahiti by Oliver (1974) and broadly reflects patterns of warfare in the most complex polities. We already saw that preparations for war included auguries and divination by special priests and pronouncements by shamans. Other ceremonies included human sacrifices to the war god Oro at principal ritual centers (*marae*). These preliminary rituals were so lengthy and public that often enemies were forewarned, and some rulers became so preoccupied with them that they ignored more secular preparations and lost the war. Protracted rituals did, however, provide time for forces to be mobilized, allies to be recruited, and deliberations to take place. Some sham wars were fought that had distinct sporting overtones.

Wars were scheduled to avoid first-fruits and harvest festivals. Pitched battles, which usually occurred on beaches, were preceded by martial music played on drums and conch shell trumpets. Armies were accompanied by priests and religious images, and ceremonies were carried out even as battle was joined. As already noted, gorgeously dressed notable warriors were conspicuous in battle, and success was reckoned as much by the killing or capture of distinguished enemies of high rank as by inflicting heavy overall casualties. Loss of important warriors could quickly dishearten their forces and cause a rout.

Elaborate peacemaking ceremonies sometimes took place after battles when there was no clear winner, but since large battles usually resulted in the resounding defeat of one side, ritual celebrations of victory were more common. Captives were sacrificed, corpses of distinguished enemies were interred in ceremonial buildings, and skulls, jawbones, and even whole bodies were kept as trophies.

Inherent in ritual were important ideological concepts. A general comment by Earle (1987:298) expresses a Polynesian ideal: "Chiefs rule not because of power, but because of their place in a sacredly chartered world order." Military success exemplified the supernatural efficacy and sanctity of elite persons and was a physical manifestation of mana, concentrated most potently in persons of the highest rank with the most legitimate claims to highest political office. But the structural logic in this association was double edged. Successful usurpers of highest titles and offices obviously manifested superior mana, so their behavior was supernaturally legitimized while the mana of losers was devalued.

VIOLENCE. Although violence is part of the conduct of war, I deferred discussing it until this point because of the common assumption that ritual or conventionalized Maya war must have been relatively nonviolent. Polynesian war, despite its ritual dimensions, often was, in fact, extremely violent. When one Tahitian army was decisively routed or forced to surrender, an orgy of slaughter and destruction often followed that included not only combatants but nearby communities and their inhabitants as well. Houses and crops were destroyed, and people of all ages and sexes who could not flee might be killed or taken captive for later sacrifice (Oliver 1974:395–98). Tongan war was similarly lethal (Gailey 1987:168–69). Even essentially egalitarian Maori war seems to have featured the butchery of surrendered or fleeing enemies, including noncombatants of all ages and sexes (Brailsford 1981; Vayda 1960).

Such violence, however, was limited to the immediate aftermath of battles. Once defeat was acknowledged, peaceful relations between conquered and conquerors were quickly established, even including the reinstatement of defeated enemy notables (as in Tahiti) who might survive to start new wars. While the internal character of Polynesian war thus failed to inhibit extreme violence, it did allow rapid reconstitution of peaceful relationships.

The current emphasis on the ritual aspects of Maya war reflects a much older anthropological tradition. As Vayda (1960:3) noted long ago, many discussions of "primitive" war seem to "disproportionately emphasize various ideological and non-utilitarian concomitants of war . . . treating only sketchily the environmental, economic, and sociopolitical setting of military activity." Ritual dimensions of Maya war are so obtrusive that it is difficult to place them in their larger sociopolitical and economic contexts. This we can do for Polynesia, and it is accordingly the focus of the most important part of this chapter.

WAR AS COMPETITION: STATUS RIVALRY. Polynesian society was strongly hierarchical. Conical clan organization was its fundamental structural principle, creating both a common thread of relationships and the basis for segmentation as populations grew in the larger island systems (Kirch 1984:31–36). Segmentation, along with polygyny, the high status of women, and bilateral descent and inheritance, created ambiguities of power and pretexts for conflicts of many kinds.

Although expressed in extremely varied ways, hierarchy stimulated intense status rivalry among highly ranked individuals and their supporting factions for titles, offices, privileges, supporters, labor, status objects, and basic resources. All accounts of Polynesian war stress status rivalry, and some (e.g., Earle 1978) single it out as the major cause of war. Great internal tensions plagued the most stratified Polynesian political systems because of the combination of "respect and reverence for hereditary rank via seniority with necessary concessions to political and economic power" (Goldman 1970: 20). We saw such contradictions in the concept of mana. To paraphrase Oliver (1974:376), serious armed conflicts, whether between or within complex Polynesian polities, expressed the ambitions of socially powerful individuals and their attempts to extend their political power and curb that of competitors.

Status-rivalry war is *by definition* internal war. It is fueled by the shared understandings of the participants concerning their respective positions within a traditional network of hierarchical social and political relationships, the associated structure of offices and titles, the behaviors and symbolic expressions appropriate to them, and the effective means by which augmentation of position and power may be sought. Such shared cultural understandings operate most immediately among people of high rank within existing political entities; the prize of successful status rivalry is control of these entities. Where such understandings are shared across political boundaries, status-rivalry war has wider political arenas; this was the situation in both Polynesia and the Maya Lowlands.

Where independent polities existed on the same or nearby islands, conflict involved status rivalry between paramounts of separate ruling lines.

Competing entities were thus both elite and territorial factions. At European contact, for example, there were four sovereign Hawai'ian polities, one on each major island. Status rivalry also was expressed in intrapolity civil wars involving elite factions with competing claims to paramount titles and offices, or fighting for independence. Very occasionally, distant island groups were conquered, as Tonga conquered parts of Fiji (one of the few possible instances of Polynesian "external" war in Otterbein's sense).

WAR AND THE SOCIAL HIERARCHY. The most complex Polynesian societies (Hawai'i, Tahiti, Tonga) were socially stratified. Members of the highest-ranked stratum were variously called *ariki, ari'i, ali'i,* and so forth (note the possible correspondence to the Postclassic Maya *almehenob,* or nobles descended from nobles, and the Classic *ahau*). They were potential "players" in the political game, themselves collectively ranked by conical clan structure with respect to titles and offices. Codes of elite comportment were widely shared, as were status symbols, so war was internal war, as we have seen. Highly ranked individuals were very jealous of insults, which could be pretexts for aggression.

Truncated from this elite stratum were the "nonplayers"—commoners (variously *manahune, tu'a,* etc.) who were essentially disenfranchised from traditional rights to land and from elite kin organization and its associated status rivalry. In Hawai'i, which has been best studied (Cordy 1981; Earle 1978; Hommon 1986; Kirch and Sahlins 1992), membership in commoner communities (*ahupua'a*) was largely defined by residence, but also by attachment to local notable individuals. Commoner families had very short genealogical depth and no important corporate functions. Interestingly though, commoners seem to have been able to change their residences and political affiliations. Various grades of minor elites and managers were intermediaries between these strata (see Spriggs 1988 for the emergence of this system).

Highborn and lowborn were ideologically linked only by the most metaphorical concepts of very distant common descent. Despite this genealogical gulf, Polynesian elites never claimed different origins from commoners, as occurred in some other ancient complex societies, including the Maya, Mixtec, and Zapotec.

"War, as the overt form of competition between greater and lesser powers, higher and lower status, indigene and invader, was thoroughly ingrained in Polynesian concepts of society" (Kirch 1984:195). Motivations for war included "struggles of rival chiefs for power, disputes as to succession, insubordination or rebellion of a subchief, or his resentment at the domination of his superior, lack of respect to a chief, disputes as to land, boundaries and property generally, the need of food and subsequent raids, abduction of or elopement with women, vengeance for the death of a relation or insult or injury inflicted upon him, and the need for human sacrifice to the gods" (Williamson 1937:3 as quoted in Kirch 1984:197).

Status-rivalry war had two basic dimensions: it continually reinforced the gulf between elites and commoners and differentiated among elites themselves. Since achievement could counterbalance hereditary rank (Earle 1978; Goldman 1970), the single most tangible expression of power was the mobilization of supporters, especially for war. From the paramount perspective, war served to maintain the status quo or to extend political influence. Lesser elites who supported paramounts sought rewards and confirmation of their positions. When lesser elites (especially junior collaterals) initiated war themselves, they sought to usurp offices of superiors or to establish independent polities. For them war was thus a vehicle of social advancement and mobility.

Similar opportunities were available to successful commoner warriors. Widespread in Polynesia was the role of distinguished warrior, known by various honorifics (*koa, toa, aito*). Although open to elites and commoners alike, distinction in war was for commoners almost the only avenue to social advancement. Privileged warrior status brought with it prestige, as well as tangible rewards and possibly the right to marry otherwise unattainable women. Distinguished warriors were much sought after by paramounts and often were attached to their households. In some of the less centralized island systems, such as the Marquesas, distinguished warriors (along with inspirational priests) "wrested substantial control of both ritual and production from the hereditary chiefs" (Kirch 1991:121).

MATERIAL REWARDS OF WAR. Much more was at stake in Polynesian war than titles, offices, privileges, and prestige. Status rivalry and the assumption of offices were inextricably linked to control of material resources. The production and redistribution of resources among elites were essential in forming, enlarging, and retaining the allegiance of political factions. Paramounts had to maintain large and impressive households for themselves and their entourages, and they also had to reward powerful subordinates or lesser relatives. All elites had to exhibit status symbols appropriate to their stations; one source was booty from successful war, which in some societies included slaves.

Earle (1978:168) has differentiated between two parallel economies for Hawai'i: the *subsistence economy* and the *political economy*. Consistent with status rivalry, he sees the commoner subsistence economy as minimizing and self-dampening, whereas the elite political economy was maximizing and self-amplifying. Into the political economy flowed the goods, labor, and services required by paramounts to fund their own establishments and to reward their followers. Material rewards might be redistributed directly by the paramount or siphoned off by privileged political subordinates, delegates, or managers. Little or nothing flowed back down to commoners, despite their participation in war. Exceptions were rewards to distinguished warriors or compensation to artisans who made status symbols, such as elaborate carvings, cloth, canoes, and gorgeous feather capes and headdresses. Because of the high redundancy of local island environments, conquest was probably not motivated by desire to control highly localized sources of nonsubsistence status materials, a point made explicitly by Oliver (1974:985) for Tahiti. The ultimate status symbols that demonstrated status and motivated competition were land and people. Successful war created complex overlapping claims on land, its products, and the labor attached to it.

In Tonga power-based claims on land and people never effectively supplanted kin-based claims (Gailey 1987). Although Tongan society was socially stratified, it had only one of the two essential elements of class structure—commoner producers *did* support elite nonproducers, but elites *could not* systematically deprive commoners of subsistence resources, even after military conquest. In Hawai'i the process went a step further. A major goal of war was control of territory and the commoners attached to it. Territorial concepts of polity seem to have supplanted kin-based ones. Paramounts were the ultimate "owners" in the sense that they asserted dominant rights of disposal over commoner lands and populations, especially those acquired by conquest. Use rights to land were delegated by chiefs and were retained by commoners through residence and contributions of corvée labor (Earle 1978:148). Even in the much less centralized Marquesas, many commoners were rendered landless by war and attached to elite households as tribute payers (Kirch 1991:127). In Tahiti the situation is less clear, but some late wars involved dispossession of losers and formation of personal estates by victors (Oliver 1974:991).

Crucial as the issues of dispossession and ownership may be for our concepts of "state" and "class," they are less so for the territorial aims of status-rivalry war. The major goal was not to destroy, drive away, or disenfranchise defeated enemies (although these sometimes occurred), but rather to reaffirm or extend paramount rights of disposal of the products of the land and the labor of those cultivating it. Whether or not commoners "owned" their lands or could be displaced with impunity is irrelevant to the fact that access to and redistribution of productive resources were essential to the political economy. In Hawai'i and elsewhere, the major reward given by paramounts in return for political support was privileged access to land and labor. Paramounts' claims to the ultimate right of disposal made such rewards possible; the ability to effectively assert such claims generated competition over the titles and offices that partly validated them.

Paramounts kept the majority of communities under their own direct control (Cordy 1981:20), delegating the rest to followers. Recipients often were close relatives, and personal "estates" were given both to elite supporters and to distinguished commoner warriors. Special managers (*konohiki*) were appointed to supervise estates. Imposition of elite proprietors by victors severed relationships between commoners and their traditional local elites, with obvious evolutionary effects. Conquest warfare in the most complex Polynesian polities essentially created a system of paramount patrons and elite clients with respect to land and labor (see Webster 1975 for a more general evolutionary discussion of this pattern). Warfare in Polynesia thus functioned to redistribute resources and to restructure social relationships.

The concept of "territorial conquest" is a slippery one under conditions of status-rivalry war. Paramounts *do* conquer territory, in the sense that they replace a competing set of elite proprietors and thus acquire the ability to dispose of the products of an enlarged political landscape and the labor of people on it. On the other hand, such conquest may not involve significant disruption of basic producers or the influx of large numbers of outsiders into conquered areas, with obvious implications for the archaeological visibility of this process.

How was it possible that commoners shared in the risks of war but not in its rewards? What rendered a lopsided system like this stable with regard to commoner unrest, especially when elites held no demographic or technological advantage of force? I think there are some obvious answers apart from the sacred and genealogical charters of Polynesian hierarchical relationships, especially for Hawai'i. First, as I have suggested for the Maya (Webster 1985), the per-capita extraction of goods and services was probably not onerous. Even if it had been, commoner communities were dispersed and often spatially isolated from one another and could not easily form collective political factions to resist elite demands on any significant supracommunity scale.

The presence of nonlocal elites and managers, along with very limited kinship depth, reduced the organizational potential for local corporate action of any kind. But more importantly, commoners had more to lose by resisting participation in elite wars than by compliance. Any small commoner group that resisted could easily be punished and dispossessed by the military force available to paramounts, limited as it was. On the other hand, neither victory nor defeat changed commoner fortunes very much, aside from the occasional violence inherent in battles and their immediate aftermaths. Peace was quickly reestablished. Victory of one's own paramount reconfirmed existing relationships and maybe even rewarded some commoner warriors. Defeat resulted in a new set of proprietors, culturally like the last, whose interests were consistent with the well-being and productivity of commoner communities. Although they situationally participated in war and were affected by it, over the short run the lot of most commoners was probably not much changed by war.

WAR AND POPULATION PRESSURE. Circumscribed island environments offer unparalleled opportunities to study the relationship between competition and imbalances between populations and resources in an evolutionary framework (Kirch 1984). Early Polynesian colonists practiced extensive agriculture and utilized wild resources. As populations grew, environments degraded, wild terrestrial resources declined, and rainfall systems of agriculture became more intensified and on many islands were supplemented by major irrigation works. These facilities, along with highly productive artificial fishponds, often were built by corvée labor at the behest of paramounts. Such processes have obvious parallels in the Maya Lowlands.

On some Polynesian islands, such as Tikopia or Easter Island, there is little question that population stress was a cause of conflict and that warfare (along with other mechanisms, such as emigration) functioned to regulate resource imbalances. Elsewhere, and particularly for the larger islands, opinion is divided. Gumerman (1986), in a general consideration of competition on island environments, sees a strong correlation between population, competition, and resource availability. Earle (1978), by contrast, flatly rejects population stress as the cause of Hawai'ian war, emphasizing status rivalry instead. Intensification of production and capital investment in modified agricultural landscapes was caused by self-amplifying demands of the political economy rather than population stress. Earle notes, however, that status rivalry is always played out under specific environmental conditions which in turn affect its forms and evolutionary potential. Kirch (1984) takes a similar position but gives environmental and demographic factors much more latitude.

Unfortunately, I found no detailed numerical reconstructions of Polynesian population density and its relationships to the resource base comparable to those available for the Maya, so claims about population pressure or the lack of it for the largest Polynesian societies are impressionistic.

It is unnecessary to try to sort out these divergent opinions here, but they do have several important implications. First, status–rivalry war is war from the top down. Information generated in the system about the desirability of war and decisions to engage in it originate on the elite level. In contrast, bottom–up information is important if war is caused in part by population pressure, which may of course be a contributing factor in status–rivalry war. Under either set of circumstances, however, warfare may occur over land and labor. Even where land was reasonably abundant, there is no

question that wars were fought between small Polynesian polities for possession of particularly productive parts of the landscape, as Vayda (1976) has
maintained for the Maori and Buck (1934) for Mangaia. In Hawai'i only
limited parts of the environment could be modified for intensive agriculture
or fishponds, and no matter why this was initially done, these areas, along
with their comparatively dense associated populations, became particularly
attractive objects of competition.

POPULATION GROWTH AND WAR. The role of population growth is less controversial. It led to the effective in-filling of most Polynesian islands and the mul-
tiplication of potentially competing political entities in the larger systems.
Political arenas thus became more complex and circumscribed. Enlargement
of the elite stratum increased demands for resources, so both production and
conflict intensified. During this process the character of war probably
changed markedly. Based partly on game-theory simulations of island evolutionary processes, Gumerman (1986) suggests that conflict tended to become more aggressive, treacherous, less profitable, and more self-defeating
as circumscription increased. In highly circumscribed environments the result might be a pattern of dynamic equilibrium characterized by cycles of
expansion and fragmentation, as described by Earle (1978:174) for Hawai'i
and Marcus (1993a) for the Maya. Such political oscillation may have characterized large systems such as Tonga and Hawai'i just before European contact changed the equation and helped "kick" both systems into more
statelike forms. As Gailey (1987:250) notes for Tonga, conquest abroad, far
from indicating effective internal political centralization, was sometimes undertaken to avoid rebellion.

MAYA/POLYNESIAN COMPARISONS:
SOME IMPLICATIONS

What have we learned from this comparative exercise? I think several implications are obvious, for the study of both Maya war and war in general.

1. War has many phases, not all of which are equally visible to archaeologists or equally significant in their effects.
2. Absence of fortifications cannot be assumed to indicate the absence of intense phases of war, including territorial conquest.
3. Dispersed settlement can be maintained even in contexts of lethal,
destructive, territorial conquest.
4. Warfare fought primarily for self-serving elite purposes may involve large numbers of commoners.
5. Even small-scale war may have important political, social, and economic consequences and functions.

6. Warfare may be ritualized internal war between culturally similar factions and still be highly lethal, destructive, and politically significant.

7. Even after violent conquest, stable conditions may be rapidly reestablished.

8. Status–rivalry war over material resources, including land and labor, can occur even in the absence of significant population stress.

9. Population growth results in more complex political arenas, which in turn can intensify aggression and ultimately can lead to destructive warfare.

10. Status–rivalry war may offer commoners few rewards, but participation in it may entail fewer risks than refusal.

11. War may have important evolutionary effects even when it does not result in successful expansion and large, stable polities.

12. Some components of warfare may have hidden functions. For example, protracted prewar ritual may be a necessary vehicle for successful mobilization.

13. Small amounts of military force available to elites may be perfectly capable of preserving the privileged status quo as long as numerically superior commoners are not hard–pressed for labor or goods and are unable to form effective political factions of their own.

The most important conclusion is that, except on the royal/ritual level, Mayanists are failing to recognize and take into account complex patterns of status–rivalry warfare and their consequences. Such warfare might have emerged very early in Maya prehistory, undergone important changes toward the end of the Classic period, and been a crucial element in the oscillation between large and small polities evident in the Maya Lowlands after AD 900 and increasingly postulated for Classic times.

By the end of the Late Classic period, the Maya version of status–rivalry war undoubtedly was more complex than that of Polynesia for many reasons. Populations were denser and political entities were more numerous, closely juxtaposed, and differentially developed. Extreme proliferation and elaboration of dynastic lines created endless opportunities for elite power seeking, and military adventures were played out on a political landscape dominated by central places that were symbols of royal dominance and hence themselves objects of competition. Protracted struggles among complex, shifting coalitions of Maya polities dominated by such Classic superpowers as Tikal, Calakmul, Caracol, and Dos Pilas are increasingly obvious in the inscriptions (e.g., Marcus 1993a; Martin and Grube 1995), although we are far from understanding their implications for sociopolitical structure.

Lest faction formation seem too much of a "top–down" process, it should be remembered that not only do leaders need constituencies, but also that constituencies need leaders. Although more difficult to document in historic and prehistoric contexts, much political maneuvering may involve active recruitment of amenable leaders by politically powerful factions. In some cases even the most exalted leaders may be veritable figureheads, as emperors were in feudal Japan, their lack of power masked behind the impressive infrastructure and rituals of the royal court.

A fascinating difference between Maya and Polynesian war is its spatial expression. For both regions it is probably more appropriate to think in terms of political centers of gravity focused on particular elite lines or individuals rather than territorial political entities. But Maya elites were more strongly "tethered" to impressive, permanent royal centers, and thus to specific segments of the landscape, and this strongly affected the conduct of war.

Other differences may lie in kinship structure. Polynesian status-rivalry war was deeply rooted in conical clan organization and its historical ramifications, but I do not attribute such organization to the Preclassic or Classic Maya. Various kinship terms are expressed in Maya texts, and rulers celebrate their parents and other kin, but long, detailed genealogical lists are unknown. It remains to be seen exactly how such relationships were structured and what their possible political implications were. The more general and obvious point is that forms of conflict we can reasonably call status-rivalry war were historically widespread in many political traditions apart from those of Polynesia and the Maya, regardless of details of kinship organization.

Although Mayanists disagree about the effects of population pressure, most acknowledge that population growth during the Classic period enhanced social circumscription, raised population densities, stimulated agricultural intensification, and was instrumental in creating the complex political arena described above. Also seemingly present, as in Polynesia, were structural features such as high ranking of women, polygyny, and tendencies toward bilateral descent and inheritance, with their implications for status ambiguity and manipulation. This was a fertile environment for endemic and ultimately self-defeating status-rivalry war, as Gumerman (1986) suggests.

Conflict intensified and assumed dimensions of mature dynastic war at least by the eighth century (Webster 1993:431). I believe, however, that the roots of such warfare extend back into the Late Preclassic times, not only in the Maya Lowlands but in Mesoamerica more generally. According to one interpretation (doubted by some epigraphers), the La Mojarra stela, an early (second century AD) royal monument in a non-Maya script, records the victory of one Harvest Mountain Lord over an erstwhile usurper—his own brother-in-law (G. Stuart 1993:110).

Mayanists differ on the utility of calling the crisis that overcame Maya polities in the eighth and ninth centuries a "collapse." Whatever we call it, warfare almost certainly contributed heavily to social and political disruption during that period. If population pressure was a factor, as it certainly was at Copán (Webster, Sanders, and van Rossum 1992), it would have exacerbated earlier patterns of status-rivalry war and created the kind of bottom-up stress that could destabilize commoner communities, adding an unprecedented element of political volatility and destructiveness.

A detailed consideration of status-rivalry war and its effects on the distinctive political landscape of the Maya Lowlands is beyond the scope of this essay. War, however, would have operated very differently at various times and places, within the contexts of different political systems. For example, the Copán polity was small enough so that some kin linkages might have integrated the whole society right up through the eighth century. The much older and larger Tikal polity might well have been more stratified, as Haviland (1992) believes.

The hypothesis that the Maya engaged in something reasonably comparable to Polynesian status-rivalry warfare raises many questions. To what extent did Maya elites share descent on an interpolity basis? How did status rivalry work in an environment of fixed royal centers and greater political centralization? To what extent did Maya lords claim rights to dispose of land and labor, and how did they reward their elite supporters? What were the dynamics of ascription and achievement in Maya society? How best do we define a Maya polity—territorially, or in terms of political allegiance and elite factions? If Maya elites pursued status-rivalry war, how is it reflected in inscriptions? All these are questions for future research.

The archaic-state concept, as noted at the beginning of this chapter, applies more problematically to the complex Polynesian societies and the Classic Maya than to the other societies discussed in this volume. If the Polynesians and Classic Maya were in some ways institutionally and organizationally more "chiefdomlike" than Egyptians or Mesopotamians, were their warfare patterns markedly different from those of archaic states as well? More broadly, is the character of warfare different in chiefdoms as contrasted with states? I think exploration of these questions requires case-by-case comparisons because the sociopolitical characters of archaic states are themselves so variable, as are their ecological settings, their associated political economies, and their degree of urbanization. Such an effort is clearly impossible here, so I will restrict my comments to the issue of status rivalry.

To the extent that some sort of kinship ranking dominates an entire system (i.e., links people from the lowest to the highest social ranks) and access to rulership is theoretically determined by some kind of principle of descent,

I would expect more intrapolity political fragility for two reasons. First, as we have already seen, political pretensions and ambitions of multiple contenders for paramount offices are fueled by ambiguities of kinship. Second, contenders for power have natural constituencies—their kinspeople—who potentially form the factions or political communities central to the definition of warfare as given above. Many scholars have noted such fragility, and the really interesting question to me is: Under what conditions does frequent, internecine warfare stimulate the development of state-type institutions? This is a subject I have explored elsewhere (Webster 1975).

In the complex Polynesian polities, kinship ranking (for all practical purposes) included only a small component of the population; the majority were effectively disenfranchised as political players (although not as warriors). In these societies the ambiguities of kinship still fueled competition at the top, but the creation and mobilization of large political factions must have proceeded quite differently.

Clearly, elite competition was a potent factor in the more stratified and bureaucratic archaic states as well, but I think the factions were more likely to be powerful families (or other institutions) and their economic or political clients, who acted largely outside a pervasive web of ranked kinship relations. To the extent that reasonably mature institutions of the state suppressed the more destructive levels of internal conflict, competition increasingly involved struggles between territorial entities, which in turn favored the development of new kinds of recruitment of soldiers and new kinds of formal military institutions.

My final observations have to do with even more basic issues relating to the archaeological record. During our seminar Flannery noted that some chiefdoms and archaic states are extremely flamboyant in their politico-religious displays while others are not. Unfortunately, archaeologists see only the most durable dimensions of display and symbolic information. Obviously, the Maya created flamboyant and durable public monuments and symbolic systems that projected royal/elite information on a scale unmatched in Polynesia. Why such contrasts exist is a significant problem in its own right. But despite this difference, I suspect that Maya and Polynesian warfare and its sociocultural settings shared much more than we presently recognize.

What really worries me is a question that ran repeatedly through my mind while reading many accounts of Polynesian war. Despite its ubiquity and importance, how would we perceive such warfare archaeologically, except where durable fortifications existed? My guess is that if we had to rely *only* on archaeological materials, we would dismiss as inconsequential one of the most important components in the structure and evolution of Polynesian society. This is perhaps the most significant lesson of all for Mayanists, and for students of prehistoric war in general.

NOTE

1.   Although the Maori retained principles of kin ranking developed before their migration to New Zealand, and certainly had chiefs, their basic sociopolitical and economic behaviors appear to me to be markedly egalitarian, not the least in warfare.

References

Abercrombie, N., S. Hill, and B. S. Turner
  1980   *The Dominant Ideology Thesis*. George Allen and Unwin, London.
Adams, B.
  1974   *Ancient Hierakonpolis*. Aris and Phillips, Warminster.
Adams, R. E. W.
  1990   Archaeological Research at the Lowland Maya City of Río Azul. *Latin American Antiquity* 1:23–41.
Adams, R. E. W. (editor)
  1977   *The Origins of Maya Civilization*. School of American Research Advanced Seminar Series, University of New Mexico Press, Albuquerque.
Adams, R. E. W., and R. C. Jones
  1981   Spatial Patterns and Regional Growth among Classic Maya Cities. *American Antiquity* 46:301–22.
Adams, R. McC.
  1962   Agriculture and Urban Life in Early Southwestern Iran. *Science* 136:109–22.
  1965   *Land Behind Baghdad: A History of Settlement on the Diyala Plains*. University of Chicago Press, Chicago.
  1966   *The Evolution of Urban Society: Early Mesopotamia and Prehispanic Mexico*. Aldine, Chicago.
  1978   Strategies of Maximization, Stability, and Resilience in Mesopotamian Society, Settlement, and Agriculture. *Proceedings of the American Philosophical Society* 122:329–35.
  1981   *Heartland of Cities: Surveys of Ancient Settlement and Land Use on the Central Floodplain of the Euphrates*. University of Chicago Press, Chicago.
  1984   Mesopotamian Social Evolution: Old Outlooks, New Goals. In *On the Evolution of Complex Societies: Essays in Honor of Harry Hoijer*, edited by T. Earle, pp. 79–129. Undena, Malibu, California.
  1992   Ideologies: Unity and Diversity. In *Ideology and Pre-Columbian Civilizations*, edited by A. A. Demarest and G. W. Conrad, pp. 205–21. School of American Research Press, Santa Fe.

Adams, R. McC., and H. Nissen
1972   *The Uruk Countryside*. University of Chicago Press, Chicago.
Adams, W. Y.
1977   *Nubia: Corridor to Africa*. Allen Lane, London.
Alden, J. R.
1987   The Susa III Period. In *The Archaeology of Western Iran,* edited by F. Hole,
        pp. 157–70. Smithsonian Institution Press, Washington, D.C.
Algaze, G.
1989   The Uruk Expansion: Cross-Cultural Exchange in Early Mesopotamian Civi-
        lization. *Current Anthropology* 30:571–608.
1993a   *The Uruk World-System: The Dynamics of Expansion in Early Mesopotamian Civi-
        lization*. University of Chicago Press, Chicago.
1993b   Expansionary Dynamics of Some Early Pristine States. *American Anthropologist*
        95:304–33.
Allchin, B., and R. Allchin
1968   *The Birth of Indian Civilization*. Penguin Books, Baltimore.
1982   *The Rise of Civilization in India and Pakistan*. Cambridge University Press,
        Cambridge.
Altenmüller, H.
1980   Markt. In *Lexikon der Ägyptologie,* edited by W. Helck and W. Westendorf, II,
        cols. 1191–94. Otto Harrassowitz, Wiesbaden.
Althusser, L.
1971   *Lenin and Philosophy and Other Essays*. Monthly Review Press, New York.
Alva, W., and C. B. Donnan
1993   *Royal Tombs of Sipán*. Fowler Museum of Cultural History, UCLA, Los
        Angeles.
Amiet, P.
1972   *La glyptique susiénne. Mémoires de la Délégation Archéologique en Iran XLIII*. Paul
        Geuthner, Paris.
Anderson, D. G.
1990   Stability and Change in Chiefdom-Level Societies: An Examination of Missis-
        sippian Political Evolution on the South Atlantic Slope. In *Lamar Archaeol-
        ogy: Mississippian Chiefdoms in the Deep South,* edited by M. Williams and
        G. Shapiro, pp. 187–213. University of Alabama Press, Tuscaloosa.
Appadurai, A.
1986   Introduction: Commodities and the Politics of Value. In *The Social Life of
        Things: Commodities in Cultural Perspective,* edited by A. Appadurai, pp. 3–63.
        Cambridge University Press, Cambridge.
Appel, J.
1982   The Postclassic: A Summary of the Ethnohistoric Information Relevant to the
        Interpretation of Late Postclassic Settlement Pattern Data, the Central and
        Valle Grande Survey Zones. In *Monte Albán's Hinterland, Part I: Prehispanic Set-
        tlement Patterns of the Central and Southern Parts of the Valley of Oaxaca, Mexico,*
        by R. E. Blanton, S. A. Kowalewski, G. M. Feinman, and J. Appel, pp. 139–
        48. Memoirs 15. Museum of Anthropology, University of Michigan, Ann
        Arbor.
1986   A Central-Place Analysis of Classic and Late Postclassic Settlement Patterns in
        the Valley of Oaxaca. In *Research in Economic Anthropology, Supplement 2: Eco-
        nomic Aspects of Prehispanic Highland Mexico,* edited by B. L. Isaac, pp. 375–418.
        JAI Press, Greenwich, Connecticut.

Apter, D. E.
1965   *The Politics of Modernization.* University of Chicago Press, Chicago.
Arnold, D.
1992   *Die Tempel Ägyptens: Götterwohnungen, Kultstätten, Baudenkmäler.* Artemis and Winkler, Zurich.
Asselberghs, H.
1961   *Chaos en Beheersing: Documenten uit het aeneolitisch Egypte.* Documenta et Monumenta Orientis Antiqui 8. E. J. Brill, Leiden.
Assmann, J.
1990   *Ma'at: Gerechtigkeit und Unsterblichkeit im alten Ägypten.* C. H. Beck, Munich.
1991   *Stein und Zeit: Mensch und Gesellschaft im alten Ägypten.* Wilhelm Fink, Munich.
1992   *Das Kulturelle Gedächtnis: Schrift, Erinnerung und politische Identität in frühen Hochkulturen.* C. H. Beck, Munich.
Badawy, A.
1968   *A History of Egyptian Architecture.* University of California Press, Berkeley.
Baer, K.
1960   *Rank and Title in the Old Kingdom: The Structure of the Egyptian Administration in the Fifth and Sixth Dynasties.* University of Chicago Press, Chicago.
1962   The Low Price of Land in Ancient Egypt. *Journal of the American Research Center in Egypt* 1:25–45.
Bagnall, R. S.
1993   *Egypt in Late Antiquity.* Princeton University Press, Princeton.
Bagnall, R. S., and B. W. Frier
1994   *The Demography of Roman Egypt.* Cambridge Studies in Population, Economy and Society in Past Time, No. 23. Cambridge University Press, Cambridge.
Bailey, F. G.
1965   Decisions by Consensus in Councils and Committees, with Special Reference to Village and Local Government in India. In *Political Systems and the Distribution of Power,* edited by M. Banton, pp. 1–20. Tavistock, London.
Baines, J.
1985   *Fecundity Figures: Egyptian Personification and the Iconology of a Genre.* Aris and Phillips, Warminster, and Bolchazy Carducci, Chicago.
1988a   Literacy, Social Organization and the Archaeological Record: The Case of Early Egypt. In *State and Society: The Emergence and Development of Social Hierarchy and Political Centralization,* edited by J. Gledhill, B. Bender, and M. T. Larsen, pp. 192–214. One World Archaeology 4. Unwin Hyman, London.
1988b   An Abydos List of Gods and an Old Kingdom Use of Texts. In *Pyramid Studies and Other Essays Presented to I. E. S. Edwards,* edited by J. Baines, T. G. H. James, M. A. Leahy, and A. F. Shore, pp. 124–33. Occasional Publications 7. Egypt Exploration Society, London.
1989a   Ancient Egyptian Concepts and Uses of the Past: 3rd to 2nd Millennium B.C. Evidence. In *Who Needs the Past? Indigenous Values and Archaeology,* edited by R. Layton, pp. 131–49. One World Archaeology 5. Unwin Hyman, London.
1989b   Communication and Display: The Integration of Early Egyptian Art and Writing. *Antiquity* 63:471–82.
1990   Restricted Knowledge, Hierarchy, and Decorum: Modern Perceptions and Ancient Institutions. *Journal of the American Research Center in Egypt* 27:1–23.
1994   On the Status and Purposes of Ancient Egyptian Art. *Cambridge Archaeological Journal* 4:67–94.
1995a   The Origins of Kingship in Egypt. In *Ancient Egyptian Kingship,* edited by

D. O'Connor and D.-P. Silverman, pp. 95–156. Probleme der Ägyptologie 9. E. J. Brill, Leiden.

1995b   Kingship, Definition of Culture, and Legitimation. In *Ancient Egyptian Kingship,* edited by D. O'Connor and D. P. Silverman, pp. 3–47. Probleme der Ägyptologie 9. E. J. Brill, Leiden.

1996   Contextualizing Egyptian Representations of Society and Ethnicity. In *The Study of the Ancient Near East in the 21st Century: The William Foxwell Albright Centennial Conference,* edited by J. S. Cooper and G. Schwartz, pp. 339–84. Eisenbrauns, Winona Lake, Indiana.

1997a   Temples as Symbols, Guarantors, and Participants in Egyptian Civilization. In *The Temple in Ancient Egypt: New Discoveries and Recent Research,* edited by S. Quirke, pp. 216–41. British Museum Press, London.

1997b   The Dawn of the Amarna Age. In *Amenhotep III: Perspectives on His Reign,* edited by E. Cline and D. O'Connor, pp. 271–312. University of Michigan Press, Ann Arbor.

1998   Prehistories of Literature: Performance, Fiction, Myth. In *Defining Egyptian Literature: Proceedings of the Symposium "Ancient Egyptian Literature, History and Forms," Los Angeles, March 24–26, 1995,* edited by G. Moers. Lingua Aegyptia Studia Monographica 2. Göttingen.

Baines, J., and C. J. Eyre
1983   Four Notes on Literacy. *Göttinger Miszellen* 61:65–96.

Baker, P. T., and W. T. Sanders
1972   Demographic Studies in Anthropology. *Annual Review of Anthropology* 1:151–78.

Bard, K.
1994   *From Farmers to Pharaohs: Mortuary Evidence for the Rise of Complex Society in Egypt.* Sheffield Academic Press, Sheffield.

Bargatzky, T.
1987   Upward Evolution, Suprasystem Dominance, and the Mature State. In *Early State Dynamics,* edited by H. J. M. Claessen and P. van de Velde, pp. 24–38. E. J. Brill, Leiden.

1988   Evolution, Sequential Hierarchy, and Areal Integration: The Case of Traditional Samoan Society. In *State and Society: The Emergence and Development of Social Hierarchy and Political Centralization,* edited by J. Gledhill, B. Bender, and M. T. Larsen, pp. 43–56. Unwin Hyman, London.

Barlow, R. H.
1949   *The Extent of the Empire of the Culhua Mexica.* Ibero-Americana 28. University of California Press, Berkeley.

Barnes, J. A.
1972   Social Networks. *An Addison-Wesley Module in Anthropology* 26:1–29.

Barth, F.
1959   *Political Leadership among the Swat Pathans.* Monograph on Social Anthropology 19. London School of Economics, London.

Baudez, C. F., and P. Becquelin
1973   *Archaeologie de Los Naranjos, Honduras.* Mission Archéologique et Ethnologique au Française Mexique, Mexico City.

Beattie, J.
1967   Checks on the Abuse of Political Power in Some African States: A Preliminary Framework for Analysis. In *Comparative Political Systems: Studies in the Politics of Pre-Industrial Societies,* edited by R. Cohen and J. Middleton, pp. 355–74. University of Texas Press, Austin.

Beaulieu, P.-A.
1989   *The Reign of King Nabonidus of Babylon, 556–539 B.C.* Yale University Press, New Haven.
Bellwood, P.
1971   Fortifications and Economy in Prehistoric New Zealand. *Proceedings of the Prehistoric Society* 37:56–95.
1979   *Man's Conquest of the Pacific.* Oxford University Press, New York.
Bender, B.
1990   The Dynamics of Nonhierarchical Societies. In *The Evolution of Political Systems: Sociopolitics in Small-Scale Sedentary Societies,* edited by S. Upham, pp. 247–63. Cambridge University Press, Cambridge.
Bennet, J.
1990   Knossos in Context: Comparative Perspectives on the Linear B Administration of LM II–III Crete. *American Journal of Archaeology* 94:193–211.
Bentley, G. C.
1986   Indigenous States of Southeast Asia. *Annual Review of Anthropology* 15:275–305.
Berdan, F. F.
1975   *Trade, Tribute and Market in the Aztec Empire.* Ph.D. dissertation, Department of Anthropology, University of Texas, Austin.
1982   *The Aztecs of Central Mexico: An Imperial Society.* Holt, Rinehart, and Winston, New York.
1987   Political and Economic Geography of the Eastern Aztec Realm. Paper presented at the 86th Annual Meeting of the American Anthropological Association, Chicago.
Bermann, M.
1994   *Lukurmata: Household Archaeology in Prehispanic Bolivia.* Princeton University Press, Princeton.
Bernard, H. R., and P. D. Killworth
1973   On the Social Structure of an Ocean-Going Research Vessel and Other Important Things. *Social Science Research* 2:145–84.
1979   Why Are There No Social Physics? *Journal of the Steward Anthropological Society* 11:33–58.
Bernbeck, R.
1993   *Steppe als Kulturlandschaft. Das 'Agig-Gebiert Ostsyriens vom Neolithikum bis zur Islamischen Zeit.* Dietrich Reimer, Berlin.
Berndt, R.
1964   Warfare in the New Guinea Highlands. *American Anthropologist* 66(4):183–203.
Bernstein, B.
1965   A Socio-Linguistic Approach to Social Learning. In *Penguin Survey of the Social Sciences 1965,* edited by J. Gould, pp. 144–68. Penguin Books, Baltimore.
1971   *Class, Codes and Control, Volume 1: Theoretical Studies Towards a Sociology of Language.* Routledge and Kegan Paul, London.
Besnier, N.
1993   The Demise of the Man Who Would Be King: Sorcery and Ambition on Nukulaelae Atoll. *Journal of Anthropological Research* 49:185–215.
Bickel, S.
1994   *La cosmogonie égyptienne avant le Nouvel Empire.* Orbis Biblicus et Orientalis 134. Editions Universitaires, Fribourg, and Vandenhoeck and Ruprecht, Göttingen.
Biggs, R.
1967   Semitic Names in the Fara Period. *Orientalia* 36:55–66.

Bisht, R.
1991   Dholavira: A New Horizon of the Indus Civilization. *Puratattva* 20:71–82.
Black, J. A.
1981   The New Year Ceremonies in Ancient Babylon: "Taking Bel by the Hand" and a Cultic Picnic. *Religion* 11:39–59.
Blanton, R. E.
1976   Anthropological Studies of Cities. *Annual Review of Anthropology* 5:249–64.
1978   *Monte Albán: Settlement Patterns at the Ancient Zapotec Capital.* Academic Press, New York.
1985   A Comparison of Early Market Systems. In *Markets and Marketing,* Monographs in Economic Anthropology 4, edited by S. Plattner, pp. 399–416. University Press of America, Lanham, Maryland.
1989   Continuity and Change in Public Architecture: Periods I through V of the Valley of Oaxaca, Mexico. In *Monte Albán's Hinterland, Part II: The Prehispanic Settlement Patterns in Tlacolula, Etla, and Ocotlán, the Valley of Oaxaca, Mexico,* by S. A. Kowalewski, G. M. Feinman, L. Finsten, R. E. Blanton, and L. M. Nicholas, pp. 409–47. Memoirs 23. Museum of Anthropology, University of Michigan, Ann Arbor.
1994   *Houses and Households: A Comparative Study.* Plenum Press, New York.
1996   The Basin of Mexico Market System and the Growth of Empire. In *Aztec Imperial Strategies,* by F. F. Berdan, R. E. Blanton, E. Boone, M. Hodge, M. E. Smith, and E. Umberger, pp. 47–84. Dumbarton Oaks, Washington, D.C.
Blanton, R. E., and G. M. Feinman
1984   The Mesoamerican World System. *American Anthropologist* 86:673–82.
Blanton, R. E., G. M. Feinman, S. A. Kowalewski, and P. N. Peregrine
1996   A Dual-Processual Theory for the Evolution of Mesoamerican Civilization. *Current Anthropology* 37:1–14.
Blanton, R. E., S. A. Kowalewski, G. M. Feinman, and J. Appel
1981   *Ancient Mesoamerica: A Comparison of Change in Three Regions.* Cambridge University Press, Cambridge.
1982   *Monte Albán's Hinterland, Part I: Prehispanic Settlement Patterns of the Central and Southern Parts of the Valley of Oaxaca, Mexico.* Memoirs 15. Museum of Anthropology, University of Michigan, Ann Arbor.
Blanton, R. E., S. A. Kowalewski, G. M. Feinman, and L. M. Finsten
1993   *Ancient Mesoamerica: A Comparison of Change in Three Regions.* 2nd ed. Cambridge University Press, Cambridge.
Blau, P. M.
1968   The Hierarchy of Authority in Organizations. *American Journal of Sociology* 73:453–67.
1970   A Formal Theory of Differentiation in Organizations. *American Sociological Review* 35:201–18.
Bloch, Marc
1961   *Feudal Society.* University of Chicago Press, Chicago.
Bloch, Maurice
1974   Symbols, Song, Dance and Features of Articulation: Is Religion an Extreme Form of Traditional Authority? *European Journal of Sociology* 15:55–81.
1975   Introduction. In *Political Language and Oratory in Traditional Society,* edited by M. Bloch, pp. 1–28. Academic Press, London.

1977a   The Past and the Present in the Present. *Man* (n.s.) 12:279–92.
1977b   The Disconnection between Power and Rank as a Process: An Outline of the Development of Kingdoms in Central Madagascar. In *The Evolution of Social Systems,* edited by J. Friedman and M. J. Rowlands, pp. 303–40. Duckworth, London.
1980   Ritual Symbolism and the Nonrepresentation of Society. In *Symbol as Sense: New Approaches to the Analysis of Meaning,* edited by M. L. Foster and S. H. Brandes, pp. 93–102. Academic Press, New York.

Boehm, C.
1993   Egalitarian Behavior and Reverse Dominance Hierarchy. *Current Anthropology* 34:227–54.

Boehmer, R. M.
1991   Uruk 1980–1990: A Progress Report. *Antiquity* 65:465–78.

Boese, J.
1989–90   *Tell Sheikh Hassan.* Archiv für Orientforschung 36/37:323–31.

Bohannan, P.
1958   Extra-Processual Events in Tiv Political Institutions. *American Anthropologist* 60:1–12.

Boltz, W.
1986   Early Chinese Writing. *World Archaeology* 17:420–36.
1994   *The Origin and Development of the Chinese Writing System.* American Oriental Society, New Haven.

Boulding, K.
1956   Toward a General Theory of Growth. *General Systems* 1:66–75.

Bourdieu, P.
1977   *Outline of a Theory of Practice.* Cambridge University Press, Cambridge.
1978–79   Symbolic Power. *Telos* 38:77–85.

Bowersock, G. W.
1988   The Dissolution of the Roman Empire. In *The Collapse of Ancient States and Civilizations,* edited by N. Yoffee and G. L. Cowgill, pp. 165–75. University of Arizona Press, Tucson.

Bowman, A. K.
1996   *Egypt after the Pharaohs 332 BC–AD 642: From Alexander to the Arab Conquest.* British Museum Publications, London.

Bradbury, R. E.
1969   Patrimonialism and Gerontocracy in Benin Political Culture. In *Man in Africa,* edited by M. Douglas and P. M. Kaberry, pp. 17–36. Tavistock, London.

Brailsford, B.
1981   *The Tattooed Land.* A. H. and A. W. Reed, Wellington.

Brandes, M.
1979   *Siegelabrollungen aus den Archaischen Bauschichten in Uruk-Warka.* Freiburger Altorientalisch Studien Band 3. Franz Steiner, Wiesbaden.

Braudel, F.
1973   *The Mediterranean and the Mediterranean World in the Age of Philip II,* vol. II. Harper and Row, New York.

Bray, W.
1968   *Everyday Life of the Aztecs.* G. P. Putnam's Sons, New York.
1972   The City State in Central Mexico at the Time of the Spanish Conquest. *Journal of Latin American Studies* 4:161–85.

Bright, C., and S. Harding
1984   Processes of Statemaking and Popular Protest: An Introduction. In *Statemaking and Social Movements: Essays in History and Theory,* edited by C. Bright and S. Harding, pp. 1–15. University of Michigan Press, Ann Arbor.

Brinkman, J. A.
1980   Kassiten. *Reallexikon der Assyriologie* 5:464–73.

Britan, G. M., and R. Cohen
1980   *Hierarchy and Society: Anthropological Perspectives on Bureaucracy.* Institute for the Study of Human Issues, Philadelphia.

Brown, P., and A. Podolefsky
1976   Population Density, Agricultural Intensity, Land Tenure, and Group Size in the New Guinea Highlands. *Ethnology* 15:211–38.

Brumfiel, E. M.
1983   Aztec State Making: Ecology, Structure, and the Origin of the State. *American Anthropologist* 85:261–84.
1992   Distinguished Lecture in Archeology: Breaking and Entering the Ecosystem—Gender, Class, and Faction Steal the Show. *American Anthropologist* 94:551–67.

Brumfiel, E. M., and T. K. Earle
1987   Specialization, Exchange, and Complex Societies: An Introduction. In *Specialization, Exchange, and Complex Societies,* edited by E. M. Brumfiel and T. K. Earle, pp. 1–9. Cambridge University Press, Cambridge.

Buck, P.
1934   *Mangaian Society.* Bulletin 122. Bernice P. Bishop Museum, Hawai'i.

Burger, R.
1992   *Chavin.* Thames and Hudson, London.

Burke, P.
1986   City-States. In *States in History,* edited by J. A. Hall, pp. 137–53. Basil Blackwell, Oxford.

Byland, B.
1980   *Political and Economic Evolution in the Tamazulapan Valley, Mixteca Alta, Oaxaca, Mexico: A Regional Approach.* Ph.D. dissertation, Department of Anthropology, Pennsylvania State University, College Park.

Cabrera Castro, R.
1991   Secuencia arquitectónica y cronológica de la Ciudadela. In *Teotihuacán 1980–1982: nuevas interpretaciones,* pp. 31–60. Serie Arqueología, INAH, Mexico, D.F.

Cabrera Castro, R., S. Sugiyama, and G. L. Cowgill
1991   The Templo de Quetzalcoatl Project at Teotihuacán: A Preliminary Report. *Ancient Mesoamerica* 2:77–92.

Calnek, E. E.
1978   The City-State in the Basin of Mexico: Late Pre-Hispanic Period. In *Urbanization in the Americas from its Beginnings to the Present,* edited by R. P. Schaedel, J. E. Hardoy, and N. S. Kinzer, pp. 463–70. Mouton, The Hague.

Calvet, Y.
1987   La phase 'Oueili de l'époque d'Obeid. In *Préhistoire de la Mésopotamie: la Mésopotamie préhistorique et l'exploration récente du djebel Hamrin,* edited by J.-L. Huot, pp. 129–51. Editions du Centre National de la Recherche Scientifique, Paris.

Campbell, J. K.
1964   *Honour, Family, and Patronage: A Study of Institutions and Moral Values in a Greek Mountain Community.* Clarendon Press, Oxford.

Campo, J. E.
1991   *The Other Side of Paradise: Explorations into the Religious Meanings of Domestic Space in Islam.* University of South Carolina Press, Columbia.

Carlton, E.
1977   *Ideology and Social Order.* Routledge and Kegan Paul, London.

Carneiro, R. L.
1967   On the Relationship between Size of Population and Complexity of Social Organization. *Southwestern Journal of Anthropology* 23:234–43.
1969   The Measurement of Cultural Development in the Ancient Near East and in Anglo-Saxon England. *Transactions of the New York Academy of Sciences,* Series II, vol. 31:1013–23.
1970a   A Theory of the Origin of the State. *Science* 169:733–38.
1970b   Scale Analysis, Evolutionary Sequences, and the Rating of Cultures. In *A Handbook of Method in Cultural Anthropology,* edited by R. Naroll and R. Cohen, pp. 843–71. Columbia University Press, New York.
1978   Political Expansion as an Expression of the Principle of Competitive Exclusion. In *The Origins of the State: The Anthropology of Political Evolution,* edited by R. Cohen and E. R. Service, pp. 205–23. Institute for the Study of Human Issues, Philadelphia.
1981   The Chiefdom: Precursor of the State. In *The Transition to Statehood in the New World,* edited by G. D. Jones and R. R. Kautz, pp. 37–79. Cambridge University Press, Cambridge.
1987   Further Reflections on Resource Concentration and Its Role in the Rise of the State. In *Studies in the Neolithic and Urban Revolution: The V. Gordon Childe Colloquium, Mexico, 1986,* edited by L. Manzanilla, pp. 245–60. BAR International Series 349. British Archaeological Reports, Oxford.
1991   The Nature of the Chiefdom as Revealed by Evidence in the Cauca Valley of Colombia. In *Profiles in Cultural Evolution,* edited by A. T. Rambo and K. Gillogly, pp. 167–90. Anthropological Papers 85. Museum of Anthropology, University of Michigan, Ann Arbor.

Carrasco, P.
1971   Social Organization of Ancient Mexico. In *Handbook of Middle American Indians, vol. 10: Archaeology of Northern Mesoamerica, Part I,* edited by R. Wauchope, pp. 349–75. University of Texas Press, Austin.
1974   Sucesión y alianzas matrimoniales en la dinastía teotihuacana. *Estudios de Cultura Náhuatl* 11:235–42.
1984   Royal Marriages in Ancient Mexico. In *Explorations in Ethnohistory: Indians of Central Mexico in the Sixteenth Century,* edited by H. R. Harvey and H. J. Prem, pp. 41–81. University of New Mexico Press, Albuquerque.

Casal, J.-M.
1964   *Fouilles d'Amri.* 2 vols. Publications de la Commission des Fouilles Archaeologiques, Fouilles du Pakistan, Paris.

Cashdan, E. A.
1980   Egalitarianism among Hunters and Gatherers. *American Anthropologist* 82:116–20.

Caso, A.
1935   Las exploraciones en Monte Albán, temporada 1934–1935. Publicación 18. Instituto Panamericano de Geografía e Historia, Mexico.
1938   Exploraciones en Oaxaca, quinta y sexta temporadas 1936–1937. Publicación 34. Instituto Panamericano de Geografía e Historia, Mexico.
Castells, M.
1983   The City and the Grassroots: A Cross-Cultural Theory of Urban Social Movements. University of California Press, Berkeley.
Castle, E. W.
1992   Shipping and Trade in Ramesside Egypt. Journal of the Economic and Social History of the Orient 35:239–77.
Champion, T., C. Gamble, S. Shennan, and A. Whittle
1984   Prehistoric Europe. Academic Press, London.
Chandler, T., and G. Fox
1974   3000 Years of Urban Growth. Academic Press, New York.
Chang, K. C.
1983   Art, Myth, and Ritual: The Path to Political Authority in Ancient China. Harvard University Press, Cambridge.
Charlton, T. H.
1972   Post-Conquest Developments in the Teotihuacán Valley, Mexico. Part I: Excavations. Report 5. Office of the State Archaeologist, University of Iowa, Iowa City.
1991   The Influence and Legacy of Teotihuacán on Regional Routes and Urban Planning. In Ancient Road Networks and Settlement Hierarchies in the New World, edited by C. D. Trombold, pp. 186–97. Cambridge University Press, Cambridge.
Charlton, T. H., and D. L. Nichols
1997   The City-State Concept: Development and Applications. In The Archaeology of City-States: Cross-Cultural Approaches, edited by D. L. Nichols and T. H. Charlton, pp. 1–14. Smithsonian Institution Press, Washington, D.C.
Charpin, D.
1980   Remarques sur l'administration paléobabylonienne sous les successeurs d'Hammurapi. Journal of the American Oriental Society 100:461–71.
1986   Le clergé d'Ur au siècle d'Hammurabi (XIXe–XVIIIe av. J.-C.). Droz, Geneva and Paris.
Charvat, P.
1988   Archaeology and Social History: The Susa Sealings ca. 4000–2340 B.C. Paléorient 14(1):57–64.
Chase, A. F., and D. Z. Chase
1987   Investigations at the Classic Maya City of Caracol, Belize: 1985–1987. Monograph 3. Pre-Columbian Art Research Institute, San Francisco.
Chase, A. F., and P. M. Rice (editors)
1985   The Lowland Maya Postclassic. University of Texas Press, Austin.
Chase-Dunn, C.
1990   World-State Formation: Historical Processes and Emergent Necessity. Political Geography Quarterly 9:108–30.
Chazan, N.
1988   The Early State in Africa: The Asante Case. In The Early State in African Perspective: Culture, Power and Division of Labor, edited by S. N. Eisenstadt, M. Abitbol, and N. Chazan, pp. 60–97. E. J. Brill, Leiden.

Childe, V. G.
1942   *What Happened in History*. Penguin, Harmondsworth.
1952   *New Light on the Most Ancient East*. Routledge and Kegan Paul, London.
Cieza de León, P.
1959 (1553)   *The Incas*. Translated by H. de Onis, edited by V. W. Von Hagen. University of Oklahoma Press, Norman.
Civil, M.
1975   Lexicography. In *Sumerological Studies in Honor of Thorkild Jacobsen on His Seventieth Birthday, June 7, 1974*, edited by S. Lieberman, pp. 123–57. University of Chicago Press, Chicago.
1987   Ur III Bureaucracy: Quantitative Approaches. In *The Organization of Power: Aspects of Bureaucracy in the Ancient Near East*, edited by M. Gibson and R. D. Biggs, pp. 19–41. Studies in Ancient Oriental Civilization 46. Oriental Institute, University of Chicago, Chicago.
1992   Education (Mesopotamia). *Anchor Bible Dictionary* II:301–5. Doubleday, New York.
Civil, M., R. D. Briggs, H. G. Güterbock, H. J. Nissen, and E. Reiner
1969   *The Series lú=ša and Related Texts*. Materials for the Sumerian Lexicon 12. Pontificium Institutum Biblicum, Rome.
Claessen, H. J. M.
1978a   The Early State: A Structural Approach. In *The Early State*, edited by H. J. M. Claessen and P. Skalník, pp. 533–96. Mouton, The Hague.
1978b   Comment. *Current Anthropology* 19:769.
1978c   Early State in Tahiti. In *The Early State*, edited by H. J. M. Claessen and P. Skalník, pp. 441–68. Mouton, The Hague.
1984   The Internal Dynamics of the Early State. *Current Anthropology* 25:365–79.
Claessen, H. J. M., and P. Skalník
1978a   The Early State: Theories and Hypotheses. In *The Early State*, edited by H. J. M. Claessen and P. Skalník, pp. 3–29. Mouton, The Hague.
1978b   The Early State: Models and Reality. In *The Early State*, edited by H. J. M. Claessen and P. Skalník, pp. 637–50. Mouton, The Hague.
Claessen, H. J. M., and P. Skalník (editors)
1978   *The Early State*. Mouton, The Hague.
1981   *The Study of the State*. Mouton, The Hague.
Claessen, H. J. M., and P. van de Velde (editors)
1987   *Early State Dynamics*. E. J. Brill, Leiden.
1991   *Early State Economics*. Transaction Publishers, New Brunswick, New Jersey.
Claessen, H. J. M., P. van de Velde, and M. E. Smith (editors)
1985   *Development and Decline: The Evolution of Sociopolitical Organization*. Bergin and Garvey, South Hadley, Massachusetts.
Clastres, P.
1977   *Society against the State*. Translated by R. Hurley. Urizen Press, New York.
Clay, A. T.
1909   *Amurru, the Home of the Northern Semites: A Study Showing That the Religion and Culture of Israel Are Not of Babylonian Origin*. The Sunday School Times, Philadelphia.
Cobb, H. (editor)
1979   *Cook's Voyages*. British Museum, London.

Cobo, B.
1990 (1653)   *Inca Religion and Customs.* Translated and edited by R. Hamilton. University of Texas Press, Austin.

Coe, M. D.
1992   *Breaking the Maya Code.* Thames and Hudson, New York.

Coe, M. D., and R. A. Diehl
1980   *In the Land of the Olmec, Vol. II: The People of the River.* University of Texas Press, Austin.

Coe, W. R.
1965   Tikal: Ten Years of Study of a Maya Ruin in the Lowlands of Guatemala. *Expedition* 8:5–56.
1990   *Excavations in the North Acropolis, North Terrace, and Great Plaza of Tikal.* Tikal Report 14. Monograph 61. University Museum, University of Pennsylvania, Philadelphia.

Cohen, R.
1978   State Origins: A Reappraisal. In *The Early State,* edited by H. J. M. Claessen and P. Skalník, pp. 31–75. Mouton, The Hague.
1981   Evolution, Fission, and the Early State. In *The Study of the State,* edited by H. J. M. Claessen and P. Skalník, pp. 87–115. Mouton, The Hague.

Cohen, R., and E. R. Service (editors)
1978   *Origins of the State: The Anthropology of Political Evolution.* Institute for the Study of Human Issues, Philadelphia.

Cohen, R., and J. D. Toland
1988   *State Formation and Political Legitimacy.* Political Anthropology VI. Series editor, M. J. Aronoff. Transaction Books, New Brunswick, New Jersey.

Collins, R.
1981   *Sociology Since Midcentury: Essays in Theory Cumulation.* Academic Press, New York.

Conklin, W. J., and M. E. Moseley
1988   The Patterns of Art and Power in the Early Intermediate Period. In *Peruvian Prehistory,* edited by R. Keatinge, pp. 145–63. Cambridge University Press, Cambridge.

Conrad, G. W.
1982   The Burial Platforms of Chan Chan: Some Social and Political Implications. In *Chan Chan: Andean Desert City,* edited by M. E. Moseley and K. C. Day, pp. 87–117. University of New Mexico Press, Albuquerque.

Cooper, J. S.
1973   Sumerian and Akkadian in Sumer and Akkad. In *Approaches to the Study of the Ancient Near East: A Volume of Studies Offered to Ignace J. Gelb,* edited by G. Buccellati, pp. 239–46. *Orientalia* 42.
1983   *Reconstructing History from Ancient Inscriptions: The Lagash–Umma Border Conflict.* Sources from the Ancient Near East 2(1). Undena, Malibu, California.
1989   Writing. *International Encyclopaedia of Communications* 4:321–31.
1993   Paradigm and Propaganda: The Dynasty of Akkade in the 21st Century. In *Akkad: The First World Empire,* edited by M. Liverani, pp. 11–23. Sargon, Padua.

Corcoran, P. E.
1979   *Political Language and Rhetoric.* University of Texas Press, Austin.

Cordy, R. H.
1981   *A Study of Prehistoric Social Change.* Academic Press, New York.

Cortés, H.
1986   *Letters from Mexico*. Yale University Press, New Haven.
Costin, C. L., and T. K. Earle
1989   Status Distinction and Legitimation of Power as Reflected in Changing Patterns of Consumption in Late Prehispanic Peru. *American Antiquity* 54:691–714.
Cowgill, G. L.
1983   Rulership and the Ciudadela: Political Inferences from Teotihuacán Architecture. In *Civilization in the Ancient Americas: Essays in Honor of Gordon R. Willey,* edited by R. M. Leventhal and A. L. Kolata, pp. 313–43. University of New Mexico Press, Albuquerque, and Peabody Museum of Archaeology and Ethnology, Harvard University, Cambridge.
1988   Onward and Upward with Collapse. In *The Collapse of Ancient States and Civilizations,* edited by N. Yoffee and G. L. Cowgill, pp. 244–76. University of Arizona Press, Tucson.
1992a   Social Differentiation at Teotihuacán. In *Mesoamerican Elites: An Archaeological Assessment,* edited by D. Z. Chase and A. F. Chase, pp. 206–20. University of Oklahoma Press, Norman.
1992b   Toward a Political History of Teotihuacán. In *Ideology and Pre-Columbian Civilizations,* edited by A. A. Demarest and G. W. Conrad, pp. 87–114. School of American Research Press, Santa Fe.
1993   Distinguished Lecture in Archeology: Beyond Criticizing New Archeology. *American Anthropologist* 95:551–73.
1997   State and Society at Teotihuacán, Mexico. *Annual Review of Anthropology* 26:129–61.
Crawford (Thompson), D. J.
1971   *Kerkeosiris: An Egyptian Village in the Ptolemaic Period*. Cambridge University Press, Cambridge.
Crawford, H.
1991   *Sumer and the Sumerians*. Cambridge University Press, Cambridge.
Creel, H. G.
1970   *The Origins of Statecraft in China, Volume One: The Western Chou Empire*. University of Chicago Press, Chicago.
Crumley, C. L.
1976   Toward a Locational Definition of State Systems of Settlement. *American Anthropologist* 78:59–73.
1987   A Dialectical Critique of Hierarchy. In *Power Relations and State Formation,* edited by T. C. Patterson and C. W. Gailey, pp. 155–69. Special publication of the Archeology Section, American Anthropological Association, Washington, D.C.
1995   Heterarchy and the Analysis of Complex Societies. In *Heterarchy and the Analysis of Complex Societies,* edited by R. Ehrenreich, C. L. Crumley, and J. E. Levy, pp. 1–5. Archeological Papers 6. American Anthropological Association, Washington, D.C.
Culbert, T. P.
1991   Polities in the Northeastern Petén, Guatemala. In *Classic Maya Political History,* edited by T. P. Culbert, pp. 128–46. School of American Research Advanced Seminar Series, Cambridge University Press, New York.

Culbert, T. P. (editor)
  1973   *The Classic Maya Collapse.* School of American Research Advanced Seminar Series, University of New Mexico Press, Albuquerque.
  1991   *Classic Maya Political History: Hieroglyphic and Archaeological Evidence.* School of American Research Advanced Seminar Series, Cambridge University Press, Cambridge.
Culbert, T. P., L. J. Kosakowsky, R. E. Fry, and W. A. Haviland
  1990   The Population of Tikal, Guatemala. In *Precolumbian Population History in the Maya Lowlands,* edited by T. P. Culbert and D. S. Rice, pp. 103–21. University of New Mexico Press, Albuquerque.
Culbert, T. P., and D. S. Rice (editors)
  1990   *Precolumbian Population History in the Maya Lowlands.* University of New Mexico Press, Albuquerque.
Dales, G. F.
  1979   The Balakot Project: Summary of Four Years Excavations in Pakistan. In *South Asian Archaeology 1977,* edited by M. Taddei, pp. 241–74. Instituto Universitario Orientale, Seminario di Studi Asiatici, Series Minor VI, Naples.
  1982   Mohenjodaro Miscellany: Some Unpublished, Forgotten or Misinterpreted Features. In *Harappan Civilization: A Contemporary Perspective,* edited by G. L. Possehl, pp. 97–106. Oxford and IBH, and the American Institute of Indian Studies, Delhi.
Dalley, S.
  1989   *Myths from Mesopotamia: Creation, the Flood, Gilgamesh, and Others.* Oxford University Press, Oxford.
  1993   Nineveh after 612 B.C. *Altorientalische Forschungen* 20:134–47.
D'Altroy, T. N.
  1992   *Provincial Power in the Inka Empire.* Smithsonian Institution Press, Washington, D.C.
D'Altroy, T. N., and T. K. Earle
  1985   Staple Finance, Wealth Finance, and Storage in the Inka Political Economy (with Comment and Reply). *Current Anthropology* 26:187–206.
Dani, A. H.
  1970–71   Excavations in the Gomal Valley. *Ancient Pakistan* 5:1–177.
Davies, C. N.
  1973   *Los mexica: primeros pasos hacia el imperio.* Serie de Cultura Náhuatl, Monografías 14. Instituto de Investigaciones Históricas, Universidad Nacional Autónoma de México, Mexico.
Davis, W. M.
  1989   *The Canonical Tradition in Ancient Egyptian Art.* Cambridge New Art History and Criticism, Cambridge University Press, Cambridge.
Day, K. C.
  1982   Ciudadelas: Their Form and Function. In *Chan Chan: Andean Desert City,* edited by M. E. Moseley and K. C. Day, pp. 55–66. University of New Mexico Press, Albuquerque.
Delougaz, P.
  1940   *The Temple Oval at Khafajah.* Publication 53. Oriental Institute, University of Chicago, Chicago.
Delougaz, P., and H. J. Kantor
  1996   *Chogha Mish I. The First Five Seasons.* Oriental Institute Publications 101. University of Chicago Press, Chicago.

Demarest, A. A.
1978   Interregional Conflict and "Situational Ethics" in Classic Maya Warfare. In *Codex Wauchope: Festschrift in Honor of Robert Wauchope,* edited by M. Giardino, B. Edmonson, and W. Creamer, pp. 101–11. Human Mosaic, Tulane University, New Orleans.
1993   Violent Saga of a Maya Kingdom. *National Geographic Magazine* 183(2):95–111.
Demarest, A. A., and G. W. Conrad (editors)
1992   *Ideology and Pre-Columbian Civilizations.* School of American Research, Santa Fe.
DeMarrais, E., L. J. Castillo, and T. Earle
1996   Ideology, Materialization, and Power Strategies. *Current Anthropology* 37(1): 15–31.
de Montmollin, O.
1989   *The Archaeology of Political Structure: Settlement Analysis in a Classic Maya Polity.* Cambridge University Press, Cambridge.
Derchain, P.
1962   Le rôle du roi d'Egypte dans le maintien de l'ordre cosmique. In *Le pouvoir et le sacré,* by L. de Heusch, P. Derchain, A. Finet, L. Flam, E. Janssens, J. Pirenne, H. Plard, C. Préaux, L. Rocher, and R. Rocher, pp. 61–73. Annales du Centre d'Etude des Religions 1. Université Libre de Bruxelles, Institut de Sociologie, Brussels.
1990   L'auteur du Papyrus Jumilhac. *Revue d'Egyptologie* 41:9–30.
Desborough, V. R. d'A.
1964   *The Last Mycenaeans and Their Successors.* Oxford University Press, Oxford.
Diakonoff, I. M.
1969   The Rise of the Despotic State in Ancient Mesopotamia. In *Ancient Mesopotamia: Socio-Economic History,* edited by I. M. Diakonoff, pp. 173–203. Nauka Publishing House, Moscow.
1974   *Structure of Ancient Society and State in Early Dynastic Sumer.* Monographs of the Ancient Near East 1(3). Undena, Malibu, California.
1985   Extended Families in Old Babylonian Ur. *Zeitschrift für Assyriologie* 75:47–65.
1990   *People of the City Ur* (in Russian). Nauka, Moscow.
Díaz, B.
1963   *The Conquest of New Spain.* Penguin Books, Baltimore.
Dirks, N.
1993   *The Hollow Crown: Ethnohistory of an Indian Kingdom.* 2nd ed. University of Michigan Press, Ann Arbor.
Donnan, C. B. (editor)
1985   *Early Ceremonial Architecture in the Andes.* Dumbarton Oaks, Washington, D.C.
Donnan, C. B., and G. A. Cock
1986   *Pacatnamú Papers,* vol. 1. Fowler Museum of Cultural History, UCLA, Los Angeles.
Douglas, M.
1967   Primitive Rationing. In *Themes in Economic Anthropology,* edited by R. Firth, pp. 119–47. Tavistock, London.
Doyle, M. W.
1986   *Empires.* Cornell University Press, Ithaca.
Drennan, R. D.
1984   Long-Distance Transport Costs in Pre-Hispanic Mesoamerica. *American Anthropologist* 86:105–12.
1991   Pre-Hispanic Chiefdom Trajectories in Mesoamerica, Central America, and

Northern South America. In *Chiefdoms: Power, Economy, and Ideology,* edited by T. Earle, pp. 263–87. Cambridge University Press, Cambridge.

1996 One for All and All for One: Accounting for Variability without Losing Sight of Regularities in the Development of Complex Society. In *Emergent Complexity: The Evolution of Intermediate Societies,* edited by J. E. Arnold, pp. 25–34. International Monographs in Prehistory (Archaeological Series 9), Ann Arbor.

Drennan, R. D., and C. A. Uribe (editors)
1987 *Chiefdoms in the Americas.* University Press of America, Lanham, Maryland.

Drewitt, B.
1967 Planeación en la antigua ciudad de Teotihuacán. In *Teotihuacán, XI Mesa Redonda,* edited by A. Ruz Lhuillier, pp. 79–95. Sociedad Mexicana de Antropología, Mexico.

Dreyer, G.
1993 Umm el-Qaab: Nachuntersuchungen im frühzeitlichen Königsfriedhof. 5./6. Vorbericht. *Mitteilungen des Deutschen Archäologischen Instituts, Abteilung Kairo* 49:23–62.

Dumont, L.
1980 *Homo Hierarchicus: The Caste System and Its Implications.* 2nd ed. University of Chicago Press, Chicago.

Dunham, D., and W. K. Simpson
1974–80 *Giza Mastabas.* 4 vols. Department of Egyptian and Ancient Near Eastern Art, Museum of Fine Arts, Boston.

Durand, J.-M.
1989 L'assemblée en Syrie à l'époque pré-amorite. In *Miscellenea Eblaitica* 2, edited by P. Fronzaroli, pp. 27–44. Università di Firenze, Florence.

Dyson, R. H.
1966 *Excavations of the Acropole of Susa and the Problems of Susa A, B, and C.* Ph.D. dissertation, Department of Anthropology, Harvard University, Cambridge.

Earle, T. K.
1977 A Reappraisal of Redistribution: Complex Hawaiian Chiefdoms. In *Exchange Systems in Prehistory,* edited by T. K. Earle and J. Ericson, pp. 213–29. Academic Press, New York.

1978 *Economic and Social Organization of a Complex Chiefdom: The Halelea District, Kaua'i, Hawai'i.* Anthropological Papers 63. Museum of Anthropology, University of Michigan, Ann Arbor.

1987 Chiefdoms in Archaeological and Ethnohistorical Perspective. *Annual Review of Anthropology* 16:279–308.

1991a The Evolution of Chiefdoms. In *Chiefdoms: Power, Economy, and Ideology,* edited by T. Earle, pp. 1–15. School of American Research Advanced Seminar Series, Cambridge University Press, Cambridge.

1991b Property Rights and the Evolution of Chiefdoms. In *Chiefdoms: Power, Economy, and Ideology,* edited by T. Earle, pp. 71–99. School of American Research Advanced Seminar Series, Cambridge University Press, Cambridge.

Earle, T. (editor)
1991 *Chiefdoms: Power, Economy, and Ideology.* School of American Research Advanced Seminar Series, Cambridge University Press, Cambridge.

Earle, T. K., T. N. D'Altroy, C. Hastorf, C. Scott, C. Costin, G. Russell, and E. Sandefur
1987 *Archaeological Field Research in the Upper Mantaro, Peru, 1982–1983: Investigations of Inka Expansion and Exchange.* Monograph 28. Institute of Archaeology, University of California, Los Angeles.

Easton, D.
1959   Political Anthropology. *Biennial Review of Anthropology* 1959:210–62.
Edzard, D. O., W. Farber, and E. Sollberger
1977   *Die Orts- und Gewässernamen der präesargonischen und sargonischen Zeit.* Répertoire Géographique des Textes Cunéiformes I. Beihefte zum Tübinger Atlas
des Vorderen Orients B7(1). Ludwig Reichert, Wiesbaden.
Ehrenreich, R. M.
1995   Early Metalworking: A Heterarchical Analysis of Industrial Organization. In
Heterarchy and the Analysis of Complex Societies, edited by R. M. Ehrenreich,
C. L. Crumley, and J. E. Levy, pp. 33–40. Archeological Papers 6. American
Anthropological Association, Washington, D.C.
Ehrenreich, R. M., C. L. Crumley, and J. E. Levy (editors)
1995   *Heterarchy and the Analysis of Complex Societies.* Archeological Papers 6. American Anthropological Association, Washington D.C.
Eisenstadt, S. N.
1965   *Essays on Comparative Institutions.* John Wiley and Sons, New York.
1969   *The Political Systems of Empires: The Rise and Fall of the Historical Bureaucratic Societies.* The Free Press, New York.
1977   Sociological Theory and an Analysis of the Dynamics of Civilizations and
Revolutions. *Daedalus* 106(4):59–78.
1980   Cultural Orientations, Institutional Entrepreneurs, and Social Change: Comparative Analysis of Traditional Civilizations. *American Journal of Sociology*
85:840–69.
1981   Cultural Traditions and Political Dynamics: The Origins and Modes of Ideological Politics. *British Journal of Sociology* 32:155–81.
1986   The Axial Age Breakthroughs—Their Characteristics and Origins. In *The
Origins and Diversity of Axial Age Civilizations,* edited by S. N. Eisenstadt,
pp. 1–25. State University of New York Press, Albany.
1988   Beyond Collapse. In *The Collapse of Ancient States and Civilizations,* edited
by N. Yoffee and G. L. Cowgill, pp. 236–43. University of Arizona Press,
Tucson.
Eisenstadt, S. N. (editor)
1986   *The Origins and Diversity of Axial Age Civilizations.* SUNY Series in Near Eastern Studies, State University of New York Press, Albany.
Ekholm, K.
1972   *Power and Prestige: The Rise and Fall of the Kongo Kingdom.* Scriv Service,
Uppsala.
Elam, J. M.
1989   Defensible and Fortified Sites. In *Monte Albán's Hinterland, Part II: The Prehispanic Settlement Patterns in Tlacolula, Etla, and Ocotlán, the Valley of Oaxaca, Mexico,* by S. A. Kowalewski, G. M. Feinman, L. Finsten, R. E. Blanton, and
L. M. Nicholas, pp. 385–407. Memoirs 23. Museum of Anthropology, University of Michigan, Ann Arbor.
el-Khouli, A. A.-R. H.
1978   *Egyptian Stone Vessels, Predynastic Period to Dynasty III: Typology and Analysis.*
3 vols. Philipp von Zabern, Mainz.
Elvin, M.
1973   *The Pattern of the Chinese Past: A Social and Economic Interpretation.* Stanford
University Press, Stanford.

1986   Was There a Transcendental Breakthrough in China? In *The Origins and Diversity of Axial Age Civilizations,* edited by S. N. Eisenstadt, pp. 325–59. State University of New York Press, Albany.

El-Wailly, F., and B. Abu al-Soof
1965   The Excavations at Tell es-Sawwan: First Preliminary Report (1964). *Sumer* 21:17–32.

Ember, M.
1963   The Relationship between Economic and Political Development in Nonindustrialized Societies. *Ethnology* 2:228–48.

Emery, W. B.
1949–58   *Great Tombs of the First Dynasty,* vols. I–III. Service des Antiquités de l'Egypte, Excavations at Sakkara, Government Press, Cairo (I), and Egypt Exploration Society, London (II–III).
1961   *Archaic Egypt.* Viking Penguin Books, New York.

Engelbach, R.
1943   An Essay on the Advent of the Dynastic Race in Egypt and Its Consequences. *Annales du Service des Antiquités de l'Egypte* 42:193–221.

Engels, D. W.
1978   *Alexander the Great and the Logistics of the Macedonian Army.* University of California Press, Berkeley.

Englund, R. K., and H. Nissen, with P. Damerow
1993   *Die lexikalischen Listen der archaischen Texte aus Uruk.* Gebrüder Mann, Berlin.

Engnell, I.
1943   *Studies in Divine Kingship in the Ancient Near East.* Almqvist and Wiksell, Uppsala.

Erickson, E. E.
1973   Life Cycle of Life Styles: Projecting the Course of Local Evolutionary Sequences. *Behavior Science Notes* 8:135–60.
1975   Growth Functions and Culture History: A Perspective on Classic Maya Cultural Development. *Behavior Science Research* 10:37–61.

Erman, A.
1923   *Aegypten und aegyptisches Leben im Altertum.* 2nd ed. Revised by H. Ranke. J. C. B. Mohr (Paul Siebeck), Tübingen. Originally published 1885.

Esson, G. M. (translator and editor)
1931   *Discourses on Salt and Iron: A Debate on State Control of Commerce and Industry in Ancient China,* chapters 1–28. E. J. Brill, Leiden.

Evans, Sir A.
1921–36   *The Palace of Minos at Knossos,* vols. I–IV. Macmillan, London.

Evans, G.
1958   Ancient Mesopotamian Assemblies. *Journal of the American Oriental Society* 78:1–11.

Evans, S. T., and J. C. Berlo
1992   Teotihuacán: An Introduction. In *Art, Ideology, and the City of Teotihuacán,* edited by J. C. Berlo, pp. 1–26. Dumbarton Oaks, Washington, D.C.

Eyre, C. J.
1992   The Adoption Papyrus in Social Context. *Journal of Egyptian Archaeology* 78:207–21.

Fairservis, W. A., Jr.
1961   *The Harappan Civilization: New Evidence and More Theory.* Novitates 2055. American Museum of Natural History, New York.

1967   The Origin, Character, and Decline of an Early Civilization. *American Museum Novitates* 2302:9–48.
1971   *The Roots of Ancient India: The Archaeology of Early Indian Civilization.* Macmillan, New York.
1986   Cattle and the Harappan Chiefdoms of the Indus Valley. *Expedition* 28(2): 43–50.
1992   *The Harappan Civilization and Its Writing: A Model for the Decipherment of the Indus Script.* Oxford and IBH, Delhi.

Fakhry, A.
1961   *The Monuments of Sneferu at Dahshur* II: *The Valley Temple I: The Temple Reliefs.* Antiquities Department of Egypt, General Organization for Government Printing Offices, Cairo.

Falkenhausen, L. von
1993   On the Historiographical Orientation of Chinese Archaeology. *Antiquity* 67: 839–49.

Falkenstein, A.
1951   Zur Chronologie der sumerischen Literatur. *Comptes Rendus du Rencontre Assyriologique International* 2:12–28.
1953   Zur Chronologie der sumerischen Literatur: Die nachaltbabylonische Stufe. *Mitteilungen der Deutschen Orient-Gesellschaft* 85:1–13.
1956–57 *Die neusumerischen Gerichtsurkunden.* 3 vols. Bayerische Akademie der Wissenschaften, Philosophisch-Historische Klasse, Abhandlungen N.F. 39, 40, 44. Bayerische Akademie/C. H. Beck, Munich.
1963   Zu den Inschriften der Grabung in Uruk-Warka. *Baghdader Mitteilungen* 2: 1–82.
1974   *The Sumerian Temple City.* Introduction and translation by M. de J. Ellis. Monographs on the Ancient Near East 1(1). Undena, Malibu, California. Originally published 1951.

Fash, W. L.
1982   A Middle Formative Cemetery from Copán, Honduras. Paper presented at the 81st Annual Meeting of the American Anthropological Association, Washington, D.C.
1983   *Maya State Formation: A Case Study and Its Implications.* Ph.D. dissertation, Department of Anthropology, Harvard University, Cambridge.
1991   *Scribes, Warriors, and Kings: The City of Copán and the Ancient Maya.* Thames and Hudson, London.

Febvre, L., and H.-J. Martin
1976   *The Coming of the Book: The Impact of Printing, 1450–1800.* Translated by D. Gerard. NLB Books, London.

Feeley-Harnik, G.
1985   Issues in Divine Kingship. *Annual Review of Anthropology* 14:273–313.

Feinman, G. M.
1986   The Emergence of Specialized Ceramic Production in Formative Oaxaca. In *Research in Economic Anthropology, Supplement 2: Economic Aspects of Prehispanic Highland Mexico,* edited by B. L. Isaac, pp. 347–73. JAI Press, Greenwich, Connecticut.
1991   Demography, Surplus, and Inequality: Early Political Formations in Highland Mesoamerica. In *Chiefdoms: Power, Economy, and Ideology,* edited by T. Earle, pp. 229–62. Cambridge University Press, Cambridge.
1995   The Emergence of Inequality: A Focus on Strategies and Processes. In *The*

Foundations of Social Inequality, edited by T. D. Price and G. M. Feinman, pp. 255–79. Plenum Press, New York.

1997　Thoughts on New Approaches to Combining the Archaeological and Historical Records. *Journal of Archaeological Method and Theory* 4:367–77.

Feinman, G. M., R. E. Blanton, and S. A. Kowalewski

1984　Market System Development in the Prehispanic Valley of Oaxaca, Mexico. In *Trade and Exchange in Early Mesoamerica,* edited by K. G. Hirth, pp. 157–78. University of New Mexico Press, Albuquerque.

Feinman, G. M., S. Kowalewski, R. Blanton, L. Finsten, and L. M. Nicholas

1985　Long-Term Demographic Change: A Perspective from the Valley of Oaxaca, Mexico. *Journal of Field Archaeology* 12:333–62.

Feinman, G. M., and J. Neitzel

1984　Too Many Types: An Overview of Sedentary Prestate Societies in the Americas. In *Advances in Archaeological Method and Theory,* vol. 7, edited by M. B. Schiffer, pp. 39–102. Academic Press, New York.

Feinman, G. M., and L. M. Nicholas

1987　Labor, Surplus, and Production: A Regional Analysis of Formative Oaxacan Socio-economic Change. In *Coasts, Plains, and Deserts: Essays in Honor of Reynold J. Ruppé,* edited by S. Gaines, pp. 27–50. Anthropological Research Papers 38. Arizona State University, Tempe.

1990　At the Margins of the Monte Albán State: Settlement Patterns in the Ejutla Valley, Oaxaca, Mexico. *Latin American Antiquity* 1:216–46.

1991　The Monte Albán State: A Diachronic Perspective on an Ancient Core and Its Periphery. In *Core/Periphery Relations in Precapitalist Worlds,* edited by C. Chase-Dunn and T. D. Hall, pp. 240–76. Westview Press, Boulder, Colorado.

1992　Human-Land Relations from an Archaeological Perspective: The Case of Ancient Oaxaca. In *Understanding Economic Process,* edited by S. Ortiz and S. Lees, pp. 155–78. University Press of America, Lanham, Maryland.

1993　Shell-Ornament Production in Ejutla: Implications for Highland-Coastal Interaction in Ancient Oaxaca. *Ancient Mesoamerica* 4:103–19.

1996　Defining the Eastern Limits of the Monte Albán State: Systematic Settlement Pattern Survey in the Guirún Area, Oaxaca, Mexico. *Mexicon* 18(5):91–97.

Fentress, M.

1976　*Resource Access, Exchange Systems and Regional Interaction in the Indus Valley: An Investigation of Archaeological Variability at Harappa and Moenjodaro.* Ph.D. dissertation, Department of Oriental Studies, University of Pennsylvania, Philadelphia.

Ferguson, Y. H.

1991　Chiefdoms to City-States: The Greek Experience. In *Chiefdoms: Power, Economy, and Ideology,* edited by T. Earle, pp. 168–92. School of American Research Advanced Seminar Series, Cambridge University Press, Cambridge.

Fesler, J. W.

1968　Centralization and Decentralization. In *International Encyclopedia of the Social Sciences,* vol. 2, edited by D. L. Sills, pp. 370–79. The Macmillan Company and The Free Press, New York.

Fine, J. V. A.

1983　*The Ancient Greeks: A Critical History.* Harvard University Press, Cambridge.

Finsten, L.

1983　*The Classic-Postclassic Transition in the Valley of Oaxaca, Mexico.* Ph.D. dissertation, Department of Sociology and Anthropology, Purdue University, West Lafayette, Indiana.

1995   *Jalieza, Oaxaca: Activity Specialization at a Hilltop Center.* Publications in Anthropology 48. Vanderbilt University, Nashville.

Fischer, H. G.
1972   Some Emblematic Uses of Hieroglyphs, with Particular Reference to an Archaic Ritual Vessel. *Metropolitan Museum Journal* 5:5–23.

1977   Gaufürst. In *Lexikon der Ägyptologie,* edited by W. Helck and W. Westendorf, II, cols. 408–17. Otto Harrassowitz, Wiesbaden.

1986   *L'écriture et l'art de l'Egypte ancienne: quatre leçons sur la paléographie et l'épigraphie pharaoniques.* Essais et Conférences, Collège de France. Presses Universitaires de France, Paris.

Fish, S. K., and S. A. Kowalewski (editors)
1990   *The Archaeology of Regions: A Case for Full-Coverage Survey.* Smithsonian Institution Press, Washington, D.C.

Flannery, K. V.
1972   The Cultural Evolution of Civilizations. *Annual Review of Ecology and Systematics* 3:399–426. Annual Reviews, Palo Alto, California.

1994   Childe the Evolutionist: A Perspective from Nuclear America. In *The Archaeology of V. Gordon Childe,* edited by D. R. Harris, pp. 101–19. University College Press, London.

1995   Prehistoric Social Evolution. In *Research Frontiers in Anthropology,* edited by C. Ember and M. Ember, pp. 1–26. Prentice-Hall, Englewood Cliffs, New Jersey.

Flannery, K. V., and J. Marcus
1976   Evolution of the Public Building in Formative Oaxaca. In *Cultural Change and Continuity: Essays in Honor of James Bennett Griffin,* edited by C. Cleland, pp. 205–21. Academic Press, New York.

1983a   The Origins of the State in Oaxaca: Editors' Introduction. In *The Cloud People: Divergent Evolution of the Zapotec and Mixtec Civilizations,* edited by K. V. Flannery and J. Marcus, pp. 79–83. Academic Press, New York.

1983b   The Changing Politics of A.D. 600–900. In *The Cloud People: Divergent Evolution of the Zapotec and Mixtec Civilizations,* edited by K. V. Flannery and J. Marcus, pp. 183–85. Academic Press, New York.

Flannery, K. V., and J. Marcus (editors)
1983   *The Cloud People: Divergent Evolution of the Zapotec and Mixtec Civilizations.* Academic Press, New York.

Folan, W. J., J. Marcus, and W. F. Miller
1995   Verification of a Maya Settlement Model through Remote Sensing. *Cambridge Archaeological Journal* 5(2):277–83.

Folan, W. J., J. Marcus, S. Pincemin, M. Domínguez Carrasco, L. Fletcher, and A. Morales López
1995   Calakmul: New Data From an Ancient Maya City in Campeche, Mexico. *Latin American Antiquity* 6:310–34.

Forge, A.
1972a   Normative Factors in the Settlement Size of Neolithic Cultivators (New Guinea). In *Man, Settlement, and Urbanism,* edited by P. J. Ucko, R. Tringham, and G. W. Dimblebly, pp. 363–76. Gerald Duckworth, London.

1972b   The Golden Fleece. *Man* (n.s.) 7:527–40.

Fortes, M., and E. E. Evans-Pritchard
  1940   *African Political Systems.* Oxford University Press, London.
Foster, B. R.
  1993   *Before the Muses: An Anthology of Akkadian Literature.* 2 vols. CDL Press, Bethesda, Maryland.
Fowden, G.
  1986   *The Egyptian Hermes: A Historical Approach to the Late Pagan Mind.* Cambridge University Press, Cambridge.
Fox, A.
  1976   *Prehistoric Maori Fortifications in the North Island of New Zealand.* Longman Paul, Auckland.
Fox, J. W.
  1987   *Maya Postclassic State Formation: Segmentary Lineage Migration in Advancing Frontiers.* Cambridge University Press, Cambridge.
Fox, R. (editor)
  1977   *Realm and Region in Traditional India.* Duke University Press, Durham, North Carolina.
Frangipane, M., and A. Palmieri (editors)
  1988   Perspectives on Protourbanization in Eastern Anatolia: Arslantepe (Malatya). An Interim Report on the 1975–1983 Campaigns. *Origini* 12:287–668.
Franke, D.
  1990   Erste und Zweite Zwischenzeit—Ein Vergleich. *Zeitschrift für Ägyptische Sprache und Altertumskunde* 117:119–29.
Frankenstein, S., and M. Rowlands
  1978   The Internal Structure and Regional Contexts of Early Iron Age Society in South-Western Germany. *Bulletin of the Institute of Archaeology of London* 15:73–112.
Frankfort, H.
  1948   *Kingship and the Gods: A Study of Ancient Near Eastern Religion as the Integration of Society and Nature.* University of Chicago Press, Chicago.
  1956   *The Birth of Civilization in the Near East.* Doubleday Anchor, New York.
Frankfort, H. A., S. Lloyd, and T. Jacobsen
  1940   *The Gimilsin Temple and the Palace of the Rulers at Tell Asmar.* Publication 43. Oriental Institute, University of Chicago, Chicago.
Frankfurter, D.
  1998   *Religion in Roman Egypt: Assimilation and Resistance.* Princeton University Press, Princeton.
Freedman, M.
  1958   *Lineage Organization in Southeastern China.* Athlone Press, London.
Freidel, D.
  1986   Maya Warfare: An Example of Peer-Polity Interaction. In *Peer-Polity Interaction and Sociopolitical Change,* edited by C. Renfrew and J. Cherry, pp. 93–108. Cambridge University Press, London.
Freidel, D. A., and L. Schele
  1988   Kingship in the Late Preclassic Maya Lowlands: The Instruments and Places of Ritual Power. *American Anthropologist* 90:547–67.
Friberg, J.
  1978–79   *The Third Millennium Roots of Babylonian Mathematics.* Research Report, Department of Mathematics, Chalmers University of Technology, Göteborg.

1994   Preliterate Counting and Accounting in the Middle East. *Orientalistische Literaturzeitung* 89(5/6):477–502.

Fried, M. H.
1967   *The Evolution of Political Society: An Essay in Political Anthropology.* Random House, New York.

Friedman, D.
1977   A Theory of the Size and Shape of Nations. *Journal of Political Economy* 85: 59–77.

Friedman, J.
1979   *System, Structure and Contradiction: The Evolution of "Asiatic" Social Formations.* National Museum of Denmark, Copenhagen.

Friedman, J., and M. J. Rowlands
1977   Notes Towards an Epigenetic Model of the Evolution of "Civilisation." In *The Evolution of Social Systems,* edited by J. Friedman and M. J. Rowlands, pp. 201–76. Duckworth, London.

Friedman, J., and M. J. Rowlands (editors)
1977   *The Evolution of Social Systems.* Duckworth, London.

Fry, R. E.
1990   Disjunctive Growth in the Maya Lowlands. In *Precolumbian Population History in the Maya Lowlands,* edited by T. P. Culbert and D. S. Rice, pp. 285–300. University of New Mexico Press, Albuquerque.

Gadd, C. J.
1963   Two Sketches from the Life at Ur. *Iraq* 25:177–88.

Gailey, C. W.
1987   *Kinship to Kingship.* University of Texas Press, Austin.

García Cook, A.
1994   *Cantona.* Salvat, Mexico.

Gardiner, A. H.
1941–52   *The Wilbour Papyrus.* 4 vols. (vol. IV by R. O. Faulkner). Brooklyn Museum, Oxford University Press, London.
1951   A Protest against Unjustified Tax-Demands. *Revue d'Egyptologie* 6:115–33.

Garelli, P.
1975   The Changing Facets of Conservative Mesopotamian Thought. *Daedalus* (Spring):47–56. *Proceedings of the American Academy of Arts and Sciences* 104(2).

Garstang, J.
1904   *Tombs of the Third Egyptian Dynasty at Reqâqnah and Bêt Khallâf.* Archibald Constable, Westminster.

Gasse, A.
1988   *Données nouvelles administratives et sacerdotales sur l'organisation du Domaine d'Amon, XXe–XXIe dynasties.* 2 vols. Bibliothèque d'Etude 104. Institut Français d'Archéologie Orientale, Cairo.

Geertz, C.
1980   *Negara: The Theater State in Nineteenth Century Bali.* Princeton University Press, Princeton.

Gelb, I. J.
1968   An Old Babylonian List of Amorites. *Journal of the American Oriental Society* 88:39–46.
1969   On the Alleged Temple and State Economies in Mesopotamia. In *Studi in onore di Edoardo Volterra* 6:137–54. Giuffrè, Milan.

1979 Household and Family in Early Mesopotamia. In *State and Temple Economy in the Ancient Near East,* vol. I, edited by E. Lipiński, pp. 1–97. Orientalia Lovanensia Analecta 5. Peeters, Louvain.

Gelb, I. J., P. Steinkeller, and R. M. Whiting, Jr.
1991 *Earliest Land Tenure Systems in the Near East: Ancient Kudurrus.* Publication 104. Oriental Institute, Chicago.

Gibson, C.
1964 *The Aztecs under Spanish Rule.* Stanford University Press, Stanford.

Giddens, A.
1984 *The Constitution of Society: Outline of the Theory of Structuration.* University of California Press, Berkeley.

Glassner, J.-J.
1986 *La chute d'Akkadé: l'événement et sa mémoire.* Berliner Beiträge zum Vorderen Orient 5. Dietrich Reimer, Berlin.

Gledhill, J., B. Bender, and M. T. Larsen (editors)
1988 *State and Society: The Emergence and Development of Social Hierarchy and Political Centralization.* Unwin Hyman, Boston.

Gluckman, M.
1940 The Kingdom of the Zulu of South Africa. In *African Political Systems,* edited by M. Fortes and E. E. Evans-Pritchard, pp. 25–55. Oxford University Press, London.
1954 *Rituals of Rebellion in South-East Africa.* Manchester University Press, Manchester.
1959 *Custom and Conflict in Africa.* Free Press, Glencoe, Illinois.
1963 *Order and Rebellion in Tribal Africa.* Cohen and West, London.

Godelier, M.
1978 Infrastructure, Societies, and History. *Current Anthropology* 19:763–71.

Goedicke, H.
1970 *Die privaten Rechtsinschriften aus dem Alten Reich.* Beiheft zur Wiener Zeitschrift für die Kunde des Morgenlandes 5. Notring, Vienna.

Goff, C.
1971 Luristan before the Iron Age. *Iran* IX:131–52.

Goldman, I.
1970 *Ancient Polynesian Society.* University of Chicago Press, Chicago.

Goody, J.
1971 *Technology, Tradition and the State in Africa.* Cambridge University Press, Cambridge.

Gorbak, C., M. Lischetti, and C. P. Muñoz
1962 Batallas rituales del Chiaraje y del Tocto de la provincia de Kanas (Cuzco, Perú). *Revista del Museo Nacional* 31:245–304. Lima.

Gould, S. J.
1985 Losing the Edge. In *The Flamingo's Smile: Reflections in Natural History,* pp. 215–29. W. W. Norton, New York.
1986 Evolution and the Triumph of Homology, or Why History Matters. *American Scientist* 74:60–69.

Graham, J. W.
1987 *The Palaces of Crete.* Revised ed. Princeton University Press, Princeton.

Green, M. W., and H. Nissen
1987 *Zeichenliste der archaischen Texte aus Uruk.* Ausgrabungen der Deutschen Forschungsgemeinschaft in Uruk-Warka 11. Gebrüder Mann, Berlin.

Grégoire, J.-P.
1962   *La province méridionale de l'état de Lagash.* Imprimerie Bourg-Bourger, Luxembourg.
Gregory, C. A.
1980   Gifts to Men and Gifts to Gods: Gift Exchange and Capital Accumulation in Contemporary Papua. *Man* (n.s.) 24:1–20.
1982   *Gifts and Commodities.* Academic Press, London.
Griffeth, R., and C. G. Thomas (editors)
1981   *The City-State in Five Cultures.* ABC-Clio, Santa Barbara.
Guaman Poma de Ayala, F.
1980 (1613)   *El primer nueva corónica y buen gobierno.* 3 vols. Edición crítica de J. V. Murra y R. Adorno. Siglo Veintiuno, Mexico.
Gumerman, G. G.
1986   The Role of Competition and Cooperation in the Evolution of Island Societies. In *Island Societies: Archaeological Approaches to Evolution and Transformation,* edited by P. V. Kirch, pp. 42–49. Cambridge University Press, New York.
Gunn, J., W. J. Folan, and H. Robichaux
1995   A Landscape Analysis of the Candelaria Watershed in Mexico: Insights into Paleoclimates Affecting Upland Horticulture in the Southern Yucatán Peninsula Semi-Karst. *Geoarchaeology* 10:3–42.
Gupta, S. P.
1978   Origin of the Form of Harappa Culture: A New Proposition. *Puratattva* 8: 141–46.
Haas, J.
1982   *The Evolution of the Prehistoric State.* Columbia University Press, New York.
Haggett, P.
1966   *Locational Analysis in Human Geography.* St. Martin's Press, New York.
Hall, J. A.
1989   Towards a Theory of Social Evolution: On State Systems and Ideological Shells. In *Domination and Resistance,* edited by D. Miller, M. Rowlands, and C. Tilley, pp. 96–107. Unwin Hyman, London.
Hallo, W. W.
1960   A Sumerian Amphictyony. *Journal of Cuneiform Studies* 14:88–114.
1962   New Viewpoints on Sumerian Literature. *Israel Exploration Journal* 12:13–26.
1963   On the Antiquity of Sumerian Literature. *Journal of the American Oriental Society* 83:167–76.
Hamayon, R. N.
1994   Shamanism in Siberia: From Partnership in Supernature to Counter-Power in Society. In *Shamanism, History, and the State,* edited by N. Thomas and C. Humphrey, pp. 76–89. University of Michigan Press, Ann Arbor.
Hammond, N.
1991   Inside the Black Box: Defining Maya Polity. In *Classic Maya Political History,* edited by T. P. Culbert, pp. 253–84. School of American Research Advanced Seminar Series, Cambridge University Press, Cambridge.
Hammond, N. G. L.
1986   *A History of Greece to 322 B.C.* 3rd ed. Oxford University Press, Oxford.
Hardacre, H.
1993   The Impact of Fundamentalism on Women, the Family, and Interpersonal Relations. In *Fundamentalisms and Society, Volume 2: Reclaiming the Sciences, the Family, and Education,* edited by M. E. Marty and R. S. Appleby, pp. 129–50. University of Chicago Press, Chicago.

Hardin, K.
1993   *The Aesthetics of Action: Continuity and Change in a West African Town.* Smithsonian Institution Press, Washington, D.C.

Harpur, Y.
1987   *Decoration in Egyptian Tombs of the Old Kingdom: Studies in Orientation and Scene Content.* KPI, London and New York.

Harris, R.
1964   The *Nadītu* Woman. In *Studies Presented to A. Leo Oppenheim,* edited by J. A. Brinkman, pp. 106–35. Oriental Institute, University of Chicago, Chicago.
1975   *Ancient Sippar: A Demographic Study of an Old Babylonian City, 1894–1595.* Nederlands Historisch-Archaeologisch Instituut, Istanbul.

Hart, H.
1948   The Logistic Growth of Political Areas. *Social Forces* 26:396–408.

Hartmann, R.
1972   Otros datos sobre las llamadas "batallas rituales." *Proceedings of the 39th International Congress of Americanists* 6:125–35. Lima.

Hartwell, R. M.
1982   Demographic, Political, and Social Transformations of China, 750–1550. *Harvard Journal of Asiatic Studies* 42(2):365–442.

Hassig, R.
1985   *Trade, Tribute, and Transportation: The Sixteenth-Century Political Economy of the Valley of Mexico.* University of Oklahoma Press, Norman.
1988   *Aztec Warfare: Imperial Expansion and Political Control.* University of Oklahoma Press, Norman.
1992   *War and Society in Ancient Mesoamerica.* University of California Press, Berkeley.

Hastings, C. M., and M. E. Moseley
1975   The Adobes of Huaca del Sol and Huaca de la Luna. *American Antiquity* 40:196–203.

Haviland, W. A.
1991   Star Wars at Tikal, or Did Caracol Do What the Glyphs Say They Did? Paper presented at the 90th Annual Meeting of the American Anthropological Association, Chicago.
1992   Status and Power in Classic Maya Society: The View from Tikal. *American Anthropologist* 94(4):937–40.

Healan, D.
1989   *Tula of the Toltecs.* University of Iowa Press, Iowa City.

Helbaek, H.
1969   Appendix 1: Plant Collecting, Dry Farming, and Irrigation in Prehistoric Deh Luran. In *Prehistoric Human Ecology of the Deh Luran Plain,* by F. Hole, K. V. Flannery, and J. A. Neely, pp. 383–426. Memoirs 1. Museum of Anthropology, University of Michigan, Ann Arbor.

Helck, W.
1972   Zur Frage der Entstehung der ägyptischen Literatur. *Wiener Zeitschrift für die Kunde des Morgenlands* 63/64:6–26.
1974   *Die altägyptischen Gaue.* Beihefte zum Tübinger Atlas des Vorderen Orients B5. Ludwig Reichert, Wiesbaden.
1975   *Wirtschaftsgeschichte des alten Ägypten im 3. und 2. Jahrtausend v. Chr.* Handbuch der Orientalistik Series 1, Subseries 1(5). E. J. Brill, Leiden.
1977   Gaue. In *Lexikon der Ägyptologie,* edited by W. Helck and W. Westendorf, II, cols. 385–407. Otto Harrassowitz, Wiesbaden.

Henrickson, E., and I. Thuesen (editors)
    1989   *Upon This Foundation: The 'Ubaid Reconsidered*. CNI Publications 10. Museum Tusculanum Press, Copenhagen.
Hindess, B.
    1982   Power, Interests, and the Outcomes of Struggles. *Sociology* 16:498–511.
Hirth, K. G.
    1987   Formative Period Settlement Patterns in the Río Amatzinac Valley. In *Ancient Chalcatzingo*, edited by D. C. Grove, pp. 343–67. University of Texas Press, Austin.
Ho, P.-T.
    1962   *The Ladder of Success in Imperial China: Aspects of Social Mobility, 1368–1911*. Da Capo Press, New York.
Hoare, Q., and G. Nowell (editors)
    1971   *Selections from the Prison Notebooks of Antonio Gramsci*. International Publishers, New York.
Hodge, M. G.
    1984   *Aztec City-States*. Studies in Latin American Ethnohistory and Archaeology, vol. III. Memoirs 18. Museum of Anthropology, University of Michigan, Ann Arbor.
Hodjash, S. I., and O. D. Berlev
    1980   A Market-Scene in the Mastaba of *D3d3-m-'nh (Tp-m-'nh)*. *Altorientalische Forschungen* 7:31–49.
Hoffman, M. A.
    1970   *Culture History and Culture Ecology at Hierakonpolis from Paleolithic Times to the Old Kingdom*. Ph.D. dissertation, Department of Anthropology, University of Wisconsin, Madison.
Hoffman, M. A., B. Adams, M. Berger, M. el Hadidi, J. Harlan, H. Hamroush, C. Lupton, J. McArdle, W. McHugh, R. Allen, and M. Rogers
    1982   *The Predynastic of Hierakonpolis: An Interim Report*. Egyptian Studies Association Publication 1. Cairo University Herbarium, Giza, and Department of Sociology and Anthropology, Western Illinois University, Macomb.
Hole, F., K. V. Flannery, and J. A. Neely
    1969   *Prehistoric Human Ecology of the Deh Luran Plain*. Memoirs 1. Museum of Anthropology, University of Michigan, Ann Arbor.
Holt, E.
    1962   *The Strangest War*. Putnam, London.
Hommon, R. J.
    1986   Social Evolution and Ancient Hawai'i. In *Island Societies: Archaeological Approaches to Evolution and Transformation*, edited by P. V. Kirch, pp. 55–68. Cambridge University Press, New York.
Hornung, E.
    1982   *Conceptions of God in Ancient Egypt: The One and the Many*. Translated by J. Baines. Cornell University Press, Ithaca.
Houston, S. D.
    1992   Weak States and Segmentary Structure: The Internal Organization of Classic Maya Polities. Paper presented at the symposium "The Segmentary State and the Classic Lowland Maya," Cleveland State University, Cleveland.
    1993   *Hieroglyphics and History at Dos Pilas: Dynastic Politics of the Classic Maya*. University of Texas Press, Austin.

Hsu, C.-Y.
1965   *Ancient China in Transition: An Analysis of Social Mobility, 722–222 B.C.* Stanford University Press, Stanford.
1986   Historical Conditions of the Emergence and Crystallization of the Confucian System. In *The Origins and Diversity of Axial Age Civilizations,* edited by S. N. Eisenstadt, pp. 306–24. State University of New York Press, Albany.
1988   The Roles of the Literati and of Regionalism in the Fall of the Han Dynasty. In *The Collapse of Ancient States and Civilizations,* edited by N. Yoffee and G. L. Cowgill, pp. 176–95. University of Arizona Press, Tucson.
Hsu, C.-Y., and K. M. Linduff
1988   *Western Chou Civilization.* Yale University Press, New Haven.
Hsu, F. L. K.
1949   *Under the Ancestor's Shadow: Chinese Culture and Personality.* Routledge and Kegan Paul, London.
Humphreys, S. C.
1977   Evolution and History: Approaches to the Study of Structural Differentiation. In *The Evolution of Social Systems,* edited by J. Friedman and M. J. Rowlands, pp. 341–71. Duckworth, London.
1978   *Anthropology and the Greeks.* Routledge and Kegan Paul, London.
Hyslop, J.
1976   *An Archaeological Investigation of the Lupaca Kingdom and Its Origins.* Ph.D. dissertation, Department of Anthropology, Columbia University, New York.
1977   Chulpas of the Lupaca Zone of the Peruvian High Plateau. *Journal of Field Archaeology* 4:149–70.
1984   *The Inka Road System.* Academic Press, San Francisco and New York.
1985   *Inkawasi: The New Cuzco.* BAR International Series 234. British Archaeological Reports, Oxford.
1990   *Inka Settlement Planning.* University of Texas Press, Austin.
Isbell, W. H., and G. F. McEwan (editors)
1991   *Huari Administrative Structure: Prehistoric Monumental Architecture and State Government.* Dumbarton Oaks, Washington, D.C.
Jacobsen, T.
1943   Primitive Democracy in Ancient Mesopotamia. *Journal of Near Eastern Studies* 2:159–72.
1957   Early Political Development in Mesopotamia. *Zeitschrift für Assyriologie* 52: 91–140.
1976   *The Treasures of Darkness: A History of Mesopotamian Religion.* Yale University Press, New Haven.
Jacobson, J.
1979   Recent Developments in South Asian Prehistory and Protohistory. *Annual Review of Anthropology* 8:467–502.
1986   The Harappan Civilization: An Early State. In *Studies in the Archaeology of India and Pakistan,* edited by J. Jacobson, pp. 137–73. Oxford and IBH, and the American Institute of Indian Studies, Delhi.
Jacquet-Gordon, H.
1962   *Les noms des domaines funéraires sous l'ancien empire égyptien.* Bibliothèque d'Etude 34. Institut Français d'Archéologie Orientale, Cairo.
Jansen, M.
1983   Theoretical Aspects of Structural Analysis for Mohenjo-daro. In *Reports on Field Work Carried out at Mohenjo-daro, Pakistan, 1982–83, by the IsMEO-*

Aachen University Mission: Interim Reports, vol. 1, edited by M. Jansen and G. Urban, pp. 39–62. RWTH/IsMEO, Aachen/Rome.

1985 Mohenjo-daro HR-A, House I, a Temple? Analysis of an Architectural Structure. In *South Asian Archaeology 1983,* edited by J. Schotsmans and M. Taddei, pp. 157–206. Series Minor 23. Instituto Universitario Orientale, Dipartimento di Studi Asiatici, Naples.

1987 Preliminary Results on the "Forma Urbis" Research at Mohenjo-daro. In *Reports on Field Work Carried Out at Mohenjo-daro, Pakistan, 1983–84: Interim Reports,* vol. 2, edited by M. Jansen and G. Urban, pp. 9–22. RWTH/IsMEO, Aachen/Rome.

1989 Some Problems Regarding the Forma Urbis Mohenjo-Daro. In *South Asian Archaeology 1985,* edited by K. Frifelt and P. Sorensen, pp. 247–56. Occasional Papers 4. Scandinavian Institute of Asian Studies, Curzon Press, London.

1992 Non-Contemporaneity of the Contemporaneous in the Indus Culture. In *South Asian Archaeology Studies,* edited by G. L. Possehl, pp. 209–22. Oxford and IBH, Delhi.

1993 *Mohenjo-daro: Stadt der Brunnen und Kanale (City of Wells and Drains), Wasserlexus vor 4500 Jharan (Water Splendor 4500 Years Ago).* Dual German-English text. Frontinus-Gesellschaft e. Verlag, Bergisch Gladbach.

Jansen-Winkeln, K.
1992 Das Ende des Neuen Reiches. *Zeitschrift für Ägyptische Sprache und Altertumskunde* 119:22–37.

Janssen, C.
1991 Samsu-iluna and the Hungry *naditums. North Akkad Project Reports* 5:3–39.

Janssen, J. J.
1975a *Commodity Prices in the Ramessid Period: An Economic Study of the Village of Necropolis Workmen at Thebes.* E. J. Brill, Leiden.

1975b Prologemena to the Study of Egypt's Economic History in the New Kingdom. *Studien zur Altägyptischen Kultur* 3:127–85.

1978 The Early State in Egypt. In *The Early State,* edited by H. J. M. Claessen and P. Skalník, pp. 213–34. New Babylon: Studies in the Social Sciences 32. Mouton, The Hague.

1980 *De markt op de oever.* Inaugural lecture, University of Leiden. E. J. Brill, Leiden.

1983 El-Amarna as a Residential City. *Bibliotheca Orientalis* 40:273–88.

Jarrige, J.-F.
1989 Excavation at Naushero, 1987–88. *Pakistan Archaeology* 24:21–67.

Johnson, A. W., and T. Earle
1987 *The Evolution of Human Societies: From Foraging Group to Agrarian State.* Stanford University Press, Stanford.

Johnson, G. A.
1972 A Test of the Utility of Central Place Theory in Archaeology. In *Man, Settlement and Urbanism,* edited by P. Ucko, R. Tringham, and G. W. Dimbleby, pp. 769–85. Duckworth, London.

1973 *Local Exchange and Early State Development in Southwestern Iran.* Anthropological Papers 51. Museum of Anthropology, University of Michigan, Ann Arbor.

1976 Early State Organization in Southwestern Iran: Preliminary Field Report. In *Proceedings of the Fourth Annual Symposium on Archaeological Research in Iran,* edited by F. Bagherzadeh, pp. 190–223. Iranian Centre for Archaeological Research, Tehran.

1978   Information Sources and the Development of Decision-Making Organizations. In *Social Archaeology: Beyond Subsistence and Dating,* edited by C. L. Redman, J. Berman, E. V. Curtin, W. T. Langhorne, Jr., N. M. Versaggi, and J. C. Wanser, pp. 87–112. Academic Press, New York.

1980   Spatial Organization of Early Uruk Settlement Systems. In *L'Archéologie de l'Iraq du début de l'epoque Néolithique a 333 avant notre ere,* pp. 233–63. Colloques Internationaux 580. Centre National de la Recherche Scientifique, Paris.

1982   Organizational Structure and Scalar Stress. In *Theory and Explanation in Archaeology: The Southampton Conference,* edited by C. Renfrew, M. Rowlands, and B. Segraves, pp. 389–421. Academic Press, New York.

1983   Decision-Making Organization and Pastoral Nomad Camp Size. *Human Ecology* 11:175–99.

1987   The Changing Organization of Uruk Administration on the Susiana Plain. In *The Archaeology of Western Iran: Settlement and Society from Prehistory to the Islamic Conquest,* edited by F. Hole, pp. 107–39. Smithsonian Institution Press, Washington, D.C.

1988–89   Late Uruk in Greater Mesopotamia: Expansion or Collapse? *Origini* 14:595–613.

Jones, C.
1991   Cycles of Growth at Tikal. In *Classic Maya Political History,* edited by T. P. Culbert, pp. 102–27. School of American Research Advanced Seminar Series, Cambridge University Press, Cambridge.

Jones, T. B.
1981   Foreword. In *The City-State in Five Cultures,* edited by R. Griffeth and C. G. Thomas, pp. ix–xii. ABC-Clio, Santa Barbara.

Joshi, J. P.
1986   Settlement Patterns in Third, Second and First Millennia in India—With Special Reference to Recent Discoveries in Punjab. In *Rtambhara: Studies in Indology,* edited by K. C. Varma, M. C. Bhartiya, L. B. Ram Anant, and T. Acharya, pp. 134–39. Society for Indic Studies, Ghaziabad.

1990   *Excavation at Surkotada 1971–72 and Exploration in Kutch.* Memoirs 87. Archaeological Survey of India, Delhi.

Julien, C. J.
1983   *Hatunqolla: A View of Inca Rule from the Lake Titicaca Region.* Publications in Anthropology 15, University of California, Berkeley and Los Angeles.

Kahn, J. S.
1985   Peasant Ideologies in the Third World. *Annual Review of Anthropology* 14:49–75.

Kaiser, W.
1987   Zum Friedhof der Naqadakultur von Minshat Abu Omar. *Annales du Service des Antiquités de l'Egypte* 71:119–25.

1990   Zur Entstehung des gesamtägyptischen Staates. *Mitteilungen des Deutschen Archäologischen Instituts, Abteilung Kairo* 46:287–99.

Kamp, K. A., and N. Yoffee
1980   Ethnicity in Ancient Western Asia: Archaeological Assessments and Ethnoarchaeological Prospectives. *Bulletin of the American Schools of Oriental Research* 237:88–104.

Kanawati, N.
1980   *Governmental Reforms in Old Kingdom Egypt.* Aris and Phillips, Warminster.

Kantor, H. J.
1992   The Relative Chronology of Egypt and Its Foreign Correlations before the
        First Intermediate Period. In *Chronologies in Old World Archaeology,* 3rd ed.,
        edited by R. Ehrich, pp. 3–21. University of Chicago Press, Chicago.
Kasarda, J. D.
1974   The Structural Implications of Social System Size: A Three-Level Analysis.
        American Sociological Review 39:19–28.
Katz, D.
1993   *Gilgamesh and Akka.* Styx, Groningen.
1995   Enmebaragesi King of Kish a Sister of Gilgameš? *Nouvelles Assyriologiques Brèves
        et Utilitaires* 2(June):24.
Kautz, R., and G. D. Jones (editors)
1981   *The Transition to Statehood in the New World.* Cambridge University Press,
        Cambridge.
Keatinge, R. W.
1982   The Chimú Empire in a Regional Perspective: Cultural Antecedents and
        Continuities. In *Chan Chan: Andean Desert City,* edited by M. E. Moseley and
        K. C. Day, pp. 197–224. University of New Mexico Press, Albuquerque.
Kees, H.
1961   *Ancient Egypt: A Cultural Topography.* University of Chicago Press, Chicago.
Keightley, D. N.
1983   The Late Shang State: When, Where, and What? In *The Origins of Chinese
        Civilization,* edited by D. N. Keightley, pp. 523–64. University of California
        Press, Berkeley.
Kelly, R. C.
1993   *Constructing Inequality: The Fabrication of a Hierarchy of Virtue among the Etoro.*
        University of Michigan Press, Ann Arbor.
Kemp, B. J.
1972   Temple and Town in Ancient Egypt. In *Man, Settlement and Urbanism,* edited
        by P. J. Ucko, R. Tringham, and G. W. Dimbleby, pp. 657–80. Duckworth,
        London.
1977   The Early Development of Towns in Egypt. *Antiquity* 51:185–200.
1981   The Character of the South Suburb at Tell el-ʿAmārna. *Mitteilungen der
        Deutschen Orient-Gesellschaft* 113:81–97.
1989   *Ancient Egypt: Anatomy of a Civilization.* Routledge, London and New York.
Kennedy, K. A. R.
1981   Skeletal Biology: When Bones Tell Tales. *Archaeology* 34(1):17–24, 51.
Kenoyer, J. M.
1991   The Indus Valley Tradition of Pakistan and Western India. *Journal of World Pre-
        history* 5:331–85.
1992   Harappan Craft Specialization and the Question of Urban Segregation and
        Stratification. *The Eastern Anthropologist* 45(1–2):39–54.
1994   The Harappan State, Was It or Wasn't It? In *From Sumer to Meluhha: Contribu-
        tions to the Archaeology of South and West Asia in Memory of George F. Dales, Jr.,*
        edited by J. M. Kenoyer, pp. 71–80. Prehistory Press, Madison, Wisconsin.
Kent, S.
1993   Sharing in an Egalitarian Kalahari Community. *Man* (n.s.) 28:479–514.
Kertzer, D. I.
1988   *Ritual, Politics, and Power.* Yale University Press, New Haven.
Khan, F. A.
1965   Excavations at Kot Diji. *Pakistan Archaeology* 2:11–85.

Kidder, A. V., J. D. Jennings, and E. M. Shook
1946   *Excavations at Kaminaljuyu, Guatemala.* Carnegie Institution of Washington, vol. 561. Washington, D.C.

Kilson, M.
1983   Antelopes and Stools: Ga Ceremonial Kingship. *Anthropos* 78:411–21.

Kirch, P. V.
1984   *The Evolution of the Polynesian Chiefdoms.* Cambridge University Press, Cambridge.
1991   Chiefship and Competitive Involution: The Marquesas Islands of Eastern Polynesia. In *Chiefdoms: Power, Economy, and Ideology,* edited by T. Earle, pp. 119–45. Cambridge University Press, Cambridge.

Kirch, P. V., and M. Sahlins
1992   *Anahulu: The Anthropology of History in the Kingdom of Hawai'i,* vols. 1–2. University of Chicago Press, Chicago.

Kitchen, K. A.
1986   *The Third Intermediate Period in Egypt (1100–650 B.C.).* 2nd ed. Aris and Phillips, Warminster.

Klochkov, S.
1982   The Late Babylonian List of Scholars. In *Gesellschaft und Kultur im alten Vorderasien,* edited by H. Klengel, pp. 149–54. Akademie-Verlag, Berlin.

Knapp, A. B.
1988   Ideology, Archaeology, and Polity. *Man* (n.s.) 23:133–63.

Knapp, A. B. (editor)
1992   *Archaeology, Annales, and Ethnohistory.* Cambridge University Press, Cambridge.

Knapp, R. G.
1986   *China's Traditional Rural Architecture: House Form and Culture.* University of Hawaii Press, Honolulu.

Kohler, J., F. E. Peiser, A. Ungnad, and P. Koschaker
1904–23   *Hammurabi's Gesetz.* 6 vols. Eduard Pfeiffer, Leipzig.

Kohr, L.
1957   *The Breakdown of Nations.* Rinehart, New York.

Kopytoff, I.
1987   The Internal African Frontier: The Making of African Political Culture. In *The African Frontier: The Reproduction of Traditional African Societies,* edited by I. Kopytoff, pp. 3–84. Indiana University Press, Bloomington.

Koschaker, P.
1942   Zur staatlichen Wirtschaftsverwaltung in altbabylonischer Zeit, insbesondere nach Urkunden aus Larsa. *Zeitschrift für Assyriologie* 47:135–80.

Kosse, K.
1990   Group Size and Societal Complexity: Thresholds in the Long-Term Memory. *Journal of Anthropological Archaeology* 9:275–303.
1994   The Evolution of Large, Complex Groups: A Hypothesis. *Journal of Anthropological Archaeology* 13(1):35–50.

Kowalewski, S. A.
1983   Valley-Floor Settlement Patterns during Monte Albán I. In *The Cloud People: Divergent Evolution of the Zapotec and Mixtec Civilizations,* edited by K. V. Flannery and J. Marcus, pp. 96–97. Academic Press, New York.
1990   The Evolution of Complexity in the Valley of Oaxaca. *Annual Review of Anthropology* 19:39–58.

Kowalewski, S. A., R. E. Blanton, G. M. Feinman, and L. Finsten
1983   Boundaries, Scale, and Internal Organization. *Journal of Anthropological Archaeology* 2:32–56.
Kowalewski, S. A., G. M. Feinman, L. Finsten, R. E. Blanton, and L. M. Nicholas
1989   *Monte Albán's Hinterland, Part II: The Prehispanic Settlement Patterns in Tlacolula, Etla, and Ocotlán, the Valley of Oaxaca, Mexico.* Memoirs 23. Museum of Anthropology, University of Michigan, Ann Arbor.
Kozloff, A. P., and B. M. Bryan, with L. M. Berman
1992   *Egypt's Dazzling Sun: Amenhotep III and His World.* Exhibition catalogue, Cleveland Museum of Art. Indiana University Press, Bloomington.
Krader, Lawrence
1968   *Formation of the State.* Prentice Hall, Englewood Cliffs, New Jersey.
Kramer, S. N.
1944   *Sumerian Mythology.* Memoirs 21. American Philosophical Society, Philadelphia.
Kraus, F. R.
1973   *Vom mesopotamischen Menschen der altbabylonischen Zeit und seiner Welt.* North Holland, Amsterdam.
1982   *"Kārum,"* ein Organ städtischer Selbstverwaltung der altbabylonischen Zeit. In *Les pouvoirs locaux en Mésopotamie et dans les régions adjacentes,* edited by A. Finet, pp. 29–42. Institut des Hautes Etudes de Belgique, Brussels.
1984   *Königliche Verfügungen in altbabylonischer Zeit.* E. J. Brill, Leiden.
Kraus, F. R. (editor)
1964   *Altbabylonische Briefe.* E. J. Brill, Leiden.
Kristiansen, K.
1991   Chiefdoms, States, and Systems of Social Evolution. In *Chiefdoms: Power, Economy, and Ideology,* edited by T. Earle, pp. 16–43. School of American Research Advanced Seminar Series, Cambridge University Press, Cambridge.
Kroeper, K., and D. Wildung
1994   *Minshat Abu Omar: Ein vor- und frühgeschichtlicher Friedhof im Nildelta.* Philipp von Zabern, Mainz.
Lacau, P.
1949   *Une stèle juridique de Karnak.* Supplément aux *Annales du Service des Antiquités de l'Egypte* 13. Imprimerie de l'Institut Français d'Archéologie Orientale, Cairo.
Lacau, P., and J.-P. Lauer
1961–65 *La Pyramide à Degrés* IV–V. Service des Antiquités de l'Egypte, Fouilles à Saqqarah. Institut Français d'Archéologie Orientale, Cairo.
Lal, B. B.
1979   Kalibangan and Indus Civilization. In *Essays in Indian Protohistory,* edited by D. P. Agrawal and D. Chakrabarti, pp. 65–97. B. R. Publishing, Delhi.
Lamberg-Karlovsky, C. C.
1985   The Near Eastern "Breakout" and the Mesopotamian Social Contract. *Symbols* (Spring):8–24.
Lambert, W. G.
1957   Authors, Ancestors, and Canonicity. *Journal of Cuneiform Studies* 11:1–9.
1960   *Babylonian Wisdom Literature.* Clarendon Press, Oxford.
1964   The Reign of Nebuchadnezzar I: A Turning Point in the History of Ancient Mesopotamian Religion. In *The Seed of Wisdom: Essays in Honor of T. J. Meek,* edited by W. S. McCullough, pp. 3–13. University of Toronto Press, Toronto.

1986   Ninurta Mythology in the Babylonian Epic of Creation. In *Keilschriftliche Lit-
        eraturen,* edited by K. Hecker and W. Sommerfeld, pp. 55–60. Dietrich
        Reimer, Berlin.

Lambert, W. G., and A. R. Millard
1969   *Atra-hasīs: The Babylonian Story of the Flood.* Clarendon Press, Oxford.

Landa, D. de
1941   *Landa's relación de las cosas de Yucatán.* Edited and annotated by A. M. Tozzer.
        Papers of the Peabody Museum 18. Harvard University, Cambridge.

Landsberger, B.
1976   *The Conceptual Autonomy of the Babylonian World.* Translated by T. Jacobsen,
        B. Foster, and H. von Siebenthal. Sources and Monographs on the Ancient
        Near East 1(4). Undena, Malibu, California. (Originally published in 1926,
        Die Eigenbegrifflichkeit der babylonischen Welt. *Islamica* 2:355–72.)

Lange, K., and M. Hirmer
1968   *Egypt: Architecture, Sculpture, Painting.* 4th ed. Phaidon, London.

Laporte, J. P., and V. Fialko
1990   New Perspectives on Old Problems: Dynastic References for the Early Classic
        at Tikal. In *Vision and Revision in Maya Studies,* edited by F. S. Clancy and
        P. D. Harrison, pp. 33–66. University of New Mexico Press, Albuquerque.

Larsen, C. E.
1983   *Life and Land Use on the Bahrain Islands: The Geoarchaeology of an Ancient Society.*
        University of Chicago Press, Chicago.

Larsen, M. T.
1976   *The Old Assyrian City-State and Its Colonies.* Akademisk Forlag, Copenhagen.
1977   Partnerships in Old Assyrian Trade. *Iraq* 39:119–45.
1982   Your Money or Your Life! A Portrait of an Assyrian Businessman. In *Societies
        and Languages of the Ancient Near East: Studies in Honor of I. M. Diakonoff,* edited
        by M. Dandamayev and J. N. Postgate, pp. 214–45. Aris and Phillips,
        Warminster.
1987a   Commercial Networks in the Ancient Near East. In *Centre and Periphery in
        the Ancient World,* edited by M. Rowlands, M. T. Larsen, and K. Kristiansen,
        pp. 47–56. Cambridge University Press, Cambridge.
1987b   The Mesopotamian Lukewarm Mind: Reflections on Science, Divination and
        Literacy. In *Language, Literature, and History: Philological and Historical Studies
        Presented to Erica Reiner,* edited by F. Rochberg-Halton, pp. 203–25. Ameri-
        can Oriental Series, vol. 67. American Oriental Society, New Haven.
1988   Introduction: Literacy and Social Complexity. In *State and Society: The Emer-
        gence and Development of Social Hierarchy and Political Centralization,* edited
        by J. Gledhill, B. Bender, and M. T. Larsen, pp. 173–91. Unwin Hyman,
        London.
1992   The Collapse of Civilizations: The Case of Mesopotamia. In *Clashes of Cul-
        tures: Volume in Honour of Niels Steensgard,* edited by J. Christian, V. Johansen,
        E. Ladewig Petersen, and H. Stevnsborg, pp. 107–29. Odense University
        Press, Odense.

Larsen, M. T. (editor)
1978   *Power and Propaganda: A Symposium on Ancient Empires.* Mesopotamia, vol. 7.
        Akademisk Forlag, Copenhagen.

Laufer, B.
1965   The Development of Ancestral Images in China. In *Reader in Comparative
        Religion: An Anthropological Approach,* edited by W. A. Lessa and E. Z. Vogt,
        pp. 445–50. Harper and Row, New York.

Leach, E. R.
1954   *Political Systems of Highland Burma: A Study of Kachin Social Structure.* Beacon Press, Boston.

Leahy, A.
1985   The Libyan Period in Egypt: An Essay in Interpretation. *Libyan Studies* 16: 51–65.

Le Brun, A.
1978   Le niveau 17B de l'Acropole de Suse (campagne de 1972). *Cahiers de la Délégation Archéologique Française en Iran* 9:57–154. Association Paléorient, Paris.

1980   Les 'écuelles grossières': état de la question. In *L'archéologie de l'Iraq: perspectives et limites de l'interpretation anthropologiques des documents,* edited by M.-T. Barrelet, pp. 59–70. Colloques Internationaux 580. Centre National de la Recherche Scientifique, Paris.

1985   Le Niveau 18 de l'Acropole de Suse. Memoire d'argile, memoire du temps. *Paléorient* 11(2):31–36.

Le Brun, A., and F. Vallat
1978   L'origine de l'écriture à Suse. *Cahiers de la Délégation Archéologique Française en Iran* 9:11–59. Association Paléorient, Paris.

Lehman, E. H.
1969   Toward a Macrosociology of Power. *American Sociological Review* 34:453–65.

Lekson, S. H.
1985   Largest Settlement Size and the Interpretation of Socio-Political Complexity at Chaco Canyon, New Mexico. *Haliksa'i: UNM Contributions to Anthropology* 4:68–75.

Lenski, G.
1966   *Power and Privilege: A Theory of Social Stratification.* McGraw Hill, New York.

Lewis, H. S.
1974a   Leaders and Followers: Some Anthropological Perspectives. *An Addison-Wesley Module in Anthropology* 50:1–25.

1974b   Neighbors, Friends, and Kinsmen: Principles of Social Organization Among the Cushitic-Speaking Peoples of Ethiopia. *Ethnology* 13:145–57.

Lichtheim, M.
1973   *Ancient Egyptian Literature: A Book of Readings I: The Old and Middle Kingdoms.* University of California Press, Berkeley.

Lieberman, S. J.
1980   Of Clay Pebbles, Hollow Clay Balls, and Writing: A Sumerian View. *American Journal of Archaeology* 84:339–58.

Limet, H.
1971   *Les légendes des sceaux cassites.* Palais des Académies, Brussels.

Linné, S.
1942   *Mexican Highland Cultures: Archaeological Researches at Teotihuacán, Calpulalpan, and Chalchicomula in 1934–35.* Publication 7 (n.s.). Ethnographic Museum of Sweden, Stockholm.

Liverani, M.
1990   *Prestige and Interest: International Relations in the Near East ca. 1600–1100 B.C.* Studies in History of the Ancient Near East 1. Sargon, Padua.

1993   Model and Actualization: The Kings of Akkad in the Historical Tradition. In *Akkad: The First World Empire,* edited by M. Liverani, pp. 41–68. Sargon, Padua.

Liverani, M. (editor)
1993   *Akkad: The First World Empire.* Sargon, Padua.

Lloyd, P. C.
1965   The Political Structure of African Kingdoms: An Exploratory Model. In *Political Systems and the Distribution of Power,* edited by M. Banton, pp. 63–112. Tavistock, London.

Longyear, J. M.
1952   *Copan Ceramics: A Study of Southeastern Maya Pottery.* Carnegie Institution of Washington, vol. 597. Washington, D.C.

Lothrop, S. K.
1937   *Coclé: An Archaeological Study of Central Panama, Part I.* Peabody Museum of Ethnology and Archaeology, vol. 7. Harvard University, Cambridge.

Lowenthal, D.
1985   *The Past Is a Foreign Country.* Cambridge University Press, Cambridge.

Luttwak, E. N.
1976   *The Grand Strategy of the Roman Empire from the First Century A.D. to the Third.* Johns Hopkins University Press, Baltimore.

Machinist, P. B.
1984/85   The Assyrians and Their Babylonian Problem: Some Reflections. *Wissenschaftskolleg zu Berlin Jahrbuch* 1984/1985:353–64.
1986   On Self-Consciousness in Mesopotamia. In *The Origins and Diversity of Axial Age Civilizations,* edited by S. N. Eisenstadt, pp. 193–202, 511–18. SUNY Series in Near Eastern Studies, State University of New York Press, Albany.
1992   Order and Disorder: Some Reflections on Mesopotamian Mythology. Manuscript on file, Department of Near Eastern Studies, University of Michigan, Ann Arbor.

Mackay, E. J. H.
1937–38   *Further Excavations at Mohenjo-daro.* 2 vols. Government of India, Delhi.
1943   *Chanhu-Daro Excavations 1935–36.* American Oriental Series, vol. 20. American Oriental Society, New Haven.

Mackey, C., and A. M. U. Klymyshyn
1990   The Southern Frontier of the Chimú Empire. In *The Northern Dynasties: Kingship and Statecraft in Chimor,* edited by M. Moseley and A. Cordy-Collins, pp. 195–226. Dumbarton Oaks, Washington, D.C.

Maekawa, K.
1987   Collective Labor Service in Girsu-Lagash: The Presargonic and Ur III Periods. In *Labor in the Ancient Near East,* edited by M. Powell, pp. 49–71. American Oriental Society, New Haven.

Maher, V.
1984   Possession and Dispossession: Maternity and Mortality in Morocco. In *Interest and Emotion: Essays on the Study of Family and Kinship,* edited by H. Medick and D. W. Sabean, pp. 103–28. Cambridge University Press, Cambridge.

Maidman, M.
1984   Kassites among the Hurrians: A Case-Study from Nuzi. *Bulletin of the Society for Mesopotamian Studies* 8:15–21.

Malik, S. C.
1968   *Indian Civilization: The Formative Period.* Indian Institute of Advanced Study, Simla.
1979   Changing Perspectives of Archaeology and Interpreting Harappan Society. In *Essays in Indian Protohistory,* edited by D. P. Agrawal and D. Chakrabarti, pp. 187–204. B. R. Publishing, Delhi.

Mann, M.
1984   The Autonomous Power of the State. *European Journal of Sociology* 25:185–213.
1986   *The Sources of Social Power, Volume I: A History of Power from the Beginning to A.D.
1760*. Cambridge University Press, Cambridge.
1987   The Autonomous Power of the State: Its Origins, Mechanisms and Results. In
States in History, edited by J. A. Hall, pp. 109–36. Basil Blackwell, Oxford.

Manzanilla, L.
1993   Los conjuntos residenciales teotihuacanos. In *Anatomía de un conjunto residencial
teotihuacano en Oztoyahualco, vol. I: las excavaciones,* edited by L. Manzanilla,
pp. 31–46. Instituto de Investigaciones Antropológicas, Universidad Autónoma de México, Mexico, D.F.

Manzanilla, L. (editor)
1993   *Anatomía de un conjunto residencial teotihuacano en Oztoyahualco.* 2 vols. Instituto
de Investigaciones Antropológicas, Universidad Autónoma de México, Mex-
ico, D.F.

Marcus, J.
1973   Territorial Organization of the Lowland Classic Maya. *Science* 180:911–16.
1974   *An Epigraphic Approach to the Territorial Organization of the Lowland Classic
Maya.* Ph.D. dissertation, Department of Anthropology, Harvard University,
Cambridge.
1976a   *Emblem and State in the Classic Maya Lowlands: An Epigraphic Approach to Territorial Organization.* Dumbarton Oaks, Washington, D.C.
1976b   Iconography of Militarism at Monte Albán and Neighboring Sites in the Valley of Oaxaca. In *The Origins of Religious Art and Iconography in Preclassic
Mesoamerica,* edited by H. B. Nicholson, pp. 123–39. UCLA Latin American
Center, Los Angeles.
1976c   The Origins of Mesoamerican Writing. *Annual Review of Anthropology* 5:
35–67.
1978   Archaeology and Religion: A Comparison of the Zapotec and Maya. *World
Archaeology* 10:172–91.
1980   Zapotec Writing. *Scientific American* 242:50–64.
1983a   Lowland Maya Archaeology at the Crossroads. *American Antiquity* 48:454–88.
1983b   On the Nature of the Mesoamerican City. In *Prehistoric Settlement Patterns:
Essays in Honor of Gordon R. Willey,* edited by E. Z. Vogt and R. Leventhal,
pp. 195–242. University of New Mexico Press, Albuquerque.
1983c   Stone Monuments and Tomb Murals of Monte Albán IIIa. In *The Cloud
People: Divergent Evolution of the Zapotec and Mixtec Civilizations,* edited by
K. V. Flannery and J. Marcus, pp. 137–43. Academic Press, New York.
1983d   Changing Patterns of Stone Monuments after the Fall of Monte Albán,
A.D. 600–900. In *The Cloud People: Divergent Evolution of the Zapotec and Mixtec Civilizations,* edited by K. V. Flannery and J. Marcus, pp. 191–97. Academic
Press, New York.
1983e   Rethinking the Zapotec Urn. In *The Cloud People: Divergent Evolution of
the Zapotec and Mixtec Civilizations,* edited by K. V. Flannery and J. Marcus,
pp. 144–48. Academic Press, New York.
1984   Mesoamerican Territorial Boundaries: Reconstructions from Archaeology and
Hieroglyphic Writing. *Archaeological Review from Cambridge* 3(2):48–62. Cambridge, England.
1987a   *The Inscriptions of Calakmul: Royal Marriage at a Maya City in Campeche, Mexico.*
Technical Reports 21. Museum of Anthropology, University of Michigan,
Ann Arbor.

1987b   *Late Intermediate Occupation at Cerro Azul, Perú. A Preliminary Report.* Technical Reports 20. Museum of Anthropology, University of Michigan, Ann Arbor.

1987c   Prehistoric Fishermen in the Kingdom of Huarco. *American Scientist* 75: 393–401.

1988   The Calakmul State and Its Expansionist Policies. Manuscript on file, Museum of Anthropology, University of Michigan, Ann Arbor.

1989   From Centralized Systems to City-States: Possible Models for the Epiclassic. In *Mesoamerica after the Decline of Teotihuacán, A.D. 700–900,* edited by R. A. Diehl and J. C. Berlo, pp. 201–8. Dumbarton Oaks, Washington, D.C.

1992a   Dynamic Cycles of Mesoamerican States: Political Fluctuations in Mesoamerica. *National Geographic Research and Exploration* 8:392–411.

1992b   Royal Families, Royal Texts: Examples from the Zapotec and Maya. In *Mesoamerican Elites: An Archaeological Assessment,* edited by D. Z. Chase and A. F. Chase, pp. 221–41. University of Oklahoma Press, Norman.

1992c   *Mesoamerican Writing Systems: Propaganda, Myth, and History in Four Ancient Civilizations.* Princeton University Press, Princeton.

1993a   Ancient Maya Political Organization. In *Lowland Maya Civilization in the Eighth Century A.D.,* edited by J. A. Sabloff and J. S. Henderson, pp. 111–83. Dumbarton Oaks, Washington, D.C.

1993b   Men's and Women's Ritual in Formative Oaxaca. Paper presented at Dumbarton Oaks conference on "Social Identity, Cosmology, and Social Organization in Formative Mesoamerica," organized by D. C. Grove and R. A. Joyce, Washington, D.C.

1994   The Collapse of Maya States: A Dynamic Process. Paper presented at the 93rd Annual Meeting of the American Anthropological Association, Atlanta.

1995a   Where is Lowland Maya Archaeology Headed? *Journal of Archaeological Research* 3:3–53.

1995b   Cinco mitos sobre la guerra maya. In *La guerra maya,* edited by E. Nalda and S. Trejo. INAH, Mexico, in press.

1995c   King Lists in the New and Old Worlds. Paper presented at the 94th Annual Meeting of the American Anthropological Association, Washington, D.C.

Marcus, J., and K. V. Flannery

1983   An Introduction to the Postclassic. In *The Cloud People: Divergent Evolution of the Zapotec and Mixtec Civilizations,* edited by K. V. Flannery and J. Marcus, pp. 217–26. Academic Press, New York.

1996   *Zapotec Civilization: How Urban Society Evolved in Mexico's Oaxaca Valley.* Thames and Hudson, London and New York.

Marcus, J., and W. J. Folan

1994   Una estela más del siglo V y nueva información sobre Pata de Jaguar, gobernante de Calakmul en el siglo VII. *Gaceta Universitaria* 15–16:21–26. Universidad Autónoma de Campeche, Mexico.

Marcus, M.

1995   Art and Ideology in Ancient Western Asia. In *Civilizations of the Ancient Near East,* vol. IV, edited by J. Sasson, pp. 2487–2505. Scribners, New York.

Marshall, J. (editor)

1931   *Mohenjo-Daro and the Indus Civilization.* 3 vols. Arthur Probsthain, London.

Martin, S., and N. Grube

1995   Maya Superstates: How a Few Powerful Kingdoms Vied for Control of the Maya Lowlands During the Classic Period (A.D. 300–900). *Archaeology* 48(6): 41–46.

Martin-Pardey, E.
1976   *Untersuchungen zur ägyptischen Provinzialverwaltung bis zum Ende des Alten Reiches.* Hildesheimer Ägyptologische Beiträge 1. Gerstenberg, Hildesheim.
Mathews, P.
1985   Maya Early Classic Monuments and Inscriptions. In *A Consideration of the Early Classic Period in the Maya Lowlands,* edited by G. R. Willey and P. Mathews, pp. 5–54. Institute for Mesoamerican Studies 10. State University of New York at Albany.
Matthews, R.
1993   *Cities, Seals, and Writing: Archaic Seal Impressions from Jemdet Nasr and Ur.* Gebrüder Mann, Berlin.
Mayr, E.
1982   *The Growth of Biological Thought.* Harvard University Press, Cambridge.
McCulloch, W. S.
1945   A Heterarchy of Values Determined by the Topology of Neural Nets. *Bulletin of Mathematical Biophysics* 7:89–93.
McDowell, A. G.
1992a   Agricultural Activity by the Workmen of Deir el-Medina. *Journal of Egyptian Archaeology* 78:195–206.
1992b   Awareness of the Past in Deir el-Medîna. In *Village Voices: Proceedings of the Symposium "Texts from Deir el-Medîna and Their Interpretation," Leiden, May 31–June 1, 1991,* edited by R.-J. Demarée and A. Egberts, pp. 95–109. Centre of Non-Western Studies, Leiden.
McEwan, G. F.
1985   Excavaciones en Pikillacta: un sitio wari. *Diálogo Andino* 4:89–136. Arica, Chile.
1991   Investigation at the Pikillacta Site: A Provincial Huari Center in the Valley of Cuzco. In *Huari Administrative Structure: Prehistoric Monumental Architecture and State Government,* edited by W. H. Isbell and G. F. McEwan, pp. 93–119. Dumbarton Oaks, Washington, D.C.
McGuire, R.
1983   Breaking Down Cultural Complexity: Inequality and Heterogeneity. *Advances in Archaeological Method and Theory,* vol. 6, edited by M. B. Schiffer, pp. 91–142. Academic Press, New York.
McGuire, R., and D. Saitta
1996   Although They Have Petty Captains, They Obey Them Badly: The Dialectics of Prehispanic Western Pueblo Social Organization. *American Antiquity* 61: 197–216.
Meadow, R. H. (editor)
1991   *Harappa Excavations 1986–1990: A Multidisciplinary Approach to Third Millennium Urbanism.* Prehistory Press, Madison, Wisconsin.
Meillassoux, C.
1978   "The Economy" in Agricultural Self-Sustaining Societies: A Preliminary Analysis. In *Relations of Production: Marxist Approaches to Economic Anthropology,* edited by D. Seddon, pp. 127–57. Frank Cass, London.
Mendelssohn, K.
1974   *The Riddle of the Pyramids.* Thames and Hudson, London.
Michailidou, A.
1989   *Knossos: A Complete Guide to the Palace of Minos.* Ekdotike Athenon, Athens.

Michalowski, P.
1983   History as Charter: Some Observations on the Sumerian King List. *Journal of the American Oriental Society* 103:237–48.
1987   Charisma and Control: On Continuity and Change in Early Mesopotamian Bureaucratic Systems. In *The Organization of Power: Aspects of Bureaucracies in the Ancient Near East,* edited by M. Gibson and R. D. Biggs, pp. 55–67. Oriental Institute, University of Chicago, Chicago.
1990   Early Mesopotamian Communicative Systems: Art, Literature, and Writing. In *Investigating Artistic Environments in the Ancient Near East,* edited by A. Gunter, pp. 56–69. Smithsonian Institution Press, Washington, D.C.
1993a   Memory and Deed: The Historiography of the Political Expansion of the Akkad State. In *Akkad: The First World Empire,* edited by M. Liverani, pp. 69–90. Sargon, Padua.
1993b   Tokenism. *American Anthropologist* 95:996–99.
1993c   On the Early Toponymy of Sumer: A Contribution to the Study of Early Mesopotamian Writing. In *Kinattūtu ša dārâti: Rafael Kutscher Memorial Volume,* edited by A. Rainey, pp. 199–233. Institute of Archaeology, Tel Aviv.
1994   Early Literacy Revisited. In *Literacy: Interdisciplinary Conversations,* edited by D. Keller-Cohen, pp. 49–70. Hampton Press, Cresskill, New Jersey.
Midant-Reynes, B.
1992   *Préhistoire de l'Egypte, des premiers hommes aux premiers pharaons.* Armand Colin, Paris.
Miller, D.
1985   Ideology and the Harappan Civilization. *Journal of Anthropological Archaeology* 4:34–71.
1989   The Limits of Dominance. In *Domination and Resistance,* edited by D. Miller, M. Rowlands, and C. Tilley, pp. 61–79. Unwin Hyman, London.
Miller, M. E.
1986   *The Murals of Bonampak.* Princeton University Press, Princeton.
Miller, N.
1984   The Use of Dung as Fuel: An Ethnographic Example and an Archaeological Application. *Paléorient* 10(2):71–79.
Miller, W. B.
1955   Two Concepts of Authority. *American Anthropologist* 57:271–89.
Millett, P.
1989   Patronage and Its Avoidance in Classical Athens. In *Patronage in Ancient Society,* edited by A. Wallace-Hadrill, pp. 15–47. Routledge and Kegan Paul, London.
Millon, R.
1973   *Urbanization at Teotihuacán, Mexico, vol. I, The Teotihuacán Map, Part I, Text.* University of Texas Press, Austin.
1976   Social Relations in Ancient Teotihuacán. In *The Valley of Mexico: Studies in Pre-Hispanic Ecology and Society,* edited by E. R. Wolf, pp. 205–48. School of American Research Advanced Seminar Series, University of New Mexico Press, Albuquerque.
1988   Where *Do* They All Come From? The Provenance of the Wagner Murals from Teotihuacán. In *Feathered Serpents and Flowering Trees: Reconstructing the Murals of Teotihuacán,* edited by K. Berrin, pp. 78–113. The Fine Arts Museum, San Francisco.

1992   Teotihuacán Studies: From 1950 to 1990 and Beyond. In *Art, Ideology, and the City of Teotihuacán,* edited by J. C. Berlo, pp. 339–429. Dumbarton Oaks, Washington, D.C.

1993   The Place Where Time Began: An Archaeologist's Interpretation of What Happened in Teotihuacán History. In *Teotihuacán,* edited by K. Berrin and E. Pasztory, pp. 17–43. Thames and Hudson, New York.

Millon, R., and S. Sugiyama

1991   Concentración de pinturas murales en el Conjunto Arquitectónico Grande, al este de la Plaza de la Luna. In *Teotihuacán 1980–1982: nuevas interpretaciones,* pp. 211–31. Serie Arqueología, INAH, Mexico.

Miroschedji, P. de

1986   Un four de potier du IVe millénaire sur le tell de l'Apadana. *Cahiers de la Délégation Archéologique Française en Iran* 7:13–46. Association Paléorient, Paris.

Moore, B., Jr.

1978   *Injustice: The Social Bases of Obedience and Revolt.* M. E. Sharpe, White Plains, New York.

Moore, S. F. (editor)

1993   *Moralizing States and the Ethnography of the Present.* Monograph Series 5. American Ethnological Society, Washington, D.C.

Moorey, P. R. S.

1978   *Kish Excavations 1923–1933.* Oxford University Press, Oxford.

1985   *Materials and Manufacture in Ancient Mesopotamia: The Evidence of Archaeology and Art. Metals and Metalwork, Glazed Materials and Glass.* BAR International Series 237. British Archaeological Reports, Oxford.

1994   *Ancient Mesopotamian Materials and Industries: The Archaeological Evidence.* Clarendon Press, Oxford.

Morelos García, N.

1991   Esculturas y arquitectura en el Conjunto Arquitectónico. In *Teotihuacán 1980–1982: nuevas interpretaciones,* pp. 193–201. Serie Arqueología, INAH, Mexico.

Morenz, S.

1969   *Prestige-Wirtschaft im alten Ägypten.* Sitzungsberichte der Bayerischen Akademie der Wissenschaften, Philosophisch-Historische Klasse fascicle 4. Bayerische Akademie/C. H. Beck, Munich.

Morley, S. G.

1920   *The Inscriptions at Copan.* Carnegie Institution of Washington, vol. 219. Washington, D.C.

Morris, C.

1967   *Storage in Tawantinsuyu.* Ph.D. dissertation, Department of Anthropology, University of Chicago, Chicago.

1972   State Settlements in Tawantinsuyu: A Strategy of Compulsory Urbanism. In *Contemporary Archaeology: A Guide to Theory and Contributions,* edited by M. P. Leone, pp. 393–401. Southern Illinois University Press, Carbondale.

1974   Reconstructing Patterns of Non-Agricultural Production in the Inca Economy: Archaeology and Ethnohistory in Institutional Analysis. In *Reconstructing Complex Societies,* edited by C. B. Moore, pp. 49–68. Supplement to the Bulletin of the American Schools of Oriental Research 20. Cambridge, Massachusetts.

1981   Tecnología y organización inca del almacenamiento de víveres en la sierra. In *La tecnología en el mundo andino,* vol. 1, edited by H. Lechtman and A. M. Soldi, pp. 327–75. Universidad Nacional Autónoma de México, Mexico, D.F.

1982   The Infrastructure of Inka Control in the Peruvian Central Highlands. In *The Inca and Aztec States, 1400–1800,* edited by G. Collier, R. Rosaldo, and J. Wirth, pp. 153–71. Academic Press, New York

1987   Arquitectura y estructura del espacio en Huánuco Pampa. *Cuadernos* 12. Instituto Nacional de Antropología, Buenos Aires.

1988a   A City Fit for an Inka. *Archaeology* 41(5):43–49.

1988b   Más allá de las fronteras de Chincha. In *La frontera del estado inca,* edited by T. Dillehay and P. Netherly, pp. 131–40. BAR International Series 442. British Archaeological Reports, Oxford.

1991   Signs of Division, Symbols of Unity: Art in the Inka Empire. In *Circa 1492: Art in the Age of Exploration,* edited by J. A. Levenson, pp. 521–28. The National Gallery of Art and Yale University Press, Washington, D.C., and London.

1993   The Wealth of a Native American State: Investment, Value and the Stimulation of Demand in the Inka Economy. In *Configurations of Power,* edited by P. Netherly and J. Henderson, pp. 36–50. Cornell University Press, Ithaca.

Morris, C., and D. E. Thompson
1985   *Huánuco Pampa: An Inca City and Its Hinterland.* Thames and Hudson, London and New York.

Morris, I.
1987   *Burial and Ancient Society: The Rise of the Greek City-State.* Cambridge University Press, Cambridge.

1989   Circulation, Deposition, and the Formation of the Greek Iron Age. *Man* (n.s.) 24:502–19.

1994   Archaeologies of Greece. In *Classical Greece: Ancient Histories and Modern Archaeologies,* edited by I. Morris, pp. 3–47. Cambridge University Press, Cambridge.

1997   An Archaeology of Equality? The Greek City-States. In *The Archaeology of City-States: Cross-Cultural Approaches,* edited by D. L. Nichols and T. H. Charlton, pp. 91–105. Smithsonian Institution Press, Washington, D.C.

Mortensen, P.
1976   Chalcolithic Settlements in the Holailan Valley. In *Proceedings of the Fourth Annual Symposium on Archaeological Research in Iran,* edited by F. Baghherzadeh, pp. 42–62. Iranian Centre for Archaeological Research, Tehran.

Moseley, M. E.
1983   Central Andean Civilization. In *Ancient South Americans,* edited by J. D. Jennings, pp. 179–239. W. H. Freeman, San Francisco.

1992   *The Incas and Their Ancestors: The Archaeology of Peru.* Thames and Hudson, London.

Moseley, M. E., and K. C. Day (editors)
1982   *Chan Chan: Andean Desert City.* School of American Research Advanced Seminar Series, University of New Mexico Press, Albuquerque.

Mote, F. W.
1968   Chinese Political Thought. In *International Encyclopedia of the Social Sciences,* vol. 2, edited by D. L. Sills, pp. 394–408. The Macmillan Company and The Free Press, New York.

Moussa, A. M., and H. Altenmüller
1977   *Das Grab des Nianchchnum und Khnumhotep.* Deutsches Archäologisches Institut, Abteilung Kairo, Archäologische Veröffentlichungen 21. Philipp von Zabern, Mainz.

Mudar, K.
1988   The Effects of Context on Bone Assemblages: Examples from the Uruk Period in Southwestern Iran. *Paléorient* 14:151–68.
Mughal, M. R.
1982   Recent Archaeological Research in the Cholistan Desert. In *Harappan Civilization: A Contemporary Perspective,* edited by G. L. Possehl, pp. 85–95. Oxford and IBH, and the American Institute of Indian Studies, Delhi.
1997   *Ancient Cholistan: Archaeology and Architecture.* Firozsons, Lahore.
Müller-Wollermann, R.
1986   *Krisenfaktoren im ägyptischen Staat des ausgehenden Alten Reiches.* Ph.D. dissertation, University of Tübingen, Tübingen.
Murra, J. V.
1960   Rite and Crop in the Inca State. In *Culture in History: Essays in Honor of Paul Radin,* edited by S. Diamond, pp. 393–407. Columbia University Press, New York.
1962a   Cloth and Its Function in the Inca State. *American Anthropologist* 64:710–28.
1962b   An Archaeological "Restudy" of an Andean Ethnohistorical Account. *American Antiquity* 28:1–4.
1964   Una apreciación etnológica de la visita. In *Visita hecha a la provincia de Chucuito por Garci Diez de San Miguel en 1567, documentos regionales para la etnología y la etnohistoria andina,* vol. 1, pp. 421–42. Casa de la Cultura, Lima.
1980   *The Economic Organization of the Inka State.* JAI Press, Greenwich, Connecticut. (Ph.D. dissertation, Department of Anthropology, University of Chicago, 1955.)
1986   The Expansion of the Inka State: Armies, War, and Rebellions. In *Anthropological History of Andean Polities,* edited by J. V. Murra, N. Wachtel, and J. Revel, pp. 49–58. Cambridge University Press, Cambridge and London, and Editions de la Maison de Sciences de l'Homme, Paris (originally in French in *Annales [ESC],* vol. 33, nos. 5–6, Paris, 1978).
Naroll, R.
1956   A Preliminary Index of Social Development. *American Anthropologist* 58:687–715.
1967   Imperial Cycles and World Order. *Peace Research Society Papers* 7:83–101.
Neely, J. A., and H. Wright
1994   *Early Settlement and Irrigation on the Deh Luran Plain.* Technical Reports 26. Museum of Anthropology, University of Michigan, Ann Arbor.
Netting, R. M.
1990   Population, Permanent Agriculture, and Politics: Unpacking the Evolutionary Portmanteau. In *The Evolution of Political Systems: Sociopolitics in Small-Scale Sedentary Societies,* edited by S. Upham, pp. 21–61. School of American Research Advanced Seminar Series, Cambridge University Press, Cambridge.
Nicholas, L. M.
1989   Land Use in Prehispanic Oaxaca. In *Monte Albán's Hinterland, Part II: The Prehispanic Settlement Patterns in Tlacolula, Etla, and Ocotlán, the Valley of Oaxaca, Mexico,* by S. A. Kowalewski, G. M. Feinman, L. Finsten, R. E. Blanton, and L. M. Nicholas, pp. 449–505. Memoirs 23. Museum of Anthropology, University of Michigan, Ann Arbor.
Nissen, H. J.
1970   Grabung in den Quadraten K/L XII in Uruk-Warka. *Baghdader Mitteilungen* 5:102–91.

1982   Die "Tempelstadt": Regierungsform der frühdynastischen Zeit in Babylonien? In *Gesellschaft und Kultur im alten Vorderasien,* edited by H. Klengel, pp. 195–200. Akademie-Verlag, Berlin.

1988   *The Early History of the Ancient Near East, 9000–2000 B.C.* Translated by E. Lutzeier and K. J. Northcott. University of Chicago Press, Chicago.

Nivison, D. S.

1959   Introduction. In *Confucianism in Action,* edited by D. S. Nivison and A. F. Wright, pp. 3–24. Stanford University Press, Stanford.

Norbeck, E.

1963   African Rituals of Conflict. *American Anthropologist* 65:1254–79.

1977   A Sanction for Authority: Etiquette. In *The Anthropology of Power: Ethnographic Studies from Asia, Oceania, and the New World,* edited by R. D. Fogelson and R. N. Adams, pp. 67–76. Academic Press, New York.

North, D.

1986   A Neoclassical Theory of the State. In *Rational Choice,* edited by J. Elster, pp. 248–60. Basil Blackwell, Oxford (originally published in 1981).

Oates, J.

1960   Ur and Eridu: The Prehistory. *Iraq* 23:32–50.

1969   Choga Mami 1967–68: A Preliminary Report. *Iraq* 31:115–52.

1977   Mesopotamian Social Organisation: Archaeological and Philological Evidence. In *The Evolution of Social Systems,* edited by J. Friedman and M. J. Rowlands, pp. 457–86. Duckworth, London.

1983   Ubaid Mesopotamia Reconsidered. In *The Hilly Flanks: Essays on the Prehistory of Southwest Asia Presented to Robert J. Braidwood,* edited by T. C. Young, P. E. L. Smith, and P. Mortensen, pp. 251–81. Oriental Institute, University of Chicago, Chicago.

1986   *Babylon.* Revised ed. Thames and Hudson, London.

1987   Ubaid Chronology. In *Chronologies du Proche-Orient,* edited by O. Aurenche, J. Evin, and F. Hours, pp. 473–82. Editions du Centre National de la Recherche Scientifique, Paris.

1993   Trade and Power in the Fifth and Fourth Millennia B.C.: New Evidence from Northern Mesopotamia. *World Archaeology* 24:403–22.

Oberem, U.

1968   Die Bergfestung Quitoloma im Nördlichen Hochland Ecuadors. *Baessler Archiv,* n.F., vol. 16, pp. 331–54. Berlin.

Oberlander, T.

1965   *The Zagros Streams.* Syracuse Geographical Series 1. Syracuse University Press, Syracuse.

O'Connor, D.

1992   The Status of Early Egyptian Temples: An Alternative Theory. In *The Followers of Horus: Studies Dedicated to Michael Allen Hoffman 1944–1990,* edited by R. Friedman and B. Adams, pp. 83–98. Egyptian Studies Association Publication 2. Oxbow Monograph 20. Oxbow Books, Oxford.

1993   *Ancient Nubia: Egypt's Rival in Africa.* University of Pennsylvania Museum, Philadelphia.

1998   *City and Cosmos in Ancient Egypt.* Athlone Publications in Egyptology and Ancient Near Eastern Studies. Athlone Press, London, forthcoming.

Oded, B.

1979   *Mass Deportations and Deportees in the Assyrian Empire.* Ludwig Reichert, Wiesbaden.

Oliver, D. L.
1974   *Ancient Tahitian Society,* Vols. 1–3. University Press of Hawai'i, Honolulu.
Oppenheim, A. L.
1975   The Position of the Intellectual in Mesopotamian Society. *Daedalus* (Spring):
        37–46. *Proceedings of the American Academy of Arts and Sciences* 104(2).
1977   *Ancient Mesopotamia: Portrait of a Dead Civilization.* 2nd ed. Edited by E. Reiner.
        University of Chicago Press, Chicago. (Originally published in 1964.)
Otterbein, K.
1968   Internal War: A Cross-Cultural Study. *American Anthropologist* 70:277–89.
1973   The Anthropology of War. In *Handbook of Social and Cultural Anthropology,*
        edited by J. Honigmann, pp. 923–58. Rand-McNally, Chicago.
Paddock, J.
1983   *Lord 5 Flower's Family: Rulers of Zaachila and Cuilapan.* Publications in Anthro-
        pology 29. Vanderbilt University, Nashville.
Parkinson, R. B.
1998   The Dream and the Knot: Contextualizing Middle Kingdom Literature. In
        *Defining Egyptian Literature: Proceedings of the Symposium "Ancient Egyptian
        Literature, History and Forms," Los Angeles, March 24–26, 1995,* edited by
        G. Moers. Lingua Aegyptia Studia Monographica 2. Göttingen, forthcoming.
Parpola, S.
1983   Assyrian Library Records. *Journal of Near Eastern Studies* 42:1–30.
Parsons, J. R.
1971   *Prehistoric Settlement Patterns of the Texcoco Region, Mexico.* Memoirs 5. Museum
        of Anthropology, University of Michigan, Ann Arbor.
Parsons, T.
1960   Max Weber. *American Sociological Review* 25:750–52.
1967   *Social Theory and Modern Society.* The Free Press, New York.
Pasternak, B.
1976   *Introduction to Kinship and Social Organization.* Prentice-Hall, Englewood Cliffs,
        New Jersey.
Pasztory, E.
1988   A Reinterpretation of Teotihuacán and Its Mural Painting Tradition. In *Feath-
        ered Serpents and Flowering Trees,* edited by K. Berrin, pp. 45–77. The Fine Arts
        Museum, San Francisco.
1992   Abstraction and the Rise of a Utopian State at Teotihuacán. In *Art, Ideology,
        and the City of Teotihuacán,* edited by J. C. Berlo, pp. 281–320. Dumbarton
        Oaks, Washington, D.C.
1997   *Teotihuacán: An Experiment in Living.* University of Oklahoma Press, Norman.
Pattee, H. H. (editor)
1973   *Hierarchy Theory: The Challenge of Complex Systems.* George Braziller, New
        York.
Patterson, T. C.
1991   *The Inka Empire: The Formation and Disintegration of a Pre-Capitalist State.* Berg,
        Herndon, Virginia.
Patterson, T. C., and C. W. Gailey (editors)
1987   *Power Relations and State Formation.* Special publication of the Archeology Sec-
        tion, American Anthropological Association, Washington, D.C.
Pendergast, D. M.
1985   Lamanai, Belize: An Updated View. In *The Lowland Maya Postclassic,* edited by
        A. F. Chase and P. M. Rice, pp. 91–103. University of Texas Press, Austin.

1986   Stability Through Change: Lamanai, Belize from the 9th to the 17th Century. In *Late Lowland Maya Civilization: Classic to Postclassic,* edited by J. A. Sabloff and E. W. Andrews, pp. 223–49. School of American Research Advanced Seminar Series, University of New Mexico Press, Albuquerque.

Peregrine, P. N.
1991   Some Political Aspects of Craft Specialization. *World Archaeology* 23:1–11.
1992   *Mississippian Evolution: A World-System Perspective.* Prehistory Press, Madison, Wisconsin.

Peregrine, P. N., and G. M. Feinman (editors)
1996   *Pre-Columbian World Systems.* Prehistory Press, Madison, Wisconsin.

Perkins, A. L.
1949   *The Comparative Archaeology of Early Mesopotamia.* Studies in Ancient Oriental Civilization 25. Oriental Institute, University of Chicago, Chicago.

Petrie, W. M. F.
1900   Sequences in Prehistoric Remains. *Journal of the Anthropological Institute of Great Britain and Ireland* 29:295–301.
1901   *Diospolis Parva: The Cemeteries of Abadiyeh and Hu, 1898–9.* Memoir 20. The Egypt Exploration Fund, London.

Pettinato, G.
1971   *Das altorientalische Menschenbild und die sumerischen und akkadischen Schöpfungsmythen.* Carl Winter, Universitätsverlag, Heidelberg.

Pierce, R. H.
1972   *Three Demotic Papyri in the Museum: A Contribution to the Study of Contracts and Their Instruments in Ptolemaic Egypt. Symbolae Osloenses,* Supplement 24. Universitetsforlaget, Oslo.

Piggott, S.
1950   *Prehistoric India to 1000 B.C.* Penguin Books, Baltimore.

Pincemin, S.
1994   *Entierro en el Palacio.* Colección: Arqueología. Universidad Autónoma de Campeche, Mexico.

Pittman, H.
1993   Pictures of an Administration: The Late Uruk Scribe at Work. In *Between the Rivers and Over the Mountains,* edited by M. Frangipane, H. Hauptmann, M. Liverani, P. Matthiae, and M. Mellink, pp. 235–246. Universita di Roma "La Sapienza," Roma.

Pokora, T.
1978   China. In *The Early State,* edited by H. J. M. Claessen and P. Skalník, pp. 191–212. Mouton, The Hague.

Polanyi, K.
1957   The Economy as an Instituted Process. In *Trade and Markets in the Early Empires: Economies in History and Theory,* edited by K. Polanyi, C. M. Arensberg, and H. W. Pearson, pp. 243–70. The Free Press, New York.

Pollock, S.
1992   Bureaucrats and Managers, Peasants and Pastoralists, Imperialists and Traders: Research on the Uruk and Jemdet Nasr Periods in Mesopotamia. *Journal of World Prehistory* 6:297–336.

Pope, M., and S. Pollock
1995   Trade, Tool, and Tasks: A Study of Uruk Chipped Stone Industries. *Research in Economic Anthropology* 16:227–65. JAI Press, Greenwich, Connecticut.

Porada, E.
1965   The Relative Chronology of Mesopotamia. In *Chronologies in Old World Archaeology*, edited by R. Ehrich, pp. 133–200. University of Chicago Press, Chicago.
1979   Some Thoughts on the Audience Reliefs of Persepolis. In *Studies in Classical Art and Archaeology: A Tribute to Peter von Blanckenhagen*, edited by G. Kopcke and M. Moore, pp. 37–44. J. J. Augustin, Locust Valley, New York.

Posener, G.
1965   Sur l'orientation et l'ordre des points cardinaux chez les Egyptiens. In *Göttinger Vorträge vom Ägyptologischen Kolloquium der Akademie am 25. und 26. August 1964*, edited by S. Schott, pp. 69–78. Vandenhoeck and Ruprecht, Göttingen.
1975   L'[anachōrēsis] dans l'Egypte pharaonique. In *Le monde grec: hommages á Claire Préaux*, edited by J. Bingen, G. Cambier, and G. Nachtergael, pp. 663–69. Editions de l'Université de Bruxelles, Brussels.

Posener-Kriéger, P.
1976   *Les archives du temple funéraire de Néferirkarê-Kakaï (les papyrus d'Abousir)*. 2 vols. Bibliothéque d'Etude 65. Institut Français d'Archéologie Orientale, Cairo.

Possehl, G. L.
1979   *Ancient Cities of the Indus*. Carolina Academic Press, Durham, North Carolina.
1986   *Kulli: An Exploration of Ancient Civilization in South Asia*. Carolina Academic Press, Durham, North Carolina.
1990   Revolution in the Urban Revolution: The Emergence of Indus Urbanization. *Annual Review of Anthropology* 19:261–82.
1993   The Date of Indus Urbanization: A Proposed Chronology for the Pre-Urban and Urban Harappan Phases. In *South Asian Archaeology 1991*, edited by A. J. Gail and G. J. R. Mevissen, pp. 231–49. Franz Steiner Verlag, Stuttgart.
1996   *Indus Age: The Writing System*. University of Pennsylvania Press, Philadelphia.

Possehl, G. L., and P. C. Rissman
1992   The Chronology of Prehistoric India: From Earliest Times to the Iron Age. In *Chronologies in Old World Archaeology*, 3rd ed., edited by R. Ehrich, pp. 465–90 (vol. 1) and 447–74 (vol. 2). University of Chicago Press, Chicago.

Postgate, J. N.
1992   *Early Mesopotamia: Society and Economy at the Dawn of History*. Routledge, London.
1993   The Four "Neo-Assyrian" Tablets from Šeh Hamad. *State Archives of Assyria Bulletin* 7:109–24.

Potter, T. W.
1980   Rome and Its Empire in the West. In *The Cambridge Encyclopedia of Archaeology*, edited by A. Sherratt, pp. 232–38. Crown, New York.

Pounds, N. J. G.
1969   The Urbanization of the Classical World. *Annals of the Association of American Geographers* 59:135–57.

Powell, M. A.
1981   Three Problems in the History of Cuneiform Writing: Origins, Direction of Script, Literacy. *Visible Language* 15:419–40.
1989–90   Masse und Gewichte. *Reallexikon der Assyriologie* 7:457–517.

Poyer, L.
1993   Egalitarianism in the Face of Hierarchy. *Journal of Anthropological Research* 49:111–33.

Pran Nath, Dr.
    1931   The Scripts on the Indus Valley Seals, with an Appendix Containing Extracts from Sumerian and Indian Literature Throwing Light upon the Words Occurring in the Inscriptions of the Indus Valley, Elam and Crete. *Supplement to The Indian Historical Quarterly* 7:1–52.
    1932   The Scripts on the Indus Valley Seals, II. *Supplement to The Indian Historical Quarterly* 8:1–32.

Price, B. J.
    1976   A Chronological Framework for Cultural Development in Mesoamerica. In *The Valley of Mexico: Studies in Pre-Hispanic Ecology and Society,* edited by E. R. Wolf, pp. 13–21. School of American Research Advanced Seminar Series, University of New Mexico Press, Albuquerque.
    1977   Shifts in Production and Organization: A Cluster-Interaction Model. *Current Anthropology* 18:209–33.

Proskouriakoff, T.
    1950   *A Study of Classic Maya Sculpture.* Carnegie Institution of Washington, vol. 593. Washington, D.C.

Puleston, D., and D. W. Callender, Jr.
    1967   Defensive Earthworks at Tikal. *Expedition* 9(3):40–48.

Quaegebeur, J.
    1989   The Egyptian Clergy and the Cult of the Ptolemaic Dynasty. *Ancient Society* 20:93–116.

Quezada, S.
    1993   *Pueblos y caciques yucatecos, 1550–1580.* El Colegio de México, Mexico.

Quibell, J. E.
    1900   *Hierakonpolis* I. Egyptian Research Account Memoir 4. Bernard Quaritch, London.

Quirke, S.
    1988   State and Labour in the Middle Kingdom: A Reconsideration of the Term [ḥrt]. *Revue d'Egyptologie* 39:83–106.

Raikes, R. L.
    1968   Kalibangan: Death from Natural Causes. *Antiquity* 42:286–91.

Rands, R.
    1952   *Some Evidences of Warfare in Classic Maya Art.* Ph.D. dissertation, Department of Anthropology, Columbia University, New York.

Rao, S. R.
    1973   *Lothal and the Indus Civilization.* Asia Publishing House, Bombay.
    1979   *Lothal: A Harappan Port Town, 1955–62.* Memoirs 78, vol. 1. Archaeological Survey of India, Delhi.
    1985   *Lothal: A Harappan Port Town, 1955–62.* Memoirs 78, vol. 2. Archaeological Survey of India, Delhi.

Rappaport, R. A.
    1971   Ritual, Sanctity, and Cybernetics. *American Anthropologist* 73:59–76.
    1977   Maladaptation in Social Systems. In *The Evolution of Social Systems,* edited by J. Friedman and M. J. Rowlands, pp. 49–71. Duckworth, London.
    1979   *Ecology, Meaning, and Religion.* North Atlantic Books, Richmond, California.

Rathbone, D.
    1991   *Economic Rationalism and Rural Society in Third-Century A.D. Egypt: The Heroninos Archive and the Appianus Estate.* Cambridge Classical Studies, Cambridge University Press, Cambridge.

Rathje, W. L.
1975   Last Tango in Mayapán: A Tentative Trajectory of Production-Distribution Systems. In *Ancient Civilization and Trade,* edited by J. Sabloff and C. C. Lamberg-Karlovsky, pp. 409–48. School of American Research Advanced Seminar Series, University of New Mexico Press, Albuquerque.

Ratnagar, S.
1981   *Encounters: The Westerly Trade of the Harappa Civilization.* Oxford University Press, Delhi.
1991   *Enquiries into the Political Organization of Harappan Society.* Ravish Publishers, Pune.

Redding, R.
1979   The Fauna Remains from Tappeh Zabarjad. In *Archaeological Investigations in Northeastern Xuzestan, 1976,* edited by H. T. Wright, pp. 91–93. Technical Reports 10. Museum of Anthropology, University of Michigan, Ann Arbor.
1981   The Animal Remains. In *An Early Town on the Deh Luran Plain: Excavations at Tepe Farukhabad,* edited by H. T. Wright, pp. 233–61. Memoirs 13. Museum of Anthropology, University of Michigan, Ann Arbor.

Redfield, R.
1953   *The Primitive World and Its Transformations.* Cornell University Press, Ithaca.

Redfield, R., and M. Singer
1954   The Cultural Role of Cities. *Economic Development and Culture Change* 3(1): 53.

Redman, C. L.
1978   *The Rise of Civilization: From Early Farmers to Urban Society in the Ancient Near East.* W. H. Freeman, San Francisco.
1991   The Comparative Context of Social Complexity. In *Chaco and Hohokam,* edited by P. L. Crown and W. J. Judge, pp. 251–81. School of American Research Press, Santa Fe.

Redmond, E. M.
1983   *A fuego y sangre: Early Zapotec Imperialism in the Cuicatlán Cañada, Oaxaca.* Studies in Latin American Ethnohistory and Archaeology, vol. I. Memoirs 16. Museum of Anthropology, University of Michigan, Ann Arbor.

Redmond, E. M., and C. S. Spencer
1994   The Cacicazgo: An Indigenous Design. In *Caciques and Their People: A Volume in Honor of Ronald Spores,* edited by J. Marcus and J. F. Zeitlin, pp. 189–225. Anthropological Papers 89. Museum of Anthropology, University of Michigan, Ann Arbor.

Reents-Budet, D.
1994   *Painting the Maya Universe: Royal Ceramics of the Classic Period.* Duke University Press, Durham, North Carolina.

Reiner, E.
1961   The Etiological Myth of the "Seven Sages." *Orientalia* 30:1–11.

Renfrew, C.
1972   *The Emergence of Civilisation: The Cyclades and the Aegean in the Third Millennium B.C.* Methuen, London.
1974   Beyond a Subsistence Economy: The Evolution of Social Organization in Prehistoric Europe. In *Reconstructing Complex Societies: An Archaeological Colloquium,* edited by C. B. Moore, pp. 69–95. Supplement to the Bulletin of the American Schools of Oriental Research 20. Cambridge, Massachusetts.

1975 Trade as Action at a Distance: Questions of Integration and Communication. In *Ancient Civilization and Trade,* edited by J. A. Sabloff and C. C. Lamberg-Karlovsky, pp. 3–59. School of American Research Advanced Seminar Series, University of New Mexico Press, Albuquerque.

1982 Polity and Power: Interaction, Intensification and Exploitation. In *An Island Polity: The Archaeology of Exploitation in Melos,* edited by C. Renfrew and M. Wagstaff, pp. 264–90. Cambridge University Press, Cambridge.

1985 *The Archaeology of Cult: The Sanctuary of Phylakopi.* The British School of Archaeology at Athens, Supplementary vol. 18. Thames and Hudson, London.

1986 Introduction: Peer Polity Interaction and Socio-Political Change. In *Peer Polity Interaction and Socio-Political Change,* edited by C. Renfrew and J. Cherry, pp. 1–18. Cambridge University Press, Cambridge.

Renfrew, C., and J. Cherry (editors)
1986 *Peer Polity Interaction and Socio-Political Change.* Cambridge University Press, Cambridge.

Renger, J.
1967 Untersuchungen zum Priestertum in der altbabylonischen Zeit. *Zeitschrift für Assyriologie* 58:110–88.

1989 Probleme und Perspektiven einer Wirtschaftsgeschichte Mesopotamiens. *Saeculum* 40:166–78.

Rhodes, P. J.
1986 *The Greek City States: A Source Book.* University of Oklahoma Press, Norman.

Rice, D. S., and P. M. Rice
1981 Muralla de León: A Lowland Maya Fortification. *Journal of Field Archaeology* 8:271–88.

Richards, A., and A. Kuper (editors)
1971 *Councils in Action.* Cambridge University Press, Cambridge.

Rissman, P.
1988 Public Displays and Private Values: A Guide to Buried Wealth in Harappan Archaeology. *World Archaeology* 20:209–28.

Rodman, W.
1993 Sorcery and the Silencing of Chiefs: "Words in the Wind" in Postindependence Ambae. *Journal of Anthropological Research* 49:217–35.

Rosaldo, R. I.
1968 Metaphors of Hierarchy in a Mayan Ritual. *American Anthropologist* 70:524–36.

Roscoe, P. B.
1993 Practice and Political Centralization. *Current Anthropology* 34:111–40.

Rosen, A. M.
1989 Environmental Change at the End of the Early Bronze Age in Palestine. In *L'urbanisation de la Palestine à l'age du Bronze ancien,* edited by P. de Miroschedji, pp. 247–55. BAR International Series 527. British Archaeological Reports, Oxford.

Rostworowski, M.
1970 Mercaderes del Valle de Chincha en la época prehispánica: un documento y unos comentarios. *Revista Española de Antropología Americana* 5:135–78. Madrid.

1978–80 Guarco y Lunahuaná: dos señoríos prehispánicos de la costa sur-central del Perú. *Revista del Museo Nacional* XLIV:153–214. Lima, Peru.

1988 *Historia del Tahuantinsuyu.* Instituto de Estudios Peruanos, Lima.

Roth, A. M.
1991 *Egyptian Phyles in the Old Kingdom: The Evolution of a System of Social Organi-*

zation. Studies in Ancient Oriental Civilization 48. Oriental Institute, University of Chicago, Chicago.

Rounds, J.
1979   Lineage, Class, and Power in the Aztec State. *American Ethnologist* 6:73–86.

Rowe, J. H.
1946   Inca Culture at the Time of the Spanish Conquest. In *Handbook of South American Indians: The Andean Civilizations,* edited by J. H. Steward, pp. 183–330. Bureau of American Ethnology, vol. 2, Bulletin 143. Smithsonian Institution, Washington, D.C.

1960   Cultural Unity and Diversification in Peruvian Archaeology. In *Men and Cultures: Selected Papers of the Fifth International Congress of Anthropological and Ethnological Sciences,* edited by A. F. C. Wallace, pp. 627–31. University of Pennsylvania Press, Philadelphia.

1962   Stages and Periods in Archaeological Interpretation. *Southwestern Journal of Anthropology* 18(1):40–54.

1979   An Account of the Shrines of Ancient Cuzco. *Ñawpa Pacha* 17:1–80.

Rowlands, M.
1985   Exclusionary Tactics in the Logic of Collective Dynamics. *Critique of Anthropology* 5(2):47–69.

Rowlands, M., and J.-P. Warnier
1988   Sorcery, Power and the Modern State in Cameroon. *Man* (n.s.) 23:118–32.

Roys, R. L.
1943   *The Indian Background of Colonial Yucatán.* Publication 548. Carnegie Institution of Washington, Washington, D.C.

1957   *The Political Geography of the Yucatán Maya.* Publication 613. Carnegie Institution of Washington, Washington, D.C.

Rudolph, S. H.
1987   Presidential Address: State Formation in Asia—Prolegomenon to a Comparative Study. *Journal of Asian Studies* 46(4):731–46.

Runciman, W. G.
1982   Origins of States: The Case of Archaic Greece. *Comparative Studies in Society and History* 24:351–77.

Russell, J. C.
1958   Late Ancient and Medieval Populations. *Transactions of the American Philosophical Society* 48(3):1–101.

Russmann, E. R.
1995   Two Heads of the Early Fourth Dynasty. In *Kunst des Alten Reiches: Symposium im Deutschen Archäologischen Institut Kairo am 29. und 30. Oktober 1991,* pp. 111–18. Deutsches Archäologisches Institut, Abteilung Kairo, Sonderschrift 28. Philipp von Zabern, Mainz.

Sabloff, J. A., and E. W. Andrews, V (editors)
1986   *Late Lowland Maya Civilization.* School of American Research Advanced Seminar Series, University of New Mexico Press, Albuquerque.

Sabloff, J. A., and J. S. Henderson (editors)
1993   *Lowland Maya Civilization in the Eighth Century A.D.* Dumbarton Oaks, Washington, D.C.

Sabloff, J. A., and G. Tourtellot
1991   *The Ancient Maya City of Sayil: The Mapping of a Puuc Region Center.* Publication 60. Middle American Research Institute, Tulane University, New Orleans.

Safar, F., M. A. Mustafa, and S. Lloyd
1981   *Eridu.* Iraq Ministry of Culture and Information, Baghdad.

Sahlins, M. D.
1958   *Social Stratification in Polynesia.* University of Washington Press, Seattle.
1961   The Segmentary Lineage: An Organization of Predatory Expansion. *American Anthropologist* 63:322–45.
1970   Poor Man, Rich Man, Big-Man, Chief: Political Types in Melanesia and Polynesia. In *Cultures of the Pacific,* edited by T. G. Harding and B. J. Wallace, pp. 203–15. Free Press, New York.
1972   *Stone Age Economics.* Aldine, Chicago.
1983   Other Times, Other Customs: The Anthropology of History. *American Anthropologist* 85:517–44.
Sahlins, M. D., and E. R. Service (editors)
1960   *Evolution of Culture.* University of Michigan Press, Ann Arbor.
Saitta, D. J.
1994   Class and Community in the Prehistoric Southwest. In *The Ancient Southwestern Community: Models and Methods for the Study of Prehistoric Social Organization,* edited by W. H. Wills and R. D. Leonard, pp. 25–43. University of New Mexico Press, Albuquerque.
Saitta, D. J., and A. S. Keene
1990   Politics and Surplus Flow in Prehistoric Communities. In *The Evolution of Political Systems: Sociopolitics in Small-Scale Sedentary Societies,* edited by S. Upham, pp. 203–24. Cambridge University Press, Cambridge.
Sajjidi, M.
1979   The Protoelamite Period on the Izeh Plain. In *Archaeological Investigations in Northeastern Xuzestan, 1976,* edited by H. T. Wright, pp. 93–98. Technical Reports 10. Museum of Anthropology, University of Michigan, Ann Arbor.
Samaniego, L., E. Vergara, and H. Bischof
1985   New Evidence on Cerro Sechín, Casma Valley, Peru. In *Early Ceremonial Architecture in the Andes,* edited by C. B. Donnan, pp. 165–90. Dumbarton Oaks, Washington, D.C.
Sanders, W. T.
1965   The Cultural Ecology of the Teotihuacán Valley. Manuscript on file, Department of Sociology and Anthropology, Pennsylvania State University, University Park.
1973   The Significance of Pikillacta in Andean Culture History. *Occasional Papers in Anthropology* 8:380–428. Pennsylvania State University, University Park.
1974   Chiefdom to State: Political Evolution at Kaminaljuyú, Guatemala. In *Reconstructing Complex Societies: An Archaeological Colloquium,* edited by C. B. Moore, pp. 97–116. Supplement to the Bulletin of the American Schools of Oriental Research, 20. Cambridge, Massachusetts.
1984   Pre-Industrial Demography and Social Evolution. In *On the Evolution of Complex Societies: Essays in Honor of Harry Hoijer 1982,* edited by T. Earle, pp. 7–39. Undena, Malibu, California.
Sanders, W. T., A. Kovar, T. Charlton, and R. A. Diehl
1970   *The Teotihuacán Valley Project Final Report, vol. 1. The Natural Environment, Contemporary Occupation, and 16th Century Population of the Valley.* Occasional Papers in Anthropology 1. Pennsylvania State University, University Park.
Sanders, W. T., J. R. Parsons, and R. S. Santley
1979   *The Basin of Mexico: Ecological Processes in the Evolution of a Civilization.* Academic Press, New York.
Sanders, W. T., and B. J. Price
1968   *Mesoamerica: The Evolution of a Civilization.* Random House, New York.

Sanders, W. T., and D. Webster
1988   The Mesoamerican Urban Tradition. *American Anthropologist* 90:521–46.
Sankarananda, S.
1962   *Hindu States of Sumeria.* Firma Mukhapadhyay, Calcutta.
Sanlaville, P.
1989   Considérations sur l'évolution de la basse Mésopotamie en cours des derniers millénaires. *Paléorient* 15(2):5–27.
Sarcina, A.
1979   A Statistical Assessment of House Patterns at Mohenjodaro. *Mesopotamia* 13/14:155–99.
Sasson, J. (principal editor)
1995   *Civilizations of the Ancient Near East.* 4 vols. Scribners, New York.
Schacht, R.
1980   Two Models of Population Growth. *American Anthropologist* 82:782–98.
Schele, L.
1991   The Owl, Shield, and Flint Blade. *Natural History* (November):6–11.
Schele, L., and D. Freidel
1990   *A Forest of Kings.* William Morrow, New York.
Schele, L., and P. Mathews
1991   Royal Visits and Other Intersite Relationships among the Classic Maya. In *Classic Maya Political History,* edited by T. P. Culbert, pp. 226–52. School of American Research Advanced Seminar Series, Cambridge University Press, Cambridge.
Schele, L., and M. E. Miller
1986   *The Blood of Kings: Dynasty and Ritual in Maya Art.* George Braziller, New York.
Schmandt-Besserat, D.
1992   *Before Writing.* 2 vols. University of Texas Press, Austin.
1993   Images of Enship. In *Between the Rivers and Over the Mountains,* edited by M. Frangipane, H. Hauptmann, M. Liverani, P. Matthiae, and M. Mellink, pp. 201–20. Universita di Roma "La Sapienza," Rome.
Schneider, P., J. Schneider, and E. Hansen
1972   Modernization and Development: The Role of Regional Elites and Noncorporate Groups in the European Mediterranean. *Comparative Studies in Society and History* 14:328–50.
Schreiber, K. J.
1987   Conquest and Consolidation: A Comparison of the Wari and Inka Occupations of a Highland Peruvian Valley. *American Antiquity* 52:266–84.
1992   *Wari Imperialism in Middle Horizon Peru.* Anthropological Papers 87. Museum of Anthropology, University of Michigan, Ann Arbor.
Schwartz, B. I.
1985   *The World of Thought in Ancient China.* Belknap–Harvard University Press, Cambridge.
Schwartz, G.
1988   Excavations at Karatut Mevkii and Perspectives on the Uruk/Jemdet Nasr Expansion. *Akkadica* 56:1–41.
Scott, J. C.
1985   *Weapons of the Weak: Everyday Forms of Peasant Resistance.* Yale University Press, New Haven.
1990   *Domination and the Arts of Resistance: Hidden Transcripts.* Yale University Press, New Haven.

Seaton, S. L.
  1978   The Early State in Hawai'i. In *The Early State,* edited by H. Claessen and
          P. Skalník, pp. 269–88. Mouton, The Hague.
Seidlmayer, S. J.
  1996   Town and State in the Early Old Kingdom: A View from Elephantine. In *As-
          pects of Early Egypt,* edited by A. J. Spencer, pp. 108–27. British Museum Press,
          London.
Séjourné, L.
  1966   *Arquitectura y pintura en Teotihuacán.* Siglo XXI, Mexico, D.F.
Service, E. R.
  1962   *Primitive Social Organization: An Evolutionary Perspective.* Random House, New
          York.
  1963   *Profiles in Ethnology.* Harper and Row, New York.
  1975   *Origins of the State and Civilization.* Norton, New York.
Sewell, W. H., Jr.
  1992   A Theory of Structure: Duality, Agency, and Transformation. *American Journal
          of Sociology* 98:1–29.
Shaffer, A.
  1983   Gilgamesh, the Cedar Forest, and Mesopotamian History. *Journal of the Ameri-
          can Oriental Society* 103:307–13.
Shaffer, J. G.
  1982   Harappan Culture: A Reconsideration. In *Harappan Civilization: A Contempo-
          rary Perspective,* edited by G. L. Possehl, pp. 41–50. Oxford and IBH, and the
          American Institute of Indian Studies, Delhi.
  1992   The Indus Valley, Baluchistan and Helmand Traditions: Neolithic through
          Bronze Age. In *Chronologies in Old World Archaeology,* 2 vols., 3rd ed., edited
          by R. W. Ehrich, pp. 441–64 (vol. 1) and 425–46 (vol. 2). University of Chi-
          cago Press, Chicago.
  1993   Reurbanization: The Eastern Punjab and Beyond. In *Urban Form and Meaning
          in South Asia,* edited by H. Spodek and D. M. Srinivasan, pp. 53–67. Studies
          in the History of Art 31. Center for Advanced Study in the Visual Arts Sym-
          posium Papers 15. National Gallery of Art, Washington, D.C.
Shaffer, J. G., and D. A. Lichtenstein
  1989   Ethnicity and Change in the Indus Valley Cultural Tradition. In *Old Problems and
          New Perspectives in South Asian Archaeology,* edited by J. M. Kenoyer, pp. 117–26.
          Wisconsin Archaeological Reports 2. University of Wisconsin, Madison.
Shanks, M., and C. Tilley
  1982   Ideology, Symbolic Power and Ritual Communication: A Reinterpretation of
          Neolithic Mortuary Practices. In *Symbolic and Structural Archaeology,* edited by
          I. Hodder, pp. 129–54. Cambridge University Press, Cambridge.
Sharer, R. J.
  1978   Archaeology and History at Quiriguá, Guatemala. *Journal of Field Archaeology*
          5:51–70.
  1990   *Quirigua: A Classic Maya Center and Its Sculpture.* Carolina Academic Press,
          Durham, North Carolina.
  1991   Diversity and Continuity in Maya Civilization: Quirigua as a Case Study. In
          Classic Maya Political History, edited by T. P. Culbert, pp. 180–98. School of
          American Research Advanced Seminar Series, Cambridge University Press,
          Cambridge.
  1995   The Beginning and End of the Copán Dynasty. Paper presented at the UCLA
          Maya Weekend, October 28, Los Angeles.

Sharer, R. J., and W. Ashmore
1987   *Archaeology: Discovering Our Past.* Mayfield, Mountain View, California.
Sharer, R. J., D. Sedat, J. Miller, A. Morales, L. Traxler, C. Carrelli, L. Centeno, and
F. López
1994   Programa de investigación de la Acrópolis temprana de la Universidad de
        Pennsylvania: informe de la temporada de 1993. Manuscript on file, Museum
        of Anthropology, University of Michigan, Ann Arbor.
Sharpe, J. A.
1987   *Early Modern England: A Social History 1550–1760.* Edward Arnold, London.
Shifferd, P. A.
1987   Aztecs and Africans: Political Processes in Twenty-Two Early States. In *Early
        State Dynamics,* edited by H. J. M. Claessen and P. van de Velde, pp. 39–53.
        E. J. Brill, Leiden.
Shimada, I.
1994   *Pampa Grande and the Mochica Culture.* University of Texas Press, Austin.
Silverman, D. P.
1991   Divinity and Deities in Ancient Egypt. In *Religion in Ancient Egypt,* edited by
        B. E. Shafer, pp. 7–87. Cornell University Press, Ithaca.
Simon, H. A.
1969   The Architecture of Complexity. In *The Sciences of the Artificial,* by H. A.
        Simon, pp. 84–118. MIT Press, Cambridge.
1973   The Organization of Complex Systems. In *Hierarchy Theory: The Challenge of
        Complex Systems,* edited by H. H. Pattee, pp. 3–27. George Braziller, New
        York.
Sjöberg, Å. W.
1975   The Old Babylonian Eduba. In *Sumerological Studies in Honor of Thorkild Jacob-
        sen on His Seventieth Birthday, June 7, 1974,* edited by S. Lieberman, pp. 159–
        79. University of Chicago Press, Chicago.
Skalník, P.
1978   The Early State as a Process. In *The Early State,* edited by H. J. M. Claessen
        and P. Skalník, pp. 597–618. Mouton, The Hague.
1983   Questioning the Concept of the State in Indigenous Africa. *Social Dynamics*
        9(2):11–28.
Skinner, G. W.
1977a   Cities and the Hierarchy of Local Systems. In *The City in Late Imperial China,*
        edited by G. W. Skinner, pp. 275–351. Stanford University Press, Stanford.
1977b   Introduction: Urban Development in Imperial China. In *The City in Late Im-
        perial China,* edited by G. W. Skinner, pp. 3–31. Stanford University Press,
        Stanford.
1985   Presidential Address: The Structure of Chinese History. *Journal of Asian Stud-
        ies* 44(2):271–92.
Small, D. B.
1994   A Different Distinction: The Case of Ancient Greece. In *The Economic An-
        thropology of the State,* edited by E. Brumfiel, pp. 287–313. University Press of
        America, Lanham, Maryland.
Smelser, N. J.
1959   A Comparative View of Exchange Systems. In *Economic Development and Cul-
        tural Change* 7:173–82.
Smith, B. C.
1985   *Decentralization: The Territorial Dimension of the State.* George Allen and Unwin,
        London.

Smith, H. S.
1972   Society and Settlement in Ancient Egypt. In *Man, Settlement and Urbanism,* edited by P. J. Ucko, R. Tringham, and G. W. Dimbleby, pp. 705–19. Duckworth, London.

Smith, M. Estellie
1985   An Aspectual Analysis of Polity Formations. In *Development and Decline: The Evolution of Sociopolitical Organization,* edited by H. J. M. Claessen, P. van de Velde, and M. E. Smith, pp. 97–125. Bergin and Garvey, South Hadley, Massachusetts.

Smith, Mary Elizabeth
1983   Codex Selden: A Manuscript from the Valley of Nochixtlán? In *The Cloud People: Divergent Evolution of the Zapotec and Mixtec Civilizations,* edited by K. V. Flannery and J. Marcus, pp. 248–55. Academic Press, New York.
1994   Why the Second Codex Selden Was Painted. In *Caciques and Their People: A Volume in Honor of Ronald Spores,* edited by J. Marcus and J. F. Zeitlin, pp. 111–41. Anthropological Papers 89. Museum of Anthropology, University of Michigan, Ann Arbor.

Smith, Michael E.
1987   Imperial Strategies in the Western Portion of the Aztec Empire. Paper presented at the 86th Annual Meeting of the American Anthropological Association, Chicago.
1992   Rhythms of Change in Postclassic Central Mexico: Archaeology, Ethnohistory, and the Braudelian Model. In *Archaeology, Annales, and Ethnohistory,* edited by A. B. Knapp, pp. 51–74. Cambridge University Press, Cambridge.

Smith, Michael E., and F. F. Berdan
1992   Archaeology and the Aztec Empire. *World Archaeology* 23:353–67.

Smith, W. S.
1949   *A History of Egyptian Sculpture and Painting in the Old Kingdom.* 2nd ed. Museum of Fine Arts, Boston, and Oxford University Press, London.

Snodgrass, A. M.
1971   *The Dark Age of Greece.* University of Edinburgh, Edinburgh.
1977   *Archaeology and the Rise of the Greek State.* Cambridge University Press, Cambridge.
1980   *Archaic Greece: The Age of Experiment.* J. M. Dent and Sons, London.
1986   Interaction by Design: The Greek City-State. In *Peer Polity Interaction and Socio-Political Change,* edited by C. Renfrew and J. F. Cherry, pp. 47–58. Cambridge University Press, Cambridge.

Sommerfeld, Walter
1987–90   Marduk. *Reallexikon der Assyriologie* 7:360–70. Walter de Gruyter, Berlin.

Sorre, M.
1962   The Concept of Genre de Vie. In *Readings in Cultural Geography,* edited by P. L. Wagner and M. W. Mikesell, pp. 399–415. University of Chicago Press, Chicago.

Southall, A. W.
1952   *Lineage Formation among the Luo.* International Africa Institute, Memorandum 31. Oxford University Press, London.
1956   *Alur Society: A Study in Processes and Types of Domination.* Heffer, Cambridge.
1965   A Critique of the Typology of States and Political Systems. In *Political Systems and the Distribution of Power,* edited by M. Banton, pp. 113–40. ASA Monograph 2. Tavistock, London.

1988   The Segmentary State in Africa and Asia. *Comparative Studies in Society and History* 30:52–82.

1991   The Segmentary State: From the Imaginary to the Material Means of Production. In *Early State Economics,* edited by H. Claessen and P. van de Velde, pp. 75–96. Transaction Publishers, New Brunswick, New Jersey.

Spencer, C. S.

1982   *The Cuicatlán Cañada and Monte Albán: A Study of Primary State Formation.* Academic Press, New York.

1987   Rethinking the Chiefdom. In *Chiefdoms in the Americas,* edited by R. D. Drennan and C. A. Uribe, pp. 369–90. University Press of America, Lanham, Maryland.

1990   On the Tempo and Mode of State Formation: Neoevolutionism Reconsidered. *Journal of Anthropological Archaeology* 9:1–30.

1993   Human Agency, Biased Transmission, and the Cultural Evolution of Chiefly Authority. *Journal of Anthropological Archaeology* 12:41–74.

Spencer, H.

1885   *The Principles of Sociology,* vol. 1. 3rd ed. Appleton, New York.

1967   *The Evolution of Society.* Edited and with an introduction by R. L. Carneiro. University of Chicago Press, Chicago.

Spores, R.

1967   *The Mixtec Kings and Their People.* University of Oklahoma Press, Norman.

1969   Settlement, Farming Technology, and Environment in the Nochixtlán Valley. *Science* 166:557–69.

1972   *An Archaeological Settlement Survey of the Nochixtlán Valley, Oaxaca.* Publications in Anthropology 1. Vanderbilt University, Nashville.

1974   Marital Alliance in the Political Integration of Mixtec Kingdoms. *American Anthropologist* 76:297–311.

1983a   Yucuñudahui. In *The Cloud People: Divergent Evolution of the Zapotec and Mixtec Civilizations,* edited by K. V. Flannery and J. Marcus, pp. 155–58. Academic Press, New York.

1983b   Postclassic Settlement Patterns in the Nochixtlán Valley. In *The Cloud People: Divergent Evolution of the Zapotec and Mixtec Civilizations,* edited by K. V. Flannery and J. Marcus, pp. 246–48. Academic Press, New York.

1983c   Postclassic Mixtec Kingdoms: Ethnohistoric and Archaeological Evidence. In *The Cloud People: Divergent Evolution of the Zapotec and Mixtec Civilizations,* edited by K. V. Flannery and J. Marcus, pp. 255–60. Academic Press, New York.

Spriggs, M.

1988   The Hawai'ian Transformation of Ancestral Polynesian Society: Conceptualizing Chiefly States. In *State and Society,* edited by J. Gledhill, B. Bender, and M. T. Larsen, pp. 57–76. Unwin Hyman, London.

Stein, B.

1977   The Segmentary State in South Indian History. In *Realm and Region in Traditional India,* edited by R. J. Fox, pp. 3–51. Duke University Press, Durham, North Carolina.

Stein, G.

1991   Imported Ideologies and Local Identities: North Mesopotamia in the Fifth Millennium B.C. Paper presented at the 56th Annual Meeting of the Society of American Archaeology, New Orleans.

1993   Ethnicity, Exchange, and Emulation: Mesopotamian–Anatolian Interaction at

Haçinebi, Turkey. Paper presented at the 58th Annual Meeting of the Society of American Archaeology, St. Louis.

1994a   Segmentary States and Organizational Variation in Early Complex Societies: A Rural Perspective. In *Archaeological Views from the Countryside: Village Communities in Early Complex Societies,* edited by G. M. Schwartz and S. E. Falconer, pp. 10–18. Smithsonian Institution Press, Washington, D.C.

1994b   Economy, Ritual, and Power in ʿUbaid Mesopotamia. In *Chiefdoms and Early States in the Near East: The Organizational Dynamics of Complexity,* edited by G. Stein and M. S. Rothman, pp. 35–46. Prehistory Press, Madison, Wisconsin.

Stein, G., R. Bernbeck, C. Coursey, A. McMahon, N. Miller, A. Misir, J. Nichols, H. Pittman, S. Pollock, and H. Wright
1996   Uruk Colonies and Anatolian Communities: An Interim Report on the 1992–1993 Excavations at Haçinebi, Turkey. *American Journal of Archaeology* 100:205–60.

Steinkeller, P.
1987   The Administrative and Economic Organization of the Ur III State: The Core and the Periphery. In *The Organization of Power: Aspects of Bureaucracy in the Ancient Near East,* edited by M. Gibson and R. D. Biggs, pp. 19–41. Studies in Ancient Civilization 46. Oriental Institute, University of Chicago, Chicago.
1989   *Sale Documents of the Ur III Period.* Freiburger Altorientalische Studien 17. Franz Steiner, Wiesbaden and Stuttgart.

Stemper, D.
1989   *The Persistence of Prehispanic Chiefdom Formations, Río Daule, Coastal Ecuador.* Ph.D. dissertation, Department of Anthropology, University of Wisconsin, Madison.

Stéve, M.-J., and H. Gasche
1973   *L'Acropole de Suse. Mémoires de la Délégation Archéologique Française en Iran XLVI.* Paul Guethner, Paris.
1990   Le Tell de l'Apadana avant les Achemenides. Contribution à la topographie de Suse. In *Melanges Jean Perrot,* edited by F. Vallat, pp. 15–60. Editions Recherche sur les Civilisations, Paris.

Steward, J. H.
1949   Cultural Causality and Law: A Trial Formulation of the Development of Early Civilizations. *American Anthropologist* 51:1–27.
1955   *Theory of Culture Change: The Methodology of Multilinear Evolution.* University of Illinois Press, Urbana.

Stol, M.
1982   State and Private Business in the Land of Larsa. *Journal of Cuneiform Studies* 33:127–230.

Stone, E. C.
1981   Texts, Architecture, and Ethnographic Analogy. *Iraq* 43:19–33.
1987   *Nippur Neighborhoods.* Studies in Ancient Oriental Civilization 44. Oriental Institute, University of Chicago, Chicago.

Strommenger, E.
1980   *Habuba Kabira: Eine Stadt vor 5000 Jahren.* Phillip von Zabern, Mainz.

Strudwick, N.
1985   *The Administration of Egypt in the Old Kingdom: The Highest Titles and Their Holders.* Studies in Egyptology. KPI, London.

Stuart, D.
1992   Hieroglyphs and Archaeology at Copán. *Ancient Mesoamerica* 3(1):169–84.

1993   Historical Inscriptions and the Maya Collapse. In *Lowland Maya Civilization in the Eighth Century A.D.,* edited by J. A. Sabloff and J. S. Henderson, pp. 321–54. Dumbarton Oaks, Washington, D.C.

1995   *A Study of Maya Inscriptions.* Ph.D. dissertation, Department of Anthropology, Vanderbilt University, Nashville.

Stuart, G.
1993   New Light on the Olmec. *National Geographic Magazine* 184(5):88–114.

Stumer, L. M.
1954   Population Centers of the Rimac Valley of Peru. *American Antiquity* 20:130–48.

Suggs, R. C.
1960   *The Island Civilizations of Polynesia.* New American Library, New York.

Sugiyama, S.
1989   Burials Dedicated to the Old Temple of Quetzalcoatl at Teotihuacán, Mexico. *American Antiquity* 54:85–106.

Sürenhagen, D.
1986   The Dry-Farming Belt: The Uruk Period and Subsequent Developments. In *The Origin of Cities in Dry Farming Syria and Mesopotamia in the Third Millennium B.C.,* edited by H. Weiss, pp. 7–43. Four Quarters, Guilford, Connecticut.

Symonds, S. C., and R. Lunagómez
1994   Settlement System and Population Development at San Lorenzo, Veracruz, Mexico. Manuscript on file, American Museum of Natural History, New York.

Taagepera, R.
1968   Growth Curves of Empires. *General Systems* 13:171–75.

1978a   Size and Duration of Empires: Systematics of Size. *Social Science Research* 7:108–27.

1978b   Size and Duration of Empires: Growth-Decline Curves, 3000 to 600 B.C. *Social Science Research* 7:180–96.

1979   Size and Duration of Empires: Growth-Decline Curves, 600 B.C. to 600 A.D. *Social Science History* 3:115–38.

Tadmor, H.
1986   Monarchy and the Elite in Assyria and Babylonia: The Question of Royal Accountability. In *The Origins and Diversity of Axial Age Civilizations,* edited by S. N. Eisenstadt, pp. 203–24. SUNY Series in Near Eastern Studies, State University of New York Press, Albany.

Tainter, J.
1988   *The Collapse of Complex Societies.* Cambridge University Press, London.

Tambiah, S. J.
1976   *World Conqueror and World Renouncer: A Study of Buddhism and Polity in Thailand against a Historical Background.* Cambridge Studies in Social Anthropology 15. Cambridge University Press, Cambridge.

1977   The Galactic Polity: The Structure of Traditional Kingdoms in Southeast Asia. *Annals of the New York Academy of Sciences* 293:69–97.

Taylour, Lord W.
1983   *The Mycenaeans.* Revised ed. Thames and Hudson, London.

Thapar, B. K.
1973   New Traits of the Indus Civilization at Kalibangan: An Appraisal. In *South Asian Archaeology,* edited by N. Hammond, pp. 85–104. Noyes Press, Park Ridge, New Jersey.

Thomas, K.
1978   *Religion and the Decline of Magic: Studies in Popular Beliefs in Sixteenth- and*

Seventeenth-Century England. Revised reprint. Penguin, London. (Originally published in 1971, Weidenfeld and Nicholson, London.)

Thompson, J. E. S.
1954   *The Rise and Fall of Maya Civilization.* University of Oklahoma Press, Norman.

Thureau-Dangin, F.
1921   *Rituels accadiens.* Ernest Leroux, Paris.

Tilly, L. A., and C. Tilly (editors)
1981   *Class Conflict and Collective Action.* Sage, Beverly Hills.

Tobler, A. J.
1950   *Excavations at Tepe Gawra,* vol. II. University of Pennsylvania Museum, Philadelphia.

Topic, J. R.
1982   Lower-Class Social and Economic Organization. In *Chan Chan: Andean Desert City,* edited by M. E. Moseley and K. C. Day, pp. 145–75. University of New Mexico Press, Albuquerque.

Tosi, M.
1977   The Archaeological Evidence for Protostate Structures in Eastern Iran and Central Asia at the End of the 3rd mill. B.C. In *Le Plateau Iranien et l'Asie Centrale des Origins a la Conquete Islamique,* edited by J.-C. Gardin, pp. 45–66. Colloques Internationaux 567. Centre National de la Recherche Scientifique, Paris.

1979a   The Development of Urban Societies in Turan and the Mesopotamian Trade with the East: The Evidence from Shahr-i Sokhta. In *Mesopotamien und Seine Nachbarn,* edited by H. J. Nissen and J. Renger, pp. 57–77. Dietrich Reimer Verlag, Berlin.

1979b   The Proto-Urban Cultures of Eastern Iran and the Indus Civilization. In *South Asian Archaeology 1977,* edited by M. Taddei, pp. 149–71. Series Minor 6. Instituto Universitario Orientale, Seminario di Studi Asiatici, Naples.

1986   The Archaeology of Early States in Middle Asia. *Oriens Antiquus* 25:153–87.

Traxler, L. P.
1996   Early Courts of the Copán Acropolis. Paper presented at the 61st Annual Meeting of the Society for American Archaeology, New Orleans.

Trigger, B. G.
1972   Determinants of Urban Growth in Pre-industrial Societies. In *Man, Settlement and Urbanism,* edited by P. J. Ucko, R. Tringham, and G. W. Dimbleby, pp. 575–99. Duckworth, London.

1990   Maintaining Economic Equality in Opposition to Complexity: An Iroquoian Case Study. In *The Evolution of Political Systems: Sociopolitics in Small-Scale Sedentary Societies,* edited by S. Upham, pp. 119–45. Cambridge University Press, Cambridge.

1993   *Early Civilizations: Ancient Egypt in Context.* American University in Cairo Press, Cairo.

Tyumenev, A. I.
1969   The Working Personnel on the Estate of the Temple of Ba-U in Lagash during the Period of Lugalanda and Urakagina (25th–24th cent. B.C.). In *Ancient Mesopotamia,* edited by I. M. Diakonoff, pp. 88–126. Nauka Publishing House, Moscow.

Uhle, M.
1902   Types of Culture in Peru. *American Anthropologist* 4:753–59.
1903   Ancient South American Civilization. *Harper's Monthly Magazine* 107:780–86.

1913   Zur Chronologie der alten Culturen von Ica. *Journal de la Société des Américanistes de Paris* (n.s.) 10:341–67.

University of Chicago
1992   *The Dictionary of the Oriental Institute of the University of Chicago*. Oriental Institute, University of Chicago, Chicago.

Upham, S.
1987   A Theoretical Consideration of Middle Range Societies. In *Chiefdoms in the Americas,* edited by R. D. Drennan and C. A. Uribe, pp. 345–68. University Press of America, Lanham, Maryland.

Valdés, J. A., and F. Fahsen
1995   The Reigning Dynasty of Uaxactun during the Early Classic: The Rulers and the Ruled. *Ancient Mesoamerica* 6:197–219.

Vallat, F.
1993   *Les noms géographiques des sources suso-èlamites.* Répertoire Géographique des Textes Cuneiformes XI. Beihefte zum Tübinger Atlas des Vorderen Orients, Reihe B, No. 7. Reichert Verlag, Wiesbaden.

van de Mieroop, M.
1992   *Society and Enterprise in Old Babylonian Ur.* Berliner Beiträge zum Vorderen Orient 12. Dietrich Reimer, Berlin.

van der Vliet, E. C. L.
1987   Tyranny and Democracy: The Evolution of Politics in Ancient Greece. In *Early State Dynamics,* edited by H. J. M. Claessen and P. van de Velde, pp. 70–90. E. J. Brill, Leiden.

van Driel, G.
1983   Seals and Sealings from Jebel Aruda, 1974–1978. *Akkadica* 33:34–62.

van Zantwijk, R.
1985   *The Aztec Arrangement: The Social History of Pre-Spanish Mexico.* University of Oklahoma Press, Norman.

van Zeist, W., and S. Bottema
1977   Palynological Investigations in Western Iran. *Palaeohistoria* 19:19–95.

Vats, M. S.
1940   *Excavations at Harappa.* 2 vols. Government of India, Delhi.

Vayda, A.
1960   *Maori Warfare.* The Polynesian Society, Wellington.
1976   *War in Ecological Perspective.* Plenum Press, New York.

Veenhof, K.
1972   *Aspects of Old Assyrian Trade and Its Terminology.* E. J. Brill, Leiden.
1980   Kanish, Kārum. In *Reallexikon der Assyriologie* 5:369–78.

Veyne, P.
1990   *Bread and Circuses: Historical Sociology and Political Pluralism.* Translated by B. Pearce. Penguin, London.

Villar, M. del
1996   La indumentaria en los cautivos mayas del Clásico. *Arqueología Mexicana* 3(17): 66–71.

Vincent, J.
1986   System and Process, 1974–1985. *Annual Review of Anthropology* 15:99–119.
1990   *Anthropology and Politics: Visions, Traditions, and Trends.* University of Arizona Press, Tucson.

Vogelzang, M., and H. Vanstiphout (editors)
1992   *Mesopotamian Epic Literature: Oral or Aural?* Edwin Mellen, Lewiston, New York.

Voorhies, B.
1989   A Model of the Pre-Aztec Political System of Soconusco. In *Ancient Trade and Tribute: Economies of the Soconusco Region of Mesoamerica,* edited by B. Voorhies, pp. 95–129. University of Utah Press, Salt Lake City.

Waddell, L. A.
1925   *The Indo-Sumerian Seals Deciphered: Discovering Sumerians of Indus Valley as Phoenicians, Barats, Goths and Famous Vedic Aryans, 3100–2300 B.C.* Luzac, London.

Wallace, A. F. C.
1971   Administrative Forms of Social Organization. *Addison-Wesley Modular Publications* 9:1–12.

Wallerstein, I.
1979   A World-System Perspective on the Social Sciences. In *The Capitalist World-Economy,* pp. 152–64. Cambridge University Press, Cambridge.
1992   The Challenge of Maturity: Whither Social Science? *Review* 15:1–7.

Walther, A.
1917   Das altbabylonische Gerichtswesen. *Leipziger Semitische Studien* 6:4–6. Leipzig.

Wattenmaker, P.
1990   On the Uruk Expansion. *Current Anthropology* 31:67–68.

Weaver, M. P.
1993   *The Aztecs, Maya, and Their Predecessors.* 3rd ed. Academic Press, New York.

Weber, M.
1946   *From Max Weber: Essays in Sociology.* Translated by H. H. Gerth and C. W. Mills. Oxford University Press, New York.
1947   *The Theory of Social and Economic Organization.* Translated by A. M. Henderson and T. Parsons. The Free Press, Glencoe, Illinois.
1951   *The Religion of China: Confucianism and Taoism.* The Free Press, Glencoe, Illinois.
1978   *Economy and Society: An Outline of Interpretive Sociology.* Edited by G. Roth and C. Wittich. University of California Press, Berkeley.

Webster, D.
1975   Warfare and the Origin of the State. *American Antiquity* 40:464–71.
1976a   Lowland Maya Fortifications. *Proceedings of the American Philosophical Society* 120:361–71. Philadelphia.
1976b   *Defensive Earthworks at Becan, Campeche, Mexico: Implications for Maya Warfare.* Publication 41. Middle American Research Institute, Tulane University, New Orleans.
1985   Surplus, Labor and Stress in Late Classic Maya Society. *Journal of Anthropological Research* 41:375–99.
1989   *The House of the Bacabs: Introduction.* Studies in Precolumbian Art and Archaeology 29. Dumbarton Oaks, Washington, D.C.
1992   Mesoamerican Elites: The View from Copán. In *Mesoamerican Elites: An Archaeological Assessment,* edited by D. Chase and A. Chase, pp. 135–56. University of Oklahoma Press, Norman.
1993   The Study of Maya Warfare: What It Tells Us about the Maya and about Maya Archaeology. In *Lowland Maya Civilization in the Eighth Century A.D.,* edited by J. A. Sabloff and J. S. Henderson, pp. 415–44. Dumbarton Oaks, Washington, D.C.

Webster, D., W. T. Sanders, and P. van Rossum
1992   A Simulation of Copán Population History and Its Implications. *Ancient Mesoamerica* 3(1):185–98.

Wei-Ming, T.
1986   The Structure and Function of the Confucian Intellectual in Ancient China. In *The Origins and Diversity of Axial Age Civilizations,* edited by S. N. Eisenstadt, pp. 360–73. State University of New York Press, Albany.

Weiss, H., and T. C. Young, Jr.
1975   The Merchants of Susa. *Iran XIII:* 1–17.

Wesson, R. G.
1978   *State Systems: International Pluralism, Politics, and Culture.* Free Press, New York.

Westenholz, A.
1984   The Sargonic Period. In *Circulation of Goods in Non-Palatial Context in the Ancient Near East,* edited by A. Archi, pp. 17–30. Incunabula Græca, Rome.

Wetterstrom, W.
1993   Foraging and Farming in Egypt: The Transition from Hunting and Gathering to Horticulture in the Nile Valley. In *The Archaeology of Africa: Food, Metals and Towns,* edited by T. Shaw, P. Sinclair, B. Andah, and A. Okpoko, pp. 165–226. Routledge, London.

Wheatley, P.
1971   *The Pivot of the Four Quarters: A Preliminary Enquiry into the Origins and Character of the Ancient Chinese City.* Aldine, Chicago, and Edinburgh University Press, Edinburgh.

Wheeler, R. E. M.
1947   Harappa 1946: The Defenses and Cemetery R-37. *Ancient India* 3:58–130.
1950   *Five Thousand Years of Pakistan: An Archaeological Outline.* Royal India and Pakistan Society, London.
1959   *Early India and Pakistan: To Ashoka.* Frederick A. Praeger, New York.
1968   *The Indus Civilization.* 3rd ed. Supplementary volume to the Cambridge Ancient History of India. University of Cambridge Press, Cambridge.

Whitecotton, J.
1992   Culture and Exchange in Postclassic Oaxaca: A World-System Perspective. In *Resources, Power, and Interregional Interaction,* edited by E. M. Schortman and P. A. Urban, pp. 51–74. Plenum Press, New York.

Whiting, R. M.
1987   *Old Babylonian Letters from Tell Asmar.* Assyriological Studies 22. Oriental Institute, University of Chicago, Chicago.

Widmer, R. J., and R. Storey
1993   Social Organization and Household Structure of a Teotihuacán Apartment Compound: S3W1:33 of the Tlajinga Barrio. In *Prehispanic Domestic Units in Western Mesoamerica: Studies of the Household, Compound, and Residence,* edited by R. S. Santley and K. G. Hirth, pp. 87–104. CRC Press, Boca Raton, Florida.

Wilcke, C.
1973   Politische Opposition nach sumerischen Quellen. In *La voix de l'opposition en Mésopotamie,* edited by A. Finet, pp. 37–65. Institut des Hautes Etudes de Belgique, Brussels.

Willey, G. R.
1974   The Classic Maya Hiatus: A Rehearsal for the Collapse? In *Mesoamerican Archaeology: New Approaches,* edited by N. Hammond, pp. 417–44. Duckworth, London.
1991   Horizontal Integration and Regional Diversity: An Alternating Process in the Rise of Civilization. *American Antiquity* 56:197–215.

Williams, B. B.
1986 *Excavations between Abu Simbel and the Sudan Frontier I: The A-Group Royal Cemetery at Qustul: Cemetery L.* Oriental Institute Nubian Expedition 3. Oriental Institute, University of Chicago, Chicago.

Williamson, R. W.
1937 *Religion and Social Organization in Central Polynesia.* Edited by R. Piddington. Cambridge University Press, London.

Wilson, D. J.
1988 *Prehispanic Settlement Patterns in the Lower Santa Valley, Peru: A Regional Perspective on the Origins and Development of Complex North Coast Society.* Smithsonian Institution Press, Washington, D.C.

1992 Modeling the Role of Ideology in Societal Adaptation: Examples from the South American Data. In *Ideology and Pre-Columbian Civilizations,* edited by A. A. Demarest and G. W. Conrad, pp. 37–63. School of American Research Press, Santa Fe.

1995 Prehispanic Settlement Patterns in the Casma Valley, North Coast of Peru. Report to the National Geographic Society, Washington, D.C.

Winter, E.
1968 *Untersuchungen zu den ägyptischen Tempelreliefs der griechisch-römischen Zeit.* Österreichische Akademie der Wissenschaften, Philosophisch-Historische Klasse, Denkschriften 98. Hermann Böhlaus Nachfolger, Vienna.

1976 Der Herrscherkult in den ägyptischen Ptolemäertempeln. In *Das ptolemäische Ägypten: Akten des internationalen Symposions, 27.–29. September 1976 in Berlin,* edited by H. Maehler and V. M. Strocka, pp. 147–60. Philipp von Zabern, Mainz.

Winter, I. J.
1981 Royal Rhetoric and the Development of Historical Narrative in Neo-Assyrian Reliefs. *Studies in Visual Communication* 7(2):2–38.

1983 The Program of the Throneroom of Assurnasirpal II. In *Essays in Middle Eastern Art and Archaeology in Honor of C.-K. Wilkinson,* edited by P. Harper and H. Pittman, pp. 15–32. Metropolitan Museum of Art, New York.

1991 Reading Concepts of Space from Ancient Mesopotamian Monuments. In *Concepts of Space, Ancient and Modern,* edited by K. Vatsyayan, pp. 57–73. Abhinav, New Delhi.

1992 "Idols of the King": Royal Images as Recipients of Ritual Action in Ancient Mesopotamia. *Journal of Ritual Studies* 6:13–42.

1995 Aesthetics in Ancient Mesopotamian Art. In *Civilizations of the Ancient Near East,* vol. IV, edited by J. Sasson, pp. 2569–82. Scribners, New York.

Winter, M. C.
1984 Exchange in Formative Highland Oaxaca. In *Trade and Exchange in Early Mesoamerica,* edited by K. G. Hirth, pp. 179–214. University of New Mexico Press, Albuquerque.

Wirsing, R.
1973 Political Power and Information: A Cross-Cultural Study. *American Anthropologist* 75:153–70.

Wolf, E. R.
1951 The Social Organization of Mecca and the Origins of Islam. *Southwest Journal of Anthropology* 7:329–56.

1982 *Europe and the People without History.* University of California Press, Berkeley.

Wolf, E. R., and E. C. Hansen
1972   *The Human Condition in Latin America.* Oxford University Press, New York.
Woodburn, J.
1982   Egalitarian Societies. *Man* (n.s.) 17:431–51.
Woolley, C. L.
1934   *Ur Excavations 2: The Royal Cemetery.* British Museum, London, and University of Pennsylvania Museum, Philadelphia.
Woolley, C. L., and P. R. S. Moorey
1982   *Ur of the Chaldees.* Revised ed. Herbert Press, London.
Wright, H. T.
1969   *The Administration of Production in an Early Mesopotamian Town.* Anthropological Papers 38. Museum of Anthropology, University of Michigan, Ann Arbor.
1977   Recent Research on the Origin of the State. *Annual Review of Anthropology* 6:379–97.
1978   Toward an Explanation of the Origin of the State. In *Origins of the State: The Anthropology of Political Evolution,* edited by R. Cohen and E. R. Service, pp. 49–68. Institute for the Study of Human Issues, Philadelphia.
1980   Past Mastery. *Comparative Studies in Society and History* 22:222–26.
1985   Excavations of IVth Millennium Levels on the Northern Acropolis of Susa, 1978. *National Geographic Society Research Reports* 21:725–34. National Geographic Society, Washington, D.C.
1986a   The Evolution of Civilizations. In *American Archaeology Past and Future: A Celebration of the Society for American Archaeology, 1935–1985,* edited by D. J. Meltzer, D. D. Fowler, and J. A. Sabloff, pp. 323–65. Smithsonian Institution Press, Washington, D.C.
1986b   The Susiana Hinterlands during the Era of Primary State Formation. In *The Archaeology of Western Iran,* edited by F. Hole, pp. 141–55. Smithsonian Institution Press, Washington, D.C.
1994   Prestate Political Formations. In *Chiefdoms and Early States in the Near East: Organizational Dynamics of Complexity,* edited by G. Stein and M. S. Rothman, pp. 67–84. Prehistory Press, Madison, Wisconsin. (Originally published in 1984.)
Wright, H. T. (editor)
1979   *Archaeological Investigations in Northeastern Xuzestan, 1976.* Technical Reports 10. Museum of Anthropology, University of Michigan, Ann Arbor.
1981   *An Early Town on the Deh Luran Plain: Excavations at Tepe Farukhabad.* Memoirs 13. Museum of Anthropology, University of Michigan, Ann Arbor.
Wright, H. T., and G. A. Johnson
1975   Population, Exchange, and Early State Formation in Southwestern Iran. *American Anthropologist* 77:267–89.
1985   Regional Perspectives on Southwestern Iranian State Development. *Paléorient* 11(2):25–30.
Wright, H. T., N. Miller, and R. Redding
1980   Time and Process in an Uruk Rural Community. In *L'archéologie de l'Iraq: perspectives et limites de l'interpretation anthropologiques des documents,* edited by M.-T. Barrelet, pp. 265–84. Colloques Internationaux 580. Centre National de la Recherche Scientifique, Paris.
Wright, H. T., R. Redding, and S. Pollock
1989   Monitoring Interannual Variability: An Example from the Period of Early State Development in Southwestern Iran. In *Bad Year Economics: Cultural Re-*

sponses to Risk and Uncertainty, edited by P. Halstead and J. O'Shea, pp. 106–13. Cambridge University Press, Cambridge.

Wrightson, K.

1982   *English Society 1580–1680.* Unwin Hyman, London.

Wrong, D. H.

1979   *Power: Its Forms, Bases and Uses.* Harper and Row, New York.

Yang, M. M.-H.

1989   The Gift Economy and State Power in China. *Comparative Studies in Society and History* 31:25–54.

Yoffee, N.

1977   *The Economic Role of the Crown in the Old Babylonian Period.* Bibliotheca Mesopotamica 5. Undena, Malibu, California.

1982   Social History and Historical Method in the Late Old Babylonian Period. *Journal of the American Oriental Society* 102:347–53.

1988a   Orienting Collapse. In *The Collapse of Ancient States and Civilizations,* edited by N. Yoffee and G. L. Cowgill, pp. 1–19. University of Arizona Press, Tucson.

1988b   The Collapse of Ancient Mesopotamian States and Civilizations. In *The Collapse of Ancient States and Civilizations,* edited by N. Yoffee and G. L. Cowgill, pp. 44–68. University of Arizona Press, Tucson.

1991   Maya Elite Interaction: Through a Glass, Sideways. In *Classic Maya Political History: Hieroglyphic and Archaeological Evidence,* edited by T. P. Culbert, pp. 285–310. School of American Research Advanced Seminar Series, Cambridge University Press, Cambridge.

1992   Reading between the Lines, Sideways, from a Distance: Anthropological Perspectives on Ancient Mesopotamian Economy and Society. Paper presented at the conference on "Documenting Cultures: Written and Unwritten in Preindustrial Societies," Columbia University, New York.

1993a   Mesopotamian Interaction Spheres. In *Early States and the Evolution of Mesopotamian Civilization: Soviet Excavations in the Sinjar Plain, Northern Iraq,* edited by N. Yoffee and J. J. Clark, pp. 257–69. University of Arizona Press, Tucson.

1993b   Too Many Chiefs? or Safe Texts for the 90s. In *Archaeological Theory: Who Sets the Agenda?* edited by N. Yoffee and A. Sherratt, pp. 60–78. Cambridge University Press, Cambridge.

1993c   The Late Great Tradition in Ancient Mesopotamia. In *The Tablet and the Scroll: Near Eastern Studies in Honor of William W. Hallo,* edited by M. E. Cohen, D. C. Snell, and D. B. Weisberg, pp. 300–308. CDL Press, Bethesda, Maryland.

1995a   Conclusion: A Mass in Celebration of the Conference. In *The Archaeology of Society in the Holy Land,* edited by T. E. Levy, pp. 542–48. Facts on File, New York.

1995b   Political Economy in Early Mesopotamian States. *Annual Review of Anthropology* 24:281–311.

1997   The Obvious and the Chimerical: City-States in Archaeological Perspective. In *The Archaeology of City-States: Cross-Cultural Approaches,* edited by D. L. Nichols and T. H. Charlton, pp. 255–63. Smithsonian Institution Press, Washington D.C.

Yoffee, N., and G. L. Cowgill (editors)

1988   *The Collapse of Ancient States and Civilizations.* University of Arizona Press, Tucson.

Young, T. C., Jr.
  1969   *Excavations at Godin Tepe: First Progress Report.* Royal Ontario Museum, Toronto.
  1986   Godin Tepe Period VI/V and Central Western Iran at the End of the Fourth Millennium. In *Ǧamdat Nasr: Period or Regional Style?* edited by U. Finkbeiner and W. Röllig, pp. 212–28. Beihefte zum Tübinger Atlas des Vorderen Orients, Reihe B, 62. Reichert Verlag, Wiesbaden.
Zimansky, P.
  1993   Review of Denise Schmandt-Besserat, *Before Writing. Journal of Field Archaeology* 20:513–17.
Zuidema, R. T.
  1964   *The Ceque System of Cuzco.* International Archives of Ethnography, Supplement to vol. 50, Leiden.

Index

School of American Research
Advanced Seminar Series

PUBLISHED BY SAR PRESS

PUBLISHED BY CAMBRIDGE UNIVERSITY PRESS

DREAMING: ANTHROPOLOGICAL AND
PSYCHOLOGICAL INTERPRETATIONS
Barbara Tedlock, ed.

THE ANASAZI IN A CHANGING
ENVIRONMENT
George J. Gumerman, ed.

REGIONAL PERSPECTIVES ON THE OLMEC
Robert J. Sharer & David C. Grove, eds.

THE CHEMISTRY OF PREHISTORIC
HUMAN BONE
T. Douglas Price, ed.

THE EMERGENCE OF MODERN HUMANS:
BIOCULTURAL ADAPTATIONS IN THE
LATER PLEISTOCENE
Erik Trinkaus, ed.

THE ANTHROPOLOGY OF WAR
Jonathan Haas, ed.

THE EVOLUTION OF POLITICAL SYSTEMS
Steadman Upham, ed.

CLASSIC MAYA POLITICAL HISTORY:
HIEROGLYPHIC AND ARCHAEOLOGICAL
EVIDENCE
T. Patrick Culbert, ed.

TURKO-PERSIA IN HISTORICAL
PERSPECTIVE
Robert L. Canfield, ed.

CHIEFDOMS: POWER, ECONOMY, AND
IDEOLOGY
Timothy Earle, ed.

PUBLISHED BY UNIVERSITY OF CALIFORNIA PRESS

WRITING CULTURE: THE POETICS
AND POLITICS OF ETHNOGRAPHY
*James Clifford &
George E. Marcus, eds.*

PUBLISHED BY UNIVERSITY OF NEW MEXICO PRESS

RECONSTRUCTING PREHISTORIC PUEBLO
SOCIETIES
William A. Longacre, ed.

NEW PERSPECTIVES ON THE PUEBLOS
Alfonso Ortiz, ed.

STRUCTURE AND PROCESS IN LATIN
AMERICA
Arnold Strickon &
Sidney M. Greenfield, eds.

THE CLASSIC MAYA COLLAPSE
T. Patrick Culbert, ed.

METHODS AND THEORIES OF
ANTHROPOLOGICAL GENETICS
M. H. Crawford & P. L. Workman, eds.

SIXTEENTH-CENTURY MEXICO: THE
WORK OF SAHAGUN
Munro S. Edmonson, ed.

ANCIENT CIVILIZATION AND TRADE
Jeremy A. Sabloff &
C. C. Lamberg-Karlovsky, eds.

PHOTOGRAPHY IN ARCHAEOLOGICAL
RESEARCH
Elmer Harp, Jr., ed.

MEANING IN ANTHROPOLOGY
Keith H. Basso & Henry A. Selby, eds.

THE VALLEY OF MEXICO: STUDIES IN
PRE-HISPANIC ECOLOGY AND SOCIETY
Eric R. Wolf, ed.

DEMOGRAPHIC ANTHROPOLOGY:
QUANTITATIVE APPROACHES
Ezra B. W. Zubrow, ed.

THE ORIGINS OF MAYA CIVILIZATION
Richard E. W. Adams, ed.

EXPLANATION OF PREHISTORIC CHANGE
James N. Hill, ed.

EXPLORATIONS IN ETHNOARCHAEOLOGY
Richard A. Gould, ed.

ENTREPRENEURS IN CULTURAL CONTEXT
Sidney M. Greenfield, Arnold Strickon,
& Robert T. Aubey, eds.

THE DYING COMMUNITY
Art Gallaher, Jr., &
Harlan Padfield, eds.

SOUTHWESTERN INDIAN RITUAL DRAMA
Charlotte J. Frisbie, ed.

LOWLAND MAYA SETTLEMENT PATTERNS
Wendy Ashmore, ed.

SIMULATIONS IN ARCHAEOLOGY
Jeremy A. Sabloff, ed.

CHAN CHAN: ANDEAN DESERT CITY
Michael E. Moseley & Kent C. Day, eds.

SHIPWRECK ANTHROPOLOGY
Richard A. Gould, ed.

ELITES: ETHNOGRAPHIC ISSUES
George E. Marcus, ed.

THE ARCHAEOLOGY OF LOWER CENTRAL
AMERICA
Frederick W. Lange &
Doris Z. Stone, eds.

LATE LOWLAND MAYA CIVILIZATION:
CLASSIC TO POSTCLASSIC
Jeremy A. Sabloff &
E. Wyllys Andrews V, eds.

Participants in the School of American Research advanced seminar "The Archaic State," Santa Fe, November 1992. Front row, from left: Kent Flannery, Richard Blanton, David Webster, Joyce Marcus, Norman Yoffee. Back row, from left: Henry Wright, Gregory Possehl, John Baines, Craig Morris, Gary Feinman. Photo by Katrina Lasko.